THE STORY OF CONSTITUTIONS

Today, 189 out of 193 officially recognised nation-states have a written constitution, and 75% of these have been ratified since 1975. How did this worldwide diffusion of constitutions come about? In this book, Wim Voermans traces the varied and surprising story of constitutions since the agricultural revolution of c.10,000 BCE. Adopting an interdisciplinary approach, Voermans shows how human evolution, human nature and the history of thought have all played their part in shaping modern constitutions. Constitutions, in turn, have shaped our societies, creating imagined communities of trust and recognition that allow us to successfully co-operate with one another. Engagingly and wittily told, the story of constitutions is vital to understanding our world, our civilisations and, most significantly, ourselves.

WIM VOERMANS is Professor of Constitutional Law at Leiden University. His research focuses on comparative constitutional law, the evolution of human groups into political societies and the genesis of constitutions, legitimacy and storytelling. Voermans has written widely on subjects related to constitutional law, including European Law, Administrative Law (and the dynamics of the Administrative State) and legislative issues. His last four books have become bestsellers in the Netherlands, selling thousands of copies over the last three years.

COMPARATIVE CONSTITUTIONAL LAW AND POLICY

Series Editors

Tom Ginsburg *University of Chicago*
Zachary Elkins *University of Texas at Austin*
Ran Hirschl *University of Toronto*

Comparative constitutional law is an intellectually vibrant field that encompasses an increasingly broad array of approaches and methodologies. This series collects analytically innovative and empirically grounded work from scholars of comparative constitutionalism across academic disciplines. Books in the series include theoretically informed studies of single constitutional jurisdictions, comparative studies of constitutional law and institutions, and edited collections of original essays that respond to challenging theoretical and empirical questions in the field.

Books in the Series

The Story of Constitutions: Discovering the We in Us
Wim Voermans

Democracy Under God: Constitutions, Islam and Human Rights in the Muslim World
Dawood Ahmed and Muhammad Zubair Abbasi

Buddhism and Comparative Constitutional Law
Edited by Tom Ginsburg and Ben Schonthal

Amending America's Unwritten Constitution
Edited by Richard Albert, Ryan C. Williams, and Yaniv Roznai

Constitutionalism and a Right to Effective Government?
Edited by Vicki C. Jackson and Yasmin Dawood

The Fall of the Arab Spring: Democracy's Challenges and Efforts to Reconstitute the Middle East
Tofigh Maboudi

Filtering Populist Claims to Fight Populism: The Italian Case in a Comparative Perspective
Giuseppe Martinico

Constitutionalism in Context
David S. Law

The New Fourth Branch: Institutions for Protecting Constitutional Democracy
Mark Tushnet

The Veil of Participation: Citizens and Political Parties in Constitution-Making Processes
Alexander Hudson

Towering Judges: A Comparative Study of Constitutional Judges
Edited by Rehan Abeyratne and Iddo Porat

The Constitution of Arbitration
Victor Ferreres Comella

Redrafting Constitutions in Democratic Orders: Theoretical and Comparative Perspectives
Edited by Gabriel L. Negretto

The Story of Constitutions

DISCOVERING THE WE IN US

WIM VOERMANS

Leiden University

CAMBRIDGE
UNIVERSITY PRESS

Shaftesbury Road, Cambridge CB2 8EA, United Kingdom

One Liberty Plaza, 20th Floor, New York, NY 10006, USA

477 Williamstown Road, Port Melbourne, VIC 3207, Australia

314–321, 3rd Floor, Plot 3, Splendor Forum, Jasola District Centre, New Delhi – 110025, India

103 Penang Road, #05–06/07, Visioncrest Commercial, Singapore 238467

Cambridge University Press is part of Cambridge University Press & Assessment, a department of the University of Cambridge.

We share the University's mission to contribute to society through the pursuit of education, learning and research at the highest international levels of excellence.

www.cambridge.org
Information on this title: www.cambridge.org/9781009385060

DOI: 10.1017/9781009385084

© Wim Voermans 2023

First published in Dutch by Prometheus, Amsterdam, the Netherlands 2019

Original title: *Het verhaal van de grondwet. Zoeken naar wij*

Translated by Brendan Monaghan

© Wim Voermans 2019, 2020

First published 2023

A catalogue record for this publication is available from the British Library

Library of Congress Cataloging-in-Publication Data
NAMES: Voermans, Wim, 1961– author.
TITLE: The story of constitutions : discovering the we in us / Wim Voermans.
DESCRIPTION: Cambridge, United Kingdom ; New York, NY : Cambridge University Press, 2023. | Includes bibliographical references and index.
IDENTIFIERS: LCCN 2023006702 (print) | LCCN 2023006703 (ebook) |
ISBN 9781009385060 (hardback) | ISBN 9781009385084 (ebook)
SUBJECTS: LCSH: Constitutional history. | Constitutions.
CLASSIFICATION: LCC K3161 .V64 2023 (print) | LCC K3161 (ebook) | DDC–dc23/eng/20230714
LC record available at https://lccn.loc.gov/2023006702
LC ebook record available at https://lccn.loc.gov/2023006703

ISBN 978-1-009-38506-0 Hardback
ISBN 978-1-009-38504-6 Paperback

To Angèle

Every self-respecting nation on the face of the earth wants to have a constitution if it does not already have one. And, with the notable exception of Great Britain, most states that have constitutions would not mind improving their existing ones. Constitutionalism in this sense is one of the dominant values of our time, all over the world. And no matter how often it seems to have been disproved by history, the belief persists that a deliberately constructed constitution is the best means available for assuring achievement of the common goals of a community.

Herbert Spiro, *Government by Constitution; The Political System of Democracy* 1959, p. 11–12

Contents

Figures

Prologue

Many prologues start off with an account of the special moment when the author came by the idea for the book. Often, during a sublime event like a gondola ride through Venice, a flash of inspiration when listening to Béla Bartók's *Bluebeard's Castle* at the Royal Albert Hall or some other momentous occasion that appeals to the imagination. In this sense, this book is bound to disappoint. I always get ideas – probably like most other people – at the most inconvenient moments, usually when I have been running for about two kilometres and have another ten to go. By the time I finally get home, I have often forgotten what the big idea was all about. I do not recall exactly when I distilled the plan for this enterprise, but it must have been a long time ago. For quite some time, I have had the feeling that something was not quite right – something in my field of study kept eluding me; things just did not add up. An uneasy – even unsettling – feeling because confronting your ignorance is quite uncomfortable if you have, like me, been working in academia for more than 30 years. Admitting: 'I just don't get it' is hard and makes you vulnerable. Still …

Law is ubiquitous; there are contracts, governments, sanctions and constitutions, and we behave as though it is the most natural thing in the world. But where does it all come from? During my studies, my professors gave a raft of explanations reminiscent of church sermons. Judging from their lectures and talks, it seemed history apparently had a design for humanity and – as we became wiser and more civilised over the course of the ages – we had increased our understanding of how to organise and behave ourselves. Law, democracy and constitutions were all products of a linear history (of ideas and civilisation) that had brought us *now* to the zenith of human development. Study and better understanding might even bring us further. This mantra was repeated time and again, until after several years I, too, started to half believe it. Were it not that as a student I happened to mix mostly with economists and students of literature, sociology and history. They had pertinent questions about these explanations of legal phenomena. However hard I tried, I could not begin giving them an answer as to why it was good to have a constitution or a legal system; why nearly the whole world had these institutions; what the economic, political or social consequences of constitutional systems were; whether it mattered which kind of systems were in place and so on. Fundamental, academic questions to which my discipline, constitutional law, seemed shy of an answer. What kind of academic discipline is unable to answer such simple questions and does not seem to be interested in them?

I later found solace with professional academic lawyers. They convinced me that it was all due to the ignominious underestimation of our discipline. The academic world has great difficulty understanding the true contribution of legal scholars and the significant and venerable interest they represent; legal scholars have an affinity with the greater dimensions of many issues – justice, legal principles and the like; we legal scholars are in close contact with a very broad constellation of principles and values that underpin our way of life. Who would not like to think this of themselves?

After my studies, I felt like an ugly duckling being warmly welcomed into the ranks of these majestic judicial swans. But after years in their midst and a career in constitutional law, the simple fundamental questions came back to haunt me. Basic questions, like, how did we end up in a world of constitutions, a world aspiring to be ruled by law? Where does this all come from? What consequences does this have?

A few years ago, I felt I finally needed to do something, whatever the risk or reputational damage. You cannot spend your entire life applying yourself to your academic comfort zone of safe research bets and innumerable meetings. Which is why I started writing this book exactly a year ago, with not much more than a hunch and a title to go on. It was to become one of the most enjoyable projects I have ever embarked upon. Not so much because I found all the answers to the fundamental questions about constitutions – I might have found a few – but because I encountered other questions and insights, both novel and familiar. Many of these were issues, themes and overall cheerful chatter with which my fellow students Els, Gosuin, Patricia, Wim, Rob, Ed, Monica, Jan, the 'Hanses', Margreet, Michel, Franke, Marco, Marinus and I enjoyed our 'fantabulous' adolescence almost forty years ago. For which I am grateful to them, besides everything else.

I am deeply indebted to the University of Leiden's wonderful Department of Constitutional and Administrative Law, which exempted me from teaching in a hectic academic year, so that I could write a book, which may not be of any use for teaching anyhow. But everyone did their bit without complaint; it is this kind of solidarity that makes our talented young group so special. I would particularly like to thank my colleagues Patricia Popelier (Professor of Public Law at the University of Antwerp), Olaf van Vliet (Professor of Social Welfare and Labour Market Policy in an International Perspective at the University of Leiden), Henk te Velde (Professor of Dutch History at the University of Leiden), Willem van Boom (Professor of Civil law at the University of Leiden at the time), Geerten Boogaard and Jerfi Uzman (professors of Constitutional Law at the University of Amsterdam and Leiden respectively),

Geerten Waling (postdoctoral researcher of Political History and Constitutional Law at the University of Leiden) and Ali Mohammad (PhD student in Constitutional and Administrative Law at the University of Leiden) for their hard work on the rough manuscript of this book at a time when it was far from finished. Seeing things through different lenses was very important. Georgina Kuipers (PhD student in Constitutional and Administrative Law) and Hugo de Vos (PhD student in Public Administration) assisted my research into the convergence of constitutions across the world. It was an immense job that had to be conducted in a limited period of time and produced interesting preliminary results. Thank you. I would also like to extend my gratitude to the Political Legitimacy Profiling Area – a collaboration between the University of Leiden's faculties of Humanities, Social Sciences, Law and Governance and Global Affairs. Its assistance and general environment both greatly supported me in recent years. Also, a *grand merci* to the Dutch Ministry of the Interior and Kingdom Relations which, like the Leiden University Profiling Area, made a financial contribution towards conducting the data analysis and the English translation. This book is the work of many people; I had the privilege of compiling it. As it is the product of the labour of so many people, I cannot thank everyone, but I must mention Wim Greijskamp, Roel Becker, Jelmer Maarsen, Rani Badloe and Abram Klop, whose indispensable services as student assistants and uncomplaining execution of all my impossible requests is much appreciated. Last but not least, I would like to thank my family. My wonderful sons Nathan and David who helped me out with economic puzzles and conundrums in the book and their patient, listening ears I filled over and over again with plans, plots and pieces of this book for more than a year at the breakfast, lunch and dinner table. And, finally, I want to thank the love of my life, Angèle. Love is all.

Leiden, September 2019

P.S. *On the translation.* The book was originally written in Dutch (*Het verhaal van de grondwet; zoeken naar wij*) and translated into English by Brendan Monaghan in 2020. Thank you, Brendan, for the splendid job you did. You were so much more than a mere translator: a co-researcher, a skilled political scientist and scholarly sparring partner to boot. The research was concluded in September 2019, even though parts of the original book were revised in order to better accommodate an international audience. This means that some wonderful new works in the field, like Linda Colley's, *The Gun, the Ship and the Pen; Warfare, Constitutions, and the Making of the Modern World* (New York/London: Liveright Publishing Corporation 2021) could not be taken on board, even though her thesis on the relationship between wars and constitutional diffusion is very thought provoking and differs from the explanation for constitutional genesis and generations given in this book.

1

Introduction

The Century of Constitutions

Was there ever a century of constitutions? Ask Americans and most of them will undoubtedly dub the eighteenth century as such. That was the era, the golden age, of civil revolutions in which the United States Constitution was conceived.[1] Many Americans, therefore, consider their constitution even to be the gold standard; it was certainly the world's first modern constitution. Many continental Europeans and South Americans would, for sure, opt for the nineteenth century as *the* century of constitutions[2] as it was the time in their national historical development when constitutions were put into place as instruments for affecting political and social change. Constitutional rules themselves were the object of political strife and constitutions were, at the time, vehicles for political and social change. Many other European and Latin American countries cemented their budding nation by enshrining parliamentary systems of government and legal systems based on the rule of law in newly adopted constitutions. In my home country, the Netherlands, for instance, the Constitution of 1814 transformed the old order of the Dutch Republic (1581–1795) into a constitutional monarchy and laid the foundations of the constitutional state the country is today. Amendments to this constitution in 1848 instituted a system of parliamentary democracy, and again in 1917, constitutional law was used to end four decades of emancipatory struggles between confessionals, liberals and socialists by introducing universal suffrage as well as equal rights for confessional education. In a host of European and American countries, constitutions were in vogue in that epoch.

However, in all fairness, only one century can be rightfully called 'the' century of constitutions, and that is the previous century. The number of constitutions increased exponentially over the last hundred years. Figures from the

---

[1]   It was ratified on 21 June 1788 and entered into force on 4 March 1789.
[2]   Sabato 2018, chapter 1 (*New Republics at Play*); Te Velde 2010, chapter 2 (*De Grondwet* – The Constitution), p. 53–73.

American *Constitute* database – which contains almost all of the world's national constitutions in force – show that at least 189[3] out of 193 official (UN recognised) national states currently have a written constitution, except for the United Kingdom and, arguably, New Zealand too, which have 'unwritten' ones.[4] And, almost all of

[3] Only 190 of them are recorded in the Constitute database. We have added UN member state San Marino, which is not included in the Constitute database, to the total.

[4] Data from *Constitute* www.constituteproject.org/?lang=en. The *Constitute* database is a wonderful collection of all the national state constitutions in the world, all recorded in certified English versions and very well organised and indexed indeed. But for all its width and comprehensiveness, it is not entirely complete. It, for example, omits UN member states San Marino (which does have a collection of constitutional documents dating back to 1600), Mali and Guinea (which have suspended their constitutions after recent regime changes). These countries do have written constitutions of some sort. *Constitute*, furthermore, includes countries which are not (recognised) national states, that is, members of the United Nations (UN) (like Taiwan, Palestine and Kosovo). Furthermore the 202 states with written constitutions recorded in *Constitute* also include Israel, Sweden, New Zealand (partially or not) and the United Kingdom. These countries do not consider themselves to have a written constitution, or at least not a constitution codified in a single constitutional document. *Constitute* lists, for example, the Magna Carta (1215) and later Parliamentary Acts with a constitutional character as the United Kingdom's constitution. In terms of intent, character and content, it is difficult to compare this thirteenth-century document and pursuant Parliament Acts over the centuries with modern constitutions, which all stem from the eighteenth, nineteenth, twentieth and twenty-first centuries. Perhaps including the Magna Carta was intended tongue-in-cheek as the British are proud that they lack a written constitution. For a clear comparison, it is maybe better to exclude the Magna Carta and the later Parliamentary Acts with constitutional characteristics. Looking at the data held in Constitute, this would then add up to 192 sovereign national states (if we include San Marino and exclude the United Kingdom) out of 193 UN member states having a written constitution – a staggering total of 99.5% of all countries in the world. Even if we were to exclude New Zealand – which we will discuss in a moment – due to the 'unwritten-ness' of its constitution the percentage would still remain at 99%. Even though the bulk of all the countries in the world have written constitutions, not all national states have codified them in a single constitutional document (or a collection of documents jointly) designated as 'the constitution'. Israel, for instance, currently has basic laws resembling a constitution which have been passed by the Knesset – the Israeli parliament – pending compilation into a constitution (Cf. Goldfeder 2013). The status of the 'constitution', 'basic laws' or 'constitutional acts' in New Zealand and Sweden is less clear. New Zealand, like the United Kingdom, always prided itself on having an unwritten constitution, but has had a Constitution Act since 1986, codifying part of its previously unwritten constitutional law and the 'semi-entrenched' New Zealand Bill of Rights Act 1990. One can argue (as does Grau 2002, notably p. 365) that these acts and the changed status of Treaty of Waitangi (the political constitution of New Zealand signed in 1840 between the British Crown and the Māori chiefs) meant that New Zealand has joined the group of countries with a written constitution. Others argue to the contrary – the Act of 1986 is a mere instrument of government, the Bill of Rights can be amended at will by parliament (even though the New Zealand judiciary considers it entrenched); New Zealand's constitution still remains largely unwritten – there is no real constitution with superior status from a constitutional convention or moment, even though New Zealanders have been debating whether to replace their current constitutional arrangement with a formal, written constitution (Cf. O'Scannlain 2005, p. 793–794.) Shades of grey, maybe. Many other countries have, like New Zealand, only partly codified their constitutional law while other parts have remained uncodified, in case law and conventions (unwritten as some would have it), but that does not mean that thereby the constitution on record is no longer a

these countries have enshrined their written constitution into a single document, with a few exceptions, like Israel and Sweden. If we were to add Guinea and Mali – which are not listed in *Constitute* due to recent regime changes, but still have a (suspended) constitution on record – to the total, this adds up to 98% of the countries in the world today having a set of written constitutional rules commonly referred to as their 'constitution'. The total would even rise to 99%, if were to include countries that have written constitutional rules – written codes establishing a legal order and political system – but that did not codify these rules into a single document.[5] The proportion would rise to 100% if the British (and New Zealanders in their wake) would finally pluck up the courage to admit that nowadays, like other countries, their most important constitutional rules are also embodied in – admittedly many different – written documents, as laws, rules and court rulings. This, of course, they are not about to do. They cherish their exceptional position, the splendid isolation of not having a *written* constitution, even though they essentially do have one. The British constitution is most certainly not an *oral* one.[6]

THE PROLIFERATION OF CONSTITUTIONS

The most striking thing about *Constitute*'s overview is that most national constitutions were enacted relatively recently.[7] Eighty-seven percent were drafted after

written constitution. Because New Zealand does have a *Constitution Act*, and did codify part of its constitutional law, one may count it as a country with a written constitution laid down in a 'core' document. We do understand this may be a bit controversial, but even then, whatever side of the argument one would choose to favour, it does have little effect on the total count – still 99% of all countries would still have a written constitution, even if we were to exclude New Zealand. Sweden, like Israel, did not enshrine its constitutional law in a single document but dispersed it over various documents or acts. The country has four constitutional laws, namely the Act of Succession (1810), the Freedom of the Press Act (1949), the Instrument of Government (1974) and the Fundamental Law on Freedom of Expression (1991). Of course, we did count Sweden as a country with a written constitution albeit for the mere reason that it has designated its most important constitutional document, the *Regeringsformen* (Instrument of Government), as the core of its constitution since 1975. But even when we were to discard Sweden and Israel as countries with 'a' (as in *one* single document) constitution from the total, and exclude the countries with an unwritten one as well, still 98% of all countries in the world could be listed as countries that have a written constitution.

5 This is essentially about two countries: San Marino and Israel. Or three, if we include the other in-between case: Sweden (cf. previous note).

6 Lijphart correctly put this into perspective: 'the distinction between written and unwritten constitutions appears to be relatively unimportant [...]' Lijphart 1999, p. 217. Cf. McLean 2018, p. 395.

7 Data from *Constitute* were also used to determine the year constitutions were adopted. Even though these dates are sometimes open to question. *Constitute* has adopted the principle of relying on countries' self-reporting: the year of adoption as stated by the country concerned is recorded in the database. This approach has limitations. Norway claims its constitution dates back to 1814, while it has only been an independent state since 1905 – since the dissolution of its union with Sweden (making its claim more flattering than factual). Following this line of reasoning, you could argue that the Polish constitution was adopted in 1791. *Constitute* until recently recorded 1815 as the year the Netherlands adopted its constitution.

1950; as many as 74% were put in place after 1975.[8] That is just the national constitutions included in this count. There are many other documents similar to national constitutions that also regulate leadership systems (political systems) and set up (parts of) legal systems. Treaties, constitutions of federated states, or fundamental rules of other regional organisations – such as the European Union (EU) – do likewise. There is much disagreement about whether these latter forms actually can rightfully be called constitutions. But even if we disregard all of these subnational and supranational basic rules, we can still conclude from what countries call their official 'national constitution'[9] that the phenomenon is found everywhere. More people currently have a constitution than a smartphone, a religion, a daily meal or a house – constitutions span the entire globe.

This is remarkable because they are a fairly modern innovation. The national constitutions we are familiar with are only about two-and-a-half-centuries old. They are relatively new compared to other political institutions, such as states and parliaments, which can trace their roots back to the Middle Ages.

Why did constitutions proliferate in such a short time? You would expect legal scholars or constitutional specialists to have a convincing explanation for that, or at least – if not – to be assiduously looking for one. But surprisingly, few explanations come from these academic quarters – and not many quests seem underway. If, for example, you were to refer to the almost fourteen-hundred-page *Oxford Handbook of Comparative Constitutional Law* (2012), currently the most comprehensive constitutional encyclopaedia, you would find almost nothing about this rapid growth[10] and little in the way of explanation. Perhaps this is because the book's mostly American constitutional experts consider this proliferation quite natural and a good development. It seems, according to many of these Handbook authors, to be more or less a consequence of the inevitable triumph of the Enlightenment, the more or less automatic course of history towards ever greater civilisation and freedom, as the German philosopher Hegel (1770–1831) had predicted more than 175 years ago.[11] As good news is no news, this proliferation seems to have remained below the radar and has gone largely unnoticed. There is possibly another, more invidious reason for

It actually dates from 29 March 1814 (the second oldest constitution in the world), but as the Kingdom of the Netherlands and the full-fledged monarchy first came into being in 1815, this is considered by some – incorrectly – the year of the constitution's adoption (see, for more details on this point, Chapter 11). The birth date was accordingly and duly corrected to 1814 in *Constitute* a few years ago. Other reported years of adoption raise questions too. There are at least three disputable cases of national constitutions' birth dates in the database: Latvia (1920 or 1991), the Netherlands (1814 or 1815) and Norway (1814 or 1905).

[8] Cf. Elkins, Ginsburg & Melton 2009, p. 41–42.
[9] Only national constitutions are included in the *Constitute* database.
[10] Stephen Holmes is a partial exception to this rule with his search for the history of ideas and development of the ideology that we refer to as 'constitutionalism': the ideal of limited government laid down in a legal constitutional document. It does not really provide an explanation for the rapid spread of constitutions. Cf. Holmes 2012, p. 189–216.
[11] Cf. Hegel 1892 (orig. 1840).

the silence: embarrassment about countries' copycat behaviour. Constitutions have come to resemble each other a great deal lately.[12] They are no longer unique products of a country's culture, history and exceptional national characteristics – as we like to think – and instead increasingly bear more resemblance to off-the-peg fashion than *haute couture*. Many hand-me-downs or constitutional transplants are uncomfortable reminders of colonialism and Western domination. Speaking of 'constitutional transplants' – which you see everywhere – seems to be considered politically incorrect in some quarters. It is true that over the past forty years, scores of Western experts and organisations have travelled to countries around the world which want to use their constitutions as tools to make the transition to liberal democracy (or the democratic rule of law[13]). They have given these countries advice but would rather not be told that their well-meaning activities have effectively exported *their* ideas and stimulated copycat behaviour. They, too, are sometimes appalled by the consequences of their efforts, especially when Western ideas and advice make their way into a constitution, but the resulting constitutional provisions are not observed or – worse still – are merely used as a fig leaf to conceal an oppressive regime's atrocities. You may wonder whether this really is due to these exported ideas, but nobody, of course, wants to be accused of latter-day constitutional colonialism.

No matter how we put it, countries around the world have been copying and pasting each other's constitutions, borrowing and transplanting stuff, or – to put it more positively – have been inspiring each other. It has certainly been a factor in the constitutional craze that has gripped the world in recent decades. Perhaps it is not such a bad thing. Drinking Coca-Cola does not automatically make you a fan of baseball, make you crave for Thanksgiving turkey or inspire the inclination to elect a president, any more than eating Gouda cheese gives you a passion for windmills or the desire to be ruled by a constitutional monarch.

The American constitutional expert Mark Tushnet, a professor at the Harvard Law School, tries to put the objections to copying into perspective:

> [...] some degree of scepticism about constitutional transplants seems to be justified. Constitutional ideas and structures might migrate, but in the process they might well be transformed to conform to the local spirit of the laws.[14]

Even something you have copied can eventually become your own. A country can assimilate constitutional ideas and structures (the separation of powers, rule of law, freedom, democratic government), with ideas and structures of this kind gradually becoming part of a country's legal and political system, and eventually its culture and identity. This does not happen automatically, as sixty years of European integration, scores of failed states, or – going farther back in time – the American Civil War

---

[12] Cf. Versteeg 2014.
[13] Even though there are certainly identifiable differences, the notion of liberal democracy is used here as a synonym for the democratic rule of law – democratic *Rechtsstaat*.
[14] Tushnet 2012, p. 211–222.

attest. It takes much time, many attempts and quite some habituation. But in this process constitutions, which are now so widespread, do have the capacity to produce *constitutional man*. 'Homo constitutionalis' – the sort of human being for whom the liberal democratic values and principles, expressed in most modern constitutions, are self-evident and incontrovertible. Beings that no longer need the norms of the constitution pointed or spelled out to them, having internalised the constitutional values in their upbringing, education and the example of others' behaviour. Nowadays, this includes many people in the west and beyond.

Why All These Constitutions?

The scant regard for this global explosion in constitutions is remarkable. Ran Hirschl, a legal scholar and political scientist, is one of the few scholars in the field who is puzzled by the lack of attention to this recent global surge.

> Although this trend is arguably one of the most important phenomena in late twentieth- and early-twenty-first-century government, the diffusion of constitutions remains largely under-explored and under-theorised.[15]

What has caused this disregard? Could it have to do with the subject? It would be unsurprising – who on earth is interested in constitutional news? Certainly not many people in Western Europe. Far from a big thrill or appealing idea, especially for young people. Constitutions rather feature as a killjoy of sorts in popular culture.

The first time I heard about constitutions, I was sitting on an uncomfortable folding seat in a huge lecture hall, with 500 other young law students. It was 1981, and the lecturer's point came across dismally in this cavernous space with cold neon lighting. It did not help that he stood glued to the lectern, head bowed, droning a prepared text. Regardless of whether it was because of this bumbling professor or the Dutch Constitution itself, it was simply and incredibly … and mind-numbingly *boring*! At secondary school we had discussed, ever so superficially, the Enlightenment thinkers, as well as some political philosophy and constitutional theory. It did not seem terribly relevant, but it was tolerable and – at times – even interesting. But *this*, this 1981 lecture, was a miserable slog through dry-as-dust concepts and ideas filled to the brim with tangles of jargon. As if that were not enough, we also had to come to terms with the inaccessible, and sometimes downright unreadable, constitutional provisions.

'No one shall require prior permission to publish thoughts or opinions through the press, without prejudice to the responsibility of every person under the law', according to the antiquated language of the Dutch version of article 7, paragraph 1

---

[15] Hirschl 2013, p. 157.

of the Dutch Constitution. Who says 'prior permission' these days? And what on earth is 'without prejudice to the responsibility'? This is, as it turns out, legalese referring to the system of constitutional limitations, which is virtually invisible to the broader public: only laws passed by parliament can set these limits. Even a well-informed lawyer will have some difficulty understanding the precise meaning of this unwieldy text, let alone laymen. This text is utterly unintelligible to them, as it was for me as a freshman in law. You need to have a lot of extra information to understand that this Dutch provision is about something as central and funda- mental as the freedom of expression; the text is the product of the constitution's historical development which explains its garbled formulation. It is no wonder that studying the constitution is not a popular pastime in the Netherlands or many other countries, even those with long-standing constitutional traditions. The older consti- tutions, like those of the United States,[16] Argentina or Canada[17] are not all that easy to read. The text does not readily speak to the hearts and minds of modern readers, even though the ideas and concepts may.

This might account for the fact that the wider public in many countries is largely indifferent to constitutional texts, but it does not explain the want of academic atten- tion. Constitutions today are studied and compared with each other more and more. There are academic series published by posh publishing houses such as Cambridge University Press, Edgard Elgar and others. There are prestigious academic journals like *The International Journal of Constitutional Law* (I-Con)[18] that has been pub- lished since 2003 with many comparative contributions. Numerous international, regional (European) and national journals and constitutional series search for pat- terns, theories, explanations based on constitutional comparisons and there are hosts of (international) conferences on the subject. Yet, from what I know, most of these journals, books and conferences say relatively little about how and why so many constitutions have come into being in recent decades. Is this because constitutional experts – mostly legal scholars – are not used to asking questions of this kind, or lack the skills to find deeper explanations? Or are these explanations simply lack- ing? That is unlikely: it cannot be down to pure coincidence that there has been an almost 75% increase in constitutions in the world over recent decades. Or is the

---

[16] Section 3 of Article III of the United States Constitution is difficult to understand without knowledge of its context. It reads: 'The Congress shall have Power to declare the Punishment of Treason, but no Attainder of Treason shall work Corruption of Blood, or Forfeiture except during the Life of the Person attainted.' Even for the most ardent originalist would have to concede that some knowledge of eighteenth century English and the meaning of the concepts expressed is needed to get what this paragraph expresses.

[17] Article 23, Section 3 of the Canadian Constitution expresses as a qualification for a senator: 'He shall be legally or equitably seised as of Freehold for his own Use and Benefit of Lands or Tenements held in Free and Common Socage, or seised or possessed for his own Use and Benefit of Lands or Tenements held in Franc-alleu or in Roture (...)'. Quite hard to read or understand for anyone, even if you are not aspiring to be a Canadian senator.

[18] Published by Oxford University Press.

astute Anglo-American political philosopher Larry Siedentop right in saying of the importance of constitutions in his book *Democracy in Europe* that we tend to be blind to the obvious?

> Few societies are good at identifying the things they take for granted. These are the things that structure their vision of the world, providing them with categories which shape their experience of fact and underpin their judgement of what is valuable. The result is that, when trying to understand ourselves, we often miss the obvious.[19]

Looking Over the Horizon

The multitalented scholar and jack-of-all-trades Ran Hirschl is one of these rare exceptions. He is not only a legal scholar, but also someone who likes to look beyond the seemingly obvious. He sees three possible explanations for the growth and increasing similarity of constitutions. Three kinds of 'stories' as he calls them.[20] The first story gives an *ideational* explanation. That is, an account which considers the meaning and quality of ideas key factors for the growth and demise of constitutions.[21] The rise and dominance of written liberal-democratic constitutions are, according to this interpretation, the result of the power of the constitutional ideas and the ideal we call *constitutionalism*.[22] Constitutionalism is the now widespread belief that it is *good and proper* for a nation to have legal rules which establish and organise a legal and a leadership system, ruled by law with government for (and ideally by) the people; for many, even amounting to the idea that nations *ought* to have constitutions. The modern version of this constitutional belief system is mainly based on the intrinsic good of individual freedom and limited government, preferably combined with (popular) elected leadership: liberal democracy. Constitutionalism as a belief[23] is closely connected to the Enlightenment's (Christian-Messianic) faith in liberation and progress; reason makes us understand our historical destiny, and (partly because of this) history is progressive, with human destiny gradually improving. The potency

---

[19] Siedentop 2001, p. 81.

[20] Hirschl 2013, p. 157–170.

[21] *Ibid.*, p. 158.

[22] *Constitutionalism* is the ideology of and faith in the functioning of constitutions. *Liberal constitutionalism* – a sub-variant – is the belief in a particular kind of constitution: those with a combination of constitutional instruments such as the division of powers, checks and balances, civil and political rights and freedoms, which offer protection against unlawful repression and warrant influence of citizens on government policy and political decision-making. The ideological aspect, according to Mark Warren, is that constitutionalism assumes 'that laws can effectively establish institutions only if they are accepted as legitimate according to widely held norms and beliefs. Constitutional protections and guarantees are ideological in this sense.' Warren 1989, especially p. 511.

[23] Brennan & Buchanan speak of (and hope for) a 'civic religion'. Cf. Brennan & Buchanan 1985, p. 150.

of this constitutional 'religion' ensures that we believers hardly question the popularity of democratic liberal constitutions because of their self-evidence.[24] Just as Christians and Muslims usually do not wonder why there are so many believers. Their belief is their truth and hence self-evident. This is why they seldom ponder why there are so many believers, and seem more preoccupied with why not *everyone* has yet seen the light. According to constitutionalism, the rise of modern constitutions is a nearly inevitable consequence of the course of history which has made us realise that freedom, rule of law, equality and fraternity are the goal of all human cooperation and society. Seen from the vantage point of this constitutional ideological account,[25] it is not at all strange that many countries have seen the light in recent years and that constitutions also increasingly resemble one another. Constitutionalism-thinkers are more interested in societies that still lack a constitution, or states that have a constitution deviating from the standard liberal-democratic arrangement.

A second explanation for the recent growth in constitutions can be found in what you could call the 'functional' stories. Our world is comprised of markets; regardless of your ideological perspective, it is evident that human society in the twenty first century is dominated by transactions and economic relations. Constitutions play an ever-greater role in this, either as a condition or as a 'tool'.[26] They resolve a number of informational and coordination problems which can impede economic growth. These include uncertainty about market development caused by unexpected nationalisations, high inflation, or sudden currency devaluations, doubts about contract enforcement and the protection of property in the absence of an efficient legal system or the unpredictability of government behaviour (things like coups, arbitrary prosecution, violence, a lack of effective, central government authority, etcetera). Uncertainties of this kind can cause producers, consumers and investors to have less confidence in a country's economic development and, consequently, to be less disposed to invest in it. Economic growth hinges on the optimist: it requires confidence in the future. Without it, economic stability can be undermined by unconstrained political and economic competition, both domestic and foreign. Constitutions function as *credible commitments* by putting in place institutions (rule of law, political accountability, enforceability of contracts, etcetera) which increase

---

[24] This Evangelical inspiration is palpable in contemporary American constitutional discussions and American constitutionalism (the ideology of constitutional governance). Cf. Compton 2014, especially p. 1–2.

[25] Fear of loss of freedom is, according to Hirschl, the main motive for constitutionalisation in this 'story': 'Even according to this prevalent narrative – resplendent as it is with myths about the liberalising power of rights, the Herculean capacities of judges, and a supposedly authentic, "we the people" quest for constitutional protection – *fear* [my italics] is a main driving force of constitutionalisation. The ineffectiveness of the Weimar Republic constitution and horrors of the Third Reich and the Nazi era are commonly invoked as a stark illustration of why strong constitutions are necessary.' Hirschl 2013, p. 158.

[26] Cf. Persson & Tabellini 2003 and Hirschl 2004, p. 82.

the predictability of market participants' behaviour, raise certainty and trust, as well as reduce arbitrary governmental behaviour; these, in turn, increase economic performance and growth. It might be a slightly dispassionate and detached account explaining the worldwide constitutional increase, lacking accolades to human elevation, culture and Enlightenment, but it is credible one in the context of a globalised economy.

Hirschl's third explanation for the proliferation of constitutions is 'politico-strategic'.[27] According to this account, constitutions are strategic instruments with which we mobilise and channel large-scale human cooperation in political communities (i.e., communities with more or less fixed leadership or authority structures). A constitution, as a 'fundamental' and written collection of politico-organisational rules, is nowadays a generally accepted normative ('legal')[28] reference point which political actors are committed to in their struggle for leadership: a document that defines the playing field, sets the rules of the game and also designates the referees and umpires. Constitutions try to provide the most acceptable (legitimate) mix of concepts (sovereignty, popular sovereignty, political identity, democracy, etcetera) rules and institutions (allocating 'remits', such as judiciary, government, legislator, voter, policeman, tax inspector) to institute sustainable political 'peace', thus enabling large-scale social coordination and cooperation.[29] The strategic aspect of it is the balancing act of reconciling and organising human collaboration as efficiently as possible – doing this better increases the competitiveness of your group – and channels the continuous struggle over interests and leadership within the group. Constitutions offer a variety of ways of achieving this balance, and several formulae (especially liberal democracy) are extremely popular – because countries have had good experiences with them.

---

[27] Or a 'realist' account, as he calls it. Hirschl 2013, p. 163 ff.

[28] 'Legal' is understood as: the rules and norms that express an expectation of *proper* behaviour ultimately enforceable by mediation of a public authority.

[29] Usually summarised as 'collective intentionality'. Searle 2004, p. 85. According to Searle, a human society's political reality is formed by adding functions and constitutive rules to collective intentionality (collective beliefs, shared attitudes etcetera within a social group). *Collective intentionality* is the energy of a society and the *functions* and *collective rules* are the direction and channels along which this energy flows. Searle 2004, p. 85–86. Incidentally, Dave Elder-Vass demonstrates that this is not unidirectional process. Collective intentionality and constitutional rules work like cyclical norm circles. He defines them as '[groups of] people who are committed to endorsing and enforcing a specific norm. As a result of sharing this commitment, each member of the group has a higher tendency to endorse and enforce the norm than they would if they had no sense (however subtle) of being part of a wider group that is committed to the norm. The consequence of their behaviour in support of the norm is to create a sense in others (and to strengthen the sense within the group) that they face a normative environment that will sanction their behaviour (positively or negatively) depending on the extent to which they conform to the norm. Through this mechanism, the norm circle has the causal power to increase the tendency of those people to conform to the norm.' Elder-Vass 2012, p. 254.

THE IMAGINED WORLD OF LAW

Hirschl's accounts provide relatively logical explanations, but they are not completely conclusive. After thousands of years of human civilisation, could the entire world have been enticed in a matter of decades by an ideologically tinted Western narrative? Are market discipline and hunger for power so great that the entire world yields to their every enticement and caprice? And, are political relations really almost inconceivable without some such legal testimonial? Probably not. Or are there, borrowing from *Hamlet*, perhaps more things at play in heaven and earth *than are dreamt in your philosophy*? Could other dimensions or causes that go beyond the exogenous factors of ideology, market or political strategy at least partially explain why the whole world has adopted constitutions?

Could it be that every human being has an intuition or sense that renders us susceptible to constitutional music? Do we have some innate instrument that enables us to play along with the music? Modern legal philosophers like John Rawls[30] and Joseph Raz,[31] as well as neurobiologists, assume that we all have an 'inner constitution', that is, a shared morality that functions as some kind of foundation based on a set of grammatical rules that enable us to rapidly learn a moral language, such as that of a constitutional system.[32] Constitutions appeal to our moral basic instincts, especially our sense of justice, and shape them in a manner that is both attractive and allows us to share them. The ideas, institutions and norms of constitutions form a language that literally speaks to the imagination. This is, maybe, the overarching, meta-story about the ins and outs of a political society, collective action and socio-economic organisation. About the *how* (how do we organise authority?, Who does what, for and with whom?) as well about the *why* (why do we consider it legitimate, why are we willing to pay the price of this kind of constitutional cooperation).[33] It is the story that tries to offer each and everyone one their due, their place in and a convincing reason for the constitutional cooperation; the grand story of who we are, what we want and where we belong.

It may be rather tenuous to conceive of constitutions as no more than a story or siren call that reels you in and gets you to take part. Something as significant and manifest as constitutional law is surely more than just a 'story' or a fairy tale? One would think so. Looking around, constitutions and their substantial impact can be seen everywhere. Imposing parliaments; judges in togas; elections; laws being made, supervised and upheld; voluminous legal codes; venerable constitutional texts in showcases. There is, of course, a big difference between the tangible reality of such things as houses of parliament and voting booths, and the imagined reality of

---

[30] Rawls 1999 (orig. 1971).

[31] Raz 1982, p. 307–330, especially p. 316 where he says: 'I attribute to Rawls is that morality is the internal constitution of the moral sense [...]'.

[32] Mikhail 2017.

[33] Hensel 2012, p. 5.

constitutional institutions such as parliaments, judges and elections. You cannot put something like an election on a table. The latter are institutional realities created by people;[34] they are abstractions and imagined representations with which we coordinate and direct our actions – forms of *collective intentionality*.[35] This fascinating phenomenon enables us as human beings to create, share and experience imagined realities, and coordinate our actions and collaborate on a large scale through them. Property, law, the state, value and money are all examples of this kind of man-made reality – institutional facts which deceptively resemble the reality of plain, empirical facts.[36] But these imagined worlds cease to exist without people, leaving only the things, the bare facts.

> Imagine there's no heaven, It's easy if you try, No hell below us, Above us, only sky [...] (John Lennon, *Imagine*, 1971)

Constitutions evoke the imagined reality of a constitutional order: a community that is committed as a political society to some kind of legal and leadership system.

This sort of imagined reality is difficult to study because its structure is complex, largely invisible and fluid, as it is made, adjusted and confirmed interactively by sharing conceptions. John Searle, the inventor of the concept of institutional facts and the way in which they shape the imagined reality of social reality, puts it thus: 'the invisibility of the structure of social reality [...] creates a problem for the analyst.'[37] You can only properly understand and describe these imagined realities from an *internal* perspective, in which you try to see everyone's experiences through their eyes – which is almost impossible and does not yield much more than an aggregate sum and snapshot of subjective observations. Conversely, an *external* perspective – examining the empirical evidence of institutional behaviour – reveals very little about the ideas and conceptions driving this behaviour – it cannot apprehend the intentionality or essence.

EMPIRICISM OF IMAGINATION

What could you do best to really understand the significance and rapid spread of constitutions or test the veracity of Hirschl's assertions? This would at the very least require delving into underlying ideas, imaged realities and conceptions. And you cannot do that without looking into the origins and meaning of the phenomenon constitution as a product of the human mind, imagination and history.[38] That is precisely what I intend to do. This book examines the story and the imagined reality of constitutions from different perspectives – through the eyes of the law, history,

---

[34] Searle 1995, p. 27–29.
[35] *Ibid.*, p. 23–26.
[36] *Ibid.*, p. 2–3.
[37] *Ibid.*, p. 5.
[38] Cf. Niezen 2010 especially Chapter 1 (*The Imagined Order*), p. 1–26.

as well as economics, political science, cognitive biology and other fields. I did not study most of these disciplines, but their insights are quite accessible nowadays.

This book attempts to 'empirically' look into the common imaginaries – the imagined worlds – of and created by constitutions[39] to uncover why we humans have adopted them *en masse*.[40] I suspect that the reason for the surge is related to the significance of constitutions for mass cooperation in societies and ensuing social necessities, as well as the way in which constitutions combine this with the idea of autonomous individuality and equality[41] to give members an acceptable place conducive of enduring mobilisation and collaboration. Constitutions are not so much an answer to ideological discussions and globalised world markets, as to the social organisation issues entailed by a rapidly expanding global population. The importance of constitutions extends much farther than their operational or functional significance (issues such as the effects of constitutions on political, legal, social or economic organisation, and who or what benefits from this) and has changed throughout history. Understanding constitutions is impossible without knowing their history. But studying their annuls is not a simple, straightforward matter. The historical development of constitutions consists of various layers of sediment which have deposited various meanings – at times on the surface, at other times hidden beneath, but always relevant.

What Kind of Imagined Worlds Are We Talking About?

That is all well and good, you will say, but the phenomenon of constitutions has been discussed very casually thus far. Before we can discover the reasons for constitutions' apparent popularity, we need at least a clear definition of the phenomenon. What do we actually mean by 'constitution'? Does this conception encompass all fundamental legal practices and norms for organising political societies' legal and leadership systems – commonly denoted as 'small c constitutions'? Or are we only referring to the so-called large C constitutions: the official, formal legally binding document that countries proclaim as 'Constitution',[42] as in the case of the 189 constitutions included in the *Constitute* database we used as a source above? Most debates on the subject indeed feature this latter category of 'formal' constitutions. One can, of course, contend whether all of these 'formal' constitutions are, in fact, real constitutions. Are they, for instance, actually observed, do they meet minimum standards, and so on. Because even though formal documents may have been proclaimed 'the Constitution' by their countries, this label says little about the practice. This kind of formal definition is unhelpful if we want to learn about the history of the

---

[39] 'Constitutional imaginaries' as Torres & Guinier label them. Torres & Guinier 2012.
[40] Or in Niezen's words: 'The ethnography of the Unknowable'. Niezen 2010, p. 1.
[41] Siedentop 2014, especially p. 349–363.
[42] Law 2010, p. 376–395, especially p. 376.

phenomenon. The tradition of solemnly enshrining legal rules about leadership and legal order of a state-based society in a single document and calling it a 'Constitution' is at most a few hundred years old. Organisational rules of this kind (small c constitutions)[43] not embedded in states, or laid down in single documents are far older.

It is no simple matter understanding what constitutions are and what they actually do. Their prescripts and rules create their own worlds. Take, for example, the legal domain: constitutional norms forge the imagined world of the law, govern the way law is made or 'found' and determine its effects. Constitutions breathe life into law and regulate it at the same time. A stunning Baron Von Munchausen performance – the braggart German soldier who claimed to have pulled himself out of a swamp by pulling his hair. Or as Mark Graber, of the Maryland School of Law, puts it:

> Constitutions provide the legal foundations for ordinary law making by establishing the rules for determining who makes the law, setting out the processes by which those governing officials make laws, and limiting the laws those governing officials enact.[44]

But the significance of constitutions extends much farther than the legal aspects. Constitutions define 'the we' of a community[45] and by this proclaim a society, its identity and regulate its rule, law and leadership.[46] The rules and norms of 'the we' usually have two dimensions: an external one (who are 'we' in relation to other people or communities – who is a member of our group and who is not?) and an internal one (how do 'we' relate to each other?). That is why we often say that constitutional rules are fundamental: they underpin our way of life in state-based societies and coordinate our complex cooperation. And they do so by appealing to our imagination. Constitutional rules and ideas literally capture the imagination: they create it. Their fundamental norms create an imagined world of a legal and a political system – an arrangement for leadership and social organisation – which enables mass cooperation in groups.

THE PERSPECTIVES AND WORLDS IN THIS BOOK

Why would you want to know more about such technical, unexciting or even boring subject? Perhaps the lack of thrill is merely a question of perspective. It may not be more than a reflection of incomprehension of one of the most important social phenomena of recent history: our unprecedented ability for mass cooperation

[43] *Ibid.*
[44] Graber 2013, p. 25.
[45] A constitution makes – constitutes – 'the we' of a constitutional community. The Australian philosopher Yarrah Hominh asks why Australians speak of 'our Constitution'. She argues, it is because 'it constitutes us rhetorically; it constitutes us ('the people') as itself an act of the people.' Hominh 2014, especially p. 42 and p. 64.
[46] Thornhill 2011, p. 8–19.

based on our common imagination that allows us to put faith in abstractions like 'law', 'authority', 'rules', 'constitutions' etcetera. Abstractions we commit to writing, imagined worlds we can share with each other in an instant (contracts, rights, rule of law) which we can employ to coordinate our efforts, channel our conflicts – with oracular linguistic concepts such as state, sovereignty, laws and authority – and mobilise us as individuals for goals which often do not even serve our individual interest. Constitutions, the system they bring into being and the law they express are fascinating phenomena, whose functioning and dynamics are poorly understood. Libraries are crammed with books on democracy and on the development of social and political systems; scores of conferences are organised on the interactions between politics and economic growth; and popular media are packed with blogs, articles and talk shows on political leaders and our political culture. We talk endlessly about the furniture, but rarely discuss the layout of the whole house.

Making Facts: Performative Expressions

Yet, it is in the layout of the house where the silent revolution is taking place: constitutions proclaiming communities around the world, defining 'the we',[47] and organising these societies' leadership and legal systems.[48] This is done in a fashion and language that the world's nations can mutually identify and recognise – and this with little more than words on paper. Constitutions might be underpinned by real military or political power, as 'realists' hasten to note, but they often overlook the fact that fundamental rules such as constitutional rules, also make this power. The constitution's voice breathes life into the society it proclaims. In this sense, constitutions are the ultimate performative expressions, as the British philosopher of language John Langshaw Austin (1911–1960)[49] termed it.[50] Constitutional texts are more than hollow proclamations; they are words that really do something – they actually create something.

Critics are bound to respond that this way of thinking is all too easy: you are trying to underscore the importance of constitutions by using rhetorical inversion. Such a distorted, artificial representation of things makes it appear as though everything begins and ends with constitutions, or in any case the fundamental rules they represent. But this is not so. Without a constitution, however ubiquitous and prominent nowadays, the sun shall rise and set and people shall get on with their lives and simply do the things that people do: get up in the morning, walk on the streets, work, start families, meet for drinks, play football on Saturdays and so forth.

---

47 Cf. note 48 and the quote from Hominh 2014 referred to there.
48 Thornhill 2011, p. 8–19.
49 Not to be confused with the English legal philosopher John Austin (1790–1859).
50 Austin 1962. Cf. Austin's follower Searle 1995, p. 34, Section 2 (*The Use of Performative Utterances in the Creation of Institutional Facts*) and more generally Chapter 3 (*Language and Social Reality*), p. 59–78.

And they would be right, if I would claim that the fundamental rules of constitutions govern our entire existence. I do not. But, on the other hand, there is no denying the fact that constitutional rules are essential to the way modern people organise their political lives, their societies. Social relations, positions, law and leadership are regulated by them. These ubiquitous constitutional rules cover large parts of our way of life nowadays and extend much farther than we normally care to think about. Take getting up in the morning, for instance. We do not usually do so of our own free will – we do so in an organised fashion, according to rules related to labour relations and the regulation of our social relationships in our market-based society. 'Well, obviously so, but surely you do not need a constitution to start a family?', one could argue. Of course not, at least not in a simple, straightforward way. But many people do make this choice dependent on first securing employment, a house and a partner. You cannot just start a family aged twelve: that is mostly prohibited by rules emanating from a legal system underpinned by a constitution. The same goes for many other social activities. Many apparently spontaneous processes in our societies are, in fact, regulated and spurred on by legal rules and norms, and, one of the central theses of this book is that law always originates from some source or form of constitutional law (i.e., the set of fundamental rules that breathes life into the very concept of law and the legal system itself). Ok. That is all well and good for legal behaviour. But surely constitutions cannot ordain the natural world? Getting up in the morning? Constitutions cannot command the sun to rise, can they? Nor can they direct the rivers to flow or the wind to blow? Of course not, but then again, on closer inspection, the pervasive constitutional rules seem to extend even here; they are ultimately the basis for commonly upheld standards of 'time', rules on time indications and time zones, not to mention daylight saving.

Without trying to sing its praises, studying the unpopular popularity of constitutions is well worth exploring. What is it that we are so partial to? Why do even inveterate dictatorships and unpleasant regimes want one? More importantly, why do authoritarian leaders nowadays mostly keep constitutions on record when they come to power? It is, at the very least, quite a risk – a collection of rules like this, pervaded with elevated ideals and lofty ambitions can come back to haunt you; like a scaffold in time it patiently awaits the demise of a tyrant. You need a wide scope to understand this. The significance of constitutions is complex; understanding this requires a clear insight into the many different aspects and meanings of constitutions, as well as a broad overview of them including their history. There are few panoptic bodies of work. Even though scores of legal scholars, political scientists, economists, historians, psychologists, sociologists and many others conduct research into our social and political lives and the role (constitutional) law, leadership arrangements, status and traditions play in this, there are few studies which synthesise these various insights. If you truly want to get to the heart of the significance of constitutions for societies, if you want a panoramic view, you will have to resort to the great works of classical antiquity, such as Aristotle (384–322 BCE), to the Enlightenment thinkers, or the eighteenth-century *Federalist Papers* – the revered series of 85 newspaper articles with which James Madison, Alexander Hamilton and John Jay attempted to persuade the American colonists to endorse their recently adopted constitution: the 'Bible' of modern constitutionalism. There are several reasons for this paucity of overviews. The first has to do with academic *specialisation*. Scholars build on each other's work and specialise, essentially resulting in them learning more and more about less and less. There are few overviews linking insights from various disciplines: writing overviews is simply not very beneficial to advancing an academic career. That does not mean we do not need them. The success of authors of wide-ranging popular science books linking such insights (Fukuyama, Pinker, Diamond, Beard and others) proves that there is broad public demand for work of this kind. And rivers of academic handbooks seem to prove an academic craving for oversight as well.

THE PECULIARITIES OF LEGAL SCHOLARSHIP

The second factor inhibiting a more fundamental examination of constitutions and their proliferation has to do with academic *traditions*. Specialisation has resulted in academic disciplines becoming ever more isolated from one another, focusing as they do on small circles of fellow specialists. Years of lectures, exams, congresses, dinners, meetings and receptions have moulded them into small introverted academic coteries and families with their own customs and language. As much as scholars and university policy makers like to talk of the great blessings of interdisciplinary and multidisciplinary collaboration, in practice this is extremely difficult to achieve. It is not so much because scholars from different disciplines are reluctant to leave their comfort zones but rather because increasing specialisation makes it more and more difficult to understand each other's language.

Legal scholars, in particular, are attached to the traditions of their discipline. Like their colleagues in other disciplines, they live in their own world, with a distinct language and scholarly ways which make it very difficult for others to understand them. An example of the kind of academic questions my colleagues and I formulate might read as follows: 'is the legal protection of citizens in small claims cases sufficient in the light of the relevant legal principles and international human rights?' It is difficult to make head or tail of at first glance and the problem is difficult to observe in the real world. At the very least, you need legal 'augmented reality' glasses to understand what it is all about. Legal scholars are usually not chiefly interested in facts and figures about the adequacy of legal protection when answering esoteric questions of this kind. Assessing adequacy is not considered the most important goal. They are far more likely to examine – often exclusively – *legal* arguments (legal rules, court rulings, 'intangible' matters such as legal principles and other legal scholars' 'authoritative' opinions) considered relevant (in the estimation of their fellow specialists) to arrive at a conclusion. This makes the study of law a very unusual discipline.[51] It is not primarily focused on the core tenets of other academic disciplines – numbers and effects, theories about relationships, like cause and effect, or patterns in processes and relationships between actors and factors. Instead, the legal discipline seems much more interested in the history of ideas, the moral quality of solutions and institutions that arbitrate between groups and individuals (political society and citizens).[52] Legal scholarship is largely inward-looking. The discipline's self-referential nature is as difficult for outsiders to grasp as it is to overcome. Legal scholarship, for instance, still largely dismisses empirical questions (like, how does the 'real' world work, what data are relevant to know about this, where to find and how to measure them?) as *'non-legal'* questions, and therefore 'irrelevant'. Empiricism, or 'real world' questions are mostly not overtly brushed aside: my colleagues and I use clever and elegant detours. Skilled legal scholars, for instance, usually insist on clear conceptions or precise *legal* definitions in discussions. This is an efficient, indirect way of excluding all manner of things not considered relevant – things beyond the legal sphere – from the exchange of ideas. Why are there so many constitutions in the world? 'You first have to have a very precise definition of "constitutions" before you can say anything about that'. Or: 'there are many different kinds of legal classification. It is all a matter of what you call "constitutions"'. Or (typically): 'Ah, the fallacy of figures! Numbers say little…' And so on and so forth. A way of ducking questions by trying to exclude them by definition or delineate them as off bounds. A side effect of this tradition is that legal scholars have become increasingly unintelligible to others and only really understand each other well. Consequently, they often only trust one other and flock together. A group with a distinct style, codes and language – prone to the formal, incomprehensible legal jargon lawyers use, known as *legalese*.[53] As a discipline,

---

[51] Andrew Coan, a professor at the University of Arizona, pulls no punches in his assessment of constitutional legal scholarship. A great deal of its discourse is not above the level of an amateur debate society, he claims: 'much of normative constitutional theory as it is presently practiced resembles a recreational debating society more than a serious effort to improve the functioning of a massively complex modern society.' He continues: 'If this seems too harsh, consider: who but an academic constitutional theorist would believe that abstractions like writtenness or binding law or popular sovereignty could shed meaningful light on how we should structure our constitutional system, without a rigorous examination of how that system functions in practice? The answer is almost certainly no one, or at least no reasonably informed person with even a modest inkling of the complexity of American government and the society it governs.' Coan 2011, p. 276.

[52] Cf. in the same vein: Law & Versteeg 2011, especially p. 1167.

[53] In his book on legalese, Adam Freedman gives many examples and points out that most of the complexity of legal text is unnecessary and the use of Latin, antiquated words and repetitions are generally superfluous. The use of legalese serves a different goal than conveying meaning or providing clarity: it tries to impose the authority of the law and the magisterial dignity of the author on you. However understanding Freedman is of the cause, his appraisal of its use is merciless: 'What distinguishes legal boilerplate is its combination of archaic terminology and frenzied verbosity, as though it were written by a medieval scribe on crack.' Freedman 2007, p. 22.

legal scholarship was until recently rather cloistered, with little interest in what outsiders had to say. Non-legal scholars are very aware of this seclusion – and often irritated by it – which legal scholars often fail to understand, as with accusations that their research is unacademic.[54]

Constitutional research is still mainly regarded as something in and of the *legal* sphere, a theme which should chiefly be researched by legal scholars. And because the academic inquiry into constitutions is still predominantly the reserve of legal scholarship, it inherits its characteristics, its preoccupations and traditions.

These peculiarities extend far beyond legal scholars' language and methods. There is also something singular about their experience of reality. Their academic education and association with other legal scholars make many of them identify themselves with the imagined world of law. Quite a few legal scholars regard the world of law as *real*. They seem no longer capable of grasping its constructed and imagined essence. In fact, rather a number of legal scholars find the metaphysical world of law *more real* than physical reality – they believe in it. One of the greatest modern legal philosophers, Ronald Dworkin, impressed many legal scholars around the world with his classic work *Law's Empire*. In the opening of the book, he loftily elucidates what he and many classically trained legal scholars make of reality:

> We live in and by the law. It makes us what we are: citizens and employees and doctors and spouses and people who own things [...] We are the subjects of law's empire, liegeman to its methods and ideals, bound in spirit while we debate what we must therefore do.[55]

Both the physical and legal world are 'real' – to Dworkin's mind – but the legal world is actually *more* important. It more or less precedes reality, it determines who we are, how we are connected, and thus what we *have* to do. This is, at the very least, a curious reversal of reality and fiction, but one that many legal scholars barely notice – in fact, most of them will feel quite at home with it. It is probably the reason why legal scholars hold so little brief for empiricism. Reality is hardly an interesting object of study because it is merely a subject of legal reality in the *realm of law*. In the eyes of many legal scholars, posing questions about real world effects

---

54 Stolker gives an illustrating overview of the characteristics of academic legal scholarship interspersed with the often witty criticism of other academic disciplines on law as a 'non-science', cf. Stolker 2014, Section 3.2 (p. 89–101 and Chapter 6 [p. 200–230]). Stolker, for instance, cites Paul Samuelson, who believes that faculties of law do not really belong at universities, because they are not academic. The relation between universities and their law school, according to Samuelson, often amounts to little more than a shared address. The ever-astute American sociologist and economist Thorstein Veblen (1857–1929) is even more scathing, saying that 'in point of substantial merit the law school belongs in the modern university no more than a school of fencing or dancing.' Veblen 2000, p. 155 cited by Stolker 2014, p. 93.

55 Dworkin 1998 (orig. 1986), p. VII.

of the law, as legal sociologists or legal anthropologists sometimes do, is to turn the matter on its head.[56] *That* is the wrong question; reality cannot instruct the law, let alone tell you anything about how the law works and the way the real world *ought* to conform to its standards.

The insularity of legal scholarship means that constitutional scholarship, which is currently still largely the domain of legal scholars, is still a relatively closed and self-contained world, with its own language and realities, which other people and other realities, approaches or (academic) perspectives do not have quick or easy access to. This detachment is sometimes due to a lack of interest and sometimes to a fear of the unfamiliar. Whatever the motive, it obviously does not further our understanding of constitutions as a contemporary phenomenon.

THE POWER OF EVIDENCE

Limited interest and tunnel vision are not the only constraints. For a great many people, there is a clear-cut reason for the existence of so many constitutions. You do not have to spend ages studying the phenomenon as it is the simple consequence of the laws of nature. The laws of our existence impel us to follow this 'constitutional' course, which we have only really come to understand in the last couple of hundred years since the Enlightenment. As is the case with other scientific discoveries, such as the law of gravity or relativity theory, we have increasingly come to understand which principles govern human societies. Constitutions are no more and no less than the outcome of natural laws governing human relationships – they express universally applicable principles. At least, in the opinion of many legal scholars. The idea of natural law as some universally applicable higher and better law, begotten by nature and rooted in the 'natural order' of things, is widespread nowadays. It is not all that surprising: its universality resonates and appeals to our shared morality. From a natural law perspective, constitutional proliferation is self-evident: it is evidence of the laws of nature at work.

In the aftermath of the Second World War, a period in which appalling human rights violations were perpetrated on an immense scale, natural rights thinking – which has been around since the Enlightenment – has assumed great importance. As states had proven unable to protect their citizens' human rights, natural law thinking took on a new dimension. What had failed after the First World War was achieved after the Second World War – global recognition of human rights was affected in the form of the Universal Declaration of Human Rights. The Declaration's significance is often downplayed by pointing out that it is not legally binding. You cannot take a case based on it to court in most countries and neither do citizens have recourse to

---

[56] Stolker even observes a certain disdain among legal scholars for legal sociologists and the like, certainly when it comes to whether the sociology of law should play a role in law school curricula. Stolker 2014, p. 271–272.

some world court. Yet this qualification fails to recognise the Declaration's special character. It was a unique event: in 1948 the *entire* world signed up to a particular portrayal of humankind and an associated articulation of the role of law and organisation of government. There is a worldwide embrace and recognition of the dictates of 'natural law' expressed as the *universal truth* that every human has inherent dignity and inalienable rights.

Preamble

Whereas recognition of the inherent dignity and of the equal and inalienable rights of all members of the human family is the foundation of freedom, justice and peace in the world, [...]

Article 1

All human beings are born free and equal in dignity and rights. They are endowed with reason and conscience and should act towards one another in a spirit of brotherhood.

You would have to be quite hard-hearted not to be touched by a text like this. The meaning conveyed by the words is, of course, not correct in any empirical sense. Looking at the real world, it is clear to see that not everyone is born free, equal, endowed with an equal amount of reason and conscience, or with the ability to behave fraternally towards their fellow human beings. But that is not the point; the text is not about objective facts, but about *truths*. It is a modern version of the preamble to the American Declaration of Independence:

We hold these truths to be self-evident, that all men are created equal, that they are endowed by their Creator with certain unalienable Rights, that among these are Life, Liberty and the pursuit of Happiness. — That to secure these rights, Governments are instituted among Men, deriving their just powers from the consent of the governed [...].

This world view, instantly recognisable to Westerners because of the Christian[57] and historical echo of their own constitutional and political development, has come to dominate the world over the past seventy years. It has been so successful that we have taken the idea of natural inalienable rights and governments requiring the consent of the ruled as really being *true* and consider it as the truth and part of reality. Even if it does not correspond to reality. Modern natural law thinking considers the rapid proliferation of constitutions, as vehicles of these values and truths, as no more than a logical and evident outcome. The only thing worth studying is the countries, groups and individuals who do *not* yet understand human history's intentions and biddings revealed to them.

---

[57] Siedentop 2014, in particular Chapter 16 (*Natural Law and Natural Rights*) and the final chapter (*Epilogue: Christianity and Secularism*).

THE STORY OF CONSTITUTIONS

In accounts of the popularity of constitutions we are not only confronted with 'stories', but with many different kinds of creeds and perceptions of the world, ideas on the ends of history as well as humankind. Ideas about living together, the goal of human cooperation, society and the organisation of leadership all have roots extending far beyond the Second World War. Bequeathed over the centuries, ideas and ideologies of this kind have become an increasingly fixed part of our collective consciousness.[58] A contingent historical development that has made us increasingly amenable to the story of constitutions. That is probably where we must look to really understand why almost the entire world has adopted constitutions. Economic, politico-strategic or ideological explanations for growth – as given by Hirschl – provide a theoretical answer to *how* the constitutional explosion could have taken place but does not conclusively account for *why* this is so. For that we do not need to consult stories about the constitution (Hirschl), but rather make an inquiry into the story of constitutions themselves. Where does the story come from, why is it such a strong story, why is it so convincing?

That requires looking beyond the commonly held view that puts the horizon of constitutionally relevant ideas in the age of Enlightenment and that traces the roots of constitutions and their conception to the end of the Middle Ages, the eve of the emergence of modern states. If we really want to know where constitutions stem from, we need to delve much deeper, and start our search – in accordance with a time-honoured tradition in constitutional theory – by looking at human nature and an inquiry into human beings as social animals.[59] Were the sixteenth and seventeenth century contract philosophers correct in surmising that over the course of our evolution we developed characteristics and properties which make us humans amenable to abstract notions like public morality, law, social classes, religion and – in a broader context – something like constitutions? Do mechanisms like constitutions, as sets of fundamental rules instituting leadership and social organisation, perhaps help us overcome inherent limitations to human cooperation? Constitutional rules do indeed seem to contain elements that enable us to cooperate on a large-scale far exceeding our neurobiological limits. Constitutions largely consist of clever mixes of elements that facilitate the two pillars of social cooperation: trust[60] and recognition.[61] They facilitate trust by making strangers' behaviour more predictable.

---

[58] Alford, Funk and Hibbing demonstrated in 2005 that ideologies are even partially genetically transferable. Alford, Funk & Hibbing 2005, especially p. 158–161 and p. 163.

[59] 'Everyone has a theory of human nature', as Steven Pinker observes in his book *The Blank Slate*. Pinker 2003, p. 1.

[60] Trust here is simply understood as what Frans de Waal defines as 'reliance on the other's truthfulness or cooperation, or at least the expectation that the other won't dupe you.' De Waal 2019, p. 167.

[61] Recognition denotes the process of a group assigning a role or identity to a group member. People are social beings and recognition is fundamental to human cooperation, and even

Abstract institutions such as law decrease uncertainty, anxiety and distrust – all of which stand in the way of large-scale human cooperation. Constitutional rules also grease the wheels of human cooperation by providing convincing common narratives about the reason for cooperation, ('good') leadership and the acceptance of authority. On top of that, constitutions confer *recognition* by defining a community – establishing the 'we':[62] the story of the group's raison d'être in relation to other groups as well as group members' roles, standing and claims within the group. Most constitutions are at heart, compelling narratives that use the elixirs of trust and recognition to enable efficient and sustainable mass cooperation; in many ways this is a kind of holy grail for human societies in a complex, globalised world; social mobilisation on the cheap. Seen in this light, it is quite understandable that just about every country in the world has started using this magic potion.

It is one thing knowing that constitutions are attractive and therefore often used, and it is quite another knowing whether they 'work' or are 'effective'. Is the constitutional magic potion a drug, a homoeopathic concoction or a real medicine? Nowadays much attention is rightly paid to the question as to whether constitutions really work. Many of the 189 (or 192) constitutions known to us are nominal or 'sham constitutions'.[63] Documents such as these are not much more than a fig leaf for regimes that fail to respect the letter and spirit of their constitutions. It is difficult to say how many sham constitutions there are, just as it is difficult to determine whether a democracy is 'genuine' or merely democratic in name. Recent research by Law and Versteeg, however, shows that there are quite a few of these sham constitutions around.[64]

A constitution that does not function, which is not 'lived', is, of course, mere fiction, no more than a tall tale. That is not how it is supposed to be. But, how do you ensure that the text of a constitution is observed? Many constitutional colleagues, including myself, tend to rush headlong into technocratic solutions. Which instrument or mechanism can we use to enforce and secure compliance? The solutions proffered to tackle non-compliance with constitutional norms are often along the lines of transnational constitutions or constitutional (supervisory) mechanisms. It is questionable whether this really helps. In a world in which we attach great importance to states' sovereignty, including peoples' right to self-determination and non-intervention in other states' affairs, solutions entailing any kind of intervention by other states hold

---

to human life. In Charles Taylor's words: 'our identity is partly shaped by recognition or its absence, often by the misrecognition of others, and so a person or group of people can suffer real damage, real distortion, if the people or society around them mirror back to them a confining or demeaning or contemptible picture of themselves. Nonrecognition or misrecognition can inflict harm, can be a form of oppression, imprisoning someone in a false, distorted, and reduced mode of being.' Taylor 1994, especially p. 25.

[62] A constant element of all constitutional imagination is the story of the 'we'. Cf. Torres and Guinier under the heading of section II: *'The Constitutional Imaginary: The Constitution As The Story Of Us'.* Torres & Guinier 2012, notably p. 1057.

[63] Law & Versteeg 2013.

[64] *Ibid.*, 2013.

little promise. Yet, there is more. This 'mechanical' kind of solution also partially fails to recognise how constitutions work. I hope to demonstrate that a constitutional story works not merely because it is legally anchored with checks and balances, but because it 'connects' with a society as a source of meaning and as an organisational mechanism. The why and how of the functioning of constitutional norms can be found largely in the story. A good constitution works by persuasion: by winning the hearts and minds of the community it creates and regulates. But how do you achieve a 'good' constitution which functions well, is persuasive and hence complied with? This is not a question of constitutional nuts and bolts, techniques or institutions. According to the former British judge and Cambridge professor Sir John Laws:

> The "good Constitution" in a democratic country seeks to balance the morality of law and the morality of government. The good Constitution can be considered at the levels of abstraction of the relationship to human rights or of the progression from parliamentary to constitutional supremacy. But [perhaps] the level of the balance between the two moralities is more fruitful. The morality of law focuses on individual rights, the morality of government on the public interest. The constant task of the Constitution is to achieve an accommodation by restraint on the part of both the judges and the executive.[65]

A *good* constitution is primarily an appeal – a story we must experience and tell each other time and again, as well as a call that we confirm with our (institutional) behaviour. Judges, laws, principles and institutions are *part* of this story, but they are not the story itself. And it is this story, the whole of it, we are going to explore in this book.

WHO IS THIS BOOK FOR?

The aim of this book is an exploration that everyone can join without much prior knowledge or legal expertise. A voyage of discovery written in a way that allows many to jump aboard, I hope. The book itself is a story. Not only to entice the reader and share my fascination with the phenomenon, but also to elucidate something: how we deal with stories, not only in a literary context, but also in law, politics, history and other contexts. For this reason, I have also tried to put the story of constitutions in a narrative form in several places. It is a narrative about a journey and at the same time an experiment in making the medium (this book) part of the message (the story of constitutions). There are perils to this endeavour: taking this path risks making the content unrecognisable both to specialists and perhaps to general interested readers. Insisting on the narrative character of constitutions and a taste for belles-lettres may put off the more traditional specialists in the field. The style of the book may easily be mistaken for frivolousness, nonchalance or theatricality. It is certainly not my intention.

This book was written in the first place for students. Not necessarily as terrifying mandatory reading material for law students, but for curious people who want to

---

[65] Laws 2012, p. 567.

learn something or know more. Someone like myself at the age of nineteen in that cavernous lecture hall at my university; the person who I still am. I know that this book is difficult to fit into current legal curricula, which pay more attention to legal aspects of constitutions. What is the legal effect of their provisions, how are they applied, how do courts treat them, etc.? Wide-ranging exploits like this one do not help aspiring lawyers win cases or become top dog in the firm. Legal curricula are already brim-full as they are, leaving little space for broad reflections on theories, the history of ideas or results of recent research on constitutional activities from other fields of academic inquiry. But perhaps we ought to re-evaluate these curricula – is this how we want academic legal studies to be? I for one believe that there is plenty of room for improvement. Academic legal research has developed in interesting ways over recent decades bringing many new insights: law students should hear of this. This would require my colleagues' assistance at home and abroad, even though this will not come easily. They, like me, are products of their classical education in the law and their law schools' traditional curricula that have a more or less fixed setup worldwide. Undoubtedly this book's approach will rub some of them up the wrong way because it is so explicitly unconventional. It contains few legal definitions and traditional constitutional debates but takes many excursions to various exotic non-legal disciplines and contains next to nothing about the role of judges, constitutional review, constitutional interpretation or the principle of legality. I do hope they will not take offence, and – most of all – not take it personally.

René Margritte (1898–1967), *Ceci n'est pas une pipe* ('La trahison des images' 1928–1929)

'Ceci, n'est pas une pipe', wrote the Belgian painter René Margritte in the sub-title to his painting. 'This is not a pipe' under a picture of a pipe in his painting 'La trahison des images' (The Treachery of Images). True to this confusing motto, this book is not a 'legal' book even though it deals with law and constitutional law. It is about the phenomenon we call constitutions and law, about the worlds they evoke and express, but it is not of that world or that world itself – not in a legal way anyway. This makes it, I believe, also accessible for students and scholars from other academic disciplines. I have tried to turn myself (and my colleagues) minds inside out in order for other to understand what goes on in lawyers' minds when they study or apply the law. How their world view relates to the real world, and how real-world views and real-world actions are shaped or affected by constitutional law and law in return.

This book might strive to be highly accessible, with an easy-going style in an attempt to appeal to a broad audience, yet its claims must still be substantiated. The price of a broad perspective is a deluge of sources. Most of them have been demoted and relegated to the endnotes, but I could not avoid including some substantia-tion in the main text. I have usually presented them as relatively short quotations. This enables the readers to assess the credibility of the argument or analysis for themselves with more ease than from a general reference to a book or article mired somewhere deep in the appendices.

I spent a great deal of time agonising over whether to banish the many quotes to the recesses of the endnotes altogether. In the end, I decided to do so only partially. The quotes in the text are not only substantiation, but also expressive voices, views with timbres revealing something of an author's character, stylistic enticements, clever and well-crafted arguments which win the reader over – precisely because of their wording. They are also part of this story, with their own role.

The book's setup is straightforward. It simply follows the trail of basic questions on where, whence, why, what and how, as they appear in our exploration. We shall look at the proliferation of constitutions in Part I, the history of constitutions in Part II, the concept and typology of constitutions in Part III, their effects in Part IV and finally, at *how* the imagined reality of constitutions works in Part V.

Constitutional Diffusion

2

Constitutions Everywhere

Our age is an age of constitutions. They are the most normal thing in the world nowadays. Nearly every country has one, as we saw in the introduction. Sometimes they are elegant, stylish and well drafted but more often they – their texts anyway – are boring, tedious or even soporific; some are recent (Thailand 2018) and a few are old (United States 1788/1789).[1] But the phenomenon itself is not all that old. The oldest surviving national constitution is 230 years old (United States), the second oldest pair is 204 years old (the Netherlands and Norway). A mere handful of states had modern constitutions at the end of eighteenth century. Now, two centuries later, 189 out of the 193 states in the world have documents with written legal rules which they use as the basic legal system to order the state. How is this possible? Constitutions have a wider range than the internet, they are as ubiquitous as t-shirts, more people in the world live under a constitution than under an actual roof. How could it come to this? This book tries to understand what it is in the constitutional formula that makes constitutions so irresistible. But maybe we are looking in the wrong direction by approaching it like this. Maybe it is not the formula of the constitution which accounts for its success. Could it not be that the proliferation of constitutions is a by-product of something else? In the same way as cathedral building, painting and modern theatre are not the outcome of some independent development, but instead are by-products of other socio-economic evolutions. These are, as economist Thorstein Veblen showed, not autonomous art-for-art's-sake developments, but rather the result of people's constant efforts to increase their status within their group by conspicuous consumption.[2] And status gives access to leadership. Does this mean we need to take our focus off the content of constitutions and look elsewhere to explain their omnipresence?

---

[1] Drafted in 1787, ratified in 1788 and came into force in 1789.
[2] Veblen 2007 (orig. 1899).

Is constitutional proliferation perhaps merely secondary to the growth and needs of world markets? Or is the rise of constitutions, to give yet another alternative explanation, a reflection of the law's importance to social relationships in our contemporary globalised world? An indirect expression of our attachment to abstract representations of justice and associated norms, which has become so important that it has started to work almost like some kind of inherited religion? In this view, constitutions almost serve as petrol stations for our legal addiction. If this is so, then it is remarkable that the we lack a 'real' universal constitution on a global level which lays down how states should organise their law and their governance structure. We may have the United Nations (UN), the Universal Declaration of Human Rights and many treaties, but they are not comprehensive arrangements for organising legal or leadership systems. All 189 (or 192) constitutions currently in force are limited to single nation states – transnational ones do not yet exist. Are national constitutions then perhaps little more than a by-product of nation states and the state-bound organisation of mass cooperation? Neither is this an entirely logical conclusion. The modern state pre-dates the first modern national constitutions by at least 150 years. In addition, around 90% of the world's national constitutions were written after 1950 and three-quarters of the world did not have a national constitution at the end of the nineteenth century, even though most of the world was already divided into nation states by then. The state-by-product explanation is thus not entirely convincing either. It is hard to imagine a post-distillation effect with a three-century interval. Are there perhaps yet other accounts for this recent rapid proliferation? Has the proliferation of constitutions perhaps coincided with the rise of democracies, as some suspect?[3]

A BY-PRODUCT OF WAVES OF DEMOCRATISATION?

The American political scientist Samuel Huntington (1927–2008) argued that modern history has seen three major waves of democratisation, with democratic governance initially rising like the incoming tide and retreating like the outgoing tide. Looking back at the past two centuries, he observes an alternation between periods in which democratic systems gained ground on non-democratic, authoritarian regimes, and periods in which democratic systems were in retreat and came under pressure. Huntington's first democratic wave surged from 1828 to 1926, the period after the great revolutions at the end of the eighteenth century in the United States and France. The first ebb, or democratic recession, was set in between 1926 and 1942,[4] when democracies declined and authoritarian regimes rose around the world. Huntington's second democratic wave occurred in the period following the Second World War, from 1943 to 1962; the era of decolonisation. At the crest of the wave, in 1962, there were 36 democracies in the world. This was followed by another decline

---

[3] Amongst others Sunstein 2001, especially in the last chapter (*Conclusion: Democracy's Constitution*).

[4] Already beginning in 1922 with Mussolini's ascent to power in Italy.

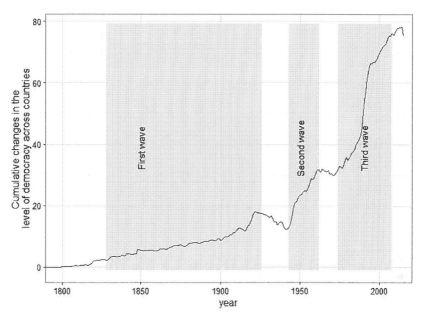

FIGURE 1 Waves of democratisation[5]

between 1958 and 1974 thanks to a combination of opposing forces, including several anti-democratic revolutions in Latin America, reducing the number of democracies to 30 in 1974.[6] The third democratic wave started, according to Huntington, with the Carnation Revolution in Portugal in 1974, subsequently breaking on Latin America, countries in Southeast Asia, Eastern Europe (after the fall of the Berlin Wall) and central and Southern Africa in the 1980s and 1990s. It peaked between 1989 and 1991.[7] The number of democracies tripled in these decades, to around 120 at the start of the new millennium. Numbers of this kind are imprecise, because they depend in part on one's definition of 'real or complete' democracy,[8] but it is indisputable that the third wave, 1974–2007, was the most successful-ever period of democratisation, regardless of one's definition. But even this third wave now seems to have crested.[9] Democracy has been in retreat over the past ten to fifteen years (Figure 1).[10]

[5] Taken from:
https://raw.githubusercontent.com/xmarquez/quick-and-dirty-democracy-scores/master/
Quick_and_Dirty_Extended_Unified_Democracy_Scores_files/figure-html/unnamed-
chunk-6-1.png (Last consulted 1 September 2019).

[6] Depending on what you mean by democracy. In 1974, there were 46 'nominal' democracies –
electoral systems with at least periodic and general elections – but only around 30 countries
actually had democracies which went hand in hand with guaranteed civil rights and liberties
(liberal democracy). Cf. for these figures Diamond 2015b, p. 141–155, especially p. 141–142.

[7] Fukuyama 2018, p. XI and p. 3.

[8] Cf. note 70.

[9] Fukuyama, p. 1–5.

[10] (Larry) Diamond 2015b, p. 153.

DEMOCRATIC RECESSION

The depth of this recession depends on how you measure it. The American organisation *Freedom House* – an independent watchdog that studies democracy, political freedom and human rights across the world – uses a seven-point scale to assess the quality of democratic systems. This rating system accords countries with the most democratic systems (free elections in a free society, that is, liberal democracy in the strictest sense) a score of one, and repressive totalitarian regimes a score of seven.[11] No recession is immediately apparent on this scoreboard. At its nadir, the global democracy score was on average 4.38 in 1974; it climbed to an average of 3.85 in 1990 and peaked at 3.22 in 2005; it reached its current score of 3.30 in 2015.[12] This represents only a modest fall of 0.08 between 2005 and 2015. Is that a real decline? According to the same figures from Freedom House, there were still 123 electoral democracies globally in 2017. Nevertheless, the organisation sounded the alarm recently. The cover of its 2018 annual report announced that democracy was in crisis.[13] The organisation's figures for that year show that, for the twelfth consecutive year, the quality of democracy has been declining in at least 113 countries, especially in terms of political and civil rights and freedoms. Later reports from 2019 onwards, using a new method to measure the quality of democracies (looking into seven dimensions), confirm this pattern of ongoing democratic backslide. Many countries have regressed from liberal democracies to 'hybrid democracies' or 'illiberal democracies', with elections reduced to little more than a polling exercise under an authoritarian system in which competition for leadership is neither free nor open and with limited or no choice between parties or candidates.[14] Seen from this angle, the past ten years have borne witness to a major recession.[15] The British newspaper *The Economist*'s democracy index shows that the number of completely free democracies in the world has fallen in recent years from twenty-eight to nineteen countries.[16] This trend seems unlikely to turn in the near future.[17]

The proliferation of constitutions appears to follow democratic trends partly, but not entirely (Figure 2). For example, many more countries have constitutions that hold democratic elections (189 with a constitution and around 123 electoral

[11] Cf. Washington: Freedom House, *Freedom in the World 2018; Methodology* https://freedomhouse
.org/report/methodology-freedom-world-2018 (Last consulted on 2 November 2018).

[12] Cf. (Larry) Diamond 2015b, p. 142.

[13] *Freedom in the World 2018, Democracy in Crisis.* Washington: Freedom House 2018. Cf. also
https://freedomhouse.org/sites/default/files/FH_FITW_Report_2018_Final_SinglePage.pdf
(Last consulted on 1 November 2018).

[14] Cf. Levitsky & Way 2010.

[15] Cf. Diamond 2015b.

[16] Cf. The Economist Intelligence Unit's Democracy Index, *Democracy Index 2017*, www.eiu
.com-/topic/democracy-index (last consulted on 2 November 2018).

[17] Cf. International Idea, *The Global State of Democracy; Exploring Democracy's Resilience.*
Stockholm: International Idea 2017.

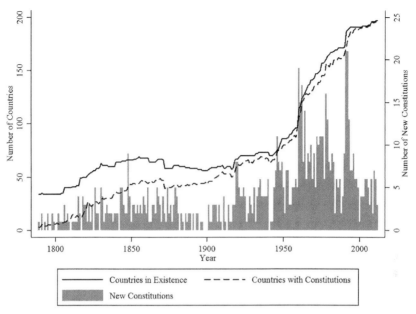

FIGURE 2 The historical development of modern constitutions[18]

democracies), let alone genuine, completely free elections. Seen in this light, the number of 'real' or truly fully-fledged democracies shrinks to somewhere between nineteen[19] and eighty-seven,[20] depending on how one computes the score. But even leaving this calculation aside, the relationship between constitutional and democratic development is still a confusing and indirect one. Constitutional proliferation only seems to follow democratic waves with a delay. Constitutional proliferation has been out of step with democratic waves, certainly in the past ten years. Unlike the democracy index, the constitution index has not fallen. Which does not say much, of course. Minor changes to existing constitutions can transform free democracies into unfree, more or less authoritarian regimes while preserving nominally free elections. This seems to be the case in Turkey, and constitutional changes in

[18] This figure is James Melton's adaptation of the diagram from Elkins, Ginsburg & Melton 2009, p. 41.

[19] Genuinely free democracies according to *The Economist*. It is difficult to compare this with Freedom House's analysis and score. *The Economist* includes far fewer countries in its comparison and computes its 'freedom' score differently – as a score on a ten-point scale. In 2017 *The Economist*'s index came up with nineteen complete democracies with scores between eight and ten. This was followed by 56 'flawed democracies' – democracies with deficiencies (scores between six and eight). Cf. *The Economist* 2017 note 87.

[20] Freedom House states in its 2018 report that 45% of the 195 countries globally (which they include in their survey) in 2017 can be regarded as genuinely liberal democracies. Cf. Freedom House 2018.

Hungary and Poland also seem to be moving them towards the category of unfree, hybrid systems (illiberal democracies).[21] Perhaps this argument can be turned on its head: apparently constitutions are unable to reverse regression from liberal democracy to less free systems.

Superficially, the development of democracies and the development of constitutions seem to follow the same path, but at least with a different cadence. Perhaps one should not look at democratic development at all if one wants to understand constitutional proliferation. Economist and political scientist Jon Elster argues that the historical development of constitutions has been on its own unique wavelength. He identifies seven more or less independent waves of constitution making,[22] which incidentally still largely ride Huntington's democratic waves. Elster adds several more, including the early constitutional waves at the end of the eighteenth century and another around 1848. He also identifies a distinct constitutional development wave in the period ensuing the First World War and after the fall of the Berlin Wall in 1989.[23] Seven waves instead of Huntington's three is a thought-provoking view and it underscores that the idea of democratic and constitutional developments possibly being correlated is probably off the mark. The evidence that modern constitutional development is directly related to democratic development, or can be explained by it in some way, is not convincing, even if we limit ourselves to the previous century.

Riding the High Billows of the World Market?

Are constitutions perhaps so in demand because of their effects on a country's economic situation? Do constitutions tread on the heels of the market? It is assumed – as in Ran Hirschl's second story – that constitutions and particularly the institutions they create have beneficial effects on economic growth.[24] Most of the effects are indirect,[25] but even so. One of these indirect economic effects is that constitutions can contribute to increasing a country's political stability.[26] Most modern constitutions do so not only by anchoring democracy, but also by guaranteeing the legality of administration, the separation of powers, and access to independent courts for

[21] Cf. Öktem & Akkoyunlu 2016; Wilkin 2018, p. 5–42.
[22] Elster 1995.
[23] *Ibid.*
[24] Hirschl 2004, especially p. 82. Stefan Voigt argues that this is inevitable: 'if constitutional rules did not have any significant effect on economic outcomes, expending effort on explaining their emergence would be pointless.' The constitutional investment alone demonstrates that this is the case. Voigt 2011, p. 206.
[25] For the role of 'constitutions', defined here for the sake of ease as a set of basic rules for a legal and political/leadership system, in markets and economic growth, cf. Weingast 1995, p. 1–31. According to Weingast, constitutions act as a system of credible commitments. Cf. chapter 22 for more on this subject.
[26] *Ibid.*

dispute settlement. Democracy regulated in this way has proved to be a demonstrable[27] and attested formula for political stability.[28] Entrenching institutional balances in a constitution with an amendment or revision procedure requiring more than a simple majority or even several procedural steps or readings for constitutional revisions, makes a political system less susceptible to fluctuation and increases the protection of minorities – who are always vulnerable in democratic systems because of their majority rule. Political stability reduces uncertainty and increases the likelihood of 'return on investment', thereby increasing the likelihood of economic growth. Constitutions and the institutions they produce (in particular, an independent judiciary) provide an answer to the problem of credible commitments.[29] To stimulate long-term economic growth, political leaders must convince and reassure domestic and foreign investors and economic actors. Constitutions can make trust grow – in each other, the government, and the future.

As briefly mentioned above, knowable and foreseeable laws and rules as well as a legal regime that allows capital formation and protects property rights are critical factors for economic growth.[30] Constitutions are highly sought after for this reason. We can also turn the evidence around again: (world) market discipline may, in turn, contribute to the proliferation of modern constitutions. All these new constitutions do not enrich or improve countries or the world automatically. When a country dons this impressive constitutional attire, it will not necessarily adhere to all the rules laid down in it or honour the commitments it has made. Globalisation and market discipline also fail to explain why, for example, so many constitutions were written between 1950 and 1962, at the depths of the Cold War, when the global market did not function nearly as well as it did between 1990 and 2010. Was this growth the result of aspirational behaviour? Or did it perhaps have more to do with collective conviction than market orientation? Neither do globalisation and market discipline offer a conclusive explanation, although it is striking that countries not dependent on the world market – due to great mineral wealth or a largely self-sufficient economy, for instance – seem to establish liberal-democratic constitutions less effectively and swiftly. We will delve deeper into the relationship between constitutions, markets and economic growth in chapter 22.

NATURE OR NURTURE?

Could the cause of constitutional proliferation be found in the law itself? In 1997, a rather obscure Mormon academic, Marianne Jennings, published an article in an

---

[27] Cooter 1999.
[28] Persson & Tabellini 2003. Cf. (Jared) Diamond 2019, p. 334–337.
[29] Constitutions are (the key to understanding) the political foundations of markets: they enable trust – the core component of free market transactions – through credible commitments. Cf. Weingast 1995, p. 2.
[30] Hirschl 2004, p. 82.

equally obscure medical journal with the remarkable title: 'Clarity of Judgement During Amoral Times in a Society Addicted to Codified Law'. Her central argument is that we have lost our personal moral compass thanks to our dependence on, our addiction to, codified law.

> Slowly there has been an evolution from a society grounded in religious values to one that remains detached and amoral. There is an addiction to positive or codified law. Codified law is the sole determinant of our standards of behaviour. [...] The addiction to codified law and individual rights at the expense of the whole leaves us with a collective lack of wisdom and judgement.[31]

It might be obscure, but it is certainly an interesting insight. Jennings uses it to develop an argument for restoring values in interpersonal relations between providers of medical service and patients, but her observation itself is most interesting. Have we grown overly dependent on the law as the way of regulating relationships in our society? The law is, of course, a very efficient way of dealing with very large groups of strangers. You do not have to continually determine how to deal with each and every stranger you come across, physically check whether someone you are dealing with can be trusted or collect information about someone from a variety of sources. Neither do you have to constantly look out for the safety of those around you, your goods or body when you are protected by the law. The law does all of these things for you – life becomes much easier. You no longer have to worry continually about all manner of things. There are, of course, drawbacks. Being highly dependent on the law sometimes makes human relationships more impersonal and the law itself can cause problems too. Life can become 'juridified',[32] and as a result, harden in several respects. 'See you in court.'

The far from obscure McGill professor Ronald Niezen calls this the silent revolution of

> [...] *legal substitution*, the processes by which formal law is introduced to or becomes dominant in societies or communities that have previously relied more exclusively on informal, customary institutions and procedures.[33]

In this process, the world becomes bureaucratised and 'disenchanted' as Weber called it,[34] as we exchange personal contact, personal qualities, honour, status and prestige for abstractions and contact is mediated by bureaucratic authorities. A shift 'from status to contract'.[35]

---

[31] Jennings 1997, especially p. 1.
[32] Teubner 1987, where he discusses the 'Juridification of social spheres'. Not a very intelligible or elegant word, 'juridification', but for want of an alternative it will have to do.
[33] Niezen 2010, p. 218–219.
[34] Weber 1973 (orig. 1917).
[35] Maine 1917 (orig. 1861), chapter V (*Primitive Society and Ancient Law*), line 101.

A SILENT LEGAL REVOLUTION?

Is this large-scale constitutional diffusion a by-product of a silent *legal* revolution? But what kind of revolution is this, we might wonder. Has it been documented, studied, analysed – do we know anything about it? Yes, we do know a little, but not all that much.[36] Studies into our increasing legal dependence are scarce,[37] even though it can be seen everywhere. The major fundamental legal theories about the law and its development are of little assistance. There are essentially only two main groups of fundamental theories about the law. The first group is the *phenomenological* group of theories, or analytic jurisprudence, as this group is commonly dubbed in legal scholarship. The second group consists of *natural law* theories. Phenomenological legal theory does not look at the phenomenon law from the vantage point of fundamental legal ideas or theories on the inner morality of law, but studies legal phenomena as they appear to us in positive sources of law. Analytical jurisprudence adopts an external point of view. It deals with law in statute books, court rulings, etcetera. In short: legal letters on paper. Many different things can be considered sources of law, like constitutions, statute laws, statutory instruments, orders, regulations, case law, legal literature, as well as customary law and legal principles etcetera. The list of legal sources is long and its outer bounds are controversial (do long-standing traditions or conventions constitute law, are recommendations by UN or Council of Europe committees' actual sources of law?). The *phenomenology* (the study of visible phenomena) we are most familiar with, from philosophers such as Husserl, Levinas and Derrida, does not consider it its task to establish causal relationships between the phenomena under examination, nor explain and consider them in the light of other grand theories. It restricts itself to observation, description and classification. This does not mean that their legal counterparts, such as the legal positivists, are mere 'superficial' observers uninterested in the outer bounds or in-depth inquiry. On the contrary: in the tradition of great legal theorists like Austin, Kelsen and Hart, legal positivists look for patterns in the legal system and try to tackle questions at the heart of the functioning of the law. They ask themselves fundamental questions like where does the force, authority and validity of the law come from? What legitimises the law's authority? How do the different sources of law relate? What is the function of the law and its prescripts? What does law intend, how does it work, what is its effect? Phenomenologists call these latter questions *intentionality* questions.

Legal phenomenology – or analytical jurisprudence – is counterposed by the natural law tradition and natural law theories. Natural law theorists assume that positive law reflects a greater idea, the will of a greater power, fundamental values or a truth. In their parlance: law is the expression of a *prepositive* order. This prepositive order may take many forms: a divine order, the law of the cosmos, a

---

[36] Niezen 2010; Pirie 2013.
[37] Teubner 1987.

'natural' order from an (imagined) primaeval or natural state, archetypical societies based social contracts, or resultant ideas about human nature, dignity and rights. The core of natural law theories always tries to assess the relative distance between the prepositive and positive order and on that basis posit the consequences. For instance, if a secular order drifts too far from the order established by god, then this can be determined and assessed as *not good*.

An illustrative, early example is that of the preamble of the Act of Abjuration by which provinces of the Habsburg Netherlands repudiated the authority of the Spanish King on 26 July 1581. They did so because they argued that the king had failed to obey his obligations under law stemming from the prepositive divine order:[38]

> As it is apparent to *all* that a prince is constituted by God to be ruler of a people, to defend them from oppression and violence as the shepherd his sheep; and whereas God did not create the people slaves to their prince, to obey his commands, whether right or wrong, but rather the prince for the sake of the subjects (without which he could be no prince), to govern them according to equity, to love and support them as a father his children or a shepherd his flock [...] And when he does not behave thus, but, on the contrary, oppresses them, seeking opportunities to infringe their ancient customs and privileges, exacting from them slavish compliance, then he is no longer a prince, but a tyrant, and the subjects are to consider him in no other view. And particularly when this is done deliberately, unauthorised by the states [general], they may not only disallow his authority, but legally proceed to the choice of another prince for their defence.

Heart-warming words which still seem to ring true. But these big words and grand legal theories offer scant help in coming to a true understanding of how law has evolved, how it functions and why we seem to have become more dependent on it. And they certainly do not tell us why there are now so many constitutions. Analytical jurisprudence and natural law theories alike are not well-suited to addressing questions on the actual purport and functioning of the law because they are largely self-referential: they try to understand and explain the law using arguments and reasoning drawn from the imagined order of the law. Theories like these are mainly the outcome of learned debates between legal insiders.

Memes?

Intra-legal explanations, like the ones underpinning constitutionalism – a branch of natural law theory – cannot fully account for the proliferation of constitutions. It is quite hard to fathom why the whole world would suddenly want to satisfy the demands of a prepositive order in the course of a few decades after failing to do so

---

[38] Cf. www.let.rug.nl/usa/documents/before-1600/plakkaat-van-verlatinghe-1581-july-26.php (last consulted on 8 February 2018), my italics. Cf. Congleton 2010, p. 201–202, and p. 418.

over thousands and thousands of years. That is why we ended up looking for more extra-legal explanations. But they are hardly conclusive either. There are many more constitutions than democracies, and constitutions seem to endure even when democracy is eroded or fails. And the proliferation of constitutions has certainly not kept pace with the development of markets or economic growth. An even greater shortcoming of these extra-legal explanations is that they hardly take any account of the normative character of constitutions, the law they express or the appeals to morality they make. This may be the key to the puzzle. Is there perhaps something in the message that constitutions convey that strikes a chord in all of us? Do we have an inherent sensitivity to them? Or did our constitutional aptitude gradually develop over time? Did constitutions cultivate their audiences over the course of history and instil a 'constitutional sense' in them. Did we gradually evolve into 'constitutional man', and have constitutions and the law they express become 'memes'? Not mere fads or ephemeral fashions, but long-lasting cultural concepts, ideas and institutions that are handed down (and honed) from generation to generation. Inherited like a 'cultural gene' as it were. Self-replicating units carrying cultural ideas like symbols, or practices, that are – even intergenerational – transmitted from one mind to another through writing, speech, gestures, rituals, or other imitable phenomena with a mimicked theme. Richard Dawkins, who formulated the concept, argues that memes, like genes, can work and replicate together as meme-complexes.[39] Mimetic transactions and transfers enable us to form complex ideas and images of reality – 'stories', 'imagined orders' – not just in and about the here and now, but over time (like life after death) and generations, and in a way that makes us believe these cultural appreciations of facts and relationships are 'objective', 'true' and 'real'. A self-reinforcing process of transferring and 'living' these concepts and ideas resulting in what the British-American academic Norman Schofield coined a 'belief cascade'.[40] The proliferation of constitutions might well be the result of mimetic mutations which may have made constitutions appealing to all kinds of countries and peoples over time, even to those previously lacking any such instrument.[41] It may even account for the fact that constitutions are now considered the 'normal' state of affairs and a standard for societies all over the world. The United States Declaration of Independence even expresses it as an obvious fact: 'We hold these truths to be *self-evident* [...]'

[39] Dawkins 2017 (orig. 1976); Dawkins 2009.

[40] Schofield 2002, p. 19.

[41] Ginsburg, Foti and Rockmore note that constitutions nowadays 'borrow' a great deal from each other, certainly when it comes to texts like 'we the people' in preambles. In a recent article they demonstrated that there are 'Memes in constitutions', that is: core components which are inherited like genetic material by other constitutions. Cf. Ginsburg, Foti & Rockmore 2014.

3

The Origin of Constitutions

The sets of fundamental rules on leadership and law we denote as 'constitutions' are in essence always about *us*. A constitution always *makes* a 'we' of some sort.[1] This is well reflected in probably the world's most famous constitutional preamble:

> We the People of the United States, in Order to form a more perfect Union [...]

A constitutional community's 'we' does not necessarily have to refer to an entire 'people', as is the case in the United States constitution. For example, the royal 'we'[2] in: 'We Carl, by the Grace of God, King of Sweden, the Goths, and the Wends [...] in the introduction of the Swedish Act of Succession',[3] or 'We, don Juan Carlos I, King of Spain, announce [...] that the Cortes have passed and the Spanish people have ratified the following Constitution',[4] or in 'We Willem-Alexander, by the grace of God, King of the Netherlands, Prince of Orange-Nassau [...]' appearing in the opening words of every Dutch parliamentary act refers to the 'we' of a community united under the government of a monarch appointed by God. The 'we' in the constitution of classical Athens referred to yet another community – that of the male citizens of the city state. The content of the 'we' in constitutional communities varies, but it is always present – explicitly or implicitly. Another common trait of all constitutions is the expression of a morality system of basic norms in a legal system and leadership (political) system in the community proclaimed as 'we'. Norms on who should do what for

---

[1] It constitutes us rhetorically, as Yarran Hominh observes. To his mind, the words of a constitution form – what J.L. Austin has called – 'a "performative utterance", i.e., words that not only just *say* something, but also *do* something'. Hominh 2014, p. 42–43 and p. 64; Much in the same vein, Mark Tushnet conceives constitutions as self-creating narratives: 'The narrative of the people of the United States must be a constitutional narrative. But, I think, not just any constitutional narrative. We are self-creating, and so have the power to reconstitute ourselves at will.' Tushnet 1997, p. 1559.

[2] This form of referral is called the majestic plural (pluralis majestatis).

[3] Of 1810. In a literal translation: 'The 1810 order of succession'.

[4] From the preamble of the Spanish Constitution of 1978.

the community and – in return – what may the community expect of its members? And, of course: who is – or are – in charge of this community? Every human group of any size has or had constitutions of this kind, constitutive agreements to shape and coordinate large-scale cooperation.[5] Their norms and rules have not always been written down or unified in a single document, but this does not mean that they are absent. They have always been present, being essential for large-scale human cooperation. It is nearly impossible for us to do otherwise – it is how *we* are.

The fundamental rules establishing legal and leadership systems (political systems)[6] in modern constitutions are primarily concerned with the 'we' of state-based societies. A state-based society entails a group of people living within the boundaries of a 'state' who in principle – according to the global community's world order[7] – are entitled to govern themselves without outside interference (sovereignty). This does not mean that there were no constitutions before states in the modern sense of the word came into being. That the fundamental rules that pre-state-based societies used to set up and enforce their legal or political systems were not usually called a constitution, does not mean that they were not constitutions. And it certainly does not mean that they are not worth studying just because they do not happen to be called or identified as such. Using a modern conception of constitutions to look back at history and concluding that there is nothing to see indicates myopia and perhaps even narrow-mindedness. If one wants to understand how constitutions work, and what their meaning and power is, then one has to examine their origins. Their roots extend much farther back in time than to the end of the eighteenth century when the first modern constitutions emerged in the United States, France and Poland. For a proper understanding of the constitutional phenomenon, one needs to turn to prehistory, the dawn of humankind, to find the origins of human communities' need to organise themselves according to fundamental and abstract normative principles. Understanding constitutions entails understanding human nature.

WHO ARE 'WE'?

Who are 'we'?[8] That is, of course, a perennial question, encompassing much more than the constitutional 'we' alone. The key to the human 'we' can be found in human evolution. We, *Homo sapiens*, are the product of several evolutionary revolutions.[9]

---

[5]   Cf. Wittington 2008, p. 282. Dicey 1889, p. 140 (CXL).

[6]   'Constitutions work by constraining, constructing and constituting politics', according to Mark Graber. The proclamation and organisation of a legal system is a part of this, particularly the constraint component. Graber 2013, p. 215.

[7]   Including the *Charter of the United Nations* and the official ('authoritative') interpretations of it, recognising the right to self-determination.

[8]   MacGregor 2018, p. XXI.

[9]   The Cognitive Revolution, the Agricultural Revolution and the Scientific Revolution. Harari 2011, p. 3.

The first of these was the Cognitive Revolution. Modern humans began to develop about 200,000 years ago,[10] evolving in East Africa, but probably also in North Africa and maybe even in the Middle East. About 130,000 years ago,[11] the first primitive 'knowing' or 'thinking' humans began to emerge: *Homo sapiens*. They spread to almost all corners of the earth from about 70,000 years BCE. *Homo sapiens* had found an evolutionary niche and mostly this happens at the expense of other species. In our case, Neanderthals were probably the greatest casualty, but we outcompeted other species too.[12] How did humankind become so successful? Is it because we learnt to control fire, were inventive and devised tools like bows, arrows, knives and spears with which to hunt? Because we learnt to cook and stay warm by wearing clothes, or – above all – because we could communicate efficiently with each other by creating sound patterns which together constituted a language? Other human species, like our cousins the Neanderthals, had these abilities too. No, there was a single unique feature which gave *Homo sapiens* a decisive advantage, enabling it to settle and stand its ground anywhere; Sapiens can communicate, plan[13] and collaborate in a way no other species can. While all other living creatures are restricted to the physical world and in principle can only communicate about it (if they can communicate at all), we 'knowing humans' can talk about things *outside* the physical world.[14] For example, the character of someone not present – an acquaintance, family member or ancestor – or fairly imperceptible patterns and relationships, like the combination of water and sun which eventually makes seeds germinate. Or that friction and sparks create fire, that roasting and boiling food increases one's chances of survival, or that bison migration has a pattern. Apart from reality, we can communicate about abstractions – spirits, drawings, images and stories – and we can also make all kinds of predictions about

---

[10] It is generally assumed that *Homo sapiens* developed from *Homo ergaster* (East Africa and the Middle East) and its Asian offshoot, *Homo erectus*. This development was probably not very linear. There is much we do not know about the early development of the species we now call *Homo sapiens*. A great deal of research is still being done into the many unanswered questions, especially in the period between 300,000 and 150,000 years ago.

[11] Richter, Grün, Joannes-Boyau, Steele, Amani, Rué, Fernandes, Raynal, Geraards, Ben-Ncer, Hublin & McPherron 2017. There are even indications and theories that *Homo sapiens* developed earlier (around 230,000–200,000 years ago) and left Africa much earlier.

[12] The success of *Homo sapiens* had a dark side, causing ecological disasters long before our era. In Australia alone, about 95% of the large animals went extinct within a few thousand years of the arrival of humans around 45,000 years ago. Even before the Neolithic Revolution really got started (12,000 years ago), sapiens had eradicated about half of all mammalian species worldwide. Miller, Fogel, Magee, Gagan, Clarke & Johnson 2005. Cf. Barnosky, Koch, Feranec, Wing & Shabel 2004, and Harari 2016, p. 72–75.

[13] The human brain is able to 'look into the future', or at least use knowledge of the past and present to make relatively reliable predictions about the future.

[14] Harari 2016, p. 149: 'Sapiens rule the world because only they can weave an intersubjective web of meaning: a web of laws, forces, entities and places that exist purely in their common imagination.' This is a very short summary of what Pinker says on the subject in Pinker 2009, particularly chapters 4 (*The Mind's Eye*), 5 (*Good ideas*) and 8 (*The Meaning of Life*); Gottschall 2012, p. 18 (the paragraph on *The Story People*) and his chapter 6 (*The Mind is a Storyteller*).

each other's reliability in the context of cooperation.[15] Trust has been an essential element on humankind's evolutionary path. Trusting others, or the future, enables specialisation. 'Go and find grains and berries. Collect wood and look after the fire. Trust me, I will defend the tribe and lead the hunt. I can ask the ancestors, who want me at this place, how to do so. Let me train and guide you; take care of me and I will take care of you. Together we will honour our ancestors and the spirits around us. And you, Shaman, drive off the forest spirits that make our children sick, tend to our wounds and tell us when to sow.' Or any variant to this formula.[16]

Specialisation, in turn, makes collective planning[17] and coordinated action possible on a truly spectacular scale. Mutual trust is the indispensable key to 'standing firm together'. Just imagine you spent all your time examining the stars or talking to the spirits in the forest, and the hunters in your tribe one day decided to banish you as a 'profiteer'. What if the group suddenly decided it had had enough of the grain storage pots you spun when you could have been out hunting? Specialising when in a group whose members you cannot trust is suicidal in the long term. The ability to 'blindly' trust each other was perhaps the biggest step humankind made – being smart on your own is no use to you at all. During the Cognitive Revolution (approximately 70,000 to 40,000 years ago),[18] our brain developed into something a little like a three-stage mental rocket. With, first, the ability to create abstract, imaginary representations and link them to present and past realities, second, communicating about this with others, and third, using this communication to measure each other's trustworthiness, enabling specialisation and improving group collaboration.[19]

These new abilities were the starting point for a second major revolution: the Neolithic Revolution. Starting around 12,000 years ago, humankind gradually exchanged its ancient, nomadic hunter-gatherer existence for a sedentary peasant life. This new phase in which we primarily cultivated and reared food instead of hunting and gathering was a consequence of our new mental faculties and not of a culturally or politically determined choice. This can be inferred from the fact that the Neolithic Revolution took place almost everywhere in the world,[20] and that an agrarian existence was essentially a step backwards. As individuals, farmers

[15] Also known as the 'gossip theory'. This theory assumes that our language, which offers so many ways of expressing abstract notions and relationships between them, developed primarily from the need to share information about each other's reliability – also in each other's absence. Reliability (reputation) and trust are the core of human cooperation. Cf. Wu, Balliet and Van Lange 2016; Dunbar 1996; Harari 2011, p. 26 ff.

[16] MacGregor 2018, chapter 1 (*The Beginnings of Belief*).

[17] Some animal species also appear to plan, for example, by stockpiling food, hibernating or migrating. But these behaviours require little 'reflection'. They are biologically motivated behaviours – instincts – and not the outcome of cognitive processes.

[18] Our brain changed over the course of our evolution. Biological and neurological changes occurred in the brain's size, disposition, functioning and pattern. Cf. Aiello 1996.

[19] The biological (neurological) and cultural process are therefore essentially conjoined. Cf. Deacon 1997.

[20] Cf. (Jared) Diamond 2005, p. 85 ff.; Roberts & Westad 2014, p. 34–39; Harari 2011, p. 87 ff.

had a harder time and survival was more difficult than in a hunter-gatherer life-style. Archaeological finds show that farmers had shorter lives and were less well-nourished and healthy than hunter-gatherers.[21] Yet, almost all of humanity switched to agriculture.[22] How come? It was certainly not the case that depletion of natural resources forced us to switch. No, we 'got caught' in this new peasant life, so to speak; it was rather like a snare snapping shut.[23] While domesticating plants and animals and the first settlements, starting about 12,000 years ago, was attractive on the short term as it brought simple and abundant supplies of food, it came at a high price. Sedentary agriculture and pastoralism demanded greater specialisation and constant attention and time – you cannot just leave your crops or flock. An agricultural existence is very labour-intensive;[24] people are not well suited to this in evolutionary terms.[25] For hundreds of thousands of years, our bodies were attuned to a hunter-gatherer existence, involving the occasional run but predominantly lazing about and strolling around – not toiling from dawn to dusk come rain or shine. This Neolithic Revolution – 'History's Biggest Fraud'[26] in the words of Harari – had para-doxical effects. There were mainly disadvantages for individuals, including all kinds of new diseases, privation, and a shorter lifespan partly thanks to the backbreaking labour; for groups however, the transition to an agricultural existence brought many benefits. The scale of operation increased in all areas. The greater food surplus increased the birth rate, and the enlarged group made even more specialisation pos-sible, resulting in more inventions and collective power, which could be utilised to expand control of the surrounding area and dominate or drive off other species and groups of people. This benefit came with a catch: there was no turning back once over the threshold of the Neolithic Revolution.[27] Not only was the group's lifestyle

---

[21] Cf. (James C.) Scott 2017 for a convincing demythologisation of the almost unstoppable 'rise-of-civilization' story after the Neolithic (Agrarian) Revolution and human health after the Neolithic Revolution, particularly p. 10.

[22] Cf. Van Schaik & Michel 2016, p. 17 ff.; (James C.) Scott 2017, p. 37–68; Harari 2011, p. 87.

[23] Cf. (Jared) Diamond 2005, p. 105–106. He concludes that agricultural food production prob-ably 'evolved' as a by-product of unrelated decisions made by hunter-gatherers, without them being aware of the consequences, let alone having the ability to control them.

[24] Aptly described in the Bible as: 'In the sweat of thy face shalt thou eat bread, till thou return unto the ground' *Genesis* 3:19 (KJV). Carel van Schaik and Kai Michel tried to prove in their book that many Biblical stories in the Old Testament are, in fact, reactions to the prob-lematic transition from a hunter-gatherer to an agrarian society. This Neolithic Revolution was a cultural quantum leap for humankind, for which the species was poorly biologically equipped. They regard the Bible as an aid – a crutch – which helps people with this adjust-ment. Cf. Van Schaik & Michel 2016, p. 17 ff.

[25] Cf. Van Schaik & Michel 2016, p. 17–25, especially p. 20–21.

[26] Harari 2011, p. 87. Van Schaik and Michel speak of 'The worst mistake in the history of the human race'. Van Schaik & Michel 2016, p. 5 ff.

[27] Reverting from an agrarian to a hunter-gatherer lifestyle is technically possible, and has occurred in human history, but is the exception. Jared Diamond demonstrates in his book *The World Until Yesterday* how altered relationships after the Neolithic Revolution made it almost impossible for groups to revert to a previous, 'paradisiacal' hunter-gatherer lifestyle. First, there is the issue of habituation – someone who has been a farmer for a long time

transformed, but individual members' relations to the group were profoundly transformed too. Abstract concepts like ownership and property came into existence,
and new forms of leadership emerged which further improved coordination of the
expanding group's activities (as well as defence against other groups).

The Leap over Dunbar's Number

As hunter-gatherers, people lived in small groups of about 20 to 50 people, who
were mostly family members. That was approximately the natural maximum size. A
group with more than 50 members becomes immobile; and it is difficult to maintain any kind of specialisation (hunting, cooking, foraging, child rearing) with less
than 20 members. A semi-sedentary existence, as many groups lived between 15,000
and 9500 BCE,[28] enables somewhat larger groups – for example, in a loose coalition
of intermittently cooperating (familial) groups. This gradual aggregation of groups
could have had various causes: exchanging goods, 'dating', intermarriage, shelter-
ing against the elements together,[29] but above all, defending and distributing stocks
and mutual defence.[30] We call these new enlarged groups 'tribes'. Initially relatively
small and bound by family ties (clans), these tribes grew steadily from 12,000 BCE.
This was partly due to a chain reaction: a larger tribe is better able to specialise
and also has numerical superiority in conflicts with other tribes. To defend yourself
from an attacking or raiding tribe you needed your own tribe, preferably bigger and
better organised than the attacker. Failing to do so probably spelled doom. In that
time strangers were certainly not given the benefit of the doubt, as possible new
best friends. We know from historical and contemporary anthropological research
that tribes are usually hostile towards one another – and when it comes down to it,
murderously so.[31] Members not only protect each other, but also claim and protect a

probably stands to lose possessions in a reversion and has probably also lost several of the
core skills needed to successfully survive in the wild. These are only the individual obstacles;
what renders reversion almost impossible is repression. Farmers appropriated land during
the Neolithic Revolution, reducing hunter-gatherers' territories. The increasing dependency
caused by specialisation (in our modern society only 2% of the population is engaged in
agriculture) makes a reversion very difficult. Diamond 2012, chapter 1 (*Friends, Enemies,
Strangers, and Traders*), especially p. 10 ff., chapter 11 (*Salt, Sugar, Fat, and Sloth*) and
Epilogue.
[28] Semi-nomadic groups have existed ever since – even today. (Jared) Diamond 2005, p. 106.
[29] As many as 400 to 500 people at the same time used to live in the Palaeolithic caves that were
discovered in Southern France.
[30] Cf. (Jared) Diamond 2005, p. 90.
[31] Jared Diamond demonstrates how territorial hunter-gatherers are and their hostile reaction to
neighbours and strangers. Diamond 2012, chapter 1 (*Friends, Enemies, Strangers, and Traders*).
Steven Pinker also points out that prehistoric nomadic groups and tribes were aggressive and
violent, in contrast to the idyllic ideas we sometimes have of them now. If anything, millen-
niums of civilisation have made us more peaceful. There has been a staggering decline in the
rates of violent deaths between prehistoric times and the present. Pinker 2011, p. 1–4 and p.
36–58.

specific territory[32] – they are territorial – and have little time for strangers. The emergence of tribes may not be much more than a side effect of the Neolithic Revolution, but it turned the whole way humans live together on its head: it literally short circuited our minds. In the hundreds of thousands of years of our hunter-gatherer existence, our brain developed the qualities required by an admittedly 'smart' but social animal to survive in a group of 20 to 50 family members. In these hunter-gatherer groups everyone was in principle equal, relationships were egalitarian, individual property did not exist (even though they were hardly hippie communes), collective protection (or flight) was simple to organise, and existential risks could be reasonably assessed. The potentially life-threatening risk of over-specialisation and excessive altruism could be obviated by the increasingly effective – that is, smart – exchange of information about each other's reliability through language, mental representation and (symbolic) communication. In the same way evolution did not equip our bodies for an agrarian lifestyle, it did not biologically fit out our brain to maintain stable social relationships in very large groups. The brain can only muster seamless cooperation with up to 148 people at a time. This cognitive-neurological limit – Dunbar's number – was established in the 1990s by the British anthropologist Robin Dunbar.[33] He calculated the maximum number of stable social relationships that our brain can process.[34] People can, of course, *know* more than 148 people, and even maintain relatively close relations with a certain 'intimacy' with them. Nowadays, we have hundreds of contacts on Facebook and LinkedIn and you can easily have hundreds of friends in a fraternity or sport club – but the Dunbar number is not about non-committal contacts of this kind. It refers to the maximum number of social contacts that you can handle in a group in which you literally live together all day.[35] You cannot just walk away from a group in which you share everything and you have to invest a great deal in the other members for reasons of self-preservation. A group upon which your survival depends. What is then the maximum number of members and related network of information exchange you can blindly rely on? In this light, 148 appears rather as a quite large number. If a group grows any larger, beyond the 148-mark, you will need 'something' to be able to keep trusting other group members whose behaviour you will not always be able to predict accurately as you grow less well acquainted with them. Cheating and distrust can easily become fatal for specialised group collaboration. Something transcendent helps – a common belief, religion, law or the like. Collective belief in abstractions of this kind can create stable mutual, 'artificial' trust in a group, even when it is no longer possible to maintain contact physically because of the size of the group.[36]

---

32   (Jared) Diamond 2012, p. 37–76.
33   Dunbar 1992 and Dunbar 1993, especially p. 686–687 on the number itself.
34   That is, the number of relationships that can be maintained intensively enough for there still to be *intimacy*. Dunbar 1998; Dunbar 1993.
35   Dunbar 1998.
36   Dávid-Barret and Dunbar 2013, p. 3–4.

Tribes usually have more than 148 members, which represents a possible problem from a neurobiological perspective. For individuals, tribes are potentially disadvantageous: there are fewer people one knows, more strangers, more danger, more aggression and violence, and less 'blind' trust. Why then did tribes come into existence? Most likely because greater large-scale cooperation gives groups competitive advantages and our mental abilities enable us to simulate trust: we can artificially make individuals overcome their fear of the unknown and strangers. As every individual has the power of imagination – the capacity for abstract and symbolic representation – and is able to communicate about it, we can imagine things beyond the physical world ('tomorrow', 'future', 'value', 'gods', 'structure of relationships'), which we can collectively believe in.[37] We can derive meaning, faith and confidence from these shared abstractions and they, in turn, can serve as the foundation of even better cooperation.[38]

EVERYTHING IS ABOUT TRUST

It is no wonder then that the first *fiduciary institutions* emerged with the formation of tribes. As set out above, abstractions such as religion, law, property, contract, etcetera and the sets of values, norms and behavioural patterns related to them, enable us to have 'artificial' trust and cooperate on a scale transcending our biological limits. No other living creature shares this capacity. Ant colonies may be large and cooperate extremely effectively, but several ant colonies cannot work together as a single super colony, any more than other social animals can escape their biological limitations.[39] People can. This is the secret of our species' success, according to evolutionary biologist Joseph Henrich: 'in the *collective brains* of our communities.'[40]

Increasing Scale

The increasing scale of human cooperation some 15,000 years ago was driven by its own dynamics.[41] Tribe formation meant that tribes had to expand into larger tribes; larger tribes had to organise themselves better to defend themselves from other groups

---

[37] We are as much 'Homo fictus' as 'Homo sapiens' according to Gottschall. Cf. Gottschall 2013, p. 4; MacGregor 2018, p. 10–11.

[38] Cf. Fukuyama 2011, p. 43.

[39] '[…] animals cannot maintain the cohesion and integrity of groups larger than a size fixed by the information-processing capacity of their neocortex.' Dunbar 1993, p. 681.

[40] Henrich 2016, p. 5.

[41] A process that Jared Diamond calls 'amalgamation'. 'Amalgamation occurs', Diamond argues, '[…] in either two ways: by merger under the threat of external force, or by actual conquest.' It is never a case of unthreatened groups joining of their own free will – this assertion is underpinned by the archaeological evidence. 'Contrary to Rousseau, such amalgamations never occur by a process of unthreatened little societies, freely deciding to merge, in order to promote the happiness of their citizens.' Diamond 2005 (orig. 1997), p. 289.

with further improvements to labour allocation and division. Over time this led to the development of *chiefdoms*, large groups working together under a more or less permanent leadership.[42] The need for even greater social stability and better (competitive) control over the natural environment subsequently impelled chiefdoms, in turn, to grow into kingships (or other forms of hereditary leadership), whence the first 'states' later arose, in which personal leadership of a group within a territory became more or less a function and leadership could ultimately also exercised by various (abstract) offices.[43] This line of political development is almost inexorable.[44] The Neolithic Revolution set forces in motion which forced humankind into political (leadership) organisation, resulting in a chain reaction of ever greater and more hierarchical forms of human cooperation. 'The necessity of politics' as political scientist Francis Fukuyama refers to this process. Although this development has not always been linear and history has a winding course, with exceptions and moments of 'relapse', it is unquestionably the common thread in the history of human societies. This history elucidates where the now ubiquitous 'state-based' societal form comes from.[45]

The almost automatic increase in scale of human cooperation is a fixed pattern in world history.[46] It happens everywhere.[47] Nowadays, only a few small groups still live as hunter-gatherers or in tribes, mostly in remote areas.[48] Larger, better organised groups generally outperform smaller, less organised ones.[49] The increasing scaling of human cooperation – at least this is the contention of much recent literature – is not just a consequence of individuals' or collectivities' will or strategy, but of a process chiefly driven by *external* factors.[50]

The fact that external factors effect greater scale does not mean that individual members of these ever-larger groups simply accepted their new fates. If the members of the new enlarged group had not seen, collectively, the added value of it or had not believed in it, then they would have certainly dispensed with it or withdrawn themselves from it.[51] Internal factors such as conviction and group feeling determine a

---

[42] As Scott demonstrates, this is not an evolutionary law, but rather a sort of social chain reaction triggered by external circumstances. (James C.) Scott 2017 (summarised in the paragraph *Thumbnail Itinerary*), p. 17 ff.

[43] The evolutionary scheme of humanity's socio-political development from groups of hunter-gatherers to tribes, then to chiefdoms and kingships and later to states has been considered the standard development since the publication of Elman Service's book *Primitive Social Organization*. Cf. Service 1976.

[44] Fukuyama 2011, Part I and II.

[45] (James C.) Scott 2017.

[46] (Jared) Diamond 2005 (orig. 1997), Part II and Part IV.

[47] (Jared) Diamond 2005 (orig. 1997). (Jared) Diamond 2012, p. 10–12.

[48] (Jared) Diamond 2012, *ibid.*

[49] Pinker says on this: 'People in all cultures feel that they are members of a group (a band, tribe, clan, or nation) and feel animosity toward other groups', Pinker 2009, p. 509; Keeley 1996.

[50] Cf. Service 1975.

[51] Scott argues that we humans, like plants and animals, have been 'domesticated' in our evolutionary process by our new, larger-scale forms of cooperation. (James C.) Scott 2017, p. 37–67.

group's continuity and strength. Members of tribes, chiefdoms or kingdoms must have been constantly cajoled to participate at the start of the Neolithic Revolution: they would have to have been continuously tempted and enticed to join such an essentially unnatural form of cooperation. Their default mindsets inclined them to renege; this made prehistoric societies quite unstable. In his book *Against the Grain*, James Scott shows how vulnerable the first states in Mesopotamia actually were and how relatively complex organised societies often collapsed and regressed to more primitive forms of collective cooperation.[52] Establishing and maintaining greater scales of human cooperation requires a durable, shared belief in its added value ('social capital'),[53] as well as members' mutual trust. Although we are not naturally able to do so, as has been outlined, we can trust people we are not acquainted with and strangers through artificial constructions, such as by constructing artificial 'families'. A religious or legal community enables you to predict other members' behaviour and establish their trustworthiness without necessarily having to know an individual member well. Trust is essential. It liberates you from having to look over your shoulder all the time, and as a rule you can be sure that tasks you have entrusted to others will actually be carried out. Trust reduces uncertainty and fear and promotes efficient collaboration.[54]

How Does Trust Work?

The importance of trust to human cooperation can hardly be overestimated: it is the foundation of coordinated large-scale human cooperation in tribes, chiefdoms, kingships and empires and, later, in states.[55] Trust is the cornerstone enabling us to cooperate on a large scale in ways far exceeding our neural capacity.[56] It is important, but also very fragile; trust might be the basis of a basically rational and strategic decision to cooperate better, but modern cognitive science has also demonstrated that it is closely linked in our brain to deep emotions such as fear, anger, sadness, joy, surprise, etcetera.; We all have very strong emotions and reactions when we are lied to or when we are deceived – something seems

---

[52] (James C.) Scott 2017, chapter 6 (Fragility of the Early State: Collapse and Disassembly), p. 183–218.

[53] Cf. Putnam 1995a and Putnam 1995b.

[54] Luhmann says on this: '[Trust] serves to surmount an element of uncertainty in the behaviour of other people which is experienced as the unpredictability of change in object. In so far as the need for complexity grows, and in so far as the other person enters the picture both as *alter ego* and as fellow-author of this complexity and of its reduction, trust has to be extended, and the original unquestionable familiarity of the world pushed back, although it cannot be eliminated completely.' Luhmann 2017 (Orig. 1973 & 1975), p. 25.

[55] Or as Solomon and Flores put it, with a nod to Thomas Hobbes: 'Without trust the corporation becomes not a community but a brutish state of nature, a war of all against all in which employment tends to be nasty, brutish, and short.' Solomon and Floris 2001, p. 5.

[56] Weber and Carter point out 'that trust is a foundational orientation between self and other.' Weber & Carter 2002, p. VII.

to really 'break' (hence 'broken trust') and it takes a long time to heal. 'For trust not him that hath once broken faith', William Shakespeare has Lady Gray say in *King Henry VI*.[57] It holds true. Broken trust results in panic-stricken reactions, emotional hurt, anger and even rage. This relates to the various aspects of trust. On the one hand, it has an *affective* dimension – the moral-emotional expectation that trust will be honoured and the belief that this is *proper* and *right* and, on the other hand, a *cognitive* dimension – the *calculated* expectation that trust will be honoured and the benefits associated with it will follow.[58] Affective trust is also needed for cognitive trust to work.[59] A leader you do not trust, a group where you do not feel at home, an exchange market you cannot rely on or even a lack of faith in the future (for example, 'declining consumer confidence') can make durable cooperation falter. That is why corruption is so detrimental to societies and political systems: it feeds a sense of a lack of trust, which impedes cognitive trust.[60] Trust contributes to the social capital[61] needed for large-scale cooperation.[62] Its presence pays dividends politically, economically and on many other fronts.[63] But you cannot simply conjure it up.[64]

However important and necessary trust in others may be, it is always a precarious and uncertain undertaking. It is essentially not much more than an optimistic prediction of other people's future behaviour – and more than anything an expectation of a favourable outcome for you.[65] But, of course, you will never know for sure what the future holds or what is really going on in someone else's mind. Your heart skips a beat in anticipation – trust is not just a calculation of probability. It is also a bit of a game of poker in which you have to guess an opponent's hand while your racing hormones, rather like screaming infants, throw you out of focus and prevent you from making the most 'rational' assessment. For emotions (anger, fear, sadness,

---

[57] William Shakespeare, *Henry VI*, 1591. Part 3, Act 4, scene 4:31.

[58] Cf. Cross 2005, especially p. 1461–1471.

[59] Cross 2005, p. 1468–1475. Affective confidence responses even precede cognitive responses (by a few milliseconds). Cf. Theiss-Morse & Barton 2017, especially p. 171.

[60] Cf. Uslaner 2017, p. 303 and p. 313.

[61] According to Robert Putnam's definition, *social capital* consists of 'features of social organisation such as networks, norms and social trust that facilitate coordination and cooperation for mutual benefit'. Putnam 1995a, p. 67; Putnam 1995b; cf. Fukuyama 2001, p. 479–480 and p. 494.

[62] Cross 2005, p. 1475–1483 and p. 1543–5144.

[63] Knack and Keefer 1997.

[64] Weber and Carter 2004, p. 154–159.

[65] Frank Cross developed a generic definition of trust. He says it comes down to: '[…] belief, attitude, or expectation concerning the likelihood that the actions or outcomes of another individual, group or organisation will be acceptable or will serve the actor's interests.' This incorporates most elements of the literature on trust from the past 40 years. Cross 2005, p. 1461. Uslaner contends that 'the decision to trust another person is essentially *strategic*,' but it has a moral dimension as well. 'Moralistic trust is a moral commandment to treat people *as if* they were trustworthy. The central idea behind moralistic trust is that most people share your fundamental moral values.' Uslaner 2008, p. 102.

happiness etcetera)[66] are inescapable biochemical reactions in your body,[67] largely beyond your control (see Chapter 24).[68] Trust is far from easy, even if you are not of a mistrustful predisposition. Trusting means surrendering control of something or someone without knowing exactly how things will turn out.[69] A representative who makes a purchase for you, someone who agrees to bake a loaf of bread for you if you give them part of your harvest, a leader who says he will protect your family if you provide services and pay taxes – situations beyond your control in which you no longer directly conduct all your own affairs. Of course, you trust to achieve or acquire things that would otherwise be out of your reach. Dependence on others and uncertainty about their trustworthiness[70] is part of the bargain.[71] Trust pays: it enables us to reach beyond our biological limits, take reasoned risks, make predictions which help us prepare for the future[72] and it contributes to economic growth and prosperity.[73]

Nature lends a helping hand when making these predictions. We are equipped with a series of neurological measuring instruments which enable us to estimate the reliability of people, things and situations; a system of pumps and valves, neurotransmitters and firing neurons in our bodies can incite our willingness to cooperate, but can, in an instant, just as easily arrest our willingness to cooperate and

---

[66] It is usually assumed that there are eight basic emotions: love, fear, joy, rage, anguish, surprise, shame and disgust. Cf. for more Levenson 1994, p. 123–126. Levenson assumes (like Ekman) that these emotions are innate products of human evolution. He is not alone in this belief, but not everyone is convinced. For what can be considered a basic emotion cf.: Ekman 1999.

[67] Our brain enables us – as social animals – to trust and measure others' trustworthiness; this capacity is also embedded in our brain's neurobiological structure. The flow of messages to the control room is largely automatic – through biochemical, hormonal reactions in our body. A number of studies have shown that, for example, the substance oxytocin (the 'love hormone') can cause changes in trust. Kosfeld, Heinrichs, Zak, Fischbacher & Fehr 2005. The Leiden professor of social and organisational psychology Carsten De Dreu and others have shown that oxytocin not only promotes cooperation, but also has a conflict-generating effect in certain cases. Oxytocin can cause members of a group to no longer want to cooperate (and hence cause a decrease in trust) so that they can defend vulnerable members of a group. Defiant group members exhibit this kind of defensive, protective (competitive) behaviour even when their self-interest is not at stake. One could call it minority protection on a hormonal-neurological level. De Dreu, Shalvi, Greer, Van Kleef & Handgraaf 2012.

[68] Dunn nicely juxtaposes these two aspects of trust: 'Trust is both a human passion and a modality of human action – a more or less consciously chosen policy for handling the freedom of other human agents or agencies. As a passion, a sentiment, it can be evanescent or durable. But as a modality of action it is essentially concerned coping with uncertainty over time.' Dunn 1990, chapter 3 *Trust and Political Agency*, especially p. 26.

[69] Barbalet 2009.

[70] Cf. Hardin 2002.

[71] Barbalet 2009.

[72] Cf. Luhmann 2017, p. 12–13, p. 17 and p. 27–29.

[73] Among other things because it lowers transaction costs (see Chapter 22). Nooteboom 2002, p. 103–108. Cf. Casson & Della Giusta 2006.

make us outrightly hostile.[74] And even though we have the ability to trust strangers, we do have to overcome many hurdles of suspicion and hesitation before we can cooperate with them.

As outlined above, people can use their imagination to help them rely on strangers, as well as unknown situations or entities. The human imagination enables us to invent things, share them and so create – reassuring and confidence-building – intersubjective realities.[75] These representations are sometimes of non-existent things, which nevertheless can be experienced collectively as being *real* and *true*.[76] This may include things like the will of the gods, the value of things, the meaning of events and representations – ideas on how we should live, how we should behave towards each other, our dues to society etcetera. Fiduciary institutions such as ownership, property, leadership as well as offices, contracts, money, marriage, edicts and the like enable us to literally make *leaps of faith*[77] and do things with outcomes we cannot assess beforehand and put trust in strangers in ways that extend beyond our biological limits.[78] Historically, it has always been difficult to tell cause from effect: did fiduciary institutions enable the Neolithic Revolution, or were they the (necessary) consequence of it? We will probably never know the full answer, but we do know that the Neolithic Revolution turned our existence upside down.[79] Everything changed, as did we.[80]

THE ETERNAL STRUGGLE FOR RECOGNITION

It is not in isolation that people weigh up the opportunities for cooperation in a group: most of all, we want to *belong*. As much as we may like seeing ourselves as independent individuals, never under the yoke of group morality, who decide for ourselves whether or not we join a group; as free-spirited and autonomous beings who decide for ourselves with whom and under what conditions we join a political community, that is not how we really are.[81] People are social animals through and

---

[74] When we lack or lose trust, a downward spiral of suspicion quickly takes hold, which is not easy to reverse. Harth & Regner 2017.

[75] Searle 1995, p. 1–5 and p. 31–34. Harari 2016, p. 150.

[76] Saler 2001, especially p. 54–55 on 'disposition theory'. Saler cites Ward Goodenough's definition of *faith*: 'propositions that people accept as true'.

[77] Möllering 2006, chapter 5, p. 105 ff.

[78] This is a considerable mental leap. For this reason, Chorvat and MacCabe also define trust as: 'the willingness to behave in such a way that only makes sense if you believe that others will reciprocate any benefits to you extended to them', Chorvat & McCabe 2006, p. 117–118.

[79] (James C.) Scott 2017.

[80] (Jared) Diamond 2002.

[81] Fukuyama says on this: 'there was *never* a period in human evolution when human beings existed as isolated individuals [...] Human beings do not enter into society and political life as a result of conscious, rational decision. Communal organisation comes to them naturally, though the specific ways they cooperate are shaped by environment, ideas, and culture.' Fukuyama 2011, p. 30.

through – we cannot live without each other. The social element of our existence is wired deep into our brain.[82] Like an invisible magnet, it draws us together and looks for groups to join. It may seem as though a group is constituted of a collection of individuals, but the group makes the individual in equal measure. Who or what an individual is and the role he or she plays in a community is largely determined by the community he or she belongs to. Individuality, like citizenship or maturity, is a *quality* that a community (such as a state) bestows on an individual member.[83] This notion runs counter to our heart-felt free-spirited individualism. Are we not all 'born free and equal in dignity and rights' – as the Universal Declaration of Human Rights proclaims – are not all men special and unique? Surely it is because of the special nature of our individuality, our *uniqueness*, that entitles us to our dignity and rights?

This is all fine and well, but the fact remains that we cannot really survive on our own. We always need help from others in some form or another.[84] There are, of course, lots of romantic stories about lonely survivors like Robinson Crusoe,[85] the Count of Monte-Cristo,[86] and their more recent counterparts Sylvester Stallone as Rambo[87] or Tom Hanks in the film *Cast Away*. Individuals who survive in harsh conditions all alone. Most appealing. The modern reader and viewer take home the message of an individual's impressive survival capacity. Yet, Crusoe would probably not have survived alone on his island in the South Pacific for long, if only because of the long-term mental effects of isolation. *Cast Away*, filmed in 2000, portrays this fairly realistically. Total isolation makes you go as mad as a March hare, it gradually drives people 'round the bend' – to the point that they experience a certain mental numbness and debilitation. And what about Rambo then? Well, in all fairness, he was, of course, a little unhinged even before his adventure started.

Ostracism

We might be able to 'survive' total isolation for a while, but it is not really 'living'.[88] We find social exclusion particularly unbearable – we are all extremely sensitive to it. Social exclusion – referred to as *ostracism* in academic literature – causes phantom pain in the same part of our brain where physical pain originates and is registered: we experience the pain of exclusion as real pain.[89] Whereas physical pain

---

[82] In the neocortex predominantly. Williams & Nida 2011, especially p. 73.

[83] Cf. (C.M.) Turnbull 1992.

[84] Pinker says on this: '[...] bands, clans, tribes, and other social groups are central to human existence and have been so as long as we have been a species.' Pinker 2003, p. 285.

[85] Daniel Dafoe 1719.

[86] Alexandre Dumas 1844.

[87] From 1982.

[88] Cf. Brennan & Buchanan 1985, p. 1–3. They too debunk the idea of the autonomous individual as the source of spontaneous economic and social order.

[89] MacDonald & Leary 2005, especially p. 218; Bernstein & Claypool 2012; Eisenberger 2012; Tchalova & Eisenberger 2017.

usually passes quickly or can be suppressed – and generally leaves little memory
of it – pain caused by social exclusion is of a less transient nature. It can also be
experienced again by recollection.[90] The pain caused by ostracism is so intense
because exclusion robs us of basic psychological needs: the need to belong, the
need for self-esteem (induced and confirmed by others' recognition), a sense of
control (over one's own destiny) and the need for a meaningful existence.[91] If we
have the slightest sense that we are being socially excluded, our response is somewhat panicked: sometimes aggressive and antisocial or sometimes overly socially
attentive and susceptible.[92] When we really are excluded, we will do everything in
our power to re-join the group.[93] This inclination works basically like an instinct – it
is our brain's default system. Whereas exclusion literally results in death for most
social animals, ostracism may lead to 'social death' for people, something we fear
on a largely subconscious level as much as death itself.[94] It is thus unsurprising that
banishment, in Antiquity and the Middle Ages, used to be feared more than corpo-
ral punishment. Even in the hyper-individualistic twenty-first century people are
extremely sensitive to exclusion.[95] Long-term exclusion has major consequences for
our psyche – it can traumatise and damage it in many different ways.[96] Social exclusion is difficult to manage and when left unchecked harms on all fronts – it frus-
trates cooperation and damages individuals. Nevertheless, social exclusion is part of
group formation processes (who does and who does not belong) – as the German
philosopher Carl Schmitt observed a century ago; nothing brings people together
quite like a strong feeling of 'us against them' or having a common foe that we can
resist or fight as friends.[97] Institutions such as the law, procedural justice, inclusive
participation mechanisms such as democracy, participation, co-determination, and
religion[98] can be used to try and soften or prevent social exclusion to some extent,
yet none of these measures are universal remedies.[99]

Nobody wants to be a truly autonomous individual; what we really want is *recognition*. People are driven by a deep instinctive desire to be a meaningful member of a
group, and to have at least some role in it. This desire for recognition (*thymos*, as the

[90] Gardner, Pickett & Brewer 2000.
[91] Lakin, Chartand & Arkin 2008; Williams & Nida 2011, p. 71–72.
[92] Williams 2007. This reaction is also called 'prosocial' (prosocial behaviour is altruistic behaviour that primarily benefits others).
[93] 'Humans have a pervasive "need to belong"', in the words of Shuo and Josephs. Shuo &
Josephs 2017, especially p. 82 (quoted) with reference to Baumeister & Leary 1995.
[94] Williams 2007 and Williams & Nida 2011.
[95] It is with good reason that bullying as is considered a particularly harmful form of social exclusion which sometimes has serious, long-term consequences for victims. Cf. Williams, Forgas
& Von Hippel 2005. This is aggravated by the fact that ostracism and bullying (as a form of
ostracism) often have a domino effect. Cf. Critcher & Zayas 2014 and Lakin et al 2008.
[96] Will, Crone, Van Lier & Güroğlu 2016.
[97] Schmitt 2007 (orig. 1933).
[98] Aydin, Fischer & Frey 2010.
[99] Van Prooijen, Van den Bos & Wilke 2004; Arfken 2013.

ancient Greeks called it) – by pursuing status, honour, fame etcetera – is a constant feature in human history. Recognition gives individuals *self-worth*[100] – warm feelings of inner fulfilment and personal value, such as pride, or experienced identity[101] – but also *dignity* – the respect of others in the group for one's role and status[102] or position.[103] Recognition forges strong links in the same way that non-recognition – humiliation, affront, exclusion, status reduction and the like – causes psychological pain and a reduction in self-esteem[104] and therefore makes for an infinite source of conflict.[105]

Knowing Your Place

Even in a group of acquaintances it can be pretty tough finding your place, let alone in a large group of strangers. Everyone still remembers the uncomfortable feeling of the first day at school, the awkwardness of introducing oneself at a new job or what it is like being a freshman or sophomore in college. Everything is new and unfamiliar, even you are in a new, as yet undefined role. You have a gnawing sense of insecurity, ignorance and feel out of place. Who are *they* and how do they see *you*? It must have felt equally awkward in the new large communities 10,000 years ago. After hundreds of thousands of years of living in close-knit family groups of hunter-gatherer bands, people suddenly found themselves shackled in societies of hundreds in their new agrarian lives. Just as we still lose our way in the confusion of thousands of people living on top of each other in a tower block, or just like we Europeans live and work in a Union of more than 400 million citizens we can barely identify with. Having strangers everywhere is both frightening and exhilarating. It puts our heads into 'overdrive'. When amongst strangers, we are constantly getting our bearings and determining our relative position to find our place. We are endlessly divining each other's social coordinates; we reconnoitre each other's roles and relationships in the group in our feverish search for *identity* – this cherished anchor of life in mass societies. Our biological drive for recognition is deep seated and only grows with any increase in the size of the group. We all suffer from a Neolithic short circuit. This is precisely the reason why we find Facebook, Twitter and Instagram irresistible.

Recognition and Value

One of the ways in which large groups of people establish their relationships and roles is by assigning 'value'. This is not an intrinsic property of objects, people,

---

[100] These feelings are partly caused by the neurotransmitter serotonin.
[101] Fukuyama 2018, p. 34.
[102] This does not have to be recorded or fixed 'somewhere'. 'Status is the public knowledge that you possess assets that would allow you to help others if you wished to' according to Pinker 2009, p. 499.
[103] Fukuyama 2018, p. 37–41.
[104] Statman 2000.
[105] Dafoe, Renshon & Huth 2014; Barnhart 2017.

events or relationships – we 'invent' it. Status, prestige, worth, dignity, glory, wealth, authority, offices etcetera are all qualities or characteristics that we as a group assign to someone or something. An example to illustrate the point:

Van Gogh
In 1888 Vincent van Gogh was living in destitution in Arles, in Southern France. He might have had many plans and the best light that he was ever to see, but his career was not going anywhere. With hindsight, we can see this as the overture of the epic biography of a tormented and great artist who saw what others did not see. A lonely hero who defied convention and decisively influenced Western painting. 'How you suffered for your sanity', Don McLean sang in his saccharine song *Vincent* about Van Gogh's martyrdom, clearly referring to Christ.[106] However this may be, it certainly did not feel that way. Van Gogh had had a litany of failed careers by 1888; he was an outcast who had set his mercurial mind to becoming a painter. Like everything else he had tried, he did so ham-fistedly. Van Gogh's biggest problem was a lack of moderation. His social standing had sunk precipitously: born into the middle classes, he had drifted to the outer fringes of society. In August 1888, going a little mad mind from sorrow and a lack of acknowledgement, he spent his last few francs painting in his cheerless room. The subject: sunflowers. He first painted twelve and then fifteen canvases. The result was not sunflowers, but colours and lines depicting sunflowers – going from full flower to seed. He used these lines and odd colour combinations to convey the 'idea of a sunflower' in a unique way – symbolising the vivacity of the sun and at the same time the disconsolation of withering and the inevitability of death. One can almost smell them. We now know this, of course, with the benefit of hindsight.

Van Gogh's raw material costs per painting for his various versions of the *Sunflowers* were roughly:

Canvas (purchased from Tasset)[107]	5.50 francs
painting materials (he painted quite thickly)[108]	2.50 francs
labour (less than 24 hours)	–
Total cost of the *Sunflowers*	8 francs per painting (around € 40 /US $ 44)

---

[106] Don McLean, *Vincent*, from the album *American Pie* 1971.

[107] Cf. the letter from Vincent van Gogh to Theo van Gogh from 3 August 1888 (number 654). http://vangoghletters.org/vg/letters/let654/letter.html (last consulted on 2 April 2019).

[108] In letter 663, Vincent van Gogh estimates that he spent five or six francs a day. We can use this to work out what he spent. He spent 1.5 francs a day on food and his rent was fifteen francs a month, or 0.50 francs a day, leaving him about two francs a day to live on. If we subtract this from the daily allowance of 5.5 francs that Vincent mentions, then the materials would have cost him a total of about 3.5 francs a day. The canvas for the sunflowers has already been included in the calculation, so I estimate that the *Sunflowers* cost around 2.5 francs per painting. Cf. next footnote for reference.

Including other costs and accommodation (about 2 francs a day) increases the total cost slightly, but not by much.[109] Van Gogh's painting business was unprofitable: there was no demand for his paintings and he hardly sold any work. He gave the 1888 version of the *Sunflowers* illustrated here to Paul Gaugin, who was visiting him. Things did not improve. Two years later, on 29 July 1890, Van Gogh committed suicide in Auvers sur l'Oise. This is an extreme instance of non-recognition: his contemporaries considered him a worthless fellow, just like his work.

Less than a century later, in March 1987, the Japanese insurance magnate Yasuo Goto paid USD 39,921,750 for Van Gogh's *Still Life: Vase with Fifteen Sunflowers* at London auction house Christie's. At the time, it was a record amount for a Van Gogh painting – a millionfold increase in value in 100 years. Bought by an insurer who was probably also looking for a certain form of recognition (prestige, reputation, status). The painting still hangs in the Seiji Togo Yasuda Memorial Museum of Modern Art in Tokyo.

Vincent van Gogh (1853–1890), *Still Life: Vase with Fifteen Sunflowers* 1888

So, value is foremost an act of recognition by a group. The current value of the painting of the sunflowers has nothing to do with the intrinsic value of the materials or of Van Gogh as a person. He is just an exception in a multitude of misunderstood

---

[109] For Vincent van Gogh's stay in Arles (and his costs of living) cf. Hulsker 1989, p. 314 and p. 352–353 (about the *Sunflowers*).

and forgotten artists past and present. This example is an extreme illustration that value is a form of 'recognition', and that recognition is a matter of *social attribution*: the value that 'we' as a group assign to something or someone. This is not limited to goods or services; value allocation extends far beyond economic relationships as economic and market relationships, which only make up a small part of social appreciation processes.

Recognition and Freedom

Recognition is essential for living together: without recognition, an individual lacks any role in society. Non-recognition can result in exclusion: in *social death*.[110] As a result, our entire existence and all of human history is dominated by the 'struggle for recognition', according to Hegel.[111] This should not be interpreted too literally as constant physical fighting or some sort of continuous death struggle. Although recognition certainly has biological roots – it is a type of instinct[112] – we can claim and receive recognition for our value, roles and identities in very rational, calm and well-considered ways. Creating and representing a social order by dividing groups into ranks and classes, allocating status and qualities (rights, powers, diplomas, honours), and through institutional mediation (authority, law, rules, offices, organs, etcetera) enables us to allocate individuals positions and meaningful roles in a group. Nowadays, recognition is not just about being allowed to partake in a group, but also about access to the levers of human society. This sometimes functions extremely subtly and almost imperceptibly. For example, you cannot see at first glance how a hermit who spends his life in prayer could be held in the highest esteem and wonder in a religious society. Hermits played an important role in the European Middle Ages. They interceded for other members of society with their prayers. It is also not immediately obvious why someone who swims against the current – say, by proclaiming a dissenting opinion[113] – or who introduces a completely different style of music or takes a new approach to the visual arts, can claim and receive recognition. Going against the grain, opposition and contrariness represent values in free societies: they are good for innovation and for confirming the value of freedom. Demanding and gaining respect for being *different* – a concept we associate with 'freedom' – is a form of recognition. The freedom so cherished in our liberal democracies is, in Isaiah Berlin's words, not much more than an echo of our deeply human need for *recognition*:

> The lack of freedom about which men or groups complain amounts, as often as not, to the lack of proper recognition. I may be seeking not for [...] security from

---

[110] Cf. Taylor who elucidates how recognition is not just a form of politeness or respect but stands for much more. Taylor 1994, p. 26.

[111] Hegel 2018 (orig. 1807).

[112] Fukuyama 2011, p. 41.

[113] For example, about the origins of constitutions.

coercion, arbitrary arrest, tyranny, deprivation of certain opportunities of action, or for room within which I am legally accountable to no one for my movements. Equally, I may not be seeking for a rational plan of social life, or the self-perfection of a dispassionate sage. What I may seek to avoid is simply being ignored, or patronized or despised, or being taken too much for granted – in short, not being treated as an individual, having my uniqueness insufficiently recognised, being classed as a member of some featureless amalgam, a statistical unit without identifiable, specifically human features and purposes of my own. This is the degradation that I am fighting against – not equality of legal rights, nor liberty to do as I wish (although I may want these too), but for a condition in which I can feel that I am, because I am taken to be, a responsible agent, whose will is taken into consideration because I am entitled to it, even if I am attacked and persecuted for being what I am or choosing as I do. This is a hankering after status and recognition [...].[114]

The desire for recognition is not some trifle, it is deeply entrenched in our brain, which is also equipped with a very sensitive radar for recognising social dominance, social status and other people's roles.[115] Our predisposition for hierarchy has far-reaching consequences. The Canadian philosopher Charles Taylor shows in his 1992 essay 'The Politics of Recognition' how modern politics revolves around the need – or even demand – for recognition. It is reflected, for example, in all kinds of emancipation claims by interest or minority groups, but also in the claims of nationalist and populist movements (what Goodhart calls the 'somewhere' people)[116] for preservation and recognition of their values, traditions and interests. Taylor argues that recognition and identity are closely linked in debates of this kind, with potentially serious consequences:

[...] our identity is partly shaped by recognition or its absence, often by the misrecognition of others, and so a person or group of people can suffer real damage, real distortion, if the people or society around them mirror back to them a confining or demeaning or contemptible picture of themselves. Nonrecognition or misrecognition can inflict harm, can be a form of oppression, imprisoning someone in a false, distorted, and reduced mode of being.[117]

---

[114] Berlin 1969.

[115] Our brains are evolutionary hardwired for social recognition, including recognising social dominance (status, hierarchies, social roles). Biochemical stimuli (in particular, the neuropeptides oxytocin and vasopressin) play a role as a hormone and neurotransmitter in activating the various parts of the brain involved in social recognition. Cf. Adolphs 2001; Insel & Young 2000; Zinc, Tong, Chen, Bassett, Stein & Meyer-Lindenberg 2008; According to Watanabe and Yamamoto, various parts of our brain – including primitive parts – are involved in recognising social structures and dominance, which shows how deeply entrenched this ability is ('the origin of the perception of dominance is a phylogenetically primitive part of the brain'), Watanabe and Yamamoto 2015 (quotation from p. 11). For a good overview cf.: Dore, Phan, Clipperton-Allen, Kavaliers & Choleris 2013 (and their expansive glossary on p. 248–255).

[116] Goodhart 2017.

[117] Henrich 1992, p. 25.

Understanding recognition – as a form of social value attribution – is important for those wanting to learn more about the meaning and functioning of constitutions. Constitutional rules are the pre-eminent instruments with which we assign value to relationships, institutions, traditions, values, characteristics and ultimately to groups and individuals. They 'organise' society, set the course in terms of who and what matters in society, and what the relationships are. They determine how, who and what 'the we' is as well as the role that 'you' play in this.

From Recognition to Legitimacy

Recognition does not just fall out of the blue. It is based upon judgments about the intrinsic value of other people and the norms, ideas, and rules which people weave together as webs of meaning.[118] Such ideas – stories – about norms, values and rules, and about roles, status and rank in a society vary over time. They give stability and strength to a community in as much and for as long as most – or the most influential – members can durably accept them, and internalise them as somehow being 'true' and 'good'. As such they serve as the foundation of sustainable cooperation. In pre-modern (tribal) societies, this recognition would mainly have had to do with the acceptance of a leader whose insight or physical strength was deemed capable of protecting members of the group, making a certain level of subordination acceptable. In more advanced societies, patterns of rank and position can be identified in a society, with classes corresponding to different roles (rights, privileges). Internalisation mechanisms in the form of sacred traditions, myths, religion, law and the like are used to make unequal relationships and leadership acceptable. Even further in the development of human societal organisation, recognition of individuals, classes and groups is transferred to abstract institutions,[119] such as 'the Republic', 'the Constitution' and 'the legislature'. Durable – internalised – patterns of recognition enjoy legitimacy.[120] That is, members of a society acknowledge the essential legitimacy of a governing system as a whole and are therefore willing to conform to its rules and norms by accepting the system as 'true' and 'good'. Today, we believe that only a liberal democracy merits durable acceptance. History shows that this form of government was certainly not the only governmental system to have been considered legitimate and generally accepted as such. Legitimacy is above all 'faith' in an order, its rules, and its values, as Max Weber showed.[121] This faith starts with recognition – our biological need to know our own value and role in a group in the form of a credible and acceptable story (see Chapter 27). Only then, Fukuyama argues, is a large group able to work together as a unit:

---

[118] Fukuyama 2011, p. 42.
[119] I use the term 'institutions' here in the sense of 'stable, valuable, repeated patterns of behaviour' accordingly to Huntington's 1973 definition, p. 12. Cf. Fukuyama 2011, p. 450.
[120] Cf. Beetham 1991, especially p. 97–99.
[121] Weber 1964 (orig. 1922), p. 382.

Recognition when granted becomes the basis of legitimacy, and legitimacy then permits the exercise of political authority.[122]

THE INVENTION OF MASS COOPERATION

Human cooperation rests on two pillars: *trust* and *recognition*. They were a matter of course, in small hunter-gatherer groups because of the small scale and familial relations. This was no longer self-evident in the new sedentary agrarian lifestyle which started around 10,000 BCE, which with the larger group composition full of strangers compromised trust and recognition. The new sizeable groups had to start organising themselves along other lines; they had to reinvent themselves.[123] The increasing scale of groups may have occurred almost automatically, but group organisation was certainly not predetermined. Group processes had a different dynamic in these new tribes of hundreds to sometimes thousands of members. The larger numbers impelled the redesign and rearrangement of relationships to work well for defence or raiding,[124] as well as for exchange, hunting, marriage, building, relocation, etcetera. The social structure of tribes – essentially cooperating family groups – initially remained relatively egalitarian, as with hunter-gatherers.[125] Cooperation was *ad hoc* and based on convenience; reciprocity (exchange of services and favours) was important and there were still hardly any differences in status or elites. These only arose when larger groups started collaborating under permanent leadership, in what are called chiefdoms. Permanent leadership enables you to organise yourself better and professionalise group functions, such as common defence. This leads to even greater specialisation in the group: leaders and soldiers require exemption from working for their own needs, necessitating the creation and distribution of shared stocks.[126] The surpluses produced by an agrarian lifestyle permit this. Taxation and distribution systems develop, giving rise to officials who levy taxes, as well as record, manage and distribute stocks. This is also accompanied by the emergence of structured systems of meaning, such as religion: a shared belief in supernatural beings or entities.[127] These strengthen mutual trust and make it easier to accede to the new hierarchical relationships in large-scale societies which

---

[122] Fukuyama 2011, p. 43.

[123] (Jared) Diamond 2005, p. 267–273.

[124] Raids in non-state societies often aimed at seizing another group's possessions but were also for safety. 'People in nonstate societies also invade for safety. The security dilemma or Hobbesian trap is very much on their minds, and they may form an alliance with nearby villages if they fear they are too small or launch a pre-emptive strike if they fear that an enemy alliance is getting too big.' Pinker 2011, p. 46. Cf. (Jared) Diamond 2005, p. 289.

[125] (Jared) Diamond 2005, p. 89–90. There is not necessarily a sharp distinction between a hunter-gatherer and an agricultural lifestyle. Both forms often occur simultaneously in early human communities. (Jared) Diamond 2005, p. 106.

[126] Roberts & Westad 2013, p. 92–94.

[127] Fukuyama 2011, chapter 4 (*Tribal Societies: Property, Justice, War*).

are so different from the equality of hunter-gatherer life. For why should I relinquish part of my food stocks that I really need? 'Because the gods require sacrifices
for your and your family's well-being.' Or: 'because we need priests to talk and pray
to the gods.' And why should I be loyal to a permanent leader? 'Because the gods
have chosen him, and he and his priests know what the gods want thanks to their
special relationship with them.' Or 'because the leader is god on Earth'.[128] As Karl
Marx famously observed, religion works as 'the opium of the people'.[129]

Chiefdoms – better organised and stronger than single tribes or family groups –
see the emergence of hierarchies and elites. A process called *social stratification*[130]
leading to a society of ranks and classes. In addition to religious opium, other 'compensation mechanisms' are used to promote acceptance of the loss of equality people were used to in their original small bands. For example, law and legal rules are
abstract expressions of notions of justice, and concepts of property and ownership –
there was usually collective ownership in tribes and chiefdoms – expressing ideas
about what is private and what is public.[131] Later still, chiefdoms grew into kingdoms, with hereditary leadership (kingship, usually grounded in religion) in which
control over a territory is established on a permanent basis. In addition to the large
scale on which kingships and kingdoms operate (thousands to tens of thousands and
hundreds of thousands of people), they see the emergence of permanent administrative centres – usually densely populated cities – from where a kingdom is ruled.
The first major cities were built around 3000 BCE in Mesopotamia, including Ur,
Uruk and Kish,[132] where palaces and temples were built for kings and priests from
their establishment.[133] These kings surrounded themselves with priests and warriors,
who were rewarded for their services and loyalty with exemptions (from taxes, for
example) and other benefits (including privileges and status). This is how ranks and
privileged classes (nobility, clergy, etcetera) developed for the first time in history.

A higher degree of political organisation brings internal and external (competitive) advantages: the new fiduciary institutions increase group cohesion. A shared

---

[128] The Egyptian pharaohs, for instance.

[129] Marx 1844.

[130] Habermas 2006 (orig. 1981), especially p. 309–310.

[131] It is clear that early forms of states and law came into being as groups grew, but it is not yet
entirely clear why. Did states, law and authority arise to prevent spirals of vengeance and
reduce violence, or to channel violence, with authorities functioning like traffic controllers
and intermediaries? The introduction of fines and compensation for crimes in old legal texts
suggests the latter. Whitman 1996, from p. 45 onwards.

[132] Incidentally, not all of the world's oldest cities are in Mesopotamia. Damascus and Aleppo
(Syria), Plovdiv (Bulgaria), Sidon and Byblos (Lebanon) and El-Faiyum (Egypt) go back even
further. They were founded between 4000 and 5000 BCE. The city of Jericho in Palestine
already existed in 9000 BCE.

[133] The first states – large territories permanently ruled by a central high-authority – also arose in
this period. They appeared in Mesopotamia around 3700 BCE, followed by Central America
only in 300 BCE, China and Southeast Asia about 2000 years ago (just before the Common
Era) and West Africa about 1000 years ago. Cf. (Jared) Diamond 2005, p. 278.

belief in abstract concepts, such as religion, law, ranks and classes, unites group members and at the same time promotes acceptance of authority and non-egalitarian relations. Belief systems of this kind also offer enormous mobilisation potential. In a politically organised society, like a city or a kingdom, a leader can demand far more of individual members than is possible in an egalitarian group. This is even more beneficial in external relations. A group with a higher degree of political organisation can produce and accumulate more resources and organise and arm itself much better in many different areas of human competition (military, economic, even in sport and culture).[134] It can thus defend itself better and it can even conquer and exploit other groups.

There is no neat chronological order in the shift to larger and more complex forms of human society.[135] There have been many hybrids and numerous shades of grey. But, history does show how trust and recognition gradually take on more abstract forms in increasingly complex societies and how these societies find themselves in a perpetual arms race of ever-improving political organisation – continuously spurred on by their innate urge for recognition.[136]

[134] (Jared) Diamond 2005, p. 90.
[135] Cf. Fukuyama 2011, p. 51–53.
[136] Fukuyama 2011, p. 41–43 (the paragraph under the title *The Struggle for Recognition*) and p. 448.

PART II

The History of the Constitution

4

Precursors

As we saw in the previous chapter, the transition to the first state-organised societies began somewhere between 9000 and 6000 BCE.[1] Collaborative entities exercising permanent control over a (not by definition consanguineous) population in a large area with distinct, complex forms of political organisation and centralised leadership. In parallel, abstract and normative notions on leadership and social organisation developed. Codes and rules on proper social and political conduct, together with authorities able to enforce them. We can identify the first contours of what will later be called 'law' in these phenomena. These first legal rules were closely linked to religion and religious rules – and would remain so for thousands of years, or most of human development.[2] It is only in modern history that a strict distinction has been drawn between them. Until a few hundred years ago, law and religion were two sides of the same coin, part of a single belief system about a society's imagined reality. For us this connection is no longer self-evident, but it is not a surprising one in the context of the wider course of history.

RELIGION

Like law, religion played – and still does play – an important, perhaps crucial role in enabling large-scale collective action.[3] Like law, religion helps reduce fear. While the abstractions of the law help us overcome our fear of strangers and enables trust beyond our biological capacity, religion helps us overcome fear of death,[4] and fear

[1] See (James C.) Scott 2017. Scott shows how during the first 3,000 years of their existence the chances of urban and state societies constantly changed. Early states were extremely fragile. That they would one day conquer the world was not written in the stars. See especially chapter 6 "Fragility of the Early State: Collapse and Disassembly" p. 183–218.
[2] Durkheim 2012. Cf. Zane 1998, in particular chapter 2 (*Law among Primordial Man*), p. 17–45.
[3] Fukuyama 2011, p. 63.
[4] Diamond argues that religion relieves a literally 'paralysing' fear of death. Our brains are capable of understanding (and predicting) that we are going to die. Animals have no fear of death. They may have an instinctive fear of danger or unpleasant experiences, but lack fear of

of the unfathomable and threatening. By sharing a faith, we also overcome our fear of each other.[5] The imagined orders of law and religion allow us to transcend the biological limits of human cooperation by a form of cultural adaptation – what Van Schaik and Michel describe as a sort of 'crutch' to assist us in our unnatural way of living.[6] In human history, law and religion are like twins, resembling each other, and usually reinforcing each other. Both law and religion have (sacred) authoritative texts, stories and symbols (more on this later), officers (priests, judges, etcetera), as well as sanctions (failure to comply with religious rules leads to sanctions including non-recognition, reputational damage or expulsion); likewise, failure to comply with legal requirements leads to forms of social reputational damage and possible exclusion. Whether one is the result of the other – whether the law comes from religion, or religion derived from early normative systems – is still difficult to determine.[7]

The first forms of law and religion were both about how we ought to live together in larger groups, according to which organisational rules, what role we, as individuals have to play, and – even if forms of subservience and relating to strangers are contrary to our nature – why we have to accept this.[8] New abstractions on good and evil, prescripts on required – unnatural – behaviour, accompanied with the reasons why.

As we will see later, these first legal rules were truly *constitutional* rules: they were about the structure of society (in particular its leadership) and the consequences of this for its members. Even more than that: these stories on proper conduct and relations created a new reality. A world of law, gods, authority and the group (identity). When looking back at the first legal rules (if they are yet called law), modern observers tend to overlook the element of competition; these rivalrous societies tried to surpass each other using their political and legal systems as a tool. Part of an arms race. Certainly from the time of the Neolithic revolution, scale and organisation have been decisive for the power of groups. Who had the best system? They probably also had the best organisation, the greatest mobilisation capacity and resources, and were able to dominate other, more poorly organised groups (by conquest, incorporation, etcetera) and also enjoyed the greatest possible amount of recognition (status, honour, glory, fame and the like). Hence political and legal organisation came with major bonuses.

This competitive notion also lies at the basis of Aristotle's comparison, in about 325 BCE, of the 158 constitutions (forms of government) of the Greek city-states

---

an 'abstract' future. 'Humans usually suffer the most from suffering they fear.' There is nothing more human than fear of death. (Jared) Diamond 2012, p. 346 ff.

5 Van Schaik & Michel 2016, p. 24–25; Pyysiäinen 2001, p. 70–93, especially p. 84–89.

6 Van Schaik & Michel 2016, p. 18–21.

7 Fukuyama 2011, p. 62–63.

8 Hirschl 2014b, chapter 2 *Early Engagements with the Constitutive Laws of Others; Lessons from Pre-Modern Religion Law,* especially p. 110–111.

known to him. Aristotle's surprisingly modern question was: which of these 158 constitutions is really the best; and which (parts of) constitutions generally deliver the best results?[9] His exercise shows that every self-respecting Greek city-state in the fourth century BCE had a set of rules about the 'we' of their society: a constitution was a permanent fixture in each of these fiercely competitive polities. It is very unlikely that they copied these rules from one other because they thought this civilised or morally correct. More likely they did so because they believed it to be useful for trade and waging war. Constitutions were tried and tested means to mobilise people and resources in order to survive, or even win, the constant internecine struggles. When a constitution has existed for some time and is a good story, people will start believing it is good or even the best.

Although many of these Greek city-state constitutions were completely or partially written – how else could Aristotle have known about their existence?[10] – they were not constitutions in a modern sense. They were not proclaimed by a constituent assembly (as far as we know); they lacked popular sovereignty and individual freedoms; they were imbued with religion and social strata; they contained many articles and prescripts that are incomprehensible to us now; and they contained many elements which would now be considered cruel and barbaric. But on the other hand, it is, of course, also a question of what you decide to call a constitution. What we call the constitution is permeated with ideology (see Chapters 1 and 21). We, today, are prone to equate what constitutions are, with what they ought to be. A constitution must be a written document, we feel, with articles on freedom, human rights, the rule of law, and democracy in order to be considered worthy of the name. Such ideological constitutional concepts (constitutionalism)[11] can make one incredibly myopic. They stand in the way of a true understanding of constitutions' earliest roots, and how the phenomenon is connected to human history. To properly understand history and estimate the different meanings of constitutions over time, one should not be blinded by modern conceptualisations. It is very interesting and instructive to know what people used to consider (the meaning of) a 'constitution'.

Aristotle considered the 'constitution of a state' and its constitutional rules to be about 'the organisation of the offices, and in particular the one that is sovereign over

[9] Aristotle 1962, *The Politics*.
[10] Students of Aristotle's Academy collected and recorded a total of 158 constitutions. This recorded collection, which survived and was studied long after Aristotle's time, has largely been lost. A few extant copies can be found in the British Museum. www.bl.uk/collection-items/the-constitution-of-the-athenians (consulted on 17 November 2018).
[11] Wittington says that constitutionalism simply consists of 'the constraining of government in order to better effectuate the fundamental principles of the political regime.' In this sense, every state and every political community has a constitution. Wittington continues: 'it can be argued that in a sense (often associated with Aristotle) every country has a constitution'. Wittington 2008, especially p. 282.

all the others."[12] In short, the organisation of society and what I have called leadership. After more than two thousand years, Aristotle's idea has lost none of its currency. The famous British constitutionalist Albert Venn Dicey (1836–1922) echoed it in his broad definition of a constitution: 'all rules which directly or indirectly affect the distribution or the exercise of sovereign power in a state.'[13] This is a sober, non-ideological perspective that looks at what constitutions *do*. In this light, foundational rules of the 'we' in a society[14] and organisation of its leadership precede eighteenth-century concepts by millennia.[15]

Princeton political scientist Melissa Lane illustrates in her book *Greek and Roman Political Ideas*[16] how modern legal definitions of constitutions make us vulnerable to myopia. It makes older 'constitutions' unrecognisable because they do not fit the detailed modern definition. Polities lacking state organisation, as we conceive it, and polities with very different ideas about the acceptability of government power and government organisation expressed in their organisational rules would – in our modern eyes – appear to lack a constitution. Undeservedly so, according to Lane. They did have constitutions; in fact, they invented them.

Omitting ancient 'constitutions' from the 'constitutional' record book risks failing to appreciate their importance. Whether or not these ancient systems of law would classify as constitutions today, they can, for starters, help us better understand the origins of the constitutional concept, how it ties in with human nature, how it helps us to coordinate our efforts in large groups, its powers, its limits and drawbacks as shown in the historical record. It may provide us with a better apprehension of how present-day constitutions, as sets of foundational rules on leadership, law and society actually work.

This requires an open-minded approach that surpasses rigid adherence to current uses of the word constitution. Modern concepts and words do not always fit older frames of thought. For instance, Melissa Lane observes that the political language of classical Greece and the Roman republic lack the word 'constitution'. *Constitutio* is first used in the Roman imperial era but referred at the time to an edict issued by an emperor rather than a set of fundamental rules about the organisation of a polity. What we mean by 'constitution' nowadays is more comparable to

[12] Nowadays, Aristotle continues, 'in every case the citizen body of a state is sovereign; the citizen-body *is* the constitution.' Aristotle 1962, *The Politics*, III.6, 1278 b6–15.

[13] Dicey 1982, p. CXL.

[14] Dicey also refers to this in a sentence directly following his famous definition above (p. CXL): 'Hence it includes (among other things) all rules which define the members of the sovereign power, all rules which *regulate* the relation of such members to each other, or which determine the mode in which the sovereign power, or the members thereof, exercise their authority.' Dicey 1889, *ibid*. In fact, Dicey's broad definition comes very close to the concept of 'constitution' employed by modern sociologists. For example, Chris Thornhill argues that a constitution is characterised by 'the fact that it refers primarily to the functions of states, and it establishes a legal form relating to the use of powers by states, or at least by actors bearing and utilising public authority.' Thornhill 2011, p. 11.

[15] Cf. Strong 1963, who also looks for the roots of modern constitutions far in the past.

[16] Lane 2014, p. 59 ff.

what was called *politeia* in classical antiquity. It too was a catch-all term, with many different connotations, but comparable to the set of values and rules we now call 'constitution'. Lane contends that politeia in a broad sense was not just about (state-based) organisation of governmental power, but also about the whys and wherefores of 'a way of life'.[17]

> The idea of the broad constitution as going beyond political organization to include the social division of labour generally – how people are procreated, educated and trained to contribute to society – would become characteristic of many Greek discussions of the 'best *politeia*'. [...] What is the relationship between a regime's way of life and its characteristic political organisation in particular? For the Greeks of the classical period, there was no single answer to that question. Rather, each kind of regime – each different *politeia* – gave its own distinctive response [...].[18]

The Greeks intently studied the diverse variants, to see whether they could learn from other communities.

PREHISTORIC CONSTITUTIONS

It is likely that constitutions – understood as foundational rules on leadership, law and society – came into existence very early in human history: at about the time the first cities appeared in around 6000 BCE. This cannot be said with certainty, because the only evidence we have is in written form – rules on leadership and legal systems handed down orally have left no traces, at least none we can chronologically pinpoint with any accuracy. The first tangible remains of prehistoric constitutions are mostly from around the time that writing was invented – the era after which the first written contracts (from 3000 BCE) surface in the area between Euphrates and Tigris rivers. In this period, the first rules about contract fulfilment and dispute settlement were written down in the trading cities of Mesopotamia. Rules about the legal rules – proto-constitutional rules. They may not have appeared out of the blue; as indicated, earlier forms on contract compliance and enforcement (as well as on leadership) may have existed before, handed down orally, as tradition or customary law. Disputes in these ancient cities would, in pre-cuneiform times (that is before writing was invented), mainly have been settled by wise men, priests, princes or kings; a famous example is 'the Biblical Judgement of Solomon'. Leading figures passed judgment as wise mediators. They did not need a written constitution to do so. Yet, it is likely that constitutions – as rules about rules – were recorded in larger communities such as cities soon after the invention of writing. Writing down constitutional rules is a very efficient and effective way of communicating in a

---

[17] Lane 2014, p. 60–61.
[18] Lane 2014, p. 61.

large community. Recording rules in this way makes it easier to access, remember and consult them, sidestepping the crackle and static associated with oral transmission ('Chinese whispers'). And it is really handy when transferring the rules from one generation to generation to the next (allowing new generations to profit from the wisdom of multiple prior generations). Harari elucidates this point with a joke about bees:

> Bees don't need lawyers because there is no danger that they might forget or violate the hive constitution. The queen does not cheat the cleaner bees of their food, and they never go on strike demanding higher wages. But humans do such things all the time. Because Sapiens social order is imagined, humans cannot preserve the critical information for running it simply by making copies of their DNA and passing these on to their progeny. A conscious effort has to be made to sustain laws, customs, procedures and manners, otherwise the social order would quickly collapse.[19]

As impressive as our brain is, it cannot store the large amounts of information needed to maintain lasting social relationships in a large-scale community (committing to memory all information on past and present exchanges, trade, neighbours, classes, status, families). Writing overcomes this shortcoming: we can use it to expand our memory and build a collective memory. For example, the incredibly complex and intricate knowledge required to maintain relationships in a large-scale collaborative community: the constitution of a community's organisation, its leadership and law, that is, its political and social order.[20] Recorded as written rules, this knowledge enables us to cooperate even better and increases our mental power exponentially by linking it up as it were.[21] Even though we lack much proof, It is highly probable that the earliest constitutions – rules on rules and rules on leadership and organisation – in Mesopotamia were somehow written down soon after their creation. However, tracing them is difficult. We have occasionally found clay tablets about (criminal) law and the settlement of certain kinds of disputes in the region, but the evidence is sporadic. These 'clay'-data carriers were vulnerable.

Nevertheless, it is clear that writing developed in Mesopotamia primarily for stock and trade administration.[22] The first legal rules found their way into these records: settled disputes were documented, as well as the grounds on which they were decided, by whom and – most of the time – with reference to the principles or

---

[19] Harari 2011, p. 135.
[20] Harari 2011, p. 136–142. Cf. Houston 2004; Steinkeller especially p. 68.
[21] Harari 2011, p. 135–142.
[22] In Uruk (Mesopotamia) temple priests developed the first (abstract) writing around 3,200 BCE to register stocks of beer, bread and herds of sheep and goats. Accounting and registration were the basis: writing made it possible to record and pass on information over time. Information could even be transferred between generations. The law also developed from this – at least our modern, written understanding of it. Finkel & Taylor 2015, p. 11–14.

rules which had been observed. In Egypt, too, writing was used to record the 'collective legal memory'. We know of references to some form of private law in Egypt, recorded in twelve books, from about 3000 BCE – even though the Egyptians did not have a real, concept of law as a distinct phenomenon in their religio-social order, separate from the other prescripts of religious and social life. They did not even have fixed words for legal or judicial matters.[23]

The first fragments of written law recognisable to us, appear on the clay tablets of Near Eastern peoples, such as the Sumerians, Babylonians, Assyrians, Elamites, and Hittites, from about 2350 BCE. We call this 'cuneiform law', recorded with wedge-shaped marks on clay tablets. The fragments that have been uncovered show that the phenomenon of written law was already widespread in the third millennium BCE.[24] It could be found in both cities and kingdoms. Despite their differences, the similarities are striking: cuneiform tablets recording law usually start with a prologue in which 1) the purpose of the recorded law is explained (peace, law, enforcement of divine will, etcetera), 2) divine authority is invoked, 3) the reader is summoned to comply with the regulations, and 4) it is declared that the rules have been decreed in the name of a ruler (a king or other leader). The direct form of address is also notable: the tablets 'talk' to the reader. We do not know very much about the government and law of the cities and kingdoms prior to 2000 BCE. Assyriology is a much younger tradition than Egyptology. Even though Egyptian hieroglyphs and Persian cuneiform script were both largely deciphered at the beginning of the nineteenth century, we have progressed much further in deciphering Egyptian texts than cuneiform script. This is undoubtedly due to the more continuous development of the pharaonic kingdoms in Egypt. We still have to uncover many of the earliest (cunei) forms of written law in the hope of discovering more about their context and their relationship.[25] For now, they are mostly mere fragments in a clay puzzle.

A first more or less coherent set of foundational rules on leadership and law, a kind of constitution, can be found in the legal code adopted by Urukagina, the ruler of the Sumerian city-state of Lagash. His *Code of Urukagina* is a prototypal constitution, which includes rules on leadership (especially government administration), social organisation and law. The code regulated a tax exemption for

---

[23] As Van Loon puts it: 'The Egyptians never developed a dedicated legal terminology. There was no conceptual uniformity within their language with regard to legal and judicial matters. Law, for instance, is translated as *hp*, but this word can also mean custom, order, justice or right. In some cases, this poses a challenge for the modern researcher, who must attempt to link the multiform accounts of Egyptian jurisdiction to modern legal categories, while also interpreting them within their own historical context. In a broader sense, Egyptian society did not have a general theory of law either, although it can be surmised from various sources that through time attempts were made in isolated cases to establish abstract legal norms.' Van Loon 2011, p. 9, referring to: Allam 2003, p. 23–24.

[24] Finkel & Taylor 2015, p. 10–22.

[25] Cf. Waerzeggers 2017; Waerzeggers 2012.

widows and orphans, compelled the city to pay funeral expenses, and obliged the rich to pay in silver (and not on credit or by barter) when buying from the poor. Powerful men (rich men or priests) were forbidden from forcing the poor to sell and so on. These surprisingly modern-sounding forms of social justice, recorded as legal rules, were enforced on authority of the ruler (King Urukagina). The code dates from around 2380 BCE and its existence was discovered – by inference – in 1877 in present-day Iraq. The actual text has not (yet) been uncovered, but rather several clay tablets containing specific references to the rules in Urukagina's legal code.

Another legal code from about the same time has been uncovered more or less intact; it was written in the reign of King Ur Nammu of Ur. The *Code of Ur-Nammu* dates from around 2050 BCE, making it the oldest surviving legal *code* – in contrast to the parts of regulations found on older clay tablets. The preamble first glorifies the great and mighty King Ur-Nammu of Ur, who decrees the laws and establishes 'equity in the land', on behalf and in the name of the gods for his subjects. Divided into 32 laws, the code's provisions deal with punishment for murder and robbery, but also family matters. The rules reflect the ordered world of the city-state, where (temple) taxes had to be paid and masters and slaves existed. But is also reveals a world where, for all the solemn invocation of gods and regal pomp, violations were dealt with in a remarkably pragmatic fashion. If, for instance, you knocked out someone's tooth, or even their eye, then you would simply be liable to pay the victim monetary compensation (laws 18 and 22) as opposed to the far harsher law of retaliation[26] ('An eye for an eye') later instituted in Babylon and the Bible (which borrowed it from the Persians). Not everything in the code has a familiar ring to us. Under the code knocking out someone's eye is about as expensive as divorcing your first wife – conflicts we would now not consider to be on par. The pragmatism of the code did not extend to adultery or other acts of indecency, which were capital offences. Inscribed on cuneiform tablets, the somewhat later *Laws of Eshnunna* (c. 1930 BCE) and the *Code of Lipit-Ishtar*, king of Isin (c. 1870 BCE) are of a similar nature. The latter includes a detailed inventory of offences and associated punishments; it reads a bit like a menu.

Probably the most renowned and comprehensive legal code of all antiquity is that of the Babylonian king Hammurabi. The *Code of Hammurabi*[27] was probably recorded in 1694 BCE and is beautifully preserved, chiselled into a 2.23-metre-high diorite stele. Discovered in 1901 in Susa, in modern-day Iran, the stele must originally have stood in the centre of Babylon. It catalogues 282 articled provisions, the majority of which are still legible.

---

[26] Lex talionis.

[27] 'Code' is a somewhat contemporary interpretation. The set of rules on Hammurabi's stele was intended foremost as instructive material for judges: an aid to judges applying the law. These judges were the actual 'bouches de la loi' (mouths of the law).

Code of Hammurabi

The engraved articles cover a variety of subjects that also give us a fascinating insight into daily life and the associated preoccupations of the densely populated city of Babylon and other cities in the Babylonian empire. Clearly people lived in close proximity to one other causing all kinds of nuisance and trouble. The great trading city was devout, had ranks and classes, officials and warlords (who enjoyed immunity), as well as an honour culture. Tax was levied on behalf of the king and male citizens owed him military service.[28] The stele gives the impression of an orderly society with detailed rules about behaviour, crimes and offences, and religious precepts. Life in Babylon, as reflected in the code, comes across as surprisingly modern in several respects; there was a social order with legal authorities, trade rules, and rules for settling claims. The biggest difference with how government organisation and law function today is the nature of the authority that formulates and enforces legal rules. The highest power – sovereignty; ultimate leadership – in the system proclaimed on Hammurabi's stele did not rest in the group, but 'outside', with the gods. Somehow, apparently, it was easier to trust each other by having a shared belief in a 'third', non-human party. This was trust in the connection, which was easier than placing your trust in a union with a human leader, who you usually did not know personally, but who you knew was subject to the same human frailties as everyone else. You could ascribe infallible qualities to god, who could evolve over time into a synthesis of society's best qualities. The upper part of the stele emphasises this by pictorially and textually emphasising the story of the divine origin of the laws written below.

The central figure on the carving atop Hammurabi's stele portrays the sun god Shamash, the supreme judge of Heaven and Earth, standing erect and handing Hammurabi a stylus. Hammurabi takes the instrument to inscribe the legal rules Shamash dictates. The image tells the story of the origin of the rules and their authority. Beneath it is a text in which Hammurabi explains in detail the divine origin of the laws and his intermediary role. He addresses the reader in a very direct and personal way.

> [...] Anu [the divine personification of the sky] and Bel [Lord of the Sky and the Wind] called by name me, Hammurabi, the exalted prince, who feared God, to bring about the rule of righteousness in the land, to destroy the wicked and the evil-doers; so that the strong should not harm the weak; so that I should rule over the black-headed people like Shamash, and enlighten the land, to further the well-being of mankind

---

[28] The laws in Hammurabi's Code are divided into seven main topics: a) *the functioning of the judiciary and capital crimes* (laws 1–25) on slander, perjury, theft, accepting stolen goods, stealing or hiding slaves, burglary, robbery, and the like; b) *military service, tenancy and leasing agricultural land* (laws 6–65) on military service, mercenaries, the immunity of warlords, agricultural duties; (laws 66–99 are missing on the stele); c) *trade* (laws 100–126) on trade missions and commercial agents, inns, bills of lading, consignment and storage of merchandise, grain and money, debt bondage; d) *morality and family and inheritance law* (laws 127–194) on adultery, rape, marital infidelity, divorce, bride price and dowry; e) *liability for mistreatment of humans or animals and the intervention of physicians* (laws 195–227); f) *trades, industries and liabilities* (laws 228–240); and finally g) on *performance during work and service activities* (laws 241–282). Classification inspired by Verdonck 2018.

[…]

When Marduk [Supreme God of Babylon] sent me to rule over men, to give the protection of right to the land, I did right and righteousness in …, and brought about the well-being of the oppressed.

The great gods have called me, I am the salvation-bearing shepherd, whose staff is straight, the good shadow that is spread over my city; on my breast I cherish the inhabitants of the land of Sumer and Akkad; in my shelter I have let them repose in peace; in my deep wisdom have I enclosed them. That the strong might not injure the weak, in order to protect the widows and orphans

[…]

The king who rules among the kings of the cities am I. My words are well considered. There is no wisdom like mine.[29]

This bronze age braggadocio reads a bit like a Trump speech, doesn't it? And the text continues in this grandiloquent vein. The whole exordium consists of 803 words, 3,856 characters (in the English translation) and reiterates Hammurabi's divine mission, wisdom and intermediary role in administering justice, and the divine origin of the legal rules. Bordering on defensive. The stele is truly verbose: we are told time and again why Hammurabi is entitled to lay down the law. So soon after the Neolithic revolution, recent memories of egalitarian relationships evidently necessitated such orotundity to provide conclusive proof of Hammurabi's prerogative. It is a textual and pictorial explanation that the great Hammurabi is actually doing nothing more than following the dictates of the supreme deity. The stele is an illustrated explanatory memorandum and blasts its trumpet over and over again: the mighty and grandiose Hammurabi is entitled and best positioned to do so. And he is surely not acting on his own accord; he is merely taking down notes from the gods.

Long, verbose and defensive, much has changed since, or has it? Maybe not as much as one would think. Modern constitutions still try to explain the reasons for their existence, for their right to be. Eighty-three percent of all constitutions nowadays are endowed with an exordium of some sort preceding the actual body of the constitution – solemn opening statements we call preambles.[30] These statements try to convince the readers or addressees of the constitution in some way or other that what follows is legitimate, right and proper. The only thing that really seems to have changed is the size of constitutional preambles: over the course of three millennia they have been reduced from Hammurabi's 808-word exordium to an average of around 300 words per constitutional preamble in 2017.[31] 'Plus ça change, plus c'est pareil' (the more things change, the more they stay the same), as the French say.

---

[29] Translated by L.W King, 1910. http://avalon.law.yale.edu/ancient/hamframe.asp (Consulted on 22 May 2019).

[30] Voermans, Stremler & Cliteur 2017, p. 15 ff.

[31] *Ibid.*, p. 21–22.

5

Etched into Collective Memory

Ancient Constitutions

The idea of God-given basic laws carved in stone is ancient and can be found in many early civilisations. Consider Yahweh giving Moses the Ten Commandments as tablets of stone, or Rome's Law of the Twelve Tables (451 BCE), bronze plaques posted at the Forum until their destruction in a Gallic raid (390 BCE). There is one crucial difference between them: the Law of the Twelve Tables largely omits gods – they are not invoked nor are they its source. The text is characteristic of the practical Romans, coming straight to the point: 'If the plaintiff summons the defendant to court the defendant shall go',[1] says the opening of table 1. No incantation, no exordium, just: 'go'. The reason for this straightforwardness is simple: the Twelve Tables were not bestowed by the gods, they were prepared by a commission. How very modern. In the newly founded Roman republic, Romans could no longer rely on a king ruling by the grace of god. They had just overthrown their last and widely despised King Tarquinius Superbus (Tarquin the Proud) in 509 BCE.[2] This obliged them to rethink many parts of Rome's law and administration. They did so by way of a rather formal procedure (a committee) and recorded the result in a formal document (the Tables). This constitutional act, in parts recognisable by contemporary standards, proclaimed both a new 'we' (organisation under new leadership) and a legal system. Despite the great differences with the present,[3] the English classicist Mary Beard is certainly right in saying that the Twelve Tables

---

[1] Table I: 'Si in ius vocat, ito.' Translation by Allan Chester Johnson, Paul Robinson Coleman-Norton & Frank Card Bourne, 1961 http://avalon.law.yale.edu/ancient/twelve_tables.asp (consulted on 24 May 2019).

[2] The Roman Republic was founded in 509 BCE, when, according to tradition, the last king of Rome, Lucius Tarquinius Superbus, was overthrown by the first consul of the Republic, Lucius Iunius Brutus.

[3] As Capogrossi Colognesi, referring to Livy, says: 'The Twelve Tables had made the will of "the people" – as embodied in the assemblies – the foundation of the legislative process, and had granted it an autonomous status.' Capogrossi Colognesi 2014, p. 87. Capogrossi Colognesi points out that there are more differences than similarities between what we now call 'law',

represent an important junction in a contingent developmental process leading to state formation and, ultimately, modern states and constitutions.[4]

THE TWELVE TABLES

The Twelve Tables were certainly not delivered to the Romans on stone tablets from upon the high skies of Anu and Bel or from Mount Sinai. Nor were they even unanimously acclaimed; they were born out of the flames of conflict. The political situation in Rome was unstable after the overthrow of the last king; the institutions, law and social organisation of the old class-based society were not adequate for the new relations.[5] Wealthy patricians had monopolised high civil, religious and military offices which enabled them to control all power and dominate the city-state of Rome. By the end of the sixth century BCE however, the city's prosperity had become increasingly dependent on the workers, small traders and artisans – the plebeians – the Roman labour class, ranking only above slaves. The Twelve Tables were the outcome of this struggle, known as the Conflict of the Orders.[6] The plebeians had tired of the exploitation and oppression they endured under the old guard and revolted. Soon after the birth of the young Republic (509 BCE), Rome was confronted with a major plebeian insurrection, the Secession of the Plebs. It was a surprisingly peaceful uprising for the day and age – the plebs went on strike. In a dramatic gesture, the plebeians abandoned the city en masse in 494 BCE, paralysing public life, in an attempt to force political change. Their protest succeeded. The plebeians were granted representatives (Tribunes of the Plebs) and their own assembly (the Plebeian Assembly, or People's Assembly);[7] the tribunes of the Plebs represented the plebeians in the general public assembly of the republic (the Centuriate Assembly)[8] which had an important – at times a final – say in most of the government business of the Roman Republic. This nominal representation did not protect individual plebeians from patrician domination and associated exploitation. The patricians were entrenched in the senate, the real centre of power in the republic, which appointed two of its members as consuls in charge of the Republic's general administration. Even with their own tribunes, the plebeians had little to no influence on decisions about public funds, law, warfare and leadership. Despite all their efforts, the plebeians made scarcely any progress after the early concessions: the doors of the senate remained firmly closed to them. In 462 BCE, the plebeian tribune Gaius Terentilius Harsa tried to pass another law limiting the consuls'

'constitutional law' and 'state' and the Roman understanding of them; in particular Roman political institutions were very different from their modern counterparts (p. 71–72).

[4] Beard 2015, p. 143.
[5] Cf. Capogrossi Colognesi 2014, p. 57–63.
[6] Beard 2015, p. 146.
[7] 'Concilium Plebis' in Latin.
[8] 'Comitia Centuriata' in Latin.

power by defining it more precisely. But senate foot-dragging until Harsa's term expired succeeded in thwarting his motion. Another major conflict seemed imminent, certainly when the plebeians also began demanding that the city's 'laws' be made public rather than kept secret so only patricians could invoke them. There was complete deadlock until the idea took hold that there should be an enquiry before any decision or arrangement was made. A time-honoured good-governance classic: buy time by study; appoint a committee. The Romans had heard of Athens' positive experiences with codified laws – the Solonian Constitution. In 454 BCE Rome sent three men to Athens to *transcribe* Solon's laws and, more generally, find out more about the way of life and the political institutions of other Greek cities. The commissioners took their time. It was two years before the embassy returned with the requested copy of the Solonian Constitution. But it paid off. The Roman Senate decided the Greek example would serve as the basis for Roman law, the only question was how to 'Romanise' it? Who would compose the first draft? The Plebeian tribunes succeeded in having a decemvirate (commission of ten men, *decemviri*) appointed for a year, tasked with drafting Roman laws (the Twelve Tables) emulating the Greek example.[9] The undertaking was considered so important that the 'regular magistrates' (consuls, proconsuls, quaestors, praetor, censor and the like) were suspended for a year (451 BCE).

The Ten-Man-Commission[10]was chaired by Appius Claudius and was – ineluctably – composed exclusively of patricians. It published a draft of Ten Tables of Laws within a year. Everyone in the city was invited to read, consider and discuss the proposed laws, which was to be followed by a general, public discussion. All very modern, as were the consequences: trouble. Whilst the decemvirate's work was much appreciated, most Romans thought it incomplete. At least another two tables were required. The following year another decemvirate was established, which had to work in far more difficult circumstances. After much controversy and even sex scandals,[11] two additional tables were completed. Along with the ten earlier laws, they were inscribed on bronze and posted at the forum in the city centre. They remained there for less than sixty years before being destroyed in a Gallic raid (or – more likely – pillaged; bronze was valuable). Their brief period at the marketplace belies the substantial influence the Twelve Tables have had in the many centuries of Roman rule and civilisation since. Their content became part of Romans' living memory, passed down from one generation to the next (both orally and in writing) and internalised. Cicero says that schoolboys at the start of the first century BCE still had to learn the Twelve Tables by rote. He complained that almost no one knew them off by heart fifty years later (c. 55 BCE). It proves yet again – there is really only one enduring grievance: everything used to be better in the old days.

---

[9] For a 'first-hand' report – 400 years after the occasion – cf. Cicero 2008, p. 51–56.
[10] The 'Decemvirate' in Latin.
[11] Beard 2015, p. 149–150.

The Twelve Tables clearly show how laws and constitutions made the transition over time from divinely mediated to human rules and how written 'legal' regulations came to play an increasing role in a society's organisation and governance. There is no mention of any god in the Twelve Tables[12] and they did not even have to explain who the 'we' was: S.P.Q.R. The senate and people of Rome – evidently. Twelve plaques enshrining and displaying a city-state's laws. After the Greek example, where constitutional experimentation had been taking place for several hundred years.

GREECE

Classical Greece could rightfully claim the title of the very first constitutional country in antiquity, were it not that Greece was not one country at the time. Ancient Greece consisted of a collection of city-states (*poleis*), colonies and settlements with a shared language, religion and culture. Between the seventh and second centuries BCE, many of the maritime and highly successful Greek city-states had collections of laws governing both city governance and relations between citizens. These laws were a patchwork of private-law rules – governing relations between citizens – and public-law rules – governing relations between citizens and government, the status of citizens and their leaders. Ancient Greeks would not have considered them a patchwork; the modern distinction between private-law and public-law rules arose at a much later date. This is, for instance, illustrated by rules governing family affairs. Nowadays the regulation of family affairs and family law is largely the domain of private law, whilst in ancient Greece it was a matter of public concern and 'public law': government played a major role in setting the rules concerning family matters since it was considered a matter of public order. In Thebes you were not permitted to start a family, let alone get married, without the permission of the king or city assembly (*ekklēsia*). If you could not find a partner, you could get an exemption from the family ban if your father promised to give his sons to the army. Adoption was often a public matter too.[13] On the other hand, things we nowadays consider almost self-evidently public and subject of governmental regulation, were not seen in the same light by the ancient Greeks. Take the administration of justice. The laws of many ancient *poleis* deemed it *not* a direct matter for the government (king, ruler, or city government), but instead one for citizens to settle through a jury, mediator or judge whom they themselves appointed. A form of dispute resolution we would now call mediation. As confusing as ancient Greek commingling of the distinction between public and private spheres can be for us, they did distinguish between legal rules of divine origin and ordinary secular rules.

---

[12] Although Table X is about sacred law (worship, sacrifices, funerals, and so on), it does not invoke the gods. Nonetheless Table VII stipulates that using magic spells or prayers, or black magic to dispatch someone is a capital offence. Hartley was, of course, correct in saying: 'The past is a foreign country; they do things differently there.' Hartley 2014, p. 1.

[13] Tomlinson 2006, p. 10.

The latter increased in step with expanding economic activity. It worked as a catalyst. Trade puts a great deal of strain on human relations and groups. How can people trust one another? In your own group or tribe, you can hold each other to account after a transaction. This is no longer possible when you have bought something from a 'stranger' in a casual place. As trade is a very attractive way of exchanging surpluses and products, and hence of increasing both parties' wealth, prosperity and well-being (trade increases your chances of survival and gives you greater control of the environment), human communities have tried to find various ways of solving its drawbacks. First, by converting occasional exchanges, in which parties more or less accidentally encounter each other, into institutionalised exchanges (dedicated marketplaces, fairs, larger gatherings) in which the presence of a crowd allowed increased social control. Later these markets became even more concentrated, allowing further control and standardisation. Markets were drawn to the cities. The French historian Fernand Braudel shows how:

> In rather minimal form perhaps, markets [...] existed in very ancient times within a single village or group of villages – the market being a sort of itinerant village, as the fair was a sort of travelling town. But the decisive step in this long history was taken when the *town* appropriated these hitherto modest little markets. [...] The *urban* market may have been invented by the Phoenicians. Certainly, the Greek city-states of about the same period all had a market on the *agora*, the central square; they also invented or at any rate propagated money, which clearly furthered the career of the market [...].[14]

Then as now, markets required rules. Not because markets could not function independently or find a balance, but simply because increasing the intensity of exchange and trade entails somehow organising the core element – *trust*. This was achieved with fiduciary abstractions and institutions: money and rules. The rise and fabulous success of the Greek city-states show how these processes go hand in hand. There was a proliferation of trading cities in the area around the Aegean Sea from the seventh century BCE. The seafaring Greeks, aided by a common language and culture (which facilitated mutual communication and hence trust) successfully utilised a new, large-scale source of wealth – large-scale overseas trade between concentrated trading centres (cities).[15] As these urban centres grew, there was a large-scale proliferation in legal rules (*nomoi*) and other fiduciary institutions. Naturally, these rules varied from place to place: every city-state had its own history and traditions. Local situations differed and accordingly, so did the law. Some city-states were literally thousands of kilometres apart. Yet, it is also interesting to look at the similarities. Unlike Mesopotamian constitutions, many of these city-state rules – which usually formed a single entity with the city-state's form of government (*politeia*) – no longer

---

[14] Braudel 1992, p. 228.
[15] Hall 2015, chapter 2 (*The Creation of Greece*) and chapter 3 (*Frogs and Dolphins Round the Pond*), p. 51–99.

referred to gods or divine origins of the laws most of the time. We know that the Greek city-states' various forms of government in the period were predominantly 'secular': they were made by humans. Religion played a much smaller role than it had in ancient Mesopotamian governance. A second striking aspect is the competition between city-states over who actually had the best laws and governance system. The ever-rivalrous Hellenes, of course, liked nothing more than a good competition (just think of the Olympic and Pythian Games),[16] but the comparisons of laws and city-states' forms of government by great thinkers like Plato and Aristotle are still extraordinary. They are enquiring quests for 'good' laws and the best forms of government, which have appealed to the imagination and served as an example right up to this day. These antique studies are all the more impressive as they were largely intended simply as comparative research into which city formula worked best. The quest for the best formula came with a bonus, for the best-organised city was most of the time also the strongest city with the best opportunities to outperform other cities or even to overpower them.

DREROS AND DRACO

The oldest *polis* legal code, or constitution, belongs to Dreros on the island of Crete (c. 650–600 BCE).[17] The code's preamble, found on a carved stone in the temple of Apollo at Delphi, states:[18]

> May God be kind (?). The city has thus decided; when a man has been *kosmos* [chief magistrate, ruler], the same man shall not be *kosmos* again for ten years. If he does act as *kosmos*, whatever, judgements he gives, he shall owe double, and he shall lose his rights to office, as long as he lives, and whatever he does as *kosmos* shall be nothing. The swearers shall be the *kosmos* (i.e., the body of *kosmoi*) […].

It is a sort of ancient one-term limit. Whoever was president or chief ruler for one term could not hold that office again for ten years. Violation of this cooling-off period was severely punished: all of the transgressor's acts were null and void, he could never hold office again, and was liable for damages resulting from his rulings (all damages awarded had to be repaid double) and the council of wise man could intervene at any time and replace him. The Dreros law does invoke God, but chiefly for form's sake as an incantation; the law itself was passed by the city.

Vastly more famous than this relatively obscure legal code is the Draconian constitution, or Draco's code. Created by the Athenian legislator Draco in about 624 BCE, we only actually know these laws from later references. As far as we know, these first Athenian laws chiefly governed criminal law. This is quite modern in itself. Draco's

---

[16] Hall 2015, chapter 7 (*The Rivalrous Macedonians*), p. 181 ff.
[17] (Michael) Scott 2016, p. 31.
[18] Meiggs & Lewis 1969, p. 2–3.

code introduced the distinction between murder (intentional homicide) and man-slaughter (unintentional homicide). It contains little about the functioning of the Athenian government. This 'Draconian constitution' does not appear to be much of a constitution at first sight. But once we appreciate its underlying intention – putting an end to the formerly common practice of taking the law into one's own hands and the disruptive consequences feuds and retaliation had on Athenian society – it gains a more familiar ring. The essence of Draco's code was twofold: halting cycles of vengeance, and prescribing that crimes and offences mentioned in the laws would be dealt with in court instead of citizens taking the law into their own hands. Various courts were also established for different kinds of offence or crime, and they were accessible to every citizen. The laws also partially ended class justice. Nonetheless, Draco's code is mainly remembered for a single quality: its 'draconian' character. Almost all violations of the rules in his law code carried the death penalty. If the Athenians had applied all these laws to the letter, they would certainly not have been able to withstand the Persian invasion in around 500 BCE thanks to a dearth of inhabitants.

THE SOLONIAN CONSTITUTION

The Draconian constitution failed to stymie internal dissension in Athens, which by the turn of the sixth century BCE was a rapidly growing and wealthy port city. This bustling *polis* was riven by constant clashes between established interests and impetuous upstarts – an age-old story in places where markets and opportunities proliferate rapidly, and everyone gets caught up in the ferment of quick profits.

Solon came to the fore in the midst of this tumultuous situation. He was a politician, poet and good legislator – a sort of cross between Confucius, King Hammurabi and King Solomon. This archetypical wise ruler, and scion of an aristocratic Athenian family, rose to prominence around 600 BCE not only as an apt army commander, but also as an adviser in a conflict between Megara and Athens over the possession of the island of Salamis. He knew better than anyone how things worked in the city – what the interests were – the landed nobility's long-standing traditions, rights and agricultural interests, and the mercantile classes' aspiration to put the *polis* on the map. Solon understood that Athens would need to bridge the differences between the city's competing factions if it were to survive the intense competition with other Greek cities.[19] It was no easy task. The power struggles between the landed aristocratic families had been partially curbed by Draco's code, but the gentry still dominated the Athenian government whilst traders, artisans and small farmers were all but excluded from it. Many ordinary Athenians were crippled by large debts and debt bondage, which was exacerbated by the nobility's (successful) litigiousness. The city was literally hamstrung. In a desperate attempt to end the upheaval, the Athenian citizenry awarded Solon autocratic powers to make a legal code which would go beyond Draco's code – new

[19]   (Michael) Scott 2016, p. 32.

laws on good, fair and just governance. Solon promulgated his revolutionary legal code in 594 BCE. Its rules were not limited solely to capital crimes but regulated just about all aspects of social life. Solon used his laws to open the city's government and public administration to all citizens. The Athenians were divided into four classes, based on property not heredity. All four groups were in principle given a say in the city's government, with the poorest classes allowed to participate in the *Ekklēsia* (popular assembly) and serving on the *Heliaia* (people's court) but barred from the other tiers of government. The *Ekklēsia* would later on serve as the cornerstone, the very foundation, of the democracy instituted by Cleisthenes from 508 BCE. Solon crafted his laws subtly, attempting to inspire the often improvident Athenians to behave with political responsibility. There were to be no political games; Solon's laws stipulated that in a political conflict every citizen must vote according to his 'conscience' and always choose the most just option above partisan interests. The laws also tried to resolve the city's rampant debt problem. They abolished all debts and debt bondage of an Athenian citizen was prohibited.[20] In addition, penalties in the Draconian code were reduced, new family and inheritance laws were introduced (allowing non-family members to inherit), parents were – how modern – obliged to have their children learn a trade, and children were, in turn, obliged to support their parents in old age. The common thread in Solon's legislation is that it forced Athenian citizens to take each other into account in order to foster and maintain harmonious and workable relations in the *polis*, or *eumonia*: good order.

Solon's laws also encompassed important economic reforms. They imposed export restrictions on agricultural products, except for olive oil. Attican produce was to feed the Atticans and not merely serve as something to be exchanged for luxury goods. Everyone was also obliged in principle to dig their own well, but those who failed to find water were entitled to use their neighbours' well. The laws contained many rules aimed at mitigating disputes between neighbours – about relatively minor matters such as planting trees and problems caused by trees, digging ditches, where to place beehives, nuisance caused by dogs, and so forth. Solon's laws also instituted a surprisingly open immigration policy: foreigners who practised a trade in the city and came to live in Athens with their whole family could obtain civil rights. We can discern without too much difficulty a city constitution in Solon's laws, even if they contained many laws that we would categorise as criminal or private law today. This do not detract from its core intention: regulating society through government intervention in a context of rules on leadership, law and society.[21]

Solon's legal code was engraved on rotating wooden rolls and posted at the agora (marketplace) where everyone could read them. They were also seen by the Roman embassy that came to study the Athenian constitution one hundred and fifty years later.

---

[20] *Ibid.*, p. 33.

[21] Lanni and Vermeule also assume that Solon's laws can be considered a constitution, like many other Greek and Roman sets of laws. They compare antique constitutions, including

Noël Coypel (1628–1707), *Solon upholds his laws against the objections of the Athenians*, c. 1672

Solon might have been wise, like the great King Hammurabi, but he was by no means modest. He praised his reforms in his poems:

> To the demos [the people] I have given such honour as is sufficient,
> neither taking away nor granting any more.
> For those who had power and were great in riches,
> I equally cared that they should suffer nothing wrong.
> Thus I stood, holding my strong shield over both,
> and I did not allow either side to prevail against justice.[22]

He was a bringer of peace who brought the Athenian aristocracy and citizenry together and wanted them to know this. For 'if someone other than I had taken power,' he boasted:

> some ill-intentioned and greedy man, he would not have been able to control the people. For had I been willing to do what pleased the opposing party then, or what the others had planned for them, this city would have lost many men.

the Draconian and Solonian constitutions, with modern constitutions in an article in the 2012 *Stanford Law Review*. There are, of course, significant differences. Classical antiquity lacked our modern political institutions and the design, classification and meaning of the law was different. A characteristic difference is that ancient constitutions were often drafted by a single individual, sometimes even a foreigner. As a rule, modern constitutions are drafted by groups or dedicated committees, and are usually adopted by delegates, who are often parliamentary representatives. What are the strengths and weaknesses of these drafting methods? A product of many minds certainly has many strengths, including a greater likelihood of enjoying widespread support, but there are situations in which a single author would be advantageous in modern relations. Cf. Lanni & Vermeule 2012.

[22] Solon, Fragment 5.1; (Michael) Scott 2016, p. 32.

That is why I made a stout defence all round, turning like a wolf among many hounds.[23]

The hounds eventually got the better of him, when a clique associated with Peisistratos usurped power in 546 BCE. By then elderly and powerless, Solon witnessed the demise of his 'third-way' politics and the moderate governance he had laboured so hard to achieve. He could not have known that his legacy had laid the foundations for Athens' zenith from 500 BCE, when after the introduction of democracy and a victory over Persia the golden era of Perikles blossomed: a period of unprecedented accomplishments in democracy, philosophy and the arts.

ARISTOTLE

The Solonian Constitution promoted unity in Athens, which facilitated social mobilisation, prosperity and order. These key factors enabled this small *polis* to withstand the mighty Persian empire[24] and become a great power for a time. Whether or not following the Athenian example, other Greek city states established constitutions of this kind too. As mentioned, the Greek philosopher Aristotle counted at least 158 of them around 325 BCE. Which one functioned best? What kind of rules made a polity strongest, happiest and most prosperous? It has remained an intriguing question to this day. Aristotle addresses it in Book II of his great work *The Politics*. His analyses are very precise and systematic – scientifically sound. By way of introduction, he argues that one, of course, needs to determine what one is talking about before embarking on a comparison. What are city-state 'constitutions' (*Politeia*)? Aristotle says that politeia are about 'the organisation of the offices [of state], and in particular the one that is sovereign over *all* the others':[25] government, including the executive and judiciary. Constitutions deal with the way in which authority and supreme power (sovereignty) is shaped. Aristotle's constitutional concept is essentially the same as Dicey's aforementioned broad definition, only it precedes it by more than two thousand years. Aristotle was confronted by great variety in the constitutions he studied, which, of course, had to do with the fact that this multitude of city-states had different societies, contexts and backgrounds. In some cases, citizens were closely bound by family ties, descent and tradition, and had a shared identity; other cities citizens did not share much more than a common defensive wall – a loose-knit collection of assorted inhabitants and communities living in the same place and sharing little in common. Aristotle gives the example of the Persian city of Babylon – part of the city was still unaware that the city had fallen two days after its capture (in 538 BCE).[26] Obviously government needs to be organised differently when citizens share little in common than when there is a close, homogeneous community.

---

[23] Solon's poem fragment 35. Cf. (Michael) Scott 2016, p. 32.
[24] Decided by the battles of Salamis (480 BCE) and Plataea (479 BCE).
[25] Aristotle 1962, *The Politics*, III.6, 1278 b6-b15. My Italics.
[26] Aristotle 1962, *The Politics*, III.3, 1276 a24-a34.

Step two of Aristotle's classification of constitutions is perhaps the most essential. In this, he addresses the aim of a constitution and the purpose of a form of government. We might be tempted to disregard this question nowadays, perhaps taking the answer for granted. Aristotle's answer starts with what sounds like a platitude: the greatest good of a form of government is 'justice', giving each their due.[27] For Aristotle, this is of supreme importance:

> This good is greatest, and is a 'good' in the highest sense, when that knowledge or skill is the most sovereign one, i.e. the faculty of statecraft. In the state, the good aimed at is justice; and that means what is for the benefit of the whole community. Now all men agree that justice means equality in some sense [...] that justice is some entity which is relative to persons, and that equality must be equal for equals.[28]

Fine. Of course. But surely this is self-evident? Not quite. Aristotle's idea of the purpose of constitutions only really becomes apparent farther in the text. What exactly does justice mean? Certainly not the identification of the individual with the community as conceived by Aristotle's teacher Plato (c. 427 – 347 BCE) in his book *The Republic*. In Plato's totalitarian utopia, property is communal and all of the community's efforts are focused on political unity, harmony and shared values: it is a community that endeavours to eliminate differences between people; what is good for the community is good for the individual and vice versa – they have to become one. Aristotle considers this an absurd goal and a misleading principle for organising a state.[29] His basic principle is that people are different and always have different needs and interests. As such, the organisation of the state must aim to recognise these differences, recognise people and, strive for the happiness and contentment of as many members of the community as possible, instead of the happiness of the community as such. Recognising differences and doing them justice is the starting point and goal of political organisation. It sounds surprisingly contemporary, especially considering modern scientific insights into the biological roots of our desire for recognition. A good state must, according to Aristotle, constantly look for the *best in* all its diverse citizens in order to turn this into the best *for all* its citizens. In this way, a polity can work towards developing some kind of happiness maximisation,[30] not for a small group, but for all citizens in a political community, a *polis*.[31]

In his third step, Aristotle takes these principles on the forms and aims of constitutions to look for patterns. He classified the Greek city-state constitutions known to him into three 'good' leadership systems (or systems of government): *monarchy* (government by a single competent leader), *aristocracy* (government by a select group

---

[27] 'Suum cuique tribuere' as the later Roman adage puts it.
[28] Aristotle 1962, *The Politics*, III.12, 1282 b14-b23.
[29] Aristotle 1962, *The Politics*, II.5.
[30] Aristotle 1962, *The Politics*, VII.13, 1332 a32-a38.
[31] Aristotle 1962, *The Politics*, VII.9, 1329 a17-a27.

of the 'best' or most competent people) and what he calls *polity* or majority rule by the citizenry. Aristotle argued that the three good forms could degenerate into three perverted forms. 'Tyranny is monarchy for the benefit of the monarch, oligarchy for the benefit of the men of means, democracy for the benefit of the men without means. None of the three aims to be of profit of the common interest.'[32] Aristotle considered democracy a perverted form of government solely focused on the short-term and short-sighted interest of those without means. There are still those, thank-fully a minority, who would concur.

One of Aristotle's greatest strengths is his appreciation that there is no one-size-fits-all constitution, even though he did favour *integrative* constitutions able to deliver the greatest happiness to the greatest number of citizens. Aristotle thinks that the most likely way of achieving this aim is through majority rule, polity, but maximal happiness of this kind might be achieved through other forms of government as well.[33] The challenge is, of course, preventing degeneration and perversion. Aristotle's prescription for this is a familiar one. He prized mixed forms of government (also known as the *mixed constitution*) in which power is divided between branches of government that keep each other in check because they can only be held temporarily and have to work together. The Greco-Roman his-torian Polybius (c. 200 – 120 BCE),[34] a great admirer of Aristotle, regarded the mixed constitution as key to the success of the Roman republic.[35] Intelligent and integrative government facilitated Roman victory in the Punic Wars against Hannibal's Carthage in the second and third centuries BCE. Rome's mixed con-stitution enabled it to utilise and deploy its human resources more effectively than its authoritarian opponent. Hannibal, a brilliant strategist, was dependent on mercenaries and allies – ultimately he simply could not match the sheer limitless resources of the 'we' of Rome.

The aim of this book is, of course, not to give a comprehensive overview of the great thinkers of antiquity but to learn more about the origin and provenance of constitutions. Aristotle's study of constitutions provides an excellent insight into this. Why do societies, like the Greek city-states, have rules to organise their government and society? What are their consequences?

Aristotle's study shows that constitutions are a solution to the organisational problem of growing and competing mercantile societies in ancient Greece. How do you take concerted action in a new environment like this? How do you deal with kin, acquaintances and strangers, and with the many conflicting interests? How do you lead a group of this kind? And how do you organise this group so that every member has a place in it and can flourish? There are essentially two

---

[32] Aristotle 1962, *The Politics*, III.8, 1279 b4-b10.
[33] Aristotle 1962, *The Politics*, IV.3, 1289 b30-1290 a25.
[34] Polybius 1923, book VI.
[35] Asmis 2005, especially p. 378.

options. Either the individual is *absorbed* by society and becomes one with it. Thus, mostly under the condition that society also commits to the fate and well-being of the individual 'family' member: the family's happiness is the family member's happiness. The community and the individual correspond entirely. Community and society become one as well. Members serve their interest by serving the group interest; failing to do so harms the group, the other members and essentially the member herself. The other option – favoured by Aristotle and his ilk – recognises that community and individual values and interests do not automatically correspond and tries to find some solution to this by making agreements about leadership, social class divisions, privileges, minority rights and so forth. The former position in which individual and community become one might initially appear to have only theoretical significance, but nothing could be farther from the truth. Major state ideologies, past and present, including theocracy as well as Communism and other humanist schools,[36] strive for exactly this kind of political and hence social unity of the group and its members. For many Christians and their leaders in early mediaeval Europe, for instance, the aims and interests of the community and its members were one and the same: serving God.[37] The modern conception of individuality was unimaginable.[38]

Aristotle is also relevant because he raises the topical issue of social engineering. Can you use rules on law, leadership and other institutions to direct and change the course of a society and markets? Or are the edifices of law and leadership not much more than the coincidental proceeds – the outcomes – of the dynamics of human society? In other words: do these institutions *matter*?[39] Do the channels of constitutions and their institutions direct the flow and course of the water, as institutionalists (old and new) believe, or is it the water current that shapes the channels? Aristotle certainly belongs to the former school; he is a neo-institutionalist avant la lettre.[40] He argues that a good, constitutional organisation of governance can shape a society's direction, provided the overall setup of this organisation is convincing, appealing and internalised:

> The same things are best for a community and for individuals, and it is these that a lawgiver must instil into the souls of men.[41]

You could put this on a modern election poster and win votes with it.

---

[36] Social and evolutionary humanism in particular. Harari 2016, p. 246–257.

[37] As Church Father Augustine wrote (and prescribed) as early as 426 CE in *De Civitate Dei*.

[38] Siedentop 2014, chapters 14 (*Fostering the Peace of God*) and 15 (*The Papal Revolution: A Constitution for Europe?*) and *Epilogue: Christianity and Secularism*.

[39] Not in everyone's view, but North argues that they *do*. Cf. his famous book on institutions North 1990.

[40] Friedland 1991, p. 223–262.

[41] Aristotle 1962, *The Politics*, VII.14, 1333 b26–b37.

PLATO AND WISDOM AS A SOURCE
OF LAW AND GOVERNMENT

Aristotle's conception of law and government as nothing more than products of human endeavour – the random outcome of a political process – has always felt a little uncomfortable, certainly for lawyers. The Australian political philosopher Tom Campbell writes that 'for many lawyers [...] the very idea that law is a manifestation or type of politics seems almost offensive.'[42] This is not a modern aversion, but an enduring attitude rooted in classical antiquity. We like to think of fundamental and legal rules as a form of higher wisdom, either of divine origin or passed down over generations from wise ancestors. This is also a cornerstone of modern common law legal systems, as found in the United Kingdom and partly in countries such as Australia, India and the United States.[43] Law is mainly derived from case law in this system – at least, in theory. It is underpinned by the idea that law arises from precedent – collections of judicial decisions. Layer upon layer of this literally 'common law' arises from tradition, custom and precedent, giving expression to a society's 'latent' wisdom.[44] Passed down from generation to generation, the law stems from a society's history and is the expression of the wisdom of centuries. It is a far cry from modern 'continental' legal systems, in which fundamental rules and legal rules are made in the present by living people and legislation is the main source of law. It does not feel right to believers in 'wise' law, like most legal scholar in common law countries, even if these days most law in these jurisdictions is also promulgated in man-made laws.[45]

The idea of seeing constitutions and law as inherited forms of wisdom and tradition, and using them as such, has many advantages. First, it gives guidance; the very survival and transmission of these organisational and legal rules has proven their worth.[46] It obviates the need for the current generation expend time and energy reinventing the wheel. Traditions, inherited wisdom and law, time-honoured forms of leadership and organisation are in this respect efficient. This guidance also binds; 'wise' inherited law confers legitimacy and socialises members of a society. Who can contradict the ancestors and long-established insights? Organisation according to long-standing practices and rules also promotes mutual trust and social cohesion and effectively appeals to our abstract imagination by referring to bygone events, departed people and the like. As a human species, we are sensitive to tradition and custom[47] and tend to regard old customs and insights as normatively binding.[48]

---

[42] Campbell 2012, p. 228.
[43] O'Scannlain 2004, especially p. 757–759 and p. 762–763.
[44] Vermeule 2007.
[45] Mattei & Pess 2008.
[46] 'Law is, of course, the result of this socially formed mentality in adapting the race to its physical surroundings, and in striving to overcome those surroundings', as Zane puts it. Zane 1998, p. 3.
[47] We are naturally sensitive to and follow custom. Cf. Amodio, Jost, Master & Ye 2007.
[48] Beetham argues that legitimacy always has a normative structure. It is always derived from rules (e.g. legal rules) that can be justified (in terms of a shared belief in them), and legitimacy

Tradition, precedent, inherited wisdom and custom have a great capacity to legiti-
mise decisions.[49]

The authors of Hammurabi's stele and the Solonian Constitution insisted that
they were *wise*. Which is hardly surprising; we are all susceptible to the self-evidence
of the relationship between law, justice and wisdom. It strikes a chord – the Platonic
chord. That law and politics needed to reflect justice and wisdom was a foregone
conclusion for the Athenian philosopher Plato (427–347 BCE). An ideal society
and perfect state[50] entail handing power to people with the capacity to govern with
knowledge and wisdom.[51] If what Plato calls the *guardians* are well prepared for
their duty to govern then they will do so wisely. These guardians must be properly
raised, educated and exempted from military training in order to be able to perform
their duties in society's interests and not merely serve their own interests.[52] It would
be best if philosophers, as the wisest and most reasonable people of all, were to rule
the state. Plato ascribes the following words to Socrates in *The Republic*.

> Unless, said I, either philosophers become kings in our states or those whom we
> now call our kings and rulers take to the pursuit of philosophy seriously and ade-
> quately, and there is a conjunction of these two things, political power and philo-
> sophical intelligence, while the motley horde of the natures who at present pursue
> either apart from the other are compulsory excluded, there can be no cessation
> of troubles, dear Glaucon, for our states, nor, I fancy, for the human race either.[53]

This idea of the wise ruler, the wise government and the wise law has survived
through to the present day.[54] It is still reflected in the idealisation of rulers and
judges, reverence for and authority of precedent, tradition and 'constructed' law
in the form of legal principles, as well as protest against transient, man-made (constitutional) law that breaks with tradition and inherited wisdom.[55] Certainly after
the emergence of large-scale societies in states and the secularisation of government, wisdom as a source of law and leadership shifted into the background.[56]

---

in the form of 'expressed consent on the part of those qualified to give it'. Cf. Beetham 1991,
chapter 3 (*The Normative Structure of Legitimacy*), p. 64–99.

[49] Weber argues that tradition confers authority and is one of the three sources of legitimacy
(alongside rational-legal and charismatic authority). Cf. Weber 1964, p. 328–329. For further
refinement, cf. Matheson 1987.

[50] Plato, *The Republic*, Volume 4, book 5, 427 e. (and Plato 1983, p. 197).

[51] Plato, *The Republic*, Volume 4, book 5, 428 b.

[52] Plato, *The Republic*, Volume 4, book 5, 428–429.

[53] Plato, *The Republic*, Volume 7, book 5, 473 d.

[54] All over the world. Chinese Confucianism has parallels with Plato's ideas and is still influential in political theory in China today. Cf. Jenco 2010.

[55] 'The great modern fallacy that a constitution can be made, can be manufactured by a combination of existing force and tendencies' as Garner says referring to Burkhardt. Garner 1990,
especially p. 52.

[56] The nineteenth century historian Burckhardt regarded the emergence of states at the end of
the sixteenth century as the root of the evil. He wrote of the perversions of state formation: 'In
this process, intellect came halfway to meet power. What power could not attain by violence,

Many people in the eighteenth century thought it a worrying development, as they witnessed reason and empirical insight supersede age-old custom and tradition. A year after the French Revolution, Edmund Burke, the Anglo-Irish father of conservatism, warned that the loss of the latent wisdom of generations even endangered the law as *law*:

> We are afraid to put men to live and trade each on his own private stock of reason; because we suspect that this stock in each man is small, and that the individuals would do better to avail themselves of the general bank and capital of nations and of ages. Many of our men of speculation, instead of exploding general prejudices, employ their sagacity to discover the latent wisdom which prevails in them.[57]

And yet, in spite of sullen nostalgia and bitter complaints, over the centuries law and constitutional law increasingly have become a human endeavour, trailing in the wake of rational humanism – a shared and profane belief which has steadily spread around the world from the late Middle Ages onwards.

intellect freely offered, in order to remain in its good graces [...] Literature and even philosophy became servile in their glorification of the state [...]' Burckhardt 1979, p. 136–137.
[57] Burke 2003, p. 74.

6

Roman Roots

On 4 September 476 CE, the Western Roman Empire formally came to an end with the deposition of its last emperor Romulus Augustulus ('Little Augustus') by the Germanic leader Odoacer. This 'fall' was not precipitated by a major conquest or victory in an epic battle, but simply because Odoacer, the new ruler after the umpteenth coup, decided to call himself the king of Italy rather than the Roman emperor. The people of Italy and other parts of this once-powerful empire were unlikely to have noticed much of the fall of the Roman Empire. Its decline had been protracted. From the end of the second century CE, Roman emperors had lost their grip on more and more parts of the empire. This crumbling edifice had been afflicted for many decades by unfortunate associations with,[1] and raids and looting by various peoples (Vandals, Visigoths and Ostrogoths, and Germans), who had also installed and toppled various (puppet) emperors. A series of warring soldier-emperors and the division of the empire into an Eastern and Western parts failed to stem the swelling chaos. After almost a millennium, mighty Rome, which had developed from a small city in central Italy into a vast empire, was no more. Its end was not sudden, nor was the blow great. The ousting of the last emperor is regarded nowadays more as a symbolic end of an empire of which little remained.[2]

---

[1] The idea that the Roman Empire collapsed from the pressure of a series of raids by Barbarian hordes is incorrect. The fall was largely due to internal factors. Cf. Omrani 2017, p. 338–339.

[2] We are also accustomed to seeing events of this kind from the perspective of contemporary conceptions of the state – a physically delimited territory in which actual authority is exercised over a population living within its borders. Hence, for *us*, the Western Roman Empire ceased to exist at the moment central authority disappeared and the integrity of the imperial borders could no longer be guaranteed. The Romans did not think about their empire in these modern state-based terms – they did so more in terms of spheres of influence, and domination of groups and peoples. A state, as a centrally governed country, fixed on a map bordered by other states, would have been a very strange idea to the Romans. Cf. A. Goldsworthy 2016, chapter XIII (*Garrisons and Raids*), p. 347–384.

From the perspective of the Eastern Roman Empire's subjects, 476 CE represented no definitive end at all. Seen from Constantinople, the overthrow of Augustulus in the West was not much more than a new incident in turbulent times. Despite its own gradual decline, the Eastern Roman Empire (also called the Byzantine Empire or Byzantium),[3] was to survive for nearly another 1000 years, until Constantinople was conquered by the Turkish sultan Mehmet II on 29 May 1453.

Whatever its importance for contemporaries, we are accustomed to regarding the fall of the Western Roman Empire as a watershed: it is the point at which the Roman Empire expired, and Western Europe descended into the dark and chaotic Middle Ages. This idea and image of degeneration is primarily the product of the great eighteenth-century English historian Edward Gibbon's magnum opus *The History of the Decline and Fall of the Roman Empire*,[4] which denotes the year 476 as a turning point in Western history. Modern historians assume that it was not so much a radical break that led to centuries of political and social chaos, but rather a much more continuous development. This continuity is clearly reflected in the way in which peoples and groups in Western Europe dealt with law and their legal order. From the early Middle Ages (500–1000), peoples in the East and West of Europe evidently continued assuming the continued existence – albeit in a virtual sense – of the Roman legal order and the associated Roman empire. As if it were still there.

Certainly in Western Europe, the *idea* of the Roman Empire and its constitution – including fundamental rules about the structure, nature and functioning of the law and legal system (in short: what the law was, who and how it bound) – was perpetuated for a long time.[5] It was like a ready-to-use template, a framework. And this is exactly what Charlemagne did when he had himself crowned Roman Emperor around the year 800. The imperial house was deemed still standing and fully furnished (with its legal system), it just occasionally remained uninhabited for extended periods of time. This idea of the still existing, albeit uninhabited house of the Roman order, is also the concept behind the *Holy Roman Empire*, which formed a kind of constitutional foundation for the mediaeval (and later) kingdoms, based on the idea that they were all part of one Roman Empire, united under one

---

[3]   The Eastern Romans incidentally continued to refer to themselves as Romans (Romaioi, Ρωμαίων) and to call their empire the 'Roman Empire'. Cf. Wickham 2010.

[4]   Gibbon 1985.

[5]   Wickham argues that the Roman Empire's most important legacy was 'the culture of the public […] The Roman Empire had a strong sense of the difference between the public, the arena of the state and the community, and the private sphere; the boundary was not drawn in exactly the same place as it is today, and there was no neat opposition between "public" and "private", but the uses of the word *publicus* were analogous to those we are used to […] *Privatus* did not denote any sort of "private" political activity, but, when used in this context, came simply to mean "powerless". Public power was all there was, even if the resources of the Roman public world were no longer available.' Wickham 2010, p. 562–563. Cf. Siedentop 2014, p. 17–18.

Roman emperor even in times when there was no longer a real empire or emperor.[6] A theoretical empire[7] with in practice hundreds – or if you counted everything – even thousands of bigger and smaller polities.[8] It was certainly a patchwork, but it was still a blanket. The idea of this ancient empire was so resilient and alive at the end of the ninth century that the first Roman-German Emperor Otto III made *Renovatio imperii Romanorum* (restoration of the Roman Empire) his personal motto from 996 and called himself 'Imperator'. This 'Holy Roman' Empire proved to be incredibly durable in one form or another – it lasted more than 1000 years, and was only dissolved in 1806. As much as the Holy Roman Empire fragmented over the centuries and the idea behind it continued to erode,[9] even at the beginning of the nineteenth century it evidently still had sufficient hold on the collective imagination and sufficient political significance for Napoleon to find it necessary to formally dissolve it in 1806.

THE ROMAN LEGAL ORDER

The culture and Roman legal order survived as a living memory[10] even after the Western Roman Empire had fallen.[11] Usually alongside or as part of new orders. The idea of a mixed or stratified legal order, a mix of Roman and local law, was familiar to the people in former Roman territories for centuries. For us, children of sovereign states, this is difficult to grasp, even in an age in which international law is

[6] The Roman Empire survived as a phantom even after its 'formal' fall, or as Voltaire so beautifully expressed it: 'Le fantôme d'empire romain subsistait' (The phantom, if the Roman Empire had survived). Voltaire 1829, p. 360.

[7] Wilson writes about this theoretical claim: 'Imperial apologists fully recognised that the Empire's territory was much smaller than the extent of the known world [...] Like the ancient Romans they distinguished between the Empire's actual territory and its divine imperial mission, which they considered limitless. French, Spanish and other western monarchs increasingly emphasized their own sovereign royalty, but this did little to diminish arguments that the emperor was still superior. Even if they acknowledged practical limits to imperial authority, most writers still believed in the desirability of a single, secular Christian leader.' Wilson 2017, p. 40.

[8] In the eighteenth century, the Holy Roman Empire consisted of approximately 1800 different territories, the majority being tiny estates owned and ruled by the families of Imperial Knights. Gagliardo 1980, p. 12–23.

[9] Voltaire quipped that the Holy Roman Empire was not holy, Roman, nor an empire ('Ce corps qui s'appelait et qui s'appelle encore le saint empire romain n'était en aucune manière ni saint, ni romain, ni empire'). Voltaire 1829, p. 238.

[10] Van Caenegem 1995, p. 44.

[11] Wickham argues that we have to learn to look at the early Middle Ages in a different light: 'That paradigm sees many aspects of late Antiquity (itself substantially revalued: the late Roman empire is now often seen as the Roman high point, not an inferior and totalitarian copy of the second-century *pax romana*) continuing into the early Middle Ages without a break. More specifically: the violence of the barbarian invaders of the empire is a literary trope; there were few if any aspects of post-Roman society and culture that did not have Roman antecedents [...] in short, one can continue to study the early medieval world, east or west, as if it were late Rome.' Wickham 2010, p. 8.

playing an ever-greater role. Roman law in antiquity (the republic and the empire) had a very different form to the law we are familiar with. It was an eclectic mix of precedent, customary rules, writings of influential lawyers and orators (like Cicero), court addresses, legal advice and opinions, court rulings and the like. There were some laws (*Leges, edicta*), passed by the senate, magistrates or later by the emperor, but they were certainly not the main sources of law. It looks like a hotchpotch from a contemporary perspective; it certainly was not for the Romans. They regarded the law in the same way as their literature and philosophy: as a tradition, part of the Roman way of life. Our ideas of state, sovereignty and ordering of a legal system were foreign to them.

The First Thousand Years of Roman Law

From tradition and edicts issued by praetors – Roman magistrates authorised to administer justice, a kind of Attorney General, Solicitor General and Lord Chancellor rolled into one[12] – we know a relatively great deal about the law of the early Roman republic. A praetor indicated in his edicts how he would administer justice for the coming year. He used them to set out his policy, as it were, and standardise (the interpretation of) parts of the law. Courts and judges adhered to this central policy when administering justice. The censors – originally magistrates who dealt with the census (and hence tax) – played a role in the legal system too; they were responsible for *supervision* (in particular with respect to morality). Government inspectors in an empire lacking police or a public prosecutor. Separate magistrates, the judges (*Iudices*), were charged with actual dispute resolution, the administration of justice. But that too was organised very differently to now. For even though there were all sorts of detailed rules about how proceedings should be commenced and conducted, how evidence could and should be provided, and so on (procedural law), there were not really institutionalised government courts. Judges in ancient Rome functioned more as arbitrators or neutral third parties, who mediated between two conflicting parties. As processes were often conducted in public, the public was able to check that everything went according to the rules. The public nature of the process had another advantage: courtroom drama educated the audience about the law.

When Rome grew into a major empire with complex trade relations, it became important for citizens, residents and trading partners to know Roman law. Not everyone could learn by being present at trials, and the volume and multitude of sources made it difficult to gain knowledge of the law. Much was done in the Republic's

---

[12] By the third century BCE, the office of praetor had been split into praetor urbi(s) or praetor urbanus and praetor peregrinus. The former dealt with case law concerning citizens of the city (Urbs) of Rome and the second with case law in disputes between Roman citizens and people who did not live in the city (peregrini).

latter period (second and first century BCE) to increase the accessibility of Roman law – impelled by economic interests. For that purpose, specialists recorded the law in books. Continuing in this tradition, later jurists such as Ulpian, Papinian, Paulus and Salvius Julianus (all of whom served the imperial state) not only recorded current Roman law, but also systematised it. One of the most influential of them was the jurist Gaius (110–180 CE), who wrote an introductory textbook, the *Institutes*, which has survived almost in its entirety. At face value this textbook could give you the impression that Roman law is first and foremost private law, regulating relationships between individuals. Constitutional law, public law and international law or the law of nations – regulating relationships between government, government institutions and individuals – seem to be of less importance. Yet, any such impression would be incorrect. Like the Greeks, the Romans dealt very differently with governance and the public domain than we do nowadays. Public affairs (*res publica*) were governed by instruments and rules which we would consider 'private law'. The governorship of a province – for example, the province of Cilicia which Cicero administered from 53 BCE – was formulated as a kind of private law agreement. Taxes were levied through tax leases, public administration relationships were often dealt with as a kind of familial relationship (at least, the hierarchical obligations associated with it), and the legions were run like large companies in the imperial era (much like large professional football clubs nowadays). Everything was simultaneously private and public. Modern distinctions between public and private law are unhelpful in understanding Roman law and especially the Roman constitution. By the first century CE, it already had developed into much more than the rules hammered into the twelve bronze tables. It was more of an amalgam of rules, edicts and writings that together stipulated the norms by which the Roman Empire and its legal system were organised and governed. This motley collection of rules, precedents, edicts, recommendations and laws are reminiscent of the United Kingdom's constitution. Dynamic for centuries, stemming from different sources, originating from different periods, written but also unwritten, and sometimes rather vague for outsiders – but no less a constitution in the sense of an arrangement of dominion (of the highest power) and organisation of government that uses the law. What must be appreciated about all these ostensibly private law rules is that Roman law was underpinned by the (constitutionally organised) power to overrule. Disobeying the rules, for example, by failing to comply with contractual agreements or not adhering to Roman morals and customs resulted in public law consequences and met with the strong arm of the law. It is especially interesting that this was also the case when the *sede vacante* of the Roman administration was seized by other authorities, kings or rulers in the early and high Middle Ages. These later rulers governed in the name of the Roman Empire and Roman administration, established themselves as the strong arm of these Roman-law rules. Besides its many private law rules, the Roman Empire did indeed have rules that were purely and simply about the relationship between the government and its citizens (public law). A legal question,

Pliny the Younger as governor of Bithynia et Pontus, submitted to Emperor Trajan at the beginning of the second century CE provides an interesting insight into this.[13] How should he – Pliny – deal with Christians and what role should he give to local customs? Treat Christians mildly and give local customs a major role, the emperor replied, who then gave a thorough explanation based on precedent and Roman-law customs.[14] Even though it was only a letter, statements of this kind by the emperor – edicts – were part of Roman law. The first attempts to actually codify parts of Roman law were made from the third century CE onwards. You can, of course, only get so far with textbooks if you want to systemise the law and make it accessible for a wide readership. The idea by the turn of the third century was to abandon annual or periodic overhauls of the law with every new praetorial edict, and to establish the totality of the law, integrated and permanent, in an all-embracing codification. This was in parallel with attempts to establish the canons of Christian doctrine in a single book and doctrine. In the late imperial period, Theodosius, the last emperor of both the Eastern and Western parts of the empire from 395 CE, tried to bring about integrated legislation for the entire empire, including the rule declaring Christianity the state religion. One of his successors, Theodosius II, subsequently tried, like the jurists of the early imperial period, to bring order to this collection of laws (*Codex Theodosianus*). That was no sinecure, as the legal code – which actually contained nothing new – took almost ten years to compile (from 429 to 438). And yet, still not all Roman law had been codified. In the Eastern Roman Empire (Byzantium) from the beginning of the sixth century, Emperor Justinian continued work on codification (and legal unity) by collecting and organising all imperial decrees. Justinian's quaestor Tribonian elaborated this in a new *Codex Justinianus* (completed on 7 April 529 CE) to which the *Novellae Constitutiones*, Justinian's own laws, were subsequently added. He also added an ordered anthology of the work of classical Roman lawyers, the *Digest* as an instruction manual. And for legal education, Tribonian wrote another accessible textbook, his own *Institutes*, which partly built upon Gaius' eponymous textbook. Together these documents form what is known as the *Corpus Juris Civilis*, the body of civil law. As it was written (and preserved) in such a complete and systematic way, the *Corpus* was accessible and also practicable for applying adaptations to Roman law in the Middle Ages in Western Europe.

---

[13] Pliny the Younger 1969, X.25 ff.
[14] Cf. (Adrian) Goldsworthy 2016, p. 255–263.

7

Mediaeval Constitutions

As we are unaccustomed to talking about the Roman Empire's *constitution*, we are
not accustomed to talking about early mediaeval constitutions in Europe either. As
explained in the previous chapter, this may have to do with the fact that the era's laws
and rules on leadership, social organisation and legal systems are unrecognisable from
a modern perspective. There are two main reasons for this difficulty in discerning constitutions in mediaeval rules and regulations on the structure of government and legal
systems. First, *states*, as we know them – delineated territories with a supreme sovereign power governing a population – did not exist in the millennium between 500
and 1500. The modern state is a fairly recent innovation that was created in principle
by the Peace of Augsburg (1555)[1] and definitively by the Peace of Westphalia (1648).[2]
Our conception of constitutions is profoundly associated with, even rooted in this idea
of states. A second factor clouding our understanding is the difficulty that our modern
eyes have in localising the core of the mediaeval dispensation's power structure. To us,
mediaeval governance structures often seem to resemble both spaghetti – everything
is connected to everything (through family ties and marriages) – and a doughnut – a
mass of dough with a hole in the middle. We can still grasp the principle of feudal
governance as it emerges from the Carolingian period (c. 750),[3] but everything seems
to disintegrate and fragment in the high mediaeval period (from about the eleventh
century). We are dazzled by the welter of relationships, liaisons, privileges, the jumble
of classes and status, heraldic forms of government and (a little later) town and city

---

[1]   After the European wars of religion had raged for more than a century, several Western
     European kingdoms and territories (most of them near present-day Germany) agreed to peace
     according to the territorial principle of 'Cuius regio, eius religio' (a ruler's right to determine
     the religion of his own state).

[2]   The Treaty of Münster, the Peace of Münster and the Peace of Osnabruck constituted this
     peace settlement.

[3]   The *First Europe*, as Van Caenegem calls the Carolingian Empire a little misleadingly.
     Van Caenegem 1995, p. 50–53.

powers and government. Again, it is mainly because we are looking through a modern 'state-based' lens and hence struggle to get the right focus, so to speak. What were the organisational principles of mediaeval law and governance? The modern answer is often something along the lines of a murky trilogy of religion, disarray and (personal) relations. The executive summary: no constitution. But this is incorrect; this trilogy actually encapsulates the old Roman Empire's three organisational principles. The European mediaeval period most certainly did have a constitutive organisational principle of government and law, but it is almost unrecognisable to us. The constitution of the mediaeval period was no more or less than that of the *Roman Empire* – the empire's old state structure, supplemented by the new state religion, Christianity. The answer to the 'we' question, which is always at the heart of constitutional law, was quite plain to a mediaeval person. The mediaeval 'we' was the 'we' of the Christian community in Europe, ruled by religious and Roman law.[4]

THE VIRTUAL EMPIRE

'Not so, absolutely not so', traditional legal scholars, especially those raised in the tradition of Carl von Savigny's (1779–1861) Historical School,[5] will argue.[6] 'Other sources of law were as important as Roman law in the mediaeval period.' For instance, local customary law, such as Salic law (the Salian Frankish civil law code) or the Saxons' customary law (the *Sachsenspiegel*),[7] recorded at the beginning of the thirteenth century, and other forms of non-Roman law, collectively called the *leges Barbarorum*.[8] This is a little odd, considering that the non-barbarian Romans had not been around for nearly 800 years by the time this name was coined. But, fair enough, other rights (hunting and fishing rights, the right to levy taxes, the right to administer justice, and so on) and privileges (tax exemptions, inheritance of titles, administrative functions) associated with the mediaeval feudal dispensation cannot be traced to Roman law.[9] Then again, this might be so, but local (customary) law had always played a prominent role in Roman law – in ancient times too. It was essentially an integral part of it. As with religion, the Romans did not interfere with

---

[4] For more about the constitutional element of mediaeval legal systems, cf. Greenberg & Sechler 2013, especially p. 1026–1043.

[5] Wauters & De Benito 2017, p. 135 ff.

[6] Greenberg and Sechler can attest that imagining the existence of a constitution even in the mediaeval period, or finding roots of modern constitutionalism in it, always generates opposition. 'A narrative that insists on the commanding presence of mediaeval theorising in the development of Western constitutionalism is not one that finds universal favour among scholars'. Greenberg & Sechler 2013, p. 1023.

[7] Wauters & De Benito 2017, p. 77.

[8] Including the *Breviary of Alaric* (*Lex Romana Visigothorum*, Roman law of the Visigoths established by Alaric II in 506) and *Lex Romana Burgundionum* (Roman Law of the Burgundians – established from the start of the sixth century). Wauters & De Benito 2017, p. 35–38.

[9] Cf. Wauters & De Benito 2017, p. 42–43.

old rights, customs and local traditions, in as much and as long as Roman authority was recognised. The Roman legal system absorbed local systems, or – for those who prefer to see things the other way around – the Roman legal system was a constitutional complement, an additional layer, on top of existing local law.

The British historian Adrian Goldsworthy illustrates this practice with the problems that the Roman proconsul Pliny the younger (61–113 CE) faced when trying a complex case during his proconsulate in Bithynia (112 CE):

> At various times Pliny consulted local laws, established practice and specific rulings including ones by Pompey, as well as several emperors, and also applied his understanding of Roman Law. In many cases these dealt with specific communities, and only occasionally were applicable to the province as a whole. Each province had its own laws, rules and conventions, and there was no attempt to impose a standard legal system and civic organisation to the entire empire, so that examples from a governor's [Pliny] past experience elsewhere were not applicable.[10]

In the Roman Empire's decentralised relations, as later in the European mediaeval period, local law was the starting point for thinking in matters of law and administration. For mediaeval people, it was quite natural that government and the administration of justice were based on age-old Roman law, bound with local law, even if the reality of the Roman empire was no more than a vague memory for rulers, kings, administrators, and judges.[11] It is hard to imagine that even when there was no longer an actual Roman empire, most mediaeval western European rulers apparently subscribed to the idea of a virtual Roman empire, at times lacking an emperor. Sometimes there was a single emperor in charge, such as Emperor Charlemagne (747/748–814 CE) or Otto I (912–973 CE) and his successors; sometimes there were several emperors; sometimes emperors shared authority with the spiritual leader, the pope; and sometimes only the pope was at the helm. And very often the emperor's throne was vacant (the doughnut situation). Francis Fukuyama shows how, after the Investiture Controversy in the eleventh and twelfth centuries, the state and church competed over the power of investiture of ecclesiastical and secular officials.[12]

---

[10] (Adrian) Goldsworthy 2016, p. 258.

[11] Greenberg & Sechler 2013, p. 1023–1025.

[12] This mainly concerned the question of who was authorised to invest senior clergy (local bishops) and the abbots and abbesses of local abbeys. Was that the worldly power (the Roman-German emperor or the English king) or the highest spiritual power (the pope)? It was essentially about total control and power over the Christian world in Western Europe, as the church had increasingly become a real centre of governmental power from the end of the ninth century. After Pope Gregory VII literally brought the Holy Roman Emperor Henry IV to his knees in a memorable incident at Canossa in 1077, the matter was finally settled half a century later in favour of this same pope. The Concordat of Worms (1122) formally granted the pope the power of investiture over the clergy, but the emperor retained an important say. He was entitled to determine the secular administrative duties of appointed bishops. This concordat was to rebound on the church: it laid the germ for the separation of church and state, a doctrine that eventually led to the church losing its position in all areas of worldly governance. Fukuyama 2011, p. 266–267.

Gradually, the church gained worldly power and increasingly acted as a state, just as the state turned more or less into a church, trying to control and wield religious power.[13] Nowadays, this seems almost unfathomable to us: worldly and religious authority as bedfellows, power structures dispersed over a patchwork of territories and rulers without the centre of gravity of a centrally-governed state – it leaves us bewildered, makes our heads spin. For mediaeval people however, it was the most normal thing in the world. They considered themselves part of a larger Christian community and felt part of a continuous history, the ancient tradition of the Roman legal and governmental order. This is reflected in mediaeval legal theory – how mediaeval people thought about the whys and wherefores of their law and government.[14] It is partly mistaken to speak of a revival of Roman law at the beginning of the twelfth century, as nineteenth-century legal historians were wont to do. Was there really a renaissance of Roman law in that period?[15] It implies that Roman law had disappeared, which does not appear to be the case, at least not in the minds of mediaeval people. Yet, from the twelfth century the first universities, which arose in Italian cities such as Bologna (1088), did start looking at Roman law differently – they returned to the source. In the newly founded European universities, the *Digest* and the *Codex Justinianus* were rediscovered and re-examined.[16] The scholars there 'revived' the rules from original Roman sources by studying and commenting on them. Like overeager grammar school students, they scribbled comments – glosses – in the margins of those old rediscovered texts.[17] It was their modest contribution to the organically growing body of Roman law.

Commentaries and the First Universities

The glosses soon developed into complete, regular commentaries for which there was great demand in the Italian cities' emerging mercantile economies. Rules of this kind give purchase to trade relations which were often overseas. In the thirteenth century, the Italian jurist Franciscus Accursius organised the profusion of glosses, numbering almost 100,000, into a sort of standard gloss, which he called the *Glossa Ordinaria*.[18]

---

[13] Fukuyama 2011, chapter 18 (*The Church becomes a State*) and chapter 19 (*The State becomes a Church*) p. 262–289.

[14] Strong 1963.

[15] An almost intact copy of part (*Institutes*) of Justinian's *Corpus Juris Civilis* was discovered in Bologna around 1070. Its significance was not much more than the rediscovery of the actual text: its principles and most important rules had never been out of currency. They were taken and copied from other forms of the *Lex Barbarorum*. Was it really a 'discovery' at all? Wauters and De Benito assert that a copy of Justinian's Digests had already surfaced in Amalfi (a town south of Naples) in the middle of the tenth century. This copy was allegedly taken as loot to Pisa in northern Italy and, possibly, thence to Bologna. The mists of time obscure what really happened. Wauters & De Benito, p. 50.

[16] Wauters & De Benito, p. 50 ff.

[17] *Ibid.*, p. 52–57.

[18] *Ibid.*, p. 53–54.

The study of Roman law at the new mediaeval universities kept pace with the development of canon law. This also had Roman underpinnings: the law and the writings of the ancient Roman censors, the magistrates who ensured compliance with moral and religious laws. Ecclesiastic or *canon law*, too, was eagerly studied, commented on and developed.[19] Schools of law like Bologna not only wrote about it, but taught it too. As a result, Bologna rapidly developed into a popular university.

Italian universities spread legal knowledge throughout Europe. After their studies at universities such as Bologna, Paris and Montpellier, lawyers found work in the service of bishops, royal courts, cities and courts, or became professors, in turn, at later universities. In the thirteenth century, universities were founded throughout western Europe, in Cambridge,[20] Orléans, Toulouse, Padua, Naples and Salamanca, followed a century later by Cologne, Heidelberg, Erfurt, Siena, Pisa, Perugia and Dublin. Universities were also founded in cities in central and eastern Europe, such as Vienna, Prague, Krakow, Budapest. The first university in the Low Countries was at Leuven (1425). These schools focused primarily on the study of Roman and canon law, which was developed by local ecclesiastical courts together with ecclesiastic councils, synods, and papal bulls.[21] As in Bologna, old texts were studied and given glosses and new commentaries, which led to all kinds of new doctrines on subjects like legal persons, unjust enrichment, property and contractual obligations, but also on political issues.[22]

Grants of Authority: Magna Carta, Bulls, Charters and Joyous Entries

Chris Thornhill, a legal sociologist and historian at the University of Manchester, contends that we should look for the start of modern constitutions in the high mediaeval period, sometime from the twelfth century.[23] It is in this same period that Francis Fukuyama marks the birth of our modern idea of legality, the rule of

---

[19] Wauters & De Benito 2017, p. 57–61.

[20] The University of Oxford – established 1096 – predates its counterpart at Cambridge. Oxford is the second-oldest university of Europe after Bologna (founded 1088).

[21] From the twelfth century, fragmented canon law was codified for the first time by Gratian in the *Decretum Gratiani*. In the thirteenth century, Pope Gregory IX had all known and applicable papal decrees compiled and recorded in the *Decretales Gregorii IX* (also known as the *Liber Extra* – 1234), the Canon (collection of key laws and legal principles) of ecclesiastic law. Pope Boniface VIII had Gregory's decretals supplemented in 1298 with the *Liber Sextus* – a compilation that was influential in canon law until the beginning of the twentieth century.
   It was only in 1917 that they were replaced by the complete codification of canon law: Benedict XV's Code of Canon Law. The mediaeval codifications were intended to support education at the newly established universities, to which copies were sent. In this way university education contributed towards standardising canon law. For an account of the lives of the colourful Gregory IX, who lived to a great age, and the later Boniface VIII – founder of the University of Rome, whose papacy was so controversial that he had to be crowned again in 1295 – cf. Norwich's entertaining 2012 papal biography, p. 183 and p. 190 ff.

[22] Cf. the website 'History of Law ('Rechtshistorie'); A gateway to legal history' www.rechtshistorie .nl/en/medieval-law (Consulted on 18 June 2019).

[23] Thornhill 2011, p. 20.

law.[24] This era, the High Middle Ages, heralds the start of the gradual development towards the modern constitution, or at least our current understanding of it. They undoubtedly have a point, but it is – as explained – a bit facile to ignore the fact that there certainly had been a systematic organisation of law, society and governmental power for the previous 750 years or so. The – admittedly fragmented – arrangement of law and government did accord authority to both centrally and locally promulgated law and rule. Understanding this clarifies how the events in this period would probably not have been regarded as a watershed by mediaeval people, but that they simply lived on in what we would call a virtual order: the Roman Empire's legal order – or rather, the continuation of its story.[25]

Not that everything stayed the same – from the twelfth century, a new wind blew through Europe: *negotiated* government. Most of us will have heard of the *Magna Carta* ('Great Charter'), in which King John of England ('John Lackland') promised his barons to govern the country according to the conditions in the charter.

Magna Carta 1215

Militarily surrounded by rebellious barons at Runnymede, a water-meadow on the south bank of the Thames near Windsor, the king signed the agreement under duress on 15 June 1215. It is undoubtedly an iconic story: a defeated king, head bowed,

[24] Fukuyama 2011, p. 271 ff.
[25] In this sense, Fukuyama's assessment of the 'reappearance of Roman Law' in the high mediaeval period may not be entirely correct. It had never disappeared. On the other hand, if Fukuyama is referring to the reappearance of the original Roman texts, then, of course, he is correct. Cf. Fukuyama 2011, p. 261 ff.

forced to recognise his subjects' rights. Many people nowadays interpret this event as the birth of individual freedoms and fundamental rights, and the first step towards constitutional rule. But this is not the document's primary purpose. 'Magna Carta wasted no time on political theory', in the words of the historian David Carpenter.[26] It is a concise document, with several financial agreements at its core, elucidating what the king could – and more especially could not – demand of his nobles. It is also about granting fishing rights, managing forests and other rights, with the intention of increasing vassals' financial strength and curbing royal arbitrariness. The document mainly granted privileges to the nobility and reconfirmed several of them. It is chiefly more minor parts of the document which subsequently gained importance, such as the right to a fair trial,[27] protection of 'church' rights,[28] limits to free men's socage,[29] and compensation for expropriation[30] (which was a more or less indirect recognition of property rights). Reading it now, you are confronted with a great deal of mediaeval preoccupations and paraphernalia. It is not immediately clear from the text why we attach such import to Magna Carta, which is still legally valid in the United Kingdom. Magna Carta's importance is not so much the moment itself, but its consequences – what later generations made of it. Or in the words of the English judge and jurist Lord (Thomas) Bingham:

> The significance of Magna Carta lay not only in what it actually said but, perhaps to an even greater extent, in what later generations claimed and believed it had said. Sometimes the myth is more important than the actuality.[31]

Perhaps it is not the text, or the rights and privileges expressed in it, but more the underlying principle of negotiated governance that has made Magna Carta such a momentous document. King John himself certainly did not believe in the myth nor in the text of the charter. From the very moment he signed the document, he did not feel bound by it as he had done so under duress. As we know, agreements resulting from mistake, fraud or threat are invalid – this was also the case in the mediaeval period. The fact that the king did not much care is perhaps the reason that the document still exists today. He did not even bother withdrawing or revoking it.

As important as Magna Carta is, it was certainly not a unique phenomenon in its time. The great charter of 1215 is not even the first charter of its kind in England; that distinction belongs to Henry I's *Charter of Liberties* of 1100, which also contained rights and privileges of the nobility and clergy. Comparable documents were

---

[26] Carpenter 1990, p. 9.

[27] For example, the right to a 'fair' trial (due process) at a permanently established court. Cf. clauses, 34, 39 and 55. An amendment to Magna Carta in 1679 also added a ban on arbitrary arrest (*habeas corpus*). It was not mentioned in the original version of Magna Carta.

[28] This is not the same as the freedom of religion, but still. Clause 1.

[29] A partial ban on forced labour. Clause 15.

[30] Clauses 52, 57 (only for Welshmen) among others and, in a sense, clause 31 too.

[31] Bingham 2010, p. 12. Cf. Spiegelman 2015, especially p. 30.

commonplace in the high mediaeval period. Many cities and countries in Europe had charters, bulls, joyous entries and privileges, in which the sovereign, usually on the occasion of his inauguration, formally confirmed, recorded or specified some kind of agreement on the legal relationship between him and the estates (clergy, nobility, common folk, townsmen and so on). Such grants of authority were the main source of institutional public law and constitutional law in several parts of the continental Europe well into the eighteenth century. Documents of this kind confirmed and reaffirmed existing rights and freedoms (enumerated as *privileges*) and, more generally, laid down the conditions to the exercise of governmental power, usually consisting of levies, taxes, and (military) services that the ruler could claim. They often contain an element of reciprocity as well. On this point, these grants of authority differed from unilateral edicts and acts promulgated by a sovereign. Multilateral grants of authority, such as bulls, charters and joyous entries,[32] were not unilaterally revocable and their enforcement was safeguarded by special guarantees.[33] They usually had to be reconfirmed and acknowledged by every new sovereign or governor at their inauguration. The sovereign could demand loyalty and obedience as long as he complied with the charter's conditions. This was of direct bearing on their reciprocal obligation in the agreement: a conditional power to rule linked to subjects' conditional loyalty. If the ruler or sovereign did not meet the conditions, subjects were – at least theoretically – freed from their oaths of allegiance to their liege and the loyalty due to him.[34] The bilateral nature of grants of authority such as Magna Carta, the Golden Bull of 1222 (Hungary), the Joyous Entry of 1356 (Brabant), the Golden Bull of 1356 (Holy Roman Empire),[35] the Carta de Logu

[32] A Joyous Entry ('Blijde Intrede', 'Blijde Inkomst' or 'Blijde Intocht' in Dutch; 'Joyeuse Entrée' in French) is the official name used for the ceremonial royal entry – the first official peaceable visit of a reigning monarch, prince, duke or governor into a city – mainly in the Duchy of Brabant or the County of Flanders and occasionally in France, Luxembourg or Hungary, usually coinciding with recognition by the monarch of the rights or privileges of the city, and sometimes accompanied by an extension of them.

[33] For example, Magna Carta provides for an independent supervisory mechanism (clause 61) – 25 barons were to monitor the king's adherence to the agreement. They were entitled to report violations.

[34] This idea is reflected in the Low Countries' Act of Abjuration of 1581, in which the States General complained that their sovereign – King Philip II of Spain – had not complied with the agreed governmental conditions. The Act of Abjuration explains how Philip had failed in his obligations to his subjects, by oppressing them and violating their ancient rights (an early form of social contract). The Act argues that Philip had thus forfeited his thrones as ruler of the provinces which had signed the Act.

[35] This Golden Bull was an important charter. It stipulated that seven (German) Prince-Electors would henceforth have the formal right to elect the king, who was then eligible to be crowned emperor of the Holy Roman Empire by the pope. They occasionally even took the title of Holy Roman emperor without a papal coronation. The Bull also stipulated that the Prince-Electors' territories should remain undivided to prevent Holy-Roman gerrymandering. The title of Prince-Elector become hereditary, on the understanding that it could only be passed down to a Prince-Elector's first legitimate son. The Bull also confirmed the

(Sardinia, 1392) and the Treaty of Tübingen (1514) are for this reason often considered precursors of modern written constitutions. The comparison is not entirely correct. Grants of authority were not intended as comprehensive arrangements establishing political or legal systems with rules on social organisation and leadership. The clauses in these mediaeval documents usually arranged only a few aspects of the feudal relationship between a sovereign or guardian and their estates. The norms for the existence and functioning of the legal system, as well as the social organisation and political system of mediaeval western European societies followed from the rules and logic of (the vestiges of) the Holy Roman Empire – the natural and hence almost invisible constitutional centre of gravity. The charters were not much more than a sort of subtenancy contracts.

Yet, something did change. From the high mediaeval period (1000–1250), forms of law came into being that extended beyond purely feudal bric-a-brac, like estates' privileges and negotiated government conditions. An early example is the *Pravda Yaroslava* (The Truth of Yaroslav the Wise; Yaroslav's Law, 1017) in which Yaroslav the Grand Prince of Kiev granted privileges to the city of Novgorod, recorded and recognised the city's existing customary law and traditions, and added rules on his method of government – about taxes, justice, the military and so on. A set of rules on the set up and operation of government. From the middle of the eleventh century, the *Pravda Yaroslava* was gradually absorbed into the *Russkaya Pravda* (The Truth of the Russians),[36] the legal code that applied in the whole federation of Kievan Rus'. Together with some Byzantine law (derived, in turn, from Roman law) and the Statutes of Lithuania (from the sixteenth century), these *Pravda* would remain part of Russian law for centuries.[37] In Serbia, the Nomocanon of Saint Sava (Saint Sava's canon of laws) was completed in 1219. It was a compilation Roman and canon law, all drawn from Byzantine texts and sources. This record of law and governance rules went far beyond Magna Carta, which is only four years older. In the principality of Catalonia, the first Catalan constitutions were promulgated in 1283, containing collections of legal and institutional rules which were constantly renewed and reaffirmed, and were ultimately important in unified Spain after the *Reconquista* (1492). Like the Serbian laws, the Catalan constitutional rules are relatively integral and less feudal: they govern many aspects of law and administration. They are also relatively independent in the sense that they are much less reliant on any underlying Roman constitution.

From the early fourteenth century, the kings of France (the Capetians) also tried to break free of the constitutional foundations of the old order by bypassing the nobility and clergy and granting liberties directly to the people. It was an attempt to strengthen royal power against the powerful high nobility and the pope. French

---

Prince-Elector's entitlement to levy tolls, administer justice, mint coins and so forth. It was in force for almost five centuries.

[36] Via the *Pravda Yaroslavichey* (The law or truth of Yaroslav's sons, 1045).

[37] Feldbrugge 2017.

sovereigns started enfranchising free cities by granting cities rights, and established the Estates General – a national assembly of the estates.[38] It gave the merchant class a place in leadership alongside the landed gentry and clergy, and allowed the king to use divide-and-rule tactics, as well as centralise governmental power, generate funds and mobilise forces in the epic attrition of the Hundred Years' War (1337–1453).[39] This protracted Anglo-French war of succession led, as did the later English War of the Roses (1455–1485),[40] the War of the Brabant Succession and the Burgundian Wars in the fifteenth century, to increased scale and centralisation of governmental and judicial authority, which were ultimately far more important to constitutional development in Europe than the Magna Carta incident at Runnymede.

The increasing scale and centralisation of governance from the thirteenth century onwards were gratefully accepted by ordinary people. It freed them from the worst of feudal arbitrariness and static, ossified relationships. Centralised government provided greater certainty, as well as better opportunities for trade, industry and prosperity, whilst at the same time giving people a little more say. The administration of justice was also increasingly consolidated.[41] Centralisation was self-reinforcing: it increased the king's capacity to fight and expand his realm, which enabled him to centralise and strengthen his power even further. This led to major changes over time.[42] It heralded a development in which the feudal idea of personal authority – governmental power as personal property – was gradually superseded by impersonal, abstract ideas on power and authority (state power, power of the people) and the abstract functioning of legal rules such as the idea that a government or ruler is bound by the law (the rule of law), and the associated idea of central and abstract administration of law (centralised, uniform administration of justice and equality before the law).

---

[38] Philip IV convoked an assembly of the estates in 1302 to aid him in his conflict with Pope Boniface VIII. He had admonished Philip in 1301 with the papal bull 'Ausculta fili' ('Give ear, my son') – a final warning to acknowledge the pope's authority.

[39] A war, mainly waged in France, between the French kings of the House of Valois and the English kings of the House of Plantagenet (descendants of William the Conqueror) – a.k.a. the Anjou dynasty – over the dynasties' conflicting claims to the French Crown.

[40] An English civil war over the English throne, fought between the mighty royal houses of Lancaster and York.

[41] In *L'ordonnance de Montils-lès-Tours*, Charles VII promulgated the codification of customary law in the provinces in 1454 and he designated the Parlement de Paris as the highest judicial body. Designating this court as the highest court established the precedence of written (in particular royal and Roman) law over other forms of (customary) law and introduced the principle of a separate supreme judicial body – as opposed to the sovereign himself. The aim of the ordinance, as expressed in Article 125, was '*abréger les procez et litiges d'entre nos subjects et les relever de mises et despens et oster toutes matières de variations et contrariétez.*' Freely translated, it can be summarised as: 'brisk and effective dispute resolution between our burghers'.

[42] Van Caenegem 1995, p. 74–78. Following the French example, Philip the Good convened a States General in Bruges for the first time in the Burgundian Netherlands on 9 January 1464. This too was part of a project to centralise the Duchy of Burgundy but resulted in greater assertiveness by the estates. Some assert that it was a prelude to the Dutch Revolt a century later.

LATE MEDIAEVAL PERIOD AND EARLY MODERN PERIOD

Centralisation

Understanding how things worked in the European mediaeval period is, as said, difficult for our modern minds. You are soon overwhelmed by the colourful patchwork of kingdoms, lordly dukes, baronies and counties flecking the map with their incessant conflicts and ever-changing borders. And, we understand mediaeval western Europeans' motivations and intentions even less. Modern concepts blur our view and seem to cut us off from a history that lasted more than a millennium. Yet, the European mediaeval period is of utmost importance in understanding why our world is pervaded by constitutions with abstract forms of governance and social organisation in accordance with a legal system's abstract norms and institutions. Apprehending this period is somewhat like viewing a pointillist painting: instead of zooming in on the details, you must step back to appreciate the coherence of the picture in its entirety. This brings the mediaeval organisation principle into focus – the remains of the Roman Empire's order – as well as the most important developments in that era: centralisation of governance and the rise of humanism. As set out above, this gradual centralisation can be seen everywhere. (Dynastic) wars drove this development – as they had earlier in China, for example.[43] Centralisation and increasing scale usually go hand in hand. Increasing scale gives competitive advantages (more land, more revenue, more military power) over other social-administrative units – facilitating their conquest or subjugation. And centralisation can help to keep larger units manageable. The idea is that it facilitates control and imposition of a ruler's will. Centralisation as a cause and effect of increasing scale is a recognisable mechanism in the late European mediaeval period. A chain reaction seemed to take place. The Tudors, for instance, asserted control over taxation and law in England at the end of the fifteenth century, after a series of foreign and domestic conflicts.[44] At the same time parallel developments unfolded in France. In the Holy Roman Empire, which governed large parts of Germany as well as all of Austria and the Low Countries at the end of the fifteenth century, future emperor Maximilian I established the *Reichskammergericht* (Imperial Chamber Court) in 1495. This court would be the Holy Roman Empire's highest judicial body.[45] It mainly applied Roman law and was primarily intended to settle incessant feudal conflicts (not only about government, but also about the formation of law and jurisdiction) in the realm. At the same time, Maximilian promulgated the *Ewiger*

---

[43] Roberts & Westad 2014, p. 136–143; Fukuyama 2011, chapter 7 (*War and the Rise of the Chinese State*), p. 110–127.

[44] Thornhill 2011, p. 77.

[45] However, this was in concurrent jurisdiction to the Aulic Council (*Reichshofrat*), a supreme court of the empire, comparable to the later Councils of State in Spain (*Consejo de Estado*, 1523), the Netherlands (*Raad van State*, 1531) and France (*Conseil d'Etat*, 1557).

Landfriede ('perpetual public peace'). This was a uniform legal arrangement, based on the earlier Golden Bull (yet another mediaeval charter), which applied in all German parts of the Empire and replaced the very diverse old Germanic peace or atonement statutes.[46] It was one of the many contemporaneous endeavours to centralise government. The Habsburgs in particular, ruling the Holy Roman Empire between 1438 and 1806 and possessing the largest empire on Earth from about 1500, after its conquests in the new world, had little option but to rationalise and centralise their form of government – if only to hold on to what they had. Unsurprisingly, a change of this magnitude was met with resistance after many centuries of decentralised feudal government. The Habsburgs' centralisation policy was the proximate cause of the revolt in the Low Countries, starting in the mid-sixteenth century.

Legal Humanism

Possibly even more important to the development of modern law – which is the central tenet of contemporary constitutions – was the rise of legal humanism at the end of the mediaeval period. Almost all present-day law, regulating relations between people, companies and governments around the world, is of legal-humanist extraction. This too seems so self-evident that it is hardly noticeable, yet it is a fairly recent innovation in the greater scheme of humankind's history. The idea that law is not a preordained emanation of God's will or decreed by history or tradition but is the work of humans, is a novelty. As is the idea that people are not merely the object of legal rules but are also subject to the law and *therefore* have rights as individuals. It was all brand-new, heretical at the time: a total reversal of the values and principles developed over the preceding millennia. As early as the fourteenth century, legal humanism started to turn the world on its head by gradually assuming that humans were able to discover, criticise and even form the law. Ultimately, at the end of the mediaeval period, this led to the radical idea that humans should be *central* to the law.

It all started quite innocently with a group of lawyers, the Bartolists (named after Bartolus de Saxoferrato 1314–1357). When the Crusades and the Renaissance led to the rediscovery of many ancient legal texts, these Bartolists attempted to bring the tried-and-tested principles of ancient Roman law in the *Digests* in line with the (legal) practices and needs of the mediaeval period (*usus modernus*).[47] A variant of this methodology was used by the Dutch school – best known from the work of Hugo Grotius. He used it creatively to link Holland's[48] legal system with the Roman

---

[46] Establishing the *Reichskammergericht* and legal standardisation also led to the introduction of a reform of judicial bodies, a more systematic approach to judicial proceedings and – ultimately – a first uniform catalogue of criminal rules laid down in the *Constitutio Criminalis Carolina* – sometimes shortened to 'Carolina' – in 1532 (named after Emperor Charles V). Cf. Thornhill 2011, p. 78.

[47] Wauters & De Benito 2017, p. 100.

[48] Holland was the predominant province in the Dutch Republic.

idea of *jus commune (Introduction to Dutch Jurisprudence*, 1619)[49] and used these communal principles of Roman law to develop international maritime law (*Mare liberum*, 1609) and the law of war and peace (*De iure belli ac pacis*, 1625); principles that could claim universality. These were the first manifestations of – humanist – international public law.

As significant as international public law is, it was not the most important out-come of legal humanism. That distinction goes to the invention of universal 'natural law' – which is legal, universally applicable and binding norms as law. Natural law reflects eternal (divinely or otherwise inspired) laws and applies – axiomatically – eternally and universally to every person, regardless of faith and origins. The idea of divinely inspired universal law was not entirely new in the mediaeval period, but the way this universal law was ascertained certainly was. It was no longer restricted to divine revelation (from the Bible or other sacred texts) and intermediaries such as oracles, diviners or priests, but could also simply be discovered by thinking for yourself, using human reason. According to someone like theologian and philoso-pher Thomas Aquinas (1225–1274), a reasonable thinking person could discover the content of natural law using his intellect and compare or even contrast them to human laws.[50] This marked a dramatic revolution in thinking about the foundations of law. Hitherto, law had been considered a matter of divine revelation, which the Church Father Saint Augustine of Hippo (354–430) had taught was mediated by the church and divinely-appointed leaders. Aquinas and other scholastics brought individual human beings on par with these intermediaries by saying that they could access knowledge of universal truths and the core of the law as well. That does not mean that Aquinas and the scholastics argued that every human being could simply know the God-given natural laws, nor that these rules were clear and unambiguous, allowing them to be expressed simply and uniformly in worldly or human laws (*lex humana*). Nothing quite this straightforward. Knowing natural law requires a great deal of study and wisdom, and always has to be applied to different situations, with the possibility of different interpretations. To reduce the chance of conflict as much as possible, Aquinas argues, people must come to agreements with their govern-ment and enter into a kind of a social contract. Public law can be based on these agreements, which then act as approved reflections on natural law. In this kind of natural law thinking, the government or state is not a necessary evil or impediment obstructing knowledge of god's will (as in Saint Augustine),[51] but rather a precondi-tion to adjusting these divine natural laws to the human scale and putting them into practice so that people, under this protection, can develop as social beings. It is

---

[49] Translated by Charles Herbert, London 1845 https://books.google.nl/books?id=8BRXAAAAc
AAJ&printsec=frontcover&dq=Introduction+to+Dutch+Jurisprudence&hl=en&sa=X&ved=
oahUKEwjH4Lnem_riAhUQesAKHY6FC5kQ6AEIKjAA#v=onepage&q&f=false.
[50] Aquinas 1265 (in particular *Prima Secundae*, Part I–II, *Summa theologiae*).
[51] Cf. Somos 2010.

a cornerstone of later thinking about the relationship between states and subjects. The people – its subjects – are not there to serve the state, but the state is there to serve its citizens. A radical reversal of the former world view in which the goals of the state, the church and the citizens were unified: they all lived to serve God. Aquinas' thinking turned the old world around and set the transition in motion to an anthropocentric world with humans at its heart.

8

Early-Modern Constitutions

The Early Modern Period started guilt-ridden.[1] At the beginning of the sixteenth century, a thousand-year-old world disintegrated. The Reformation spread like wild-fire across Western Europe after Luther's protest (1517), tearing apart the Christian community, and resulting in almost two centuries of rebellion, religious struggles, and political conflicts. Old connections were lost, but new worlds also arose, bringing new opportunities, discoveries, conquests and wealth. It was an exciting period in which everything changed, and many old certainties vanished. Fragmenting mutual trust set in motion a feverish search for new forms of recognition and identity, and new (political) stability. These troubled times left deep scars in the collective psyche.

This includes, for example, the young King Charles IX of France, responsible for the Saint Bartholomew's Day Massacre (starting on the night of 23 to 24 August 1572). He ordered – or at least approved – the wholesale slaughter of tens of thousands of Huguenots (French Protestants) in Paris and the rest of France. Charles was haunted by the event. Two years later, he was bedridden with tuberculosis and slowly going mad from guilt. According to the French historian Charles de Lacretelle:

> Frightful memories haunted him in his bed, which was always bathed in blood; he would, but could not tear himself from that place. Often his looks were wild, like those of a man who thinks himself chased by avenging ghosts [...].[2]

[1] The early modern period is conventionally regarded as running from the fifteenth to nineteenth century – starting around the fall of Constantinople in 1453 and ending around the French Revolution. The era heralded the start of European colonisation and the Reformation, resulting in the European wars of religion. Central authority gained in importance in most European states; states emerged, and many countries developed into modern nation states.

[2] From the English translation in: The Last Days of Charles IX, *Christian Secretary* (1822–1889), 13 May 1842, Hartford Vol. 5(9) *American Periodicals*, p. 4. Original French: '[D]'affreux souvenirs persécutaient sa pensée dans un lit toujours baigné de sang. Il voulait en ne pouvait pas s'arracher de cette place. Souvent ses regards étaient égarés, comme ceux d'un homme qui se croit poursuivi par des ombres vengeresses.' Lacretelle 1814, p. 421.

Charles IX 1550-1574

To his nurse – a Protestant woman he had been able to save from the carnage of that August night – young Charles deliriously cried:

> Ah, my dear! What bloodshed! What murders! [...] What evil counsel I have followed! O my God, forgive me! I am lost! What is to become of us? What should we do? I know all too well: I am lost.[3]

Deranged and racked by guilt, Charles died on 30 May 1574, aged just 23, less than two years after the horrific events.

The turmoil and divisions unleashed by the reformation corroded communities' cohesion. New ideas about leadership and social organisation and law took hold. It was no longer possible to rely on the old invisible structures of the Roman Empire's legal organisation and the like. Luther's protest and the Protestation at Speyer (1529)[4] proclaimed the legal fall of the Roman Empire. These new ideas contained a different conception of humans, rational humanism, which emphasised

---

[3] Original French: 'Ah! ma mie', lui disait-il, 'que j'ai suivi méchant conseil! Mon Dieu, pardonne-le moi, fais-moi grâce! Je ne sais où j'en suis. Que deviendra tout ceci? Que faire? Je le sens bien, je suis perdu.' Lacretelle 1814, p. 422.

[4] The Imperial Diet at which German evangelical rulers protested against the reversal of the freedom of faith promised by the leaders of the Holy Roman Empire three years previously.

autonomous thinking people. Whereas the mediaeval conception of humans was essentially that of a kind of servile ecclesiastic ant, humans were regarded as possessing mental superpowers in this new age. These powers enabled humans to know God's will, infer natural laws (and even moral and natural law), and in a certain sense be autonomous and choose wisely. These two conceptions of humans could not be farther apart, and the change was exceptionally swift. Whilst this new conception may not have come entirely out of the blue in intellectual circles, for most people in the early sixteenth everything changed very abruptly over the course of a few decades. This caused psychological, social and political stupefaction.

THE STATE AS A BY-PRODUCT?

The roots of the modern constitution are usually sought in the Early Modern period (1450–1800). This is unsurprising as the kind of fundamental rules for legal, social and political organisation that emerged in this period were more like the sets of rules we now regard as a constitution than their antecedents. But, it is a persistent misconception to infer that fundamental rules of this kind did not exist prior to the early modern period or could not exist without the social and political organisational principle that emerges in this period – the state. This is not the case: states existed long before the early modern period, even if they did not always go by this name.[5] The early modern period did not occasion much more than a *new conception* of the state.[6] The emergence of states was not new; rather the conception of humankind and the notion of leadership and justice was. It was an unprecedented revolution, propelled by the printing press,[7] which precipitated a complete metamorphosis of world view and a radical break with old and familiar paradigms on the relationship between governments and citizens and the role of law.[8] In a certain sense, the modern conception of the state is a by-product of this. Roberts and Westad, the authors of *The Penguin History of the World*, write:

> [...] the authority of states, and therefore the power of their governments, waxed in these years. It is important *not to be misled by forms*. For all the arguments about who should exercise it, and a mass of political writing which suggested all sorts of limit on it, the general trend was towards acceptance of the idea of legislative authority – that is, Europeans came to feel that, provided that the authority of the state was in the right hands, there should be no restriction upon its powers to make laws. Even given the proviso, this was an enormous break with the thinking of the past. To a medieval European the idea that there might not be rights and rules

---

[5] Scott 2017, p. 12–17 and Skinner 1978, p. IX. Skinner shows that the history of change(s) and the concept of state is one of 'historical semantics' (p. X and Conclusion in his book).

[6] A development that had started in the West-European Renaissance. Cf. Skinner 1978, *ibid.*

[7] Cf. Ferguson 2017, chapter 16, for more about this.

[8] Mediaeval universalism was exchanged for an international order of sovereign states. Cf. Sheehan 2015, especially p. 381.

above human interference, legal immunities and chartered freedoms inaccessible to change by subsequent law-makers, fundamental laws which always be respected, or laws of God which never could be contravened by those of men, would have been social and juridical, as well as theological, blasphemy.[9]

The existence of states was not a prerequisite to these new notions or rules and the formation of states, and the emergence of sovereign states was not an independent phenomenon, but rather a reaction of groups and countries grappling with an over-reaching process of centralisation and the resultant increased conflict.[10] The Peace of Augsburg (1555) and the Peace of Westphalia (1648) – to which we owe much of our modern concept of states – provided a mainly pragmatic response to contain the consequences of religious conflict, centralisation tendencies and wars of conquest. We will never know with certainty exactly how cause and effect are related. Were the European wars of religion in the sixteenth and seventeenth centuries reactions to longer-running centralisation of government – as was, for instance, the case in the Spanish Netherlands – or did these conflicts impel states to organise themselves even more centrally and effectively?[11] In other words: did these conflicts result from, or rather catalyse, the process of centralisation that engendered modern states and modern government? What about the new humanist conception of humankind? Was it the catalyst, cause or effect? Whatever the case, the combination of centralisation, new state formation and radical ideas culminated in a new central idea on governance: the idea of the necessity of (contractually) constraining governmental power with certain conditions and requirements, especially legal requirements and conditions.[12] The idea of a constitution as it emerged in the Age of Enlightenment.

THE ENLIGHTENMENT

The British historian and expert on the sixteenth and seventeenth centuries, Jonathan Israel, regards the Enlightenment not so much as an era of change, but as a change of era; a change of overall mentality:

> All societies, of course, rely heavily on myths, revelations and basic concepts explaining the principles and justifications on which they are organized, concepts which, in the nature of things, are in varying degrees shared and disputed. Tension rises in proportion as the range of disagreement widens in relation to the spectrum

---

[9] Roberts & Westad 2013, p. 574. My italics.
[10] Such as the Schmalkaldic War (1546–1552), the Thirty Years' War (1618–1648), the Eighty Years' War (1568–1648), and the English Civil War (1642–1651).
[11] Cf. Van Caenegem 1995, chapter 5 (*The foundation of the modern state*), p. 72–90, especially p. 88–90.
[12] Demands and conditions imposed on (increasing) governmental power traditionally took a different form in China. A ruler (emperor) was not heir to legal rules, but rather forms of wisdom, tradition and administrative mores through his and his civil service's (Confucian) education and instruction. Cf. Fukuyama 2011, p. 298 ff. and Scott 2016, p. 75.

of consensus. But a potentially revolutionary change can arise only with major and thoroughgoing questioning of the validity of justifications and legitimizations that previously commanded wide respect and veneration [...].[13]

Israel's central proposition is that – as the European Enlightenment demonstrates – the institutions, social hierarchies, status and market relations on which society is based can only be stable if a society's accounts and justifications ('stories') of these relationships, are widely shared and accepted. Otherwise society disintegrates and there is revolution. Israel argues that this is an almost inevitable consequence of the Enlightenment in the ensuing centuries. Whether it is possible for revolution to proceed from not much more than changing world views and the power of ideas, or they are the invariable result of changing social or production relations is a question that has been debated for a long time. Resolving it is beyond the scope of this book. It is in any case clear that the Enlightenment clearly shows the power of constitutional stories.

The exact dates of the age we call *the* Enlightenment are contentious. The period covers a relatively long period, and only the end is easily determined: the last decade of eighteenth century – some even contend exactly in the year 1789. A good candidate for the start of the period would be René Descartes' philosophical proposition: *Cogito ergo sum,*[14] although some, especially in the Anglo-Saxon world, argue for a later date (somewhere between 1720 and 1725).[15] Descartes' 'I think, therefore I am' recognised that people can 'know' and experience things through their own reason and intellect – autonomously. According to this self-evident axiom, human beings are no longer puppets of external forces, but independent entities with their own souls and wills, capable of making choices. It is this kind of radical insight that so draws us to the Enlightenment, an era abounding in new ideas about the design, organisation and cohesion of human societies and their governments. How do you shape a society in which humans are the centre of the world view? Which structures and institutions can contribute to a new balance? Which convincing (constitutional) story goes with this? Three main lines of thought in political (constitutional) theory and philosophy surfaced in the seventeenth and eighteenth century:

a. **sectoral autonomy and self-determination** (sovereignty of ideas and proto-democratic ideas);
b. **social contract** (government by popular mandate, conditional government); and – closely related –
c. **individuality and individual freedom** postulate (human beings as individuals, responsible and endowed with authority over their own destiny).

---

[13] Cf. Israel 2006, p. 4.
[14] René Descartes, *Principia Philosophiae*, 1644. However, the statement did not originate in this book. It made its debut was seven years earlier in Descartes' *Discours de la Méthode*, 1637, in French: *Je pense donc je suis.*
[15] Pinker 2018, p. 8. Incidentally, Pinker argues that we are still in the midst of the Enlightenment.

Sectoral Autonomy and Self-determination: The State

One of the first problems Enlightenment thinkers encountered with their humanist ideas was the will of groups in society. How can unity and cooperation be maintained in societies when there are manifestly different views on faith and (related) governmental authority? How is a polity to be governed in which Descartes' autonomous and independent individuals think differently about anything and everything? What is the future direction of polities when governmental authority is no longer legitimised by the existence of a single, indivisible Christian community (*Res publica Christiana*) united under the – formal, perhaps even virtual – authority of the Holy Roman Empire?[16] One of the first practical answers came soon after the first wave of religious conflicts, in the aforementioned Peace of Augsburg (1555). The *Cuius regio eius religio* ('whose realm, his religion') guideline allowed a ruler to dictate the religion of his state, and therefore the kind of authority exercised. This transformed the exercise of authority from something that was in principle universal (Roman-Christian) to something territorial. Contemporaneous political thinkers, such as the French writer Jean Bodin (1530–1596), gave this new practice theoretical underpinnings. He argued that the territorial principle was not simply accepted at Augsburg for expediency's sake, it was *morally justified*. 'State' leaders and rulers have an absolute and eternal right to exercise supreme power without interference of others – sovereignty – Bodin wrote in *Les six livres de la république* in the latter part of the sixteenth century.[17] He argued that sovereignty, as a state's absolute and eternal power, is not subordinate to any external or higher authority, and is necessary to maintain order and tranquillity in a political system. In his eyes, protracted (religious) conflicts, such as the French Wars of Religion 1562–1598,[18] could only be settled by a strong central authority. To this end, a ruler must be able to exercise absolute power and use the state's sovereign power. The idea of sovereign power and sovereign states, autonomous and fully entitled to govern themselves without external interference, was to become a guiding principle in the Peace of Westphalia in 1648, which largely brought the European wars of religion to an end. This influential principle has remained a keystone of international law to this day, as expressed in the Charter of the United Nations, for example.

Social Contract

The idea of a social contract implies that a government owes its authority to some kind of agreement it has concluded with its citizens. The members of a society relinquish some of their natural liberties in exchange for the government's protection.

---

[16] Thornhill 2011, p. 93–95.
[17] 'La souveraineté est la puissance absolue et perpétuelle d'une République [...]' Bodin 1993, Chapitre (Chapter) VIII *De la souveraineté* (*On Sovereignty*), p. 111.
[18] The Edict of Nantes, signed by King Henry IV in 1598, ended the conflict. It gave the Huguenots a certain degree of freedom of religion and protection in safe havens.

The idea has a universally recognisable ring to it: this powerful notion of consensual entry of autonomous individuals into society embodied in the contract metaphor is still attractive to us today – despite the fact that we now know that there has never been any such mythical contract and people have never roamed the world as totally free, isolated, noble savages – Rousseau's proverbial unspoilt individuals.[19] No matter. The idea of a social covenant – with its recognisable echo of God's covenant with humanity in the Old Testament – it still extraordinarily appealing to this day. The whole idea of a reciprocal agreement between government and citizens also implies that it can be terminated. It is a conditional exchange: if the government does not adhere to the conditions of the contract, members of society no longer have to uphold their side of the bargain – obedience to the government. Suspension of obedience played a major role in events like the Dutch Revolt and the American Revolution. Reciprocity and conditionality of government rule were expressed as principles in the Act of Abjuration (1581), and subsequently influenced the American Declaration of Independence (1776) too. These new ideas spread quickly and caught on. Writers like Beza (*Du droit des magistrats* 1574) and (the anonymous) Brutus (*Vindiciae contra tyrannos* 1579, 'Defences [of Liberty] against Tyrants') were in the vanguard of this new contract thinking. These so-called monarchomachs, writing at the end of the sixteenth century, still based most of their arguments and theory on the Bible and other religious works. This changed with later contract thinkers such as Thomas Hobbes, John Locke and Jean-Jacques Rousseau. They based their theories on the contract between government and citizens on human nature and human history. In doing so, they expanded the theory from a mere right to resist to an all-encompassing theory of a social contract between government and citizens, in which government's role is primarily to be of service.

One of the great monuments of contract theory is Thomas Hobbes' book *Leviathan*, published in 1651.[20] Hobbes (1588–1679) did not have a very high estimation of human beings. Like a dark echo of his own times (the English Civil War), Hobbes has a gloomy view of humans as selfish and fractious creatures who could never survive outside the control of an organised society. Everything goes awry when humans are left to their own devices; in our original state, our natural state, Hobbes famously states, life is 'solitary, poor, nasty, brutish, and short'. The (leader of a) state – the Leviathan[21] – has to protect people against each other and themselves. To this end, individuals in a society must enter into a social contract in which they empower the state to rule over their opposing and conflicting interests, in exchange for freedom. Hobbes' contract entitles the state to use force to coerce individuals, if

---

[19] Cf. Fukuyama 2011, chapter 2 (*The State of Nature*).
[20] Complete title: *Thomas Hobbes: Leviathan, or The Matter, Forme & Power of a Common-Wealth Ecclesiasticall and Civil*, 1651.
[21] Named after the biblical sea monster (Psalm 74: 13–14; Job 41; Isaiah 27: 1).

necessary. People give up freedom not only out of necessity, but also conditionally. Hobbes says in his Jacobean English:

> [...] that a man be willing, when others are so too, as far-forth as for peace and defence of himself he shall think it necessary, to lay down this right to all things, and be contented with so much liberty against other men as he would allow other men against himself. For as long as every man holdeth this right of doing anything he liketh, so long are all men in the condition of war. But if other men will not lay down their right as well as he, then there is no reason for any one to divest himself of his; for that were to expose himself to prey, which no man is bound to, rather than to dispose himself to peace.[22]

His younger countryman and contemporary John Locke (1632–1704) had a more favourable conception of humankind. He believed that humans entered the world as a 'blank slate' (*tabula rasa*) and were not necessarily driven by evil. In his great work *Second Treatise of Government* (1689), Locke assumed there was no need for incessant internecine warfare in humans' original state of nature – as suggested by Hobbes – but that members of a society come together to form a state of their own volition. They are not forced by their corrupt nature to enter into a social contract, but consent to do so, reasoning that they can better serve their interests within the community. It is a question of standing strong together and pursuing individual interests through the public interest. This requires a leader as a sort of neutral referee ('neutral judge') able to protect individual interests and 'life, liberty and wealth' in a commonwealth. The state must constantly strive to secure citizens' freedoms and interests. For Locke, state action – the exercise of governmental authority – is only legitimised insofar as the public interest is served by securing citizens' natural rights. The later French writer Jean-Jacques Rousseau (1712–1778) concurred. He also believed that political power – expressed, for example, in mandatory legal rules – can be traced back to citizens in a society once having consented to a social contract. From their state of nature, they entered into an agreement with the government to protect their individual liberties. In this contract, they submitted to the *volonté générale* or 'general will'. It is this general will that legitimises every form of power or law and – concerned as it is (or should be) with the public interest – protects everyone's natural freedom.[23] But Rousseau goes further than Locke: the government does not stop at striving to promote the public interest and protecting individual rights – Rousseau does not differentiate between them. To his mind the general will *is* the public interest and therefore protects everyone's rights and interests – they are one and the same. A will of the people that fails to serve the public interest and thereby protect the rights of all is essentially no longer a general will. This curious reasoning would subsequently become highly influential.

---

[22] Hobbes 1651, chapter XIV.
[23] Rousseau 1762.

Individuality and Individual Freedom

A third Enlightenment theory is closely related to the concept of a social contract: the idea that every human being possesses inherent dignity and certain inalienable, individual fundamental freedoms. This is a completely self-evident concept to us nowadays, but it is a relatively recent invention[24] and a radical break with mediaeval thinking on the nature and essence of human beings and human societies.

We have already seen above that we are social beings thanks to our neurobiological predisposition and evolutionary development.[25] Humans depend on a group for basic necessities and survival. In the Enlightenment, however, a number of political philosophers assumed the polar opposite. Man is by nature an autonomous individual, they thought; he is a *noble savage* (as Rousseau called it) in his state of nature, who enters into voluntary relationships with other people. According to Rousseau we were all free and good in this state of nature; it was society that corrupted us. As proof, he adduced the existence of 'savages' and 'primitive tribes' which Europeans had first come into contact with during the voyages of discovery in the seventeenth and eighteenth centuries. In his *Discourse on the Origin and Foundations of Inequality among Men*, Rousseau wrote in 1755:

> The example of savages, who have almost all been found at this point, seems to confirm that the human race was made to remain in [a state of nature] always; that this state is the veritable prime of the world; and that all subsequent progress has been in appearance so many steps toward the perfection of the individual, and in fact toward the decrepitude of the species.[26]

Hence, history – civilisation – has perverted us. A surprising number of people still believe in this good state of nature to this very day. 'Man is born free, and everywhere he is in chains', Rousseau despairs in his book *Du contrat social* (1762).[27] This is because the rights that people are naturally endowed with and that everyone can know because they are self-evident (the rights to life, freedom and material possessions) are vulnerable, as are their individual bearers. It is easy to ignore and suppress these rights, even though the aim and rationale of all governmental authority is to *recognise* and guarantee individual freedom.

The essential step of recognising individual dignity and freedom is often implicit in Enlightenment contract philosophers' writings. It is probably because they regard it as a rather self-evident truth: a law of nature. This self-evidence can be seen, for example, in the aforementioned United States Declaration of Independence (1776):

> We hold these truths to be self-evident, that all men are created equal, that they are endowed by their Creator with certain unalienable Rights, that among these

---

[24] Cf. Siedentop 2014, p. 349–363.
[25] Cf. Fukuyama 2014, p. 8–9.
[26] Rousseau 1755, p. 131.
[27] Published in English as *The Social Contract*; cf. book II, chapter 5.

are Life, Liberty and the pursuit of Happiness. — That to secure these rights, Governments are instituted among Men, deriving their just powers from the consent of the governed [...].

All core elements of contract thinking are concisely condensed in this text, and the postulate of the individual in society and government is expressed.

How do you ensure that a government best protects citizens' vulnerable liberties, and that living together under a government does not deprive us of our rights, causing us to regress and degenerate and reducing our interests to mere administrative concessions? Like a modern Aristotle, the French political philosopher Charles de Montesquieu (1689–1755) compared several systems of government known to him in his book *De L'Esprit des Loix*[28] (*The Spirit of the Laws*)[29] to assess which is best suited to preserving and safeguarding citizens' liberties. Government power is by its nature a constant threat to individual freedom. Montesquieu concludes that a system in which government powers are separated is best suited to protecting citizens' freedom and equality. The division of government into a legislative, executive and judicial branch – the separation of powers (*trias politica*) as it became known after Montesquieu[30] – ensures that these powers can hold each other in check and prevent abuse of governmental power, which is always a danger when there is a concentration of power.

Establishing individual civil rights and freedom as the foundational principle not only gives government a (new) goal, it also sows the seeds of egalitarian participatory thinking in which free and equal citizens have an equal share in government. This was to become the basis of the modern conception of democracy.

Although the idea of free individuals with natural rights and freedoms appears to be self-evident and true, as expounded above, there is actually nothing self-evident about a society in which individuals, deemed equal and free in principle, would voluntarily unite under a government on condition of protecting their natural freedoms and rights. Human history has produced few, if any, such instances. The 'general principles of Civil Liberty' that ensue from 'what reason and equity, and the rights of humanity give' as the British political philosopher Richard Price expressed it in 1776,[31] do not automatically follow from the nature of things (there is no equality in 'nature') – they are

---

[28] Spelled *Lois* in modern French.
[29] Montesquieu 1748.
[30] A tripartite separation of powers does not exist anywhere in Montesquieu's work as a concept. In his discussion of the English constitution in *The Spirit of the Laws* Montesquieu discerns three sorts of power in states: legislative, executive and judicial. (Book XI, chapter 6). 'When the legislative and executive powers are united in the same person, or in the same body of magistrates, there can be no liberty; because apprehensions may arise, lest the same monarch or senate should enact tyrannical laws, to execute them in a tyrannical manner. Again, there is no liberty, if the judiciary power be not separated from the legislative and executive. Were it joined with the legislative, the life and liberty of the subject would be exposed to arbitrary control; for the judge would be then the legislator. Were it joined to the executive power, the judge might behave with violence and oppression.' Montesquieu 2001, Book XI, chapter 6 (*Of the Constitution of England*), p. 173.
[31] Cf. Price 1776, who was very popular during his lifetime.

contrivances, cultural artefacts.[32] Claiming that individual human rights emanate from the nature of things is 'rhetorical nonsense, nonsense upon stilts' as Jeremy Bentham scoffed at the end of the eighteenth century.[33] Just as there is nothing 'natural' about claims to exercise the highest offices of government (sovereignty) over a territory (state) without interference. They are all products of a very specific history of ideas that is closely linked to Christian teachings and culture. The British political scientist Larry Siedentop demonstrates that individuality, individual fundamental freedoms and the accompanying ideas of state administration and law are recent inventions:

> Like other cultures, Western Culture is founded on *shared beliefs*. But in contrast to most others, Western beliefs privilege the idea of equality. And it is the privileging of equality – of a premise that excludes permanent equalities of status and ascriptions of authoritative opinion to any idea or group – which underpins the secular state and the idea of fundamental or 'natural' rights. Thus, the only birth right recognised by the liberal tradition is individual freedom. Christianity played a decisive part in this. Yet the idea that liberalism and secularism have religious roots is by no means widely understood.[34]

Hence, Enlightenment philosophers were partially mistaken. People are not biologically predisposed to survive as individuals. There are also no natural rights that we have borne latently for 10,000 years, just as there are no visible boundaries running across the landscape delineating states. Nor is sovereignty an unchanging, empirically observable quality, regardless of how many sashes, crowns, sceptres or other regalia you amass. All those things – individuality, rights and freedoms, states, sovereignty and the like – are cultural artefacts, fabrications and fictions that enable us to trust and literally know our place, and hence collaborate on a large scale and in ever-changing circumstances.

THE INFLUENCE OF THE PHILOSOPHES

The Enlightenment Philosophers introduced radical new ideas, without much empirical evidence, ideas which can only be properly understood in the context of their specific Western European historical development. They have had unprecedented influence. These ideas are discernible in just about all constitutions currently in force.

---

[32] Hunt 2007, especially p. 26–34 and p. 121–126.

[33] 'Natural rights', according to Bentham, were 'simple nonsense: natural and imprescriptible rights, rhetorical nonsense, – nonsense upon stilts.' This nonsense has unpleasant consequences. 'What then, was their object in declaring the existence of imprescriptible rights, and without specifying a single one by any such mark as it could be known? This and other to excite and keep up a spirit of resistance to all laws a spirit of insurrection against all governments....' In Bentham's view, rights are 'the fruits of the law, and of the law alone. There are no rights without law – no rights contrary to the law – no rights anterior to the law.' From the pamphlet written by Jeremy Bentham in 1795 (but only published in French in 1816 and in English in 1824) 'Nonsense upon Stilts, or Pandora's Box Opened, or The French Declaration of Rights prefixed to the Constitution of 1791 Laid Open and Exposed' reprinted in: Bentham 2002, p. 319–375, (quotes from p. 329–331).

[34] Siedentop 2014, p. 349. My italics.

How did intuitive insights of this kind, ultimately incorporated in constitutions, conquer the world? The answer is not difficult for 'believers': the world has simply seen the light. But on closer examination things are less straightforward. Why did the world view and political philosophy of Chinese thinkers such as Zhu Xi (1130–1200) and Wang Tingxiang (1474–1544)[35] and Taoism[36] – influential in the Song and Ming dynasties – not conquer the world? They too are based – perhaps more credibly – on the natural order of things. Why did Brahman, Buddhist, Islamic or Orunmila[37] world views and conceptions of humans and their accompanying political theories not prevail? Is it because dominant Westerners wrote world history? Did they force their own perspective on others and make their world view and conception of humans a generally accepted reality through a process of the genealogy of power?[38] Has this conditioned us to refuse to acknowledge as constitutions fundamental rules about law, leadership and social organisation within state boundaries that lack these elements of the voluntary association of free individuals and statehood, rejecting them as inadequate?[39] It is a possible explanation, but the reasons are still largely a mystery.

It is not the case that Enlightenment thinking on the constitution in the seventeenth and eighteenth centuries met with immediate approval and led to changes in existing political practices. The radical ideas and works of Enlightenment thinkers – the *Philosophes* – were as controversial as they were widely read, despite relentless efforts to supress their work. Western Europe was in the process of recovering from the wars of religion and conforming to the new state order. Ideas and concepts about states, humanism, individuality and freedom spread around the world in the wake of the voyages of discovery, wars of conquest and colonisation. Initially, the new 'we' of humanism was only translated into new rules for social order: the state-based order (initially, mainly empires and kingdoms) and the contingent concept of governmental sovereignty. It is the formula of the Peace of Augsburg and the Peace of Westphalia. The concept of humanism governed relations between societies but was less influential within them. It was almost 150 years before the humanist formula, as liberal humanism, made more normative inroads into the political relations between citizens and government.

FUNDAMENTAL ORDERS AND GOVERNMENT INSTRUMENTS

The interlude was not without precursors. One of the first new-style constitutions, entitled *Fundamental Orders*, belonged to the English colony of Connecticut. This North American outpost was, of course, hardly sovereign. As such, the fundamental rules on

---

[35] Cf. Kim 2007, p. 108–125.
[36] Taoism, or Daoism, teaches that everything in the world is in perfect harmony according to a dynamic order in continuous flux. The balance is constantly changing, and nothing can exist without its opposite. If someone goes along with the flow of change and lives in unity with nature, they can become a perfect, immortal human with the help of knowledge and wisdom.
[37] The Orisha of wisdom, knowledge and divination originally from West Africa.
[38] Cf. Foucault 1977 (orig. 1975).
[39] Weiler 1999.

its political, legal and social organisation could hardly be called a real constitution in the modern sense of the word. This is not how they see things in Connecticut. It had always been an independent state, Connecticuters would say; this fact just dawned a little late on the English. The Fundamental Orders were promulgated as self-determination documents by the Puritan Connecticut Colony Council on 14 January 1639. Even though the document has strongly theocentric features, the elements of modern thinking in it are conspicuous. This is clear in an excerpt from the preamble:

> [We, the Connecticut colonists,] do therefore associate and conjoin ourselves to be as one Public State or Commonwealth; and do for ourselves and our successors and such as shall be adjoined to us at any time hereafter, enter into Combination and Confederation together, to maintain and preserve the liberty and purity of the Gospel of our Lord Jesus which we now profess […].

An expression of the principle of voluntary association in order to protect the freedom of religion and worship. The document continues:

> […] as also, the discipline of the Churches, which according to the truth of the said Gospel is now practiced amongst us; as also our civil affairs to be guided and governed according to such Laws, Rules, Orders and Decrees as shall be made, ordered, and decreed as followeth :[…].

Public affairs settled by laws and regulations enacted by representatives and applied by magistrates appointed by the people. This was unprecedented. New post-reformation conglomerations – states – organising themselves and coming up with and recording principles and rules according to which they were to be organised and led. Chris Thornhill argues convincingly that the dual exigencies of replacing the defunct medi-aeval legal and constitutional frameworks (of the old Roman Empire), and strengthening governmental power to curb polarisation in societies and withstanding competition with other states, impelled more and more of these new states in Europe to *positivise* their constitutional law by putting it in writing.[40] This was also new in a world accustomed to common and religious law, in which communication was mainly oral or via images and other expressions. In this period, just after the invention of the printing press, written communication, including of the legal kind, could take place much faster, as well as in a much more abstract form. This also applies to communicating the new dispensation within states.[41] Throughout Europe written constitutions were promulgated which, like the Orders, primarily focused on organising leadership – government and governmental power. They contained little about the relations between governments and citizens. They were *instruments of government*.

---

[40] Thornhill 2011, p. 95–96.
[41] Ferguson shows how the speed of communication and thus of interaction and networking increased exponentially with the invention of printing. He argues that the Reformation would not have been possible without the printing press. Ferguson 2017, p. 82–100. Cf. Choudhry 2006.

9

Generations

The First Generation of Monarchical Constitutions

At the end of the sixteenth and seventeenth centuries, rules and documents emerged that start to resemble what we would now call a constitution. Written documents with norms codified as legal rules on the functioning of government – rules on power and its exercise. They were not conferred by a divine being or handed down as tradition but promulgated by people in the present for people in the present. Representations of a new beginning in a man-made order, contained in a written document. The earliest instances – the Union of Utrecht and the Act of Abjuration in the Netherlands, and the Fundamental Orders in Connecticut – are still highly instrumental in nature: nuts and bolts of government operation. We would not really recognise them as fully fledged constitutions nowadays. As we saw at the end of the previous chapter, they are 'instruments of government'. These instruments were primarily focused on who does what in government administration and were less concerned with 'why' and 'for what'.

Even England once had a written constitution of this kind. The *Instrument of Government* was the English Protectorate's state regulation under Oliver Cromwell, in force between December 1653 and May 1657. The forty-two articles, drafted by the Parliamentarian Major-General John Lambert, laid down the principles of state administration. After the execution of Charles II in 1649 and the dissolution of the monarchy, the leadership of the Commonwealth of England (also called the English Republic) had to be arranged post-haste. The provisions of the *Instrument of Government* mainly attempted to restore order after the turmoil of the English civil wars. For this reason, the *Instrument* is more like an emergency state regulation than a modern constitution. It hardly makes mention of relations between government and citizens, apart from rules on the composition of a single representative body. Words like 'individual' or 'freedom' are nowhere to be found, and are similarly absent in its successor, the *Humble Petition and Advice*, which gave Lord Protector Oliver Cromwell even more powers from May 1657 onwards. Yet, they certainly contain the germs of the modern constitution: they are written, temporal legal rules for a legal system and leadership with territorially delimited authority. In a certain sense, the Union of Utrecht (1579) of the Dutch Republic (after 1581), and the Treaties and Constitutions of the Zaporozhian Sich in Ukraine (1710) can also be regarded as examples of written, early modern constitutions of this kind.

The first written early-modern constitutions, with their emphasis on strong government, engendered a reaction in the legal doctrine: the idea that government is always subject to 'fundamental laws'.[1] The idea, partly derived from mediaeval natural law that government power by its very nature is always limited by inviolable, natural rules and laws, was shared by a number of influential lawyers in this period.[2]

This idea of legally constraining governmental power with fundamental rules is reflected, for example, in the Swedish *Regeringsform* (Instrument of Government) of 1634 – a written constitution promulgated by the *Riksens ständer* (Riksdag of the Estates; a kind of parliament or assembly of the estates). For instance, Article 5 of this constitutional regulation stipulates that the Privy Council must ensure that the king rules in accordance with the law of the land and there must be 'constant care for the rights, dignity and advantage and welfare of King and People'.[3] In the subsequent *Regeringsform* of 1719, the power of the Swedish king was further curtailed. He became more or less the chair of a collegiate council of ministers whose members were appointed by the *Riksdag* (parliament). Sweden is also one of the very first countries in the world to enact a law on the freedom of the press (1766), the rules of which by their very nature restrict governmental power. It's still a cornerstone of the current Swedish constitution.

The idea of fundamental laws with rights of citizens limiting government is also clearly reflected in the English *Bill of Rights* (1689). After King James II was replaced with the co-regency of King William III and Queen Mary II in what was called the Glorious Revolution, in 1688, governmental power was permanently bound to the law and limited by citizens' fundamental freedoms in the *Bill of Rights*. The example of binding of royal power to the law (no longer as a royal favour in the form of privileges) was imitated in many European kingdoms in the seventeenth and eighteenth centuries. A series of constitutional arrangements of this kind were promulgated. It is the first generation of real – that is to say, recognisable to us – constitutions that the American constitutionalist Stephen Holmes calls 'monarchical constitutions'.[4]

---

[1] '[…] the aftermath of the Reformation in many societies saw the formulation of a strong doctrine of fundamental laws (*leges fundamentales*), which, often sustained by ideas of natural law, was used to express the form and content of state power. This theory, based in the claim that states were defined and constrained by a distinct and stable body of inviolable legal norms, clearly had its origins in the judicial ideals of the Middle Ages, and it reflected the mediaeval belief that regal power was curtailed by customary rights and privileges.' Thornhill 2011, p. 103.

[2] For example, the Englishman Richard Hooker and Frenchmen Jean du Tillet, Innocent Gentillet, Pierre Rebuffi and Théodore de Bèze. Cf. Thornhill 2011, p. 105–110.

[3] Thornhill 2011, p. 135.

[4] Holmes 2012, p. 200–201.

10

Second Generation

Revolutionary Constitutions

France was supposed to have a monarchical constitution after the upheavals of the summer of 1789. At least that was the original idea. Slowed down by a convoluted passage of two turbulent revolutionary years,[1] the new National Constituent Assembly finally adopted a constitution on 3 September 1791. The Declaration of the Rights of Man and of the Citizen (*Déclaration des droits de l'homme et du citoyen*), which had been adopted in August 1789, became the preamble of this new constitution. The Declaration is a poetic text that concisely expresses the new ideas and principles of this novel form of government.[2] The Marquis de Lafayette – one of the aristocratic leaders of the French Revolution[3] – submitted a draft text of the declaration to the newly established National Assembly (*Assemblée nationale*) on 11 July 1789 (on the eve of the Storming of the Bastille). He drew inspiration from the 1776 United States Declaration of Independence. Lafayette knew the document well, having befriended General Washington and other prominent thinkers and politicians during the American War of Independence whilst fighting on the side of the insurgents.[4] The revolutionary nature of his proposal for a French declaration immediately caused controversy. It ascribed government sovereignty to the people

---

[1] The National Assembly had already established a twelve-member Constitutional Committee on 14 July 1789 (coincidentally the day the Bastille was stormed). After heated debates and failing to convince the Assembly of its proposals, it was soon succeeded by a second Constitutional Committee. It presented proposals in 1790, which were examined by a Committee of Revisions, after which the first French constitution was adopted on 3 September 1791.

[2] In that same year, 1791, Thomas Paine published his influential pamphlet (book) *Rights of Man* in response to Edmund Burke's public rejection of the French Revolution. He clearly expounded the new revolutionary ideas, which he had corresponded about with George Washington. Lafayette was undoubtedly familiar with its ideas. Paine 1969 (orig. 1791).

[3] Marie-Joseph Paul Yves Roch Gilbert du Motier, better known as the Marquis de Lafayette.

[4] He even had the concept of the Declaration of the Rights of Man and of the Citizen read to Thomas Jefferson, who would later become the president of the United States. Jefferson was Ambassador to France at the time (1789) – living in the Hôtel de Langeac in Paris – and made a number of proposals, including his hobbyhorse: that a new constituent assembly should

(popular sovereignty), lighting a fire beneath the Ancien Régime, and it introduced several completely novel ideas on natural law and the nature of human beings as an eternal truth and the foundation of all state administration.[5] At this time, Louis XVI still ruled France by the grace of god. It is no small miracle that, in the midst of the revolutionary turmoil and heated, sometimes chaotic, debates,[6] the National Constituent Assembly succeeded in adopting a text based on Lafayette's proposal within a month (August 1789) – the Declaration of the Rights of Man and of the Citizen (see image on the next page) – which, like its American counterpart, stirs hearts and minds to this very day with words that literally appeal to the imagination:[7]

> The representatives of the French People, formed into a National Assembly, considering ignorance, forgetfulness or contempt of the rights of man to be the only causes of public misfortunes and the corruption of Governments, have resolved to set forth, in a solemn Declaration, the natural, unalienable and sacred rights of man, to the end that this Declaration, constantly present to all members of the body politic, may remind them unceasingly of their rights and their duties; […]
>
> In consequence whereof, the National Assembly recognises and declares, in the presence and under the auspices of the Supreme Being, the following Rights of Man and of the Citizen:

1. Men are born and remain free and equal in rights. Social distinctions may be based only on considerations of the common good.
2. The aim of every political association is the preservation of the natural and imprescriptible rights of Man. These rights are Liberty, Property, Safety and Resistance to Oppression.
3. The principle of any Sovereignty lies primarily in the Nation. No corporate body, no individual may exercise any authority that does not expressly emanate from it.
4. Liberty consists in being able to do anything that does not harm others: thus, the exercise of the natural rights of every man has no bounds other than those that ensure to the other members of society the enjoyment of these same rights. These bounds may be determined only by Law […].[8]

---

meet at specific times (every generation) to revise the initial constitution. 'The dead should not govern the living.' But he was no more successful in convincing people of this idea in France than he had been in the thirteen colonies. Schama 1989, p. 374–375.

5 An example of 'cognitive constitutionalism': the conscious organisation of a state according to certain 'rational' principles. Cf. Holmes 2012, p. 202–203.

6 Schama 1989, p. 370–374.

7 The definitive text was displayed on two painted stone tablets, a reference to Moses' Ten Commandments hewn into stone tablets. For more on this parallel, cf. Ezrahi 2012, p. 64 and Ribner 1993.

8 The text contains seventeen provisions. This is only an excerpt. The Declaration of the Rights of Man and of the Citizen is one of the three texts that serve as a preamble of the current French Constitution of the Fifth Republic (1958). In 1971, the Constitutional Council ruled that the Declaration was an integral part of French constitutional law. *Conseil constitutionnel,*

Jean-Jacques-François Le Barbier (1738–1826) *Déclaration des droits de l'homme et du citoyen*

The Assembly was so enraptured that it was dumbfounded by the king's reluctance to grant it his immediate approval. His misgivings are quite understandable in hindsight. The Declaration did away with everything Louis XVI stood for in a single stroke: it

Décisions no. 71–44 *DC* 16 juillet 1971 and no 73–51 *DC* du 27 décembre 1973. www.conseil-constitutionnel.fr/en/declaration-of-human-and-civic-rights-of-26-august-1789.

expresses a totally different 'we' to the Ancien Régime 'we'. Louis' contemporaries were rather less clement. In September, tension again mounted. On 5 October 1789 a starving crowd of Parisian women, led by the Marquis de Lafayette, marched on Versailles to petition the king[9] and compelled him to return to Paris and sign the Declaration. It proved to be a defining moment, a point of no return in the French Revolution.

As always, the devil is in the details. Whilst the basic principles of the Declaration were soon agreed upon, the specifics of the new form of government were much more contentious. It took the National Assembly another two years to reach agreement on the text of the constitution it had promised before the summer of 1789. Two tumultuous years in which one political movement after another vied for political ascendency, the country virtually descended into civil war, foreign interference reached a crescendo, and political leaders rose and fell in rapid succession. The world looked very different by the time the constitution was adopted at the start of autumn 1791. Many French people must have thought: 'was the summer of 1789 only two years ago?'

After the king's failed flight to Varennes, he was brought to the Constitutional Assembly as a prisoner on 14 September 1791 to swear an oath of allegiance to the long-awaited constitution, turning France into a constitutional monarchy. It was a painful discomfiture for the great scion of the House of Bourbon, which had ruled the country for two centuries. Louis, the last king in an almost thousand-year-old tradition of uninterrupted monarchy in France, the absolute ruler of France by the grace of god, was forced to swear allegiance to a charter that deprived him of the splendour of his office. Just sign on the dotted line, Sire; he was utterly humiliated. And yet, he did – partly at his wife's insistence – in the hustle and bustle of the Constitutional Assembly that fateful Wednesday. Dressed like an ordinary citizen, he accepted the new French constitution and promised:

> to maintain it at home and defend it against attacks from abroad and to use all the means it places in my power to execute it faithfully.[10]

A national celebration ensued. Even though the oath had been partially coerced, and the country was in ruins, everyone had to know about it. Four days later, a hot-air balloon draped in tricolours floated triumphantly above the Champs-Elysées announcing the king's official acceptance of the constitution.[11] Flags were flown throughout the country and there was celebration and dancing.

---

[9] They took him to the Tuileries Palace in Paris, so that he could once more live amongst his people, with whom he was so closely connected (or ought to be). Ironically, the palace at Versailles had been built to protect the king from turmoil in Paris – as it was so often the scene of upheaval.

[10] As cited by Schama 1989, p. 484. The original French text: 'J'accepte, [...], la Constitution; je prends l'engagement de la maintenir au dedans, de la défendre contre les attaques du dehors et de la faire exécuter par tous les moyens qu'elle met en mon pouvoir.'

[11] There were soaring expectations. Illustrations were published in newspaper articles with the text: 'Ô la bonne Constitution, que la Constitution Française! Elle assure notre bonheur et

The euphoria was short-lived because the forces at motion were by then inexorable. Less than a year later, on 22 September 1792, the newly elected National Convention proclaimed the French Republic. The year-long experiment with constitutional monarchy had ended in failure,[12] yet it would prove to be an important step in the country's subsequent development.[13] The proclamation of the Republic in 1792 changed the character of the Constitution of 1791. It became a revolutionary constitution until its replacement by the Constitution of 1793[14] on 24 June the following year. This latter constitution came replete with modern, radical ideas, such as direct elections to the National Representation (with a parliamentary term of just one year) by all citizens aged 21 and older. It included a series of fundamental freedoms (such as the right to equality, liberty, security and property)[15] and lofty goals ('the aim of society is the common welfare').[16] The Constitution of 1793[17] never came into force and after the Reign of Terror (1793–1794), led by Maximilien de Robespierre, it was soon replaced by the much more conservative Constitution of the Year III on 22 August 1795.[18] This 1795-*Thermidor constitution* turned back the clock:[19] it paid lip service to popular sovereignty,[20] but democracy and the people were no longer the central themes. It laid much less emphasis on fundamental freedoms – the list is considerably shorter than in 1793 – and a greater emphasis on security, and independence of the judiciary

---

celui de nos enfans' (Oh the good Constitution, the French Constitution. It ensures our and our children's happiness). The illustration and text can be found on the Gallica website: https://gallica.bnf.fr/ark:/12148/btv1b52504671b.r=constitution?rk=21459;2 (Consulted 27 April 2018).

[12] Entitled '*L'échec de la monarchie constitutionnelle*' (The failure of the constitutional monarchy), the French Wikipedia page gives a laconic explanation: 'Ce régime constitutionnel échoue rapidement, car il révèle très vite ses défauts' (this constitutional system swiftly failed because its faults were soon revealed). https://fr.wikipedia.org/wiki/Constitution_fran%C3%A7aise_du_3_septembre_1791#L%E2%80%99%C3%A9chec_de_la_monarchie_constitutionnelle (consulted on 14 March 2018).

[13] Thornhill argues that the Constitution of 1791 highlighted what France stood for, what the public interest was, and who was responsible for it. Thornhill 2011, p. 218–219.

[14] Also known as the Constitution of the Year I or the Montagnard Constitution, after the *Montagnards*, a political group in the National Assembly, whose members sat on the highest benches. The architects of the Montagnard constitution were Maximilien de Robespierre – leader of the Montagnards – and the very young Louis Saint-Just (who would not live to be older than 27), both of whom also served on the executive Committee of Public Safety. This committee's rule gave the public little safety and culminated in the Reign of Terror – the revolutionary Terror of 1794 with its numerous arrests, show trials and guillotine executions of political opponents.

[15] Cf. Article 2.

[16] Article 1. http://chnm.gmu.edu/revolution/d/297.

[17] Also called the Jacobin Constitution.

[18] Time was literally reset in revolutionary France on 21 September 1792, the day that the monarchy was abolished and the republic proclaimed. It marked the first day of *Year I*.

[19] Named after the month of the uprising and the overthrow of the Jacobin terror: *Thermidor*. On 9 Thermidor (27 July 1794), the most powerful figure in the revolutionary government, Robespierre, was arrested and he was executed the following day.

[20] Cf. Article 6 and Article 17.

and the right to a fair trial; the latter was a reaction to the judicial arbitrariness of the Reign of Terror. The 1795 constitution remained in force until Napoleon Bonaparte's coup d'état in 1799.

REVOLUTIONARY CONSTITUTIONS: A NEW BEGINNING

The end of the eighteenth century was the era of constitutional revolutions.[21] Characteristic of the epoch's 'revolutionary constitutions' is how they set out to start a new era in history. The Ancien Régime was cast aside as the wrong vision and governance structure; a new era was ushered in.[22] Revolutionary constitutions – by no means all born in an actual revolution – radically broke with the past and established a completely new legal and governing system according to a different world view, a different conception of humans. Time itself was reset in this new world to Day One;[23] synchronised with the new dawn of humankind.[24] Discontinuity.

A new era in history had hitherto been inconceivable. For instance, the Dutch Act of Abjuration (1581) or the English Bill of Rights (1689) in no way disputed the continued existence of the legal or governance system.[25] At most, they supplemented or criticised it. The United States Constitution, on the other hand, represents a new beginning.

> We the People of the United States, in Order to form a more perfect Union, *establish* Justice, insure domestic Tranquility, *provide* for the common defence, *promote* the general Welfare, and *secure* the Blessings of Liberty to ourselves and our Posterity, *do ordain and establish this Constitution for the United States of America.*[26]

The 'people' created a new constitutional order on that day on 17 September 1787.[27] This act of creation was firmly grounded in the present, paid no heed to the past and was only concerned with the future.

Civil rights and fundamental freedoms usually have a central role in these revolutionary constitutions. Enlightenment ideas, especially the liberal-humanist doctrine, became increasingly important in politics over the course of the eighteenth century. They fell on fertile ground in the new state-based societies in which relationships and the nature of governmental authority had changed considerably. Leadership and governmental authority within these new states were gradually becoming more

---

[21] Somewhere between 1770 and 1790. Thornhill 2011, p. 219.
[22] Thornhill calls it an '*ex nihilo* justification' that could already be seen in the 'state constitutions' of the colonies that would later form the United States of America. Thornhill 2011, p. 190.
[23] '*Stunde* o' (Stunde Null) as the Germans say.
[24] This literally happened in France – cf. note 471.
[25] The preamble of the *Bill of Rights* simply states: 'An Act declaring the Rights and Liberties of the Subject and Setleing the Succession of the Crowne'.
[26] My italics.
[27] It was ratified on 21 June 1788 and entered into force on 4 March 1789.

abstract and less personal.[28] From time immemorial to the mediaeval period (and beyond), authority and governmental power had primarily been a private matter concerning individuals; governmental power (administration, taxation, regulations and to some extent, the administration of justice) was more or less a form of private ownership. From the mediaeval period, the fief or domain governed by rulers or office-holders was often actually their property, whether or not it was leased or 'leant'. Whoever was on this property was a vassal of the lord (duke, count, knight, bishop, etcetera). This property could also be transferred, inherited or confiscated.

Everything changed in the seventeenth and eighteenth centuries, actually quite swiftly. The idea of governmental power as personal property with rights (privileges, tokens, vassals' obligations) was exchanged for an idea of state and government as abstract entities. For example, a state became an administrative area with more or less fixed boundaries that were not regularly redrawn after every marriage or military campaign. Governmental power was increasingly authority limited by rules and exercised by an office; it was no longer property or dependant on the whims or preferences of a particular person, and it was no longer dependent on any single person's fortunes. It was not inherited or bestowed but passed on or granted according to (usually) written rules. This also includes the idea that a ruler – usually a king at the time – was not there for himself, his family or god, but only held office to serve his subjects and guarantee their liberties and rights. It was a Copernican revolution in thinking about state administration, shifting the starting point from the rulers to the ruled and their liberties. This new paradigm is clearly reflected in the revolutionary constitutions of the United States of America, the French Constitution of 1791 or that of Saint-Domingue (present-day Haiti) of 1801.

The Polish-Lithuanian Commonwealth's Great Sejm adopted a similar constitution on 3 May 1791 in the form of a 'Government Act' (*Ustawa rządowa*). The Polish-Lithuanian constitution – inspired by the American example – introduced a constitutional monarchy and a modern governmental system based on popular sovereignty and the separation of powers. It was a vain attempt to preserve the commonwealth's crumbling independence which was rapidly succumbing to the ambitions of neighbouring states and its kings were effectively picked by the Russian tsar. About a year and a half after the constitution's adoption, it was repealed by a competing parliament, the Grodno Sejm (1793), and the sovereign state of Poland soon entirely disappeared from the map (1795).

A similar kind of regression came about in Sweden. The aforementioned *Government Form* of 1719 (revised in 1720) had greatly limited the royal power. For a few decades, Sweden functioned as a constitutional monarchy, with the king acting as a kind of chair of the Council of Ministers and the ministers appointed by the Riksdag. The Riksdag also discussed and engaged in the adoption of laws and

---

[28] A process of ever-increasing political abstraction, as Thornhill calls it. Thornhill 2011, p. 159–160.

could even introduce bills. This configuration was comparable to that of the United Kingdom at the time.[29] But as in Poland, Sweden's parliamentary constitution was revoked. After a coup d'état on 19 August 1772, Gustav III repealed the constitution of 1720 and largely restored absolute monarchy. The Riksdag of the Estates was disbanded and could only reconvene if convoked by the king. And the king was once again in charge of his ministers whom he could from that point onwards appoint and dismiss at his leisure. However, he still relied on the Riksdag approving the budget and needed its cooperation to adopt and repeal laws.

The Corsican constitutions of 1755 (when for a short time Corsica became a republic independent of Genoa before its incorporation into France in 1769) and 1794 were also pervaded with the spirit of the new era.[30] The latter even introduced universal suffrage for property owners. The Northern-German kingdom of Prussia also functioned as a constitutional monarchy, despite lacking a written document that was a proper constitution. Although the *Allgemeines Landsrecht* of 1794 was not a formal constitution in the sense of a state dispensation, it does contain an abstract conception of the state, as well as a modern notion of human rights based on every individual's natural freedom.[31]

The revolutionary spirit swept over Europe and other parts of the world spawning – mostly short-lived – revolutionary constitutions in its wake. And even though most of these constitutions did not survive, the ideas they expressed did.

---

[29] Sweden also had two rival political factions in parliament: the Caps (*Mössorna*) and the Hats (*Hattarna*). Cf. Thornhill 2011, p. 170.

[30] Van Caenegem argues that the governments of Prussia and Austria at the end of the eighteenth century were examples of enlightened absolutism. Van Caenegem 1995, p. 129 ff.

[31] This emphasis on fundamental freedoms – the civil rights citizens are naturally endowed with as individuals – is also found in the Dutch revolutionary constitution: the Constitution of the Batavian Republic of 1 May 1798. Protection of natural rights is at its heart, as can be ascertained in the preamble: 'The Batavian People, constituting an indivisible State, and realising that the main depravity of all Governments is in the disregard of the natural and hallowed rights of Man in Society, declares the following propositions to be the legitimate basis upon which It establishes its Constitution, and as rules to which It wants to change its civil and political relations.' This is a nice summary of the revolutionary fervour of the era's constitutions: people, state and nation, a reference to natural rights and the task entailed for the newly abstract office of government, the legal basis and the new insights born out of the necessity to change the existing order. The new human, in his new place. The Batavian Constitution of 1798 is largely forgotten nowadays in the Netherlands. The constitutional history of the Netherlands according to conventional scholarship and wisdom starts on 29 March 1814 when the Constitution of the Kingdom of the Netherlands was adopted – it's still in force today. This consignment to oblivion is undoubtedly related to the Constitution's problematic establishment (by two referendums, the latter involving coercion), the turbulent times in which it was drafted and its short lifespan. In 1801, barely three years after its proclamation, it was repealed. It had hardly any legal effect but all the more so as an idea.

11

Third Generation

Restoration Constitutions

Unrest breeds more unrest. The French constitutions of 1793 and 1795 and the new order exacerbated the contradictions and turmoil more than they ameliorated them. Even the revolutionaries' success in maintaining power and increasing support and acceptance of the new ideas, at home as well as abroad, failed to restore peace. The revolutionaries grew ever more radical, extreme, bordering on paranoid under the Jacobin-dominated Committee of Public Safety's Reign of Terror (1793–1794). Even a constitution brimming with lofty ideals, principles and rights has little power as a document when confronted by abuse of authority and popular rage. The Committee of Public Safety's successor, the five-man collegiate body called the Directory, had difficulty overcoming continuing internal disputes and costly foreign conflicts. Was the revolutionary order simply too new, implemented too abruptly or too far ahead of its time? It is hard to say. The revolutionary ideas did mobilise the French people, even resulting in military success. Yet, the ongoing internal conflicts due to sustained political strife weakened the French government on many different fronts.

The new constitution imposed by Napoleon after a coup d'état at the end of 1799 (the Constitution of the Year VIII) solved this problem in one fell swoop. Following the example of the Roman Republic, which was greatly admired at the time, France was to be led by a three-man Consulate. Like a latter-day Caesar, Napoleon Bonaparte held all real power, but the constitution gave France what it yearned for after ten revolutionary years: peace and order. Bonaparte was the First Consul; the other two consuls played a marginal role. Despite being the result of a seizure of power, the new order paid shrewd lip service to the past, enabling Napoleon to obscure its provenance. He allowed the widely admired Emmanuel Joseph Sieyès, one of the first revolutionaries who wrote the influential revolutionary pamphlet *What Is the Third Estate?*, to draft a constitution.[1] When a college of 500 delegates

---

[1] Published in January 1789, seven months before the outbreak of the revolution and an important source of inspiration for the events culminating in the Tennis Court Oath.

rejected it, Napoleon proposed his own text, which was approved by an overwhelming majority in a referendum.

Napoleon's constitution of the year VIII was a clever mix of old and new. It upheld the revolutionary confiscation of property, as well as the strict laws forbidding the return of émigrés (predominantly nobility). But, it also contained new 'stabilising' elements: a single-person executive, legislative power controlled by the consul, an influential administrative advisory body – the Council of State (*Conseil d'État*), composed of influential lawyers acting as a revamped privy council. The state finances were modernised, as was the rest of the state apparatus – in particular, the law and administration of justice.[2] The Constitution of the Year VIII is one of the first in Europe to focus on meritocratic administration by experts: capacity and skill served as the guiding principles for recruitment to government service, instead of birth or descent. The revolutionary motto *Liberté, Égalité, Fraternité* ('liberty, equality, fraternity') was, however, quietly dropped. Neither does it contain any reference to universal natural human rights; the new, sober state administration also dispensed with the Declaration of the Rights of Man and of the Citizen. Whilst French men still had nominal universal suffrage, it was no more than a sham democracy: the First Consul and his followers determined who would be admitted to the representative organs.[3] Many even doubt whether the constitution of 1799 made France a constitutional state – a state governed by the rule of law – which had been a key revolutionary ambition.[4]

Much was – intentionally – unclear in the new constitution. Napoleon felt that:

A constitution should be short and obscure. It must be made in such a way as not to hamper the action of government.[5]

---

[2] In 1800, Napoleon convened a committee of eminent jurists including Jean-Étienne-Marie Portalis and Napoleon's fellow consul Jean-Jacques Régis de Cambacérès to draft a civil code codifying much existing customary civil law (including the Customs of Paris – a compilation of customary law maintained since 1510 – and much Roman-French law and Chancellor d'Aguesseau's decrees, maintained since c. 1731). The civil code was introduced in 1804. This is followed by the codification of the criminal code in 1810. Both codes were highly influential on private and criminal law in the nineteenth century in Europe and – due to colonisation – far beyond.

[3] Of which, the senate was initially the most important.

[4] Thornhill argues that the Napoleonic constitutions did indeed preserve the revolutionary achievements of the French constitution of 1791 in particular, including the idea of the rule of law. 'Even after the constitutional reforms of 1802, when the authoritarian powers of the Napoleonic executive were reinforced, it is doubtful whether Bonapartist rule fell completely outside the pattern of constitutional governance. Indeed, his elevation to imperial grandeur after 1804 did not mean that Napoleon governed wholly without parliamentary checks, and his regime preserved (albeit highly limited) countervailing powers in the state [...] At Napoleon's first accession to power, however, the constitutional dimensions of his regime were clear and pronounced.' Thornhill 2011, p. 223. He precedes to argue that in several respects '[...] Napoleonic government remained within the category of constitutional rule.' Thornhill 2011, p. 225. For a less sanguine appraisal, cf. Bernard 2017.

[5] In the original French: 'Il faut qu'une constitution soit courte et obscure. Elle doit être faite de manière à ne pas gêner l'action du gouvernement.' Soullier 1852.

This Napoleonic constitution attempted to reconcile the old and the new, and fuse good, trusted administrative traditions and the legitimacy and authority of a time-honoured administrative culture with the new ideas on freedom and governance bound to the law. It was to be widely imitated, even after the fall of the French Empire in 1814, when all of Europe had become acquainted with the new ideas. There was a proliferation of constitutions designed according to this synthesis of old and new elements. They were particularly popular in the Europe of kingdoms in the first period of the restoration after 1815. These early-nineteenth-century constitutions were not monarchical constitutions along eighteenth-century lines, but rather 'restoration constitutions'; partial restoration of venerable institutions (monarchy) and familiar (religious and secular) authority, but bound in new relations.[6] Royal power was not so much limited as recast, re-established and redesigned as part of a strong state with a strong executive.[7] The new dispensation entailed both limitation (conditional and limited allocation of authority) and reinforcement of power.[8] It is a form of instrumental constitutionalism. The constitution centralised state power and restructured the state system and administration.[9] Some reassuring old furniture in a new house, you might say.

An early example is the 1807 Constitution of the Kingdom of Westphalia. Napoleon imposed this constitution on the Confederation of the Rhine after his victory at Austerlitz. This first German Constitution – the result of the Treaties of Tilsit – established the new kingdom of Westphalia. It was an unprecedented innovation. It had hitherto been inconceivable to simply create kingdoms or monarchies, which were God-given, and it required at the very least incumbent spiritual and secular leaders' recognition. None of which bothered Napoleon in the slightest. The conqueror of a new Europe established new kingdoms, installed kings, crowned himself king of Italy and then emperor of the French in a ceremony at Notre-Dame de Paris, with Pope Pius VII a passive onlooker. This was a profound affront to the crowns of Europe.[10]

The Westphalian constitution had marked revolutionary features.[11] It introduced freedom of religion, equality before the law, economic freedoms and abolished many of the aristocracy's privileges as well as serfdom. Government operation was also organised according to the new principles. It instituted the tripartite separation of powers, modernised the administration of justice and codified and modernised private law (the law governing relations between citizens) along French lines. Even though the artificial kingdom of Westphalia was short-lived (expiring in 1813), its

---

[6] Cf. Meadwell 2001, especially p. 173.
[7] Cf. Thornhill 2011, p. 228 who talks of the 'restoration constitution' to indicate the French post-Napoleonic constitution.
[8] Thornhill rightly characterises this type of constitution as 'monarchy limited and intensified'. Thornhill 2011, p. 228–240.
[9] Thornhill 2011, p. 220.
[10] Lawday 2007, chapters 8 and 9, especially from p. 147.
[11] Cf. Grothe 2005, p. 1–19 on p. 6.

constitution has had profound and lasting influence in Germany. It was a source of inspiration for the Bavarian constitution of 1808 and the constitution of the Grand Duchy of Frankfurt of 1810,[12] influenced German officials and intellectuals long after 1813,[13] and had consequences up to 1848.

The Westphalian constitution was one of the first in a wave of constitutions to inundate the world at the start of the nineteenth century. They tried to create a new order based on new, enlightened insights.[14] This includes the influential constitution of Cádiz (1812), which transformed Spain and the Spanish Empire into a constitutional monarchy based on new liberal principles for two years.[15] Like its Westphalian counterpart, its short lifespan belies its abiding influence. It was briefly reinstituted between 1820 and 1823, during the *Trienio Liberal* – three years of regained freedom after an uprising in 1820 – and re-emerged for a third time – briefly – in 1836 and 1837, whilst the Spanish constitution of 1837 was being drafted,[16] which itself is regarded as an attempt to restore the constitution of Cádiz.

But the Constitution of Cádiz has had the greatest influence chiefly outside Spain. After the liberal revolution of 1820, Portugal adopted a constitution in 1822 based on the liberal Cádiz approach; it affirmed the separation of powers, a role for parliamentary representation, fundamental freedoms, and a modern legal system. This Portuguese constitution was in its turn an important step towards newly independent Brazil's constitution, which was adopted in 1824. The greatest consequence of the Constitution of Cádiz was on the new independent republics that supplanted the former Spanish colonies in Latin America between 1809 and 1833. This includes the constitutions of Chile (1833),[17] the Republic of Colombia (*Constitution of Cúcuta*, 1821), the Federal Republic of Central America (1824), Bolivia (1831) and Uruguay[18] (1829).[19] The venerable Constitution of Cádiz continued to be a key source of inspiration for constitutional development in Latin America throughout the nineteenth century.[20]

---

[12] Grothe 2005, p. 10.

[13] *Ibid.*

[14] Cf. For a historical overview, Constitutions of the World Online, which presents the results of the project *The Rise of Modern Constitutionalism, 1776 – 1849* www.modern-constitutions.de/nbu.php?page_id=f430314067d0b98efac2049c65113d41 (Consulted on 30 April 2018).

[15] Its official title is the Political Constitution of the Spanish Monarchy (*Constitución Política de la Monarquía Española*) Cf. Mirow 2015.

[16] In its turn, it was replaced by the more liberal constitution of 1845.

[17] This constitution, which includes many recognisable elements of the French Thermidor constitution of 1795 (authoritarian presidentialism and an oligarchic parliamentary system), survived until 1925, making it to this day South America's longest-surviving constitution. Gargarella argues that this is mainly due to its clever design: 'On the one hand, the Constitution organised its system of rights according to the needs and demands of the Catholic Church: Only the Catholic Church was recognised and accepted [...]. On the other hand, the Constitution made all the different institutional powers dependent on the will of a hyperpowerful president.' Gargarella 2016, especially p. 100.

[18] Cf. Bewes 1920, p. 60–63.

[19] Cf. Sabato 2018, p. 38–40.

[20] Mirow 2015, chapter 6, especially p. 237–238.

A SERIES OF CONSTITUTIONAL MONARCHIES

The need for formative constitutions on the European continent grew even stronger after the fall of Napoleon. Restoration constitutions came to be regarded as the remedy for shaping the changed relations of a new Europe devised at the Congress of Vienna (1814–1815). The nineteenth century was to see the flowering of constitutionalism in Europe.[21] Constitutions were regarded for almost a century not only as instruments of political change, but also as instruments capable of averting political tensions in a rapidly changing world. In his book *Phantom Terror*,[22] Adam Zamoyski lucidly describes how post-Napoleonic generations lived in incessant dread. Nothing seemed sacred, certain or safe after the Jacobin and Napoleonic carnage. Zamoyski argues that Europe endured a protracted crisis between 1789 and the democratic revolutions of 1848. Rulers were bedevilled by political paranoia and were constantly fearful of the danger of insurrection, subversion of the current social order and (Jacobin) terror, which they feared could break out at any time. A strong monarchical and constitutionally-anchored authority was regarded as the only effective remedy to persistent danger of this kind.[23] These constitutions used legal rules to codify law from venerable traditions and mix them with new ones and by this 'constitute' and cement pacifying legal, social and political orders. This made a constitution more than collection of legal rules or political principles: it established the nature of the nation and described its 'constitution'. As part of the judicious and measured peace of 1815 (the 'Concert of Europe' organised at the Congress of Vienna), old empires and monarchies continued, and were sometimes re-established or newly invented. This was often affected with a constitution. It would be superfluous to mention all of them here; most failed to survive to the present.

Innovative Restoration

On that day an Assembly representing the United Netherlands' convened at the Nieuwe Kerk in Amsterdam to consider a draft prepared by a Royal Constitutional Committee.[24] The authoritarian and bad-tempered Justice Minister Van Maanen – who had served under Napoleon rule and was versed in it – had already let it be

[21] For an insight into the proliferation of constitutions in the nineteenth century, cf. Dippel 2004.
[22] *Phantom Terror: The Threat of Revolution and the Repression of Liberty 1789–1848*, Zamoyski 2014.
[23] Cf. Constant 1997 (orig. 1806–1810).
[24] The first Constitution of 1814 was prepared by a constitutional committee established by William I – who had proclaimed himself Sovereign Prince of the United Netherlands at the end of 1813 – and chaired by Gijsbert Karel van Hogendorp. The latter had been working in secret on a draft constitution for a sovereign principality of the United Netherlands during the final years of French rule. This basic text was opportune, greatly expediting the matter. A complete text was produced in March 1814 – less than four months after William had embarked in the Netherlands and agreed to act as its sovereign prince.

known that there was to be no discussion. Of the 600 notables invited, 474 were present; the newly arrived prince spoke and Van Maanen, who had been a member of the constitutional committee, gave a brief explanation of the constitution's design. Then it was put to a vote without debate or further ado: Ayes 448, Noes 26. Everything was done and dusted within an hour and a half.

Typical of the period, the 1814 Constitution enshrines a mix of old and new elements. It clearly bound government to the law,[25] recognised the 'invaluable advantages of civil freedom and personal safety' and granted a number of fundamental freedoms (prohibition of arbitrary arrest, access to justice),[26] freedom of religion and confession.[27] It furthermore recognised a role for the people in governing the state[28] and separated governmental power into executive,[29] legislative[30] and judicial[31] branches. This 1814 Constitution, like the other constitutions in the post-Napoleonic period, focused on strong central authority and strong monarchical rule. Numerous articles conferred the Sovereign Prince and from 16 March 1815 King William I[32] supreme governmental power and other important executive responsibilities, including supreme authority over colonies and overseas state assets[33] and finances,[34] authority over foreign affairs (including conclusion and ratification of treaties),[35] issuing currency,[36] command of the fleet and armed forces,[37] and the

[25] The 1814 Constitution is permeated with this idea. The whole concept of the document is that state powers are bound to the rules contained in it – constitutional law and the law based on it. The constitution's intention to bind to the law is explicit in article 72 and article 104, but in general is implicit in the rest of the document.

[26] All from article 101 of the 1814 Constitution.

[27] Articles 134 and 135 of the 1814 Constitution. Other forms of freedom of expression, such as the freedom of the press, petition and so on were only introduced in 1815 Constitution of the United Kingdom of the Netherlands at the insistence of the southerners.

[28] Article 52 of the 1814 Constitution is the most 'venerable' and stable provision in the Dutch Constitution: 'The States General shall represent the entire people of the Netherlands.'

[29] The 1814 Constitution conferred the Sovereign Prince executive authority in many areas. This authority extended beyond merely implementing laws. The Constitution also conferred many general implementation responsibilities and powers to the monarch. Cf. Articles 36, 37, 39, 41 and 50 of the 1814 Constitution.

[30] Cf. Articles 68 to 71 of the 1814 Constitution.

[31] Cf. Articles 101 and 105 of the 1814 Constitution.

[32] The European powers at the Congress of Vienna decided to grant William this elevation. The Congress decided to unite the Northern and Southern Netherlands (approximately contiguous with present-day Belgium) under the newly established crown of the Kingdom of the Netherlands. King William I was also made Grand Duke of Luxembourg by the same decision. A proclamation in the Government Gazette of 16 March 1815 (Bulletin of Acts & Decrees 27) informed the people of the Netherlands of the new situation. From that moment, the Netherlands was a Kingdom. William I was officially inaugurated in Brussels on 21 September 1815, after the adoption of the 1815 Constitution.

[33] Cf. Article 36 of the 1814 Constitution.

[34] Cf. Article 40 of the 1814 Constitution.

[35] Cf. Article 38 of the 1814 Constitution.

[36] Cf. Article 41 of the 1814 Constitution.

[37] Cf. Article 39 of the 1814 Constitution.

right to declare war and make peace.[38] There were great expectations of strong government. Several of the drafters had had first-hand experience of the French Empire's effective governance from the Netherlands' incorporation into the empire in 1806.[39] It contrasted sharply with the atrophied and ineffective governance that had blighted the late Dutch Republic. However much the drafters wanted a restoration in form, they certainly did not want to tamper with the innovation of French-style governance along Napoleonic lines.

Meanwhile in Norway…

Norway's first constitution also dates from this period. It was adopted on 17 May 1814, about two months after the adoption of the Dutch Constitution. The rapid pace of political development meant that it was done post-haste. Norway had hitherto been part of the Kingdom of Denmark, which had allied itself with France – against the wishes of the Norwegians. After the French defeat at Leipzig in autumn 1813, the Norwegians had a brief outburst of national consciousness thanks to a Swedish naval blockade of the Danes. At a summarily convened Constituent Assembly (*Riksforsamlingen*) in Eidsvoll, the Norwegians proclaimed their own kingdom under regent Christian Frederik and give themselves a constitution. The adventure only lasted a few months, as Norway entered into a personal union with Sweden in November 1814 – which part of the Constituent Assembly had incidentally called for in the spring. It would take another 91 years for the Norwegians to secede from Sweden and reclaim their actual independence, although they kept their 1814 constitution on record and intact during the time of the union. The Norwegians mark the events of 1814 by celebrating Constitution Day on 17 May. This instance clearly illustrates how constitutions and nation-building go hand in hand.

The Dutch Constitution of 1814 was also rapidly overtaken by facts on the ground. The European powers convened the Congress of Vienna to hammer out how to organise a post-Napoleonic Europe after Napoleon. They decided in March 1815 to merge the former Dutch Republic and Austrian Netherlands into a buffer state to frustrate French imperial ambitions. The decision was mainly impelled by the Hundred Days – Napoleon's final military campaign[40] after his return from exile on Elba. Constitutional arrangements went less smoothly this time; much had to be hurriedly improvised in the new kingdom. The revised Constitution of 1815 proved

---

[38] Cf. Article 38 of the 1814 Constitution.

[39] Such as the influential C.F. (Cornelis Felix) van Maanen, who had been Louis Napoleon's Minister of Justice and Police (from 1807) and also served as the new kingdom's Minister of Justice between 1814 and 1842. He was not unique. Several members of the 1814 Constitutional Committee had also served in the French (and sometimes even the Batavian) era and later served as ministers in the new kingdom, including G.W. (Gustaaf Willem) baron van Imhoff, C.Th. (Cornelis Theodorus) Elout and W.F. (Willem Frederik) baron Röell.

[40] Culminating in the Battle of Waterloo and Napoleon's final defeat on 18 June 1815.

to be a hard-won compromise.[41] Mutual misunderstanding and distrust resulted in a voluminous text abounding in impenetrable and ambiguous compromise texts. Eighty years later, the Dutch constitutional lawyer Buijs complained that it 'distinguished itself by nothing so much as the laxity of its editing'.[42] The process was beset with irritation and frustration. Part of the reason was certainly the prospective king's imperiousness. Having already been proclaimed king by the European powers in Vienna, he was less accommodating towards the southerners than he had been towards the northerners in 1813 and 1814 when he was still unsure of his position. Cultural differences also played a role. This sleight of hand is known to posterity as *Arithmétique hollandaise* (Dutch arithmetic). The 1815 Constitution was ill-starred. The United Netherlands was to disintegrate within fifteen years, with the outbreak of the Belgian Revolution in 1830. This was not thanks to the constitution or its troubled inception, but it certainly did not help prevent the rift.

Imposed constitutions – as the constitution of the United Netherlands of 1815 was to a certain extent – usually have little binding force, and have difficulty coming to life, so to speak. This may explain why hardly any attempts were made to defuse the rising tensions between the Northern and Southern Netherlands between 1830 and 1839 by revising the constitution and – thereby – reorganising relations. The pre-existing constitutional order had little effect on the Belgian Revolution. The southerners – the Belgians – were unconcerned about its legal details when they seceded in 1830. They acted as if the whole Constitution of 1815 was simply non-existent to them anymore; they did not bother amending or revising it, neither did they wish to discuss bilateral matters with the rump Netherlands. It was largely left to the great powers of Europe (with a superannuated Talleyrand in a leading role)[43] to decide

---

[41] In the Northern Netherlands, the 1815 constitution was prepared and adopted as a revision of the 1814 constitution. In the Southern Netherlands, the constitution was presented to the population in a kind of referendum and thence to a popular assembly in Brussels. As said, this could not have been done in any other way – the southerners were not yet part of the constitutional order. Although the Dutch tried their best to engage their Belgian counterparts in the preparations, the Belgians kept opposing and voting down drafts for the revised Constitution of the Kingdom. In a new, final attempt to get it adopted delegates of the Belgian people were invited to great constitutional assembly Brussels to vote on it yet again. The king and his party were furious with the backtracking Belgians – who were perhaps not so much manipulative and devious as politically inexperienced (ruled by foreigners for more than 200 years) and disorganised. They had trouble coordinating their position and struggled to respond to royal pressure. Perhaps they chose the only sensible option; they stayed away. One sixth of the delegates at the great constitutional assembly in Brussels – mostly southerners – did not attend in silent protest. This created a major problem in both terms of quorum and majority for the already enraged royal camp. They decided to get 'creative' by adding the votes of the absentees to the ayes in order to get the 1815 Constitution adopted. And even though the southerners have ever since called this form of manipulation '*Arithmétique Hollandaise*' (Dutch Arithmetic) the constitution of the United Kingdom of the Netherlands was duly enacted on 24 August 1815 in Brussels. Cf. Voermans 2018, p. 12–13.

[42] My translation of Buijs 1883 (Dutch original), p. 229.

[43] This French statesman, who had played an active role in and survived the French Revolution, Directory, Consulate, Empire and restored monarchy, was 76 years-old by this time. Lawday 2007, chapter 21 (*Last Performance*).

how to deal with the consequences of the Belgian secession, partly thanks to Dutch obduracy. In a way, the Belgian case was referred back to the Congress of Vienna, where the idea of a United Kingdom of the Netherlands had been born.[44] The existing constitutional order toppled under the weight of political developments. This fate was shared by many post-Napoleonic constitutions: many of them were revoked from 1818 onwards.[45]

The same fate also awaited France's imposed constitution, the Charter of 1814 which – under the guise of mediaeval privilege – had 'restored' the Bourbon monarchy and created a constitutional monarchy. The reactionary king Charles X was deposed in July 1830 and replaced by the 'citizen king' Louis Philippe and a more liberal constitution.[46] There were uprisings and revolutions throughout Europe in 1830, which the anti-Napoleonic allies succeeded in suppressing. In a remarkable pattern, revolts broke out simultaneously in nineteenth-century Europe. The next stop would be the one of the Revolutions of 1848.

---

[44] The Talleyrand partition plan for Belgium, partially based on ethnic borders, was very modern. It was rejected by the other great powers. The Free State of Antwerp would have deprived the industrialising and richest part of Belgium – the francophone area, now called Wallonia – from access to the sea.

[45] The year of the Congress of Aix-la-Chapelle, the first of a series of conferences convened by the great powers of the Congress of Vienna. This system, called the Concert of Europe, continued until the 1840s. The period from 1815 to 1848 is also known as the *Age of Von Metternich* – after the influential Austrian chancellor Prince Klemens von Metternich, the linchpin in the Concert of Europe. A paranoid fear of insurrection and revolution led to political and civil liberties being curtailed in favour of strong and effective monarchical rule. Zamoyski 2014.

[46] After a brief three-day revolution on 27, 28 and 29 July, known as the *Trois Glorieuses*.

12

Fourth Generation

Liberal Constitutions

1848: A NEW SOCIAL ORDER. THE ASCENT OF PARLIAMENTS

In early spring 1848, Europe was buffeted by a perfect storm – 'a moment of madness', in the words of Aristide Zolberg.[1] In what is known as the 'Springtime of Peoples', a broad civil movement revolted against Europe's autocratic, and by then downright repressive regimes, many of which were the product of the Congress of Vienna of 1815.[2] Citizens demanded democratic reforms, participation in government and liberal constitutions. The spirit of liberty, equality and fraternity returned from its long banishment within a few months or even days.

The first eruption is on 12 January 1848 in Palermo, Sicily. A group of Italian nationalists led by Giuseppe Mazzini, the founder of *Giovine Italia* (Young Italy), rose against the Bourbon king Ferdinand II's reactionary regime. They aimed to force him to grant a constitution and thus spur the unification of Italy.[3] After brief success, with rebellion spreading throughout Italy, the uprising was crushed with Austrian help. Short-lived constitutions and new liberties[4] were granted in various Italian kingdoms. Next, the unrest spread to France. Just over a month after the Italian uprising (23 February 1848), an uprising sparked by the prohibition of a benefit banquet caused the fall of the Guizot government. The proximate cause of this outdoor dinner party was far from frivolous: organising banquets was one of the few ways of circumventing the severe restrictions on political freedoms. It was one of the reactionary French government's many repressive measures at the time to stamp out all dissent. The situation spiralled out of control, royalist troops refused to intervene,[5]

---

[1] Zolberg 1972, p. 183 ff.
[2] *Ibid.*
[3] Sperber 2005, p. 116 ff.
[4] Naples and Piedmont were granted a constitution in March.
[5] Bugeaud, commander of the royal security forces in Paris, intervened too late – or rather, he failed to intervene at all, whilst barricades were being erected everywhere. Bugeaud claimed that the royal orders reached him too late and his troops had been obliged to wait too long for

and the king abdicated. The Second Republic was proclaimed on 25 February, and a new constitution was introduced, granting many individual fundamental freedoms and direct universal suffrage to men over the age of 21. This constitution, however, proved unable to end the unrest in Paris, which continued for most of the rest of the year. A workers' uprising from 23 to 26 June of that year resulted in bloody riots.[6] Approximately 10,000 people were either killed or injured at the hands of the National Guard, sent in to quell the rebellion.

The unrest in France spread within two days to Belgium, where there were only a few disturbances in Brussels, and the Grand Duchy of Baden in what is now Germany. A popular assembly abolished the Baden nobility's privileges, demanded popular sovereignty and a liberal constitution (a revision of the 1818 constitution) on 27 February 1848. The violent uprising in Baden spread in turn to Bavaria and Prussia, where liberal-democratic uprisings broke out in mid-March.[7] At this point, events in continental Europe spiralled out of control. Lajos Kossuth demanded democratic government in Hungary, peasant revolts erupted in Silesia and Galicia, and a German national assembly in Frankfurt pressed for universal suffrage and a united Germany. A proletarian revolution broke out in the Rhineland with similar demands.[8] The rebellion swept on to Bohemia, Moravia and even Vienna. Klemens von Metternich, the architect and enforcer of the Congress of Vienna and Chancellor of the Austrian Empire for 39 years, was forced to resign and flee in disgrace. 'Everything is lost!' he wrote in stupefaction to friends.[9] The world of the Congress of Vienna had indeed come irrevocably to an end.

Whilst the Prussian king made concessions to demonstrators in Berlin, the unrest in the Austro-Hungarian empire proved more difficult to contain. Venice proclaimed itself the Republic of San Marco, Lombardy joined the uprising, and the Hungarians declared independence. There was also unrest in Bohemia and Moravia. A pan-Slavic congress convened in Prague at which the empire's Slavic peoples demanded the restructuring of the Habsburg Empire as a federation of autonomous peoples.[10] The mighty Austro-Hungarian empire, which dominated most of South-eastern and central Europe, tottered. Even despite a second uprising in Vienna that year, it preserved its integrity and regained control through a

---

supplies and ammunition. Bugeaud's justification is not very convincing. Cf. Sperber 2005, p. 116–117; Zamoyski 2014, p. 483–484.

[6] Author George Sand participated in the *June Days uprising* (French: Les journées de Juin). Standing on the top of a barricade, she shouted to a friend: 'N'est-ce-pas que c'est magnifique, n'est-ce-pas que c'est beau!' (Isn't this magnificent, isn't this beautiful!) As cited by Figes 2019, p. 131.

[7] Sperber 2005, p. 117.

[8] They even dreamt of merging with the Netherlands and Belgium.

[9] Zamoyski 2014, p. 486–487.

[10] They wanted to transform the Habsburg Empire into a 'a federation of autonomous peoples.'

combination of concessions (including granting universal suffrage in places) and military intervention (with Russian aid). It was so successful that the new emperor was able to nullify all the preceding months' concessions before the end of the year.

RISE OF NATIONS

Despite incumbent governments or their successors thwarting[11] many of the 'constitutional' revolts[12] and largely repudiating their constitutional proceeds, they did produce enduring results in several cases. What was going on? Why did things boil over from Wexford[13] to Calabria and from the Baltic Sea to the Ionian Sea – and as far afield as New Zealand (1852)[14] and Argentina (1853)?[15] Truly convincing explanations are difficult to come by and even more so for why the rebellions followed each other in such quick succession. Several of them certainly have common causes: revolts against the conservative Austrian Empire and its retainers.[16] And the rebellions can also in part be attributed to resistance to the exploitation of the proletariat and workers' abominable living and working conditions resulting from the industrial revolution. 1848 was also the year of Karl Marx and Friedrich Engels' *The Communist Manifesto*, although the rebellions were certainly not triggered by this document; the first workers' revolts merely rode on the coattails of the 1848 revolutions.

1848 does mark a period when constitutions were conceived or rediscovered as instruments of national liberation.[17] Hitherto, states had chiefly been territories

---

[11] Thornhill argues that most of these constitutional revolutions were not successful – and certainly not on the long term. *Ibid.* I think this only applies to the short term. The revolts initiated a development that would lead to changes over time. The Italian and German uprisings were the prelude to the unification of Italy and Germany a few decades later. This was also accompanied by constitutional changes.

[12] Concessions in the form of constitutional guarantees and freedoms were the aim of most of these revolutions. That is why Thornhill calls the rebellions the 'constitutional revolutions of 1848.' Thornhill 2011, p. 241.

[13] The place where the Young Islander rebellion started in Ireland, before proceeding to County Kilkenny and County Tipperary. https://en.wikipedia.org/wiki/Young_Irelander_Rebellion_of_1848 (consulted 24 October 2018).

[14] The New Zealand Constitution Act 1846 was an attempt to give New Zealand self-government. It was a little premature for the European powers. After the document was withdrawn, the New Zealand Constitution Act 1852 was enacted (entering into force in 1853), giving New Zealand a measure of self-government and a parliament (an elected lower chamber and an appointed upper chamber) with legislative authority. Westminster (London) retained control of the executive.

[15] The Argentine Constitution of 1853 is a truly liberal constitution, in the sense that it grants fundamental freedoms and introduces a separation of powers.

[16] In reality, the Holy Roman Empire had been defunct since the beginning of the nineteenth century – formally at least, since the Congress of Vienna (1815). The ensuing peace treaty dissolved the entity and left it to the emperors of Austria to settle the venerable mediaeval empire's estate. In the nineteenth century, there was still what Wilson termed the empire's 'afterlife'. Wilson 2016, p. 663–676. Cf. Van Hooff 2018.

[17] 'In particular, this period saw a widespread inflation of the concept of national sovereignty, in which, in conjunction with rights, the idea of national self-legislation began to act as

controlled by governments whose borders had been drawn by the major powers at
the Congress of Vienna in 1815. States increasingly began to reinvent themselves in
this period into imagined political communities[18] of 'nations'.

The idea of a nation as denoting a group or a population that feels connected
by language, culture, race, kinship, common history or any other trait. The traits
themselves do not really matter a great deal. The concept of nation is mainly about
self-image – the 'we' – and the connectedness and solidarity it gave rise to. A nation
is not about what a group or population actually 'is', but what this group 'wants to
be', what it wants to do together. Or as Ernest Renan explained to an audience of
baffled Dutch students in a lecture hall in Leiden in 1877: the 'nation' is about the
connection between all the great things you have done together, and above all about
the greater things you still want to do.[19]

This desire to be together,[20] live together in a state of connectedness, and freely
determine the conditions of living together, gained momentum in this period.
The idea of this interconnectedness and a political society's social capital grew in
strength. Whilst the state was still a vehicle for nation-building in the early nineteenth century, as illustrated by the example of the Napoleonic administration in
France,[21] the roles were reversed from the middle of the nineteenth century: nation
formation was increasingly seen as a development that preceded, or should precede, state formation.[22] The consequences of this metamorphosis in thinking about
states and political societies as nations, and the desire for freedom it engendered,

the leading impulse of inclusionary political formation. This reached an apotheosis in the
(largely unsuccessful) constitutional revolutions of 1848, when in many European societies
the demand for constitutional formation and rights-based representation coincided with an
impetus towards the construction of states founded in more fully and cohesively integrated
national societies.' Thornhill 2011, p. 240–241.

[18] 'Imagined community' in Benedict Anderson's words. (Benedict) Anderson 1991 (orig. 1983.)

[19] My rendering of 'avoir fait de grandes choses ensemble, vouloir en faire encore'. Cf. www
.bmlisieux.com/archives/nation04.htm for the original text (consulted on 5 May 2018). My
translation is based on Renan's more extensive explanation: 'Une nation est une âme, un
principe spirituel. Deux choses qui, à vrai dire, n'en font qu'une, constituent cette âme, ce
principe spirituel. L'une est dans le passé, l'autre est dans le présent. L'une est la possession en
commun d'un riche legs de souvenirs; l'autre est le consentement actuel, le désir de vivre
ensemble, la volonté de continuer à faire valoir l'héritage qu'on a reçu indivis.' Cf. Renan 2018
(orig. 1882), part III.

[20] 'Le désir de vivre ensemble' ('[…] avoir fait de grandes choses ensemble, vouloir en faire
encore […]'). Renan 1882, chapter III.

[21] Breuilly 2011 – and Stedman, Jones & Claeys 2011, part I (*Political thought after the French
Revolution*).

[22] It is important to distinguish between the concept of nation and *nationalism*. The latter is,
in short, the ideology that asserts that the state (as a territory) and the nation *must* coincide,
that the two must have a one-to-one relationship. Nation must also be distinguished from the
principle of nationality. Breuilly argues that the principle of 'nationality' is based on several
coherent principles: 'humanity is divided into nations; nations are worthy of recognition and
respect; recognition and respect require autonomy, usually meaning political independence
within the national territory.' Breuilly 2011, p. 77.

extended well beyond Europe. In Latin America, a series of new states and republics with liberal constitutions came into being on the back of this new thinking.[23] These new constitutions were also a way of claiming and marking sovereignty.[24] This phenomenon of state formation by constitution also emerged in Europe. In response to several external factors and foreign powers' claims, Switzerland consolidated its right to self-government in its 1848 constitution, which made the country an independent confederation. Just as Belgium had proclaimed itself an independent state and monarchy in its 1831 constitution. For the same reason, the Greeks drafted their first constitution in 1822 (amended in 1823 and 1827) in an effort to achieve independence from the Ottoman Empire.[25] Given this background, the peak in constitution writing around 1850 is unsurprising.[26] The period marks the birth of parliaments as truly representative bodies, with powers of effective oversight and instruments to control government (budget, ideas on accountability etcetera) on behalf of the people.[27] Many political freedoms date back to this era in which parliaments rose and the seeds for later fully integrative democracies were planted.

---

[23] Sabato 2018. Gargalla 2014, p. 9–11.

[24] Elkins, Ginsburg & Melton 2009, p. 41–42.

[25] The French Thermidor constitution of 1795 was an important source of inspiration for the Greek constitution of 1822.

[26] Cf. figure 3.1 Elkins, Ginsburg & Melton 2009, p. 41.

[27] In the Netherlands, 1848 marks the birth of the modern parliamentary system. In October of that year the government finally persuaded the king to agree to a new, liberal constitution. It gave parliament more influence, limited the king's power and granted citizens new rights and freedoms. The turmoil in Europe must certainly have been one of the reasons for the king's sudden change of heart; until then he had refused to countenance change and had obdurately thwarted constitutional modernisation. The rise of the liberals under the leadership of the constitutional reformer Johan Rudolph Thorbecke (1798–1872) was undoubtedly an additional factor. The most important innovation in the Constitution of 1848 was the introduction of direct elections to the House of Representatives, Provincial Councils and municipal councils. However, political franchise was still subject to property qualifications, only entitling a small proportion of the population to vote. The elected House of Representatives had more effective control from 1848, thanks to its right to amend bills as well as its right to effectively contribute to budget formulation – by law, the budget had to be submitted yearly for parliamentary approval (including parliamentary input). Parliament was also granted the right of inquiry, and Senate sessions were made public. Equally importantly, the 1848 constitution limited the king's power by introducing political ministerial responsibility. Ministers were henceforth answerable to parliament, rather than to the king, for their policies. Royal power was further reduced by curtailing the king's independent, constitutional governmental powers. It is also fundamentally important that fundamental freedoms enabled citizens to participate and partake in forming public opinion and political processes. This includes the prohibition of censorship and freedom of expression, the freedom of association, assembly and religion and the freedom of education (both teaching and learning). It is these rights in particular that make the Dutch Constitution of 1848 a prime example of this period's liberal constitutions.

13

Fifth Generation

Imperial Constitutions

The legacy of liberal constitutions and the rise of national consciousness might have been expected to cause Europe after 1848 to fragment into smaller new states claiming the right to self-government, as happened in Belgium and the Czech lands. Instead the reverse occurred: states in Europe merged into larger units and sometimes even into global empires. In various places, this was caused by demands for national unification. German and Italian unification between 1860 and 1870 entailed the absorption of an array of small and middling states and kingdoms into a single, large entity, greatly increasing the scale of cooperation.[1] The new 'we' of these unified states, as free nations, had the wind in its sails; it enabled them to consolidate and direct the forces of collective collaboration and social energy both inwardly and outwardly. This was essential: the global empires at the end of the nineteenth century were pitted against each other in a relentless struggle in a rapidly globalising world. Industrialisation and colonisation went hand in hand. In the competition for raw materials, markets and world power, superpowers vied for spheres of influence and territory, most dramatically in the Scramble for Africa.[2] The new world of global empires impelled states to acquire size, power and a global network. This was the greatest challenge for colonial neophytes like Germany, Italy and Belgium, and to a certain extent France. They brought all their new imperial achievements to

---

[1] In Thornhill's words: 'the imperial period after 1870 normally saw a striking acceleration in the process of political inclusion and intensification in European societies. [...] most constitutions of imperial Europe, with significant variations, promoted the tentative beginnings of mass-political organization, and an increase in parliamentary competence and party-political organisation and inclusivity usually accompanied this process. Throughout Europe, thus, the imperial period brought both an extension of national franchises and a correlated consolidation of domestic statehood.' Thornhill 2011, p. 258.

[2] *The scramble for Africa*, Wettlauf um Afrika or *partage de l'Afrique*. Cf. Ferguson 2003, p. 222–225.

bear, including a greater scale of collaboration, growing social identity and national consciousness.

Constitutions played an important role in this increase in scale. They united these new nation states and promoted national awareness, enabling identity-based, social mobilisation.[3] Constitutions of this period told, as never before, the story of the new 'we'.

ITALIAN *RISORGIMENTO*

This was anything but a smooth process. The pain of Italian unification (*Risorgimento*), involving at least three wars with foreign powers (especially Austria and France) is magnificently conveyed in *The Leopard*, a novel about this period. 'Bad times, Your Excellency', Father Pirrone says to the prince of Salina, Don Fabrizio Corbera, on their drive to the capital, Palermo, when they see the nationalist rebels' bonfires burning on mountain tops.[4] It was May 1860. An army of 'Red shirts' led by the nationalist Garibaldi had raided Sicily and besieged Palermo, where the Austrian-backed Bourbon King Francis II of the Two Sicilies was ensconced. The repressive and arch-conservative[5] Bourbon regime had lost all popular support, enabling Garibaldi's modest band of nationalist volunteers to defeat a numerically superior royal force. The Risorgimento was a struggle for self-determination and national autonomy rather than a struggle for new civil rights or another form of government. The Italians strove for self-government and preservation of their traditions, the right to live as they saw fit on their peninsula, which had been dominated by foreign powers for centuries. Even the prince of Salina's young nephew Tancredi, prince of Falconeri, joined Garibaldi, despite having much to lose as a member of the old nobility and the Bourbon Ancien Régime in the uncertain future of the new nationalist and possibly republican regime.

> 'You're mad, my boy, to go with those people,' Don Fabrizio prince of Salina says to his nephew Tancredi. [...] 'A Falconeri should be with us, for the King.'
>
> Tancredi answers: 'For the King, yes of course. But which King?' [...] 'Unless we ourselves take a hand now, they'll foist a republic on us. If we want things to stay as they are, things will have to change.'[6]

The events of 1860 precipitated new wars on the Italian peninsular, culminating in the annexation Rome in 1870. The former papal state was made the new capital of the unified kingdom of Italy, which had been proclaimed in 1861. The

---

3   Cf. (Eugen) Weber 1959 & (Max) Weber 1976 (orig. 1909).
4   Tomasi di Lampedusa 2007 (orig. 1958), p. 13–14.
5   Italians were particularly grieved by Ferdinand II's bloody repression of the 1848 uprising, also aided by Austria. He ordered the bombardment of the insurgents, causing many civilian casualties. This earnt him the nickname king 'Bomba'.
6   Tomasi di Lampedusa 2007 (orig. 1958), p. 19.

papal administration was restricted to the Vatican City and from 1871 the new king, Victor Emmanuel, reigned over almost all of modern-day Italy. The struggle for the Risorgimento, dating as far back as 1815, had finally been accomplished.[7]

Italian politics may have been united, but the new kingdom's constitution was as fragmented as the various stages of the struggle for independence and Italian unification. Its constitutional foundation was the *Statuto Albertino* – the constitution King Charles Albert had conceded to the Kingdom of Sardinia in 1848. This was a basically liberal constitution with a few fundamental freedoms (freedom of press, freedom of association, and equality of all citizens before the law), but with a very limited franchise (only 3% of the population was entitled to vote). The Statuto Albertino was precipitated by the revolutions of March 1848 but drew more inspiration from the French constitution of 1830 than from more modern liberal constitutions, such as the Swiss or the Dutch one (both revised in 1848). The king and his government were still at the heart of the Albertine Statute (constitution). It was the king who appointed the senate, and ministers were responsible to the king, not to the Chamber of Deputies. The document may not have been overly progressive, but it was certainly very Italian as well as being very well-known. From 1865, the Statuto Albertino served as the entire Kingdom of Italy's basic law, or pseudo-constitution. It was primarily intended as an arrangement to facilitate the *transformismo* (the transformation of all Italian-speaking areas into a single kingdom). The realities of Italian political life changed without concomitant constitutional changes. In much of Europe, including Italy, ministerial responsibility gradually shifted at the end of the nineteenth century to the elected parliament. The electoral franchise gradually expanded too. The old house of the Statuto Albertino accommodated the new political realities well into the twentieth century.

GERMAN UNIFICATION

A similar unification process took place in Germany between 1848 and 1871. As noted in the previous chapter, there had been uprisings in various German-speaking cities (Berlin, Frankfurt) in March 1848. These were primarily directed against the system of governance that had been imposed by the Concert of Europe – based on the divine right of kings – and the dominance of the great German powers (Prussia and Austria). They initially met with success. As noted, Frederick William IV granted Prussia a liberal constitution after the 1848 uprising, and the Frankfurt Parliament produced

---

[7] After 1871, Italy continued to claim Italian-speaking territories south of the Alps under Austrian rule. Italian irredentism aimed to unite all Italian-speaking peoples in an Italian state, continued to agitate for 'reconciliation' with Trentino (populated by Italians, except for German-speaking South Tyrol) and Istria (predominantly populated by Slovenes and Croats, apart from Trieste and part of the coast) until the First World War. It largely succeeded after an extended struggle.

a constitution for the 39 states of the German confederation.[8] The Constitution of the German Empire, also known as the Frankfurt Constitution or Constitution of St. Paul's Church, was intended to be a constitution for a unified German nation state. At the time, Germany was a patchwork of German-speaking kingdoms, principalities and other areas, dominated by Prussia and Austria. The 1849 Constitution, adopted by the Frankfurt Parliament, proclaimed the unification of Germany and King Frederick William IV of Prussia as its emperor. Frederick William IV rejected the title of Emperor of the Germans as not the Parliament's to give. In any case, he had already reversed the constitutional reforms of 1848 at home by this time. The Frankfurt Constitution was a bit of a poisoned chalice to the ambitious and authoritarian Prussian monarchy. It would have firmly bound royal power to this pan-German Parliament, rendered the Prussian king more or less a figurehead and encumbered the monarch with the challenge of dealing with 'other' German states' aspirations.

Whereas the populace of the German-speaking world increasingly subscribed to liberal freedoms, liberal governance and unification, the powers-that-be of the various states were less sympathetic towards these ideas, fearing loss of position and power. The Frankfurt Constitution of 1849 was nothing more than an aspiration and a dead letter for quite some time, partly thanks to its rejection by other major German kingdoms after 1850. The requisite momentum and solidarity for unification under the new system came only after the defeat of Austria (in the Austro-Prussian War of 1866) and France (in the Franco-German War, 1870–1871) when, with calculated political manoeuvring by statesmen such as the Prussian Chancellor Otto von Bismarck (1815–1898), finally most of the German states could be enticed to unite. After the Prussian victory over France at the Battle of Sedan (September 1870), King Wilhelm I of Prussia was proclaimed German Emperor at the Hall of Mirrors in the Palace of Versailles on 18 January 1871. This indignity gnawed at the French soul. To the extent that the French exacted retribution for this indignity by insisting, nearly 50 years later, that the peace treaty after First World War be signed at the same place.

The proclamation of the German Empire in 1871 finally brought the aspirations of 1848 to fruition: a unified Germany under Prussian leadership. The new relations were formalised in the Constitution of the German Empire (*Verfassung des Deutschen Reiches*), which was established on 16 April 1871.[9] It was not a liberal constitution like the Frankfurt Constitution; the imperial constitution invested more in unification than in freedom. It contained hardly any fundamental rights or political freedoms and although it certainly enshrined the idea of the rule of law, the document mainly facilitated a strongly autocratic central government and accorded little power to the chamber of representatives (the *Reichstag*) or the Federal Council (the

---

[8] The German Confederation, created by the Congress of Vienna, was an association of 39 states, presided over by Austria.

[9] Based on the North German Constitution that Bismarck had written during his vacation in 1866.

Bundesrath). Nevertheless, the German Empire was not a really strong state[10] with a strong central authority, partly because the federal states retained much authority and self-rule. The imperial constitution was in many respects a rather laboured attempt to amalgamate entities that were not yet one. It was an attempt to respond to the Pan-Germanism that enjoyed such popularity at the time – this movement aimed to unite all German-speaking peoples in a single, independent nation state. The aspiration for group freedom and national self-determination was not easy to reconcile with individual freedom and democratic governance – an eternal dilemma.

In his novel *The Magic Mountain*, the German writer Thomas Mann has two scholars explore opposing positions.[11] Naphta is a cynical Jesuit; Settembrini is a humanist and romantic idealist. How do large-scale groups, such as states, and individuals relate to one other?

Naphta argues that state-based societies dehumanise people in a certain sense. They partially eliminate the individual – moral – choice between good and evil. This only leaves a simple choice:

> The Beyond is absorbed into the Here, [...] man ceases to be the theatre of a struggle between two hostile principles, [...] the conflict subsists merely between his individual and his collective interest; and the will of the State becomes, in good pagan wise, the law of morality. Either one thing or the other.[12]

This is too much for Settembrini:

> I protest against the imputation that the modern State means the subjugation of the individual to evil ends! [...] Democracy has no meaning whatever if not that of an individualistic corrective to State absolutism of every kind. Truth and justice are the immediate jewels of personal morality. If, at times, they may appear to stand counter, even to be hostile, to the interests of the State, they may do so while all the time holding before their eyes her higher, yes let us boldly say, her spiritual weal. [...] The Renaissance and the intellectual revival are personality, freedom, and the rights of man.[13]

But Naphta brings him back to earth:

> I was already tolerably aware that what is called liberalism – individualism, the humanistic conception of citizenship – was the product of the Renaissance. But the fact leaves me entirely cold, realising as I do, that your great heroic period age is a thing of the past, its ideals defunct, or at least lying at their latest gasp [...]

---

[10] Thornhill goes so far as to call it a weak state. He illustrates this argument with the persistent failure of the empire's tax reforms. Attempts to introduce federal (inheritance) taxes were a perennial bone of contention, even causing the government to collapse in 1909. Thornhill 2011, p. 263–264.

[11] In the novel protagonist Hans Castorp spends lots of his time with his fellow-patients Naphta and Settembrini at a Swiss tuberculosis clinic in the Alps. Mann 1960 (orig. 1924).

[12] Mann 1960, p. 399.

[13] *Ibid.*

You call yourself, if I am not mistaken, a revolutionist. But you err in holding that future revolutions will issue in freedom. [...] the principle of freedom has outlived its usefulness. [...] Liberation and the development of the individual are not the key to our age, they are not what our age demands. What it needs, what it wrestles after, what it will create – is Terror.[14]

Ominous words on a classic conflict of positions in Western political thinking which was about to politically materialise – even explode – in the twentieth century.

THE SPANISH, FRENCH AND RUSSIAN GLOBAL EMPIRES

From 1870, imperial constitutions with a greater emphasis on strong government than on individual liberties proliferated across Europe. These constitutions tried to exploit nation building's mobilising power. Strong nations, of course, had economies of scale in the imperial contest taking place around the world in the globalised economy.[15] Constitutional reforms in Russia from 1861 (the abolition of serfdom, curtailment of noble privileges and local self-government, and centralisation of government and the administration of justice) were also attempts to consolidate imperial power and thus strengthen the Russian state internally, making it stronger and more competitive externally.[16] In the long term, these reforms gave parliament its first modicum of power in Russia. The Russian Revolution of 1905[17] led to constitutional reform in October 1906, including the establishment of the State Duma (parliament), which drafted a number of fundamental laws giving the Duma a very modest voice in governing the Russian state.

France also gained a constitution with imperial characteristics in this era – despite the collapse of the Second Empire (1852–1870) after by the Germans in 1870.[18] In that same year the Third Republic was proclaimed, and a new constitution was promulgated in 1875. Its focus was less on the great republican principles (popular sovereignty, democracy, rights and freedoms, etcetera) than on stability, strong government and a strong state.[19]

---

[14] *Ibid.*, p. 400.
[15] Ferguson calls the period from the mid-nineteenth century to the First World War 'the first era of globalisation'. Ferguson 2009, p. 290. Cf. Ferguson 2008, part I, chapters 1–5. Ferguson has an interesting theory that expiring and declining empires are a major source of large and violent conflicts. Cf. Figes 2019.
[16] Thornhill 2011, p. 267–268. After the Crimean War (1853–1856) debacle, Russia quickly adapted to the new situation by embracing major reforms from 1861 (including military reforms). It met with success: between 1861 and the beginning of the twentieth century, Russia consolidated and strengthened its position as an imperial power. Cf. Frankopan 2015, p. 292–293 and for the effects of Russian reforms: chapter 16 *The Road to War*, especially p. 294–313.
[17] After Russian defeats by Japan in 1904 and 1905.
[18] The collapse was precipitated by the French defeat at Sedan and the capture of Emperor Napoleon III first by the Germans and then by the French.
[19] '[...] the 1875 constitution of France had a clear similarity with other constitutions of this era in that it was intended to institute a technical order of governance above the primary conflicts of society.' Thornhill 2011, p. 271–272. Cf. (Eugen) Weber 1976.

The Spanish 'imperial' constitution of 1876 also strove for internal pacification and stability in order to give external strength in a changing world. After a series of constitutional experiments (even including a short republican period from 1873 to 1874), the Spanish document of 1876 was primarily pragmatic. It accorded parliament (the *Cortes*) some influence, but for the most part instituted strong government, eschewing grandiose language and principles which had given rise to past conflicts. An imperial constitution in nature, although it would be reasonable to wonder what was so 'imperial' about the constitution of a country that was a shadow of the powerful colonial empire that until some 50 years previously had held sway over much of the Americas.[20] The Spanish constitution of 1876 had little influence in the New World. Despite the flame of liberty having been extinguished in many parts of Latin America,[21] the region's constitutional development was still largely inspired by the liberal constitution of Cádiz from the turn of the century.[22]

The imperial constitutions of the last quarter of the nineteenth century were essentially a mishmash of governmental instruments. Devoid of big ideas and focused on short-term power and stability, they proved incapable of sustainably organising inclusive and stable political societies. Imperial constitutions left unresolved many social issues – groups' claims and emancipation, expansion of franchise, individuals' position and equal rights, etcetera. They led to major conflicts at the beginning of the twentieth century which fatally undermined most of these empires. However eclectic these imperial constitutions were, there is a striking pattern. Why did so many countries adopt each other's constitutional architecture around 1870?[23] This is all the more surprising because these constitutions' governmental underpinnings contained scarcely any compelling ideologies or ideas. What was so attractive about them? Their results? Or did it involve less conscious processes, more the result of the global market's vagaries and competitive forces propelling countries and empires in a certain direction, like some kind of politico-economic law of nature? Why do they so emphatically follow each other's example? This question is also relevant to the constitutional currents and trends in the twentieth and twenty-first centuries.

---

[20] Cuba and Puerto Rico were the only remnants of the Spanish empire in the Americas after 1865. Spain also retained the Philippines and Guam in Asia, several small islands in the South Pacific, and Spanish West Africa, Spanish Guinea, Ceuta and Melilla in Africa.

[21] Mirow 2015. Cf. Smith 2016.

[22] Mirow 2015.

[23] The constitutions of Canada (Constitution Act 1867) and Australia (Commonwealth of Australia Constitution Act 1901) can also be included in this period. Like the Constitution Act of New Zealand, they were forms of mixed government in which London retained significant influence over government. As in New Zealand, they too contained few individual freedoms. They were imperial constitutions that chiefly established a system of government. This does not mean that New Zealand, Canada or Australia lacked any individual fundamental freedoms – they simply were not derived from their own constitutional documents. Tonga (1875) and Luxembourg (1868) also promulgated constitutions that established a monarchical system of government with a strong executive.

14

Sixth Generation

Leviathan Constitutions

Historians will contend that how the First World War (1914–1918) started is not really the big question – it is why the conflict got out of hand so quickly.[1] Some argue it was inevitable;[2] others regard it as the result of an accident that spiralled out of control. Either way, it is clear that superpower rivalry had turned international politics into a powder keg, needing no more than an angry young man like Gavrilo Princip to spark an inferno.[3] In four years, the First World War lay waste to the world. Global trade was more than a quarter lower in 1918 than in 1914. Vanquished countries' gross national product tumbled by a third. States were 'the graves of nations' after the catastrophe.[4] The significance for the end of the conflagration is as contentious

---

[1] Tuchman 1976, p. 88 ff. (Section entitled *Outbreak*). For someone who argues that the First World War was inevitable: Cf. Ferguson 2007, in particular part II (*Empire-States*).

[2] Ferguson 2007.

[3] The Serbian nationalist Gavrilo Princip's assassination of Archduke Franz Ferdinand of Austria on 28 June 1914 in Sarajevo was the proximate cause of the First World War because the great powers immediately activated a series of interlocking alliances, turning a local, Balkan affair into a European, or a global one for that matter. Those who do not believe in coincidence argue that this vindicates their case: how else could it be? Naysayers argue it is a textbook example: the attack succeeded thanks to a series of coincidences. History might have been dramatically altered if events had unfolded slightly differently. Just take the initial failure of the attack. One of Princip's accomplices hurled a hand grenade at the Archduke's car but missed his target and only injured three officers. In a situation as tense as in Sarajevo in 1914, harbouring a profusion of fanatical Serbian nationalists, it would have been expedient for the heir presumptive to abort his visit at this point. But Franz Ferdinand did not. He initially wanted to complete his tour of the city but had second thoughts and decided to visit the hospital first. His driver took a wrong turn and brought the Archduke directly past a delicatessen Princip had just left (having decided to go home). The twenty-year-old – an inexperienced marksman, rejected for military service – sprang into action, firing three shots at point-blank range. The royal couple were fatally wounded; the Archduke having been hit in the jugular vein and his wife having sustained abdominal injuries. What if the driver had not made a wrong turn, or Princip had not bought a sandwich at that delicatessen and so on? Perhaps it would have happened a week later in equally inane circumstances, or perhaps not. We shall never know.

[4] Alfred Döblin, cited by Ferguson 2006, p. 217.

as its beginning. Technically, hostilities ceased on 11 November 1918, at 11 a.m., Paris time, as agreed in the armistice signed by the Germans and the Allies in a railway carriage near the French town of Compiègne. But some argue this was merely an interlude of some twenty years, before hostilities resumed in 1939.[5] In any case, the end of the First World War meant the demise of several global empires, including Austria-Hungary, tsarist Russia, and the Ottoman and German empires. It also partially ended the worldwide struggle to participate in or control parts of world trade. Globalisation almost came to a standstill in 1918.[6] Europe was left largely in ruins and the rest of the world was paralysed; states were compelled to reinvent, overhaul, develop and consolidate themselves at breakneck speed in this vacuum. They needed all the manpower, capital, natural and other resources within (range of) their borders.

The nature of states changed rapidly in this period. Not only did new states emerge from the debris of the old empires,[7] it was the nature of state-based cooperation above all that changed. After the First World War, states and governments intervened ever more in the lives of their citizens, penetrating society's deepest nooks and crannies. Whereas the state had mainly provided a stage for social and economic cooperation in the nineteenth century, it increasingly became a fellow player – an active participant – on this stage from the beginning of the twentieth century. The relationship between government and citizens was completely transformed in many Western countries. The world entered an age of state-led mass cooperation; it moved from cooperation between groups and nations in growing empires to the new 'we' of mass cooperation within states. For a variety of reasons, governments tried to mobilise the masses – a 'levée en masse'.

In post-war Europe and elsewhere, the state became an important player in economic processes in many places; as an investor, (economic) regulator, co-partner, mediator in labour disputes, or state monopolist.[8] It sometimes took control of entire markets. This new activism required greater sums of capital than ever before. Funds were raised by taxing citizens and companies, borrowing or 'creating' money using new monetary policy. States had increasingly intimate relations with their citizens: they reared and educated them, deployed them and involved them more closely in policy. Citizens became an integral part of these states. Nationalism was fostered to

---

[5] Ferguson argues that the world's great powers were engaged in a continuous global conflict for about a hundred years (approximately the entire twentieth century), ultimately leading to the (ongoing) fall of the West as the dominant world power. Ferguson 2006, p. 71. It is a rather bleak and apocalyptic, but highly readable account which appeals to our shared intuitive fear of the end of the world. Meadwell contends that the events of the first half of the twentieth century are not much more than the tail end of the 'long nineteenth century' in Europe, which he asserts started in 1789 and ended in 1945 from a political-historical perspective. Meadwell 2001, p. 189.

[6] Cf. Ortiz-Ospina & Roser 2018.

[7] Finland, Estonia, Latvia, Lithuania, Poland, Czechoslovakia, Yugoslavia, etcetera.

[8] 'The state, thus, became an effective party in industrial conflict', according to Thornhill 2011, p. 276.

increase cohesion, solidarity and, above all, the mobilisation potential. As citizens, individuals became part of the state machinery.[9] New electoral systems – universal suffrage emerged as the cornerstone of representative democracy in many Western states – and new emancipatory arrangements (such as according equal rights to socio-political groups like workers, ethnic or religious groups)[10] enabled states to exploit new possibilities, means and sources of power on an unprecedented scale. This altered the boundaries between the public and private domain. As at the end of the previous century, constitutions were used as a vehicle for the new, even larger 'we'. They had little choice, according to Thornhill:[11]

> [...] states were forced to develop constitutional mechanisms to exercise their power at an exponentially heightened level of societal inclusivity and generalisation.

You might say with the benefit of hindsight that this was a doomed experiment. As a rule, a system that reduces people to mere pawns in a feverish contest between states inevitably leads to catastrophe. The interwar period was certainly still a world which largely revolved around states and superpowers – it was primarily focused on masses and socio-political realignment, and not on individuals. It was also the era of labour movements, mass movements and mass-based political parties.[12] More than previously, individuals derived their identity from the group, nation and state they lived in, which also entailed that they were partially at the state's service. But, this is not very different to how contemporary states function. The modern interventionist welfare state was essentially invented directly after the First World War. Despite an ideologically driven eschewal of the term 'welfare state' in some quarters, this is exactly what most contemporary states still are. The big difference between the interwar period and the present is the organisation of the international domain. International institutions and public law were at the time rudimentary and – crucially – consensual: a system of well-disposed cooperating states and peoples, skewed by Western and Allied overrepresentation. It was with good reason that the new international organisation charged with maintaining world peace after the First World War was called the League of Nations. The League was created as a referee to maintain the order established by the Paris Peace Conference in 1919, based on the American President Woodrow Wilson's Fourteen Points. A mediator and no more than that. The League's guiding principle was nations' right to self-determination; the arbiter was given no means to act. The honourable intentions of 1919[13] had tragic and

---

9   This is magnificently portrayed in Charlie Chaplin's film *Modern Times* (1936) in which an assembly-line worker frantically tries to keep up with and gets stuck in a giant factory machine.
10 Religious groups and workers, for instance, in the Netherlands after 1917. Cf. Andeweg & Irwin 2014, p. 24–25.
11 Thornhill 2011, p. 275.
12 Duverger 1954.
13 The Dutch historian Geert Mak gives an interesting account of the peace negotiations in Versailles in 1919 in his book *In Europe*. Given from the perspective of the British delegate

unintended consequences and were unable to curb the downward spiral of rampant nationalism, the rise of totalitarian states, instability, conflict and ultimately another global war. An immutable law of history is that the future always surpasses our imagination.

1918–1939: THE DEMOCRATIC-CORPORATIST CONSTITUTIONS OF THE INTERWAR PERIOD

Old constitutional foundations were cast aside for new ones. Only a single European state, Italy, retained its old constitution during this period (the *Statuto Albertino* of 1848), but only in a formal sense.[14] Mussolini's seizure of power in 1922 gave Italy a fascist regime. The liberal *Statuto Albertino* was substituted for *corporatism*. This is a system of group or sectoral governance in which representatives of unified economic, industrial, agricultural and professional groups – corporations – are assigned an important co-legislative role in governing economic and social life. It was a kind of middle way between a liberal-capitalist and a socialist-communist system of government and market organisation. This development profoundly altered the contents of the Italian constitution. But unlike Italy, many other countries did in effect promulgate new constitutions. And whether communist, liberal or corporatist (or with elements thereof), almost all these new constitutions – with the possible exception of the Austrian Constitution of 1920[15] – radically changed relations between governments and citizens.

The Russian Constitution of 1918 was the most radical one, overhauling all property and production relations (by expropriating them) and giving the working class – at least, nominally – power in the Supreme Soviet (people's assembly) and the Polit Bureau (the highest organ of the Communist Party). It is the first instance of a Communist constitution. The Mexican Constitution of 1917[16] drew inspiration from the Russian Revolution and the new political system, without Mexico becoming a fully-fledged communist state.[17] The new German republic's Weimar Constitution not only had

Nicolson, it is a vibrant illustration of the negotiators' enthusiasm, but also their naivety and amateur approach. Mak also devotes attention to Marcel Proust, ever the probing enquirer of the human mind and motives, who wanted to know very precisely from Nicolson what the atmosphere and relations were like. Proust was probably one of the few contemporaries who suspected how serious the psychological devastation must have been. Mak 2007, p. 126–129.

[14] The Statuto Albertino was only abrogated in 1948.

[15] Austria promulgated a constitution with strong constitutional guarantees and a constitutional court based on the American system in 1920. It was heavily influenced by one of its most important drafters, the legal philosopher Hans Kelsen, who believed in constitutional depersonalisation of the state. Like citizens and society as a whole, the state should be bound by the law, but should adopt a 'neutral' attitude towards citizens and their society, and not interfere excessively in social and economic processes.

[16] All mineral resources (in particular, oil reserves) were declared state property.

[17] The Mexican Constitution of 1917 was very influential on other Latin American countries' constitutional development in the twentieth century, as the Cádiz constitution had been in the nineteenth century. Cf. Mirow 2015, p. 237.

more liberal roots and established a democratic constitutional system of government, but also contained the corporatist or syndicalist elements ('group rights') so characteristic of the period. For instance, the Weimar Constitution of 1919 instituted the *Zentralarbeitsgemeinschaft*, a public institution that functioned as a central platform for tripartite labour consultations between government, employers (employers' associations) and employees (trade unions). Similar organisations still exist in some European countries, such as Italy. Constitutions like the Weimar Constitution and the Mexican Constitution attempted to reconcile capitalist-liberalism and socialist-communism by instituting regulated capitalism in a parliamentary democracy.[18] This third-way approach gained popularity and was widely copied – for instance, many countries in Latin America followed the Mexican example. The Brazilian Constitution of 1934 has an extensive chapter on the organisation of socio-economic life.

Another feature of post-First World War constitutions is their emphasis on inclusive representative democracy – usually parliamentary democracy – based on periodic universal suffrage. The new constitutions were in most cases 'democratic'. Their conception of democracy is rather different to our current understanding. The overarching idea of these first democratic constitutions does not seem to have been that citizens – out of respect for their individual autonomy – should decide government policy through their votes. The thinking at the time was rather more that citizens should be involved in government policy 'as a group' through their collective votes, doing justice to their group rights, interests and identity. This 'democracy' enabled the state to function like the mythical giant Leviathan – the monster king consisting of countless tiny people like the illustration on the cover of Thomas Hobbes' eponymous book of 1651.

Many new states and constitutions emerged from the debris of the empires of Central and Eastern Europe after the Paris Peace Conference of 1919: Estonia (1917), Latvia (1922) and Lithuania (1922), Poland (1921), Finland (1919), Romania (1923), the Kingdom of Serbs, Croats and Slovenes (1920, the Kingdom of Yugoslavia from 1929),[19] Czechoslovakia (1920),[20] Georgia (1921)[21] and Ukraine (1918).[22] They all had modern constitutions, based on democratic governance.[23] It is noteworthy how these new states all opted for a constitution to institute the new structure for leadership, legal and – usually also – socio-economic organisation. Henceforth, state formation and constitutions would appear to go hand in glove.

---

[18] Grimm considers this kind of constitution of the 'Social or Welfare State Constitution' type. Grimm 2012, p. 124.

[19] The Vidovdan Constitution of 28 June 1920 – repealed in 1931.

[20] This leap year constitution of 29 February 1920 replaced the provisional constitution of 1918.

[21] This constitution had a very short lifespan – just four days. Probably a world record. Independent Georgia's constitution was established on 21 February 1921. Soviet troops overran Georgia on 25 February and the Soviet Union immediately annexed the country.

[22] This constitution had a brief lifespan too. Ukraine was annexed by Russia in 1919 – Western Ukraine became part of Poland from 1921 to 1939.

[23] Papuashvili 2017.

Like Italy, Spain and Portugal followed a corporatist course in the interwar period. Portugal, in contrast to Italy and Spain, formalised this in its constitution (1933), which Salazar's dictatorial regime used to control Portugal from then on. Spain, like Italy, maintained its essentially liberal-democratic constitution (of the Second Republic) that was adopted in 1931. This constitutional arrangement was similar to the Weimar Constitution. In another parallel with Italy, it was little more than a fig leaf for a fascist regime after the Spanish Civil War (1936–1939), giving all power to the dictator Franco. A situation that continued until his death in 1975.

1917–1945: SOCIALIST INFLUENCES

Mexico set the seal on its revolution (1917),[24] and Lebanon (1926) and Ireland (1937) marked their independence with a constitution. Apart from attempting to free the state from the church, the Mexican Constitution's socialist characteristics are particularly noteworthy. It contains a right to free, non-religious education, rights for workers, restrictions on large-scale landownership, restrictions on foreign landownership. Designed as a democratic constitution, it includes popular representation and universal suffrage. The edifice was impressive, but the furniture never arrived – Mexico immediately became a one-party state. The Institutional Revolutionary Party monopolised the system from the outset, and Mexico would endure many decades of semi-authoritarian government.[25]

Lebanon has certainly not been a one-party state since 1926, but its electoral system cannot directly be characterised as proportional representation. The 1926 Constitution[26] uses a complicated system of proportional representation of confessional groups (Christians and Muslims) in an attempt to achieve a balanced reflection of groups in the representative bodies. That was by no means a modest feat in Lebanon, as subsequent history has shown.

The Irish Constitution of 1937 is, in a sense, also a child of its time. Despite containing far fewer socialist elements than the Mexican or Weimar constitutions, it also regulates rights to natural resources and property,[27] and demands the loyalty of all Irish citizens to the state.[28] It is, in any case, also a democratic constitution: 'Ireland is a sovereign, independent, democratic state.'[29] Like many other countries

---

[24] Originally *Constitución Política de los Estados Unidos Mexicanos* (Political Constitution of the United States of Mexico) of 5 February 1917, nowadays commemorated as a national holiday, *Día de la Constitución* (Constitution Day).

[25] The *Partido Revolucionario Institucional*, PRI.

[26] Modelled on the French Third Republic's constitution (1870).

[27] The Irish Constitution, articles 10 and 11.

[28] *Ibid.*, article 9, third paragraph, stipulates: 'Fidelity to the nation and loyalty to the State are fundamental political duties of all citizens.'

[29] *Ibid.*, article 5.

in the period, it became a republic in 1937. The most common form of government before the First World War had been monarchy, which was rapidly exchanged for other forms of popular government in this period. 'Government by the people' became the premise. Fifteen monarchies were disbanded between 1900 and 1917, and thirty-two monarchies ended in the period 1917–1918. Another twelve monarchies were overthrown between 1919 and 1939.[30]

---

[30] Information from the Wikipedia page 'The Abolition of Monarchy'. https://en.wikipedia.org/
wiki/Abolition_of_monarchy (Consulted 4 June 2018).

15

The Seventh Generation

Liberation Constitutions

Eleven months before the fateful Japanese attack on Pearl Harbor, the American president Roosevelt addressed Congress. On 6 January 1941, a few weeks before his third inauguration as president, he made a visionary promise to the world:

In the future days, which we seek to make secure, we look forward to a world founded upon four essential human freedoms.

The first is freedom of speech and expression — everywhere in the world.
The second is freedom of every person to worship God in his own way — everywhere in the world.
The third is freedom from want — which, translated into world terms, means economic understandings which will secure to every nation a healthy peacetime life for its inhabitants — everywhere in the world.
The fourth is freedom from fear — which, translated into world terms, means a world-wide reduction of armaments to such a point and in such a thorough fashion that no nation will be in a position to commit an act of physical aggression against any neighbour — anywhere in the world.

That is no vision of a distant millennium. It is a definite basis for a kind of world attainable in our own time and generation. That kind of world is the very antithesis of the so-called new order of tyranny which the dictators seek to create with the crash of a bomb.

To that new order we oppose the greater conception — the moral order. A good society is able to face schemes of world domination and foreign revolutions alike without fear.

This extraordinary speech laid the foundations of new moral order, built on four core freedoms for every human being, which, after an exceptionally hard-fought struggle, would be taken up around the world within a decade. The speech is also noteworthy for what it did not say; the freedoms were not attributed to divine authority and lacked any reference to a state of nature or prehistoric contract. There was no mention of traditions, teachings or ideas derived from the course of history. There was nothing about states, nations or groups. The only subjects were the entire world and 'every person'. The new 'we' of this (Four) freedom order included everyone everywhere in the world; it was ahistorical and 'universal'. These were a new kind of freedom, not part of the standard repertoire of classic political freedoms and civil rights (such as the freedom of association and assembly, the prohibition of arbitrary arrest, equality before the law, and the like) that developed from the Enlightenment in the West over the previous 250 years. Although two of Roosevelt's freedoms (the freedom of expression and the freedom of religion) do bear some similarity to their antecedents, they are fundamentally different because of their unconditionality. They apply at all times and places. Regardless of government, nationality, and religion. The freedoms take human equality as being almost self-evident: they assume that every person is reasonable and may hold an opinion or conviction. The final two freedoms place the world citizen in his physical environment: the freedom from want and the freedom from fear. Governments must work to ensure citizens have a healthy and peaceful life, free of fear. A final noteworthy feature is that the freedoms referred to in the speech did not exist heretofore, they did not come from anywhere – from some or other 'truth' that had descended from upon high. Roosevelt said that developing them was the task entrusted to his generation. A universal, humanist appeal for a new moral order that would keep (or take) us out of the sway of tyranny. Roosevelt did not live to see his new moral order, dying on 12 April 1945.[1] His wife Eleanor played an important role in establishing the Universal Declaration of Human Rights. This was the United Nations' humanist human rights manifesto which was adopted by the General Assembly on 10 December 1948. It was and still is upheld by the entire world, and has been the undisputed basis, at least in theory, of Roosevelt's world order for more than 70 years. Its core value is expressed in the Declaration:

> All human beings are born free and equal in dignity and rights. They are endowed with reason and conscience and should act towards one another in a spirit of brotherhood.[2]

Many today are gloomy about the state of the world order. The Second World War, the war to end all wars, has been followed by many others. Misery, hunger, oppression, suffering and sorrow are still manifest in every corner of the world – not to mention injustice. Yet there also is another, more positive story. The new world order's humanist principles are seldom disputed, and there have been no conflicts on a global scale since 1945. Humankind has certainly made progress over the past 70 years, although it ought not simply be attributed to fundamental freedoms or a new world order under the aegis of the United Nations. The liberal humanism expressed in the Universal Declaration of Human Rights appears to have triumphed as an idea and

---

[1]   At the start of his fourth term as President of the United States.
[2]   Article 1.

conception of humankind.[3] It vanquished other ideologies, such as (equally anthro-pocentric)[4] communism, fascism,[5] (liberal) nationalism and theocentric ideologies.[6] The past is, of course, a poor guide to the future. This is certainly true of something as inherently fragile as a world order built on 'soft' values, voluntarily endorsed by disparate countries and states in the context of major differences in perspective and political direction. Still, it is the light, ideologically-neutral configuration of the UN and the Declaration – the 'soft' side – which seems to be key to success thus far. When one of the framers of the Universal Declaration of Human Rights was asked which fundamental principles and ideas the Declaration was based on, he responded diplomatically and wittily: 'no philosophy whatsoever'.[7] This ideological neutrality certainly contributed to the wide endorsement of the Declaration in 1948,[8] even if it bears many recognisable traces of the intellectual history it hails from.[9]

1945–1950: ALLIED GIFTS OF FREEDOM

General Douglas McArthur, to whom Japan surrendered in 1945, was a man who liked to get things done. When Japanese constitutional reform ran aground,[10] he had his own staff draft a constitutional convention to underpin democracy and freedom. It took them a mere six days, using a 1939 book on constitutions in the world, and translation took another four days. It was immediately presented to dumbfounded Japanese officials. Despite its unpalatability to the Japanese 'imperial' government – it was based on popular sovereignty – it was duly approved by a newly elected parliament.[11] The new constitution entered into force on 3 May 1947. The Peace Constitution, as it is also known, exudes the spirit of Roosevelt's freedoms, even explicitly mentioning them.[12] It also expresses a – now

---

[3] Steven Pinker is convinced of Enlightenment's victory. His substantial argumentation for the triumph of humanism, human reason and science comprises fourteen chapters and nearly 300 pages (of the book's 556 pages). It is a worthwhile and uplifting read. Cf. Pinker 2018. Cf. chapter 23 in which humanism is re-examined.

[4] Ideologies that place humans at the centre of their world view and aspirations.

[5] Harari calls them variants of humanism: social humanism (communism) and evolutionary humanism (fascism), in addition to the aforementioned liberal humanism. Harari 2016, p. 246–257.

[6] In which a divinity is the source and inspiration of (the governance of) a society or group.

[7] John Humphrey, as cited by Pinker 2018, p. 419.

[8] Of the 58 countries in the UN General Assembly which adopted the Declaration (resolution 217) at the Palais de Chaillot in Paris on 10 December 1948, 48 voted in favour and none against. Only the Soviet bloc (Russia and its Eastern European satellite states), communist Yugoslavia, Saudi Arabia and South Africa (which had just instituted apartheid) abstained and two members did not vote at all.

[9] Simmons 2011, p. 5–6.

[10] A Japanese commission worked for four months from the end of 1946 to early 1947 on rewriting the old imperial Meiji constitution (1889), but McArthur rejected the timid proposals.

[11] www.crf-usa.org/election-central/bringing-democracy-to-japan.html (Consulted 25 May 2018).

[12] The preamble literally refers to them: 'We recognise that all peoples of the world have the right to live in peace, free from fear and want.'

customary – confidence in the ability of a written legal document like a constitution to function as a durable guide to a country's future political and social development. Although the emperor is retained as the formal and ceremonial head of state, highest power and exclusive legislative power is conferred on the directly-elected Diet (parliament).[13] The constitution enshrines a modern democratic parliamentary system with a separation of powers and the exercise of all governmental power is bound by law (rule of law). Fundamental human rights – to be ensured by the Japanese government and state – are at the heart of it. This kind of constitution would become widespread in the years after the Second World War. The Japanese constitution contains another extraordinary feature, which it eloquently expresses:

> The fundamental human rights by this Constitution guaranteed to the people of Japan are fruits of the age-old struggle of man to be free; they have survived the many exacting tests for durability and are conferred upon this and future generations in trust, to be held for all time inviolate.[14]

Constitutional revision is permitted,[15] but not of the fundamental freedoms laid down, for example, in Chapter III of the constitution. This does not mean that these rights cannot be altered in any way, but that the essence of these freedoms is inviolable.

The constitution of West Germany, which entered into force at midnight on 23 May 1949,[16] contained a similar constitutional 'lock'. An eternity clause[17] ensures that certain parts of the German Constitution (*Grundgesetz*, Basic Law) can never be removed, including the fundamental freedoms.[18] Like its Japanese counterpart, the German constitution defines the universal nature of fundamental freedoms or human rights (this term refers to the fact that everyone is endowed with them):

> The German people therefore acknowledge inviolable and inalienable human rights as the basis of every community, of peace and of justice in the world.

The German Constitution made the German Federal Republic an independent democracy and a constitutional state with a separation of powers and in which everyone is bound by the law. This document, which paved the way to German post-war

---

[13] Article 41.

[14] Article 97.

[15] Article 96.

[16] The constitution was drafted by Germans to a far greater degree than was the case in Japan. General Lucius D. Clay assembled a group of German experts at the Herrenchiemsee castle in Bavaria in August 1948 (*Verfassungskonvent auf Herrenchiemsee*). Reportedly powered by copious quantities of broth, they developed Germany's constitutional order after the Second World War. As in Japan, they completed their task at breakneck speed – in less than two weeks.

[17] Article 79.

[18] Cf. articles 1 to 20 of the German Constitution.

self-rule, also has a few additional conditions. The German Constitution provides that human rights are universal in nature, and thus also apply to the German constitutional order. But, the Constitution stipulates, if these rights are violated, as happened in the 1930s, then Germans are no longer obliged to follow the laws or orders emanating from government or state, and are entitled to resist if there are no other options available within the system.[19] It is, in a manner of speaking, a universal emergency brake on the system.

These post-war constitutions may originally have been imposed by the Allies,[20] but the passage of time has made them very much part of Germany and Japan, and they have both stood the test of time as constitutional systems.

Many constitutions promulgated in the aftermath of the Second World War have a strong emphasis on universal human rights. They figure in them as expressions of the human dignity that every person is endowed with and entitled to, everywhere in the world, regardless of their background; they are inalienable and take precedence over the authority of national states. The Taiwanese (1947), South Korean (1948) and Indian (1949)[21] constitutions are prominent examples of this kind of universalist rights-based constitution. The novelty of these constitutions is that, in addition to classic individual rights with restraints on government – creating government-free spheres – they contain an increasing number of adhortative freedom rights; basic rights in the form of claims, creating governmental obligations (education, safety, health care, and so on). The Italian constitution of 1948[22] has an impressive list of freedoms in response to the aberrations of Italy's recent fascist past – particularly notable are its 'social' freedoms. These fundamental social rights entitle Italian citizens to government action to secure basic living conditions. What use is an abstract freedom of speech if you cannot read or write; or a right to assembly and demonstration if you are forced to work a seven-day week or simply cannot afford to travel to a demonstration? The Italian Constitution of 1948 includes rights to health care, social security, education, fair pay, collective bargaining, a (limited) right to strike, form trade unions, workers' participation, and so forth. The socialists and communists who were in power at the time left an indelible mark on the text. Yet unlike many countries in Central and Eastern Europe, Italy did not promulgate a communist constitution in 1948, instead developing a predominantly liberal-democratic constitutional system, which was primarily overseen by the constitutional court (*Corte costituzionale della Repubblica Italiana*) in the first years after the Second World War.[23]

---

[19] Article 20.
[20] Elkins, Ginsburg and Melton regard the Japanese and German constitutions as imposed constitutions. Elkins, Ginsburg & Melton 2009, p. 199.
[21] It is also an example of a 'decolonisation' constitution.
[22] Promulgated by the constitutional assembly on 22 December 1947.
[23] Thornhill 2011, p. 322–333.

1950–1960: COMMUNIST CONSTITUTIONS

Many countries behind the Iron Curtain after the Second World War promulgated communist constitutions[24] – including Albania,[25] Bulgaria,[26] Hungary,[27] Yugoslavia,[28] the German Democratic Republic (East Germany),[29] Poland,[30] Czechoslovakia,[31] and Romania[32] – usually variations on the 1936 Stalinist Soviet constitution. A hallmark of this kind of constitution is that the state is granted complete control over the market and economy (and therefore of society) and is dominated by a single party: the communist party. Furthermore, communist constitutions have no separation or division of governmental power; popular power is unified, expressed by a single party and an indivisible government that expresses the popular will and serves and protects the people. Communist constitutions revolve around the link between ideology, society, politics and economy.[33] They are not an end in themselves but a means of establishing the dictatorship of the proletariat. In this type of political regime, the separation of powers is usually scornfully dismissed as an outmoded form of 'bourgeois constitutionalism'.[34] An independent judiciary and free judicial review do not play a significant role in this system. Like other parts of government, the judiciary is at the service of the popular will, mediated and expressed by the communist party. Communist constitutions contain extensive catalogues of citizens' rights and freedoms, but these are usually not rights to freedom from state interference,[35] but social rights creating state obligations. Government is not the greatest danger to individual freedom in the communist dispensation, but rather market participants, producers and other economic actors. They are the ones that must be controlled, regulated and put in their place by government. For example, the Hungarian Constitution of 1949 instructs courts to 'punish the enemies of the working people'.[36] These constitutions are about the needs of the working class as a 'whole', which always precede the needs of individuals, whether workers or not. Communist constitutions are means to a greater end. They are only intended for a transitional period, as the first Chinese Constitution of 1954, inspired by the Russian Constitution, expresses:

---

[24] Or 'socialist' constitution. Grimm 2012, p. 128 ff.
[25] 1946, replaced in 1976.
[26] The Stalinist 'Dimitrov' constitution of 1947.
[27] 1949 and 1972.
[28] 1946, replaced in 1953, and again in 1963 – supplemented by the substantial amendments in 1967, 1968 and 1971.
[29] 1949, replaced in 1968.
[30] The 'Small Constitution' of 1947, replaced in 1952 – completely revised in 1976.
[31] 1948, replaced in the 1960s.
[32] 1948, replaced in 1952 and again in 1965. This high turnover rate is typical of communist constitutions. Cf. Brunner 1997.
[33] Simons 1980, p. XIV–XV.
[34] Thornhill 2011, p. 327; Brunner 1977.
[35] Brunner 1977, p. 137–140.
[36] Article 41.

The basic needs of the state in the transition period and the common aspiration of the masses of the people to build a socialist society.[37]

They were not much more than a step on the way to a communist utopia which would not require a constitution thanks to completely fair relations of production and the dictatorship of the proletariat. In this light, a constitution can be seen as merely a component of a programme of comprehensive national change, re-education and reorganisation. Constitutions of this kind[38] and the model of state order and utopianism they expressed held great appeal far into the 1970s.[39] This model came to be regarded as a failed experiment when its underpinning ideology collapsed in 1990. Even China, one of the few remaining countries with a nominally communist constitution (it is still a one-party state), has drastically changed its original design since 1982.

1960–1970: POST-COLONIAL CONSTITUTIONS

The Charter of the United Nations contains a right to self-determination for peoples.[40] This was not a new principle in 1948. It had been regarded – especially by the United States – as a guiding principle in the world order ever since the First World War, but only gained momentum after the Second World War due to a combination of factors.[41] After colonies in the Americas gained independence in the eighteenth and nineteenth centuries, a wave of decolonisation swept Africa and Asia from 1945. The harbingers were the Japanese-occupied 'orphaned colonies' of German-occupied European powers in Southeast Asia. Sukarno and Hatta proclaimed the independent Republic of Indonesia in the former Dutch East Indies in August 1945. A month later Hô Chí Minh proclaimed the Democratic Republic of Vietnam in French Indochina. Dutch and French military intervention in their respective colonies only delayed full independence – Indonesia gained international recognition in 1949 and Vietnam in 1954.[42] The biggest of them all, of course, was India, which gained independence on 15 August 1947, the day that the United Kingdom transferred legislative sovereignty to the Indian Constituent Assembly – eighteen years after India had proclaimed itself

---

[37] From the preamble. Cf. www.un.org/en/charter-united-nations/. Consulted 1 September 2018.

[38] As well as China and the aforementioned countries, Cuba (1959, subsequently 1976), Laos (1991), North Korea (1948) and Vietnam (1946, 1959, which also applied to South Vietnam after its incorporation in 1975, 1980, 1992 and 2014) have communist constitutions. There have been communist constitutions in many other places such as Afghanistan, Angola, Cambodia, Congo, Ethiopia, Mongolia, Somalia and so forth.

[39] Niall Ferguson points out that we often risk forgetting how successful communism was in the 1950s and 1960s. In 1950, it even seemed likely that communism would spread to most of the world's population. Ferguson 2016, especially p. 249–264.

[40] Article 1, second paragraph: 'To develop friendly relations among nations based on respect for the principle of equal rights and self-determination of peoples, and to take other appropriate measures to strengthen universal peace'.

[41] Cf. Thürer & Burri 2008.

[42] Vietnam only regained its territorial integrity in 1975, after the defeat of American-backed South Vietnam.

independent.[43] From this time in the late forties, old colonisers around the world were sent packing. There had only been 56 independent states in 1910; that number had risen to 142 by 1970. Decolonisation added another 36 new states by 2000. Nearly all of them promulgated a constitution, almost as a matter-of-course. In 1973, the Czech political scientist Ivo Duchacek observed that:

> Over two-thirds of the [world's] existing national constitutions were drafted and promulgated in the last three decades.[44]

Hence, the vast majority of existing constitutions are both relatively recent and the result of the formation of new states, most of which are products of decolonisation. The post-independence constitutional process was often fitful. In most cases, the new countries adopted large parts of the former coloniser's constitution and constitutional system. This was regarded sometimes as an expression of conservatism, and sometimes as an inheritance or dowry. Sir William Dale wrote in 1993 that the British Empire had 'left some 50 specific legacies: every Commonwealth State, a written constitution, or the means of receiving one'.[45] These constitutions were sometimes drafted in consultation with commonwealth countries, or sometimes by London alone, as a 'parting gift'. In Dale's estimation: 'Whitehall lawyers must have drafted at least 33 complete and final independence constitutions during the period, to say nothing of a deluge of intermediate instruments'.[46]

　　Most of these post-colonial constitutions were liberal-democratic ones inspired by the system of the former colonising power. This kind of 'intra-imperial isomorphism',[47] as it is known in the jargon, was not always very successful. Hessebon argues that what he calls 'hand-me-down constitutions' did not work well in Africa because they were not sufficiently adapted to the new social and political dynamics and contexts.[48] Most of the new constitutional democracies were consequently discarded by military coups and dictatorships.[49] In a second wave from the late 1960s to the early 1980s, many African constitutions were increasingly adapted to the realities of (one-party) authoritarian systems. This development subsequently gave rise to the third wave of African constitutional promulgation between 1985 and 2000, which replaced these authoritarian constitutions with multi-party democracy and institutions that foster greater political stability by instituting strong, centralised government (a powerful executive) and firmly secured fundamental freedoms. Much of sub-Saharan Africa is now in its fourth wave of constitutional promulgation,

---

[43] At the 1929 Lahore session of the Indian National Congress, the *Purna Swaraj* declaration, or 'Declaration of the Independence of India' was promulgated, in which India proclaimed its independence from the United Kingdom.

[44] Duchacek, as cited by Go 2002, p. 558; cited by Beer 1979, p. 8.

[45] Dale 1993, especially p. 67.

[46] *Ibid.*

[47] Cf. Go 2002, p. 559.

[48] Hessebon 2014, p. 186.

[49] Mbaku 2013, especially p. 160.

in which many countries are trying to curb their powerful executives and reduce abuse of governmental power and corruption by decentralising and putting greater emphasis on the role of minorities and ethnicity in order to protect fundamental freedoms and human rights.[50] This constitutional learning curve would seem to be a good development: constitutions are evolving from poor-fitting fast fashion into well-tailored costumes. On the other hand, it is also an interminable business that undermines the stability that a constitution can give to a political system as well as the values it represents. A constitution is little use as a jukebox.[51]

Newly independent countries in Southeast and South Asia have followed a similar route. Although the constitutional examples of the United States (particularly in the Philippines) and France (in Indochina – present-day Vietnam, Laos and Cambodia) were important in some new independent, post-colonial states,[52] the British 'Westminster Export Model' held sway in this region too.[53] A parliamentary governmental system in which the powerful executive is formally subordinate to the legislature (parliament), which also controls (budgetary) legislation and the broad outlines of policy. The whole system is overseen by a judge charged with ensuring that both government and citizens abide by the law. Few of these new constitutions were durable, often for the same reasons as in Africa.[54] Most of these post-colonial constitutions took far too little account of the multi-ethnic character of post-colonial societies. The interests of ethnic and cultural minorities were soon compromised in dispensations where simple majorities decided policy and law.[55] This sometimes resulted in tribalism. The search for constitutional legitimacy has been and continues to be a constant problem in many Southeast Asian countries.[56]

1974–1978: POST-DICTATORIAL CONSTITUTIONS

In May 2017, Portugal won the Eurovision Song Contest with Salvador Sobral's beautiful song *Amar Pelos Dois*.[57] It was a major event because Portugal had never

---

[50] Hessebon 2014, p. 190–195.

[51] Fombad 2014.

[52] Indonesia is one of the few countries to tread its own path straight after decolonisation. The federal constitution of 1949/1950 introduced a presidential system with some parliamentary characteristics. It established a strong central executive with a limited separation of powers. But Indonesia also became a dictatorship within ten years, when Sukarno suspended both elections and the 1950 constitution in 1959, proclaiming himself president of Indonesia's 'guided democracy'.

[53] Tan 2002, especially p. 10–12.

[54] Tan 2002, p. 41.

[55] A society based solely on 'individual equality' is not yet a just or inclusive society. 'Group equality' is also an important factor, along with pluralism (i.e., respect for differences and different groups). Or as Rosenfeld puts it: 'Comprehensive pluralism is, in principle, better suited than liberalism to do justice to minority group equality claims based to a large extent on difference.' Cf. Rosenfeld 2011, p. 93. Cf. Moyn 2018.

[56] Croissant 2014.

[57] Love for Both of Us.

been ranked higher than sixth place in the previous 48 editions. Yet, Portugal's Eurovision entry which gained the country last place in 1974[58] is far more significant to Portuguese people than Sobral's triumph in 2017. On that fateful day of 24 April 1974, a radio station in Lisbon broadcast Paulo de Carvalho's melancholic fado *E Depois do Adeus* (And After The Farewell). De Carvalho's 'farewell' had the same effect as the aria *Amour sacré de la patrie* (The sacred Love of the Fatherland)[59] had on the Belgians in 1830: a secret code word which signalled the beginning of an uprising. Farewell to Caetano's dictatorial regime (successor to the even more infamous Salazar), farewell to poverty, oppression and drawn-out military conflicts in Africa. It sparked a largely non-violent revolution. Despite a ban, people took to the streets, protesting and putting carnations into the barrels of soldiers' rifles (earning the popular uprising name of the Carnation Revolution). The soldiers did not act – partially because the uprising was preceded by a military coup. At half past four in the morning of 26 April, its leader, Major Otelo Saraiva, announced that Caetano had been overthrown and the uprising had succeeded. The first free, democratic elections were held in 1976.

Portugal was not the only country to throw off the shackles of a dictatorial regime in this period. The same also happened in Spain (1975), Greece (1973/1974) and Turkey (1983), resulting in a proliferation of post-dictatorial constitutions (Portugal 1976, Spain 1978, Greece 1975, Turkey 1982).[60] These constitutions are similar to the 'rights-based' constitutions that had been adopted in many European countries straight after the Second World War in response to abuses and state repression. Somehow these countries had missed the boat back then. Chris Thornhill says of them:

> [...] some European societies preserved an under evolved rights fabric after 1945 [...] Generally, states that had not followed the pattern of constitutional transition and rights-based political abstraction after 1945 [...] proved particularly susceptible to crises of legitimacy.[61]

These European post-dictatorial constitutions have been reasonably successful. Some forty years later, most of them are still in force and have contributed to the fact that at least Spain, Greece and Portugal have grown into free and stable democracies which soon acceded to the European Union.[62]

That these constitutions are a kind of latter-day variant of the constitutions promulgated after the Second World War is indicated not only by their universalist

---

[58] Held on 6 April 1974 in Bristol in the United Kingdom. Competition was incredibly fierce that year. The Swedish group Abba won with *Waterloo*.

[59] From Daniel François Esprit Auber's opera *La Muette de Portici* (*The Mute Girl of Portici*) performed in Brussels on 25 August 1830.

[60] Adopted during the 1980–1983 military regime.

[61] Thornhill 2011, p. 342.

[62] Greece in 1981, and Spain and Portugal in 1986.

features, but also by the fact that – like Japan and Germany – some of them have a constitutional 'lock' to prevent them from ever relapsing into misrule and dictatorship. The Greek Constitution expresses this in the following terms:

> Observance of the constitution is entrusted to the patriotism of the Greeks who shall have the right and the duty to resist by all possible means against anyone who attempts the violent abolition of the Constitution.[63]

Not only are Greeks entitled to resist the violation of the constitution, they are positively obliged to do so.

This spirit of freedom is undoubtedly also the cause of the continuing decline in the number of monarchies. As noted above, nearly 50 monarchies were disbanded between 1900 and 1940; on a conservative count, another 55 kings, princes and emperors received marching orders in the period 1940–2000. Monarchy was reduced from the dominant form of governance to the exception over the course of the twentieth century.[64]

---

[63] Article 120, fourth paragraph.

[64] There were still thirty hereditary monarchies and four non-hereditary monarchies in world in 2018. This figure gives a distorted impression because it includes only a few medium-sized countries (Saudi-Arabia, Japan, Spain and so on), sixteen members of the Commonwealth are linked to the British crown (ranging from medium-sized countries like Canada to tiny Grenada), and numerous small to minute kingdoms, duchies and the like (Eswatini, Monaco, Bhutan, Tonga, Liechtenstein, Brunei, Kuwait and so on). Monarchy has become largely symbolic in most countries; monarchs who are absolute rulers have become a rarity, but are still found in Saudi Arabia, Bahrain, Brunei, Oman and Qatar. Almost all remaining monarchies are constitutional monarchies.

16

The Eighth Generation

Liberal-Democratic Constitutions

Fast forward to 1989. At 6:57 pm on 9 November of that year, the Berlin Wall fell. All it took was a simple announcement by an East German government spokesperson, Günter Schabowski, that every East German citizen could henceforth travel freely to the West. With that message he had unwittingly triggered a chain reaction that ended the Cold War within a few days, bringing down the Iron Curtain and doing away with almost all communist regimes in Europe (and well beyond) within a year. This relatively non-violent revolution spread like wildfire across the communist world. Its similarity to the 1848 revolutions is often remarked upon: it was a 'critical juncture'[1] at which the whole of history – suddenly – veered in a new direction.[2] It also appeared to mark the end of the titanic struggle between the humanist ideologies that so profoundly shaped political developments in the nineteenth and twentieth centuries. Of the three humanist ideologies – social, evolutionary and liberal humanism[3] – only liberal humanism seemed to survive intact.

In his famous essay *The End of History?* (1989) Francis Fukuyama writes on this turn of events:

> What we may be witnessing is not just the end of the Cold War, or the passing of a particular period of post-war history, but the end of history as such: that is, the end point of mankind's ideological evolution and the universalisation of Western liberal democracy as the final form of human government.[4]

---

[1] This refers to the phenomenon of 'brief phases of institutional flux – referred to as critical junctions – during which more dramatic change is possible.' Cf. Capoccia & Keleman 2007, especially p. 341.

[2] More technically, the concept of critical juncture refers to 'situations of uncertainty in which decisions of important actors are causally decisive for the selection of one path of institutional development over other possible paths.' (…) 'A sort of "distal historical causation": events and developments in the distant past, generally concentrated in a relatively short period, that have a crucial impact on outcomes later in time.' Cf. Capoccia 2016, chapter 5 *Critical Junctures*, p. 89–90.

[3] Harari 2016, p. 246–257.

[4] Fukuyama 1989, p. 4. Elaborated in Fukuyama 2012, particularly p. XI and XII and part V.

Western liberal democracy as the ultimate concept of governance and political ideology to end all others?[5] A provocative thought.[6] On whichever side of the debate
one stands, the fall of the Berlin Wall did indeed spell the end of many communist
regimes in Central and Eastern Europe, spawning many new states and ultimately
about twenty new constitutions. Almost all of them were in the liberal-democratic
mould: parliamentary democracies combined with the rule of law, constitutionally
guaranteed separation of powers and individual fundamental freedoms.

Not everywhere was change unleashed precipitously on 9 November 1989. In
Poland, change to the communist (Leninist) constitution of 1952 (personally
approved by Stalin) was already initiated by amendments in 1970 mandating the
Polish Council of State to oversee the constitutionality of laws. It was the prelude
to a separate Constitutional Tribunal in 1982 and later a full constitutional review
of legislative and administrative acts in which individual (human) rights played an
increasingly important role. And forms of independent (constitutional) review had
also already enabled the judiciaries of Yugoslavia and Hungary to break free of the
party-dominated complex of legislative and executive even before 1989.

Yet, the fall of the Berlin Wall was still a shock. The sudden collapse of the
old regimes sometimes created a political vacuum. A multitude of longstanding
national and regional aspirations and claims was ignited more or less overnight. Old
states like the Soviet Union and Yugoslavia fragmented, and new states were formed
from their remnants. The process was peaceful in most cases, but Yugoslavia's dis-
integration into six or seven new states incited bitter civil wars. All these new states,
of course, promulgated their own, usually new, constitutions. These constitutions
were designed as a kind of bulwark to prevent any repetition of the past, which is
reflected in the Romanian Constitution (1991):

[5] Liberal democracy is a paradoxical concept. It is a political system in which protecting (individual) freedom is paramount and is combined with a system of decision-making based on the
consent of each individual. Individual freedoms and claims are inevitably not entirely compat-
ible with political (majority) decision-making exigencies in most cases. There is a continual
need to try and reach a balance. Fierlbeck and many others point out that liberalism and
democracy are quite distinct concepts. Liberalism is a substantive category which assumes as
its starting point the freedom and equality of people (at least before the law); its most important
value is coexistence in a society. Conversely, liberalism is 'a procedural system constructed to
recognise formally the principle that political legitimacy was grounded upon the consent of
each citizen.' Fierlbeck 2008, p. 77.
[6] Fukuyama's idea is often misunderstood. 'End' in his 'End of history' is a sort of a pun on
words. He uses the word in a double sense: 'the End' as something coming to an end, and 'the
End' as the goal of something – for instance, history. Mueller in 2014, explains that Fukuyama's
end 'formulation was derived from Hegel, and it has generally been misinterpreted. He did
not mean that things would stop happening – obviously a preposterous proposal. Rather, he
contended that there had been a profound ideological development. With the demise of communism, its chief remaining challenger after the extinguishment earlier in the century of
monarchy and Fascism, liberalism – democracy and market capitalism – had triumphed over
all other governmental and economic systems or sets of ordering principles.' Mueller 2014,
p. 35 ff.

Romania is a democratic and social state, [...] and the ideals of the Revolution of December 1989, [...] shall be guaranteed.[7]

As well as in the Bulgarian constitution (1991):

No part of the people, no political party nor any other organization, state institution or individual shall usurp the expression of the popular sovereignty.[8]

Formulae intended to exorcise the spirits of the past. The newly formed states are almost all democracies, at least this aspiration is written in their constitutions. But constitutions are, of course, not magic wands. Establishing the principle of democratic government in a constitutional regulation does not make it a fact.[9] The journey towards democracy and democratic governance has been a process of trial and error in many new states, sometimes failing or simply not occurring, as in Belarus[10] or Azerbaijan.[11]

Years of dictatorial rule often entail these countries lacking relevant experience in democratic governance and elections. They have few political parties, and these parties are young. There is little trust in government and governmental institutions – or fellow citizens and the law. Individual freedom and a free market economy are also brand new and untested. The new constitutions are vehicles for change, as is association with other, more mature free democracies in Europe. Thirteen former Warsaw Pact countries have acceded to the European Union (EU) since 2004. This 'deal' seemed to be to everyone's benefit at the outset: it enlarged the internal market, strengthened the EU (also politically) and the accession countries have been able to consolidate their liberal democracies and increase their economic prosperity. Accession was also intended to prevent relapse. EU membership is, as it happens, conditional. Membership candidates are required to meet the Copenhagen criteria,[12] requiring prospective countries to have stable institutions guaranteeing democracy, the rule of law, respect for human rights and minorities and a well-functioning free-market economy able to cope with free competition. These requirements are permanent and apply after accession too. For most of the newcomers, their new liberal-democratic constitutions were the keys that unlocked the EU gates. Constitutions that were not up to scratch were swiftly adapted to EU requirements.

Thirty years after the fall of the Berlin Wall, many of the 'liberated' countries still have a multitude of political and administrative problems, and the relationship between the new and older EU members is not always simple or harmonious.

---

[7] Article 1, third paragraph.
[8] Article 1, third paragraph.
[9] As Ernest Gellner demonstrates in his book *Conditions of Liberty*. Gellner 1994.
[10] 1994 constitution.
[11] 1995 constitution (revised 2016).
[12] Adopted by the European Council in Copenhagen in 1993 and the European Council in Madrid in 1995.

Despite the ensuing disenchantment, much has been achieved. Most of these new states have grown into stable liberal democracies, with reasonably functioning free markets that have brought significant economic prosperity. It was not written in the stars and this outcome was hardly inevitable in 1990. It certainly cannot be attributed solely to the (new) liberal and democratic constitutions of the 1990s. As noted, constitutions are not magic wands. Yet, these constitutions have played an indirect and intermediary role in establishing and maintaining mutual trust, as well as (political) trust in institutions. And, we know that trust in institutions is important for market opportunities and market growth in a free market economy.[13]

THE FALL OF THE BERLIN WALL: CONSTITUTIONS 1989–2018

The events of 1989 certainly did not hail the end of history (as Fukuyama's *End of History* is often misapprehended),[14] nor the end of constitutional history for that matter. The 'Berlin Wall wave' of liberal-democratic constitutions[15] appears to be predominantly a regional phenomenon, mainly limited to Central and Eastern Europe. It chimes with the other – often silent – constitutional revolutions taking place around the world at this time, although these often seemed to have been triggered by other causes, contexts and reasons. More than half of all the constitutions in the world – 102 in total – were promulgated over the past thirty years,[16] and only the birth of about a quarter of these new constitutions can be directly be attributed to the desire for 'liberation' through a new political system.

Over the course of recent decades, the desire for a liberal democracy has by no means always been the motivation for a new system, nor was its adoption the only principal choice. A small study we conducted in 2018 at Leiden University revealed that this was – as indicated – only so in a quarter of the cases. Even though the motives for amendments or new constitutions are notoriously ambiguous and difficult to uncover, we were able to demonstrate that new constitutions since 1989 seem more often to be impelled by external factors, rather than internal (i.e., principled, ideological) ones. These external factors include events like the fall of dictatorships (19%), the end of civil wars or internal conflicts (21%), and the proclamation of new states or (regained) independence (14%). Many of these factors, of course, overlap, but the study shows that the reasons for promulgating constitutions – which are largely liberal-democratic in nature these days (see Chapter 19 Convergence) – are diverse, and certainly not always the result of any widespread, shared or deep-rooted belief in the desirability of liberal democracy.

[13] Cf. McAllister 1999.
[14] Fukuyama's 'end' did, as explained above, not merely refer to the 'conclusion' but – in a Hegelian/Marxist sense – to the *goal* of history. Cf. Fukuyama 2018, p. XII.
[15] A third wave according to Thornhill. Cf. Thornhill 2011, p. 355 ff.
[16] Total in June 2018.

DEMOCRACY WITHOUT FREEDOM:
THE RISE OF ILLIBERAL DEMOCRACY

In 1997, the American journalist Fareed Zakaria wrote an oft-quoted article 'The Rise of Illiberal Democracy' in the magazine *Foreign Affairs*. Written ten years after the fall of the Berlin Wall, he exposed the Achilles heel of constitutional liberal democracies. Using examples from Africa and Latin America, he illustrated that countries have made the transition to democracy but have certainly not always become true liberal democracies. Zakaria concluded that for a number of these new democracies:

> Constitutional liberalism has led to democracy, but democracy does not seem to bring constitutional liberalism.[17]

Zakaria coined the term *illiberal democracies* for these countries where democracy is not accompanied by constitutionally guaranteed freedom. He considers illiberal democracies lacking the rule of law the worst of two worlds:

> Democracy without constitutional liberalism is not simply inadequate, but dangerous, bringing with it the erosion of liberty, the abuse of power, ethnic divisions, and even war.[18]

As early as 1997, Zakaria noted that they were growing alarmingly in number.[19] They were mainly concentrated in Africa, the Middle East, Central Asia and parts of Latin America at the time.[20] This is still the case twenty years later,[21] although many more regions are now facing declining freedom and democracy. Freedom watchdog Freedom House's reports show that the trend is expanding, intensifying and accelerating.[22]

---

[17] Cf. Zakaria 1997, especially p. 28; and more recently (Larry) Diamond 2015a.

[18] Zakaria 1997, p. 42–43.

[19] 'Illiberal democracy is a growth industry' Zakaria argued. Zakaria 1997, p. 24.

[20] Even in the past ten years there has been a liberal-democratic recession, a relapse into illiberalism and a decline in democracy, as Larry Diamond has shown in a recent article. This has mainly been caused by inequality (in rights, opportunities and income), diversity, corruption and abuse of power. (Larry) Diamond 2015b, p. 142–155. Cf. Puddington 2015 for a similar analysis.

[21] Cf. Zakaria 2007. Rocha Menocal, Fritz & Rakner 2008. Cheeseman 2015. Cf. Freedom House watcher Erik Meyersson's blog 'Which country has the most illiberal democracy in the world?' 2015 (based on Freedom House analyses and measurements) https://erikmeyersson .com/2015/06/18/which-country-has-the-most-illiberal-democracy-in-the-world/ (Consulted on 9 June 2018).

[22] Freedom House has been tracking the state of freedom and freedoms in the world for more than a quarter of a century and publishes annual reports on the subject (*Freedom in the World*). In 2017, for the twelfth consecutive year, the annual report recorded a decline in freedom and democracy on all fronts. Freedom House also noted an acceleration in the recession. According to Freedom House's criteria, 45% of the countries in the world in 2017 were completely free, 30% were partially free and 25% were unfree. The figures look less flattering when seen in terms of population. Thirty-nine percent of the world's population live

Much constitutional promulgation in the years 1989–2018 occurred in countries now experiencing declines in liberal-democratic political systems (including the problems of illiberal democracy). To understand this development, we have to look at where the 102 constitutions promulgated in this period come from. Figures from the past thirty years show that forty-five countries on the African continent passed new constitutions, twenty-five in Europe, twenty-four in Asia, seven in Latin America, and one in Oceania. Most of the constitutions in Europe from this period are directly related to the fall of the Berlin Wall and new state formation. But where do all the new constitutions in Africa,[23] Asia, Latin America, and Oceania come from?

Unlike in Europe, there is no single cause. Various reasons have played a role, often in conjunction with each other. Looking, for example, at the reasons in Africa – where most of the recent constitutions have been promulgated – gives a varied impression (Figure 3).

Dictatorships, Islam, the Arab Spring,[24] the desire for liberal democracy, but also the establishment or consolidation of authoritarian regimes all have played a part – in short, everything.[25] The same goes for Asia. Anyone trying to make sense of this will observe a fitful pattern of growth spurts, with an oscillating process drifting towards liberal democracy – this can also be seen in some Latin American countries[26] over the past 75 years. Large parts of Western Europe have followed a similarly winding path over the past 150 years. A country or region does not usually convert all at once to democracy or respect for human dignity and protection of fundamental freedoms. It is usually a long and painful process involving much trial and error.

The above assumes – with some facileness – that liberal democracy, embedded in a constitution, is or should be the ultimate goal of a country or nation's political development. This is philosophically untenable because history simply has no 'objective' goal or point on the horizon we are all working our way towards.[27] But it is undeniable that increasing numbers of countries, for whatever reason, are saying that they want to be a liberal democracy – certainly since the Second World War. And the number of countries actually succeeding in this goal, even bearing liberal democratic recession in mind, is growing.[28]

---

in freedom, 24% live in partial freedom and 37% are not free – they live in an unfree country. Freedom House, *Freedom in the World* https://freedomhouse.org/report/freedom-world/freedom-world-2018 (Consulted 10 June 2018). Cf. Puddington 2015, p. 122 for the situation in 2014.

[23] Cheeseman 2015.

[24] A series of uprisings, protests and revolutions against autocratic regimes in the Arab world that began in Tunisia on 18 December 2010.

[25] Of Freedom House's twelve 'Worst of the Worst Regimes' in 2018, seven were on the African continent. Freedom House 2018.

[26] Cf. Picado 2004, p. 28–31 and Nogales & Zelaya-Fenner 2013.

[27] Li-Ann Thio claims that this model does not fit some countries, as they are more inclined towards forms of 'mixed constitutionalism'. Thio 2012, p. 137–138.

[28] Pinker 2018, especially p. 418–420.

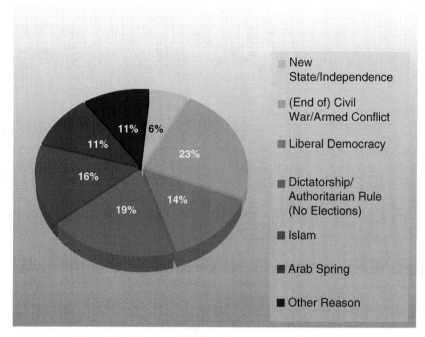

FIGURE 3   Constitutions in Africa 1989–2018

It is particularly notable that almost all countries that nowadays aspire to or want (variants of) liberal democracy embed their intention in a legal document: a constitution. Ever greater numbers of formal constitutional liberal democracies are emerging. Although liberal democracy, as a political system that combines periodically elected leadership with guaranteed individual freedom, is certainly not practised everywhere, it seems to have become at the very least a common, global frame of reference. It is almost a global public belief[29] as to how and according to which values and conditions government power can be exercised. For this reason, it might be better to see most constitutions as articles of faith committed to writing rather than as achieved or unachieved political practices. Constitutional, liberal-democratic developments in Africa and Asia started later and with shorter transitions than, say, Latin America and Europe. Moreover, external factors and actors have perhaps played a greater role in Africa and Asia than in transitional processes in Latin America and Europe, where an analysis by the researchers Rocha Menocal, Fritz and Rakner in 2008 shows that it was primarily internal political actors which incited the transition.[30] To this day, the role of the global community and major

---

[29]   Cf. Law & Versteeg 2011.

[30]   Their research shows that: '[...] in the Eastern European and Latin American experiences, where democratisation transitions were driven mostly from within. In contrast, in Asia and especially in Africa (and possibly low-income and aid-dependent countries elsewhere),

powers in liberal-democratic transitions in African and Asian countries has been considerable. It is therefore unsurprising that such a rapid transition, sometimes involving external pressure, has not directly led to the peaceful, inclusive and prosperous societies promised by the ideal of constitutionally embedded, liberal democracy. Democracy, freedom and inclusiveness have a complex relationship, and their forces are difficult to balance durably. Zakaria shows how democracy can quickly degenerate into uncontrollable, freedom-sapping political competition when a culture of trust, solidarity and tolerance is lacking.[31]

A constitution is only able to do so much, and certainly cannot dictate the culture within which it is situated. Constitutional norms and institutions can act as catalysts or stabilisers because their norms are adopted as the common reference points required to build a liberal-democratic constitutional culture in a country. Gradual development – sometimes via 'hybrid' regimes[32] – and consolidation are the instruments which moderate downward spirals and create courses down which the constitutionally-embedded ideals of liberal democracy can be achieved.[33] Countries use different and often constitutional forms to achieve this. Over the last thirty years, constitutions have tried to promote public mutual trust through various inclusivity mechanisms (recognising minorities, ethnicity and religion, as well as increasing participation and emancipation of groups).[34] Attempts have also been made to develop a constitutional identity.[35]

Ethnically diverse countries in particular often have emancipatory constitutions. Another way to try to steer the forces of young, constitutionally embedded liberal democracies is by giving them 'flexible constitutions'. Constitutions must be able to be adapted to new circumstances more often and faster than in the past[36] as things are changing faster. Although one of the core functions of constitutions is to accord sustainability and structure to a political system,[37] rigidity can have a conflict-generating effect. A firm constitutional structure that is also adaptable can cushion growth spurts and introduce a learning element into a constitutional-political system.[38] The large number of constitutions that have been promulgated around the world in recent years indicates that countries and states have great confidence in the

---

external actors played a much stronger role in these political transformations. [...]' Rocha Menocal, Fritz & Rakner 2008, p. 30.

[31] 'Political competition that is so divisive can rapidly degenerate into violence. Opposition movements, armed rebellions, and coups in Africa have often been directed against ethnically based regimes, many of which came to power through elections.' Zakaria 1997, p. 35–36. Cf. Snyder 2000.

[32] Rocha Menocal, Fritz & Rakner 2008, p. 29.

[33] Zakaria 1997, p. 40–43 and Rocha Menocal, Fritz & Rakner 2008, p. 29–40.

[34] Budryté 2011.

[35] Cf. Jacobsohn 2012.

[36] Cf. Ginsburg 2011, p. 117–120.

[37] Ginsburg 2011, p. 112–114 and Elkins, Ginsburg & Melton 2009, p. 12–19 and p. 33–34.

[38] Passchier 2017.

capacity of constitutions. Yet, this power is questionable. Constitutional norms have a limited capacity to make political and social reality and bring about transitions, certainly over a short time span. It is noteworthy that constitutions are nowadays invariably involved in processes of this kind. Their norms articulate and reconfirm the values and principles of the system they are trying to establish. They do little more at times, but certainly no less.

ISLAMIC CONSTITUTIONS

Liberal democracy and state religion[39] are uneasy bedfellows. Until recently, religion played a role in all aspects of life in many countries. Only a few centuries ago, many countries had a state religion.[40] From North (Sweden) to South (Greece), and East (Russia) to West (Ireland), most countries in Europe had state churches by the nineteenth century.

Most countries in Europe and the Americas have gradually disestablished official state religions over the past 200 years. They were incompatible with the widespread principle of religious freedom and even less so with emerging humanist liberal ideas and concomitant secularisation. Spain was one of the last countries in the EU where the state religion, introduced under Franco, was disestablished in 1978.

State religions do still exist, mostly in Islamic countries in the Middle East, North Africa and Southeast Asia. The constitutions of 23 countries proclaim Islam as the state religion:[41] Afghanistan, Algeria, Bahrain, Bangladesh, Brunei, Egypt, Iran, Iraq, Jordan, Kuwait, Libya, Malaysia, the Maldives, Mauritania, Morocco, Oman, Pakistan, Qatar, Saudi Arabia, Somalia, Tunisia, the United Arab Emirates and Yemen.[42] Constitutions of this kind can therefore be considered 'Islamic constitutions', although this does not mean that all Islamic laws, in particular the Islamic legal system (sharia), are fully applicable in all these countries.[43]

The past century has brought great changes in most Islamic countries. Many were once part of large empires (including the Ottoman Empire) or were colonised or

---

[39] Also referred to as 'established religion'.

[40] There were exceptions to this rule, like the Netherlands, where the Dutch Reformed Church, whilst certainly privileged, never became the state religion over the course of more than 400 years.

[41] Which does not imply that Islam is only the state religion in these countries. Islam is the *de facto* state religion in Sudan, for example, but it is not designated as such in the constitution. It is an important element in seventeen of the world's newest constitutions (1989–2018), mostly in Africa and the Middle East.

[42] United States Commission on International Religious Freedom www.uscirf.gov/reports-briefs/spotlight/did-you-knowmuslim-constitutions (Consulted 1 June 2018).

[43] Several countries still include sharia protection clauses in the constitution, although this phenomenon seems to be declining; it is certainly more controversial nowadays than before. Cf. Lombardi 2013. Cf. Vikør 2016 for the situation in Egypt and a discussion of its 2012 constitution (p. 219–220).

dominated by Western imperial powers; and when these empires collapsed, they were caught in the midst of turbulent processes of nation and state formation and were coveted by rival superpowers.[44] Finding a balance in relations that have often been imposed by foreign powers and dealing with democracy and liberalism, whose values have sometimes clashed with existing or traditional structures, has proved difficult. It has been particularly challenging to accord (religious) minorities a place in the constitutional framework and adequately protect them, even where a modern constitutional organisation of the political system has been pursued.[45] Finding a workable relationship between state and religion has also been challenging. How should secular leaders relate to faith, Islamic law, and their 'subjects'?[46] How free are the state and its subjects in relation to religious rules and principles? What kind of leadership is needed, what are the guiding values?[47] These have become major, controversial issues in the context of advancing secularisation and the rise of liberal-democratic ideas.[48] The American Islam researcher Clark Lombardi says in a recent article:

> During the pre-modern era, many Muslims embraced a principle that state law is legitimate only if it is consistent with Islamic legal principles. Whatever consensus existed in the pre-modern era about Islamic legal authority has collapsed. Muslims in every country today are contesting basic questions of Islamic law—questions of Islamic authority, questions of interpretive method, and questions about what types of law a state can legitimately enact without violating the fundamental principles of *sharia*.[49]

This contest has resulted in various outcomes: An Islamic Revolution in Iran (1979); civil wars in Afghanistan, Yemen and Sudan; and paroxysms of political unrest in Pakistan and other countries. A striking number of Islamic countries in the Middle East and Africa have recently tried to use new constitutions to find a new balance. This has certainly not been a panacea. As expounded above, and regardless of the promises of travelling constitutional miracle doctors and foreign advisers, constitutional liberalism and democracy do not always bring about peaceful relations and political stability.[50] Liberal-democratic constitutions are usually not the reward, but rather the investment. They give a society an appetite for more. Perhaps the seven

---

[44] Cf. Frankopan 2015, chapter 23 (*The Road of Superpower Rivalry*).
[45] *Ibid*, chapters 24 (*The Road to Catastrophe*) and 25 (*The Road to Tragedy*).
[46] Vikør 2016, p. 219–220.
[47] Zakaria 2004, especially p. 7–9.
[48] Cf. Mallat 2012. Mallat discerns three arcs of crisis. The first is the region covering Afghanistan, Pakistan, India and surrounding countries; the second is Iran (in relation to Saudi Arabia and Iraq); and the third is Israel and its environs. The issues are different in each of the 'arcs'. Mallat 2012, p. 1287–1290. Samuel Huntington argues that these crises are not accidental hot spots, but front lines of a clash of civilisations that has been taking place in the aftermath of the struggle between the great ideologies of the Cold War. Cf. Huntington 2011 (orig. 1996).
[49] Lombardi 2013, p. 644.
[50] Cf. Emon 2010.

new constitutions emanating from the Arab Spring, which spread across the Arab world in the early 2010s, should be seen in this light.[51]

CONSTITUTIONS THAT ARE NOT STATE-BASED?

Constitutions currently correspond almost invariably with national states. Almost every state has one and nowadays state formation is always accompanied by constitutional formation, as the historical overview has demonstrated. But, how about the converse; can entities other than states also have constitutions? Most certainly. Federated states and regions often have constitutions, although we do not call them national constitutions. Private organisations also sometimes call their basic rules constitutions,[52] even if they are of a very different nature to their public namesakes. Can international organisations, such as the European Union, have a constitution like a state? European constitutionalists like German Dieter Grimm argue that they can in theory.[53] Others, like Grimm's originally South African colleague Joseph Weiler, beg to differ; he is horrified by the idea of a constitution as no more than a technocratic project, lacking a people, popular will, nation or state. A constitution without a people, without a 'we', is a project with a gaping void at its heart.[54] Frenchman Olivier Beaud tried to contextualise the intellectual posturing that reached a crescendo in the run-up to the plan for a 'stateless' European constitution around 2004:

> The continental European tradition is distinctive in that it considers the concept of state itself as being presupposed by the concept of constitution. [...] According to this tradition, then, the state has in some sense become a sort of second nature of modern constitutional law.[55]

That did not stop the Europeans from trying at the dawn of the new millennium. The plan for a constitution for the European Union was brought about by the many enlargements (a club of six Western European countries has grown into a continent-wide union of nearly thirty states) and the expanding reach of European Union policy. The mass of treaties had become labyrinthine and decision-making

---

[51] Although its effects are certainly not always easy to understand from a Western perspective. Fadel 2016. Fadel argues that we try to understand developments in the Arab world too much from a liberal world view and against the background of Western developments in the relationship between church and state – that is, through the lens of Western political history. This does not help to elucidate what is happening, say, in Egypt at the moment. Cf. p. 505–506.

[52] Cf., for example, the Constitution for Buddhist Brotherhood Society University of Colombo (USA).

[53] Grimm 2011.

[54] Weiler 1999.

[55] Beaud 2012, p. 271–272. In that sense, for the difference between 'rule of law' and 'Rechtsstaat' (as it is called in German and Dutch speaking countries), cf. Barber 2003. These two concepts differ again from the French concept of 'l'État de droit' – which basically conveys the same notion (government rule bound by law – rule by law and not by men).

procedures an inscrutable morass which only specialists could navigate. The EU was criticised for its lack of democracy, transparency and efficiency. In reaction to this, the European Council adopted the 'Laeken Declaration' in 2001, also with a view to the forthcoming accession of ten new member states. Part of this plan was to arrive at a single systematically ordered treaty for the EU. The document was to be called a 'constitution' and would be drafted by a constitutional convention (following the example of the American Philadelphia Convention of 1787),[56] in the hope of giving the treaty and the EU some kudos. The appellation 'constitution' was controversial from the outset because the 'Treaty establishing a Constitution for Europe' – as the document was ultimately called – was, of course, not a constitution in the classical sense. The EU is not a state and there is no 'European people' with an independent claim to sovereignty. The decision to call the document a constitution was interpreted in the feverish debate leading up to the adoption and ratification of the treaty as a political preference, a devious prelude to transforming the EU into a superstate which would quash member states' hard-fought national sovereignty and independence. Most member states and European citizens were opposed to any such development: they did not want to live in a single European state as a single European people under a – democratically elected – EU administration. After the European Constitution was rejected referendums in two (founding) member states (France and the Netherlands) in 2005, an interim solution was engineered after an interval of several years: the rejected draft constitution was recast in the classic form of a treaty that – as the preamble says – was not drawn up 'by' the European people but on behalf of the citizens and states of Europe.[57] This Lisbon Treaty (2007) has largely the same content as the rejected European Constitution, but anything too reminiscent of a traditional constitution was quietly discarded. To exorcise any residual memories of the rejected document, everything was well-mixed resulting in a circumlocutory treaty text packed with unintelligible compromises. Joseph Weiler lampooned it in the following terms:

> No convention, no European Philadelphia, no Constitutionspeak. At best, a good old treaty, masquerading as a constitution.[58]

---

[56] The European Convention – chaired by the former president of France, Valéry Giscard d'Estaing – met between February 2002 and July 2003. The 217 delegates represented member states, accession states, national parliaments, the European Parliament and the European Commission. The final document was a concept for a new treaty for the European Union. This document was the basis of a subsequent intergovernmental conference, which sat from 4 October 2003 to 18 June 2004. It produced the draft *Constitutional Treaty* which was approved by the European Council and the Foreign Ministers in Rome later that year, and finally submitted to the member states for ratification.

[57] The 'EU people' do not exist under the EU treaties. The EU Treaty itself only mentions 'the peoples of Europe' (Article 1, Treaty on European Union).

[58] Weiler 2005, quote from p. 176.

The institutional reforms of the EU that had been deemed necessary in 2001 – democratisation, increased transparency and a separate catalogue of fundamental rights and political freedoms – were implemented in the Lisbon Treaty,[59] which was constitutional in all respects except its name.

MULTI-LAYERED LEGAL ORDERS

The debacle of the European constitution shows something else too. Nowadays, we live in multi-layered legal orders in which law is no longer only formed and determined by national states, but to a considerable extent also transnationally and internationally. There has, of course, always been international treaty law, but it has undergone an immense increase in scale in recent decades. International law is becoming more and more important. In many parts of the world, modern citizens largely rely on international human rights treaties, such as the International Covenant on Civil and Political Rights (1966), and (in Europe) the European Convention for the Protection of Human Rights and Fundamental Freedoms (ECHR, 1950), for the protection of their individual fundamental freedoms. Human rights cases can be brought before international tribunals and courts, such as the European Court of Human Rights in Strasbourg. Constitutions are no longer the only source of protection of individual freedom or unique pillars in a legal system. Constitutional orders seem to be slipping their state moorings – legal systems are no longer confined to states. We will return to this in Chapter 19.

---

[59] Entered into force in 2009.

17

What Are the Lessons of History?

What does the history of constitutions teach us? That is a very difficult question. Can the past teach us anything at all?[1] Probably not.[2] But perhaps that is not the primary importance of historical analysis. Historiography is not so much about how things once were, but more about who we now are and how we now view things. Histories are always representations of the past to which we assign significance ('important', 'explanation', 'valuable', 'related to', 'explanatory', and so on) relevant to the present. Stories[3] about historical events show how what is self-evident today was not always so. Historically, it is far from self-evident that people must live in states or organise their cooperation around written constitutional rules. Neither was there any historical necessity for us to develop in this way. Constitutions are the product of historical contingency – series of incidents that are not necessarily linked building on one other.[4] Constitutions are not the result of historical laws or enlightened revelations that teach us history's intentions for humanity. As what 'is' does not automatically follow from what 'ought to be', neither does what now 'is' necessarily follow from what once 'was'.

---

[1]   'History does not repeat itself, it merely rhymes.' This aphorism is attributed to Mark Twain, despite not being found in his work, which does not make it any less true, of course.
[2]   Burckhardt for one is rigorous in his assessment of history, whilst offering solace: 'history is actually the most unscientific of all the sciences, although it communicates so much that is worth knowing.' Burckhardt 1979 (orig. 1905), p. 121.
[3]   Currie and Sterelny note that 'we take it as obvious that historians and historical scientists construct narratives'. Currie & Sterelny 2017, p. 15.
[4]   Cf. Sterelny 2016. Sterelny elucidates how contingent historical development is not the same as a series of successive random events. Relationships and patterns can certainly be discerned in which one event or development is decisive for another. This is the case in path dependency in which past choices or events influence the course of subsequent developments, mainly because the initial choice precludes or hinders certain options.

So, none of that. Nevertheless, the long history of constitutions does exhibit patterns. Its earliest roots were in the Middle East and Europe, and they have now spread to all corners of the earth. We live in a world filled with constitutions.[5]

A close examination of the long history of constitutions does reveal more clearly what constitutions actually do. Invariably they proclaim rules on leadership and social organisation, and give rules on a legal system as well. They breathe life into the phenomenon 'law' and create a legal order with 'meta-rules'.[6] Law greases the wheels of societies; it supports large-scale cooperation by creating artificial trust which can be derived from all manner of abstractions and assumptions. Such as assuming that you and others must adhere to important suprapersonal, common standards. Or that people in a society (ought to) have different roles and positions and that the rules of the law can 'create' these roles and positions in the form of institutions, authority, offices and rights. Constitutions perform the magic of the law; they impart the collective belief in its operation and value. The story of constitutions symbolises the world of law – a story told as a written text. Constitutions, law and written language go hand in hand nowadays. And, whilst it is certainly not impossible that unwritten ones existed, there are no longer large-scale legal systems based purely on oral traditions. Written constitutions are far more durable and less vulnerable to information loss during transfer.

The long history of constitutions also shows 'how' they effect the leap of faith from the here and now to the world of law. This vault always starts with the definition of a 'we', however implicit, which is indispensable. Large-scale communities that exceed the Dunbar number do not arise spontaneously. 'There are no societies', the political economist Elster remarks, 'only individuals who interact with each other.'[7] Collaborative communities, such as those associated with a legal system, a market or a state, are proclaimed or declared. They need a convincing story, an appeal that touches members' hearts, to maintain collaboration and the trust this requires. If you scratch beneath the surface, it soon becomes apparent that constitutions are much more than collections of arid legal rules. They are social mobilisation vehicles that combine clever blends of fiduciary institutions, recognition and recognition mechanisms (how does an individual relate to the community?[8]) in a

---

[5] Cf. Lane 1996 for more on the global trend impelling countries to codify their constitutional law in a single written constitutional text.

[6] The rules on legal rules, so to speak. 'Rules of recognition', according to the British legal theorist Herbert Hart. Kelsen calls them *Grundnormen* ('basic norms' in German). Meta-rules should not be conceived of as a list of regulations or rules (codified or not) but rather as a complex of abstractions and ideas necessary for the recognition of the concept of law. In other words, the abstract recognition that law exists and has the capacity to influence relationships and behaviour and create institutions – in short, the idea that law exists and is *in force*. A basic concept of this kind is essential to a legal system. Cf. Kelsen 1961 (orig. 1945), p. 110–111 and Hart 2012 (orig. 1961), p. 92.

[7] Elster 1989, p. 248; Smilov 2013, p. 630–633.

[8] Cf. Chapter 6 for more on this topic.

convincing story to forge human collaboration. This story functions as communal 'cement',[9] telling us who we are, why we belong together, and how we collaborate (according to which structure). Constitutional rules can designate abstract, collective norms (precepts and prohibitions) as constitutional norms or rules to which everyone in the community is bound.

The history of constitutions also shows how constitutions originally appealed to the combined 'we' of the religious community and the political community (tribe, kingdom, city or region) for the acceptance of the authority and binding of the law.[10] Early constitutions needed a great deal of proof for law to be accepted and binding. This is aptly illustrated by the emphatic tone and style of Hammurabi's stele, and the 'story' of the Law of Moses. The way these rules were promulgated also illustrates legislators' desire to convince the population: they are recorded on imposing structures in prominent locations (a marketplace, central square or something similar), for everyone to see, read and behold, often accompanied with pomp and ceremony.

The role of religion as the connecting element of a legal community's 'we' diminished over time. The legal community's new 'we' first became the state community, then the political state community (nation), and finally the human (global) community. These various forms of the 'we' do not succeed each other discretely. There is no clear 'end' of one period and start of a 'new' period – they are often interwoven and blend into one another. Many of the world's constitutions contain elements and features from various periods; they consist of layers, although different periods certainly have specific accents. Accents that I have highlighted and used to show the genesis of constitutions over succeeding generations.

Over time, constitutional norms have increasingly become a collaborative platform: a locus where normative notions of leadership and law are forged into large-scale cooperation. Thus, optimally employing a society's energies and – by creating a stable political society and effective legal order – offering advantages and better opportunities in the perennial competition between human groups. This has become increasingly depersonalised and more and more efficient over time: notions of normative cooperation have grown more abstract and shifted more from the physical to the imagined world. The functioning of law, democracy and the judiciary, the authority of legislative bodies, holding elections, the reprehensibility of nepotism and corruption, the importance of transparency, depersonalised government in the form of symbolic offices with powers (ministers, mayors, financial watchdogs) are just a few examples of the process of political and legal abstraction. We accord meaning (authority, etcetera) to things (institutions) that do not exist in the physical

---

[9] *Ibid.*
[10] Finnis 2011 (an adaptation of a previous article published in 1984). Finnis demonstrates that legal theory is also part of social and political theory in this respect. As is the converse: 'Law is one of the paradigms of political authority'. Finnis 2011, p. 61.

world, which we nevertheless accept as fairly self-evident conditions for our own lives and coexistence in society.[11]

The history of constitutions is above all a history of ideas. Ideas matter: they are a formative force and often drive events.[12] And they rarely simply fall out of the sky. Like historical developments, ideas are contingent. Thoughts, notions and theories respond to, build on, and mix with each other. The Enlightenment and Enlightenment political thinkers' ideas moulded the history of modern constitutions. Sets of political ideas about the source of state and governmental power, the essence of humankind, contract theory, individuality and fundamental freedom.[13] Enlightenment ideas can be reduced to one core concept: every person is endowed with the capacity to think and reason, which enables everyone to contemplate their existence and shape their destiny. This world view, known as 'rational humanism', wrests control of destiny from God and places it firmly in the hands of humankind.

Baruch Spinoza (1632–1677) is an important, perhaps the most important, nexus in this history of ideas, despite his occasional absence from annals of the great 'philosophes' of political theory.[14] Spinoza connects the mediaeval idea of a universe controlled by God and the associated concept of natural law – as a reflection of divine law – with Descartes' idea of a thinking, independent 'I': *cogito ergo sum*.[15] I think, therefore I am; therefore, I can devise everything I can or want to be. Spinoza combines these ideas: our mind is the result of a divine spark. Like Prometheus, we have all received the divine fire. Everyone can use reasoning to discover for themselves how God and nature work, what kind of order they form, and what this order signifies.[16] The longer and more coherently we think, the better we can understand

---

[11] As Thornhill puts it: 'If we assume that modern differentiated societies demand, and in fact can only effectively utilise, power as an autonomously abstracted and replicably inclusive phenomenon, the institutions of legitimate constitutional rule can be observed as normative principles that the political system of modern society produces or externalises *for itself* in order to heighten the societal abstraction of its power and to fulfil the complex requirements for positive statutory laws and rulings that characterise modern societies. The primary norms of constitutional order are thus best explicable within an exclusively internalistic and sociological paradigm.' Thornhill 2011, p. 373.

[12] Pinker 2018, p. 349. 'There can be no better proof of the power of ideas than the ironic influence of the political philosopher who most insisted on the power of vested interests, the man who wrote that "the ruling ideas of each age have ever been the ideas of its ruling class." Karl Marx possessed no wealth and commanded no army, but the ideas he scribbled in the reading room of the British Museum shaped the course of the 20th century and beyond, wrenching the lives of billions.'

[13] Yaron Ezrahi considers the idea – the fiction – of the human being as an individual detached from the group the basis of the evolution of the whole idea of liberal democracy and its associated moral and legal order. 'Disembedded individualism is a necessary fiction for the evolution of liberal democracy and its moral and legal order.' Ezrahi 2012, p. 34.

[14] For instance, there is no reference to Spinoza in Rosenfeld & Sajó 2012.

[15] Spinoza 2008 (orig. 1677), *The Ethics*, particularly part V (*Of the Power of the Understanding, or of Human Freedom*). Cf. Spinoza 2002.

[16] Spinoza concludes in his theo-political treatise that 'revealed knowledge has no overlap with natural knowledge' and that 'each person must be allowed to make up his own mind, being

this meaning. Spinoza's 'rational (legal) humanism' enjoins a journey of discovery in our own brain, with the implicit promise of linear development towards a better 'I' and a better 'we'. This is thinking and reasoning as a secular form of prayer; hunting for treasure using the secret map concealed in your head. It is a very powerful idea – amenable to a wide audience. The currents of colonialism, world conflicts and globalisation helped it on its way and spread this belief to all four corners of the world.

The history of constitutions also shows that processes of state formation and constitutional formation only started to coincide as a fixed set in the past century. It is very tempting to read all sorts of laws or patterns into this observation. Some modern observers are adamant that states cannot exist without a constitution, or vice versa. Or that there must be at least a sense of community, a people, a *demos*, a nation, an idea of shared destiny that precedes any notion of a constitution. Others argue that sovereignty and self-determination come before everything. Many contemporary constitutions may well be built on the foundations of sovereign states, or notions of nations or peoples, but this does not imply that something like a constitution is per se dependent on this. That constitutions do not as yet exist outside or above states does not prove it is not possible. The past teaches that constitutions – as rules about a community's leadership, social organisation and legal system – once existed separately to the 'state' or '(popular) sovereignty'. Besides, the history of constitutions does not dictate what constitutions 'ought to be', or the minimum conditions required to promulgate one. Joseph Weiler pokes fun at muddled normative approaches of this kind, saying that:

> [...] in many cases, constitutional doctrine presupposes the existence of that which it creates.[17]

Constitutions, like states, are belief systems. Therefore, if we were all to believe that a stateless (global or otherwise) constitution was a good idea and an appealing story, then it would surely be feasible to devise one. Many international treaties already contain traditional constitutional elements, such as fundamental freedoms, an independent judiciary and notions of the binding nature of law.[18] Whether we would (or ought to) want to live according to these non-state constitutions is another matter.

---

enabled to interpret the foundations of the faith according to his own understanding.' The 'freedom that the revealed divine law grants to everyone' implies that 'this freedom can be granted without harm to the peace of the State or the status of the sovereign, but further that it must be granted, and can't be taken away without great danger to peace and great harm to the whole republic.' 'I begin with the natural right of each person. [...] No law of nature obliges anyone to live according to someone else's understanding; everyone is the defender of his own freedom.' Baruch Spinoza, Preface, in: *Treatise on Theology and Politics* (Original title: *Tractatus Theologico-Politicus*). Cf. Spinoza 2017 (orig. 1670), p. 7 and p. 11 ff. Cf. Spinoza 2002.

17   Weiler 2001, especially p. 56.
18   De Wet 2012.

There are more and more constitutions – in reality, every state in the world has one – and they are growing increasingly similar. There seems to be convergence. The historical overview shows three main models. The first is the 'theistic' constitution, based on the idea that a community, empire or state (in short: a polity) is governed by God's will and laws, whether or not through human mediation. The second model is the 'socialist/communist' constitution as a set of rules for the journey to communist utopia via the dictatorship of the proletariat. Finally, there is the 'liberal-democratic' constitution. This model has become dominant in the past thirty years. Theistic and socialist constitutions are on the wane nowadays, becoming exceptions. Most countries have liberal democratic constitutions, which increasingly seem to resemble each other. The Australian constitutionalist Jeffrey Goldsworthy even sees a common model emerging:

> [...] the migration of constitutional ideas through judicial borrowings has facilitated the emergence, in a variety of jurisdictions, of a *common liberal democratic model* of constitutionalism.[19]

Certainly since the Second World War, the idea of a liberal (democratic) constitutional structure[20] has been increasingly espoused. This idea, or ideology, vests faith in a leadership and justice system bound by law and recognising, with minimal variation, universal human dignity, and a government that protects individual rights and freedoms as 'pre-positive' freedom axioms. The maximal variant uses the mechanism of elections to accord individual members of society a meaningful role in leadership selection and participation in allocating public funds (liberal democracy). Many states with liberal-democratic constitutions fall short of these ideals, but it is telling that so many states nevertheless endorse – or at least aspire to – this ideal and model. What other reason would there be for them to keep a constitution of this kind in the books? The provenance of liberal-democratic constitutions is unambiguous: they are the product of humanist (legal) rationalism, specifically liberal humanism as it developed in Western Europe from the seventeenth century. This is not an interpretation or form of cultural determinism, but a factual observation. Just as there are countless opinions on Hollywood films, and we know that many Hollywood films do not even come from Hollywood in Los Angeles, but it is indisputable that Hollywood is where the format comes from.

Clearly, various generations exist in modern constitutional history – periods of development of the rational-humanist constitutional model in which certain (new) features emerge or acquire a particular accent.[21] This is not only of academic

---

[19] (Jeffrey) Goldsworthy 2006, especially p. 115. My italics.
[20] Cf. Chang & Yeh 2012.
[21] My classification and categorisation of periods and constitutions differ from the economist and political scientist Jon Elster's waves of constitution making cited above. He discerns eight waves of constitution making, starting in 1780. These waves largely correspond to my generations, but he excludes monarchical and imperial constitutions. His waves also refer to

interest. As already observed, the idea of these generations enables a better understanding of modern constitutional history through its phases. It does not imply that every constitution exclusively bears features of the period in which it was promulgated. The Constitution of the United States is a revolutionary constitution, but it has also been a liberal and essentially a democratic constitution from its inception. Most constitutions have various features and layers, rather like layers of sediment from various periods.

moments at which various constitutions in the period were written, but he is not always conscious of the substantive features and similarities of the documents concerned. Elster poses an important question: why does there seem to be a rhythm in constitution making? Why do countries appear to decide to promulgate constitutions (of a certain kind) simultaneously? Elster 1995, p. 368–370.

PART III

Concepts, Shapes and Types of Constitutions

18

What Is a Constitution?

On 13 February 2008, the British Justice Secretary, Jack Straw, made a speech at the George Washington University in the United States in which he announced:

> The next stage in the United Kingdom's constitutional development is to look at whether we need better to articulate those rights which are scattered across a whole host of different places, and indeed the responsibilities that go with being British. [...] We can learn a great deal from the United States example, and particularly with regard to the enviable notion of civic duty that seems to flow so strongly through American veins [...].[1]

Straw's gambit might have seemed uncontroversial enough to his American audience, but it caused great indignation at home. Many Britons are proud of their country's lack of a written constitution. In an article in the *Independent* explaining why the United Kingdom did not need an instrument of this kind, Nigel Morris sniffed: 'essentially because the country has been too stable for too long.'[2] To the likes of Morris, a written constitution is something more suitable for countries incapable of maintaining sustainable, stable political relations without artificial intervention. Straw's plans for something as primitive as a written constitution for the United Kingdom simply did not pass muster.

Taking pride in lacking a written constitution is an unusual – and perhaps even refreshing – stance in a world dominated by these documents. It is also a good example of the British penchant for exceptionalism ('splendid isolation'). But is it actually correct? Does the United Kingdom really lack a written constitution? It is certainly not the case that the United Kingdom has always been so politically stable that it did not need any written rules on state organisation. In the aftermath of the

---

[1] Quoted by Peter Hoskin, (Coffeeshop blog), *Towards a written constitution?* 14 February 2008
    https://blogs.spectator.co.uk/2008/02/towards-a-written-constitution/ (consulted 16 June 2018).
[2] Nigel Morris, 'The Big Question: Why doesn't the UK have a written constitution, and does it
    matter?', *Independent*, 14 February 2008.

English Civil War in the seventeenth century, the Bill of Rights (1689) was drafted during the Glorious Revolution. These written rules were intended to ensure peaceful and politically stable relations in King William and Queen Mary's new monarchical regime, laying the foundations of British parliamentary democracy, which prevail to this day. Many other documents – still in force – also contain rules which are considered written constitutional rules in the United Kingdom. These include the Magna Carta (1215), guaranteeing a number of fundamental freedoms and privileges; the Case of Proclamations (1611), limiting the Royal Prerogative; the Act of Settlement (1701) on succession to the throne and judicial independence; the Reform Act (1832) on parliamentary organisation and elections; the Parliament Act (1911) on the powers of the chambers of parliament; the Representation of the People Act (1918) on electoral law; the Parliament Act (1948) on the powers of the House of Lords; the recent Human Rights Act (1998), incorporating of European human rights into British law; and the Constitutional Reform Act (2005), establishing the British Supreme Court. In this light, Dicey's classic definition[3] would give the United Kingdom at least ten written constitutions, or constitutional documents.[4] They have simply not been merged into a single document and, most significantly, are not considered a 'constitution' or 'constitutions' by the British. The United Kingdom is hardly unique in this; Sweden and Israel do not have a single constitutional document referred to as *the* 'constitution', although they seem to be less preoccupied by labels.

Anyway, it seems only fair to conclude that all countries nowadays have written constitutional rules of some sort; only some countries do not call them a 'constitution'. Why bother? What is in a name? Quite a bit, actually.

CONSTITUTION, CONSTITUTIONAL RULES: WHAT IS IN A NAME?

We have thus far not really considered an accurate definition of the concept constitution. This has been a deliberate strategy. Debates about definitions are mind-numbingly tedious, causing historical myopia. They are also sometimes confusing because definitions are pervaded by normative elements about what a constitution ought to be. But after a long journey through constitutional history, we can no longer avoid saying something about modern constitutional concepts or definitions. What do we mean by constitutions nowadays? Do we mean the same phenomenon or various things?

---

[3] 'All rules which directly or indirectly affect the distribution or the exercise of the sovereign in a state.' Dicey 1982 (orig. 1889). Cf. chapter 5.

[4] There are possibly more, including the Assize of Clarendon (1166), Laws in Wales Acts (1536 and 1543), Petition of Right (1628), the Habeas Corpus Act (1679), the Acts of Union (1707, 1800 and 1801), etcetera.

The Meaning of Constitution

What does the word itself mean? The first two definitions of constitution in the Oxford English Dictionary are:

> 'A decree, ordinance, law, regulation; usually, one made by a superior authority, civil
> or ecclesiastical'; and: 'The way in which anything is constituted or made up [...]',
> 'Physical nature or character of the body in regard to healthiness, strength, vitality, etc.'
> The first definition associated with state organisation is relegated to the third position.
> 'The mode in which a state is constituted or organized; especially, as to the location of
> the sovereign power, as a monarchical, oligarchical, or democratic constitution.'

The more technical definition is relegated to seventh place: 'The system or body of fundamental principles according to which a nation, state, or body politic is constituted and governed.'

This latter definition contains the word 'fundamental', referring to the basis or foundations. This constitutional association with something fundamental or fundamental law can also be found in other European languages. In German 'constitution' is *Grundgesetz* (basic law), in Norwegian and Danish a constitution is called *Grundlov*, in Dutch *grondwet* and in Swedish *grundlagar*: all refer to 'ground'. Constitutions and constitutional law are – therefore – also referred to as fundamental law, and 'basic law'.

There is also a more historic element in the term. The word 'constitution' comes from the Latin *constituere*, meaning something like 'establish', 'appoint', 'form', or 'assemble'. It was already used in the Roman Empire in the first sense to refer to an emperor's edicts, a very different kind of statute to what we would understand by constitution. Constitution usually bears the meaning 'frame' – the basic set-up, 'skeleton' or framework of an entity. In this sense, it is usually used to indicate fundamental rules on the form of government. 'Constitution' (French and English) refers to this idea of a 'frame', as does *constitución* (Spanish), *costituzione* (Italian), *constituição* (Portuguese) or *Verfassung* (German, especially in Austria and Switzerland).

As the British example shows, there is no uniform, universal definition of the concept constitution. The significance of a constitution is first and foremost a matter of self-interpretation. What does a country, author or anyone else think the definition is or ought to be?[5]

Rules with a Higher Status

Not everything is subjective though. Regardless of how a constitution is defined, it never just means any set of statutes, regulations or law. When we deem a set

---

5   Including Dixon and Ginsburg: 'Perhaps the most straightforward way in which to define the
     constitutional domain is by reference to the text of legal instruments that are expressly labelled
     by their drafters as "constitutional".' Dixon & Ginsburg 2011, p. 4.

of rules a constitution, it always has a foundational connotation. A constitution has a higher status than other legal rules in our eyes. It is a solemn, lofty kind of law, usually preceded by an overture in the form of a preamble. When we refer to *the* Constitution (and not constitutions in general) most jurisdictions capitalise the instrument to accord it respect. This to underscore that this kind of law precedes state institutions, proclaims the political, administrative and legal system and endows it with authority. As constitutions have a foundational function, constitutions almost invariably have a higher status than other rules or legal norms in a legal system. A constitution is usually regarded as supreme law or paramount because it is the cornerstone of the entire order. The legal norms of a constitution give legal force to all other norms, enabling the creation and application of legal norms. The Austrian legal philosopher Hans Kelsen (1881–1973) goes as far as asserting that a constitution has a legally higher status than ordinary laws by logical necessity. Without a higher status, a constitution could be disregarded by any ordinary law or judicial decision. Kelsen argued that without this higher status, a constitution is no longer a constitution; without a higher status, it is meaningless.[6] Or, as the United States Supreme Court stated in its 1803 ruling in the case *Marbury v. Madison*:

> The constitution is either a superior, paramount law, unchangeable by ordinary means, or it is on a level with ordinary legislative acts, and, like other acts, is alterable when the legislature shall please to alter it.
>
> If the former part of the alternative be true, then a legislative act contrary to the constitution is not law: if the latter part be true, then written constitutions are absurd attempts, on the part of the people, to limit a power in its own nature illimitable.[7]

Constitutional Entrenchment by Way of Complex Amendment Procedures

A constitution is thus a form of basic law with a higher status.[8] This status may be protected by the constitutional amendment or revision procedure.[9] Most of the world's constitutions have strict requirements for amendment or revision[10] and

---

[6] Cf. Kelsen 2008 (orig. 1929), p. Cf. Kelsen 1967 (orig. 1960 [1934]), p. 263–266. Cf. Troper 2005.

[7] Marbury v. Madison, 5 U.S. (1 Cranch) 137; 2 L. Ed. 60 (1803), *U.S. Lexis* 352.

[8] Grimm 2012, p. 109–114.

[9] Some argue that constitutions ought to be difficult to amend if they are to maintain their constitutional nature. Cooter, for instance, considers the essence of a constitution that it is 'more general' than other laws, has 'precedence' over ordinary laws, and is *more difficult* to amend. Cooter 2000, p. 1. Cf. Gilbert 2017.

[10] Some countries, like Austria, Bulgaria, Costa Rica, Nicaragua and Spain, distinguish between a constitutional *amendment* and a constitutional *revision*. Constitutional 'revisions' often imply more substantial changes and therefore require higher thresholds for adoption than a mere constitutional amendment, writes the International Idea 2014 report on Constitutional Amendment Procedures. 'Such a distinction follows the assumption that the authority to

cannot simply be amended or revised by a simple majority vote in parliament, an executive decision or a judicial ruling.[11] Procedural requirements, like supermajority votes, double-decision rules, or reference to the people or states (provinces/regions), aim to prevent constitutional amendments from being taken too lightly by simple majorities or without in-depth debate.[12]

A wide variety of amendment/revision procedures try to make countries think twice or deeply before changing the constitution.[13] The American Constitution, for instance, can only be amended through a two-step procedure: a law proposing an amendment must be passed with a two-thirds majority vote by Congress (or a convention of states),[14] and then ratified by a three-quarters majority of states.[15] Many countries have amendment procedures to entrench constitutional content.

Procedural entrenchments of this kind are put in place to 'rigidify' a constitution – making amendments cumbersome in order to protect the constitution's fundamental rules from ill-advised, arbitrary change. Rigid revision procedures come in many shapes and sizes.[16] They sometimes involve supermajorities (a three-fifth majority requirement, such as in the Slovakian Constitution, or, more commonly forms of the two-thirds majority requirement), or various readings (or cooling-off periods). Occasionally they involve substantive entrenchment, with the constitution determining which parts may and may not be amended.[17] A famous example of this

---

amend a constitution implies the introduction of adjustments, modifications or changes within the constitution but does not include the power to exchange/replace it or its original structure.' International Idea 2014, p. 6.

[11] Amendment is not the same as interpretation. Judicial interpretation can admittedly result in constitutional provisions being applied or understood in a completely different way to their authors' intentions. Nevertheless, interpretation lacks the intention and authority to change the constitution.

[12] In Hungary, the Constitution may be amended by a simple two-thirds majority in the unicameral legislature (the House of the Nation). There is a low threshold for amending the constitution, especially as the electoral system makes it relatively easy for a ruling party to achieve a supermajority. Indeed, as the International Idea 2014 report on Constitutional Amendment Procedures notes, 'since the spring of 2010, Hungary's *Fidesz* government has been dismantling the system of constitutional checks and balances to create a state that centralizes political control in the hands of one political (coalition) party. Twelve constitutional amendments in the first year of governing removed most of the institutional checks that could have stopped what the government did next, which was to install a new constitution that has been regarded by many as weakening Hungary's democracy and its rule-of-law standard.' International Idea 2014, p. 13.

[13] Albert 2019.

[14] Called for by two-thirds of the state legislatures. Article V United States Constitution.

[15] More precisely: according to article V of the US Constitution, an amendment must be ratified by either – as determined by Congress – the legislatures of three-quarters of the states or state ratifying conventions in three-quarters of the states in order to become part of the Constitution. Cf. Tushnet 2009b.

[16] Cf. Dixon 2011; Böckenförde 2017.

[17] Cf., for instance, article 288 of the Portuguese Constitution, which bans amendments on many issues like national independence, the unity of the state, the republican form of government, the separation between church and state, citizens' rights, freedoms and guarantees, the rights of workers, workers' committees and trade unions, etcetera. In 2014, more than 70

is the aforementioned *eternity clause* in the German Constitution, which prohibits changes to fundamental elements of the constitution, such as fundamental rights and the structure of the state and the rule of law.[18]

Modern constitutions often combine procedural and substantive hurdles to prevent ill-considered constitutional changes, such as the Constitution of Guinea-Bissau.[19] Putting constitutional norms too firmly under lock and key, on the other hand, risks ossification: constitutional rules that are difficult or impossible to adapt to changing circumstances and exigencies of changing times.[20] If a constitutional order becomes too rigid it also risks being rendered unusable and irrelevant. In the worst case, the basic rules of the game are adjusted outside the constitutional framework. This is not necessarily disastrous,[21] but an increasingly obsolete constitution is of no use to anyone and ceases to be a constitution at a certain point. Many countries try to balance structure and adaptability in the design of their constitutional revision procedure. The German constitutionalist Karl Loewenstein argued that a measure of flexibility works best:

> the process of constitutional amendment everywhere is best kept sensibly elastic, neither too rigid to invite, with changing conditions, revolutionary rapture, nor too flexible to allow basic modifications without the consent of qualified majorities.[22]

Another reason to keep constitutions 'living' is the passing of generations. One of the founding fathers of the United States, Thomas Jefferson, wrote a famous letter to James Madison on the possibility of constitutional revision, and the need for flexible amendment procedures, saying that 'the dead should not govern the living'.[23] At least not without good reason.

---

constitutions around the world included such unamendable provisions. The content of these provisions differs widely from country to country. Examples of immutable provisions include national unity (Indonesia), the status of religion (Tunisia), the multi-party system (Romania), the democratic or republican form of government (France), electoral rights (Brazil), basic human rights (Germany) and presidential term limits (Honduras). International Idea 2014, p. 8–10. The number has even gone up. In 2018, the Constitute database reported 78 constitutions with unamendable provisions (41% of all constitutions) – or seventy-seven, if we contend (as some do) that article V of the US Constitution is amendable too.

[18] Article 79, paragraph 3.
[19] Articles 128 to 131 of the Constitution.
[20] Gilbert 2017.
[21] Passchier 2017; Schwartzberg 2014 including chapter 6 *Constitutionalism without Supermajorities*.
[22] Loewenstein 1951, p. 215. For a detailed description of the origin and problems of qualified majorities (supermajorities), including in establishing and amending constitutional rules, cf. Schwartzberg 2014.
[23] Jefferson's aphorism in his letter to James Madison from Paris on 6 September 1789 was actually slightly different. He put it even better (but less concisely): 'The question Whether one generation of men has a right to bind another, seems never to have been started either on this or our side of the water. Yet it is a question of such consequences as not only to merit decision, but place also, among the fundamental principles of every government. […] I set out on this ground which I suppose to be self-evident, "that the earth belongs in usufruct to the

A common flexible variant at the present time is a 'normal' parliamentary procedure followed by a referendum: a review procedure used in Ireland, Côte d'Ivoire,
Djibouti and Guinea. An amendment procedure of this kind allows a constitution
to be strong enough to offer shelter, whilst moving with the prevailing winds without breaking. 'A good constitution tilts without tumbling over', according to the
American game theorist and legal scholar Robert Cooter.[24]

A constitution lacking forms of procedural entrenchment can also be fundamental or of a higher order, although this may invite difficulties.[25] The Indian
Constitution of 1949 permits amendment by simple parliamentary majority –
which is essentially still the case.[26] An amendment procedure of this kind risks,
as Hans Kelsen predicted, piecemeal destruction of a constitution. A constitution
is essentially degraded to the level of an ordinary law if parliament can amend it
with simple majorities at will – however democratic the decision may be. This
may be undesirable as it strips the constitution of its fundamental character. The
Indian Supreme Court concurred, ruling in 1973 in the case *Kesavananda Bharati
v. State of Kerala*[27] that certain parts of the constitution could not be amended by
a simple parliamentary majority. The court argued that the unchangeable basic
structure of the Indian Constitution included norms about the rule of law, the
independence of the judiciary, the doctrine of the separation of powers, federalism, secularism, sovereignty and the republican form of government, the principle
of democracy, the parliamentary system, the principle of free and fair elections,
and so on.

The Constitution as a Legal Obligation

Another core tenet of the concept constitution is the idea of 'legal obligation'. The
rules in a constitution are compulsory: they are legal norms that must be observed. A
constitution lacking legal obligation or merely seen as a set of grandiloquent appeals
and precepts to which no one feels bound, is not a real constitution. This is true
regardless of the definition used.

Une constitution est un corps de lois obligatoires, ou ce n'est rien.[28]

---

living;" that the dead have neither powers nor rights over it.' *The Letters of Thomas Jefferson
1743–1826.* www.let.rug.nl/usa/presidents/thomas-jefferson/letters-of-thomas-jefferson/jefl81.php
(Consulted 18 June 2018). Cf. Sunstein 2009, Introduction *Jefferson's Revenge.*
[24] Cooter 2000, p. 372. Cf. Gilbert 2017.
[25] Cf. Gilbert 2017.
[26] Article 368 Constitution of India.
[27] Supreme Court of India (Constitutional Bench) 24 April 1973, His Holiness Kesavananda
Bharati Sripadagalvaru and others. v. State of Kerala and Anr. (1973) 4 *SCC* 225.
[28] Emmanuel Joseph Sieyès, proceedings of 5 August 1794 (*Amande* – Almond), *Opinion de
Sieyès sur les attributions et l'organisation du jury constitutionnaire proposé le 2 thermidor*, prononcée à la Convention nationale le 18 du même, l'an III de la République, dans *Moniteur*,
Séance du 18 thermidor an III, p. 1311. Sieyès 1794.

as the great French revolutionary, the Abbé Sieyès, observed as early as 1794: 'a constitution is a body of obligatory laws or it is nothing at all'. A constitution establishes first and foremost a 'legal order'.[29] It is a set of rules with one shared and central objective: making the law and legal order it proclaims legally binding. In modern constitutions this usually coincides with the idea of the rule of law, often but not necessarily supplanting the idea of being governed by human or 'divine' leaders. There are still constitutions that establish a legal order with norms aiming to bring citizens together, but in which the rule of law[30] has not (completely) replaced 'rule by men'. China is one such example.[31]

The Constitution as a Creation

As well establishing a legal order, modern constitutions create and regulate governmental power.[32] Contemporary constitutions establish government (the function of leadership) in a state and organise it by a conscious act of creation. Constitutions occasionally assume that something already existed which can be built upon – a pre-existing structure of a state, a body of states, regions or provinces,[33] peoples, existing laws and traditions, etcetera. Yet, however commonplace and sensible this may seem, it is actually the exception. Most of the world's constitutions give the impression that the state system it proclaims is completely new and nothing existed hitherto. They are predominantly *ex nihilo* creations that organise the future and create a new 'we'. If the past is mentioned, it is mostly in a preliminary statement such as a preamble. Even if a constitution does not change the current situation

---

[29] It therefore necessarily has a *legal* character – the essence of a constitution is largely dependent on it. Cf. Grimm 2012, p. 105–108.

[30] When the Constitution for the Commonwealth of Massachusetts (adopted 1780) was established, the future president of the United States, John Adams, wrote of the purpose of the constitution's system of government: 'to the end it may be a government of laws, and not of men.'

[31] Mazur & Ursu 2011. They assert on page 376: 'In particular, the absence of a true rule of law in China seems to defy conventional wisdom about the necessary institutional prerequisites for successful economic development.'

[32] Dixon and Ginsburg call this: '[…] the role of constitutions in both "checking" and "creating" government power.' Dixon & Ginsburg 2011, p. 4.

[33] An example is Article 124 in the Dutch Constitution: 'The powers of provinces and municipalities to regulate and administer their own internal affairs shall be delegated to their administrative organs.' The word 'delegated' is a somewhat misleading, legalese translation of the Dutch word 'overgelaten' in the article which actually means 'left up to'. The constitutional wording here indicates that provinces and municipalities existed before the constitutional order of 1814 and already possessed autonomous powers. Saying that the regulation and administration of their internal affairs is 'left up to' provincial and municipal authorities recognises their (pre-existing) autonomous self-rule. The constitution of 1814 'recognises' provincial and municipal self-rule and assigns it a place in the new dispensation. Recognition is, of course, an act of creation. Without recognition in 1814, the municipalities and provinces would have been unable to act and decide legally, no matter how long they had existed.

or its norms are merely a logical continuation of the past, it is often presented as something novel. Thus, the Swedish Instrument of Government of 1974 stipulates: 'The King or Queen who occupies the throne of Sweden in accordance with the Act of Succession shall be the Head of State'.[34] Sweden has been a monarchy with a monarch as head of the state since the sixteenth century – this has not only been so since 1974. The 2011 Constitution of Hungary says something similar: 'Hungary shall be an independent, democratic rule-of-law State'.[35] Despite any shortcomings in practice, Hungary was already a democratic constitutional state before 2011.

Constitutions create the universe of law – they create the legal system's virtual, imagined order and determine how it works. A sort of a judicial 'Big Bang'. Once established by a constitution, legal systems determine who is authorised to do what and under what conditions within the legal community it defines. Who exercises power, with what kind of authority? Who is entitled to collect and distribute resources? How can people be mobilised and deployed, under which kind of obligation? Legal systems also lay down how law itself is formed (or 'found'), applied and interpreted, who occupies which public offices, which resources offices may use, they even extend to issues like how we gain and assess status (diplomas, recognition, through to orders and electoral rights). Above all, constitutional rules determine the 'official' story of the 'we' of the state, the 'we' of society, the 'we' of the legal system.[36] This ensures that we perceive the legal and leadership system established by the constitution as 'real', official, authentic, valid and (therefore) binding. It does not always work, but it is what constitutions try to achieve: imprinting the real, official story.

Constitutions are by no means always the alpha and omega of the rules that determine who can do what and under what conditions in a state. Most countries have other – fundamental – rules in addition to their constitution: The *Constitution Outside the Constitution*.[37] Forms of constitutional law resulting from long-standing traditions, time-honoured practices, customs or 'conventions'. The latter are mostly unwritten practices of constitutional behaviour that have been followed so consistently and which are believed to have such force that they are generally considered to govern constitutional behaviour.[38] Conventions are often engrained in the

---

[34] Article 5.

[35] Article B.

[36] What Law calls a constitution's *ideological narrative*: 'It is a core function of constitutions to justify the existence and organisation of the state.' Law 2016, p. 153.

[37] Cf. Young 2007; Tushnet 2012, p. 224–225.

[38] Legal scholars agree that it is actually quite difficult to pinpoint what a constitutional convention is. What, for instance, distinguishes a mere social convention, like say, not eating soup with your bare hands at official dinners, from a real constitutional convention? '[C]onstitutional convention', Jaconelli argues, 'is to be limited to those social rules that possess a constitutional – and not merely a political – significance.' Jaconelli 2005, p. 151. A somewhat circular line of reasoning. More to the point is Jaconelli's analysis that there is a *conceptual gap* between law and conventions – they each perform different functions, have different contexts, and cannot be simply be lumped together. Jaconelli 2005, p. 153–156. The key difference is

constitutional system itself and are so strong that it is very difficult to deviate from them. For example, New Zealand has an unwritten convention on caretaker government that a government must significantly constrain its decision-making if it loses the confidence of the House of Representatives, despite having full legal powers to govern.[39] Another convention in the Land of the Long White Cloud is the practice that the sovereign only acts on the advice of ministers, subordinating the queen's legal powers (and those of her representative in New Zealand, the governor-general) to cabinet, notwithstanding the fact that there is no 'legal' obligation to do so.[40]

Such extra-constitutional constitutional rules and norms are a widespread phenomenon in constitutional systems. Organic laws (as laws relating to the organs of state are referred to in many continental systems), statutory interpretation laws,[41] unwritten law, legal principles, court rulings, conventions (customs that impart legal duty), precedent (as with convention, cases in which authorities believe should be dealt with in a certain way again in the future) and (more morally binding) traditions[42] and customs. The British State Opening of Parliament and the accompanying Queen's Speech are, for instance, steeped in ritual and custom, with pomp and pageantry ranging from a grand carriage procession, a royal 'hostage', the searching of the cellars,[43] the royal regalia (the royal crown, the ceremonial Sword of State

---

that constitutional conventions 'bind' differently to ordinary legal rules and are complied with on a different footing. In the words of Marshall: 'No general reason needs to be advanced to account for compliance with duty-imposing conventions beyond the fact that when they are obeyed (rather than disobeyed, rejected or changed), they are believed to formulate valid rules of obligation.' Marshall 1984, p. 210. Cf. the TeAra website https://teara.govt.nz/en/constitution/page-2 (consulted 6 November 2019).

[39] In my home country, the Netherlands, the 'convention of 1922' is an example of a constitutional convention. This rule dating back to 1922 prescribes that when the Dutch House of Representatives has been dissolved for elections, an outgoing cabinet does not await the electoral results (and see if it can hold onto power) but resigns on the eve of the elections. A somewhat less strictly observed convention – and more controversial – is the 'convention of 1966', which holds that a newly-elected House of Representatives can only produce a cabinet of a single political combination and that negotiations after the fall of a cabinet cannot result in a new cabinet coalition of a completely different political hue. The idea of it stands to reason, but there is a lot of controversy in the Netherlands on the question whether it is really a rule or a constitutional convention. Conventions are often moving targets, and – especially in political arenas – controversial.

[40] Cf. the TeAra website https://teara.govt.nz/en/constitution/page-2 (consulted 6 November 2019).

[41] Laws with provisions binding institutions, especially judges, in their interpretation of legislative acts. This kind of act is quite common in (former) commonwealth countries, for example, Australia's the Acts Interpretation Act 1901, the Interpretation Act 1985 in Canada, the General Clauses and Interpretation Ordinance 1966 in Hongkong, the Interpretation Act 1999 and the Interpretation Amendment Act 2005 in New Zealand and many others. A Dutch example is the venerable, almost forgotten, *Wet Algemeene bepalingen* (General Provisions Act) of 1829.

[42] For more on the nature and development of traditions, cf. Hobsbawm & Ranger 1984.

[43] In 1605 Guy Fawkes and the Gunpowder Plotters tried to assassinate king James I by blowing up the houses of parliament on the occasion of the King's speech to parliament. A memorable event. The British have commemorated the failed attempt every year since on Guy Fawkes Day (5 November).

and the Cap of Maintenance) to the slamming parliament's doors and knocking on them with black rods. These customs and traditions – however strange as they may appear at first sight – express, more than anything, historical bonds and lineages in a political society, a veneration of (the wisdom of) past generations; they define and underline the 'we' of the constitutional community.

In every country, there are more constitutional rules and norms than the provisions contained in the written constitution. Constitutional rules outside the constitution are somewhat confusing, especially the so-called unwritten ones. Do these unwritten constitutional rules and principles have equal status and the same binding force as the written kind? Are they all part and parcel of the same constitutional system, or are unwritten constitutional rules and principles, like respect for human dignity, the right to life and freedom or the independence of the judiciary,[44] even more fundamental than written constitutional rules? Do they precede the written, man-made, part of the constitution and take precedence over its norms?[45] For this reason, some countries distinguish between constitutional law and 'extra-constitutional law' or 'supra-constitutional law'. Sometimes this is to denote that extra or supra-constitutional norms are part of the whole of the constitutional system, sometimes to underscore that these norms precede and therefore may trump positive constitutional norms and law. Or, as is the case in some anglophone legal systems, it serves to emphasise that present-day, positive (constitutional) law builds on common law. As Trevor Allan explains:

> In anglophone legal systems, the common law provides a constitutional foundation for legitimate government. It embodies a tradition of governmental compliance with the rule of law, subjecting official decisions and actions to independent judicial scrutiny. The evolution of common law principle, prompted by changing moral attitudes within society at large, provides for the adaptation of traditional values to present conditions. It enables the abstract clauses of a "written" constitution to acquire new meaning and gives an "unwritten" constitution its principal legal content. [...] In a common law legal order, authoritative texts – whatever their formal status – are interpreted as elements of that larger constitutional design. Their true meaning and legal consequences are always matters of conscientious moral

---

[44] Cf., for an interesting recent case, the *Semenyih Jaya Sdn Bhd v Pentadbir Tanah Daerah Hulu Langat* judgment in which the Malaysian Apex Court struck down a law requiring High Court judges presiding over contested land acquisition cases to be bound by the assessments of lay assessors in their judgments. A law that ran counter to the principle of the independence of the judiciary – a principle that, according to the Apex Court, forms part of the 'basic features' of the Constitution. Case [2017] 3 MLJ 561 (Federal Court). Cf. Tay 2019, p. 115–116.

[45] In his famous article on common law and legislation (Harvard Law Review 1908) Roscoe Pound opposes the idea of unwritten (natural) law principles trumping legislation. He argues that '[...] the purely personal and arbitrary character of all natural law theories, demonstrates the impossibility of maintaining any such doctrine.' Ideas of this kind can be harmful, Pound continues, 'there are those who maintain there are extra-constitutional limitations upon legislative power, and some such feeling on the part of judges contributes not a little to the current attitude toward legislation.' Pound 1908, p. 393.

judgment, undertaken within the context of a strong legal tradition: The exercise of power is everywhere subject to moral scrutiny and the standing requirement of reasoned justification.[46]

However noble the intentions of these distinctions may be, they are often confusing. Discussing how norms, principles, precedents, conventions or common law precede, inspire or trump written constitutions ignores the fact that it is the constitution itself that actually breathes life into a legal system. Without a constitution of any kind, there is no law, no legally binding effect of whatever norm in the first place. Constitutions are fundamental to the existence of legal systems: they proclaim them. Unwritten law, principles, and what have you are thus always and per se part of a country's constitutional system; without the edifice of the constitution there would be no legal system. For stars to shine, there needs to be a firmament.

The distinction between constitutional and extra-constitutional law is also often used to elucidate who makes these rules,[47] even though not always in enlightening ways. The political scientist David Law's distinction between 'large-C' and 'small-c' constitutions is more useful to help us distinguish sorts and shapes of constitutional law. A large-C constitution, according to Law, is a formal, legal document that confers on itself the status of supreme or fundamental law, regulates (state) power, and protects its supreme status by imposing requirements on amendments. A small-c constitution:

> [...] consists of the body of rules, practices, and understandings, written or unwritten, that actually determines who holds what kind of power, under what conditions, and subject to what limits.[48]

Almost all of the 192 constitutions included in the Constitute database in 2018 are both large-C and small-c constitutions. This distinction also shows that small-c constitutions preceded formal, state constitutions by millennia. Aristotle's Greek city-states' constitutions, for example, or the constitution of the Holy Roman Empire were certainly not large-C, but small-c constitutions they were. In sum: a constitution is either a document a country or state refers to as such, or a set of fundamental rules about leadership and a legal system of a community with a higher status than normal laws and hence more difficult to amend.[49] Or both.

---

[46] Allan 2007, p. 185. In Allen's view: 'the common law is prior to legislative supremacy, which it defines and regulates.' Allan 2001, p. 271. Jeffrey Goldsworthy debunks this 'confusing' idea of 'common law constitutionalism'. He feels it threatens or promises to 'replace legislative supremacy with judicial supremacy. Instead of Parliament being the master of the constitution, with the ability to change any part of it (except, perhaps, for the doctrine of legislative supremacy itself), the judges turn out to be in charge.' (Jeffrey) Goldsworthy 2007, p. 205–206.

[47] Cf. Tushnet 2012, p. 228–230. Neither does he consider the distinction enlightening in all respects.

[48] Law 2010, p. 376.

[49] Cf. Dixon & Ginsburg 2011, p. 4–5.

Calling a document a constitution is, of course. not very significant in itself. Nigeria, Sudan and Russia have documents that are both large-C and small-c constitutions, brimming with fine words, but they fail to live up to them. Promising all manner of things which the government does not deliver, they jostle for first place in the 'sham constitutions' rankings[50] (see Chapter 21). And what about North Korea and China? They have constitutions too, but both lack the rule of law, and are what are termed undemocratic, unfree, one-party states.[51] A *real* constitution is, of course, not just any document; nowadays it is fairly generally accepted that a 'real' constitution also embodies a universal ideal: a government serving its citizens whilst protecting their inalienable rights and freedoms, elected leaders abiding by the law, the distribution of governmental power amongst different agencies, and an independent judiciary settling disputes.[52] In short: constitutions that comply with the tenets of constitutionalism, the ideology that plays such a major role in contemporary constitutional theory (see the next section). This also explains why the question 'what is a constitution?' does not stop at an academic, disengaged debate. It touches hearts and minds. The dimensions of a constitution as both an aspiration and a practice, as idealism and reality are all intertwined in its conceptual formation.[53] This is contentious territory.[54] As with football, music and politics, it is difficult to discuss what a constitution 'is' without a notion of what it 'should be'. It is problematic, but perhaps also the beauty of the subject.

APPROACHES TO CONSTITUTIONAL LAW

As so often in the study of law, there is no clear, uniform and single definition of 'a constitution' or 'constitutional law' for that matter. When it comes to defining legal concepts and definitions, legal scholars are like doctors around a sickbed: they disagree on much if not everything. But they concur on one thing: small-c and large-C constitutions are insufficiently revealing. It is a far too formal and coarse distinction, failing to take into account the 'essence' of a constitution. To avoid getting ensnared in such discussions, the *Oxford Handbook of Comparative Constitutional Law* devotes hundreds of pages to conceptualising constitutional law. However valuable these learned analyses may be, they leave interested onlookers baffled. It is useful to know that there are really only three kinds of basic approaches to the question of what constitutions are: formal, material and ideological. 'Formal approaches', encountered above, conceive of a constitution as a law, or several

---

[50] Law & Versteeg 2013, p. 899.
[51] Cf. Wen-Chen & Law 2018.
[52] Law & Versteeg 2011.
[53] Holmes 2012.
[54] 'A substantive definition is impossible', Van Maarseveen and Van der Tang lamented, after having tried their best. Van Maarseveen & Van der Tang 1978, p. 232.

laws, with a special status.[55] The special status of a law of this kind can be indicated by various things, such as the special promulgation (or the special enactment[56] or revision procedure), the name of the document ('Constitution', 'Grundgesetz', 'Constituição' and so forth), its special (hierarchical) position in relation to other legislation, or a combination of these elements. This conception of constitutions is very much a formal approach, largely overlapping with the large-C definition, in which a constitution is defined by external characteristics (procedure, external or outward characteristics). The second approach conceives of constitutions 'substantively' as systems of rules aimed at establishing and delimiting governmental power.[57] 'Functional' or 'substantive' approaches (like that of the small-c constitution) consider a constitution to be primarily a set of rules aimed at attributing and delimiting governmental powers, and regulating and delimiting the exercise of public power of any kind.

THE BELIEF IN CONSTITUTIONALISM

The 'political' or 'ideological' concept closely links the phenomenon constitution to ideal types of a political society's functioning in a state. Approaches of this kind consider constitutions primarily as a political act, one in which a constitution is seen as the expression of the will of a sovereign people or nation to manifest itself (self-determination, sovereignty), proclaiming an independent political unit (state) and organising its leadership and legal system independently (constitutional autonomy).[58] In most cases, this line of thinking does not consider constitutions just any political act, but acts with distinct ideological underpinnings. The best-known instance of this approach, 'constitutionalism' is not primarily concerned with addressing the question what a constitution actually *is*, but rather what a constitution *ought to be*. One of the basic constitutionalist principles is that a people ought to have a certain form of constitution with a particular form.[59] In the words of the American political scientist Walter Murphy:

> Constitutionalism is a normative political creed that endorses a special kind of political order, one whose principal tenet is as follows: Although government is necessary to a life that is truly human, every exercise of governmental power should be subject to *substantive* limitations and obligations.[60]

---

[55] For the Austrian philosopher of law Hans Kelsen, the fact that a constitution takes precedence over a parliamentary law – to which it is hierarchically superior – is the essential characteristic of a constitution. Kelsen 1967 (orig. 1960 [1934]), p. 263–266.

[56] For example, by a constituent assembly.

[57] The difference between a 'constitution in a formal and in a substantive sense'. Grimm 2012, p. 106.

[58] Cf. Weiler 2003.

[59] Henkin 1994, p. 40–41.

[60] Murphy 2007, p. 6.

Constitutionalism is the political belief in government constrained by rules (especially the rule of law).[61] Constitutional ideology also fits well with a number of modern democratic theories based on the equality of all individuals as the source of, and
endowed with, the individual fundamental freedoms that are the core value and
starting point of a just society. But constitutionalism is as diverse as its adherents.[62]
There are myriad perspectives, but no conclusive definition. It is rather like art or
literature, as the human rights philosopher Louis Henkin puts it:

> Constitutionalism is nowhere defined. [Yet] we speak of it as if its meaning is self-
> evident, or that we know it when we see it.[63]

Murphy says supporters mostly agree on two things: a) governmental power must be
'limited' and minorities must be protected (at the very least procedurally), and b) it
must serve the well-being of citizens.[64] It goes without saying that this normative theory
is incompatible with totalitarianism and highly authoritarian forms of government.[65]

There are several variants of constitutionalism, including 'negative constitutionalism' which is predominantly focused on what a government is not allowed to
do, government abstinence. 'Positive constitutionalism' is more focused on human
development and the active role this demands of government to create the conditions for all to fully enjoy their fundamental freedoms.[66] Modern welfare states, for
instance, try to put this conviction into practice, often with constitutions requiring
them to do so.

Constitutionalism is not a phenomenon but a conviction, or a 'belief', as Murphy
sees it.[67] Believers sometimes fanatically express this belief, not as one idea amongst
many, but as *the* truth, the product of an irrefutable emanation, the outcome of
history.[68] It is difficult to debate with believers. Constitutionalism, as the dominant

---

[61]   Cf. Warren 1989, p. 511. There are again various views on this. Ten observes: 'In the spe-
     cific context of the United States of America, constitutionalism is often associated with issues
     related to the correct method of interpreting the Constitution, and to the role of the Supreme
     Court in constraining legislation. According to the doctrine of "originalism," the Constitution
     is to be interpreted by a historical inquiry into the concrete intentions of the framers, even
     though they used abstract moral principles in formulating constitutional clauses.' Cf. Ten
     2012, especially p. 493.
[62]   Thomas Grey calls it 'one of these concepts, evocative and persuasive in its connotations yet
     cloudy in its analytic and descriptive content, which at once enrich and confuse political
     discourse.' Grey 1979, p. 189.
[63]   Henkin 1994, p. 40.
[64]   Murphy 2007, p. 6–7.
[65]   In Murphy's words: 'Moreover it coexists uneasily with its usual bed partner, representative
     democracy, which would impose few substantive limitations on the people's freely chosen
     representatives.' Murphy 2007, p. 7. Cf. Kahn 2003.
[66]   There are other variants, such as the distinction between *legal constitutionalism* (which seeks
     guarantees primarily in legal institutions) and *political constitutionalism* (focused primarily on
     democracy and power sharing). Bellamy 2007.
[67]   Cf. Warren 1989, p. 511.
[68]   *Ibid.*

school in constitutional law, certainly sometimes hinders academic research in this regard. Hence, it is unsurprising that the best research and the most fundamental insights into the nature and effects of constitutions are not from legal scholarship, but (as we will see in Chapter 21) from political science, political economy, sociology and the cognitive sciences (including social psychology). Legal scholars often seem to have difficulties transcending their views in this respect.

SHAPES, SIZES AND TYPES

Constitutions come in all shapes and sizes. The classical distinction is between written and unwritten constitutions, although unwritten constitutions hardly exist any longer. This distinction in most cases actually refers to the difference between constitutions contained in a single document (single document constitutions) and constitutions distributed over several sources, including principles, customs, traditions and documents including court rulings (multiple document/instrument constitutions). This does not mean that they are unwritten (they usually are), but that they are not recorded in a single authoritative or official document with precedence over other (similar) documents.[69] Another well-known distinction, mentioned above, is between easily amendable 'flexible' and difficult-to-change 'rigid' constitutions.[70] This continuum extends from the easily-changed Indian Constitution[71] at one end to the rigid Japanese Constitution[72] at the other end.

Examining the different kinds of political society organised by a constitution produces a distinction – discussed above – between liberal-democratic constitutions (with purely democratic and purely liberal constitutions as sub-variants) and social constitutions (with welfare state constitutions and socialist or communist constitutions as sub-variants).[73]

Constitutions can also be distinguished in terms of effectiveness; are constitutional norms respected or not? Loewenstein, for one, distinguishes between *normative* constitutions (when political reality conforms to constitutional rules), *nominal* constitutions (when a polity wants to conform to the rules but – for socio-economic or other reasons – is unable to do so) and *semantic* constitutions (when constitutional rules only reflect political reality without imposing binding rules on it – mere instruments of the incumbent).[74] Chapter 21 deals with this subject in more detail.

---

[69] Cf. McLean 2018, p. 396 ff.

[70] Wheare 1966, p. 15–19. Albert 2019.

[71] Article 368 of the Indian Constitution allows the constitution to be amended when a majority of both Houses of Parliament approve an amendment 'by a majority of not less than two-thirds of the members of that House present and voting'.

[72] Article 96 of the Japanese constitution provides for an amendment procedure that requires a two-thirds majority on a proposal in parliament followed by a nationwide referendum to ratify the proposal.

[73] Cf. Grimm 2012.

[74] Loewenstein 1957, p. 147 ff.

There is also a distinction (in addition to the many others still to be mentioned)[75] between '*fresh-start*' and *revised constitutions*.[76] A fresh-start constitution establishes an entirely new (political, governmental or legal) system, or a new form of government (or both). Constitutions of this kind are usually, but not always, born of revolution. Revolutionary constitutions radically break with the old state of affairs, replacing them with new relations and new powers.[77] They sometimes even claim to be a new epoch in history. A revised constitution only adapts an existing one. The constitutions of the United States (1787/1788) and the First French Republic (1792) are, for instance, clearly revolutionary. The constitutions of South Africa (1994) and Germany (1949) are examples of fresh-start constitutions which were not promulgated in a revolution. How should the Swiss Constitution of 2000 or the Dutch Constitution of 1815 be regarded: did they start afresh? Some claim that they did, but the Dutch Constitution of 1815 was – as we have seen – more a revision of the 1814 constitution in terms of procedure and content than anything else.[78] The Swiss constitution of 2000 is – to be frank – not much more than a millennial makeover of its predecessor of 1874, although some would disagree. Here again, everything depends on how you want to see things.

To better understand how constitutions come about Bruce Ackerman – professor of Law and Political Science at Yale Law School USA – has suggested that there are actually three different *paths* to constitutionalism in the modern world. In his words:

> Under the first [path], revolutionary outsiders use the constitution to commit their new regime to the principles proclaimed during their previous struggle. India, South Africa, Italy and France have followed this path. Under the second, establishment insiders use the constitution to make strategic concessions to disrupt revolutionary movements before they can gain power. Britain provides paradigmatic examples. Under the third, ordinary citizens remain passive while political and social elites construct a new constitution. Spain, Japan and Germany provide variations on this theme.[79]

CONSTITUTIONAL ARCHETYPES AND A UNIVERSALIST INTERNATIONAL CONSTITUTION

It is not hard to distinguish even more types of constitutions, but this may not be very worthwhile. Distinctions can become eclectic, superficial and unhelpful for understanding. To avoid this, David Law argues that you need to look beyond the surface

---

[75] For an overview of more types cf. Grimm 2012.
[76] Approximately the distinction between what are called 'foundational and modifying constitutions'. Grimm 2012, p. 108.
[77] Cf. Arendt 1974.
[78] Cf. Chapter 11, section *Innovative restoration.*
[79] Ackerman 2005, p. 705.

of a constitution's articles and rules to ascertain its type. He asserts that constitutions essentially express a story: they somehow justify a polity's existence and organisation. Every constitution contains a society's unique ideological narrative, but regularities and fixed patterns can be discerned in all these stories.[80] Law identifies three archetypal constitutional narratives: the *liberal, state* and *universalist* type.

> Each is defined by a particular type of justification for the existence and organisation of the state, and each draws nourishment from a different legal tradition. The liberal archetype owes a historical debt to the common law tradition and legitimates the state by placing limits upon its authority. The statist archetype draws disproportionate support from civil law countries and generates legitimacy for the state by invoking notions of community and nationhood that bind the people to one another and to their government. The universalist archetype, the newest and most prevalent of the three, [...] conditions the legitimacy of the state upon adherence to norms of a supranational character.[81]

Nowadays, countries like Armenia derive many of their 'constitutional' rules and freedoms, which had previously been derived from national constitutional law, from international treaties and agreements. Armenian citizens are as, if not more, dependent for the protection of their fundamental freedoms on the European Convention on Human Rights and its court in Strasbourg than on the catalogue of national fundamental freedoms in the Armenian Constitution. In the European Union, the EU Treaties serve as a framework for the constitutional systems of its member states.[82] Noting that the EU is becoming an organisation that operates vis-à-vis its citizens as a federation in all but name is absolutely no exaggeration or extreme position, however politically taboo it may be (the dreaded 'F-word'). The German constitutionalist Dieter Grimm therefore argues that 'a new type of constitution is emerging: the international constitution as opposed to the national constitution' (see chapter 16 for more on this subject).[83] Whether you think it a good or horrific idea is also a question of semantics. 'Whether or not it is indeed correct', Grimm notes of the impending international constitution, 'depends largely on the meaning of "constitution".'[84]

[80] Grimm also categorises constitutions according to their underlying legitimising principle. He arrives at a different categorisation and distinguishes between constitutions based on absolute (supra-individual) truths (religious God-given truth or secular truth like the vision of a perfect society or based on an idea of the ultimate goal of history) on the one hand and constitutions based on the principle of 'consensus' (such as the principle of democracy) on the other. Grimm 2012, p. 114–115.
[81] Law 2016, p. 161.
[82] For its constitutional character, cf. Rosas & Armati 2012, especially p. 1–7, chapter 1 (*What Constitution?*) and p. 7–19.
[83] Grimm 2012, p. 131.
[84] *Ibid.*

19

Constitutional Kinship

The number of constitutions is growing – as we saw above – and their similarity is increasing too. No matter which perspective we employ, however many types we want to distinguish, or whatever concepts we care to apply: all of them are written, almost all of them in a single document, they all establish a legal and governance system (leadership system), and hardly any lack the standard four elements of the liberal-democratic formula (the rule of law, democratic governance, separation of powers and individual fundamental freedoms). There is no denying that constitutions are converging. But, if we are going to be totally honest, is a global outlook like this a fair method of comparison? You can, of course, always see similarities when you want to – it all depends on your perspective. If you were to fly in a hot air balloon seventy metres above Red Square in Moscow during the Liberation Day Parade – which I would not recommend – all the marching soldiers would look exactly the same. You might be able to spot small differences between the colours of uniforms here and there, but they would otherwise seem identical from this distance. If the balloon were to descend to two metres above the soldiers' heads, then you would see how different all the soldiers were, even if they did manage to keep in step. This also applies to constitutions: the closer you look and the more you know, the more apparent the differences become. And, of course, the key point is: what is most interesting thing about comparing constitutions: the similarities or the differences?[1]

How does one come to know anything about the differences between constitutions with all their apparent similarities? Is there anything like, say, a *normal-difference pattern* (a kind of standard deviation) between national constitutions or aspects of them? Not as far as I know, at least not for whole constitutions. How do you go about constructing a good analysis of similarities and differences? With *comparative law*? This is often done; specialists group countries' constitutions together and make qualitative statements about them. But can you really make scientific inferences

---

[1] Dixon & Ginsburg 2011, p. 6–7.

from something like this? The bulk of these studies only involve small groups of constitutions – predominantly the usual suspects from the West[2] – and the comparative dimensions they encompass are mainly a question of taste. Which characteristics do the comparators deem important to compare? There is often a haphazard element about it. If you compare twenty songs with styles you happen to like or consider important (say: rock, country, classical and chanson), then the outcome of the exercise will tell you very little about types of music as such – or about similarities or their frequency. Analyses like these tell you something about the preference of the author. Only the comparison of many more songs – preferably all – could really tell you something about styles.

For constitutional comparison this sort of analysis is now possible. As we are able to make much larger comparison sets in constitutional research these days, we can also try delving more deeply into constitutional similarities and differences.[3] Not by comparing constitutional systems of countries as a whole – which produces mind-boggling combinations of elements and dimensions due to the entanglement with the specifics of a country's political system, history, culture etcetera – but as a limited comparative exercise on the specifics, concepts and characteristics in the constitutional text itself. What kind of patterns can we discern? To examine this, we may use a method similar to that for determining language differences between countries. There are currently about 3,700 living languages.[4] Eighty of the largest languages are spoken by 80% of the world's population, while only 0.2% of the world's population communicates with the 3600 minor languages. Of the eighty largest languages, thirteen stand out, being spoken by more than 60% of the world's population.[5] If we divide the number of languages by the number of countries (80/193) this results in a 'correspondence rate' of 42% – the proportion of countries in the world that 'share' a language. Countries also use different currencies. The United Nations recognises 180 currencies as legal tender.[6] Yet, the American dollar alone is the official currency in 22 countries, twenty European countries share the Euro, and the British pound sterling is used in Britain and

---

[2] Hirschl 2014b, p. 4–5. 'Selection biases abound', according to Hirschl, in what he calls 'armchair' (comparative) constitutional research.

[3] Cf., for instance, Goderis & Versteeg 2013 and Hirschl 2014b, p. 272–273.

[4] That is the number of *official* languages, but there are many more. In his book *The World Until Yesterday*, Diamond says that about 7,000 languages are currently spoken in the world (7,111 according to the *Ethnologue Languages of the World* website – cf. next note). (Jared) Diamond 2012, p. 395. He is also worried about the speed at which languages are disappearing. Cf. (S.) Anderson 2010.

[5] Minor languages are disappearing quickly. Roughly 40% of the 7,111 languages listed on the *Ethnologue Languages of the World* website are now endangered, often with less than 1,000 speakers left. According to some estimates, as many as half of the world's remaining languages may go extinct by the end of the twenty-first century. Krauss 1992, p. 6. Just 23 languages account for more than half the world's population. www.ethnologue.com/guides/how-many-languages (consulted 10 November 2019). Cf. (S.) Anderson 2010.

[6] https://en.wikipedia.org/wiki/List_of_circulating_currencies (consulted 23 January 2019).

at least four other territories of the United Kingdom. Subtracting countries with shared currencies leaves us with around 124 different currencies and 69 countries with a shared currency. Applying these figures to the total of 193 countries results in a correspondence rate of about 36%. But what do this correspondence rate tell us – if anything?

Even lawyers – not usually the world's most well accomplished mathematicians – can sense that this kind of calculation does not really work. The fact that there are 80 major languages does not mean that countries actually 'share' them; and the existence of 124 different currencies says more about the differences between currencies than about what is 'shared'.

It is perhaps even more difficult to compare constitutions and their inter-relationships. What does it mean, for example, if a comparison between two constitutions shows that they differ for 33% and share 67%? They could easily be in the same *family*,[7] sharing a common heritage, both belonging to the liberal-democratic family or the aforementioned Cádiz family, for instance. Similarities do not say much – comparisons looking for similarities are invariably about what has been declared to be analogous – what is regarded as a similarity. When looking for meaningful constitutional affinities or similarities it is crucial to accurately select the characteristics, dimensions and subjects you want to compare. If you really want to know more about similarities and differences between constitutions, you will have to include many constitutions and many characteristics in the comparison. Some will say that this is undesirable as it is much too ambitious and will fail to produce results. Yet, academic curiosity naturally compels us to compare all the world's constitutions, especially as a comparison of this kind is now possible – at least at a textual level – thanks to the compilation of all national constitutions in the *Constitution* database. What can be done, must, of course, be done – unwillingness to compare and know is the worst of all academic errors.

COEFFICIENT OF RELATIONSHIP

If you want to compare constitutions based on relational characteristics, it may be worth looking at how this is done in other disciplines, such as biology, which has developed a *coefficient* to measure relatedness. The *coefficient of relationship* is used in biology to determine the biological relationship (the degree of consanguinity) between two individuals. The coefficient of relationship between two living beings depends on the proportion of genes they have in common. For example, the coefficient of relationship between a father and daughter is 0.5, because the daughter inherits half of her genes from her father. The other half of her genes comes from her mother: the coefficient of relationship between mother and daughter is

[7] Cf. Jackson 2012.

therefore also 0.5, and between grandmother and daughter is 0.25. The coefficient of relationship between full siblings is 0.5. Siblings inherit half of their genes from each parent, but not exactly the same half, so full siblings share on average 50% of their genes. The proportion for direct family relationships is therefore on average 50% or higher. To come to know more about relatedness you have to include the elements genetic variation and heredity. Not all characteristics are inherited in the same way, for instance, some variations are unique. You may not have to worry about that at first in constitutional kinship comparisons as the comparison set is relatively small (192 constitutions) with wide-ranging 'chromosome pairs' usually dating to different periods. They are all written, use language as their means of expression, and are structured and segmented, one way or another, in sections (chapters, articles, sections, etcetera) with various recognisable and classified – or classifiable – categories. The aforementioned *Constitute* database, which includes all of the world's 194 (192 in the corrected total)[8] national constitutions in official English translation, has categorised their contents by subject into 11 main categories and 54 subcategories, making it possible to search and compare them. The website includes 65 categories, but classification can be extended further. Based on the *Constitute* classification, we[9] conducted our own constitutional kinship[10] research and arrived at a total of 320 different categories of elements *frequently* found in constitutions. An element had to appear at least in five constitutions to be considered 'frequent'; we considered elements which occurred less frequently than this threshold more or less unique.[11]

A list of elements like this made it easier to search for similarities and even relationships between constitutions. We were able to dig even deeper: many similarities and a high coefficient of relationship could indicate constitutional kinship or 'familial' relationships. One of our findings has already come up in this book: constitutions from a particular *generation* commonly share characteristics. Apart from a search for generational kinship you can also look at substantive kinship of constitutions. Which substantive characteristics do they share, which patterns can be discerned? Aristotle did so in his comparison of Greek city states' constitutions. Looking at types of government in these constitutions, he arrived at a typology of governance

---

[8]   The *Constitute* database, by the end of 2018, recorded more national constitutions than there actually were UN nations – there were only 192 truly national constitutions in total at the time. Cf. note 3 in Chapter 1.

[9]   Political scientist, public administration specialist and legal researcher Georgina Kuipers, lawyer and public administration specialist Abram Klop, public administration specialist Hugo de Vos and myself.

[10] A *kinship* coefficient is a simple measure of relatedness, defined as the probability that a pair of randomly sampled homologous (paired chromosomes found in the same place) alleles (possible variations of a gene) are identical by descent.

[11] We used the Principle Component Analysis (PCA) method to structure the dimensionality of the data, which made it more suited to reading patterns from the constitutional comparison frequency analysis.

systems (see Chapter 5). Looking for patterns you can also look at the types of norms expressed in constitutions. What kind are they? Do they establish institutions, such as offices or bodies (legislative, judicial, administrative or other bodies); do they delineate procedures, or fundamental freedoms? To do this in detail you would, of course, have to check this article by article. And this might blur the comparison. The number of articles varies enormously between constitutions – from 372[12] in the Indian Constitution to 7 in the American constitution – as does the length of provisions and the number of topics per article.[13] For this reason, Elkins, Ginsburg and Melton use a method that solely characterises constitutions' legal content by *topic*. In 2009, they compared 148 constitutions based on 92 characteristics which give them an impression of the breadth of constitutions; do these include many or few topics, and what kind of topics? On this basis, they then examined whether a constitution's breadth was an indication of its longevity[14] (see Chapter 21).

WHICH TOPICS ARE MOST COMMON?

Today, with the texts of all 192 constitutions available, we can go even further than in 2009. Using Elkins, Ginsburg and Melton's method as an inspiration, we conducted a comparison in 2018 employing a category list of 320 elements (topics) applied to an adjusted total of 192 national constitutions from the *Constitute* database.[15] Which topics headed our list as recurrent features of a constitution? First, on our frequency scoreboard were the provisions on revising the constitution (192 times), followed by provisions on the structure of the legislature (190 times), judiciary (190 times), administration (ministers/cabinet 188 times; head of state 185 times), freedom of religion (184 times), freedom of expression (183 times) and so on. Not only does the list of categories allow one to look for frequency, it also permits one to examine relatedness or even kinship of constitutions. If a pair or group of constitutions shares many topics (a high similitude frequency), this may be seen as a first indication of substantive relatedness – or even of kinship or familial relationship – if the pattern is repeated in other constitutions in a systematic or regular way. On the other hand, if a constitution contains many elements seldom encountered elsewhere that might indicate singularity (Figure 4).

Our analysis revealed some interesting patterns in this respect. First of all, more than half of all 192 national constitutions share 149 elements of the 320 topics in the list. This not yet mean a great deal in itself but it does suggest a formula. More significantly, the vast majority of countries share the most important

---

[12] According to a conservative calculation – it contains many schedules.
[13] Since 1789 constitutions have contained an average of 14,000 words and devoted between 260 and 320 words per topic. Elkins, Ginsburg & Melton 2009, p. 105.
[14] Elkins, Ginsburg & Melton 2009, especially p. 104–105 and Chapter 2.
[15] There are more national constitutions in this set than the 189 written constitutions codified in one document – cf. note 3 in Chapter 1.

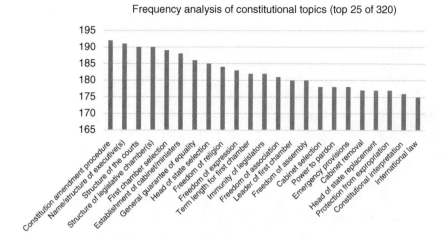

Frequency analysis of constitutional topics (top 25 of 320)

FIGURE 4 Frequency analysis of constitutional topics

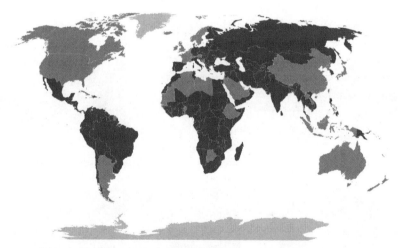

FIGURE 5 Countries whose constitutions share more than 87% of the top
seventy-five elements

elements of a liberal-democratic constitutional model (the rule of law, electoral democracy, democratic control, division of powers and fundamental freedoms). These liberal-democratic elements are overrepresented in the seventy-five most shared topics (see Figure 5). The countries shaded blue in the figure below have more than 87% of the top seventy-five constitutional elements represented in their constitution.

The fact that so many countries share more than 87% of the top seventy-five elements is certainly an indication of some sort of kinship (which would start at

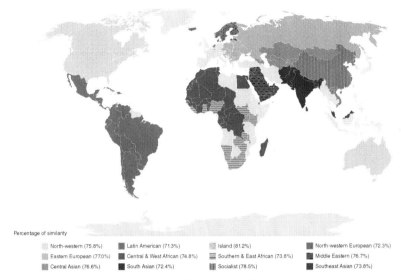

Percentage of similarity

North-western (75.8%)	Latin American (71.3%)	Island (81.2%)
Eastern European (77.0%)	Central & West African (74.8%)	Southern & East African (73.8%)
Central Asian (76.6%)	South Asian (72.4%)	Socialist (78.5%)

North-western European (72.3%)
Middle Eastern (76.7%)
Southeast Asian (73.8%)

FIGURE 6 Constitutional families

more than 50% relatedness). There are many constitutional brethren, so to speak. These coefficient of relationship scores can also be used to try to distinguish constitutional families. One could, for instance, contend that a group of constitutions constitutes a *family* if this group of countries shares more than 75% of their constitutional characteristics. This gave us twelve constitutional families worldwide. Figure 6 shows the various *families* – the percentages listed next to the groups in the key pertain to similarity *within* the group.

CONVERGENCE?

The historical survey in Part II of this book and the kinship analysis above indicate a pattern in which constitutions appear to have come to increasingly resemble each other over time.[16] Law and Versteeg examined this phenomenon between 1946 and 2006, and concluded that:

> […] the vast majority of constitutions have converged upon a generic core of rights-related provisions that is gaining in both popularity and scope over time.[17]

More and more constitutions are of the liberal variety. Constitutions based on other ideologies have become rarer, as have mixed forms – such as the Mexican

---

[16] Cf. Elkins, Ginsburg & Melton 2009, who use a similarity index for a longitudinal equation, p. 25–29 and p. 148–149.
[17] Law & Versteeg 2011, p. 1243.

constitution of 1917, for instance, or Germany's 'Weimar constitution' of 1919.[18] Not only in terms of fundamental freedoms, but also in regard to governmental structures (government bodies and institutions), constitutions are drawing closer to each other. Tom Ginsburg observed in 2012 that more and more constitutional courts are emerging across the world, in step with an increase in judges' powers of constitutional review.[19] Democratic instruments and governmental systems too seem to be becoming more alike. Representative democracy, based on the idea of popular sovereignty and electoral equality, has all but prevailed over all previous conceptions of the authority and legitimacy of rule. Conceptual models of government in constitutions seem to have boiled down to basically three forms, parliamentary, presidential and semi-presidential regimes.[20] A driver for this is that constitutions nowadays seem to be subject to fashions and trends, such as the widespread introduction of Councils for the Judiciary in European countries over the past twenty years. Countries borrow and replicate elements from each other over short periods of time, resulting in steady constitutional convergence. As awkward and uncomfortable as this may be, Rosenfeld and Sajó write in the introduction to their major *Handbook of Comparative Constitutional Law* that:

> Constitutional borrowing and transplantation of constitutional norms, structures, doctrines and institutions is a fact of life, regardless of ideological or theoretical objections to these practices [...].[21]

And we will have to deal with it as a fact of life. According to David Schneiderman:

> Comparative constitutionalists traditionally have been preoccupied with the identification of difference and similarity between *families* of national constitutional systems. [...] Today, the dominant trend among comparative constitutionalists is to seek out not just differences and similarities, but *convergence*.[22]

At least, *if* you believe the phenomenon exists, if you believe it *is* a fact of life. The critical Canadian comparative legal scholar, Pierre Legrand, is having none of it. He considers the whole idea of convergence as ridiculous nonsense. The fact that rules and concepts in constitutions sometimes bear a resemblance indicates very little – it is merely superficial – and soon results in tunnel vision:

> [...] rules and concepts alone actually tell one very little about a given legal system and reveal even less about whether two legal systems are converging or not. They may provide one with much information about what is apparently happening, but they indicate nothing about the deep structures of legal system [...].[23]

[18] *Ibid.*
[19] Ginsburg 2012.
[20] Lijphart 2004, especially p. 101–103.
[21] Rosenfeld & Sajó 2012 intro, p. 13.
[22] Schneiderman 2011, p. 189; my italics.
[23] Legrand 1996, especially p. 56.

'Dicit Legrand'. It goes without saying that if you stare long and deeply enough, everything eventually looks different – as in the case of the soldiers on Red Square. Legrand's refreshing and contrary attitude is a reiteration of a long-running and drawn-out controversy between comparative legal scholars. Back in 1974, Alan Watson wrote a book entitled *Legal Transplants*. In it he demonstrated that modern legal systems increasingly adopt each other's solutions, concepts and rules be it as sources of inspiration, of 'legal borrowing', or simply as out-and-out 'legal transplants'.[24] This ruffled several legal sociologists' feathers, who reproached Watson for committing the fallacy of assuming that people who drive a Toyota Prius will be the same kind of people, or at any rate will behave like 'Prius people' in the long run. In short, Watson was accused of failing to take social variables into account. As the otherwise congenial American legal sociologist Robert Seidman put it curtly: Watson's outcomes were 'either trivial or banal'.[25] Seidman received widespread support.[26] Why? Taking a leaf out of someone else's book appears an innocent enough phenomenon. Perhaps it had to do with Max Weber's warning about comparative studies: to get to know a culture you should not look for analogies and superficial parallels, but rather singular characteristics.[27] It was probably the Zeitgeist too; the 1970s were a time of post-colonialism, the Cold War and ideological spheres of influence. Legal transplantation reeked of the export of Western ideas and ideologies, and post-colonial interference – potentially impeding countries' control of their destinies. The law is not just any old object, Legrand protested, it is part of a broader social context, a legal culture: 'a matter of myth and narrative.' He argued that legal transplants are not only undesirable, but also impossible.[28]

Things are less charged these days. Much is shared, borrowed, adopted and studied in comparison in constitutional law in recent years. Discrete terminology is used to steer clear of the overheated Watson-Legrand debate. Most authors agree that there is certainly convergence, but that is not so much a case of transplantation and copying, as of inspiration, working with what could be called a common 'gene pool',[29] bricolage (as with IKEA furniture),[30] and borrowing. These effects do not result in identical outcomes everywhere, but borrowed or adopted elements (such as fundamental

---

[24] Watson 1974.

[25] Seidman 1975, p. 682–683.

[26] For an overview cf. Cairns 2013, p. 637–696.

[27] 'Comparative study [sh]ould not aim at finding "analogies" and "parallels", as is done by those engrossed in the currently fashionable enterprise of constructing general schemes of development. The aim should, rather, be precisely the opposite: to identify and define the individuality of each development, the characteristics, which made the one, conclude in a manner so different from that of the other. This done, one can then determine the causes which led to these differences.' (Max) Weber 1976, p. 385.

[28] Legrand 1997, p. 111.

[29] Saunders 2009.

[30] Frankenberg 2010.

freedoms, democratic instruments, or institutions such as constitutional review) can have a catalytic effect.[31] Adoptions can result in adjustments and reforms, and make systems learn from each other.[32] Constitutional ideas migrate,[33] making constitutions around the world increasingly similar. It is a somewhat uncomfortable development in a world in which we would like every constitution, like every national flag and anthem,[34] to be a unique expression of tradition, culture and shared values, but there is no getting around the fact that constitutions are becoming more generic.[35]

This might perhaps detract from the uniqueness of constitutions[36] and, in turn, possibly from the esteem in which societies hold modern written constitutions as the symbol of national self-awareness, the right to self-determination and independence.[37] Convergence and the concomitantly generic nature of constitutions can be at the expense of the normative and integrative power of its norms.[38] For, if documents of this kind are merely borrowed or second-hand, how can 'we' still feel at home in their order? How can we still *believe* in them?

To be able to accept a constitutional system and the regime it expresses communities and countries use distinct narratives, stories that try to convince us that the constitutional system deserves our support. We do this by claiming that government power originates from the people, or that authority is derived from traditions or superhuman categories or values. Constitutions are not just random inventions, or ideas of any group of people that happens to be assembled in a constituent assembly; we like to associate them with rules we have 'uncovered' in our traditions, echoes of earlier writings, wisdom bequeathed by earlier generations, even voices from the beyond.[39] This idea of the law being impersonally 'uncovered' – the fiction of it already having

---

[31] Teubner 1998.

[32] Elkins & Simmons, 2005.

[33] Choudhry 2006.

[34] Incidentally, many national flags consist of minimal variations of red, white and blue and – I am writing this during the 2018 World Cup Soccer in Russia – national anthems have substantial similarities too.

[35] Law & Versteeg 2011, p. 1243–1244.

[36] Which sometimes takes the form of constitutional 'exceptionalism': the conviction that the historical development and characteristics of a constitutional order make it extraordinary or exceptional in comparison with other countries' constitutions and it should therefore be safeguarded against 'universalist' influences. Cf. Versteeg 2014, p. 1641 ff.

[37] Hensel 2012, p. 5.

[38] If constitutions have such potential. Grimm argues that they do, albeit indirectly. Grimm 2005.

[39] Even though constitutions can be used to transfer intergenerational wisdom. Constitutional rigidity can, for instance, ensure that tried and tested formulae and structures cannot simply be cast aside but leave space only for well-considered new insights. Cf. Tremmel 2017, p. 4–17 who illustrates this by quoting Thomas Jefferson in a letter dated 12 July 1816 to Samuel Kercheval. Jefferson writes that constitutional rigidity always means that we will have to live with small imperfections, but 'I know also, that laws and institutions must go hand in hand with the progress of the human mind. As that becomes more developed, more enlightened, as new discoveries are made, new truths disclosed, and manners and opinions change with the change of circumstances, institutions must advance also, and keep pace with the times.' Tremmel 2017, (his) footnote 64.

been in existence – is a method that has certainly not only been employed in common law to increase the acceptability and authority of the law. This kind of 'ethos' is also important for the acceptance of a constitutional order. Convergence, indiscriminate borrowing and adoption do not fit into this image of constitutions as manifestations of something higher and superhuman. Yet, it is irrefutable that modern constitutions are human creations – the outcome of political processes – however much difficulty some people (often lawyers) may have with this.[40] Constitutions are not 'uncovered', they are made.[41] They are drafted, constructed and designed, with all the attendant consequences.[42] In Tom Ginsburg's words:

> Design implies a technocratic architectural paradigm that does not easily fit the messy realities of social institutions, especially not the messy process of constitution making.[43]

This, of course, does not chime well with the romantic ideal of the dawning of the constitution that ushers in a glorious future for all.

Global Constitutions?

Is there going to be a single universal[44] one-size-fits-all constitutional arrangement, a 'common liberal democratic model of constitutionalism' in the not-too-distant future, as predicted by Jeffrey Goldsworthy?[45] The most important question is, of course: is that desirable? Would a global model not be exceedingly bland? Might a global constitution ultimately not lead to the rule of mediocrity, to sub-optimal solutions and low levels of protection?

It may be so, but perhaps it is out of our hands. Some argue that the globalisation of constitutional law is an inevitable result of the currents of international cooperation and economic relations, privatisation and digitisation.[46] Others take the view that national constitutional systems must counteract this and 'channel' the globalisation of constitutional law in their own constitution to prevent a possible 'race to the bottom'.[47]

---

[40] 'For many lawyers, law is respectable and politics is not. To some of these the very idea that law is a manifestation or type of politics seems almost offensive', says Tom Campbell. Campbell 2012, p. 228.

[41] Pitkin 1987.

[42] Ginsburg 2012.

[43] Ginsburg 2012, p. 1.

[44] Cf. Elkins, Ginsburg & Melton 2009 who argue that a universal constitutional model has actually been around since the rise of the modern state at the end of the eighteenth century ('no universal model existed until the rise of the modern state at the turn of the eighteenth century'), p. 41.

[45] (Jeffrey) Goldsworthy 2006, p. 115.

[46] As by Teubner 2004.

[47] Tushnet 2009a.

The globalisation of constitutions does not only flow one-way, with influences from outside or above pervading a constitutional order through popular ideas and conventions, such as the International Covenant on Civil and Political Rights, or the European Convention on Human Rights. International law – treaty law in particular – has constitutional effects too.[48] These treaties are increasingly adopting characteristics hitherto exclusive to the national-constitutional domain: the hierarchy of norms, directly enforceable claims and individual rights, international tribunals, judicial review, and suchlike.

The globalisation of constitutions and the constitutionalisation of international law are not uncontentious. There is much discussion, including about what exactly the 'globalisation' of constitutions is. There are two approaches. The first is global constitutionalism as a project.[49] Its central question is how we can use the ideas of constitutionalism to improve institutions for 'global governance'. Constitutionalism is used here as 'a resource for entrenching for global best practices in limited government and market reforms'.[50] This is somewhat comparable to off-the-peg clothing. The second approach is 'constitutionalism as critique' in which constitutionalist ideas serve more as a benchmark for national constitutions, resulting in an increasingly common source of shared constitutionalist values. The 'New Constitutionalism' school is an example of this approach. Its spiritual progenitor, Stephen Gill, argues that the whole idea of constitutionalism is protecting liberties by restraining political power.[51] In a globalising world, much power – including political power – is exercised supranationally on world markets and it is important to guarantee individuals' fundamental freedoms on this plane. Constitutionalism should be focused on its ends (restraining power) rather than being bound to states – which are becoming a less decisive factor in determining citizens' fates and freedoms. New constitutionalism can be seen in various national and international phenomena, such as treaties with guarantees that are as difficult to change as those in constitutions, the rise of international human rights courts and tribunals,[52] market-friendly human rights in economic treaties and regional trade associations, as well as non-discrimination guarantees for foreign investors in national constitutions.[53] This approach is mainly about constitutionalist reactions to globalising markets.[54] It elicits fierce criticism. Is it not a kind of non-committal wishful thinking? Does this globalising phenomenon really exist? Can constitutionalism be apportioned into separate parts? Is it not better to see it as an interconnected whole, the result of a historical development, bound

---

[48] De Wet 2012.
[49] Schneiderman 2011, p. 189.
[50] *Ibid.*, p. 190.
[51] Gill 2007.
[52] Such as the European Court of Human Rights (ECHR) and the Inter-American Court of Human Rights (CIDH).
[53] Moyn 2018.
[54] Cf. Hirschl 2014a.

to the fate of specific states and peoples? According to some, constitutionalism as constitutions without a *demos* (people) – whom constitutions emanate from, are intended for and are subject to – is entirely impossible.[55] That is why the whole idea of a constitution without a state is problematic in their eyes.[56]

Wishful Thinking?

Is the world coming together? It is something many of us like to believe in. Converging constitutions appeal to warm sentiments of unitedness. But does it hold true? In a critical article, 'The Limits of Constitutional Convergence' from 2011 Rosalind Dixon and Eric Posner express some doubts. Are constitutions really converging, they ask (where is the actual evidence?) and if they are, is it a mere temporal effect or a permanent one?[57] For the answer to that last question they look into the 'why', into the underlying motives and mechanisms that make countries attune their constitutions. If it is merely lip service of some kind driving the process, then convergence will slow or even decrease over the course of time. If countries are truly committed to learn from each other's best practices, spurred on by competitive forces or 'superstructures' (like globalisation, common technological developments) or even downright forced (by international organisations or military force) the temporal effects of convergence may play out differently.[58] They assert that we should critically look at these mechanisms driving convergence and the effects in the long run, rather than make wishful and broad 'arm chair' statements about it. In their words:

> [...] if constitutional convergence based on these mechanisms is in fact as broad and inevitable as some suggest, therefore, constitutional decision-makers should have much greater pause than currently as to the scope of useful forms of constitutional comparison – at least by them, rather than scholars.[59]

And follow it up with a warning:

> [...] The more such mechanisms apply, the less likely it is, in any given context, that even an apparent global "consensus" on a particular constitutional question will actually provide useful information about constitutional morality or consequences.[60]

---

[55] Cf. Newton 2006. He says on p. 336: '[...] constitutions do more than charter the organs of state; they also purport to define (or set terms for the formation of) the political subjectivity of society and of its members: they constitute the political collectivity and individual subjects alike from the multitude (which in its plural, polymorphous flux is always there, "before" and "underneath" particular political subjectivities). The institutions of power and political subjectivities are necessarily correlative.'

[56] Beaud 2012, p. 272–273.

[57] Dixon & Posner 2011, p. 400–402.

[58] *Ibid.*, p. 402–404 and p. 421–423.

[59] *Ibid.*, p. 423.

[60] *Ibid.*

Sobering thoughts indeed. How about these underlying intentions and constitutional morality? How can we (get to) know them?

CONSTITUTIONAL IDENTITY

The *intentions* behind constitutions usually embody more than some tool kit with a random assortment of legal elements with which a legal system and the machinery of government can be constructed in any old way.[61] Technocratic bricolage is soulless; constitutions represent values. One of the tenets of modern constitutions is that they bind a society by establishing and articulating its core values. Constitutions around the world attempt to convince their society why it is important and good to work together according to the constitution's formula. Why you can trust each other and your leaders in a constitutional community; why and how you will be treated and recognised in a fair way, if you participate. Constitutions tell a story that appeals to your psyche, morality and imagination (see Chapter 28). A story that rests on the group's distinctiveness, identity and shared values. Constitutions articulate group identities and values in order that we internalise this identity and strengthen it where possible, so that we feel at home in the larger story of the constitutional community of values, in this constitutional order.[62] It is a two-way process: the story and its values become part of us and we – as a people or group – become part of the story of this particular constitutional order, enabling us to cooperate better and on a larger scale.[63] This identity element of constitutions is very coveted: it has great potential to mobilise people.[64] Yet, it is also invidious: identity is not only about core values and belonging, but also who and what does *not* belong.[65] We often see this reflected in constitutional preambles – like the Surinamese preamble:

> We, the People of Suriname,
>   inspired by the love for this Country and the belief in the power of the Almighty and guided by the centuries-long struggle of our people against colonialism,

---

[61] Cf. Lindahl 2013b.

[62] According to Schechtman's narrative view of identity, experiences and events (relationships with others, one's own experiences of right and wrong) can acquire another meaning for individuals by being placed in the context of a larger story that connects them. Schechtman 1996. Cf. Ricoeur 1992.

[63] Cf. Hans Lindahl, who sees constitutions as doing two things. First: 'constitutions include rules that empower legal behaviour in the sense of behaviour that is commanded, prohibited, or permitted', but second and far more importantly: 'a constitution empowers *a collective self* in that it opens up a realm of joint action under law. And this entails opening up the first-person plural perspective: "we together"'. Lindahl 2013, Chapter 3 (*Identity of Legal Collectives*), p. 99–100; my italics. Cf. Rosenfeld 2010, p. 27–36 (section 1.2).

[64] Cf. Lindahl 2007.

[65] Lindahl says: 'a constitution structures the ongoing legal process of inclusion in and exclusion from a collective self. [...] a constitution is the master legal rule for inclusion in and exclusion from a legal order'. Lindahl 2013, p. 100. Collective 'self-inclusion goes hand in hand with excluding the 'other'. Cf. Ricoeur 1992. Cf. Schmitt 2007.

which was terminated by the establishment of the Republic of Suriname on 25 November 1975, taking the coup d'état of 25 February 1980 and the consequences thereof, conscious of our duty to combat and to prevent every form of foreign domination, resolved to defend and protect the national sovereignty, independence and integrity [...]

On the other hand, maybe you should not expect too much pedagogic value from a constitutional text. In the words of the former ECHR judge and constitutionalist Sajó, the text itself can only do little:

> The text itself has only limited potential for forging identity. A legally binding document is but a first step on the long and winding road from a political design for collective identity to a socially embedded institution that actually fosters such identity.[66]

Yet, constitutions do have a role to play in bridging the gap between the collective imagined identity and the subjective identity. Constitutions *make* identities, both *collective* ones like 'nation', 'people', 'empire', 'republic', 'legal order' etcetera, and *individual* ones like 'citizen', 'national', 'voter' and so on. All of these attributed identities are intended to interact with your subjective identity and your own experience of selfhood. Constitutional identity can be used to try to influence the experience of selfhood.[67]

Knowing how this forging of identity works is, of course, worth something in a world of constitutions. Quite a bit has been written about constitutional identity in recent years. Not always all that comprehensibly, if you ask me, but perhaps it is just me. What does constitutional identity actually mean? It is certainly controversial.[68] Constitutional identity is about features of a constitution that are both characteristic of and essential to a system.[69] Sometimes this identity is interpreted as something normative, as Michel Troper does:

> Constitutional identity results from [...] certain principles which can be posited as essential and as such distinguishable from other constitutional norms and which can be relied upon to protect the integrity of the constitution in cases in which it confronts threats that might erode its vital bond to the people or nation it is meant to serve.[70]

He puts it on a par with the basic structure of a constitution – a core structure of values that offers protection and must itself be protected.[71] This makes constitutional

---

[66] Sajó 2005, especially p. 243.
[67] Referring to Ricoeur's categories of sameness and selfhood, Rosenfeld says: '[...] constitutional identity can be constructed on the basis of sameness or of selfhood, or more precisely, based on the dynamic interaction between projections of sameness and images of selfhood.' Rosenfeld 2010, p. 27.
[68] Rosenfeld argues that constitutional identity is 'an essentially contested concept', as is the concept democracy. Rosenfeld 2012, p. 756.
[69] Cf. Jacobsohn 2006, especially p. 361–362.
[70] Troper 2010, p. 202.
[71] Cf. Müller 2018.

identity more than a label or a slogan for a politically desirable result.[72] But can any more be said about constitutional identity in an objective sense? Not according to the Harvard professor Laurence Tribe:

> [T]he very identity of "the Constitution" [… is] itself a matter that cannot be objectively deduced or passively discerned in a viewpoint-free way […].[73]

But that is too easy. You have to look further than this, in the opinion of Tribe's colleague Gary Jacobsohn. If you want to know something about the identity of a constitution, then you have to examine the order's self-image. What or whom do they want to be as a community? Answering this not only requires an examination of the text, but of what does not work – the disharmonies in and around a constitution. Are there paradoxes in the constitutional text, alternative views on the order's offices and procedures, competing visions of what are described as the 'common' traditions and legacies? Second, what is the relationship between the constitution and social reality? Where are the fault lines, the confrontations between norms and practice? Jacobsohn argues that this is the only way of learning more about a country's constitutional identity.[74]

None of these types, models and identities, however, will directly help us to understand what constitutions actually are. That requires more than simply knowing where they come from, or the various meanings we ascribe to them today. It requires above all knowing what constitutions *do*. And that is what we will explore in Part IV of this book.

---

[72] Jacobsohn 2006, p. 361.

[73] Tribe 1983, especially p. 440.

[74] Jacobsohn 2010, p. 129–130. Jacobsohn distinguishes different types of constitutional identities such as 'militant' and 'acquiescent' constitutions of the German, French, American, British, Spanish and post-colonial models, as well as revolutionary, patented, transitional and transnational constitutions. Cf. Jacobsohn 2012.

PART IV

Effects

20

What Does a Constitution Do?

Are you better off with a constitution? Heroic paintings, public holidays commemorating constitutions, statues, songs, hymns and even pop songs[1] suggest an affirmative. Perusing the countless preambles and reading the high hopes expressed in lofty language points to a similar conclusion too. The expectations of constitutions are usually high, which is probably why there are so many of them. But what can be said about the results? Are you really better off with a constitution? What happens when you have one? What does it do? As we know, they sometimes do nothing. 'Sham constitutions', whose norms are not complied with, were discussed briefly above. Naturally, this is never supposed to happen. Constitutions of this kind do not have any measurable effect, regardless of their pledges. But serious constitutions do; effectivity is the whole point of them. But what kind of consequences and effects do constitutions have; what is their consequence, meaning, their substance? And, how can we deduce and uncover them? These are the questions addressed in this chapter. It will follow a general approach as examining the effects and meanings of constitutions involves questions that are sometimes impossibly broad, nebulous and all-encompassing. This often involves questions that go beyond constitutions, even touching on issues about the effects of the entire phenomenon law.

In the face of it, constitutions are written texts expressing legal norms. These norms say something about how things ought to be. The first step in learning about their consequences and effects is examining whether the norms contained in constitutional provisions are complied with. Do government institutions, politicians, citizens and society do what the constitution requires? This is quite difficult to measure. Do you only look at violations? Or court cases? And if this is possible, what does it mean? For example, the Dutch Constitution regulates the freedom of the press (freedom of expression) with the following, somewhat antiquated text:

---

[1] Including The Who, 'Won't Get Fooled Again' (no. 9) from the 1971 album Who's next. 'I'll tip my hat for the new constitution; Take a bow for the new revolution, Smile and grin at the change all around […].' The song was banned in South Korea for being inflammatory.

No one shall require prior permission to publish thoughts or opinions through the press, without prejudice to the responsibility of every person under the law.

Compliance to this norm indicates little about the effect or meaning of freedom of expression in the Netherlands. The article is seldom used. Of the approximately 17 million court cases in the country over the past twenty years, twelve or so cases have involved this article. Experts know that this has to do with the European Convention on Human Rights, which has a provision on the freedom of expression which Dutch courts can apply directly.[2] This provision is invoked more than ten times as often in court cases.[3] What does this say about compliance with the freedom of the press in the Dutch Constitution? Is it no longer important? Or does it really still matter? I would think so. This example illustrates that constitutions are about more than just legal rules whether or not they are observed, as with many other laws. As well as their function as legal rules, constitutional rules have another, higher purpose: they are expressions of a larger idea. A constitution's legal norms and rules are linked with values, principles and ideas such as freedom, democracy, recognition of law and the rule of law, and individual recognition. Besides legal rules, a constitution also enshrines 'system rules' establishing a legal and/or political system. Constitutions protect citizens from their government, but at the same time their rules create the government. These rather quixotic dimensions of a constitutional order make delineating the consequences of constitutions an uphill task.[4] Constitutions are aggregations of various phenomena whose effects, let alone causal relationships, are very difficult to disentangle.[5]

Relatively little is known about whether constitutions matter, and their direct or indirect consequences. This is surprising to say the least, considering their long and deep historical roots and the unprecedented popularity of the instrument.[6] A dearth of data, interconnectedness of factors, complexity, invisible factors, path dependency, historical contingency and evidence pointing in all directions often conspire to make the subject slip like desert sand between researchers' fingers.

---

[2] Article 10 ECHR.

[3] Article 10 of the ECHR is mentioned 219 times in the content indication of the judgments in the Dutch *Rechtspraak.nl* database. Article 7 of the Dutch Constitution is mentioned a mere eleven times (consulted 8 January 2019).

[4] As is the case with the law in general. Cf. Bogart 2002, in particular chapter 3 (*The Complexities of Assessing Impact*).

[5] Law says: 'Constitutions are complex phenomena with a host of potential causes and effects that can interact or conflict with one another and evolve over time in ways that are difficult to predict. It is a daunting task to identify [...] the underlying causal mechanisms and chains of causation'. Law 2010, p. 388.

[6] More and more research has been conducted in recent decades, as we have seen above. Ginsburg and Huq recently published a book devoted entirely to constitutional achievements and consequences. Ginsburg & Huq 2016. They also concede that it is a broad and elusive subject which is difficult to research.

21

The Legal Meaning of Constitutions

If *anything*, a constitution creates a legal system. A legal system may already have existed, but a constitution breathes new life into it by defining it. Constitutions past and present contain meta-rules about the 'we' of a legal community, what the law is, who is involved in its formation and enforcement, and how we are bound by it. Those who are willing to look beyond or willing to read between the lines of constitutions will certainly find plenty of evidence to this effect.

Oddly enough, legal scholarsthe experts on legal rulesusually do look at the matter in this light. They have the distinction between 'formal' constitutions, codified in a single document (called 'a constitution'), and 'material' constitutions (collections of fundamental constitutional rules) drummed into them during their studies, and are taught never to confuse the two. Legal scholars, especially in Europe, are also taught that constitutions are fairly recent inventions and that the origins of the law can only be traced back to private law, the law on relationships between individuals. Conventional distinctions of this kind have been rendered all but obsolete nowadays. The difference between formal and material constitutions has become utterly blurred, now almost every state in the world has chosen to codify the bulk of its constitutional rules into a single written document. And the idea that private law is at the root of all law and all legal systems is at least a questionable, largely unsubstantiated theory, if not downright incorrect.

CONFUSING FIELDS OF LAW

Conventional doctrines and distinctions of this kind impede rather than contribute to the understanding of what constitutions do. Similarly, definitions of fields of law are sometimes unintentional obstructions. For example, it is common for legal doctrines to divide legal systems into fields of law. They mostly include private law (involving relationships between individuals), criminal law (rules on criminal behaviour), administrative law, tax law, cartel and competition law, international law, EU law (in Europe) and so forth. Generally calm and sensible legal scholars can get very agitated about the boundaries between these fields. It is not because they are short-sighted but because of the illustrious cultures and traditions represented by these fields. What is the relationship between the various specialisms; what is the basis of what; which areas of expertise matter in practice (and therefore to the profession)? These are often questions of hierarchy as well, entailing differences in status.

One of the most important classifications assumes that private law is the general, 'common' law and thus functions as 'basic law'. It is always in force, has the longest lineage, and as the nineteenth-century German legal scholar Friedrich Karl von Savigny demonstrated, precedes states and constitutions considerably. Many who concur with Von Savigny and the so-called Historical School of Jurists consider the fundamentals of this basic private law rules to emanate from Roman law,[1] endowing it with a kind of universal character. It has always existed; the Romans simply codified it as inherited wisdom.[2] Supporters of this idea of private law as general, foundational law assume that societies always have had private law, and that private law is always in force, regardless of other forms of order by public law. This 'general' (private) law in societies existed even without governments and states. It is the basis onto which the rest was subsequently added. According to this way of thinking, private law is pre-constitutional.[3] But, in fact, it is not. Ancient law also needed constitutional institutions, authority, an imagined legal order of some sort to implement 'private law rules', despite of course lacking any clear distinction between public (constitutional) and private law rules at the time. This distinction is a modern, nineteenth-century invention. There was never a total absence of institutions in ancient times, as the Code of Hammurabi (eighteenth century BCE) shows. Part 5 of the code, for instance, requires judges (who evidently existed) to write down their judgments:

> [...] present his judgment in writing; if later error shall appear in his decision, and it be through his own fault, then he shall pay twelve times the fine set by him in the case, and he shall be publicly removed from the judge's bench, and never again shall he sit there to render judgment.[4]

---

[1] Wauters & De Benito 2017, p. 1 and p. 135–136.

[2] Taco Terpstra shows in a recent study of trading communities in the Roman Empire that it did not work like this. Roman-era traders in the Mediterranean basin often relied on their own rules and trusted networks (of family and acquaintances) to implement and enforce their contracts rather than the rules and institutions of Roman law. The state-based institutions and rules were not always available or usable due to wars and shifting boundaries. In periods when 'official' rules and institutions could not be used, trust in abstract rules and institutions was replaced with trust in kin relations and acquaintancesthey fell back on standards known to them from common practices and customs in their trusted networks. This was, in fact, a sort of retreat to the Dunbar number (see Chapter 3). Cf. Terpstra 2013.

[3] Terpstra, for one, shows that Roman private law in antiquity was certainly not pre-constitutional. Terpstra 2013.

[4] L.W. King's English translation on the Yale University website (Avalon project) http://avalon .law.yale.edu/ancient/hamframe.asp (consulted 1 July 2018).

What kind of law is this? 'Civil procedural law', contemporary legal scholars would say, 'this rule should be seen in the context of the ensuing private law dispute settlement rules in the document.' But that is rather a modern extrapolation, of course, cramming these rules into the mould of our present concepts and understanding. Rules like this may fall within the scope of private law nowadays, but what we see above is the official establishment of a judicial system, invoking legal qualities and status (judge, judgment, judge's bench), directives on how to settle disputes and sanctions (removal of judges, fines) according to foreseeable, officially enacted rules (codification). Without the prerequisite legal and leadership systemestablished by a constitution these words would be incomprehensible abstractionsmere puffs of hot air.

It is useful to examine a second example, as an isolated instance is not in itself instructive. Take Article X of the Gortyn Code, from Crete in the fifth century BCE (see image below), which reads:[5]

> As long as a father lives, no one shall purchase any of his property from a son, or take it on mortgage; [...].

This is surely private law? It is about ownership and selling, even though the rest of the article is about inheritance law. This, too, would constitute private law of a kind in our modern day and age. But not necessarily so in antiquity.

The Gortyn Code

---

[5] From the Fordham University website https://sourcebooks.fordham.edu/ancient/450-gortyn .asp (consulted 1 July 2018).

FRUITS OF A CONSTITUTION: CREATING A LEGAL SYSTEM

Indeed today, the Gortyn Code rule can be considered a private law norm, despite the reductionism involved. But we always need to keep in mind that Gortyn, like Hammurabi's Babylon, had no concept of private, criminal, or public law; these polities were not states in a modern sense, and certainly lacked a formal constitution as we know it today. Looking at early instances through the lens of contemporary concepts clouds our vision.[6] Projecting our modern concept of law onto the past adjusts the realities of another era to our contemporary ideas.[7]

This, moreover, conceals what the Code of Hammurabi and the Gortyn code do: they create a world. A world of law a legal system in which abstractions such as judges, written verdicts, possessions, the sale of property and mortgages operate. Naming them 'constitutes' them and creates them in the world of law. Constitutions do not make this world and legal system literally or physically (which is impossible anyway). Sometimes they seem to do no more than acknowledge or incorporate 'pre-existing' institutions (courts, judges, mediators, priests and the like) or 'prior' law (inherited law, customary law, divine law or law 'uncovered' through legal wisdom). But in order to function all of these previously existing things must be recognised someplace; the legal system has to be defined, established, organised and have 'life breathed into it' somewhere. It does not appear out of thin air even if the very first constitutions, such as the Code of Hammurabi, like to present it in this way. Constitutions create and organise legal systems, even though they do not always (seem to) do so explicitly in their texts.

As fish do not know that they swim in water, neither do we … We are mostly unaware of living in imagined legal and political worlds created by conscious constitutional acts, often codified in constitutions, as we are so accustomed to doing so. The world of law, of mass societies under abstract leadership in states, has become a matter, of course, to us. But these worlds are by no means self-evident, certainly not from an historical perspective. Francis Fukuyama gives an insightful comment on the genesis of the world of law:

> The original understanding of the law as something fixed either by divine authority, by custom or by nature, implied that the law could not be changed by human agency, though it could and had to be interpreted to fit novel circumstances. With the decline of religious authority and belief in natural law in modern times, we have come to understand the law as something created by human beings, but only under a strict set of procedural rules that guarantee that they conform to a broad social consensus over basic values. The distinction between law and legislation now corresponds to the distinction between constitutional and ordinary law, where the former has more stringent requirements for enactment, such as supermajority voting. In the contemporary United States, this means that any new

---

[6]   Cf. Pocock 1987, p. 1–5 and p. 27–29.

[7]   Cf. Floyd & Stears 2011, p. 1–9.

law passed by Congress must be consistent with a prior and superior body of law, the Constitution, as interpreted by the Supreme Court.[8]

Many people to this day still find it hard to stomach the idea that the law is a product of human creation. The American philosopher of law Jeremy Waldron is astounded by the widespread resistance to conceiving law as the work of humans. He considers this especially so in Common Law jurisdictions:

> [...] the sentiment widespread among twentieth-century legal scholars that the character of Common Law systems is changing for the worse as legislation crowds out the more endogenous and traditional bases of legal growth. Statutes, we are told, 'have no roots' and are often 'hastily and inconsiderately adopted'. [...] 'Choking on Statutes' the title of the first chapter of Guido Calabresi's book on courts and legislationis an apt motto for this sort of attitude. [...] Among some Common Law jurists, this attitude crystallizes in a curious, almost snobbish reluctance to regard legislation as a form of law at all.[9]

But law, like the constitutional rules which bring it to life, has, of course, always been the work of humans. It is the product of human hands, passed on from person to person, without divine intervention or prerequisite maturation. These rules do not need fertile ground to work, other than the collective conviction that the imagined world of the constitutional order is real and true (see Part V) and the legal system and law based on it 'binds' as law. In other words, that its rules and orders must be obeyed and merit observance. Nothing more is required: no demos, state or other condition.[10] The conviction, the collective belief, is decisive.

The essence of this conviction is *that* the constitutional order binds as law, as a collection of obligations and commands. For someone like Van Alstyne, a constitution needs to be hard law, or otherwise it is not a real constitution.[11] The essence of a constitution depends on this legal character, he observes:

> It is the idea of the constitution as hard law, [...] law as meaning reliable law and law that is reliable partly because it is not easily altered, law that is hard with *all* the implications of hard law.[12]

This reasoning cannot be turned on its head: a constitution does not necessarily expire all at once if its norms are no longer respected as law or if individuals or groups are no longer convinced of the value of compliance. As long as a group, even a minority, succeeds in imposing its will and conviction on a majority whether through coercion, repression or even manipulation a constitution, even an unjust

---

[8] Fukuyama 2011, p. 246.
[9] Waldron 1999, p. 9.
[10] Saskia Sassen seems to assume in general terms that the principle of territoriality is a condition for the functioning of a constitution. Cf. Sassen 2008.
[11] Van Alstyne 1987, p. 174–183.
[12] *Ibid.*, p. 179–180.

one, can endure. There are many such examples in history. It is certainly true that
a constitutional order based on a tiny minority of adherents is not sustainable in the
long run. But the empirical evidence indicates that the world has and has had many
instances of constitutions which have not enjoyed the support of a broad majority of
the population. This does not always result in immediate repercussions. Revolutions
or reform are often slow in coming. The idea that a constitution's norms bind as law
does not develop overnight; nor can it be extrapolated from an opinion poll and
the idea itself is rarely subject to a parliamentary vote. It develops in a process taking many years or even centuries. But ultimately a constitution ceases to be a *real*
constitution when over an extended period of time it no longer binds as law and/or
people are no longer convinced of the value of compliance. The exact point when
an old constitution loses its effect is difficult to measure.[13]

EFFECTIVENESS?

Constitutional norms create political and legal systems and provide (institutional)
rules of conduct, but none of this gives much indication of their effectiveness.[14]
Whilst not all of a constitution's norms have to be observed and a constitution
does not require every single citizen's endorsement to exist, apply and work, non-
compliance with its norms logically undermines the whole idea and its raison
d'être.[15] Yet, non-compliance is, of course, quite common. A 'total-compliance' constitution does not exist. Numerous factors can cause differences to arise between the

---

[13] As in the case of the Dutch magistrate and minister Cornelis Felix van Maanen. This future
Minister of Justice of the Netherlands was the chief justice at the imperial Court of Justice in
The Hague when Napoleon lost the Battle of Leipzig in mid-October 1813 and French forces
began withdrawing everywhere in Europe. The French legal system and the Constitution of
1804 (the year XII) were still in force in the Netherlands. The lost battle at Leipzig did not have
a direct effect on pending legal cases, collection of claims, transfer of real estate, the significance of subpoenas, drafting of notarial deeds, and conducting exams and awarding diplomas
by Leiden University. The legal system, created by the 1804 Constitution, composed by the
defeated and fleeing emperor, was still in force. A power vacuum developed over the course
of November. Naturally, things could not just continue regardless. This was a challenge for
Van Maanen. As a faithful servant of the Empire, he dreaded the consequences of the demise
of Napoleonic authority. He feared the population would run amok in the resultant vacuum
and there would be general chaos. So, he stayed on his post. Van Maanen was still reporting
to the imperial justice minister in Paris days after the departure of the French civil authorities
from the Netherlands. Only the arrival of the invading Russian Cossacks at the heart of The
Hague made him realise that his loyalty to the French emperor might no longer be realistic.
But still Van Maanen doggedly continued his work at the Court of Justice as if a change of
regime had not taken place. He would continue to do so for almost another month. Anecdotal
proof that the fundamental laws and structures created by constitutions are tenacious because
their consequences extend into society's deepest nooks and crannies.
[14] Stringham 2015, p. 9–20 and more in general chapter 2 (*Beyond the Deus ex Machina Theory
of Law*).
[15] Andrea Pozas Loyo argues that: 'norm-behaviour congruence [is] a necessary but not sufficient
condition' of constitutions. Pozas Loyo 2016, especially p. 34.

letter of the (constitutional) law and events in the real world. For example, one of the first articles in the Japanese Constitution prohibits the country from having armed forces, yet the country has had a substantial military force for over fifty years: the Japanese Self-Defense Forces (JSDF).[16] Even though it is contested as to whether they are really unconstitutional (of course, they are), the reason for the deviation from the letter of the law is obvious: sheer physical preservation dictates that Japan must be able to defend itself in some way.[17]

CONSTITUTIONAL PERFORMANCE

Thus, a constitution's norms are not always complied with or observed, but how much does this matter? Complying with a constitutional text to the letter is not a goal or a measure of success in itself. It gives little indication of a constitution's performance.[18] Some constitutional texts such as those of Norway, Belgium and the United States are centuries-old. The older a constitutional text is, the more time has passed between the world when it was adopted and current circumstances. The passage of time makes it ever more likely that the old text can no longer be applied to the letter or complied with without any translation to the present.[19] Even if you are an ardent adherent of *originalism* (the constitutional orthodoxy requiring a constitution be interpreted according to its original intention and literal text see Chapter 28), you cannot halt the march of time. Time moves forwards and changes the context of constitutional norms.[20] This does not mean that old constitutions are less successful or usable than new ones.[21] On the contrary, a constitution's age is often an indication of its effectiveness and durability; of its overall endurance.[22]

How can you tell whether a constitution is functioning properly and whether its norms are effective? You could try measuring everyone's beliefs, using a survey or something similar ('Are you convinced by the Constitution? Why, or why not?'). This is, of course, impracticable, as well as absurd. It would be better to look at other things to assess a constitution's performance and success. The American

[16] Article 9.
[17] 'A constitution is not a suicide pact', as Judge Arthur Goldberg expressed it in the United States Supreme Court *Kennedy v. Mendoza-Martinez* ruling, 372 US 144 (1963). Cf. Posner 2007 (orig.). 1972, p. 679–688 and Müller 2018.
[18] Ginsburg & Huq 2016.
[19] Cf. George Tsebelis and Dominic J. Nardi's amusing research which demonstrates that the longer constitutions are poorly observed, the more must be changed, even if they have a rigid review procedure. This makes sense, if you think about it. Tsebelis & Nardi 2016.
[20] Brest 1980.
[21] Elkins, Ginsburg and Melton point out that 'the statistical analysis suggests that the primary effect of time on the efficacy of constitutional rights is maturation. As constitutional rights get older, the constitutional promises tend to improve performance.' Elkins, Ginsburg & Melton 2016, p. 264–265.
[22] Hirschl 2009, especially p. 1353.

constitutionalists Ginsburg and Huq argue that a constitution's 'success' depends on several factors. First, success can be assessed according to an internal or external perspective. You could say that a constitution is a 'successful' project if it achieves the constituent legislator's intentionsdistilling and disseminating the constitutional ideas convincingly (internal perspective). Or more generally, when it succeeds in binding government to law, establishes an effective judicial system, brings about peaceful political and social relations, effectively protects fundamental freedoms, guarantees democracy, and so forth (external perspective).[23] Second, constitutional 'success' is not a binary question of compliance or non-compliance to the literal text, but rather a question of the degree of compliance. Total compliance is probably unachievable, but the greater the gap between the world of constitutional norms and reality, the less likely it is that these norms are successful and the lower a constitution's performance, with sham constitutions (dealt with below) at the unsuccessful end of the spectrum. Third, measuring a constitution's success requires patience. A constitution's real success can only be measured over the longer term. Incidents, controversy, accidental neglect of constitutional norms, or the occasional obsolete norm say very little in themselves about overall constitutional success over time, even though commentators are liable to foretell the impending doom of the whole constitutional system when mishaps occur. To really measure a constitution's success, you always have to look at the mid-range. Ginsburg and Huq argue that this means a period covering a substantial number of years, preferably several decades.[24] They also assert that, alongside these perspectives, four kinds of aspects or criteria are indicative of constitutional success. First, (sociological) 'legitimacy': how does a constitutional system perform in terms of imparting the shared faith to a substantial section of the population that the constitution deserves respect and loyalty.[25] Second, 'political channelling': to what extent does a constitution manage to peacefully settle potentially violent political conflicts through constitutional institutions. Third, 'control over agency costs': related to the institutionalisation of government. Does a constitutional system succeed in preventing the functioning of offices and organs from becoming 'personal' and/ or 'self-enriching' property of a person or clique? Fourth, to what extent does a constitution create valuable, 'suitable public goods', things and interventions that would not occur spontaneously without constitutional institutions, such as public order and safety, dykes, protected conservation areas, defence, clean air and the like.[26] Taken together, Ginsburg and Huq have developed a valuable yardstick, but it is, of course, difficult to use in the day-to-day political and legal practice of constitutional life.

---

[23] Ginsburg & Huq 2016 *Introduction*, especially p. 6–10.
[24] *Ibid.*, p. 15.
[25] *Ibid.*, p. 15–16.
[26] *Ibid.*, p. 15–23.

SHAM CONSTITUTIONS

Constitutions around the world are full of high-minded ideals and intentions that are not always achieved. Sometimes these goals and promises were not even ever intended to be met. For example, the Eritrean Constitution recognises freedom of expression, religion, and conscience. The North Korean Constitution enshrines the freedom of the press, freedom of expression, freedom of association and assembly, and freedom of movement and residence. These are dead letters, because in reality Eritrea and North Korea are repressive dictatorships whose subjects can at most dream of such rights. These constitutions' authors did not even intend to work towards these rights when they were formulating these lofty sentiments. Such constitutions are called *sham constitutions* (or façade constitutions)[27] that fail to do what they ought to do: adjust political reality to the letter of the constitution and provide citizens with the rights and guarantees they promise. As we have seen above, the capacity of constitutional documents is limited and vulnerable. Constitutions are often no more than parchment barriers,[28] as James Madison put it, between rightful and legitimate use of power and its abuse of it. And there will, of course, always be a discrepancy between the constitutional ideal, and existing practice and political reality.[29]

What is important is how big this gap is, or how big it is allowed to grow. Whichever perspective one cares to adopt, at a certain point it becomes undeniable that a constitution has degenerated from a real to a sham or façade constitution. Law and Versteeg developed an indicator in 2013. They consider a constitution 'sham' when there is excessive non-compliance with its provisions. They tried to establish this gap by examining the relative distance between the words and provisions of a constitution and existing practice. An increase in the magnitude and frequency of this distance indicates an increase in the likelihood that a constitution is sham.[30] These distances are best illustrated by juxtaposing several constitutional systems. Law and Versteeg compared the fundamental freedoms in 729 constitutions belonging to 188 countries (existing or historical, between 1946 and 2010) to the quantitative data (mainly) from social science research on these countries' compliance with these freedoms. This is a limited quantification because it excludes constitutions' vital institutional provisions (the role of the judiciary, the legislature, executive powers

---

[27] Law & Versteeg 2013.
[28] Madison 1987 (orig. 1788).
[29] Law & Versteeg 2013, p. 868–872.
[30] They also make a further classification. Some constitutions promise a great deal, others less (high or low de jure rights); some states observe them to a high degree (high de facto rights protection), others do not or less so (low de facto rights protection). When a great deal is promised and delivered Law and Versteeg speak of a 'strong constitution'. When little is promised but a great deal is delivered, they speak of a 'modest constitution'. And when little is promised and delivered, they speak of a 'weak constitution'. A sham constitution then is one that promises a great deal but delivers very little.

and so forth). Nevertheless, their analysis certainly gives a good indication of the real state of these constitutions. Their worst ten sham constitutions (the 'Hall of Shame') in 2010 was led by Nigeria in first place, followed by Eritrea, Myanmar, Sudan, Russia, Sri Lanka, Ethiopia, Vietnam, Congo (Kinshasa), Afghanistan and Pakistan. You may wonder how North Korea could possibly not have some place of honour in the Hall of Shame. The reason is simple: some countries' constitutions are so bogus that there is not even any data on complicity with their provisions. Even without such data, North Korea is a prime candidate for the Hall of Shame in this regard.[31] The research also shows that the number of sham constitutions increased sharply between 1981 and 2010 and most of them can be found in Africa and Central and Southeast Asia the regions which have witnessed the greatest constitutional production since 1989. This is hardly reassuring. As with the relationship Law and Versteeg established between the length of constitutional freedom catalogues and actual freedom: countries with extensive fundamental freedoms in their constitutional catalogues usually have more political violence and (state) terror.[32] For instance, torture seems to occur more often in countries with a constitutional prohibition of torture than in other countries.[33] It would appear that repressive regimes use their constitutions for window dressing to boost their legitimacy.

ENDURANCE

As well as establishing legal systems, constitutional norms also create leadership or political systems. They do so by creating leadership institutions (agencies, authorities and offices, such as parliaments, governments, ministers) and rules for their composition and functioning (elections, appointment and dismissal, rules on roles, information provision, accountability). These constitutional norms are much more than survival kits to get from one election to the next. The whole idea of a constitution is to give structure to a political system, and for the constitutional norms to create a framework endowing a political system with solidity.[34] This is one of the key reasons why constitutional rules enjoy a higher status than other legal rules, alongside their often rigid, difficult revision procedures. The more solid and rigid they are, the more certainty they give. Conversely, you might infer the success of a constitution from its age and durability: its endurance. One could argue that the longer

---

[31] Even a casual perusal of its constitution reveals many constitutional provisions that are blatantly disregarded. For example, article 17: 'Independence, peace and friendship are the basic ideals of the foreign policy and the principles of the external activities of the Democratic People's Republic of Korea.' Article 67: 'Citizens are guaranteed freedom of speech, the press, assembly, demonstration and association. The State shall guarantee the conditions for the free activities of democratic political parties and social organizations.'

[32] Law & Versteeg 2013, p. 1219–1220; Cf. Tsebelis 2017.

[33] Cf. Law 2010, especially p. 382 where Law cites several studies that seem to suggest a negative relationship between formal constitutional rights (protection) and actual compliance.

[34] Levinson 2012, p. 364.

a constitution has survived, the more successful it is, otherwise it would have been discarded. It is tempting to think of constitutions ageing like fine wine, as some kind of attested formula. Unfortunately, like wine, constitutions also risk spoilage over the years. A rigid revision procedure can cause a constitution to become outdated, rendering it obsolete and irrelevant.[35] Despite the need for structure and some rigidity, it is also important for constitutions to have some flexibility and adaptability, especially in rapidly changing times.[36] The golden mean is structure and adaptability in just the right proportions. In the words of Robert Cooter, 'a good constitution tilts without tumbling over'.[37]

THE DEAD SHOULD NOT GOVERN THE LIVING

Thomas Jefferson and James Madison had a famous discussion about finding this balance over two centuries ago. Madison was a delegate at the Philadelphia Convention that drafted the United States Constitution, and Jefferson was one of the chief architects of the United States Declaration of Independence. Both are considered Founding Fathers of the United States. After the Constitution had been drafted, Jefferson was appointed as American ambassador in Paris, where he wrote a famous letter to James Madison in September 1789. In it, he seemed to doubt the wisdom of the new United States Constitution's rigid amendment procedure. It stipulates that a proposal for an amendment must be adopted by Congress and ratified by three-quarters of the States. This is a formidable hurdle; perhaps it is too much of a good thing. It could stifle constitutional changes for decades. A constitution, Jefferson wrote, should not be in force for longer than one generation. Jefferson used an actuarial formula to calculate the length of a single generation and came up with about nineteen years. Every generation should be able to make their own constitutional mark. '[The] dead should not govern the living', Jefferson wrote.[38]

Madison begged to differ, arguing instead that a constitution had to be durable. This gives institutions and rules time to mature and consolidate, gradually gaining in authority and compliance. The essence of a constitution's fundamental rules is that they endow a polity with structure and stability. Madison argued that time is a crucial element and durability an intrinsic value in this process.[39] A constitution must be able to 'survive'. But adaptability is equally important as it prevents these

---

[35] Passchier 2017, p. 1–4.
[36] Scheuerman 2002.
[37] Cooter 2000, p. 372.
[38] Thomas Jefferson to James Madison, 6 September 1789. *The Letters of Thomas Jefferson 1743–1826* www.let.rug.nl/usa/presidents/thomas-jefferson/letters-of-thomas-jefferson/jefl81.php (consulted 10 July 2018). Cf. Sunstein 2009, Introduction *Jefferson's Revenge*.
[39] James Madison's reply to Thomas Jefferson, 4 February 1790 www.constitution.org/jm/17900 204_tj.txt (consulted 10 July 2018).

rules imposing the will of the dead on the living. In *The Origins of Political Order*, Francis Fukuyama shows how essential the balance between a political system's structure (in the form of strong institutions) and adaptability is for its odds of survival.[40] Too little adaptability is fatal, as is too little stability. A balancing act of this kind is just as important for constitutions.

But how do constitutions adapt? They do so in various ways. First, by use of their formal amendment procedures. Most of the world's constitutions have amendment procedures; amendmentsor, when very substantial, 'revisions' usually have to follow a special procedure, often involving multiple parliamentary votes and requiring a parliamentary supermajority. Early generations of constitutions (between around 1810 and 1880) tend to be highly rigid in this respect. They include various, stacked procedural hurdles, such as numerous readings, and prerequisite supermajorities. Constitutional generations after the Second World War tend to have slightly more flexible revision procedures overall, including differentiation of revision procedures with different revision procedures demanding and less demanding for various parts of the constitution.[41]

Age Matters

Zachary Elkins, Tom Ginsburg and James Melton's 2009 book *The Endurance of National Constitutions* proves James Madison right.[42] The dead do govern the living, and maybe there is not much wrong with that. Elkins and his co-authors looked into the life cycles of around 935 past and current constitutions between 1789 and 2006[43] and concluded that a constitution's endurance does matter. There are:

> significant associations between long-lived constitutions and various social and political goods including rights protection, democracy, wealth and political stability. Countries with enduring constitutions are richer and more democratic.[44]

Old age comes with benefits. The older a constitution, for example, the higher the likelihood of a country having a high gross national product. We should be careful when interpreting the results of this research that we do not get ahead of ourselves. Are the consequences and relationships observed directly related to the constitution? Or are these consequences and links a result of a combination of factors, some

---

[40] Fukuyama 2011, especially p. 452–457 and p. 458–459.
[41] Research by Reijer Passchier shows that around 60% of all constitutions from after the Second World War are equipped with a 'differentiated' revision procedure. Passchier 2015. Cf. https://papers.ssrn.com/sol3/papers.cfm?abstract_id=2693493 (consulted 10 July 2018). Cf. Albert 2018. Cf. Albert, Kontiadēs & Fotiadou 2017.
[42] Elkins, Ginsburg & Melton 2009, p. 30 ff.
[43] *Ibid.*, p. 50–51. Their data set consisted of 189 current constitutions and 746 historical constitutions (which were retracted, expired or superseded; in any case no longer valid).
[44] This is how Ginsburg summarises the 2009 study by Elkins, Ginsburg & Melton. Ginsburg 2011, p. 114.

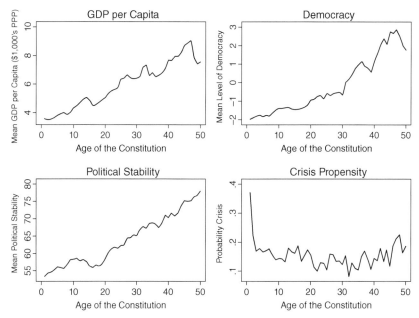

Figure 7 Mean select economic and political variables
Source: From Elkins, Ginsburg and Melton 2009, p. 32

of which we are unaware? And, in addition, what is cause and what is effect? Many countries with venerable democratic traditions have relatively old constitutions; they often do not have big wealth inequalities and their residents are on average relatively prosperous. What, then, is the relationship between the age of a constitution and a country's level of prosperity in these cases? Not a straightforward, unidirectional or causational one most likely. You cannot remove democracy and income differentials from the equation, or sweep them under the carpet, when looking at constitution-prosperity relations. Prosperity and welfare depend on many variables. Moreover, what is the consequence of what? Could it be that countries which have long had a socially peaceable climate, suffered few large social cleavages, enjoyed relatively modest wealth inequality and a culture of wealth redistribution are also more likely to be democratic and to adopt a constitution that will last?[45] Do peaceful and stable political communities breed enduring and stable constitutions or does it work the other way around? Or, more likely, does it work both ways?

Whatever the case may be, Elkins, Ginsburg and Melton demonstrate in their 2009 study that there is a significant positive correlation between the age of a constitution on the one hand and the per capita gross national product, democracy and political stability in a country on the other (see Figure 7). There also seems to be an

---

[45] For the many different relationships between income inequality, democracy and democratic participation, and constitutions cf. Dawood 2007. (Jared) Diamond 2019, p. 336–337.

(albeit modest) negative correlation between the age of a constitution and the likelihood of a political or economic crisis. The likelihood of a crisis seems to decrease
with the age of a constitution.[46]

All asides aside, in sum a constitution's endurance does appear to really matter,
as Madison had anticipated. On the other hand, it turns out that Jefferson was not
incorrect either. Elkins, Ginsburg and Melton's study also shows that the mean
lifespan of a constitution is exactly what Jefferson had calculated in Paris: nineteen
years.[47] How prophetic.

THE SELF-ENFORCING CONSTITUTION

Constitutions do not automatically endure. For them to survive, their norms have
to be upheld somehow or another. Who acts as the policeman or inspector? One
obvious answer is: the judiciary, or one of the other branches of government. As
well as and preferably the people, 'politics', or even *all* members of a constitutional
society. In this respect, there are more than enough inspectors and guardians to go
around. But it is not so simple. As systemic laws, constitutions are always susceptible
to political majorities and power. Constitutions provide no physical protection; the
Chilean constitution was powerless to protect President Allende when mutinous
troops burst into the presidential palace on 11 September 1973. No one was able
to prevent president De Gaulle from unconstitutionally forcing direct presidential
elections via a referendum in 1962.[48] And who can prevent presidents Erdogan,
Putin or the Philippine and Hungarian governments changing their constitutional
systems to better suit themselves? Certainly not the judges, supervisors or officials
they have dismissed or intimidated. Not to mention fascist and communist regimes
in the twentieth century. Constitutions really are no more than fragile parchment
barriers; checking political power with constitutional norms is a bit like reasoning
with your head in a crocodile's mouth,[49] or taming a bear bare handed. If a constitutional system is to become durable it will need to be self-enforcing to some extent. It
must consolidate itself and gradually mature into common heritage. Larry Diamond
argues that this consolidation requires:

---

[46] But, once again, you can wonder whether this is a result of the constitution or mature democ-
      racy. David Runciman shows in his book *The Confidence Trap* that democracies are good at
      dealing with and overcoming crises. Contrary to what you might expect. Then again, the same
      book shows that they are bad at preventing crises. Runciman 2013.
[47] Cf. Elkins, Ginsburg & Melton 2009, p. 3 and p. 207.
[48] De Gaulle called a referendum in which the French people approved a revision to the French
      Constitution enabling direct presidential elections. This was in violation with the constitu-
      tional revision procedure laid out in the French constitution. The *Conseil constitutionnel* (the
      French Constitutional Court) and the government had protested against De Gaulle's course
      of action prior to the referendum, but the referendum and constitutional revision were effectu-
      ated all the same.
[49] Free rendition of Churchill's (apocryphal) words in the film *The Darkest Hour* (2017).

[…] elites, organisations, and the mass public must all believe that the political system they actually have in their country is worth obeying and defending. […] consolidation occurs when citizens and politicians know 'that political conflict will be resolved according to the established norms and that violations of these norms are likely to be both ineffective and costly'.[50]

But how do you get the constitutional public to realise and believe that by calmly trusting in the principle 'today me, tomorrow you'[51] a constitutional system will ultimately benefit everyone? This will rely on finding clever ways of making a constitutional system self-enforcing. Constitutions need to find an optimum in which preserving the constitutional order is in everyone's interest as well as forge a minimum level of self-enforcement. A critical level for which we cannot solely depend upon referees, supervisors and guardians. Mittal and Weingast contend that two things are needed for a constitutional system to become self-enforcing,[52] and thus durable:

> […] at a given moment, all actors must find it in their interests to adhere to the constitutional rules, and as circumstances change, they must be able to adapt policies and institutions to maintain that stability over time. Incentives are central to both parts of the definition: Actors out of power must have incentives to pursue their goals within the system, and political officials must have incentives to honor the rules.[53]

Something for everyone. For a constitutional formula to keep working everyone must potentially be able to benefit from the system, and it must respond to everyone's motives for compliance. Mittal and Weingast add several important limiting conditions. The constitutional rules must really govern and supervise political power and not make it an 'all-or-nothing' game. Leaders must be restrained from making deals with cliques, monopolising or 'buying' power,[54] and bypassing the rules of the system. Minorities must be able to force majorities to comply with the constitutional rules (consensus condition) and have the opportunity to serve their interests and pursue their goals, even when they are not in power. Finally, the system as a whole must be able to adapt to changing circumstances (adaptive efficiency).[55] This is a tall order; it is hardly surprising that things sometimes go wrong.

---

[50] (Larry) Diamond 1999, p. 66 (including a reference to Linz & Stepan 1996, p. 5).

[51] From the Latin: 'Hodie mihi, cras tibi.'

[52] Cf. Graber 2013, p. 242–243. Graber asserts that a constitutional system is self-enforcing if constitutional procedures are set up so that, on balance, plausible answers can be found to interpretation differences on constitutional norms or issues over the years that participants in the discussion recognise as fair and reasonable (p. 242 and 243).

[53] Mittal & Weingast 2011, especially p. 282–283.

[54] What is called '(re)patrimonialisation'. Fukuyama 2011, p. 454.

[55] Mittal & Weingast 2011, p. 297–298.

In short, a constitutional system's survival requires trust in the system and trust in the 'others'. This does not happen automatically and certainly not overnight. Time and experience[56] are important factors in achieving a self-enforcing equilibrium.[57]

The likelihood of more or less spontaneous compliance with constitutional norms increases when the rules are clear and when it is also clear what happens when these rules are not observed (procedures, sanctions, etcetera). Compliance increases when constitutional rules are embraced by various groups in society and are seen as legitimate and binding rules of law. Finally, compliance is helped if enforcers of the constitutional rules are actually prepared to act in the event of non-compliance, knowing that in principle they can count on acceptance.[58]

Spontaneous compliance through self-enforcement is good and important – referees, overseers and repression on their own will not suffice – but this does not imply that guardians, judges and enforcers are unimportant to the system. You will always need constitutional police. It is best to establish a network of prevention and control mechanisms (checks and balances), as most modern constitutions do, at all levels of government and governmental action to prevent constitutional rules, especially individuals' rights and freedoms, falling victim to rulers' caprice.[59] For this reason, many modern constitutional systems have various forms of distribution of powers, involving modes of division of governmental power into legislative, executive and judicial branches. In these systems each branch of government is conferred separate powers or forced to work together to exercise its legislative, executive or judicial function.

The classic separation of powers into three branches of government (the *trias politica*) prevents a corrupting concentration of power and makes it possible for the three branches to monitor each other, thus acting as each other's referees. There are many variants. Some countries assign the judiciary sometimes even a separate constitutional supreme court the role of the ultimate interpreter and arbiter as to the issue whether constitutional law applies, how it is to be interpreted, whether it has been violated and what the consequences should be (*judicial primacy systems*). In other countries, parliament is the ultimate guardian of the constitutional rules (*parliamentary primacy systems*). Many modern constitutions contain a multitude of independent regulators beyond the purview of the traditional branches of government, including electoral boards (overseeing elections), audit offices, ombudsmen, and human rights commissioners, most of them monitoring agencies primarily charged with reporting. Monitoring bodies from beyond the national constitutional system, such as the United Nations Human Rights Committee or the European Committee on Social Rights, are increasingly common. All of them are constitutional watchdogs

---

[56] 'Maturation', as Elkins and others sum it up. Elkins, Ginsburg & Melton 2016, p. 264–265.
[57] Weingast 1997, especially p. 262.
[58] Elkins, Ginsburg & Melton 2009, p. 76–77.
[59] Kokott & Kaspar 2012, especially p. 796.

entrusted with keeping an eye on things. They are certainly flourishing, despite their effectiveness remaining unclear.[60]

Strict compliance with constitutional rules is, of course, not an end in itself. Constitutional rules only command and merit compliance if they are the *right* rules. Thomas Jefferson for one even argued that we should resist them if they are not:

> A strict observance of the written law is doubtless one of the high duties of a good citizen, but it is not the highest. The laws of necessity, of self-preservation, of saving our country when in danger, are of higher obligation. To lose our country by a scrupulous adherence to the written law, would be to lose the law itself, with life, liberty, property and all those who are enjoying them with us; thus absurdly sacrificing the ends to the means.[61]

Words which ring true through the ages.

---

[60] Flinders is critical of this development. He poses the rhetorical question: has 'the transition from "representative" to "monitory" democracy, which is reflected in an increasingly dense and aggressive "accountability industry" (constitutional watchdogs, audit processes, ethical guardians, investigatory agencies, regulatory boards, freedom of information legislation, quasi-judicial commissions, etc.), [...] actually contributed to the erosion of public support for politicians, political processes, and political institutions?' Flinders 2011, p. 595–596 ff.

[61] Cited in Brest, Levinson, Balkin, Amar & Seigel 2006, p. 65–67.

22

Economic Aspects

There is in fact no such thing as an unregulated financial market, as any student of ancient Mesopotamia – or Adam Smith's Scotland – knows. [But] the rule of law has many enemies. One of them is bad law.

Niall Ferguson[1]

We live in a world of markets[2] – yet another omnipresent phenomenon in our world today. These are usually 'free' markets in which supply and demand determine which products (goods, services, etcetera) are produced at what price. In principle, supply and demand in a free market economy are matched by private actors (consumers and producers) in an open process of free competition. Because we as individuals tend to make rational choices and operate efficiently – individuals strive for utility maximisation (convenience, low prices, high returns and so forth) – freely operating supply and demand in an open market of any size brings about greater efficiency, more utility and an increase in value. On balance, large groups act more rationally than a single individual.[3] This is the miracle of Adam Smith's 'invisible hand': the unseen self-regulating effect of a market in which every individual pursues her self-interest but in doing so creates collective prosperity.[4] Free markets not

---

[1] Transcript of Niall Ferguson's lecture *The Darwinian Economy*, the Reith Lecture 2012, recorded at The New York Historical Society in New York and broadcast on BBC Radio 4 and the BBC World Service on Tuesday, 26 June 2012. www.bbc.co.uk/programmes/articl es/3XhZsLTM18KBQX6C97w8K6z/niall-ferguson-the-darwinian-economy (consulted on 13 July 2018).

[2] We live in a 'transactional society'. Cf. Kehoe, Ratzan & Yiftach 2015, p. 2–3.

[3] 'Methodological Individualism'. Cf. Towfigh 2017, p. 18–19.

[4] Smith says: '[E]very individual who employs his capital in the support of domestic industry, necessarily endeavours so to direct that industry, that its produce may be of the greatest possible value [...] By preferring the support of domestic to that of foreign industry, he intends only his own security; and by directing that industry in such a manner as its produce may be of the greatest value, he intends only his own gain, and he is in this, as in many other cases,

only create prosperity, they also produce – it is assumed – (more) liberty.[5] Free markets strengthen individual autonomy, increase individual freedom of choice (which also increases the 'value' of individual freedom), and ensure a positive interaction between civil virtues,[6] legal rights (like ownership) and freedoms with economic freedom.[7]

Well … do they really? Some people, including historian Bas van Bavel, argue that free markets actually ultimately obstruct freedom and equality.[8] There is plenty of material for passionate discussions. The debate on whether free markets promote democracy is equally heated. Seymour Lipset suggested in 1963 that there was a connection between economic growth and democracy,[9] providing a possible proof of modernisation theory.[10] This is a theory which asserts that there is a direct link between economic development and the kind of political system a country has. The higher a country's level of economic development, the more likely it will be to develop a stable, consolidated democratic political system.[11] Thomas Piketty, celebrated author of the bestseller *Capital in the Twenty-First Century*, begs to differ at the end of his book:

> […] a market economy based on private property, if left to itself, […] contains powerful forces of divergence, which are potentially threatening to democratic societies and to the values of social justice on which they are based.[12]

Whatever the risks in the long run may be, it does seem firmly established that there is a strong correlation between a country's economic development and democracy, albeit it not the extent of a deterministic, almost causal relationship as conceived by Lipset.[13] There is lively academic debate about the mechanics of the interaction

led by an *invisible hand* to promote an end which was no part of his intention.' Smith 2003 (orig. 1776), p. 571–572. My italics.

[5] Milton Friedman's 1960s claim that economic development seems to go hand-in-hand with political freedom has been substantiated in many studies and cases since, even though it does not always seem to work this way. Sometimes the freedom-prosperity engine just fails to start or runs out of steam for some or other (unexpected) reason. The dynamics of this nexus still elude us sometimes. Hayek 1960; Roll & Talbott argue that political freedom and democracy *cause* economic prosperity and (eventually) health. Roll & Talbott 2003, p. 76–77 and p. 84–85. 1962.

[6] Cf. McCloskey 2006.

[7] Cf. Benyishai & Betancourt 2010.

[8] Van Bavel 2016.

[9] Lipset 1963.

[10] Lipset 1959.

[11] *Ibid.*, p. 75.

[12] Piketty 2014, p. 571.

[13] 'Thriving markets and economic growth do not produce democracy', according to Weingast. 'Instead, both democracy and markets require the limit condition. Countries that have devised means to satisfy the limit condition can therefore sustain both democracy and the market.' The limiting condition is, for one, the constitutional rules governing and controlling the exercise of power (cf. the section in the previous chapter on self-enforcing constitutions). Weingast 2016a, especially p. 272.

between markets, freedom, democracy and institutions like the law. I will not dwell on this subject and only discuss it briefly and superficially, not only because I am not familiar with all of the latest developments in political economy, but also because it is not directly relevant to the purposes of this book. What is important in this chapter is the role of constitutions and constitutional rules in and their significance to markets and economies.

Constitutions and constitutional rules are significant to economic life in two ways: as a *condition* and a *factor*.[14]

THE CONSTITUTION AS A CONDITION

It goes without saying that our lives are not entirely determined by markets, goods and transactions, but markets and the economy are very important. The course of a person's life is greatly affected by their wealth, opportunities (education, information, income), and risks they run or attributed to them (illness, background, network, business risk, etcetera). Personal destiny really does depend on market forces. Adam Smith's conventional economic theory assumes that a free market basically gives everyone equal, 'fair' (optimal) opportunities thanks to market forces. Open competition on a free market is supposed to result in an equilibrium between supply and demand – also increasing general prosperity. In a system of 'natural freedom' – with minimal governmental intervention – rational market participants create added value on aggregate by pursuing their self-interest, hence contributing towards the interest of all by increasing prosperity.[15] Adam Smith famously wrote that (*The Wealth of Nations*):

> It is not from the benevolence of the butcher, the brewer, or the baker, that we expect our dinner, but from their regard to their own interest.[16]

In theory a free market gives fair opportunities to all participants and regulates itself without governmental interference.[17] There is just one snag: in practice they don't.

---

[14] Relations between constitutions and economics are studied in what is called 'constitutional economics'. This field of research has two traditions or schools. The first school conducts normative research using modern social contract theories to try to understand how optimal equilibriums can be achieved in (parts of) constitutions and how constitutional rules can be improved (above a Pareto distribution). The second, positive school is less concerned with formulae, and instead tries to understand the (economic) effects of constitutional rules, and how the rise and change of constitutional rules can be explained or understood. This tradition coincides with my theme 'constitution as a factor'. Cf. Voigt 2011, especially p. 205–206.

[15] The pursuit of self-interest is a key feature of human nature. People are 'rational utility maximizers in *all* areas of life, not just in "economic" affairs […]', as Posner puts it. Posner 2007, p. 4.

[16] Smith 2003 (orig. 1776), *The Wealth of Nations*, book I, chapter II (*Of the Principle Which Gives Occasion to the division of Labour*), p. 23–24.

[17] In Adam Smith's words: 'All systems either of preference or of restraint, therefore, being thus completely taken away, the obvious and simple system of natural liberty establishes itself of its own accord. Every man, as long as he does not violate the laws of justice, is left perfectly

Contrary to what is sometimes claimed,[18] (large-scale) markets cannot entirely regulate themselves, at least not completely and durably. Free markets do not always generate fair and certainly not equal opportunities. This is what Piketty, of course, is hinting at. The economic history of the past two centuries, the heyday of wealth creation by industrialisation, is littered with the victims of exploitation, inequality and economic crises. The invisible hand sometimes deals heavy blows. This does not necessarily imply that the idea of free markets and open competition is a failure. It is just things get in the way: obstacles and intervening factors which frustrate equal opportunities and fair and open competition and thus obstruct the potential of fair distribution of wealth for all. Markets can fail to fulfil their potential because they are distorted by unfair competition, in the form of market dominance, price-fixing or unfair use of public funds or goods (natural resources, the environment).

To generate optimal added value markets must be as free as possible, but without any regulation they can cease to function properly due to what economists call 'market failure'.[19] This term denotes distortions of the free market principle causing markets to no longer do what they are supposed to do – generate maximum prosperity from which all can benefit. Preventing and remedying such distortions requires some kind of governmental intervention, nowadays mostly based on constitutional rules and institutions (offices, authorities, powers, rule-based interventions with public resources, regulation etcetera). Political debates in modern states are invariably about how far government market-regulation should go, from neo-liberal minimalism to socialist maximalism, and every imaginable variation between them. There is hardly anyone nowadays who seriously argues that markets can regulate themselves without any government intervention. Governments, rules and market interventions are needed to take corrective measures. Free markets probably could not even exist without them. In political economist Barry Weingast's words:

> Universally in today's developed world, governments provide [...] market infrastructure, and no market economy exists without it.[20]

free to pursue his own interest his own way, and to bring both his industry and capital into competition with those of any other man, or order of men.' Smith 2003 (orig. 1776), book IV, chapter IX, p. 873.

[18] Weingast castigates the widespread notion that free markets can exist without governments and governmental control as a 'neoclassical fallacy'. Weingast 2016b.

[19] In general, causes of market failure are divided into four groups: a) abuse of market power (monopolies or cartels – i.e., unfair pricing agreements), b) uneven allocation of externalities/external effects (such as pollution, and antisocial behaviour – matters outside the demand-supply situation with an effect on price), c) unequal access to public goods (such as defence, dykes, education and so forth. When these goods are not available on equal terms and non-competitively to market participants, they can disrupt markets through free-rider behaviour), and finally d) asymmetrical information (for example, when a market participant or a group has more information than others). Cf. Veljanovski 2010, p. 20–22.

[20] Weingast 2017, p. 2.

Free market economies do not operate in a vacuum, but in the controlled conditions created by states, law, governments and interventions. Constitutions play an important, perhaps even indispensable, role in this.[21] Rational market participants want to be able to look into the future: they want to have certain basic certainties, know the risks, and be sure that contracts will be honoured, investments will provide returns, and money and property value and are protected. Constitutions' rules on leadership and legal systems, and the resultant legal certainty, solve the problems of anarchy, such as violence, looting, corruption and abuse of power, and the absence of authority to enforce contracts or, more generally, legal rules.[22] First and foremost, constitutions provide stability[23] in the form of a reduction in uncertainty and an increase in predictability.[24] Constitutions that succeed in doing so act as *credible commitments*[25] which are important for market participants and investors. Commitments like these reduce risk, raise trust and certainty, thereby increasing opportunities for economic growth. Canadian constitutionalist Ran Hirschl even sees the law and legal certainty and legal protection provided by constitutions as critical preconditions for economic growth:

> Two critical preconditions for economic development are the existence of predictable laws governing the marketplace and a legal regime that protects capital formation and ensures property rights. The entrenchment of constitutional rights and the establishment of independent judicial monitoring of the legislative and executive branches are seen as ways of increasing a given regime's credibility and enhancing the ability of its bureaucracy to enforce contracts, thereby securing investors' trust and enhancing their incentive to invest, innovate, and develop.[26]

One of the reasons for the great global popularity of constitutions in recent times is that:

> political leaders of any independent political unit want to promote sustainable long-term economic growth and encourage investment that will facilitate the prosperity of their polity.[27]

[21] *Ibid.*, p. 6.
[22] North, Wallis and Weingast argue that controlling violence and anarchy logically involves three things: 1) the police and army are controlled by politics, 2) politics (the political system) is governed by a number of institutions (including rules) and motives which restrict the illegal use of power and violence, and 3) for a political group or party to maintain power requires the support of representatives of social and political interests and these interests must (continue to) be represented. Government must not be restricted to serving the private or personal interests of the parties in power or their members ('rent-seeking politics'). North, Wallis & Weingast 2009, p. 22.
[23] Cf. Mittal & Weingast 2011.
[24] Max Weber argues that predictability and certainty are the foundations of successful 'capitalist free markets'. Cf. (Max) Weber 1972 (orig. 1922).
[25] In North and Weingast's words: 'For economic growth to occur the sovereign or government must not merely establish the relevant set of rights, but must make a *credible commitment* to them.' North & Weingast 1989, p. 803. My italics. Cf. Weingast 1993, p. 286–311.
[26] Ran Hirschl 2004, p. 82.
[27] *Ibid.*

THE CONSTITUTION AS A FACTOR

Do constitutional rules effect markets and the economy? Most certainly. Stefan Voigt reasons that they would be rather pointless if they did not – (the hope of) beneficial economic effects also largely explain the proliferation of constitutions:

> if constitutional rules did not have any significant effect on economic outcomes, expending effort on explaining their emergence would be pointless. However, there is now substantial evidence that constitutional rules do have important economic effects.[28]

This is a somewhat indirect explanation, in my opinion, unlikely to prove much in itself. Trade and free markets that brought prosperity existed before constitutions became omnipresent. But Voigt's question does point in the right direction. Why would you want something like a constitution from an economic perspective? It is costly to draft, generates incessant discussion before it can be agreed upon, and myriad procedural obstacles must be overcome before its promulgation. And when a constitution finally enters force, many expensive institutions must be established, such as parliaments, courts and councils – not to mention the civil servants needed to run the show. Why do countries do it?

The first motive was elucidated above: constitutional systems act as credible commitments,[29] on the condition, of course, that they are combined with the rule of law.[30] A constitutional system promises domestic and foreign market participants that the market they want to trade on or invest in is reliable; that market relationships are governed by predictable legal rules and law, that the government enforces these rules and guarantees fair dispute settlement. A commitment of this kind reduces uncertainty, improving market growth. The converse is also so: uncertainty raises prices, lowers investment readiness and increases transaction costs. As market success and political success are nowadays almost regarded as extensions of one other, reducing transaction costs is a particularly compelling motive for having a constitutional system.[31]

Transaction costs[32] are all the costs a market participant must incur before a transaction can be completed. In their book *Law and Transaction Cost in the Ancient Economy*, Kehoe, Ratzan and Yiftach show, as a case in point, how prohibitively expensive and difficult trade relations were in classical antiquity. In the Roman Empire it was difficult to bring buyers and sellers together and ascertain information about each other. Transport was expensive and dangerous, and the government was unreliable and thoroughly corrupt. Officials had to be paid for literally everything. As

---

[28] Voigt 2011, p. 206.
[29] North & Weingast 1989.
[30] North, Wallis & Weingast 2009, p. 115.
[31] They decrease uncertainty, thereby increasing confidence, resulting in lower transaction costs. Cf. Nooteboom 2002, p. 103–108.
[32] A term coined by the renowned economist Ronald Coase. Cf. Coase 1960, especially p. 15 ff.

if this were not enough, delivery was uncertain, payment transactions complicated and – when things went wrong, as they often did – dispute resolution (supposing you could even find a judge) was so expensive that people usually only threatened with legal action but rather settled out of court.[33] The entire market mechanism in the Roman Empire largely depended on informal contacts and norms, the bonds of trust in families and trade networks, and traditions.[34] It was a paragon of inefficiency. And Rome was about the most open and prosperous market in all antiquity. The ancients were not ignorant of these impediments – Athens was acutely aware of them by the fourth century BCE. Kehoe, Ratzan and Yiftach show how the city-state cleverly managed to attract foreign investors with clear-cut, knowable rules and a reliable (or at least reasonably predictable) judicial system.[35] In the end, of course, this system could not in itself protect Athens' mighty market from foreign invasions. Rules and judges were, at the time, no match for soldiers' boots

Transaction Costs

Whilst transactions are still costly, on balance the array of institutions established by modern constitutional systems do reduce these costs.[36] Not only in an absolute sense, but more especially in a relative sense. The costs of producing goods and services are not solely determined by capital, labour and natural resources, but also by the costs of establishing and protecting property and property rights and fulfilling (contractual) agreements. The restrictions imposed by current institutions on transactions may appear to raise the costs of products and services, but transactions are – as a result of them – smoother, faster and more reliable, allowing transaction volumes and confidence to increase. In modern open economies with large trading volumes, transaction costs can be incorporated relatively easily in the cost price without a major impact on competitiveness.

Modern institutions,[37] including constitutional legal systems with all their seemingly expensive regalia, are thus very efficient – certainly in an historical perspective.[38] They 'depersonalise' trade and settlement – in that you do not know or need to know the other party personally – with the guarantee that a third party (court, arbitrator, state body or the like) can enforce fulfilment of the transaction.[39] This is not only reassuring, but also lowers costs. Robert Nozick demonstrated in 1974

---

[33] Kehoe, Ratzan & Yiftach 2015, p. 15–27.

[34] Networks that operated on what would nowadays be call 'distributed trust', with kinship, relationships and reputation as enforcement mechanisms. Cf. Botsman 2017, p. 8 ff.

[35] Kehoe, Ratzan & Yiftach 2015, p. 17.

[36] North 1990, especially p. 11–12. North summarises Coase's ideas from Coase 1960 and his classic: Coase 1937.

[37] This is taken here as a society's rules, or more formally: 'the behavioural limitations designed by people who determine human interaction'. North 1990, p. 3.

[38] Even if you include all decision-making costs. Cf. Mueller 2003, p. 627–628.

[39] As Douglass North puts it: 'impersonal exchange with third-party enforcement'. North 1990, p. 35.

that the costs of establishing and maintaining a legal system with property rights are much lower than the costs incurred in an anarchic situation to protect property by force.[40] This holds at all levels. For instance, it saves an inordinate amount of hassle when a buyer can safely presume that a vendor's scales have been calibrated by an officially recognised independent entity. Otherwise you would have to lug your own scales around with you and haggle endlessly. Institutions like legal systems are indispensable. In the words of Nobel Prize winner Douglass North, they are 'the critical underpinning of successful modern economies.'[41] At any rate, that is the theory. Can it be seen and measured in practice? This has proven difficult. And perhaps it is the wrong way of posing the question. Let me try to explain.

Tiebreaker?

The tiebreaker rule was adopted in 1970. At score of 6-6, a set is determined by one more game, a tiebreaker, with points counted using ordinary numbering (1, 2, 3). Each player serves two consecutive points in a tiebreaker. The tiebreaker is won by the first player to score seven points and at least two points more than their opponent. Otherwise, it continues beyond seven points and the first player to score two points more than their opponent wins. Has this relatively transparent institution improved tennis? It is hard to tell. The 1970 Wimbledon Men's singles final between John Newcombe and Ken Rosewall is like a slow-motion film in comparison with the 2018 men's singles final between Novak Djokovic and Kevin Anderson. Newcombe and Rosewall positively lumbered across the court – it was more like walking interspersed with the occasional clumsy leap. Djokovic and Anderson served much faster than their colleagues in 1970, were constantly on the move, used short sprints to command every inch of the court, and served far fewer faults. The game is much quicker than it was in 1970, it is more enjoyable, more attractive, and far more people watch it. Players earn astronomically more than Newcombe and Rosewall ever did. Tennis has become a popular sport, involving large amounts of money, and eye-watering earnings. How did the tiebreaker rule contribute to this development? Or, if you consider this too vague: is it possible to determine how the rules of the game have contributed – in sporting or economic terms – to tennis' success? It goes without saying that many factors contributed to the success of the sport, not just these rules. Equipment, subsurface, technology and strategy, training methods, diet, construction, media development, global information and media networks, etcetera. How and to what extent the (peculiar) rules of tennis[42] contributed to this

---

[40] Even though they are often invisible. Something like 'the invisible hand of the state' operates in modern market economies. Nozick 2002 (orig. 1974), chapter 5 (*The State*), especially p. 118–119.

[41] North 1990, p. 35.

[42] The scoring (15, 30, 40) in games comes from the value of a coin (15 *derniers*) originally used per point in the mediaeval French game *jeu de paume* ('game of the palm').

success is very difficult to determine.[43] Rules are important, but they do not make the game. Hence, finding a direct causal link between these rules and tennis' success is virtually impossible; at most, there may be some correlation here and there. The idea behind the tiebreaker rule was to increase a game's tempo – something you might be able to measure. Did games get shorter? And what effect did this have on the attractiveness of the sport? Incidentally, the longest tennis game ever played was at Wimbledon *after* the introduction of the tiebreaker rule. Isner and Mahut spent more than eleven hours on the court in 2010, in a match that went on for three days.[44] This spectacle certainly did nothing to diminish the popularity of tennis.

THE CONSTITUTION AS A CATALYST

The most direct effect constitutional rules have on economic relations is increasing mutual trust. Stable market transactions are based on trust, and our neurobiological disposition (Chapter 3) makes it difficult to build trust and maintain it with strangers. The fiduciary institutions of the law enable abstract trust. The vulnerability of trust – 'trust comes on foot but leaves on horseback'[45] – is overcome by abstract notions of law, legal certainty and institutions (enforcers, authorities, regulators, courts and so on) that channel the mostly state-based monopoly on the use of force. Trust generates more trust, reduces transaction costs and encourages reciprocity, enabling us to collaborate better and develop collective goods (infrastructure, education, social services, environmental protection).[46] Constitutions work more or less like catalysts in this regard.

Some of the effects of parts or aspects of constitutions on economic life we can measure more directly. As noted in the previous chapter, for instance, the age of constitutions seems to have a positive correlation with per capita gross national product (GDP).[47] Alvaro Montenegro identified another peculiar correlation in 1995: short constitutions with few articles are usually associated with a higher per capita GDP and, conversely, long constitutions with many articles are associated with a lower per capita GDP.[48] Tsebelis and Nardi come to the same conclusion twenty years later. Not only did they observe an association between longer constitutions and a lower per capita GDP, but also more corruption and amendments than in the case of short constitutions.[49] Long constitutions are even more likely to be amended more frequently than short ones, despite any constitutional rigidity.[50] Brevity is

---

[43] Tennis is the fourth biggest sport in the world. Around 1.2 billion people regularly play or watch tennis (2012 estimate). www.quora.com/How-many-people-play-tennis-worldwide The tennis industry is worth billions of euros/dollars.

[44] Eventually, Isner won the fifth set – to which the tiebreaker rule does not apply – 70–68.

[45] A Dutch saying.

[46] Kahan 2003, especially p. 102–103.

[47] Elkins, Ginsburg & Melton 2009, p. 31–32.

[48] Montenegro 1995, especially p. 169.

[49] Tsebelis & Nardi, especially p. 474.

[50] Tsebelis 2017.

indeed the soul of wit. But, it is still best not to jump to conclusions. Longer constitutions are themselves the product of something, such as a culture of low mutual trust, as Montenegro's research shows. We often try to avert distrust with long contracts and equally lengthy constitutions.[51] It is difficult to determine causal relations in this respect and to accurately pinpoint what is related to what.

But difficulties of course 'are but the dares of fate' and should never discourage us.[52] Undeterred Torsten Persson and Guido Tabellini researched the economic effects of constitutions in 2002.[53] Rather than looking at entire constitutions, they focused on parts of them, such as electoral system rules and systems of government. They did so in eighty-five countries between 1960 and 1988. The results are interesting. Countries with a first-past-the-post electoral system, for instance, had lower public expenditure (around 3%) than countries with proportional representation, but social security expenditure overall was 2–3% higher. Furthermore, countries with a first-past-the-post electoral system often have a slightly smaller budget deficit than countries with a proportional representation (around 1–2% smaller). Another striking result is that the smaller a constituency is, the more corruption there is. A less easily interpretable result is that labour productivity is positively correlated to the number of directly elected representatives. Subsequent research has corroborated these results.[54] It is important to bear in mind that these effects are mostly not direct, autonomous consequences of electoral systems, and have an indirect association.[55]

The observed effects of constitutional rules on governmental systems are equally interesting. In terms of government spending, for example, Persson and Tabellini see differences between presidential and parliamentary systems. Government spending is around 6% lower in presidential than in parliamentary systems; and the latter have welfare states that are 2–3% larger on average than in presidential systems. Corruption is slightly lower in presidential systems, but otherwise, presidential and parliamentary systems do not differ greatly in this regard.[56] Whilst these results are certainly interesting, they do not say much about the overall effect of constitutions as a whole.

An Echo Chamber of Freedom?

The aforementioned Douglass North (1920–2015) believes that institutions – defined as rules of the game – are important for society's economic and political success. In

---

[51] Montenegro 1995, p. 169. Montenegro asserts that this also explains why countries with many lawyers have lower economic growth: distrust. Cf. Murphy, Shleifer and Vishny 1991.
[52] From the poem, 'Being Alive', by Ella Wheeler Wilcox (1850–1919) published in, *The Art of Being Alive*. New York, London: Harper 1914, II.
[53] Persson & Tabellini 2003, par. 9.11, p. 212–215.
[54] Blume, Müller & Voigt 2009.
[55] Persson & Tabellini 2004, p. 76 and p. 94–96.
[56] Cf. Persson & Tabellini 2003, par. 9.1.2, p. 215–217.

his book *Institutions, Institutional Change and Economic Performance*, published in 1990, he says: 'institutions reduce uncertainty by providing a structure to everyday life.'[57] Institutions matter – they are, so to speak, the political economy's river bed: they may not determine the speed, volume or temperature of the flow, but they do determine the course.

Constitutions are packed with rules of this kind, *hence* determining our economic and political life to a large extent. The freedom, rights and rules enshrined in modern liberal constitutions actually work as a precondition for free markets, economic growth and greater prosperity. These constitutional rules are the foundations. Some disagree stridently with this conception, including William Riker. He considers it far too simplistic – and even deterministic. Constitutions do not produce free markets and free people: free people and free markets produce constitutions.[58] An argument that provides plenty of food for thought and is a classic to boot. As Marx and Engels wrote in the *Communist Manifesto* in 1848, rules do not change the world, or economic (production) or social relations. Legal rules are mere products of the (bourgeois) production and property relations they codify:

> […] jurisprudence is but the will of your class made into a law for all, a will, whose central character and direction are determined by economic conditions of existence of your class.[59]

Or, then again, perhaps not? Scholarship is sometimes like hopscotch. In 2014, Alfonso-Gil, Lacalle-Calderón and Sánchez-Mangas tried to look a little longer and farther back at these effects.[60] They examined the effect of civil liberties – usually the core of a modern constitutional order – on economic growth (GNP) in 149 countries over a period of more than a century (1850–2010).[61] And what did they find? Their study observed that increases in civil liberty correlated with GNP growth.[62] Roll and Talbott have demonstrated that over the past decades political freedom and democracy, nowadays always enshrined in constitutions, *cause* increases in

[57] North 1990, p. 3.
[58] Riker 1976, p. 13: 'Does constitutional structure cause a political condition and a state of public opinion or does the political condition and a state of public opinion cause the constitutional structure? […] Constitutional forms are typically derivative. It seems probable to me that public opinion usually causes constitutional structure, and seldom, if ever, the other way around.'
[59] 'But don't wrangle with us so long as you apply, to our intended abolition of bourgeois property, the standard of your bourgeois notions of freedom, culture, law, etc. Your very ideas are but the outgrowth of the conditions of your bourgeois production and property, just as your jurisprudence is but the will of your class made into a law for all, a will, whose central character and direction are determined by economic conditions of existence of your class.' Marx & Engels 1888 (orig. 1848), chapter II (*Proletarians and Communists*).
[60] Alfonso-Gil, Lacalle-Calderón & Sánchez-Mangas 2014.
[61] Generally understood as the limitation of governmental power as a whole (not as a collection of specific fundamental freedoms). The researchers used the XCONST variable of the Systemic Peace project's Polity IV data.
[62] Alfonso-Gil, Lacalle-Calderón & Sánchez-Mangas 2014, p. 446.

economic prosperity.[63] It is a little over-optimistic to directly infer that this is incontrovertible proof that constitutionally protected rights are the measure of the market. But, conversely, it is unlikely that these countries truncated civil liberties or political freedom every time they had an economic downturn. Quite the opposite. Roll and Talbott show that anti-democratic events and reduction of political freedom are invariably followed by a reduction in growth,[64] even though not always a sustained one. At the face of it: freedom does seem to pay off. Enshrining it in a rigid constitution – as a guarantee against political upheaval and whims of the day – is not a bad idea. From a purely economic point of view, it makes sense.

---

[63] Roll & Talbott 2003, p. 76–77 and p. 84–85.
[64] Roll & Talbott 2003, p. 84.

23

Political Aspects

FRIENDS?

The perennial question of all political society is: 'to cooperate or not to cooperate?' Even though collaboration comes naturally to us, it is still hard to do. Because we are hardwired to distrust strangers, we need information on the reliability of others before we can make common cause with people we do not know. This creates incessant and major problems: information on trustworthiness is hard to come by, we tend to misread it and all kind of biases get in the way – as Malcolm Gladwell shows in his book *Talking to Strangers*.[1] To make matters worse: cooperation is not a free choice; we must work together in order to survive. This means that our days are spent worrying about others' trustworthiness, weighing the information they give us, before we can make some sort of informed decision. Sound strategies are of the essence. The gullible will most likely get cheated; the overly suspicious will lose out as well. And it is not a one-off game – we need to bond with different people at different times to best serve our interests. But work together with whom? Which alliance works best? When and for how long? We are constantly pondering our best cooperative chances, forever triangulating and assessing incomplete and mostly distorted bits of information. It is a wonder we can sleep at all if not for the miracle of taking risks and the wonder of leaps of faith.

When cooperative information comes from many different sources, things can get mindbogglingly complicated. An episode of the epic sitcom *Friends* illustrates the agony resulting from strategic complexities of this kind.[2] Joey's best friend and flatmate Chandler is in a secret relationship with their neighbour Monica, who is also his friend Ross' sister. Joey is in the know and has agreed to keep mum. In this

---

[1] Gladwell 2019.
[2] Episode 14 (production number 467664), season 5, 'The one where everybody finds out', first aired in 1999.

episode from 1999, Monica's flatmate Rachel and her former flatmate Phoebe find out about Monica and Chandler when they happen to visit the flat opposite the building and see Monica and Chandler kissing. After a hilarious bit of confused questioning, they tell Joey what they know. Joey is relieved. Assured that enough people know, he feels that he can finally inform other friends – including Ross – about the relationship. Not being the brightest of sparks, he has struggled to keep the secret. But Phoebe and Rachel – a bit put out at being left out of their best friends' secret for so long – decide not to confront Chandler and Monica and play dumb in order to wind up Monica and Chandler. They insist that Joey holds his tongue, which completely bewilders him. In the key scene, Joey is flummoxed by the complexities of the strategic combinations.

RACHEL: Phoebe just found out about Monica and Chandler.

JOEY: You mean how they're friends and nothing more? (Glares at Rachel.)

RACHEL: No. Joey, she knows! We were at Ugly Naked Guy's apartment [apartment opposite Rachel and Monica's apartment] and we saw them doing it through the window. (Joey gasps) Actually, we saw them doing it up against the window.

PHOEBE: Okay, so now they know that you know and they don't know that Rachel knows?

JOEY: Yes, but y'know what? It doesn't matter who knows what. Now, enough of us know that we can just tell them that we know! Then all the lying and the secrets would finally be over!

PHOEBE: Or, we could not tell them we know and have a little fun of our own.

RACHEL: Wh-what do you mean?

[a little later, when Joey has admitted to Monica and Chandler that Phoebe and Rachel know about the relationship because they saw them kissing from the opposite flat]

JOEY: I'm sorry! But hey, it's over now, right? Because you can tell them that you know they know and I can go back to knowing absolutely nothing!

MONICA: Unless…

JOEY: No! Not unless! Look this must end now!

MONICA: Oh man, they think they are so slick messing with us! But see they don't know that we know that they know! So…

CHANDLER: Ahh yes, the messers become the messies!

[…]

Joey is overwhelmed by the combinations. He wants to stay friends with everybody (general peace), which will require him to enter an alliance of some sort to prevent him breaking his personal promise not to tell the secret. But his friends have their own interests too – Joey's choices depend on theirs, which raises all kinds of dilemmas and makes decision making – in view of the various consequences – very hard. Translated into a simple scheme, the following sets of consequences might unfold:

	Joey tells the truth	Joey keeps the secret
Rachel and Phoebe tell the truth	Monica and Chandler will not be able to play their trick ('mess with the messies') – Everybody will be a little annoyed but not overly.	Monica and Chandler will be able to play their trick ('mess with the messies') but probably on an already overwhelmed Joey. General peace (friendship) is compromised.
Rachel and Phoebe keep the secret	Monica and Chandler will be able to play their trick ('mess with the messies') on Rachel and Phoebe. General peace (friendship) is compromised.	Monica and Chandler will not be able to play their trick ('mess with the messies'), Joey's conscience is still burdened and general peace has in reality been compromised (if all friends are being secretive their friendship is no longer 'genuine' – it is no longer an honest bond).

Nobody can win in this situation, but everyone owning up would seem the most logical strategy as it would cause the least harm. But that would, of course, not be very funny. Joey, Rachel and Phoebe choose a different course of action in this episode of Friends.

Dilemmas like this are classic elements of comedies – for good reason. They pique our interest and make us laugh because we recognise conundrums like this in our own lives. Every choice depends on what others do, and deciding whether or not to collaborate depends on 'reading' the other, on incomplete information, and even on ignorance and taking a risk. Even game shows use this format of expounding collaborative strategies.

> In the finale of ABC's reality show *The Bachelor Pad* (2010–2012) the winner could pocket a $250,000 prize in a final test. The two finalists, 'were forced to go into separate rooms and decide whether they wanted to "keep" or "share" the final prize. If they both picked 'share', the money would be split evenly between them ($125,000 each). If only one picked 'share' and the other 'keep,' the keeper gets the entire prize ($250,000) and the other (the weeper) gets nothing. If they both pick 'keep,' then neither gets the cash and it is split among the other losing contestants (about $14,000 each).[3]

---

[3] http://freakonomics.com/2010/09/17/the-prisoners-dilemma-makes-a-reality-tv-appearance/. (consulted 12 December 2018)

The snag, of course, was that neither finalist knew what the other would do. A classic instance of what economists call a prisoner's dilemma and the collaborative theory associated with it: game theory.

Constitutional Game Theory

Game theory is a branch of mathematics and economics focused on decisions. The prisoner's dilemma involves a hypothetical cooperative conflict. Two armed-robbery suspects were both carrying a weapon when they were arrested; they were apprehended separately and have not been able to communicate. The prosecutors offer each prisoner a bargain. They can either betray the other by testifying against them, or cooperate with the other suspect by remaining silent. The possible outcomes are:

- If A and B each betray the other, each of them serves two years in prison,
- If A betrays B but B remains silent, A will be released and B will serve three years in prison (and vice versa),
- If A and B both remain silent, both of them will serve only one year in prison (on the lesser charge).

Set out in a scheme:

The Prisoner's Dilemma

	B stays silent (cooperates)	B betrays A (defects)
A stays silent (cooperates)	Both serve 1 year	A serves 3 years, B goes free
A betrays B (defects)	A goes free, B serves 3 years	Both serve 2 years

Prisoner's dilemma payoff matrix

This very American example invites you to consider the Nash equilibrium.[4] What is the best thing an apprehended suspect can do? What is the optimal strategy: a cooperative strategy (remaining tight-lipped) or a non-cooperative strategy (confessing)?

---

[4] A proposed solution of non-cooperative games devised by John Forbes Nash Jr., a Princeton University fellow and Nobel Prize laureate in economics, and the main character in the

On the face of it, it may be best for both suspects to stay tight-lipped (lenient punishment), but if one of them confesses – abandoning the cooperative strategy of keeping mum, so to speak – she can expect no punishment at all and maximises her benefit through selfishness. Selfishness 'logically' offers the greatest reward in this game. In reality, however, people seem more prone to display a systemic bias towards *cooperative* behaviour, in this and similar games, despite what is predicted by simple models of 'rational' self-interested action.[5] Actual cooperative decisions do not blindly follow simple one-off, rent-seeking paths.

Whilst most of us will rarely be involved in armed robberies, we are constantly confronted with dilemmas of this kind. What do we do if we all agree to cook for each other and do the washing-up, but someone ducks her duty after eating like a king at communal meals? And what if we enter the Tour de France and cycle head over head the Alpe d'Huez climb, trying to catch up with a runaway Chris Froome, but a cyclist evades front work, saving his energy for a blistering final sprint to win the leader's jersey and the stage. How do you deal with this? And what on Earth does this have to do with constitutions? Everything.

Constitutions, as expounded, are always about the 'we' – rules on a group, group decisions and the role of individual group members. Constitutions define a political arena, where distribution decisions[6] are taken by and for a group (and usually in its name). This always leads to contention. How do we coordinate our efforts? When do we work together? How do we deal with members who do not acquiesce in majority agreements? Who gets what? Who does not get what? Why? It is like an infinite episode of *Friends,* and endless *Bachelor Pad* show. Like life itself, which constantly plays tricks with the dualism of our basic neurological disposition. On the one hand, we are evolutionarily predisposed to pursue our self-interest and on the other hand, we are inherently altruistic[7] – and we depend on trust and recognition for cooperation.

The Minimax Constitution

Cooter shows in his 2000 book *The Strategic Constitution* how most of the big constitutional theory questions – 'what is a good constitution?' – can be attributed and boiled down to simple game-theory questions. Prisoner's dilemmas always play a role

biographical film *A Beautiful Mind* (2001). He developed them in his Ph.D. Dissertation entitled 'Equilibrium points in n-person games', Nash 1950 and 'Non-Cooperative Games' Nash 1951.

5   Fehr & Fischbacher 2003.

6   This is what all political processes are about according to Lasswell's famous definition: 'Who gets what, when, how?' Lasswell 1936.

7   Hofman 1981 and Gintis, Bowles, Boyd & Fehr 2003. There is still debate as to whether altruism is an innate trait, or a form of intelligent group behaviour (*reciprocal altruism*: self-sacrifice

in drafting constitutions. Freedom, whether or not constitutionally protected, gives individuals the liberty to choose, follow their preferences and satisfy their desires. This condition also contributes optimally to economic growth and prosperity because only free markets can match supply and demand efficiently and maximise utility.[8] But individual freedom can often only be achieved collaboratively, by limiting governmental power, for instance, restricting political distribution decisions that impinge on the scope of individual decisions. Government power, on the other hand, is itself a highly sought-after commodity because being in charge allows you to capitalise your own, short-term selfish (group) interests and try to expropriate the jackpot – a proportion of market revenues.[9] To prevent this, the future constitutional community must somehow try to limit political power now and in the future by binding its exercise to law and legal rules. But, it is certainly not a foregone conclusion that justice will prevail in a contest with power. Spain had no fewer than 43 coups between 1814 and 1923;[10] and Paraguay has had 19, Japan 11 and Haiti 27 coups in the last 200 years.[11]

Cooter concludes that the first goal of a constitution must therefore be:

> [...] to impose the rule of law and protect the liberty of citizens. Game theory provides a useful restatement of this goal. A player who follows the *minimax* strategy in a game minimises the maximum harm that he can suffer.[12]

A 'minimax constitution's' equilibrium:

> [...] minimises the harm when the worst political possibilities materialise. The minimax constitution pursues the classical political goals of security, legality, and liberty.[13]

Everyone would like a minimax constitution like this. It meets the moral precepts of a catalogue of great thinkers, including Immanuel Kant's categorical imperative (a generalised test of your decisions and actions: would you arrive at the same decision if it were to apply to everyone?),[14] John Stuart Mill's harm principle (freedom

---

for reasons of kinship or in the hope of being paid back in kind). The articles cited show that altruism, contrary to what might be expected (survival of the fittest), has evolutionary advantages; altruism might thus be innate.

[8] Cf. Leitzel 2015, p. 4–6.

[9] Barry Weingast puts in in the following terms: 'the fundamental political dilemma of an economic system is this: a government strong enough to protect property rights and enforce contracts is also strong enough to confiscate the wealth of its citizens.' Weingast 1995, p. 1.

[10] According to the table in Cooter 2000, p. 11 (who quoted *The Economist* in 1992).

[11] Cf. the Wikipedia overview of coup d'états https://en.wikipedia.org/wiki/List_of_coups_d%27%C3%A9tat_and_coup_attempts_by_country#Austria (Consulted 19 July 2018).

[12] 'In a zero-sum game, minimising the maximum harm is equivalent to maximising the minimum payoff. Thus the minimax constitution can also be described as the maximum constitution.' Note 26, Cooter 2000, p. 11.

[13] Cooter 2000, p. 11–12.

[14] Finding moral good by generalising your own interests, principles and motives for action (maxims). Kant summarises it as: 'I ought never to proceed except in such a way that I could

should only be limited to prevent harm to other individuals),[15] and John Rawls' veil of ignorance (how would you organise a just society if you were ignorant of your own situation?).[16] But perhaps it is too good to be true. Achieving such ideal equilibriums requires reasonable, rational and honest people. This cannot be said of all of us and certainly not all the time. A succession of recent Nobel Prize winners has shown that our behaviour is sometimes also motivated by less noble motives. The game is marred by people who secretly peek from behind the veil of ignorance, thinking 'to hell with Kant's moth-eaten imperative or a hippyish harm principle': I'm not sacrificing any of *my* freedom for some greater good; that's just the way some of us are.

Richard Thaler (Nobel Prize laureate in economics 2017) wrote an entertaining and good book on this subject: *Misbehaving*. He shows how many modern economic and political theories assume reasonable, rational people and rational human behaviour (Adam Smith's rational *homo economicus*), but, in fact, *real* people's behaviour is often far from rational.[17] We have limited ability to act rationally (bounded rationality) because we are constantly inclined to completely misjudge risks and overestimate ourselves, causing us to negotiate ineptly (bounded self-interest). On top of this, we have a limited capacity to control ourselves (bounded willpower).[18] We 'misbehave' all the time and do not suddenly stop doing so when having to make important political decisions, not even when making the most fundamental of all political decisions: a constitution.

If you try to make forecasts in economics or politics and you want to calculate them according to some formula or (economic) model, you will soon be confronted by humanity's irrational side. You can use the law of large numbers to partly filter this out. On balance, the irrationality of a few people does not hinder the (predictable) rationality of large groups due to a mechanism we also call the wisdom of the crowds; the concept of the *homo economicus*. On balance, we will act rationally. Even so, forecasting is still difficult, as Buchanan and Tullock illustrated in their 1962 classic *The Calculus of Consent*.[19] This is because masses are not the starting point; all forms of economic or political cooperation start with cooperation between two or more individuals. And it is not just something we do easily or right away. We need to be seduced, enticed, lured into 'what is in it for me?' We work together by exchanging goods and services in our mutual desire to gain something – to benefit ourselves. This is no different in economic cooperation than in political or collective

---

also will that my maxim should become a universal law.' ('[...] ich soll niemals anders verfahren, als so, daß ich auch wollen könne, meine Maxime solle ein allgemeines Gesetz werden.') Kant 2011 (orig. 1786), p. 33.

[15] Formulated by Mill (who never used the term harm principle) as 'the only purpose for which power can be rightfully exercised over any member of a civilised community, against his will, is to prevent harm to others.' Mill 2002 (orig. 1859), p. 8.

[16] Rawls 1999 (orig. 1971) p. 19.

[17] Thaler 2015, chapters 7 to 13, and in particular chapter 13 (*Misbehaving in the Real World*), p. 115–124.

[18] Sunstein, Jolls & Thaler, especially p. 1477–1479.

[19] Buchanan & Tullock 2007 (orig. 1962).

action, despite it sometimes taking a little longer in the latter to work out what everyone's benefit is, what the interests are, and which utility is being maximised.

Adam Smith's classical economic-theoretical assertion that the pursuit of your individual interest almost automatically serves the general interest (by increasing prosperity) is not so self-evident in the political and constitutional world. Yet, economic laws can still help improve understanding and prediction of the course and outcomes of collective action, including in political processes. When you realise that individuals can and want to pursue collective utility maximisation, you can also calculate how, driven by economic motives, they try to do so efficiently and optimally. Buchanan and Tullock attempt in their 'public choice theory' to use maximisation and efficiency theories to calculate, understand and predict in models how and where people in a competitive politico-economic community achieve an equilibrium. This also involves game theory,[20] but also shows that the shortest route to the sacred minimax constitution cannot be found or calculated directly. If it were possible, we would immediately introduce this constitutional optimum everywhere as a blueprint.

The problem is that there is a difference in approach between the political and economic worlds. Smith's economic law asserts that pursuing your own short-sighted interest is not possible at the expense of all other market participants, as was assumed in economic theories before Smith.[21] Instead, other participants potentially benefit from your behaviour thanks to an increase in general prosperity. If the pie grows, there is more to be shared out and everybody may benefit. But does this rationale apply to a political society too? The economic approach to (political) collective action processes (*the utility maximising approach*) maintains that individual utility maximising behaviour best serves general prosperity and hence also the public, general interest. The *power maximising approach*, on the other hand, assumes that collective decision-making processes are a zero-sum game: one person's gain is another's loss. Perhaps the truth is somewhere in the middle. It is difficult to know because the picture is (further) muddled by a phenomenon called 'group dynamics'. Buchanan and Tullock conclude at the end of their book that political communities are complex and multifaceted. They contend that their theory on political processes shows:

> [...] that individuals are the only meaningful decision-making units, that these individuals are motivated by utility-maximising considerations, and that they are well informed and fully rational in their choices. Yet we know that 'groups' do exist as something apart from the individual members, that individuals are motivated by many considerations, and that individuals are far from being either well informed or rational in their political behaviour. [This] would seem to restrict severely the descriptive, explanatory, and predictive value of our theory.[22]

---

[20] *Ibid.*, p. 19–22. Cf. Fukuyama 2011, p. 448.
[21] As described by Thomas Malthus in his pamphlet *An Essay on the Principle of Population* in 1798. He assumes that prosperity must necessarily decrease if population growth increases, due to finite resources. For this reason, we call this approach 'Malthusian'.
[22] Buchanan & Tullock 2007 (orig. 1962), p. 297.

It is just not possible to predict or calculate the best choice, a constitution's mini-max option. And it would not even desirable to boot; constitutional rules are not collective or public choice algorithms. Constitutions are not about the outcomes of political decision-making – they do not prescribe solutions – but rather accom-modate and channel conflict of interest resolution and political processes. Ginsburg and Huq aptly note that:

> Successful constitutions channel conflict through formal political institutions, as opposed to forcing antagonists to take disagreements to the street.[23]

Minimax is a procedure rather than a solution.

CONSTITUTIONAL ARCHITECTURE FOR DIVIDED SOCIETIES

Constitutional arrangements try to reconcile the pursuit of individual or factional interests and the importance of larger-scale cooperation. As we have seen, individu-als and smaller groups do not automatically bridge this gap and embark on the unknown travails of cooperation on a larger scale. We are naturally conservative, attached to the things and people we know.[24] Individuals have to be convinced – by making them believe in the material benefits of the new form of cooperation and order. This can be done by calculation, proving the benefits of the new form of cooperation. Large-scale and convincing proof to join is best achieved by making an appeal that appeals to everyone – connecting with something everyone believes in. If the new community has a shared religion, it can be said that the new larger-scale order has God's blessing or has been ordained by God. If you live in the world guided by science, rationality and an anthropocentric world view, then these elements can be used to show the added value of larger-scale cooperation and order: your invest-ment in large-scale cooperation – renouncing some of your freedom – ultimately pays off (protection, improved competitive capacity of your group as a whole, reduc-tion of the costs of conflict). As Alexis de Tocqueville (1805–1859) observed, if you are led by rational considerations, then cooperation in a larger group under consti-tutional rules is often a form of *enlightened self-interest*.[25]

Bridging Differences

It is one thing wanting to reconcile individuals and a large-scale society's interests and quite another actually doing so. Aligning individual interests and desires one-on-one with those of large groups of individuals as a group is a logical impossibility – even for

---

[23] Ginsburg & Huq 2016-*introduction*, p. 18.
[24] Cf. on this subject Amodio, Jost, Master & Ye 2007 and Fowler & Schreiber 2008, p. 912–914. Cf. May 2018, p. 120–121.
[25] Tocqueville 2002 (orig. 1835 and 1840), p. 595 where he says: 'The Americans, on the contrary, are fond of explaining almost all the actions of their lives by the principle of interest rightly

an instant. It is completely impossible. Myriad utopian experiments (including of the communist and fascist variety) claiming to unify individual and state interests offer ample proof: state-based communities of this kind always rapidly degenerate into repressive regimes. All that can be done is to try to recognise and reconcile individual and collective interests, for example, by looking for an acceptable compromise (which, incidentally, does not have to satisfy everyone). This primarily involves reconciling the opposing interests of large groups, and channelling conflicts so that differences do not undermine a community's collective capacity to cooperate.

Modern constitutions contain a multiplicity of rules designed to reconcile social differences for exactly this reason. However, constitutional ambitions and results vary widely. Some constitutions aspire to little more than acting as a peace treaty to defuse or freeze (recent) conflicts, such as East Timor's 2002 constitution. Constitutions like these attempt to induce loose forms of cooperation in a new federative association, combining it with some form of institutionalisation of political, cultural or ethnic differences.[26] Other constitutions go further and try to actually reconcile groups in a new (federative) association (e.g. South Africa 1996)[27] and, whilst recognising differences and identities, try to meld them in a single nation.[28] It goes without saying that this requires far more than soothing words in a constitution, but it is noteworthy that the constitutions of many post-conflict countries in the past few decades predominantly focus on safeguarding and consolidating peace.[29] Constitutions and constitutional arrangements are increasingly used as 'social cement'.[30] They have become a popular medicine to overcome and cure political, ethnic, religious or cultural cleavages and conflicts. As a result, a thriving pharmaceutical industry has taken root, dispensing constitutional remedies across the world. Since the fall of the Berlin Wall, international organisations, sponsors and experts have jostled at the bedside of revamped states with diagnoses and prescriptions which they believe will do just the trick. They have been particularly prominent at times of great change in societies: in the aftermath of the Balkan wars, during the accession of eastern and central European countries to the EU, and during and after the Arab Spring.

---

understood; they show with complacency how *an enlightened regard for themselves* constantly prompts them to assist each other, and inclines them willingly to sacrifice a portion of their time and property to the welfare of the State' (my italics). Cf. De Waal 2019, p. 30 ff.

[26] Wallis mentions a series of countries in which traditional socio-political groups maintained a formal and protective role in the new political dispensation, including Palau, Tonga, Vanuatu and so on. Cf. Wallis 2014, p. 332.

[27] The preamble contains a brief and meaningful reference to the past: 'We, the people of South Africa, Recognise the injustices of our past; Honour those who suffered for justice and freedom in our land; Respect those who have worked to build and develop our country; and Believe that South Africa belongs to all who live in it, united in our diversity.'

[28] Cf. the different forms of constitutional bargains discussed in the contributions to Choudhry and Ginsburg 2016.

[29] Samuels 2006.

[30] Freely adapted from Jon Elster 1989, whose metaphor primarily referred to rationality and not to constitutions.

Constitutional Formulae

What kind of constitutional arrangement – what kind of medicine – works best for a given situation? How do you resolve political conflicts, especially in deeply divided or segmented societies, in a peaceful and durable manner? Any remedy of this kind will mainly revolve around finding a good balance between majority and minority interests. Can constitutional rules on fair (democratic) decision-making prevent minority or individual rights from being trampled underfoot? The most common solution is the concept of the democratic constitutional state (or liberal democracy): the combination of a democratic system with the guarantee of limited government (bound by the law and separation of powers), protected individual and group rights (human rights, fundamental freedoms) and independent judicial arbitration. Democratisation and judicialisation – forces that certainly do not always coexist harmoniously.[31] For which form of democracy (a majoritarian or consensual system, such as consociational democracy) is most suited,[32] which electoral system (universal suffrage, plurality voting in single-member electoral districts, proportional representation and so on) is best fitted, or which government system (presidential, parliamentary, power sharing or power concentrating,[33] centralised or decentralised and so on) fits best? Which position and role are to be conferred on the independent judiciary in relation to democratic political bodies? Which modality of judicial review is optimal? And how do you best guarantee all of this in a constitution?[34] There are many conceivable – and passionately contested – formulae. It is not certain which works best,[35] but some kind of constitutional philosopher's stone is in great demand – a constitution that brings eternal peace to the constitutional community and joy to the world for that matter, with no more than the written word.

---

[31]　Shapiro and Sweet 2002. Isaiah Berlin concisely expresses the paradox: 'there is no necessary connection between individual liberty and democratic rule. [...] This connection [...] is a good deal more tenuous than it seemed to many advocates of both.' Berlin 1969, p. 130–131. Francis Sejersted argues that they are essentially two different concepts of freedom: 'The rule of law and democracy correspond to the two different concepts of liberty, the negative, which makes liberty dependent on the curbing of authority, and the positive, which makes it dependent on the exercising of authority.' Sejersted argues that these concepts are (quoted by Berlin), '"two profoundly divergent and irreconcilable attitudes to the ends of life." The claims of each of them have, however, "an equal right to be classed among the deepest interests of mankind."' Sejersted 1997, p. 131.

[32]　Lijphart 2004, p. 97.

[33]　Also called centripetal.

[34]　Horowitz, an advocate of plurality voting systems and presidential government, recommends strong and firmly embedded constitutional institutions – such as a constitutional court – to maintain balance in the system. Horowitz 2014. As well as the rather older Horowitz 1991.

[35]　Lijphart – challenged by people like Horowitz – is less cautious. Based on his own study of thirty-six democracies around the world, he rejects Horowitz's predilection for power-concentrating majoritarian systems: 'In sum, power sharing has proven to be the only democratic model that appears to have much chance of being adopted in divided societies, which in turn makes it unhelpful to ask constitution writers to contemplate alternatives to it.' Lijphart 2004, p. 99. Cf. Choudhry 2010 *introduction* (and in particular p. 15–26 for a summary of the Lijphart-Horowitz debate).

PART V

The Imagined Order of the Constitution

24

The Constitution's Beating Heart

Emotions

In our minds, constitution is a 'good word'. It has favourable emotive properties, like freedom, justice or democracy. Therefore, the word is retained, or adopted, even when the association between the utterance 'constitution' and the behavioural response it elicits [...] becomes entirely baseless.

Giovanni Sartor[1]

Emotions are not the first thing that comes to mind when you wonder where modern constitutions come from and how they work. Surely, they are products of rationality, proceeds of the Enlightenment and well-considered projects designed to restrain passions? Fear, hatred, self-centredness, disgust, revulsion and paranoia are all potentially incendiary emotions. Like passion,[2] they can threaten the stable order of human communities, and cause or aggravate conflicts. Whilst emotions are not necessarily at odds with reasonable, well-considered behaviour – they produce many good and wonderful things – they can get out of hand, and obstruct our reasonable, calm judgment.[3] This has cast emotions in a bad light in discussions about the nature and structure of polities and constitutions.[4] When it comes to something as important as state administration, emotionality and impulsive behaviour are regarded for the most part as primitive, infantile and sometimes downright dangerous. They can easily lead to remorseless popular fury, derelict nationalism, riots, bloody revolution and wars.

Our turbulent nature can only be kept in check by rationality and restrained by reason. This is why we like to bind our better, rational selves to the mast of sensible

---

[1] Sartor 1962, p. 855.
[2] Understood as intense emotion.
[3] Cf. Spinoza 2008 (orig. 1677), part III (*The Origin and Nature of Emotions*). Cf. Spinoza 2002.
[4] Cf. Barbalet 2001 (orig. 1998), especially p. 13–20 (*The expulsion of emotion from sociology*) and Berezin 2002.

constitutional arrangements. But, this is only one side of the coin. Rationality and emotions – the biochemical reactions induced independently of our explicit will that effect on our mental state – are not opposites.[5] People are social beings 'reliant on both emotionality and reasoning' in the words of political scientist George Marcus in a recent book on political and legal aspects of *Passions and Emotions* (which doubles as the book's title).[6] Our esteem for rationality, reason and wisdom inclines us to (prefer to) forget that emotions are at the root of most of what we do.[7] They even control our cognitive abilities.

This does not mean that we merely follow our hormonal impulses or heartbeat, but that they prompt or play a role in our choices. Who goes to a clothes shop and rationally calculates which item of clothing is optimal, given your objectified bodily requirements (cooling, heating, protection), combined with medium-term strategy (climate development, sustainability, geographical location and financial resources), and costs (purchase, depreciation, production)? Nobody. Whilst these considerations may play a role, they do not explain your preference for leopard prints or paisley neckties. Nor do they explain why, considering the problem of covering distance in the shortest possible time at the lowest possible cost, the best colour for your next car should be metallic blue marine, or why a particular film, song or exciting book should cheer you up and measurably increase your productivity. Even Sheldon Cooper from the *Big Bang Theory* cannot explain that one. We adore blue, like certain brands for reasons that are difficult to explain and fall for the *je ne sais quoi* qualities of certain people or things.

Preferences, intuitions, affections, (unreasoned) fears, disgust and horror determine our choices, actions and lives. We are rational, but calm consideration of benefits and drawbacks certainly does not always precede our behaviour. Recent research has demonstrated that most of our judgments and decisions are unconsciously

---

[5] Jack Barbalet: 'Emotions [...] are continuous with the operations of pervasive social institutions. Conventional representations of emotion are blind to these emotions. These emotions render especially absurd the idea that reason and emotion are opposed'. Barbalet 2001 (orig. 1998), p. 61 (chapter 2 *Emotion and rationality*, p. 29–61 is entirely devoted to this theme). Harari asserts that feelings are a form of evolutionary rationality which enables us to make lightning-quick calculations of probability. 'Feelings are [...] not the opposite of rationality – they embody evolutionary rationality.' Harari 2018, p. 47. Most cognitive scientists nowadays subscribe to this assumption. Cf. Levenson 1994 and Ekman 1999.

[6] Cf. Marcus 2013, p. 127.

[7] As mentioned in previous chapters, there are eight basic emotions: love, fear, joy, anger, sadness, surprise, shame and disgust/aversion. At least, we usually assume so. Cf. Levenson 1994, p. 123–126. However, many emotions you distinguish depends on what you want to call them – how you want to classify them. Emotions are relatively universal, although there are cultural differences in how emotions are expressed in public. Neither are emotions unchangeable. They are the product of our evolutionary development. Emotions are mainly processed in the amygdalae, deep in the brain's temporal lobe, which are part of the limbic system. The amygdalae make connections between information from various senses and associate it with emotions. This is how our brain constantly assesses which emotional reaction is most useful or appropriate in a given situation. Pinker 2009, p. 369 and p. 371–372.

(intuitively) made.[8] About 95% of all our thinking and acting is on autopilot.[9] But it does not *feel* like that – as we often reason with hindsight and try to rationalise intuitive decisions in retrospect.[10] A rational retrospective interpretation.[11] As children of the Enlightenment, we have great regard for rationality, but it is, in fact, not such an elevated quality. Saying that someone acts rationally only means that someone has or gives sufficient reasons for her action.[12] It is not a substantive statement. Rational action is not much more than explained action, giving reasons that can convince others that there were reasons – which is not the same as 'objective' or 'true' reasons and arguments.[13] In addition, we only have a limited ability to act rationally. It simply is not possible to keep our emotions under control and suppress our impulses continually.[14] It is not simply a question of culpable weakness of character, but a fact we must take into account in understanding law, politics and economics. The completely rational human being, the *homo economicus* does not exist. Our will-power, rationality and ability to serve our enlightened self-interest – as Tocqueville put it[15] – are limited.[16]

---

[8]   Cf. Kahneman 2003. Kahneman shows that human cognition – our reasoning – uses two systems. The first system generates intuitive/automatic impressions based on perceptions or thoughts. This is independent of our will and is not usually verbally explicit. The second system generates judgments/assessments which are always conscious and explicit (whilst they might not be expressed). Judgments produced by the second system are based on impressions from the first system or deliberate reasoning. Many judgments by the second system are direct translations of impressions from the first system ('intuitive judgments'). In some cases, the second system monitors immediate action based on impressions from the first system, but less than you might think (and hope). Kahneman's research shows that 'the [second system's] monitoring is normally quite lax, and allows many intuitive judgments to be expressed, including some that are erroneous.' Kahneman 2003, p. 451. Cf. Thaler & Sunstein 2009, p. 19–22.

[9]   Sajó 2011, p. 16 with a reference to Bargh & Chartrand 1999.

[10] Whether or not as a correction of an intuitive impression, or impulse. Cf. Kahneman 2003, p. 451; Gladwell 2006; Sunstein & Thaler 2008.

[11] Empirical research shows that even judges – who are also human – often rely on first impressions, intuition and 'feeling' when judging cases. This is an uncomfortable realisation, although the consequences are not disastrous. Guthrie et al. argue that acknowledging this is the first step towards solving associated problems – particularly tunnel vision and lack of self-control. Cf. Guthrie, Rachlinski & Wistrich 2007.

[12] Elster 2009, p. 2.

[13] Literary theorist Walter Fisher argues that rationality and reason – giving good reasons – are essentially a form of rhetoric. People are storytellers who communicate and reason through stories they draw from history, culture, perceptions of facts and representations (ideas, imagined worlds and so on). 'Rationality is determined by the nature of persons as narrative beings – their inherent awareness of *narrative probability*, what constitutes a coherent story, and their constant habit of testing *narrative fidelity*, whether or not the stories they experience ring true with the stories they know to be true in their lives [...].' Fisher 1989 (orig. 1987), quote from p. 5. Cf. p. 57.

[14] Cf. Kenny 2003 (orig. 1963).

[15] Tocqueville 2002 (orig. 1835 and 1840), p. 595.

[16] Thaler argues that our rationality has 'three bounds: bounded rationality, bounded willpower, and bounded self-interest.' Until recently, he continues, 'in law and economics these properties of humans had therefore assumed to be thoroughly unbounded.' Thaler 2015, p. 258. Sen 2010, p. 176–177.

Emotions are not simply a hindrance, or something to be curbed; they have very positive aspects too. Feelings of connectedness, trust, moral behaviour, values and charity enable us to work together on a large scale. Notions of shared identity, solidarity and justice can unite groups of people and act as a guiding light for a political or legal order. Emotions are essential for social structures and organisations, inspiring a sense of trust and recognition,[17] which gives them a great deal of potential for social mobilisation. You can also direct them. National states use compulsory education, an official language, cultural education, conscription and other institutions to cultivate emotional (state) solidarity. They also use language, art, literature, music, national symbols, museums and historiography to induce people to identify with the state.[18] A state that feels like 'home'. The political institutions of modern nation states have emotions embedded in them.[19] Constitutions are part of this formula. Emotions are crucial to truly understanding how constitutions work, and why they are so sought-after.[20] Regarding them purely as rationally conceived formulae ignores essential questions: how do they touch us, how do they appeal to our hearts, from which sentiments do they arise?

András Sajó – formerly a judge at the European Court of Human Rights and a constitutional scholar – wrote a book about this entitled *Constitutional Sentiments*. One of his central propositions is that:

> [...] constitutions reflect a selection of the emotional experiences of a given community. What is seen in constitutional law to be the expression of rational considerations, and is legitimized as such, is to a considerable extent the interplay of emotions reflected in public sentiments, and in particular fear. The rationality of a constitutional solution originates partly in its capacity to handle constitutional sentiments – passions in particular.[21]

Constitutional sentiments have two very distinct elements. On the one hand, they are fed by strong feelings of justice, they are about passionate ideas about who we are, where we come from, where we should be heading, and how we should organise ourselves, according to which principles and rules. As I said, emotions of this kind have a great capacity to mobilise and unite people. Exhorted by abstract concepts such as self-determination, people, nation, freedom, law and justice, (legal)

---

[17] Lewis and Weigert call them 'social emotions'. Lewis & Weigert, 2012, especially 26.

[18] Berezin 2002, p. 43.

[19] 'The modern nation-state contains emotions within political institutions', according to Berezin 2002, p. 43. Cf. Nussbaum 2013.

[20] Emotions are not fixed, tangible 'things', but rather complex reciprocal processes: they are blends of the feelings associated with emotions and what we culturally attribute to those emotions (including their appreciation). Sajó summarises this concisely: 'Most emotions are blends of the related feelings and cultural ascriptions; that is, a complex of the blend receives a common name which has feedback and other regulatory consequences. The blend reflects cultural influences and is organised by the self-concept of the person.' Sajó 2011, p. 17. Cf. Pinker 2009, p. 364-370.

[21] Sajó 2011, p. 114.

protection and the like, they can increase our confidence in our fellow constitutional human beings and help us accept (new) social and political orders. But, we
are also liable to get carried away by these same emotions. They can turn into all-
consuming passions that hinder our collective capacity for sober judgment.

A LATE SESSION

Is it a good idea for an inexperienced assembly to extend a sitting into the small
hours when the delegates have had too much to drink and in the midst of a crisis?
Was what happened on the night of the fourth of August 1789 'wise'?

> The recently proclaimed French National Assembly met that evening and night in
> the chic Salle des Menus Plaisirs in Versailles, after delegates had forced its convoca-
> tion at a nearby tennis court on 20 June. Its members were as inexperienced, nervous
> and restless as school children. Hardly surprising though: no one had any political
> experience, as the Estates General had not been convened in more than a century
> and a half.[22] France essentially lacked a political culture other than a philosophical
> debate culture, rather reminiscent of a common room packed with sophisticates,
> which had thrived in the seclusion of small Parisian salons. The air was buzzing with
> excitement – which had been further heightened by the maelstrom of events after
> the fall of the Bastille and subsequent skirmishes across the country[23] – when the oh-
> so-green delegates took their places on the benches beneath the soaring gilded vaults.

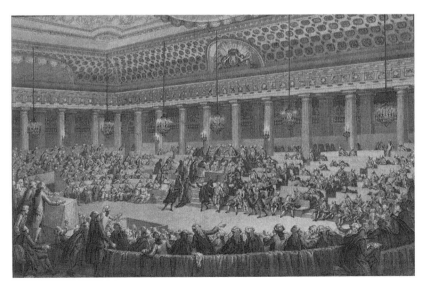

Charles Monnet (1732–1808), *Meeting of the Night of 4 August 1789*

[22] The Estates General had last been convened in 1614.
[23] A wave of revolt and destruction swept through France in July 1789 and there was much dis-
      satisfaction with the failure to draft the constitution promised in June. Revolutionaries like

It started with a bummer. The session was about the extremely dull but pressing issue of taxation. Foreign military adventures, bad harvests and years of financial and economic mismanagement had left France bankrupt. The delegates' pledge at the Versailles tennis court a few months earlier to promulgate a new constitution with a modern monarchical dispensation and a new tax system would have to wait. Preventing the country descending into financial chaos urgently required the extension of existing taxes. It would have been irresponsible to suspend taxes in the interim. The new constitution was making no headway anyway, even with the popular Marquis de La Fayette, the hero of the American War of Independence, in the drafting committee. So the session of 4 August got off to a difficult start, with much lamenting of the economic slump and tedious technical debates about the country's financial state. Then, all over sudden, the spark was ignited when the Viscount de Noailles (La Fayette's brother-in-law) took the floor. In a classic instance of revolutionary rhetoric, he told the assembly that it was pointless tinkering in the margins. Grousing about these old taxes was merely treating the symptoms; a radical change of tack was needed: a new order with new relations had to be introduced.[24] And there was not a moment to be lost, with the danger of insurrection and discord.[25] 'The kingdom', Noailles said, 'stands at a crossroads of total social destruction, or a government whose example will be admired and imitated throughout Europe'.[26] The effect on the chamber was electrifying. Delegates from all estates were in a state of exhilaration and used emotional language and grand gestures to renounce their ancient rights and privileges. In the space of just a few hours, the nobility and clergy – theatrically outbidding one another – cast their centuries-old entitlements, tax exemptions, titles and rights onto the revolutionary cast bonfire. It was, in Simon Schama's words:

[…] a mixture of apprehension and demonstrative patriotism that swept up the noble and clerical deputies of the National Assembly on the night of the fourth of August.[27]

Mirabeau ascribed this delay to deliberate foot-dragging and a conspiracy against freedom and the people. Cf. Elster 2007, especially p. 76–77.

[24] 'Le but du projet d'arrêté que l'Assemblée vient d'entendre est d'arrêter l'effervescence des provinces, d'assurer la liberté publique, et de confirmer les propriétaires dans leurs véritables droits.' (The aim of the project for a decree that the Assembly has just heard is to halt the disturbances in the provinces, assure public liberty, and confirm the legitimate rights of proprietors.) In: *Acts of the National Assembly of 4 August 1789.* (*Grands moments d'éloquence*). Cf. www2 .assemblee-nationale.fr/decouvrir-l-assemblee/histoire/grands-discours-parlementaires/target-noailles-et-aiguillon-nuit-du-4-aout-1789#prettyPhoto (Consulted 31 August 2018). Translation Paul H. Beik 1970.

[25] 'D'après tous les différends qui ont existé entre les représentants de la Nation, les campagnes n'ont connu que les gens avoués par elles, qui sollicitaient leur bonheur, et les personnes puissantes qui s'y opposaient.' (All things considered, all these differences of opinion here in the people's assembly meant that the country has not had any dedicated delegates representing the people's welfare, but rather powerful people who resisted it.) Source: *ibid.* My translation.

[26] 'le royaume flotte, dans ce moment, entre l'alternative de la destruction de la société, ou d'un gouvernement qui sera admiré et suivi de toute l'Europe.' *Acts Assemblée Nationale* 4 August 1789.

[27] Schama 1989, p. 370.

Even a deputy as progressive as the Marquis Lally-Tollendal grew increasingly uneasy with the patriotic inebriation which seemed to take hold of his fellow delegates' judgment in the small hours. He tried to quell this intoxication by passing an urgent note to his friend the Duc de Liancourt, who was presiding over the session. 'They are not in their right minds,' he exhorted, 'adjourn the session.'[28] But the genie was out of the bottle. 'Instead, the sunrise shone through the windows of the Salle des Menus Plaisirs as deputies wept, embraced, sang, and surrendered themselves to the patriotic rhapsody.'[29]

Much could be said about this event, but it certainly was not wise in the short term.[30] France suffered a financial implosion, the economy was disrupted further, and state administration was destabilised. It also marked an historical turning point: the session represented the end of a thousand-year-old model of the monarchic-feudal polity's social order. All of this was brought about by some five hours of 'revolutionary drunkenness'. Its ramifications can still be felt to this day.

You might think that the delegates would have learnt from the upheaval of the night of the fourth of August 1789 that it was perhaps better to sit when well-rested, sober, calm and thoughtful – and maybe to leave out the singing. Hardly. Less than two weeks later – after six days of tumultuous and chaotic preparation this time – they were once again swayed by their passions in the splendid Menus Plaisirs hall, resulting in an equally sublime accident. On 26 August 1789, the delegates adopted the *Déclaration des droits de l'homme et du citoyen* – a text that is still regarded today as *the* archetype of human rights documents.

Constitutions are not just the result of mathematical calculation – emotions play a role, just as they do in all human thought and action. It is perhaps not so such a bad thing and is actually very understandable. The subject of constitutions (living together) and the appeal they make to our inner psyche, touches our deepest fears (loss of our lives and the lives of loved ones, loss of property and life to tyranny and violence), our desire for recognition (who are 'we', and who am I in this 'we'? What is expected of me?) and our need for certainty and trust (who can I or we trust? Who or what is protecting me?).

[28] *Ibid.*, p. 372.
[29] *Ibid.*
[30] King Louis XVI was having none of it. He refused to approve the revocations that same day, writing in a – for him – emotional letter to the Archbishop of Arles: 'Je ne consentirai jamais à dépouiller *mon* clergé, *ma* noblesse.' (I shall never consent to a decision that robs me of *my* clergy and nobility.) He continued, betraying his totally incorrect assessment of the situation: 'Si la force m'obligeait à sanctionner, alors je céderais, mais alors il n'y aurait plus en France ni monarchie ni monarque.' (I shall resign if I am forced to approve this, but then there shall no longer be a monarchy or a monarch in France.) They were prophetic words. It was all in vain: the genie was out of the bottle. Louis reluctantly agreed on 5 October 1789 but failed to carry out his threat. It was carried out for him a few years later.

COGNITIVE SCIENCE AND THE KEYS OF HUMAN NATURE

Economist and political scientist Jon Elster has been writing interesting pieces on the role of rationality and emotions in constitutions for forty years.[31] Despite his many contributions to the subject, he is not (yet) very prominent in the canons of constitutional legal literature. It is a pity, as he is one of the most significant contemporary constitutional thinkers, in my opinion. It is probably not easy for the average constitutionalist to place this former Marxist, non-lawyer, European (Norwegian), who considers emotions in constitutional projects, proverbs, the latest development in cognitive sciences, and also quotes the giants of French literature (Montaigne, Stendahl, Proust and so on) left, right and centre. This is certainly not only the result of a preference for the familiar, petty prejudices, or the dominance of ideological approaches in the discipline (especially in constitutionalism), but rather because many constitutional scholars believe they can only make well-founded statements about the cognisable, rational aspect of constitutions and constitutional arrangements. Emotions are – certainly for most legal scholars – slippery, creepy and not really cognisable or scientifically comprehensible, or so it seems. Against this backdrop, trying to fathom whether and how emotions play a role in human decisions, and certainly in a monumental decision like a constitution, is regarded in the profession as a speculative, perilous undertaking. This is an understandable attitude – until recently there was little more to know and say about emotions and our deepest motivations than unsubstantiated generalities and clichés.

Things have changed. Research in the (still young) field of cognitive science has in a short time yielded many new insights into human nature, emotions and how our psyche and human reasoning function.[32] These findings are highly relevant to constitutional scholarship. All major thinkers in the field of constitutional law – from Hobbes to Rousseau, from Montesquieu and Locke[33] to Rawls and Fuller – base their theories on (the design of) constitutions and the law on basic assumptions about the essence and functioning of human nature. Their assessments were mainly intuitions – hypotheses they could not usually prove.[34] They supported them with

---

[31] Cf. alongside the aforementioned publications, Elster 1979; Elster 1999; Elster 2000 and Elster 2017.

[32] Cf. Fleming 2013 who looks closely at recent insights into the nature of passions and emotions, including human motivations, and the role they play in law and politics.

[33] Locke: 'The state of nature has a law of nature to govern it, which obliges every one: and reason, which is that law, teaches all mankind, who will but consult it, that being all equal and independent, no one ought to harm another in his life, health, liberty, or possessions [...] [and] when his own preservation comes not in competition, ought he, as much as he can, to preserve the rest of mankind, and may not, unless it be to do justice on an offender, take away, or impair the life, or what tends to the preservation of the life, the liberty, health, limb, or goods of another.' Locke 1689, *Second Treatise*, §6.

[34] De Brito Machado and Cavalcanti Ramos demonstrate that the great philosophers were often not far off the mark; modern neuroscientific studies confirm many (but not all) of their impressions, but now with evidence based on empirical research. De Brito Machado Secundo & Cavalcanti Ramos Machado 2017. Cf. Pinker 2018, p. 10.

more or less persuasive examples and common sense reasoning.[35] Everyone knows that people are all born good (Rousseau), people can pose a danger to each other (Hobbes),[36] and we are capable of mutual altruism (Locke). Science has progressed and we have been able to actually test some of these hypotheses. We now know (a little) more and understand (a little) better how our bodies and minds work and what that means for human cooperation and social order.

The recent proceeds of the cognitive sciences certainly deserve a place in constitutional debates for, if constitutions are about anything, then they are about human nature. And human nature is, we know, not only rational. We will soon agree with Elster that making constitutions is not a purely rational exercise.[37] Yet, we still try to understand these choices rather artificially in this sense. Most of the academic literature on constitutions focuses in some way on the question whether constitutional choices or choices based on a constitution are well considered and sensible – ideologically (has the constitutionalist ideal been well interpreted?), economically (is it a good basis for efficient market organisation and its regulation?)[38] or politico-strategically (is it a good basis for a durable social and political order and its regulation?). We assume that constitutions consist of rational choices which we can reconstruct and understand, even though all sorts of other things such as emotions play a role.

Rational choice theories (including the aforementioned public choice theories)[39] assume that people and groups of people make choices that are somehow the result of a calculation based on objective information about the world around us. These choices involve making a logical connection between an (individual, group or institutional) interest, and maximising this interest (or satisfying a demand) in competition with other interests in a community. All these elements can be determined and considered relatively objectively in rational choice theories. The more and the better informed you are about the world around you, your own interests and the interests of others, the better you will be able to make a 'good' or 'rational' decision. And, to boot, you can calculate or extrapolate where things went wrong. Sub-optimal results are the consequence of either too little information, or sloppy or poor calculation. For instance, if the National Assembly representatives had reflected a little longer, they might have realised that their actions on the night of the fourth of August 1789 would probably not have the most optimal outcome, considering the challenges they were actually faced with. For the sake of convenience, I assume that few delegates deliberately sought state bankruptcy, economic stagnation and social

---

[35] Often a fallacy, but it is an oft-used rhetorical trick.
[36] Hobbes thinks humans have two, seemingly incompatible aspects, a kind of duality: 'both sayings are very true; That Man to Man is a kind of God; and that Man to Man is an arrant Wolfe.' Hobbes 'wolfe' alludes to Roman playwright Plautus' verse: 'lupus est homo homini' (man is a wolf to man) in his play *Asinaria*. Cf. Hobbes 1651 (orig. 1642), quote from the dedication to 'the Right Honourable, William, Earle of Devonshire'.
[37] Elster 2017, p. 143–144.
[38] Cf. Frerichs 2017.
[39] Cf. chapter 23 of this book and for an extensive overview Mueller 2003.

chaos.[40] Emotions and passions can reinforce ideas and increase a sense of interconnectedness and altruism.[41] But they can also obstruct reasonable calculations due to misinformation, incorrect evaluation and hasty decisions (increased risk of being incorrectly or imperfectly informed).

This is why constitutional law literature of an economic slant often calls for the control of passions and emotions when making important choices. They argue that constitutions must give precedence to common sense and not to passions, which must be kept in check by constitutional legal norms. Political philosopher Friedrich Hayek argues that constitutions are primarily an 'appeal from the people drunk to the people sober'.[42] As the American constitutionalist Holmes poetically puts it:

> A constitution is Peter sober while the electorate is Peter drunk. Citizens need a constitution, just as Ulysses needed to be bound to his mast. If voters were allowed to get what they wanted, they would inevitably shipwreck themselves. By binding themselves to rigid rules, they can avoid tripping over their own feet.[43]

Disaster can only be prevented by expressing the constraints of rationality in constitutional rules.[44] It sounds convincing and has certainly been internalised by many wise scientists, administrators and politicians – there is no place for emotional impulses in the crucible of the common good. But, it is not how we work.[45] It is a myth, or in the words of the aforementioned Sajó:

> In the myth of reason, emotions are presented as separate from reason; passions' interference in reasoning, even if irresistible, is only a troubling external nuisance. Law is described as a mechanism to counter such interferences, institutionally

---

[40] Not even M. le comte Stanislas de Clermont-Tonnerre, who expressed at a subsequent session of the Assembly the ancient idea that things must sometimes get worse before they can get better. Amidst increasing turmoil in France, he uttered the prophetic words: 'l'anarchie est un passage effrayant, mais nécessaire, et c'est le seul moment où l'on peut arriver à un nouvel ordre de choses.' (Anarchy is a frightening but necessary phase and the only moment to bring about a new order.) Comte de Clermont-Tonnerre, *Archives Parlementaires*, Séance du lundi 19 Octobre 1789, 461, Série I 1787–1799, Paris 1875–1888. My translation.

[41] There are basically two types of altruism: *nepotistic altruism* (kin-related, family love) and *reciprocal altruism* (based on the reciprocal trading of favours). Pinker 2003, p. 242–243.

[42] Hayek 1960, p. 268.

[43] Holmes 1988, p. 196.

[44] This is why there is a consensus in much constitutional literature on the wisdom of using constitutional arrangements to keep certain decisions outside the political arena (where fickle voters and their representatives are in charge), for example, the protection of minority interests. People with very little faith in voters' rational capacity (essentially their fellow citizens) will be more inclined to isolate certain decisions from the electorate/politics through constitutional norms and transfer them to independent specialists, such as judges (who are highly esteemed by legal scholars). For these balances: cf. Consani 2015.

[45] Pinker contends that the opposition between emotions and rationality is a false distinction, a product of Romanticism. Yet the idea enjoys widespread credence, in academia too. 'Most scientists tacitly accept the premises of Romanticism even when they disagree with its morals. The irrational emotions and the repressing intellect keep reappearing in scientific guises'. This casts undue suspicion on emotions and blinds us to their role in cognitive processes.

reinforcing reason's shelter. This isolationist position, based on the reason-emotion divide, is unsustainable. The scientific evidence indicates that reason and emotion operate interactively in human decision-making and in the actual process of legal institution-building.[46]

EMOTIONAL RATIONALITY

People are not adding machines that make a rational, logical deductions based on objectively known facts and information. When people make assessments and take decisions, they colour the information they receive from their senses and act on desires which do not always coincide with their enlightened self-interest. We buy things that are too expensive, constantly consume unhealthy food and drinks, lose our patience and are angered or frightened for no real reason. In short, we are continuously driven by all manner of impulses, in a warped representation of the world and our self-interest. Welcome to the world of what is now called the *belief-desire theory* (BDT) of human action.[47] This theory shows that human calculation and consideration arise in a different way than rational choice theory supposes. This does, however, not directly condemn 'non-rational-calculus-outcomes' as 'irrational', unwise or incorrect decisions or choices.[48] According to BDT, emotions are the product of mental, cognitive processes, which consist of subjective perceptions of reality (convictions/beliefs) and personal desires. Emotions work as our intellect's software modules.[49] We do not calculate the optimal course for our actions in ones and zeros.[50] We choose what, based on our impressions and preferences, we consider to be the best course or solution. Elster summarises this as follows:

> We *explain* actions by assuming that among the options people believe to be available to them, they choose the one they believe will provide the best way of realising their desires, or ranks highest in their preference order. Thus, the antecedent mental states of action are beliefs and desires.[51]

'The problem with the emotions is not that they are untamed forces or vestiges of our animal past; it is that they were designed to propagate copies of the genes that built them rather than to promote happiness, wisdom or moral values.' Pinker 2009, p. 370. Cf. Sen 2010, p. 49–51.

[46] Sajó 2011, p. 11.

[47] Cf. Reisenzein 2009, especially p. 6–7.

[48] But it is still a kind of calculation, according to this theory. Beliefs and desires are regarded as information, which are processed by the brain as sets of symbols into instructions. Pinker refers to belief-desire theories as 'computational theory of mind'. Pinker 2009, p. 25.

[49] Pinker argues that 'emotions are adaptations, well-engineered software modules that work in harmony with the intellect and are indispensable to the functioning of the whole mind.' Pinker 2009, p. 370.

[50] I have disregarded the issue of intentionality of thinking and acting. It simply underlines how very different logical human reasoning is from machine logic.

[51] Elster 2017, p. 134.

If we want to understand how people make decisions and we want to predict their actions, an ex-post rational explanation risks being reductive and inaccurate (as is, for instance, demonstrated by the inability of classical economic models to forecast economic crises). If we really want to get to grips with how people decide, on what grounds and what basis, we also need to look at underlying impressions, perceptions and desires.[52]

IMAGINED REALITY – THE CONSTRUCTION OF SOCIAL REALITY

Beliefs and desires arising from emotions do not play some minor part in a society's constitutional rules, they are their cornerstone.[53] Constitutions are products of our imagination and create an imagined reality, an intangible social reality, that serves as the organisation, precept and value reference point of human cooperation.[54] They address our minds, their rules articulate mental representations of the organisation of social cooperation.

In the Introduction and Part I of this book we saw that our species has several unique characteristics relative to other living beings. We can see things that do not exist and communicate with each other about them. These are not mere fantasies or myths: we can talk about our mental, abstract representations as though they were real. We can even construct imaginary worlds which we accept as reality. In his book *The Construction of Social Reality*, the American philosopher John Searle demonstrates how we do so.[55] Humans use their unique language to construct intersubjective social realities and string them together into stories evoking invisible worlds which we find so convincing that we take them as true and real – making them reality. These invisible worlds include imagined orders, such as religion, money, units of time, economic value, government, the state or nation and indeed … the law.

Imagined orders form an intermediate category between the world of objective facts and the entirely subjective experiences of feelings and emotions. They are not individual but rather collective conceptions that we share and confirm time and again as 'true' and 'real'.[56] For instance, 'states' do not exist in physical reality. Satellite pictures of the Earth do not record borders anywhere. They do show rivers, mountain ranges and even walls, but the exact borders of the world's approximately

---

[52] The branch of psychology focused on understanding human behaviour based on the belief-desire model is sometimes referred to as folk psychology. Cf. Pinker 2009, p. 63.

[53] This idea is also called the 'social life of emotions'. Tiedens & Leach 2004, especially p. 2–3.

[54] Cf. Searle 1995, p. 4–5 and chapter 2 p. 31–57. Niezen 2010, chapter 1 (*The Imagined Order*), p. 1–28.

[55] Searle 1995.

[56] Yaron Ezrahi argues that collective imagination is a process of: 'composing, decomposing, and recomposing the fabrics of images, metaphors, narratives, symbols, metaphysics, fantasies, common-sense facts, popular views of science, social values, shared fears and emotions, and other cultural and experiential materials – a process that continually produces configurations that fulfil diverse needs and functions.' Ezrahi 2012, p. 37.

193 states are nowhere to be seen. You would have to imagine the borders for yourself because these borders only exist as a collective conception. Figments of our imagination. Incidentally, the imagined order of what a state is consists of much more than mere borders. It is connected to notions of groups of people, inhabitants with a special relationship to a particular territory, who, perhaps for this reason, also know better than others – non-residents – how to live in this area. The imagined order of the state is strong because it is shared by many people and is therefore constantly confirmed.[57] This meaningful and valuable (imagined) reality is also connected to collective moral judgments. We not only experience the existence of states, we now also think they *ought* to exist – that the inhabitants of this particular collective – 'state' – have a claim on a territory's natural resources, should enjoy some sort of autonomy and sovereignty, may never be attacked unprovoked by other nations, have something to say about their own fate, and so on. Imagined orders are ubiquitous and they are so strong that it is difficult for many people to accept that they are not much more than the product of our imagination.[58] They feel 'real' – very much as a sort of existential belief. Yuval Harari expresses this uncomfortable feeling in his book *Homo Deus*:

> People find it difficult to understand the idea of 'imagined orders' because they assume that there are only two types of realities: objective realities and subjective realities. In objective reality, things exist independently of our beliefs and feelings. [...] Subjective reality, in contrast, depends on my personal beliefs and feelings. [...] Most people presume that reality is either objective or subjective, and that there is no third option. Hence once they satisfy themselves that something isn't just their own subjective feeling, they jump to the conclusion that it *must* be objective. If lots of people believe in God; if money makes the world go round; and if nationalism starts wars and builds empires – then these things aren't just a selective belief or mine. God, money and nations *must* therefore be objective realities.[59]

[57] They are self-referential, according to Searle 1995, p. 32–34. Niezen 2010, p. 1–28.
[58] Harari claims there is even an 'iron rule of history that every imagined hierarchy disavows its fictional origins and claims to be natural and inevitable'. Harari 2011, p. 148.
[59] Harari 2016, p. 143–144. My italics.

25

The Roots of the Tree of Knowledge

VIA EMOTIONS AND SENTIMENTS TO MORALITY

Constitutional norms create the imaginary world of law and political (leadership) order: a story spanning the gap between emotions, sentiments[1] and social order (the 'we'). Emotions and sentiments enable us to assess not only our physical environment and act accordingly, but also to vet our relationships with others, even to value our own thinking and conduct – that is, morality. We now know that moral awareness comes from our social instincts, as Charles Darwin (1809–1882) – the founder of evolutionary biology – demonstrated. They are important for group survival.[2] The social instinct is a biological predisposition which works in roughly the same way as our language instinct.[3] This capacity is still relatively unfixed at birth; it is an

---

[1] There is a difference between the two: emotions are about the way of feeling; sentiments are the feeling itself.

[2] Darwin 1981 (orig. 1871), p. 96–97 and p. 161–164 (elaboration of his earlier observations in *Origin of Species*, 1859); Cf. Swaab 2014 (orig. 2000), especially Chapter XIV (*Moral Behaviour*).

[3] Pinker 2007a in which Pinker elaborates Noam Chomsky's theories of language as instinct. Cf. Chomsky 2005. Darwin established as early as 1871 that morality works similarly to a social instinct. (Charles Darwin 1981 [orig. 1871], p. 96–97). Modern evolutionary biologists are finding an increasing amount of evidence underpinning this, although not yet conclusively. Marc D. Hauser, author of *Moral Minds* 2006 (New York: Harper Collins) claimed to have found conclusive evidence, but he appeared to have manipulated various parts of his research and received a stern reprimand from Harvard University and other research committees for scientific misconduct and resigned his position as professor at Harvard in 2011. *Moral Minds* was incidentally not one of the publications in question but was, of course, indirectly tainted by the scandal. So, morality is not an instinct after all? It is better not to jump to conclusions. Like Darwin, evolutionary biologists assume in broad lines that morality is innate like a kind of instinct. We do not yet know exactly how it works. Regarding human morality as an innate, biological adaptation – and not a mere learned behaviour – is called 'moral nativism'. Cf. Joyce 2014, especially p. 262 (and other contributions in the series entitled *Behavior*, published in De Waal 2015; Joyce 2006; Dwyer 2006). John Rawls draws a parallel between the basis of human morality and the language instinct ('sense of grammar') in his argumentation. Rawls 1999 (orig. 1971), p. 46–47.

'instinct' to acquire a skill – an art.[4] Which is not to say you are born a blank slate (tabula rasa):[5] it all depends on what you do with it.

Moral judgments of approval and disapproval, about right and wrong, fair and unfair[6] are individual mental processes that arise from individual impressions and experiences. Our aptitude and imagination allow us to communicate and share judgments of this kind. Seeing or ascertaining other people's emotions and moral judgments can cause resonance behaviour or resonance emotions (seeing people cry makes you sad, cheerfulness is contagious). This can happen spontaneously or be induced by transmitting a representation of an emotion of this kind (as a story or image).[7] Someone other than the person experiencing the emotion can feel it as well thanks to our capacity for empathy.[8] Certain judgments, arising from individual emotions, can be elevated to normative *public* sentiments – shared moral values: public standards on how things should be done. As Sajó puts it:

> Emotional interactions and social narratives about emotions result in widespread and repetitious individual feelings, which become socially observed and recognised as normative public sentiments.[9]

Such public sentiments do not arise overnight. They are often the product of long historical developments and are usually internalised gradually through narrative transfer, long-term imitation (tradition) and reconfirmation.[10] That repetition and recognition can at some point make habits function as law (norms) or that precedents and traditions assume a connective function in society are good illustrations of the process known as *constructive sentimentalism*.[11] It usually takes time for such sentiments to be internalised, but sometimes it can happen quite quickly. Public sentiments and values are sometimes invented right under your nose and presented

---

[4] 'An instinct to acquire an art' as Pinker calls it. Pinker 2007a, (title of the first paragraph), p. 1.

[5] Pinker 2003.

[6] Prinz 2013, especially p. 3 and p.13. Views differ on whether emotions are part of, precede, or result from a moral judgment. Prinz maintains that moral judgments contain emotions, but longer-standing moral *values* become independent sentiments ('dispositions to feel emotions') preceding moral judgments – they are elevated to the level of the software itself. Prinz 2013, p. 7.

[7] This resonance takes place in mirror neurons. Rizzolatti, Sinigaglia & Anderson 2008.

[8] Cf. Davis 2004.

[9] Sajó 2011, p. 25.

[10] Public sentiments are not universal. According to the latest insights in evolutionary biology, they do not have a fixed, unchanging core (discoverable, say, by self-examination) as conceived by natural law thinkers in the tradition of Hobbes, Locke and Rousseau (and even Rawls). 'It follows that contemporary evolutionary biology cannot be used to arrive at a universally valid definition of the way humans ought to live: today's life sciences are not conceptually suited to become the basis of a "natural law" akin to the theological doctrines of the past.' Gruter & Masters 1986, especially p. 154. As with language, we seem to have a basic aptitude for morality. An innate ability that works like an instinct and is developed by stimulation and learning. Cf. Hauser 2006 and Joyce 2006.

[11] Prinz 2013, p. 13.

as venerable, historically-developed traditions – therefore worthy to be upheld.[12]
A good example is the American Pledge of Allegiance, the custom of expressing
allegiance to the United States flag and republic by saluting the flag with the right
hand over the heart every morning. The time-honoured custom of the Pledge was
only 'invented' in 1892 as part of an advertising campaign to promote the sale of
flags to celebrate the fourth centenary of Columbus' landfall in the Americas.
Starting out as a gimmick, the Pledge was observed in more and more schools and
institutions as a public rite, until it was eventually solemnly adopted by Congress as
a long-standing national tradition during the Second World War.[13]

Public sentiments and values can also change quickly and completely within
one or two generations, such as the relationship between parents and children or
the sexes (or what the sexes are), or how we should behave in the public sphere
(violence, smoking, alcohol and driving). They are not fixed and are malleable to
some extent. They may even be imposed by norms – such as legal rules – envisaged
to change public sentiments and values. As controversial as imposed public morality
may be, it does quite often work.

The conversion of legal rules to public morality is no mean feat. But when governments or authorities succeed in elevating legal rules to public sentiment, they have
well and truly hit the jack pot, finding a way into the hearts and minds of members of
society. Their ideas and policies on morality have become the group members' internalised morality. This is the greatest prize for any modern administrator. Instilling
your rules, laws and policies in public sentiments allows you to achieve your goals
virtually without cost or effort – you hardly need any policemen, inspections or other
institutions to enforce rules that people have made their own.[14] This sounds much

---

[12] Hobsbawm & Ranger 1984 (orig. 1983).

[13] The pledge reads: 'I pledge allegiance to the flag of the United States of America, and to
the republic for which it stands, one nation under God, indivisible, with liberty and justice
for all.' The original text – based on a pledge version devised by Captain George T. Balch –
was composed by Francis Bellamy, giving it the name the Bellamy Salute. The Pledge of
Allegiance was actually popularised by a campaign by the magazine *The Youth's Companion*
to commemorate the fourth centenary of the European discovery of the Americas by selling
Star-Spangled Banners to its subscribers so that public schools across the country would be
adorned with American flags on Columbus Day. Even though originally intended as a way
of boosting flag sales in 1892, its gravitas increased dramatically in 1942, and even more so
in 1954, when Congress became involved. Congress added 'One nation under God' to the
original text and congressional sessions since that moment open with the recital of the Pledge
by all members, placing hand over hart and standing to attention, as do meetings of many
lower tiers of government and private organisations. Recitals are also regularly scheduled in
most public schools and are a requirement at naturalisation ceremonies. Recital of the Pledge
is so widespread that most Americans know it better than the United States Declaration of
Independence or the United States Constitution. See the recent study of 2017 by the Annenberg
Public Policy Centre of the University of Pennsylvania 'Americans Are Poorly Informed About
Basic Constitutional Provisions' www.annenbergpublicpolicycenter.org/americans-are-poorly-
informed-about-basic-constitutional-provisions/ (consulted 19 November 2019).

[14] Such as our self-evident life with and in the phenomenon 'national state'. Mabel Berezin
argues that 'the modern nation-state contains emotions within political institutions', but they

easier than it actually is because our inner morality works like a mirror. Public morality, expressed in such things as legal rules, and personal morality should not diverge too greatly. There must be some congruence with our own moral intuitions. 'It is prohibitively difficult to sustain law against morality', Sajó comments.[15] And he is right. But neither is it necessary for all rights, as a set of norms and rules on personal, institutional and leadership behaviour, to correspond perfectly to everyone's personal moral intuition. Individual morality is a little malleable. But how and to what extent?

For centuries, philosophers of law have pondered over the relationship between individual morality and (established or constructed) forms of public morality, such as the law. We have not been able to reach a definitive conclusion. A well-known example is the debate between American professor Lon Fuller of Harvard University and British professor Herbert Hart of the University of Oxford. In a famous 1958 article (published in the lion's den, the *Harvard Law Review*), Hart takes the view that there is no evidence of any necessary link between the law and its moral justification; the law knows no minimum morality.[16] The law continues to exist – and be enforced – when it does not correspond to public morality or an individual's sense of justice, Hart observes. Fuller takes a quite different perspective. He considers the law and legal rules not so much as an arbitrary set of norms and rules, but rather as a form of societal organisation. Fuller argues that law is the enterprise of subjecting human conduct to the governance of rules.[17] This requires a legal system meeting certain minimum conditions. An essential precondition for this is the recognition of the rule of law in a society. On top of that, Fuller argues, legal rules must also meet at least eight basic criteria of inner morality to be recognised as such. They must be general, promulgated, prospective, clear, non-contradictory, practicable, durable and actually enforced, and not retroactive.[18] If legal rules fail to meet these criteria, this will lead (in the long term) to social resistance and more and more members of society no longer feeling morally obliged to comply with the norms and rules. Law is a two-way process, according to Fuller. 'The functioning of a legal system depends upon a co-operative effort – an effective and responsible interaction – between law-giver and subject.'[19]

Who is right? After decades, the jury is still out. At the very least, the debate is living proof of the importance of emotions in law. The exchange of views on these

are almost invisible. 'Emotions of membership are rarely transparent except under conditions of threat from internal or external forces.' External threats can stir up national emotions that may encourage community members to defend their state, or, in the event of internal threats, induce them to put a particular party in charge to achieve domestic order or fair relations. Cf. Berezin 2002, p. 43.

[15] Sajó 2011, p. 25.

[16] Hart's clear answer to whether the law 'must satisfy a moral minimum in order to be a law' is in the negative. Cf. Hart 1958, p. 601.

[17] '[A] system for subjecting human conduct to the government of rules.' Fuller 1969a, p. 46.

[18] *Ibid.*, p. 41–94.

[19] Fuller 1969a, p. 219.

issues between otherwise impeccably polite and affable legal scholars is punctuated with large words and bitter reproaches. Hart's adherents view Fuller's supporters as dreamers and idealists, slipshod thinkers unable to distinguish between the world as it *ought* to be and as it *is*. The Fuller camp counters with examples of tyrannical law, the horrors of the Second World War and failing legal systems – in short, reproaching Hart adherents for being blinkered when reflecting on the validity of the law.

There is, of course, something to be said for both positions. They are also partly talking at cross purposes. Lon Fuller's wish list is, of course, quite American and specific to his time. And no matter how much Hart tries to steer clear of the question of a requisite minimum in morality for the law to be valid, he cannot avoid facing up to the fact that the validity of the law relies on some form of acceptance by those bound by it. Incidentally, he has an elegant solution to this: the overall acceptance of the entire legal system.

RULES OF RECOGNITION

Hart argues that, from an external point of view, 'the foundations of a legal system consist of a situation in which the majority of a social group habitually obey the orders backed by threats of the sovereign person or persons'.[20] This is sufficient for implementation, but not for validity. For a legal system to be truly *valid* – and be accepted as legitimate – requires a certain degree of internalisation and identification with the legal subjects. Legal systems always depend on a meta rule: a 'rule of recognition' as Hart calls it.[21] This rule of recognition implies overall acceptance that there is such a thing as law – as a system of abstract norms and rules – to which you are bound (whether or not you agree with it), which is generally observed and provides criteria determining which norms and rules are valid (that is, binding) law and which are not.[22] Hart's rule of recognition is rather similar to what Austrian legal philosopher Hans Kelsen famously called a *Grundnorm* (Basic norm). Kelsen also wanted to steer clear of the question of the kind of content law must have before it can really be called law. An unsolvable question in scholarly terms.[23]

THE ELEGANT SIMPLICITY OF POSITIVE LAW

Scholars like Austin, Hart and Kelsen argue that understanding the law and its operation principally requires examination of how the law appears to us as an observable

---

[20] Hart 2012 (orig. 1961), p. 100.

[21] *Ibid.*, p. 100–101.

[22] Hart assumes a union of primary legal rules (with behavioural norms and orders) and secondary legal rules (rules which determine how law is formed, amended, recognised and applied) for the latter aspect. *Ibid.*

[23] Kelsen asserts on the morality of justice: 'No other question has been discussed so passionately; no other question has caused so much precious blood and so many bitter tears to be shed; no

phenomenon: as positive law.[24] Kelsen regards the law as a hierarchically-ordered system of mutually-progressing norms and legal rules to which judicial institutions (offices, authorities, courts) give effect, in the form of sanctions, applications, rulings and the like in in a legal order. The law is what it is. The phenomenon can no longer be studied rationally once you start mixing it with your own judgments of right and wrong because the worlds of what is and what ought to be become entangled.[25] The validity of the law does not depend on whether it meets a minimum standard of morality or justice, but on what we have agreed to. An abstract basic agreement, a basic norm, which recognises the legal order. Kelsen thinks there is no absolute, perennial standard of justice which can be used to measure whether or not the law is good or should be valid.[26]

Neither is Lon Fuller, who assumes that law can have minimum validity requirements, able to avoid the fact that you cannot shop around in law, picking and choosing parts that match your moral tastes or persuasions. A legal system as a whole would have great difficulty functioning if everyone relied solely on their own sense of morality to decide which law they were bound to, even if based on Fuller's 'objective' minimum criteria. To counter this, Fuller posits that legal systems rely on a reciprocity principle according to which:

> [...] on the one hand, the lawgiver must be able to anticipate that the citizenry as a whole will accept as law and generally observe the body of rules he has promulgated. On the other hand, the legal subject must be able to anticipate that government will itself abide by its own declared rules when it comes to the judgment of his actions [...].[27]

And this is the point at which Fuller, Hart and Kelsen's worlds seem to meet. Reciprocity or (formal) recognition for that matter of the legal system as a whole is a prerequisite for the validity of law. When it comes down to this Hart, Fuller and Kelsen's views are not all that divergent.

Certain subjects are best avoided at birthday parties, weddings and evening get-togethers after football matches: taste in music, political preferences and – above all – anything related to law and justice. As an Austrian, Hans Kelsen would have had plenty to explain in a local football club canteen. People have passionate opinions about law and its morality. 'Morality is a subject that interests us above all others',

other question has been the object of so much intensive thinking by the most illustrious thinkers from Plato to Kant; and yet, this question is today as unanswered as it ever was.' Kelsen 1971, especially p. 1.

[24] Kelsen 1967 (orig. 1960 [1934]), p. 67–69.

[25] *Ibid.*

[26] Kelsen: 'If the history of human thought proves anything, it is the futility of the attempt to establish, in the way of rational considerations, an absolutely correct standard of human behaviour [...] If we may learn anything from the intellectual experiences of the past, it is the fact that only relative values are accessible to human reason [...] Absolute justice is an irrational ideal or, what amounts to the same, an illusion – one of the eternal illusions of mankind.' Kelsen 1971, p. 20.

[27] Fuller 1969b, p. 24 and Fuller 1969a, p. 217 and p. 219.

David Hume wrote in 1739.[28] Little has changed since then. Hart and Kelsen may maintain that law can only be known rationally by studying valid legal norms, but in doing so they miss something: the interaction of individuals (individual morality) and the law (as an expression of some kind of public morality). A 2004 study by Oliver Goodenough and Kristin Prehn shows how people come to normative judgments through emotions and intuition, and that these judgments play a role in how we deal with the law and experience what the law is.[29] The law is not so much 'something' or an 'object', but rather more a 'process'. As a system of 'belonging', the law not only judges us – we constantly judge the legal system. The people applying, interpreting, forming, finding and implementing the law have these emotions and intuitions too. We require that those responsible for administering the law (try to) ignore or resist these emotions and intuitions. We need them to act dispassionately, even if it is nearly impossible. We must prevent, as legal economist Posner puts it: 'dangerous intrusions of emotion into the judicial process'.[30] Be that as it may, we sometimes do try somehow or another to assimilate legal emotions, deep-seated feelings of justice with existing law. A judge, for instance, may every so often 'discover' a legal principle; an existing law may be reinterpreted due to changed (legal) conceptions; or longstanding practices may on occasion be deemed 'law'. And sometimes existing rules even cease to be applied because they are considered obsolete[31] or run contrary to legal principles. Although it is not so that everyone may decide, based on their own moral insights, whether they are bound by the law, we have already seen that there is an interaction between sentiments of justice and the law. Constitutional rules and their messages operate in this sphere, beyond legal positivists' field of vision.

DOES NATURAL LAW EXIST?

Is the imagined world of law based solely on some esoteric sort of formal recognition as Hart and Kelsen argue or is there more to it? Are there deeper roots? Does the validity of a legal system's rules perhaps stem from higher, metaphysical, universal principles or norms beyond the law? Emanations of basic principles, norms and ideas about justice shared by all people at all times. Roman orator, politician and philosopher Cicero (106–43 BCE) thought so:

> There is a true law, a right reason, conformable to nature, universal, unchangeable, eternal, whose commands urge us to duty, and whose prohibitions restrain us from

---

[28] Hume 2004 (orig. 1739–1740), Book III (*Morals*), part I, section I.
[29] Goodenough & Prehn 2004.
[30] Posner 1999, especially p. 327.
[31] Obsolete acts – when not repealed – may fall prey to 'desuetude' a doctrine that causes statutes or legal principles to lapse and become unenforceable by a long habit of non-enforcement or passage of time. See, for instance, the Hackney Carriage Act 1879 in India. It was repealed in 2017 but had already been a dead letter for some time. An example from my home country the Netherlands is the 1829 General Provisions Act, which is still in force but no longer observed.

evil. [...] This law cannot be contradicted by any other law, and is not liable either to derogation or abrogation.[32]

Plato before him and an array of thinkers after him (Augustine of Hippo, Thomas Aquinas, Grotius,[33] Hobbes, Locke and Rousseau) assumed the intuitive idea that there are superhuman rules and principles – arising from the cosmic, divine or natural order – which can be known through revelation or reason and precede existing law:[34] *natural law*.

Seventeenth-century philosopher and former captain in the English Civil War, John Locke, thought anyone guided by reason and using common sense could know natural law:

> The state of nature has a law of nature to govern it, which obliges every one: and reason, which is that law, teaches all mankind, who will but consult it, that being all equal and independent, no one ought to harm another in his life, health, liberty, or possessions … [and] when his own preservation comes not in competition, ought he, as much as he can, to preserve the rest of mankind, and may not, unless it be to do justice on an offender, take away, or impair the life, or what tends to the preservation of the life, the liberty, health, limb, or goods of another.[35]

In short, everyone is independent (free) and equal, and the natural law of reason shows that nobody should harm another person and we must protect each other as much as possible. This natural law is to be found in the nature of things and is discoverable to any reasonable and receptive person. It sounds familiar. The whole idea is closely linked to Christian teaching – revelation through prayer (bringing knowledge of God's will). Locke substitutes it with revelation through thinking (uncovering the laws of nature and natural law). Whilst the natural law of gravity discovered in the same period by Isaac Newton is universal and immutable, opinion is very divided about what the state of nature and natural law are. The task of unambiguously establishing natural law has proved to be anything but easy. Even the thinking of Locke's contemporary Hobbes, who also experienced the horrors of the English Civil War, led to radically different insights about the state of nature and natural law. Hobbes concurs that reason makes people sense that there is a right to life, and we have a duty to respect each other's rights,[36] but these rights are constantly under attack. As free individuals in our state of nature, we do not protect each other as allies, but rather are at each other's throats as

---

[32] (Quote from) Cicero 1841, *Treatise on the Republic*, III, XXII, 33, p. 270; Cf. Cicero 2008, p. 68–69.

[33] For Grotius, much of Roman law also expressed natural law. Cf. Strautman 2015.

[34] Which is why it is also called 'prepositive'.

[35] Locke 1689, § 6.

[36] Hobbes considers the 'law of Nature' (*lex naturalis*), the first law, to be: 'a precept, or general rule, found out by reason, by which a man is forbidden to do that which is destructive of his life, or taketh away the means of preserving the same, and to omit that by which he thinketh it may be best preserved.' Hobbes 1651, chapter XIV, p. 80.

opponents. Hobbes famously argues that the state of nature is not paradise but hell on earth, with:

> no knowledge of the face of the earth, no account of time, no arts, no letters, no society, and which is worst of all, continual fear and danger of violent death, and the life of man, solitary, poor, nasty, brutish, and short.[37]

This unsustainable situation inevitably impels people into a political community united under a leader: the Leviathan. A community (commonwealth) with a strong leader is able to do what free individuals' selfishness precludes: provide protection. In exchange, members accept the ruler's dominion (therefore relinquishing some freedom), albeit conditionally.[38] Whereas Locke's natural law holds that free individuals compel each other to recognise and protect each other's rights in order to remain free, Hobbes's natural law does not signify much more than a fearful trust construction to secure the individual's right to life through a community – a misanthrope's world view.

Diametrically opposed to these ideas is the eighteenth-century Franco-Swiss prodigy Jean-Jacques Rousseau's conception of the state of nature and natural law. His state of nature is truly a paradise. People were free and good in that state; we would return to it like a shot, given half the chance. He finds 'proof' for the actual existence of the state of nature in the lives of the primitive tribes Western Europe had just discovered around the world at that time. 'The example of savages', Rousseau writes, 'who have almost all been found at this point, seems to confirm that the human race was made to remain in [a state of nature] always; that this state is the veritable prime of the world; and that all subsequent progress has been in appearance so many steps toward the perfection of the individual, and in fact toward the decrepitude of the species.'[39] So living in large communities has literally corrupted us. Rousseau's idea of the state of nature and the life of primitive tribes is, of course, highly idealised and romanticised – despite quite a number of people in back-to-nature movements today who still strongly believe in it. Yet, it is as unrealistic as Hobbes' unremitting anarchy. There never was a state of nature in which we

---

[37] Hobbes 1651, chapter XIII (*Of the Natural Condition of Mankind as Concerning their Felicity and Misery*), p. 78.

[38] Hobbes expresses this conditionality as a second law: 'that a man be willing, when others are so too, as far-forth as for peace and defence of himself he shall think it necessary, to lay down this right to all things, and be contented with so much liberty against other men as he would allow other men against himself. For as long as every man holdeth this right of doing anything he liketh, so long are all men in the condition of war. But if other men will not lay down their right as well as he, then there is no reason for anyone to divest himself of his; for that were to expose himself to prey, which no man is bound to, rather than to dispose himself to peace. This is that law of the Gospel: "whatsoever you require that others should do to you, that do ye to them." And that law of all men, quod tibi fieri non vis, alteri ne feceris.' Hobbes 1651, chapter XIV, p. 80–81.

[39] Rousseau 1755, volume 2, p. 65.

lived freely and independently as individuals and which we voluntarily left, on some kind of contractual basis, to enter a community that was supposed to guarantee our natural rights.[40] In the words of Francis Fukuyama:

> Everything that modern biology and anthropology tell us about the state of nature suggests the opposite: there was *never* a period in human evolution when human beings existed as isolated individuals [...] Human beings do not enter into society and political life as a result of a conscious, rational decision. Communal organisation comes to them naturally, though the specific ways they cooperate are shaped by environment, ideas and culture.[41]

There was no state of nature – neither an idyll nor a hell. No more than there is natural law 'etched' somewhere, like some law book packed with universal rules of life, on everyone's mental bookshelf. There is simply no such thing as innate knowledge of universally applicable natural law in the form of a set of cognisable, concrete norms and rules that can serve as a moral compass and frame of reference for our decisions. Legal behavioural researchers Gruter and Master observe that:

> contemporary biology cannot reveal a universally valid "natural law" to guide our legal and political decisions and institutions.[42]

Observations of this kind vex people who strongly believe in universal 'natural' values, such as universal human rights. It just cannot be true! It is yet more proof of how modern science assumes a kind of omniscience. 'Scientism', Simon sniffs in his book *Universal Rights and the Constitution*[43] – a misguided, excessive belief in science. Anybody can see that there are universal rights, scholars like Simon will point out. Just take the Universal Declaration of Human Rights, or any other of the myriad international Human Rights Treaties currently in force. The existence of these omnipresent rights flows from the moral (and actual) imperative to hold the ever-present threat of barbarism at bay. Such arguments may not in themselves prove that everyone is born with an in-built natural law manual, but rather that 'all men are born natural-law jurists', as Rommen puts it.[44] The existence of natural law, the essence of universal

---

[40] Although we now know that people never lived solitary lives and did not negotiate a cohabitation contract in some kind of marketplace, the contract thinkers did understand – intuitively – how the biological mechanism of mutual altruism worked. Pinker argues that: 'reciprocal altruism, in particular, is just the traditional concept of the social contract restated in biological terms. [...] Of course, humans were never solitary (as Rousseau and Hobbes incorrectly surmised), and they did not inaugurate group living by haggling over a contract at a particular time and place. Bands, clans, tribes, and other social groups are central to human existence and have been so for as long as we have been a species. But the *logic* of social contracts may have propelled the evolution of the mental faculties that keep us in these groups.' Pinker 2003, p. 285.

[41] Fukuyama 2011, p. 30.

[42] Gruter et al. 1986 p. 153.

[43] Simon 2014, p. 118–119.

[44] Rommen 1947, p. 266.

human rights, is based on faith[45] rather than facts.[46] Law and human rights are neither innate nor the product of metaphysical revelation: they are a product of human
conception. Modern legal theory too – even in an era that appears to attach such
importance to universal human rights – seems to have abandoned the natural law
approach to law. Influential philosopher of law Ronald Dworkin (1931–2013) explains
why it has become de rigueur for legal scholars to no longer take natural law seriously:

> [N]o one wants to be called a natural lawyer. Natural law insists that what the law
> is depends in some way on what the law should be. This seems metaphysical or at
> least vaguely religious. In any case it seems plainly wrong. If some theory of law is
> shown to be a natural law theory, therefore, people can be excused if they do not
> attend to it much further.[47]

UNIVERSAL MORALITY?

Does this ring the death knell of natural law as an inspiration for law, and a source of
constitutional rules and, more generally, of law? Perhaps not quite.[48] Enlightenment
thinkers' assessment of 'nature' might not have been correct, but modern insights into
human nature show that Hobbes, Locke, Rousseau and other thinkers of their ilk had
a decent intuitive conception of human nature.[49] The keystone of natural law – that
people have a universal, shared morality – is a plausible idea, recent cognitive studies show. As elucidated in Chapter 3, our morality does not appear to be extraneous;
people seem to have an innate aptitude, a social instinct,[50] for morality.[51] Roughly analogous to our linguistic ability, this hereditary trait is an aptitude trained by learning.[52]

45　Stephen Hopgood already regards (international) human rights as a form of *secular belief*:
　　'derived from natural law principles sanctified in a moment of creation, of "constitution",
　　when an "unmoved mover", an unquestionable authority, a secular god, authorises all subse-
　　quent rules.' Hopgood 2013, p. 122.
46　Legal philosopher Jeremy Waldron warns us that it is also unwise to try to base human rights
　　on – indisputable – universal natural law claims: 'the shift from "natural rights" to "human
　　rights" marks a loss of faith in our ability to justify rights on the basis of truths about human
　　nature.' Waldron 1987, p. 163.
47　Dworkin rejects this simplistic argumentation, a consequence of labelling, later in the article.
　　Dworkin 1982, quote from p. 165.
48　Cf. Dworkin, who gallantly admits that: 'if [it] is correct, that any theory which makes the
　　content of law sometimes depend on the correct answer to some moral question is a natural
　　law theory, then I am guilty of natural law.' *Ibid.*
49　Cf. Pinker 2003, p. 285 and Pinker 2018, p. 10–14.
50　This instinct is related to our capacity for empathy: we can empathise with someone else – put
　　ourselves in their situation. Empathy not only enables us to imagine what it is like to be in
　　someone else's shoes, it can also inspire compassion and sympathy – wanting to help or com-
　　fort the other person. De Waal 2019, p. 88–93.
51　There is still a lack of consensus on this matter, with debate between 'moral nativists' who argue
　　that morality is a biological adaptation and 'spandrel theorists' who counter that it is merely a
　　by-product of our psychological faculties. The former seems to be slightly in the ascendant. Cf.
　　Joyce 2014, especially p. 262–266; Suhler & Churchland 2011; Murrow & Murrow 2013.
52　Joyce 2006; May 2018, p. 78–80.

The process is fairly automatic and intuitive; little training is needed to be able to make moral judgments. John Mikhail, professor at George Town Law School, contends that every normal person is innately endowed with moral grammar rules.[53] His colleague and fellow-American John Rawls (1921–2002) had anticipated this.[54] This inborn grammar explains our amenability to norms, such as how things should be. Legal norms – norms telling us how to behave – adroitly exploit this aptitude: our moral grammar rules enable us to easily understand the message of law and legal norms. Mikhail thinks that this basic aptitude[55] is fertile ground on which to establish a legal system:[56]

> Ordinary individuals are intuitive lawyers, who possess tacit or unconscious knowledge of a rich variety of legal rules, concepts, and principles, along with a natural readiness to compute mental representations of human acts and omissions in legally cognisable terms.[57]

THE GOLDEN RULE

Moral judgments are a product of our emotions, as we saw. Influenced by imitation and social narratives,[58] they can become so widespread that they grow into socially recognised, normative public sentiments. The process is clear, but is this morality also substantive? According to the biological laws, our human social instincts are subject to, it is. Charles Darwin said on this subject:

> [...] the social instincts [...] with the aid of active intellectual powers and the effects of habit, naturally lead to the golden rule, 'as ye would that men should do to you, do ye to them likewise';[59] and this lies at the foundation of morality.[60]

---

[53] Mikhail 2017, chapter 5 (*The Moral Grammar Hypothesis*), p. 101 ff. Pinker 2003, p. 166.

[54] In *A Theory of Justice*, 1971. Rawls 1999 (orig. 1971), p. 47.

[55] Mikhail 2017, p. 307 ff. It is in effect a new kind of evidence for the assumptions underpinning the ideas of natural law and universal human rights. Mikhail: 'Linguists and cognitive scientists have argued that every normal human being is endowed with innate knowledge of grammatical principles – with a specific genetic program, in effect, for language acquisition. Both the classical understanding of the law of nature and the modern idea of human rights [...] rest at bottom on an analogous idea.' Mikhail 2017, p. 317.

[56] Michael Guttentag, professor at the Loyola Law School in Los Angeles goes a step further. 'Is there a Law Instinct?' he wonders in an eponymous article in 2009. He thinks there is: 'the neuroanatomy of human social behaviour all suggest that humans have an innate predisposition to rely on legal systems to organise their social behaviour. Evidence from the historical and anthropological records and considerations of the evolutionary viability of a law instinct are consistent with the law instinct hypothesis.' Guttentag 2009, quote from p. 328.

[57] Mikhail 2017, p. 101.

[58] 'Narratives' refers here to the narrative nature of human communication in which we simultaneously give meaning to and explain actual or imagined events. 'Narrative explanation does not subsume events under laws. Instead, it explains by clarifying the significance of events that have occurred on the basis of the outcome that has followed. In this sense, narrative explanation is retroactive.' Polkinghorne 1988, p. 21 and Czarniwska 2014, p. 7–8.

[59] *King James Version*, Luke 6:31.

[60] Darwin 1981 (orig. 1871), p. 106.

Our social instincts of self-preservation and reciprocal altruism bring us to a form of basic rational morality,[61] which develops into a habit and becomes 'hereditary' over generations.[62] Memes, as these phenomena are known, were already discussed in Chapter 2. As nice and comforting as the idea is that humanity has some kind of common-sense basic morality, it does not entail any such thing as timeless or objectively cognisable moral values. Doubting Thomases, including what are called *error theorists* (an easily misread term), argue that acknowledging the existence of common-sense morality essentially implies acknowledging objective moral values.[63] This flies in the face of human history and our present condition which prove that there are no such timeless, universal values, or at least none that can be objectively established.[64] The content of public values varies from time to place. Ethicist John Mizzoni wonders in a 2009 article what Charles Darwin would have made of this postmodernist, false-theoretical objection that 'objective values are not cognisable'.[65] Mizzoni argues that Darwin would likely have said that we probably cannot know these values objectively or empirically, but that we do *feel* them. We can discern these values with our emotions. It is in large part our moral sense that tells us what we should do, even though we do not always do so.[66]

MORALITY UNDER HUME'S GUILLOTINE

That the aptitude for morality does not produce the same results everywhere would not have come as a surprise to Darwin. The aptitude for language, our language instinct, has not led us to all speak the same language. For Darwin, morality may come from our social instincts, but it is formed and given substance by our intellectual abilities and habits. It is an aptitude that is trained and practised until it is internalised. This is also how public, shared morality comes about – rather like a shared language: acquisition, practice and habit. As András Sajó pointed out above, public sentiments, as a set of values and guidelines for action, can only really arise through observance and compliance. Normative frameworks arise from long-term habits, or ways of doing things.

A classic phenomenon in law is that norms and legal rules can arise from customary practices. Common law, derived from traditions and time-honoured customs, is considered an important source of law in almost all legal cultures. You can use

---

[61] Hoffman: 'Reciprocal altruism is itself a kind of pre-moral sentiment, requiring the ability to give and accept benefits with an anticipation of a promised return.' Hoffman 2011, quote from p. 487.

[62] 'Habits, moreover, followed during many generations probably tend to be inherited.' Darwin 1981 (orig. 1871), p. 164. Cf. Gommer 2011, p. 54–60, paragraph 2 of chapter III (*Deriving norms from facts*).

[63] Joyce 2001, p. 60–61 and chapters 1, 2 and 6.

[64] Mackie 1977.

[65] Mizonni 2009, especially p. 131.

[66] *Ibid.*

customary law to build upon earlier generations' insights and wisdom. Such tried-and-tested formulae provide purchase. People are creatures of habit, trusting the familiar and depending on routines.[67] This propensity, coupled with our innate sense of morality, makes us regard traditions or habits as how things ought to be in a relatively short time. German sociologist and scholar of civilisation Norbert Elias published a seminal work on the subject in 1939. Taking Desiderius Erasmus's 1530 etiquette handbook,[68] Elias demonstrated that some habits and customs, regardless of their origins, start functioning as norms and the rules of etiquette for civilised behaviour at a certain point. One example is table manners, like not eating the bread someone else has already taken a bite of, not gulping wine before wiping your greasy lips, not playing with your knife, not spitting or emitting any form of body fluids or gases for that matter, and so forth. These rules originally developed at more well-to-do tables for health reasons or conflict avoidance.[69] Elias dubbed this process 'sociogenesis'.[70]

It might be commonplace for customs to become norms, but the phenomenon is controversial in the law, or even a bone of contention known as the *is-ought problem* or Hume's guillotine.[71] Logically, what 'ought to be' does not automatically follow from what 'is'. In his book *A Treatise of Human Nature* (1739), the Scottish philosopher David Hume expressed his amazement that so many of his colleagues seemed to make this logical error. Taking an existing situation – an empirical statement about what is – they deduced what ought to be.[72] Which is, of course, a fallacious. The fact that it is raining does not mean it ought to rain. Or the fact that Brazil had 2093 million inhabitants in 2019 does not automatically mean it ought to have this number of inhabitants (or more, or less). Even if someone thinks the country is full or overpopulated[73] they will know that this cannot be deduced from the present size of the population. These are easy examples. But can the Swedish habit of shaking hands also mean that people ought to shake hands in Sweden?[74] What if you are a devout Muslim and your faith bars you, as a woman, from shaking a man's hand – even at a job interview? At this point it becomes more difficult for many people to separate the worlds of 'is' and 'ought' with Hume's guillotine. Indeed, these worlds have a great deal to do with each other. 'The "is" can sometimes inform the "ought," according to American judge and behavioural scientist Morris Hoffman.[75] How

---

[67] Amodio, Jost, Master & Ye 2008 and May 2018.

[68] Desiderius Erasmus, *On Civility in Children*, 1530.

[69] Elias 2000 (orig. 1939), p. 48–60 and p. 99–109.

[70] *Ibid.*, p. 109 (for the definition) and – for the preliminary treatise – chapters 1 and 2 of part I (*On the Sociogenesis of the Concepts of "Civilization" and "Culture"*).

[71] Also known as the naturalistic fallacy.

[72] Hume 2004 (orig. 1739–1740), Book III (*Morals*) part I, section I.

[73] Navneet, K., 2014, 'Overpopulation and Sustainability Crisis in Brazil', https://crisisinbrazil .weebly.com/population.html (consulted 8 October 2018).

[74] See www.nytimes.com/2018/08/16/world/europe/sweden-muslim-handshake.html (consulted 8 October 2018).

[75] Hoffman, 2011, p. 501.

things ought to be shapes the world around us: we colour steak (grey-brown) and tomato juice (brownish) red because we believe they should be red. To say nothing of our appearances. What is and ought to be may be logically distinguishable, but they are intertwined in our emotional minds. We can hardly perceive without emotion or judgments: normativity, judgments and values are closely linked to our perception, they are difficult to separate and study separately.[76] This can get in the way of and blur any attempt to look for common 'basic' values or 'shared normativity', as you try to do in a constitution.

ARE CONSTITUTIONAL RULES REFLECTIONS OF BASIC MORALITY?

Sajó argues that groups' public sentiments lead to moral judgments and 'normative, moral frames' of how leadership should be organised and how group members should relate to each other. As he puts it:

> These moral frames, which animate the moral solutions of constitutional law, reflect moral emotions.[77]

Interactions of individual moral judgments inspire public sentiments – especially trust and recognition. Constitutions are based on specific public sentiments – constitutional sentiments. Determining them is not a simple matter of a show of hands or counting heads.[78] Neither are they the result of calculating the greatest good for all, utility maximisation, or pursuing a constant Pareto optimum in which no one in society can improve her position at the expense of someone else. Moral judgments are individual judgments that become public sentiments and group judgments. This process involves a leap of faith – which is notoriously difficult to nail down or predict. Public sentiments must be recognisable; otherwise group members' moral judgments may cause them to cease identifying with them and even resist them at some point. The matter is complicated by public sentiments not being a simple reflection of a universal basic morality – sentiments and values develop. They can totally change over time. Take, for instance, the idea of the equality of all humans. It would have been dismissed out of hand as absurd and ridiculous in the Roman Empire,[79] whereas it is lauded as a 'universal' principle nowadays.

---

[76] Elqayam & Evans 2011.

[77] Sajó 2011, p. 25.

[78] Mila Versteeg shows in a recent article how countries' most highly prized public values (measured by questioning more than half a million respondents) are not reflected in constitutional choices and norms (the public sentiments). 'The link between nations' specific constitutional choices and their citizens' values has generally been weak or nonexistent [sic].' Cf. Versteeg 2014, p. 1.

[79] Cf. McLynn 2010.

26

Constitutions as Vehicles for Legitimacy

Everyone has a built-in morality antenna. But is it always turned on? Do we think much about good and evil, and whether we live by fair rules in an acceptable system? There are days, I must admit, that I am not at all preoccupied by such thoughts: wonderful, carefree days when I just go with the flow.

The more you think about it, the stranger it seems. Why do intelligent, freedom-loving people in societies like the ones we live in – with myriad opportunities for personal enrichment, satisfaction and instant gratification – obey all kinds of oppressive norms and rules that restrict this freedom and the associated opportunities? Is it fear of sanctions?[1] Reputational damage?[2] Herd behaviour?[3] Combinations of enlightened, strategic, long-term self-interest?[4] Or simply to be spared the hassle? It is an eternal question which, oddly enough, is usually reversed: why do people *not* obey rules?[5] This is a little peculiar, to say the least. Why does disobedience to rules and norms so fascinate us in academia, from criminology to legal theory; in government policy, from more bobbies on the beat to zero tolerance; and in popular culture, from Robin Hood to the Godfather? In a genuinely free society, *disobedience* should, in fact, be less surprising than law abiding behaviour. How come free people in free societies obey norms and rules en masse? Laws and rules they barely know – at least, have mostly not read. Autopilot, unquestioned and subservient observance of public rules and laws by almost everybody without having to be continuously shadowed by a policeman. How is this possible?[6] Indeed, disobedience to laws and rules is actually the exception: just look around you.

---

[1] Cf. Tyler 2006, especially p. 22–25; Robinson & Darley 2003, Pinker 2011, p. 529–547.
[2] Cf. Sacconi 2007.
[3] Tyler 2006, *ibid.*; Wittberg 2006, p. 25–43.
[4] Tyler 2006, p. 171–174; Tocqueville 2002 (orig. 1835 and 1840), p. 595.
[5] Wingrove, Korpas & Weisz 2011.
[6] For more on this phenomenon cf. Hughes 2018.

How is this possible? Scholars argue that the main reason we swiftly and almost automatically accept laws and rules from the appropriate authorities (institutions upon which we confer this status) is because we come to morally identify with them.[7] We share the collective belief that rules which have been appropriately established and enforced by the appropriate institution are legitimate – that is, acceptable. The legitimacy of a political or legal system is not a fixed trait, but a (process of) collective conviction. At the beginning of the twentieth century, Max Weber insightfully observed that:

> The basis of every system of authority, and correspondingly of every kind of willingness to obey, is a *belief*, a belief by virtue of which persons exercising authority are lent prestige.[8]

According to Weber, acceptance of authority and obedience to rules results from a *belief in legitimacy (Legitimitätsglaube)*. This belief concurs with our conviction that the authority instructing us to do or not do things is entitled to do so and has the proper credentials to demand obedience. For example, because an authority can invoke a legal power, based in a valid legal system (rational-legal authority), refer to traditions (traditional authority), or fall back on the (emotional) charisma of its leader (charismatic authority).[9] The legitimacy of imposed norms and rules involves more than individual conviction. For a political or legal system to be able to build on durable obedience, the acceptance belief – legitimacy – must be 'socialised'[10] so that it is a generally accepted belief in a society that authorities' orders must be obeyed.[11] Legitimacy is not an object, it primarily expresses a sense of propriety: an ongoing process of legitimacy.[12]

This also partly explains the role and popularity of constitutions. They are the ultimate vehicles of legitimacy.[13] Constitutions proclaim a legal system, establishing a basis for rational legal authority, and at the same time try to convince us that the form of authority (leadership) advocated in the constitutional system has the best credentials.[14] Like the now widely-held belief that government authority exercised according to cognisable and authorised rules is preferable to the capricious dispositions of a great leader – even if he was once revered or is God's anointed one. The

---

[7] Cf. Luhmann 1969, p. 34–35. Luhmann also refers to 'internalisation' in this connection (p. 35). Sometimes this requires the 'neutralisation of personal motives', p. 250.

[8] (Max) Weber 1964 (orig. 1922), p. 382.

[9] (Max) Weber 1964 (orig. 1922), p. 328–329.

[10] Tyler 2006, p. 176–178. Cf. Easton 1975, especially p. 448.

[11] For the relationship between legitimacy and political trust cf. Thomassen, Andeweg & Ham 2017.

[12] Beetham argues that legitimacy has a normative structure. Beetham 1991, p. 64 ff. He argues that we deem authority legitimate when: 1. it is derived from and exercised in accordance with rules ('legality'), 2. these rules are applied by the appropriate authority and for appropriate reasons in accordance with current social views on acceptable government ('normative justifiability'), and 3. when there is 'express consent or affirmation of appropriate subordinates, and by recognition from other legitimate authorities' ('legitimation'). Beetham 1991, p. 15–20.

[13] Cf. Ginsburg & Huq 2016, *Introduction*, p. 16–17.

[14] Habermas speaks in this context of discursiveness (and the discourse theory) of the law and constitutions: 'discourse theory of law conceives constitutional democracy as institutionalising – by

idea of 'a government of laws and not of men'[15] is an example of a socialised concept of legitimacy, although it is not recognised everywhere.[16] Constitutions also use other stories and ideas in their attempt to convince us that the politico-legal organisation systems they proclaim are worthy of acceptance. Take the widely accepted story about the connection between geography and social organisation: the 'state'. The idea that a group found within a particular physical boundary which unites politically is therefore entitled to certain claims, such as free leadership selection, self-rule, territorial and even (cultural) identity claims (bundled up in the concept of 'sovereignty').[17] Then, there is the idea that governmental authority should not be concentrated in the hands of a single person or body, but must be shared in order to be and remain acceptable (the concept of division of powers, like trias politica). Or the idea that it is preferable to somehow involve the people effected by decisions in decision-making (democracy). And, finally, the idea that majority decisions must always respect minority interests, even individual ones (human rights) for a system to gain durable acceptance. A lofty idea, recognising the inherent rights and dignity of every person, which is always vulnerable to incumbent rulers or majorities. But even without these Angel's choirs, powerful enough on its own as a form of sensible precautionary pragmatism: today's minorities are often tomorrow's majorities.

Constitutions use these 'stories'[18] in constant effort to convince us that the outcomes of the politico-legal social system they establish are worthy of support, acceptance, and obedience. By telling the story time and time again, and even by criticising it, it is confirmed by real behaviour, fully or partially translating it into reality and making it part of ongoing practice.[19] This further increases our willingness to accept – our belief in – the systems and norms of the constitutional order.[20]

---

way of legitimate law (and hence by also guaranteeing private autonomy) – the procedures and communicative presuppositions for a discursive opinion- and will-formation that, in turn, makes possible (the exercise of political autonomy and) legitimate law-making.' Habermas 1996, p. 437.

[15] According to tradition, these words were introduced into the Massachusetts constitution in 1780 by founding father and future president of the United States, John Adams (1735–1826; president 1797–1801). Article XXX of the 1780 text states: 'In the government of this commonwealth, the legislative department shall never exercise the executive and judicial powers, or either of them; the executive shall never exercise the legislative and judicial powers, or either of them; the judicial shall never exercise the legislative and executive powers, or either of them; to the end it may be a government of laws, and not of men.'

[16] In China, for example. Traditional 'Confucian' thinking – which is still influential in China – teaches that the law can never rule by itself. Government is the work of men; wisdom – and not (only) the law or justice – is its guiding principle. Cf. Seppänen 2016, p. 30–33.

[17] Flathman 2012, p. 678 ff.

[18] Or 'rhetoric' as someone like Nick Turnbull would call it. (N.) Turnbull 2010.

[19] Chris Thornhill argues that the reflexivity constitutions produce is essential: 'The functional and reflexive reserves of legitimacy produced by constitutions are among the main reasons why modern society is able to exist, politically, in a functionally and differentiated and pluralistic [way].' Thornhill 2010, p. 52.

[20] Cf. Graber 2013, p. 215.

27

The Story of the Constitution

[…] stories make societies work better by encouraging us to behave ethically.

Jonathan Gottschall[1]

STORYTELLERS

'In the beginning was the Word' is the opening of the gospel of John. Spot on: we experience our world through our senses, emotions and intellectual capacities, and communicate about reality and imagined realities through the medium of stories.[2] We use sounds, gestures, facial expressions, painting, carving, film, writing, jumping, singing, playing and dancing to convey narrative units and bits or sometimes even reams of meaning to each other. Narratives mobilise, motivate and inspire collaboration. Conversely, they can also obstruct cooperation. Narratives are 'coloured' forms of enhanced information transfer. Stories allow us to intersubjectively transfer information about real or imagined realities and events to each other and give meaning to these experiences at the same time.[3] This generates shared representations of what we experience as true, real, exciting, beautiful, valuable, sacred and important. Harari argues that it is the attribution of meaning that makes storytelling such a powerful weapon:

> Meaning is created when many people weave together a common network of stories. […] Sapiens rule the world because only they can weave an intersubjective web of meaning: a web of laws, forces, entities and places that exist purely in their common imagination. This web allows humans alone to organise crusades, socialist revolutions and human rights movements. […] No other animal can stand up

---

[1] Gottschall 2013, p. 134.
[2] For more detail about the (evolutionary) background of storytelling cf. Boyd 2009.
[3] Jonathan Gottschall sees people as storytelling creatures: stories make us human. The human mind is organised for stories. Gottschall 2013, in particular chapter 5 (*The Mind is a Storyteller*).

to us, not because they lack a soul or mind, but because they lack the necessary imagination.[4]

The American professor of communication Walter Fisher has investigated *how* we tell stories. What does this form of communication involve? Everyone can tell stories, but not every story is credible. Take the stories spouted by some grumpy uncle or neighbour who pontificates endlessly at get-togethers about the exchange rate, the national football team's performance, the economy or politics. An inveterate misanthrope who always knows 'how things will turn out', despite the repeated failure of his forecasts. The point is: not every story is considered real, true or worthwhile. Even the word itself is charged – calling someone a storyteller is certainly not always a positive qualification. It can also refer to a blatherer or windbag: someone who talks long-windedly with no real substance. We are certainly not overly enamoured of stories in academia.[5]

Fisher shows in his 1987 book *Human Communication as Narration* that a story must be able to convince to convey an experience in a truly meaningful way.[6] This is simply how we work: 'Humans are... storytellers' Fisher says.[7] We experience our world in stories and we convey our experience of reality to each other through stories.[8]

Not that all experiences and meanings assigned to them are equally valuable: not all stories are convincing. Only stories we consider likely or reliable – based, for example, on good reasons or arguments – convince us, and are able to move the recipient in some way or another, or possibly even impel her into action. This is not restricted to stories based on objectively observable facts or logically-correct deductions; stories appealing to a collectively-experienced emotion (such as the story of the refugee toddler Aylan Kurdi who drowned on a beach in Bodrum, Princess Diana's death, and the Shakespearean Brexit drama) are equally capable of touching and mobilising people.

We are also adroit at assessing the plausibility of stories. Fisher argues that we are all equipped with senses to assess the veracity of stories. People have an 'inherent awareness of *narrative probability*' which can determine whether a story is coherent and consistent. We constantly test (each other's) narrative fidelity, checking 'whether or not the stories they experience ring true with the stories they know to be true in their lives'.[9] We use this reliability check to assess how a story fits with our own truths

4   Harari 2016, p. 146 p. 149–150.
5   Cf. Aunger 1995.
6   Fisher 1989 (orig. 1987), p. 5.
7   *Ibid.*
8   This is the essence of Fisher's 'narrative paradigm'. Fisher 1989 (orig. 1987), p. 5. 'The narrative paradigm proposes that human beings are inherently storytellers who have a natural capacity to recognize the coherence and fidelity of stories they tell and experience.' Fisher 1989 (orig. 1987), p. 24.
9   Fisher 1989 (orig. 1987), p. 5.

and experience of reality.[10] It is an in-built credibility radar, so to speak. We test a story on various criteria before being persuaded: is it correct, does it touch us, and who is actually the storyteller? Aristotle apprehended in the fourth century BCE that the persuasiveness of a narrative or argument largely depends on three dimensions: the quality of the *logos*, its reason or logical argumentation; the *pathos*, the emotions it evokes, such as anger, fear, joy or pride; and finally the *ethos*, the speaker's quality and authority – whether she is honest, credible, respectable, reputed and so forth.[11] When deciding whether to believe a story, we look further than just the substantive arguments and the facts. This certainly does not mean that we are irrational or essentially depend on our gut feelings, but that our rationality, our reasoning, is a 'narrative rationality'. Fisher says that we reason by, with and based on stories, with which we can subsequently identify, at least if we believe in them.[12]

THE CONSTITUTION: A COMPELLING STORY

It is an uncomfortable fact, but people really are gullible; we like to believe in things. This includes things we cannot actually perceive – like God, historical events, life after death, fame, characters and events in myths and parables – but which have 'something to tell' all of us. We have a 'narrative' way of thinking and kind of logic.[13] This is reflected in how we constantly coordinate our stories about reality and experiences of reality. A single reality does not exist; our experience of reality is filtered, and information about it is coloured, given meaning and transmitted in a manner that touches, fascinates and is taken on board by another person.

We align and tune our impressions and experiences with conventions, agreements about things we consider 'real'. Take, for example, our perception of colours. We can, of course, see them, but we do not all share exactly the same perception. Which is why we have assigned names to particular light reflections;[14] such as green or blue. Historically, the Japanese language did not distinguish between green and blue. It lacked a word for green, which was regarded as a shade of blue.[15] The Japanese have recently chosen a word for green.[16] A bit like Korean (and some

[10] Fisher: 'The world as we know it is a set of stories that must be chosen among in order for us to live life in a process of continual re-recreation.' *Ibid.*
[11] Aristotle 2018, p. 12 (1356a, 1–5): 'Of the means of persuasion, that proceed through speech, there are three kinds (*eidos*). For some depend on [1] the character of the speaker, some on [2] disposing the listener in some way, and some on [3] the argument itself, due to its showing or appearing to show something.'
[12] Fisher 1989 (orig. 1987), p. 66 and p. 192–194.
[13] Roland Barthes: '[narrative] is present at all times, in all places, in all societies; indeed narrative starts with the very history of mankind; there is not, there has never been anywhere, any people without'. Barthes 1975, especially p. 237.
[14] Pinker 2007b, p. 114 ff.
[15] The Japanese word for blue is: *Ao.*
[16] *Midori.*

Southern-African languages), which does not draw a clear distinction between blue and green. Koreans solved this by having separate words for the blue of the sky and of the ground, bringing the language a bit closer to the story many other cultures tell about these colours. There are many more narrative conventions of this kind which 'tweak' our experience of reality. Stories about the meaning of sounds, language, and words or about value, money, the future and who or what is important. But also, about the how and why of large-scale societies, leadership, a group's cohesion, identity, the meaning and course of history, an individual's role, the value of art,[17] the exhilaration of a song, and – last but not least – the story about the law.[18]

The Oxford Dictionary of English defines 'story' in four senses. Its third definition comes closest to the sense in which we are using the word: 'an account of past events in someone's life or in the development of something.'[19] This definition is excessively restrictive in several senses. Contrary to what is implied above, stories are not restricted to 'past events'; they can be situated in the present or future too. Stories are also far more than mere accounts: they have the potential to captivate. Stories can induce emotions, and therefore effect our biochemical system (through fear, sadness, joy), motivate us, and mobilise us, which helps shape cooperation and history. And not just in the way that fables, legends, myths, books, films or lyrics can make you think or touch you. Our greatest stories are so strong that we accept them as truth and reality: they can actually change the world.[20]

We live in a story. A story of imagined trust (law, shared identity and so on), status differences (fame, authority, and so forth), and myriad empirically invisible relationships in the associated virtual world of markets, contracts, money, and economic value allocation. Superficially, you only see how billions of people drive goods to and fro, commute to offices five out of seven mornings, punch letters on a keyboard attached to some kind of light box, eat in groups, or throw a ball at each other. Behaviour of this kind can only be understood by knowing the underlying story; the story of the modern market economy based on the belief in a better future and progress, or the story of the utility of investing in it, and the story and idea of universal trust – that a symbolic act (a contract) can establish a reciprocal agreement between two strangers. The story of the market economy motivates actions (investment, transactions, the use of abstract means of exchange such as money, and so on), but it also

---

[17] Pinker thinks that the value of art is not in beauty itself, but mainly in the status it expresses ('conspicuous consumption'). Pinker 2009, p. 500–501 and p. 521–523.

[18] Cf. Zane 1998, orig. 1927.

[19] *Oxford Dictionary of English*, Oxford: University of Oxford Press. The present online version of OED (consulted 25 October 2019).

[20] Ezrahi distinguishes between performative imagination (representations, stories – 'political imaginaries' – which incite action and create social and political facts), and reflective imagination (a kind of feedback mechanism in our imagination, a reflection in which past experiences are interpreted in light of current interests, feelings and emotions). The two sides of the 'story' or imagination that I have tried to capture in the distinction between stories as a motive and the motive made in or by stories. Ezrahi 2012, p. 37–40.

informs the motives (belief in the future, trust in strangers, reciprocity of claims). The story makes the imagined reality of the market economy, which has major consequences for our behaviour and the way we cooperate and organise the world (and do all manner of things).

JUSTICE

Perhaps even bigger is the story of justice. The great narrative of how we ought to behave towards one other: good and evil, and what is fair and unfair. A story that touches all people. Religious books have an endless amount to say on the subject; justice is woven into the core of myths, sagas, fairy tales and legends. It is the second best-selling hit in narrative world history, pipped at the post by the love story.

Although its content varies over time, we are touched – in fact, moved – by stories about injustice. Whilst we are certainly not the only primate to be upset by unfair treatment, humankind is so sensitive to it that we are even affected by stories about justice. Our great stories about injustice are mostly not solely about unfair treatment, which can enrage capuchin monkeys too,[21] but also the tragic forms of non-recognition of our position in the group, which we find excruciating.[22] Stories of saints and martyrs dying for beliefs and visions which were not recognised by the authorities of their time, or of leaders such as Simon Bolivar, Toussaint Louverture, Nelson Mandela and Gandhi who resisted oppression, which is another form of non-recognition of claims. Their visions, speeches and beliefs, their analysis and accounts of injustices, their example, moved and motivated people and ultimately changed world views and the fates of the peoples whom their addresses were directed at.

Even fictional accounts of injustice can have deep impacts. Harriet Beecher Stowe's fictional story *Uncle Tom's Cabin*[23] hit home in the United States. It changed the American view of slavery and contributed to its abolition. Likewise, other great stories about social injustice, such as Victor Hugo's *Les Misérables*[24] or Charles Dickens' *Oliver Twist*[25] sparked broad social debate about injustice and its resolution.

And even a dream, may have a powerful appeal.

I have a dream that one day this nation will rise up and live out the true meaning of its creed: 'We hold these truths to be self-evident: that all men are created equal.'
I have a dream that one day on the red hills of Georgia the sons of former slaves

---

[21] Cf. De Waal 2019, p. 187–190 on the 'aversion to unfairness' in monkeys that he and Sarah Brosnan discovered.

[22] As we have seen above, the far-reaching and damaging consequences of non-recognition on individuals were until recently underestimated in social psychology. Cf. Williams, Forgas & Von Hippel 2005.

[23] Beecher Stowe 1852.

[24] Hugo 1862.

[25] Dickens 1838.

and the sons of former slave owners will be able to sit down together at a table of brotherhood. I have a dream that one day even the state of Mississippi, a state, sweltering with the heat of injustice and sweltering with the heat of oppression, will be transformed into an oasis of freedom and justice. I have a dream that my four little children will one day live in a nation where they will not be judged by the colour of their skin but by the content of their character. I have a dream today.

Stories about law and justice do not get more stirring than Martin Luther King Jr.'s 1963 story – if you ask me.[26] It spread across the world: a dream that has yet to become reality, and still tugs at your heartstrings. Stories about justice make our hearts throb, our limbic system churn, and our neocortex flare; we cannot abide injustice.[27] Stories about the imagined world of law try to address and overcome the problem of exclusion and unfair treatment (non-recognition), as well as our fear of strangers (distrust). We do so by telling each other that everybody matters, that we all have a significant role: be it as members of a religious community, be it as people endowed with a soul and thus inalienable rights, be it as parties to a contract who can depend on the other party fulfilling its obligations, or be it as members of a (political) community who can rest assured that a stranger will not break into your home, steal your properties or kill you or your loved ones. Stories we regard as reality, which can serve as a foundation for further growth.

THE STORY OF THE CONSTITUTION

The essence of every constitution is a story of this kind. A story about who we are as a community and as individuals, how we are organised, and about the role the moral system of law plays in our relationships. The story of the constitution is a story about leadership, how 'we' are able to collaborate on a large-scale and all have a place in this collaboration, with its 'fair' relations established by the constitutionally embedded story of the law. The story of the law is about justice which connects our social, political and individual roles in the greater constitutional story through the conception of a legal order.[28] Constitutional stories and fictions about the past,[29] present and future try to persuade us and make us believe in the imagined reality

---

[26] Martin Luther King Jr. delivered his speech *I Have a Dream* on 28 August 1963 at a protest rally at the Lincoln Memorial in Washington DC attended by some 200,000 people.

[27] For more about the neurobiological basis of feelings of justice cf. Gruter et al. 1986 and more recent Yoder and Decety 2014. Cf. research by Singer et al. showing which empathic, neural reactions occur (in particular affective and aggressive emotions, such as feelings of revenge) when people experience injustice. Singer, Seymour, O'Doherty, Stephan, Dolan, & Frith 2006.

[28] Lindahl: 'a constitution structures the ongoing legal process of inclusion in and exclusion from a collective self. [...] a constitution is the master legal rule for inclusion in and exclusion from a legal order'. Lindahl 2013b, p. 100.

[29] Constitutions also record the story of the past. Kim Lane Scheppele: 'Constitutions in their moments of creation cannot be inspired solely by imagined futures. Perhaps even more crucially, they encode imagined pasts', Scheppele 2008, p. 1380.

of this constitutional leadership and legal order, and their claims. In his book with the provocative title *Constitutional Law as Fiction*, American legal scholar Lewis LaRue claims:

> [...] that the proud towers of the law are built not on the level bedrock of 'fact' but on the perplexed terrain of 'fiction' [...].[30]

LaRue argues that constitutional law is about convincing the public[31] – 'telling stories' as convincingly as possible.[32] This conception, of course, goes against the grain for many people. Something as important and solemn as a constitution surely cannot be reduced to nothing more than a story, a mere fiction? You can see the reality of constitutional law all around you. The Supreme Court of Kenya has seven justices and a building. Likewise, there is a European Commission and an EU Council of Ministers. Both are headquartered on Rue de la Loi in Brussels, where officials, commissioners and ministers go about their business, and the press reports on their meetings and press conferences. The pomp and circumstance of the State Opening of Parliament with the Queen's speech in the United Kingdom, with the Queen arriving in the horse-drawn State Coach carrying the Imperial State Crown, the crowds thronging the route, the robes, maces, the joint session of parliament. This is as real as it gets.

Well, not entirely. Erecting a grand building at the heart of Nairobi or Brussels, riding around in a carriage or assembling in a mediaeval hall does not make a Supreme Court of Kenya, European Commission, king or the Houses of Parliament. Only when meaning is assigned to these buildings, parades and assemblies do they become the institutions we are familiar with and consider to be true. The act of assigning this meaning – institutional facts – gives *brute facts* an extra dimension, authority, value, 'existence'.[33] The fictions of institutional facts give rise to the 'augmented reality'[34] of a constitutional order and a legal system.[35] This is not a one-off event or narration, but an ongoing process and continuous story. Constitutions incessantly try to convince us, seduce us, make us believe in, and establish the political and legal system, the story expressed by the constitutional rules. This is the story that we not only have a 'self', individuality and identity, but also that all

---

[30] LaRue 1995b, p. 8. White 2011, who regards the law as a language and judgment medium for maintenance and 'repair of human community' (especially 398–399, quote from p. 402). Cf. Edwards 2010, especially p. 884 and p. 886–891 (the article deals largely with the question of which stories are valid in the law – and not with the story of the law itself).

[31] LaRue 1995b, p. 11: 'Without persuasion, law could not be law, and without fiction, there would be no persuasion'; cf. LaRue 1995a, especially p. 1285–1286. LaRue draws on Kenneth Burke's five ratios of action (Burkes 'pentad'): 'the actor, the act, the scene, the instruments, and the goal'. K. Burke 1945, p. 341 (in the section entitled *Meanings of 'Constitution'*).

[32] Morawetz 1997.

[33] Searle 1995, chapter 2 (*Creating Institutional Facts*), p. 31–57.

[34] The enchanted world, as Charles Taylor calls it. Taylor 2007, e.g. p. 152. Taylor argues that we currently live in a progressively disenchanted world.

[35] Burke speaks of: 'Constitution as enactment'. K. Burke 1945, p. 340.

of us constitute a 'we', and that we must trust each other, that we all have a role, that we must obey rules, at least the ones we consider law, that cooperation and leadership are necessary, and that leaders – somehow or another – must be obeyed. Constitutional fictions and stories try to make music on the strings of the morality instrument embedded within each of us. These fictions and stories sing a siren song that tries to seduce us time and again to experience as real and true and accept the imagined reality of the constitution – with its story about cooperation, leadership and law – and make *performative imaginaries* from it.[36]

---

[36] Ezrahi's rather long but precise definition of performative (political) imaginaries is: 'Political imaginaries, […] refer to fictions, metaphors, ideas, images, or conceptions that acquire the power to regulate and shape political behaviour and institutions in a particular society. The power of some such political fictions to become politically productive by generating performative scripts that orient behaviour and pattern institutions is grounded, among other things, in their apparent congruence with aspects of political and social experience and expectations, their compatibility with norms that appear to legitimate their power, and their (unphilosophical) tolerance for inconsistencies. Although initially political fictions commonly suggest empirically baseless fabrications, some gain sufficient credibility and adherence to attain the status of performative imaginaries that produce behaviour that, in turn, affirms them.' Ezrahi 2012, p. 3.

28

Appealing to the Imagination

Constitutional Experience

Seeing how constitutions appeal to the imagination with their stories means looking a little further than rules on paper, authorities (judges, politicians and so on), and even history. Constitutions tell a story that tries to convince us and explains the division of roles in a social order, how this enables us to collaborate well, and what – in this context – is 'your' role in the 'we' of this order. With this constitutional 'imaginary',[1] constitutions forge and spin the 'we' of the order it evokes in the same way a storyteller can conjure up a lifelike, imagined world before a critical audience. This is more difficult than it seems. The audience must have some prior knowledge; explanations must be in familiar language; and – like a class or theatre audience – the audience does not sit still all the time. It has a thousand questions. The listener wonders: why should I abidingly trust this arrangement? How does it relate to my interests? How do I stand out in this constitutional world? Can I rely on other members of the 'we' of this constitutional order adhering to the order's principles and norms? Will they grant me the place I have been promised? Excitable basic emotions wreak emotional havoc on the listener: 'yes… but what if…?' This is why the storyteller has to pull out all the stops, using imagery, rhetoric,[2] text, icons, music, visions and symbols.[3] The constitutional storyteller repeats her story time and time again, constantly appealing to common sense, stressing emotions,[4] harping on about traditions and values. She drills her audience ad nauseam, until it can sing about the

---

[1] 'The constitutional imaginary', Torres and Guinier assert, is 'composed of those sets of values and institutions comprising the empirical and symbolic aspects of our social life. This imaginary gives us a way of understanding the social world and our place in it.' Torres & Guinier 2012, p. 1052–1072, especially p. 1054. Cf. Blokker & Thornhill 2017a, p. 11–14.

[2] For the importance of rhetoric in political arenas and political development, cf. Te Velde 2015. English translation forthcoming.

[3] Cf. K. Burke 1989.

[4] Sajó says that 'emotions participate in building the constitution and a culture of constitutionalism, and these creatures of constitutional sentiment patrol emotion display. This position contradicts the myth of law as reason […]'. Cf. Sajó 2011, p. 11.

new 'we' in unison, rattle off its tenets like a catechism, the *Iliad*, or Queen's 'We Are The Champions'. When the penny drops, a constitution can really start doing its work. German professor of history Silke Hensel explains:

> Constitutions can only do justice to their central tasks of legitimising and integrating political communities and their institutions if their normative rules and offered meanings are accepted and practiced in the social reality, if communication about fundamental values and patterns of behaviour takes place between the rulers and the ruled. This permanent process of conveying and securing the basic patterns of socio-political arrangements and loyalty has a subjective dimension that is conveyed through symbols, because symbols help to give a structure to reality.[5]

The public is brought up in the story of the constitution until its conception is experienced as real and true, or at least is considered to be true. Until you actually believe it. In this regard, constitutional stories and the idea of the law resemble religion.

A neat theory, but is it demonstrable? What does the oscillating process of the story of the constitution look like? What should one expect? Not much has yet been written about this most essential element of the functioning of constitutional systems and the law they proclaim. Fortunately, there are some recent helpful studies we can learn from thanks to the significant advances in cognitive sciences.[6] There are few of them. Why? Perhaps little thought had been devoted to this subject because it all seemed so self-evident. Why would you wonder about such matters as constitutional or legal imaginaries? Why ponder on judges wearing long robes, on ceremonies involving a hereditary leader transported to a mediaeval hall in a richly adorned coach? Or muse on the question why members of parliament and ministers are required to swear an oath of office, why we stand in front of a judge, stand to attention when the national flag is raised, why the seating of parliament is set up as it is, why equestrian statues invariably raise their hands ...? Surely, it is just the way things *are*? But then again, maybe not. All these formal, symbolic acts might appear self-evident, but they mask a host of interesting phenomena, many of them constitutional, and worthy of study. Why are we so disposed towards stories like this, how does our constitutional imagination work? What emotions do they evoke and how do such stories move us or fail to do so? What happens in and after a story of this kind? People unfamiliar with the constitutional imagination do not understand the constitutional experience – and that is essentially how we deal with constitutions and constitutional law. There is also no constitutional law without constitutional experience. Sociologist Paul Blokker says this experience is a kind of process:

> Constitutional *experience* consists of an on-going process of imagining and performing the constitutional – through fictions, metaphors, images, and conceptions – and in this depends on political imaginaries that shape and limit

[5]   Hensel 2012, p. 5.
[6]   Cf. Otten, Sassenberg & Kessler 2009. Particularly Wenzel's interesting 2009 contribution, which focuses on the law.

views of the possible, but that equally provide the basis for re-imagining the constitutional order.[7]

TEXT

How can we understand the constitutional experience in concrete terms? Does it follow from the text itself? Written constitutions consist of letters and words on paper. They are rarely moving.[8] Certainly, constitutional texts can occasionally be poetic, such as preambles (more on this in a moment), but for the most part constitutions consist of dry, business-like texts, primarily focused on an expert and initiated readership. They are not the kind of texts you read for fun or that stick in your mind like a catchy melody. The 1996 South African Constitution is an excellent example of an accessible and simply written constitutional text, yet I cannot imagine anyone snuggling up in bed with a mug of cocoa to read the following:

Article 168 Supreme Court of Appeal

[...] 3.a The Supreme Court of Appeal may decide appeals in any matter arising from the High Court of South Africa or a court of a status similar to the High Court of South Africa, except in respect of labour or competition matters to such extent as may be determined by act of Parliament.

This text is, of course, not intended for idle leisure. The text of most of the world's constitutions functions like a rule book in football, basketball or tennis. It is undoubtedly important – but not as important as the game and definitely not as an end in itself. The literal texts of constitutions are better understood as reference works. They are part of the story, not the constitutional experience itself. There is much more to the story, the experience than can be deduced from the text. The story of the constitution therefore cannot be identified with the text, which is only one minuscule part of it – the legal manifestation, the rules of the game. 'Constitutional truths, are neither majoritarian nor textual', according to Richard Weisberg, who examined the relationship between constitutional texts and constitutional experiences in 1986. He argues that constitutional experiences do not stem from the text, but 'like Sundays, they are embedded as "ideas" in communities.'[9]

Yet, some legal scholars still focus principally on the literal texts of constitutions, for example, in the United States. A debate has been raging there for decades on the correct form of (judicial) constitutional interpretation.[10] Should you interpret the text literally as it was written and intended by the drafters of the constitution, more than

---

[7] Blokker 2017, especially p. 174–175.

[8] Cf. Weisberg 1986, especially p. 993–994. Weisberg shows that constitutional experience *does not* stem from the text. This has been the case since the founding fathers of the United States constitution drafted this text ('Faith in language was foreign to them').

[9] Weisberg 1986, p. 994.

[10] Tushnet 2009b, p. 242 ff.

200 years ago (the *originalist position* or *originalism*)?[11] Or should you consider the constitution as an historical, living document (*living instrument position*),[12] embodying ideas which must constantly be rethought and reinterpreted in the light of changing circumstances?[13] It is no small matter for many Americans, and the vehemence of the debate can only be understood in the context of the protestant *sola scriptura* culture. For many – often deeply-religious – Americans, their constitution is comparable to a biblical text: its words are revelations.[14] They are truths given to humanity in the same way as the Laws of Moses. You cannot simply pick and choose Eternal Truths, seeing whether and how they fit in modern circumstances. They must be applied literally.

Be this as it may, even the text of the brief United States Constitution is hard to read for modern readers – and hence difficult to understand and apply in the here and now. Everyone knows the clarion call of its opening words: 'We the people [...]', but it is no more than an introductory statement: a preamble. It does not contain rules, just some guiding principles. The body of the American constitutional settlement is not very accessible. Try reading and understanding these sections:[15]

3. No Bill of Attainder or ex post facto Law shall be passed.
4. No Capitation, or other direct, Tax shall be laid, unless in Proportion to the Census or Enumeration herein before directed to be taken.[16]

Fully understanding the above without prior legal training is an impressive feat. And no matter how much Americans might revere their constitution, they are largely unfamiliar with its text[17] – which can also be said of any other country,

[11] Cf. Harvard professor of constitutional law Jack Balkin's criticism in 2005. He objects to the apparent sympathy the United States Supreme Court started showing for 'originalism' around this time. Balkin argues that original meaning and intention should not be confused with literality – taking the original text literally. 'Original meaning does not mean original expected application. For example, the Constitution bans cruel and unusual punishments. But the application of the concepts of "cruel and unusual" must be that of our own day, not 1791.' Balkin 2005 (web magazine). Cf. www.slate.com/id/2125226/ (Consulted on 12 October 2018). Cf. Tushnet 2009b, p. 258–262 on 'original understanding'.

[12] The result of 'many minds' in the words of Cass Sunstein. Sunstein 2009, p. 7–10.

[13] Cf. Chief Justice William Rehnquist's controversial article in the 1970s, in which he, as a member of the US Supreme Court, went against the then almost self-evident idea that the constitution is not based on its literal text, but on its original spirit and intention in a modern context. Rehnquist's greatest objection to the 'notion of the living Constitution is that it seems to ignore totally the nature of political value judgements in a democratic society. If such a society adopts a constitution and incorporates in that constitution safeguards for individual liberty, these safeguards indeed do take on a generalised moral rightness or goodness. They assume a general social acceptance neither because of any intrinsic worth nor because of any unique origins in someone's idea of natural justice but instead simply because they have been incorporated in a constitution by the people.' Rehnquist 2006, especially p. 412.

[14] In general 'Americans revere their Constitution', as Sunstein puts it. Sunstein 2009, p. 210.

[15] Article I, section 9.

[16] Text quoted from http://constitutions.com/ (consulted on 12 October 2018).

[17] The Annenberg Public Policy Center of the University of Pennsylvania discovered in their 2017 annual civic knowledge survey that Americans are poorly informed about basic constitutional provisions. The Annenberg Constitution Day Civics Survey finds that more than

incidentally.[18] It may matter little – the message is what counts – but it was still ignominious for a presidential candidate to let slip that he did not even know how many articles his country's constitution had. At a meeting with republican senators in July 2016, presidential candidate Donald Trump solemnly promised that as president he would always defend article XII of the constitution.[19] It sounds like a reassuring commitment, except the United States Constitution does not have an article XII; it only has seven articles, followed by twenty-seven amendments. Trump presumably had one of the amendments in mind.

WORDINESS

Most constitutional texts are tedious and inaccessible. They are technical, jargon-laden, sometimes dated, and often their obscurity is exacerbated by being the product of hard-won compromises, resulting in a linguistic tangle. Most of them tend to be lengthy and verbose.

The inordinate length of many constitutions is certainly not conducive to their readability. In 2016, political scientists Tsbelis and Nardi of the University of Michigan examined the length of the constitutions of members of the Organisation for Economic Co-operation and Development (OECD).[20] Iceland had the shortest constitution in their study, with 4090 words (twelve to fifteen pages of A4 paper; less text than many a Monday newspaper). The longest text they encountered was the towering Mexican Constitution, with 50,700 words – more than ten times the length of its Icelandic counterpart. Their conclusion is surprising: the longer a constitution is, the worse its performance. Tsebelis and Nardi argue that the length of a constitution correlates negatively with a country's economic and – indirectly – political and governmental performance.[21] It remains to be seen whether this really is

half of Americans (53%) incorrectly think it is accurate to say that immigrants who are here illegally do not have any rights under the United States Constitution; more than a third of those surveyed (37%) cannot name any of the rights guaranteed in the First Amendment; and only a quarter of Americans (26%) can name all three branches of government. See www .annenbergpublicpolicycenter.org/americans-are-poorly-informed-about-basic-constitutional-provisions/(consulted 18 December 2019).

[18] The Dutch, for instance, seem to be poorly acquainted with their 200-year-old constitution too. A study commissioned by the Ministry of the Interior and Kingdom Relations in 2008 shows, as we saw in chapter 1, that almost all respondents considered the constitution important, but 84% of them indicated having little or no knowledge of its contents. A test confirmed these results: more than 94% of the participants 'failed' (with fewer than three correct answers) when answering six simple questions about the constitution. TNO/Nipo, *De Grondwet: Wat weet en vindt de Nederlander?* (The Constitution: what do Dutch People know and think of it?) The Hague 2008. Cf. Oomen & Lelieveldt 2008.

[19] Hughes 2016.

[20] Tsebelis & Nardi 2016. They did not examine constitutions from across the world, only those of the thirty-six member states of the Organisation for Economic Cooperation and Development (OECD), all relatively developed countries. It certainly gives a representative impression.

[21] *Ibid.*

a pattern, but lengthy texts certainly do not contribute to accessibility. At first glance, this seems difficult to reconcile with Elkins, Ginsburg and Melton's observation that constitutional texts have increased in length over the centuries.[22] The trio ascribe this to the increasing complexity of the sphere constitutions regulate. Modern government is far more comprehensive than it was a few centuries ago, meaning more subjects require regulation, which entails more text. The world champion is the Indian constitution, with more than 140,000 words; and the shortest one Elkins, Ginsburg and Melton encountered was Mauritania's 1985 constitution (replaced by a longer one in 1991), with just 865 words – 3 sheets of A4 paper at most. The average length of constitutions between 1789 and now is around 14,000 words.[23]

These mountains of words are difficult to access for the general members of the constitutional community, let alone to understand and know by heart. As said, it is probably not so problematic that people do not know a constitutional text. The public is usually familiar with a constitution's basic ideas and central tenets. Public information initiatives aimed at increasing public awareness of the content of constitutional texts by translating them into simpler language are laudable but not terribly effective. It is not in the words. The text does not create the constitutional experience, however exquisite it may be.

PREAMBLES

Not all texts in constitutions are technical or soulless. Some sections try to appeal directly to the imagination. Who is not touched by the first lines of the American constitution, 'We the people of the United States…'?[24] This text is so stirring that many other countries have adopted it in declarations preceding their constitutions.[25] Statements preceding a constitutional text, 'preambles',[26] are a popular means nowadays of concisely highlighting the ideas behind a constitutional system. They are usually fine texts, which briefly explain the idea of and reason for a constitution: why has it been drafted, by whom and why in this fashion? Preambles are meaningful expressions, often echoes of the 'we'

---

[22] Elkins, Ginsburg & Melton 2009, p. 104–105.

[23] *Ibid.*, p. 105.

[24] The text was written by Governor Morris (1752–1816). The first draft, written in August 1787, was far less stirring: 'We the people of the states of New-Hampshire, Massachusetts, Rhode-Island […] do ordain, declare and establish the following constitution for the government of ourselves and our posterity.' After discussion arose as to whether the people in the various states could be lumped together in this fashion, Morris elegantly sidestepped the issue in his final draft by simply removing the names of the states.

[25] Although this exemplary effect has declined in recent years. Cf. Law & Versteeg 2012.

[26] Preambles – 'any statement that follows the title of the constitution and that precedes the numbered articles' – are popular. Whereas only about 69% of constitutions had a preamble in the nineteenth century, the proportion increased to 83% in the second half of the twentieth century. No less than 93% of constitutions promulgated between 2000 and 2016 had a preamble. Cf. Voermans, Stremler & Cliteur 2017, p. 15 (for the definition) and p. 18 (for the numbers).

of the constitutional legal order. They refer to the connecting – religious, ideological, republican, monarchical, etcetera – core values; history or national characteristics; the desire to live together; the claim to self-determination and sovereignty; and ideology.[27] Preambles try to speak or sing to, exhilarate, or plug away at the public's emotions. A good example is the preamble to Bhutan's 2008 constitution (see below).

Preamble to Bhutan's 2008 constitution

---

[27] Voermans, Stremler & Cliteur 2017, chapter 3.

The text uses letters, language and tone in an attempt to elicit readers' affinity, reinforced by its rich crimson-and-gold margins. 'Don't be afraid and be glad you can trust this wonderful constitutional community' – emotions of this kind. You would have to be made of stony stuff for this to leave you cold.

HAPPY AND SAD CONSTITUTIONS

This is all most interesting – but is it possible to measure whether the words of a pre-amble have any effect, and, if so, what it is? For example, how happy does it make you? Of course, feelings of joy and happiness vary from person to person. Some people are delighted by everything, even a bad television series, or spring storm. And you are not going to convince misanthropes and curmudgeons with a bit of joyful text. 'There's just no pleasing some people', Brian points out in the Monty Python film *Life of Brian*.[28] American scientists Ginsburg, Foti and Rockmore gave it a shot in 2014, using a sentimental analysis of preambles to measure how 'happy' a text was.[29] They scored constitutional texts on several happy words in their preambles and used a complex, impressive calculation formula:

$$\frac{\left(\mathrm{hf;avg}\,(c)\right) = \sum w\,\mathrm{in}\,N(c)\,h(w)\,fc(w)}{\sum z\,\mathrm{in}\,N(c)\,fc(z)}$$

The underlying idea is simple and highly original.[30] The more positive words, such as wisdom, fortunes, blessings, happiness and well-being (see the example of Bhutan) in a text, the happier it is. Perhaps this increases a constitution's capacity to mobilise citizens and encourage unified collaboration (which they did not investigate).

You can, of course, try to touch people with drama and tragedy, as the 2017 Thai Constitution does:

> May there be virtue. Today is the tenth day of the waxing moon in the fifth month of the year of the Rooster under the lunar calendar, being Thursday, the sixth day of April under the solar calendar, in the 2560th year of the Buddhist Era.
>
> His Majesty King Maha Vajiralongkorn Bodindradebayavarangkun is graciously pleased to proclaim that the Prime Minister has respectfully informed that since Phrabat Somdet Phra Paramintharamaha Prajadhipok Phra Pokklao Chaoyuhua graciously granted the Constitution of the Kingdom of Siam, B.E. 2475 (1932), Thailand has continuously and always maintained the intention to adhere to a democratic regime of government with the King as Head of State. Even though Constitutions have been annulled, amended and promulgated on

---

[28] To the cured leper complaining about his alms. Monty Python, *Life of Brian* 1979.
[29] Ginsburg, Foti & Rockmore 2014, p. 305–340.
[30] *Ibid*, p. 340.

several occasions to suitably reorganise governance, there was still no stability or order due to various problems and conflicts. At times, those events degenerated into Constitutional crises which cannot be resolved. This was partially caused by there being persons ignoring or disobeying governance rules of the country, being corrupt and fraudulent, abusing power, and lacking a sense of responsibility towards the nation and the people, resulting in the ineffective enforcement of law. It is, therefore, necessary to prevent and rectify these matters by reforming education and law enforcement, and strengthening the system of merits and ethics. Other causes are governance rules which are inappropriate to the situation of the country and the times, the prioritisation of forms and procedures over basic principles of democracy, or the failure to effectively apply, during the crises, existing rules to individuals' behaviours and situations, the forms and procedures of which differ from those of the past.

It laments 'problems', 'conflicts', 'crises', 'corrupt', 'fraudulent', 'ineffective enforcement of law' and 'failure'. Not the happiest nation on the planet, the Thai, judging from their preamble. Preambles are often summaries of the story of the constitution. From an academic perspective, a preamble's legal significance is actually the least interesting question. It causes you to stop listening to the siren call – what the story has to tell you.

A PICTURE IS WORTH A THOUSAND WORDS[31]

The story of the constitution is about more than just a text. It is expressed in wordless ideas, rituals, symbols and images too.[32] Like the Babylonian king Hammurabi, whose divine investiture is depicted on his stele above his laws. He had the stele installed in the busiest market in the city for everyone to see. Everything from flags and paintings to songs sung together about great constitutional ideas, such as freedom, equality and historical struggle, are part of what is called the 'constitutional imaginary'.[33] These kinds of visual or audible representations impress and *also* tell the story. Amongst all the techniques of constitutional interpretation and scholarly debate, we tend to lose sight of these forms of transmission or constitutional communication, but constitutions' visual language (iconography) is certainly as interesting as their texts.

Using images to express ideas about authority and values is so self-evident to us that we hardly think about it. The iconography of (constitutional) law – from the

---

[31] A relatively recent saying which seems to have come from the advertising industry at the start of the twentieth century.

[32] Czarniwska 2014, p. 1.

[33] In the words of Torres and Guinier: '[t]he constitutional imaginary is composed of those sets of values and institutions comprising the empirical and symbolic aspects of our social life. This imaginary gives us a way of understanding the social world and our place in it.' Torres & Guinier 2012, p. 1052–1072, especially p. 1054. Blokker and Thornhill 2017a, p. 11–15 (in particular the section on 'constitutional imaginary').

design of courtrooms and parliaments, uniforms, state portraits, livery collars to judges and lawyers' wigs and gowns – merits in-depth research, I believe, to shed a little more light on our perceptions of legal and constitutional authority. The story of the constitution is directly related to the imaginaries of constitutional law.[34] It is chiefly through these imaginaries, ranging from statues to paintings and everyday public rituals and symbols (ballot boxes, the Leader of the Opposition, maces, state carriages, insignia, national flags, national emblems)[35] that we propagate the ideas and message of the constitutional order and the law. Most of us are aware of these ideas through education, theatre, film, television, illustrated or print material, and so on.[36] The text of the constitution plays but a modest role in this transmission of these representations. This method of transmission does sometimes affect the message itself. Over the past hundred years, people in the West have increasingly come to experience the story of the constitution as the story of rebellion, liberation, individuality as identity and human equality as a core value,[37] with voluntary, contractual association (governed by solemn constitutional rules) as the basic principle of leadership and group experience, based on law and imagined empathy (through the idea of state and nation).[38] This symbolic story[39] has spread across the world on the wings of all sorts of mass communicated representations.[40] Visual language is perhaps the key to answering the question why constitutional ideas and rules have spread so rapidly; images easily cross language barriers. The dissemination potential of constitutional imaginary through iconography may well be greater than that of language.

ICONOGRAPHY

Two examples illustrate this well. The first is the image of the constitution as a solemn contract, an oath of union between the various sections or classes in society. The second – more indirectly linked to the constitution – is the illuminating light of human reason, referring to historical revelation and the linear development of human rationality: the idea of humanist messianism that places faith in the ability of our increasing and improving knowledge to improve and therefore understand the purpose of history.[41] It is similar to how many religions teach that prayer can bring

---

[34] Douzinas & Nead 1999.
[35] Cf. Gusfield & Michalowicz 1984.
[36] *Ibid.*, p. 417–443.
[37] Cf. Hunt 2008, p. 33 and p. 35 ff. Polkinghorne 1988, p. 146 ff. ('*Narrative and the self*').
[38] 'Imagined communities' that Benedict Anderson argues are capable of generating imaginary empathy which can lead to real solidarity. (Benedict) Anderson 1991 (orig. 1983), especially p. 25–36.
[39] Cf. Corwin 1936, when he refers to the symbolic dimension of the American constitution as a 'symbol and bulwark of a previously achieved order of human rights' (p. 1072).
[40] Cf. Loughlin 2015.
[41] The 'Weltgeist' ('world spirit') enables us to attain self-awareness and (dialectical) deepening of insight through which we can attain freedom. Hegel 1892 (orig. 1840), *Introduction*. 'These endowments [have] put our species on a moral escalator', Pinker says. Pinker 2003, p. 168.

you closer to God (and His intentions). Particularly at the end of the nineteenth century, images of pacts, oaths and enlightened speeches spread across Europe and the United States. Their symbolism is still easily recognisable.

Many of us know Jacques-Louis David's painting *The Oath of the Tennis Court*, reproduced on the cover of this book. It is an iconic depiction of a legendary event. David also made a drawing in chalk (see below), recalling the events of Saturday, 20 June 1789. King Louis XVI had originally convened the French Estates General in early Spring of that year, but it had become hopelessly bogged down. Perhaps such endless delays were only to be unexpected of an assembly with deputies of the French Estates (orders) that had not been convened in living memory. As the Estates proved unable to agree upon procedural matters, the king deferred formally convening the assembly, which also included the Third Estate (the peasants and bourgeoisie). Delegates of the Third Estate – economically powerful but virtually unrepresented under the Ancien Régime – grew increasingly restive, suspecting royal obstruction. The session, initially scheduled on 24 April 1789, kept getting postponed, leaving the bourgeois representatives pointlessly kicking their heels for more than two months in Versailles. Finding the hall where the Third Estate met closed on the king's orders,[42] delegates decided to take matters into their own hands. Frustrated and angry, they and their sympathisers[43] decamped to the adjacent royal tennis court. On the initiative of Jean-Joseph Mounier, a moderate representative from Grenoble, they preceded to swear an oath. The delegates vowed not to separate until they, as the National Assembly (Assemblée nationale) settled a new constitution for the kingdom. The print brims with symbolism: the spirit of the new times streams through the open windows, shafts of the light of reason crown the delegates' heads, three estates united; everything in the print points upwards, towards the light of the future and edification. The occasion was presided over by Jean-Sylvain Bailly, an astronomer and mayor of Paris, who can be seen reading out the oath on a table at the centre of the painting.[44] He has put one hand on his heart, which Simon Schama calls 'the gesture *par excellence* of Rousseauan sincerity'.[45] It is said that the delegates in this scene are imitating the Oath of the Horatii – three Roman brothers' oath to defend their city – a famous painting composed five year previously by the same Jacques-Louis David.[46]

[42] This was probably due to a misunderstanding. On 20 June 1789, the Third Estate deputies and their supporters, who by this time had declared themselves the 'Nation' and National Assembly, found the door to the Salle des Menus Plaisirs (the hall where they met) locked because workmen were adjusting the interior and the stage for the upcoming *séance royale*. In line with the decisions taken by the joint assembly (Estates General) on 17 June. The deputies feared chicanery and yet another attempt to thwart their convocation. Cf. Schama 1989, p. 305–307.

[43] Primarily the lower clergy and nobility (576 in total).

[44] One delegate, Joseph Martin-Dauch, did *not* take the oath. He is depicted in the lower right corner of the print, huddling in his chair, arms crossed over his chest, signifying his uncompromising refusal. Cf. Schama 1989, p. 420. Martin-Dauch is no longer depicted in David's later, unfinished painting. His eccentric refusal was subsequently interpreted as a betrayal of the revolution in 1793.

[45] Schama 1989, p. 420–421.

[46] *Ibid.*

Jacques-Louis David (1748–1825). [Drawing of the] *Oath at the Tennis Court.*
Photo © Château de Versailles, Dist. RMN-Grand Palais / Christophe Fouin

The model of groups and classes spontaneously coming together in a popular
assembly to give their country a new constitution was widely imitated. For instance,
the Polish-Lithuanian Commonwealth's new parliament (*Sejm*) assembled on 3

Kazimierz Wojniakowski (1771–1812). *The passing of the 3 May Constitution*

May 1791 to swear allegiance to the new constitution it had just approved.[47] This is also magnificently and symbolically represented in a painting by Wojniakowski (see above), with light descending from high windows – the light of reason – hope and high expectations of the future, unity and loyalty.

Such images of oaths of alliance, assembly and freedom have etched the idea of the constitution into the collective memory.

GRAND OATHS AND MUTUAL TRUST

Swearing oaths of allegiance started with collective vows at constitutional assemblies but extended over time to personal oaths of allegiance to the constitution. The best known of these are oaths of office – the affirmation of officials, such as presidents, parliamentarians and judges, of allegiance and fidelity to the constitution. Like in many other countries, in the United States the Oath or Affirmation to support the Constitution is mandatory under the Constitution.[48] Without it, Members of the House of Representatives may not exercise their office. The representatives-elect usually take their oath during the first day of a new Congress, when the House organises itself. After the Speaker is elected, the Member with the longest continuous service (the Dean of the House) administers the oath to the Speaker. Upon taking office they swear or promise:

I, [AB], do solemnly swear (or affirm) that I will support and defend the Constitution of the United States against all enemies, foreign and domestic; that I will bear true faith and allegiance to the same; that I take this obligation freely, without any mental reservation or purpose of evasion, and that I will well and faithfully discharge the duties of the office on which I am about to enter. So help me God.[49]

The Members of the House of Representatives take the oath as a group in a ceremony before the Speaker, often accompanied by relatives or close friends. In my home country, the Netherlands, oaths and promises are sworn individually. Upon accepting office, each Member of the Dutch Parliament swears or promises allegiance to the king and the Constitution and pledge that they will faithfully discharge their duties.[50] Even though the king is not present, the whole inauguration

---

[47] What is called the 'Governance Act' (*Ustawa rządowa*).

[48] United States Constitution, Article VI, clause 3.

[49] Title 5, Section 3331 of the United States Code. Article VI of the US Constitution does not specify the text of the oath or affirmation – it merely requires an oath of support of the Constitution to be taken (or affirmation to that effect). The text of the oath was elaborated in the United States Code. Different formulae have been used over time, but the text quoted here is the text in use since 1966.

[50] Article 60 of the Dutch Constitution and Wet beëdiging ministers en leden Staten-Generaal, *Stb.* 1992, 120 (Law on the inauguration of Ministers and Members of the States-General, *Official Bulletin* 1992, 120).

ceremony is a solemn moment. The oath or affirmation in the Netherlands is read out in its entirety and the parliamentarian, raising his right arm, forefinger and middle finger, declares: 'So help me God Almighty!' ('This I declare and promise!'). Parliamentarians who ignore the letter of the constitution, or even want to scrap parts of it, have little to fear as it entails no sanctions and they will not be prosecuted. The primary significance is symbolic. This is not so for American presidents, who take an oath of office which can incur sanctions when violated. Despite the pragmatic brevity of the United States Constitution, it includes the president's oath of office in its entirety:

> I do solemnly swear (or affirm) that I will faithfully execute the Office of President of the United States, and will to the best of my Ability, preserve, protect and defend the Constitution of the United States.[51]

The presidential oath is given extra weight by being publicly administered by the Chief Justice of the Supreme Court, and the president placing his left hand on the Bible and raising his right hand. The president almost always concludes with the words 'So help me God', an extra-constitutional tradition (the words are not in the constitutional text) that George Washington started at his inauguration in 1789. There have been a few exceptions, including Theodore Roosevelt in 1901. He concluded with 'And thus I swear'.[52]

In spite of their scant legal significance, oaths matter as public expressions of loyalty. They are expressions of solidarity and loyalty to the 'we' of a constitutional, political and/or legal community. A good example inspires imitation. A community's sense of solidarity is strengthened by political and community leaders swearing allegiance to the constitution and thus to the community. It confirms its existence and emphasises its importance, as does the above-mentioned pledge of allegiance to the flag and country. It conforms the mutual bond and stimulates members' disposition to cooperate. This be positive – promising to work together – but also negative: if you promise to cease doing something or solemnly declare that you will distance yourself from certain things or promise to cut personal ties or loyalties. Many countries have oaths or affirmations of integrity for parliamentarians, administrators

---

[51] Article II, section 1, paragraph 8 United States Constitution; with the enigmatic capitalisation of 'Ability'. American presidents take the entire oath in person (sometimes in an amusingly halting way) and non-compliance incurs sanctions. These sanctions can be triggered not only by violating the oath. A president can only be dismissed after a conviction for 'Treason, Bribery, or other high Crimes and Misdemeanours' (Article II, section 4; 'impeachment').

[52] Americans take the oath of office and the way it is said very seriously. For example, activist atheist Michael Newdow filed a lawsuit against Chief Justice John Roberts, seeking to prevent him from saying 'So help me God' at Barack Obama's inauguration as president. 'So help me God' is not part of the formula in the constitution. Newdow argued that incorporating it in the oath was unconstitutional. The courts ruled against him both in 2009 and 2013. Cf. Bishop 2007.

and officials. Oaths can also be exclusive. In Lithuania, for example, you are not allowed to participate in parliamentary elections if you are bound to a foreign power by an oath of allegiance.[53]

Revolutions and radical regime changes are particularly rich seams of visual language, symbolism and grand public displays. In the French Revolution at the end of the eighteenth century, revolutionaries went to town with liberty trees, the Cult of the Supreme Being, all manner of references to the (perceived) beneficence of nature and humans' state of nature, and images of liberty, equality and fraternity.[54] This was an attempt to unite French society under the banner of the new order after overthrowing a thousand-year-old Ancien Régime which had rendered society rather disjointed. It was an onerous undertaking. Significantly, these frenetic attempts to convince the populace took their inspiration from history, particularly from classical antiquity – or at least, an eighteenth-century version of it.[55] Neoclassicism even continued in the Napoleonic Empire. People are naturally inclined towards the old and familiar: it takes a great deal to entice them into a new world.

CONSTITUTIONAL RITUALS AND CONSTITUTIONAL PATRIOTISM

Many countries underline the importance of their constitution with public rituals expressing appreciation, or even love, of it. Some countries, from Mexico[56] and Norway[57] to Fiji,[58] have a Constitution Day, celebrating the adoption of the constitution as a national holiday. Almost a third of countries with a constitution commemorate its adoption some way or another;[59] almost a quarter of countries with a national holiday.[60] Perhaps not everyone can imagine such devotion to abstract ideas about public order and principles laid down in written texts. Yet as early as 1758, Rousseau emphasised the importance of festivities, parades, symbols

---

[53] Article 56 of the Lithuanian Constitution states: 'Any citizen of the Republic of Lithuania *who is not bound by an oath or pledge to a foreign state*, and who, on the election day, is not younger than 25 years of age and permanently resides in Lithuania, may be elected a Member of the Seimas.' (My italics). This provision is, of course, all about Lithuania's difficult (historical) relationship with the Russian Federation.

[54] Cf. Schama 1989, who talks of 'Acts of Faith' and 'acting citizens'. Cf. p. 400–436 for examples of the new symbols and visual language of the French revolution.

[55] Cf. Ezrahi 2012, p. 64–65.

[56] *Día de la Constitución* commemorates the adoption of the Constitution on 5 February 1917.

[57] The *Syttande mai* celebration (17 May, commemorating the adoption of the constitution of 17 May 1814).

[58] On 7 September.

[59] Fifty-eight countries.

[60] Approximately forty-seven countries.

and other public rituals in bringing together and maintaining public communities, including constitutional communities.[61]

We live by symbols[62]

As United States Supreme Court judge Oliver Wendell Holmes noted in 1920. Flags, singing together, public exhibitions of constitutional texts,[63] monuments, obelisks (see below, the 2008 Monument to the Turkmenistan Constitution), and coats of arms alluding to the country and constitution.

Constitution monument Turkmenistan

Rituals and symbols facilitate individual members' identification with the community and the values, principles and ideas it represents.[64] They make you feel at home in this community and make it feel like some kind of extension of yourself.[65] This kind of identification can, in turn, make us come to regard constitutional

[61] Cf. Daley 2016, especially p. 620 and his reference to Rousseau and d'Alembert's correspondence in 1758.

[62] The sentence continues: 'and what shall be symbolised by any image of the sight depends upon the mind of him who sees it'. Wendell Holmes 1920, p. 270.

[63] In recent years there has been a discussion in the Netherlands about the way in which the Act of Abjuration is exhibited at the National Archive in The Hague. Some people do not think it is exhibited prominently enough. There will be a permanent exhibition from 2020 onwards.

[64] Ginsburg & Huq 2016-*introduction*, p. 17.

[65] A sentiment reflected in communitarian ideology: '[...] Community membership as a kind of extension of one's own self.' Cf. Sen 2007, p. 32–33.

norms, ideas and values as 'normal', the 'normal way of doing things'; 'habitus' as the French sociologist Pierre Bourdieu (1930–2002) calls it.[66]

You can even extend this further: not only feeling familiar but positively *loving* a constitution. The German philosopher Jürgen Habermas promotes the idea of constitutional patriotism – love of the constitution inspiring identification with its values and institutions – as an alternative to nationalist patriotism.[67] Excessive patriotism has a dark side, Habermas observes, and nation states, the object of national patriotic love, are losing importance in a rapidly internationalising world. In his view, love of transnational values, anchored in constitutions, is perhaps more in keeping with the spirit of the times. The jury is still out on this, to put it mildly.[68]

Be this as it may, a constitution is not much use if it amounts to little more than a dead letter. For a constitutional system's ideas, principles, norms and values to function – that is, organise large-scale cooperation by giving confidence and recognition – its story must live in the hearts and minds of people belonging to the group. This means it has to be told time and time again, being endlessly repeated and passed on by all available means: imagery, sound and imaginary representations until it takes root and is accepted as true and normal. Until it is *internalised.*[69]

Princeton University sociologist Kim Lane Scheppele has observed an intriguing paradox. You probably do not notice much about a truly 'living' constitutional order. It is considered 'normal' and the 'normal state of affairs' – a habitus. Scheppele wrote in 2017:

> Constitutions – or at least successful constitutions – manage to create their own social life. They do so by naturalising, channelling and/or legitimating power. Successful constitutions extend the idea of constitutionalism beyond any constitutional text and beyond the directly regulated political classes into a broader social world in which constitutional ideas shape social expectations and understandings, and come to be taken for granted.[70]

Her colleague Mark Graber, a legal scholar, concurs that a constitution only really comes to life when it is permanently fixed in the hearts and minds of members of the constitutional community.[71] When

---

[66] Bourdieu 1987.
[67] Cf. Habermas 1993, especially p. 128 and p. 132. Müller 2010.
[68] Cf. Abraham 2007.
[69] People can internalise norms through socialisation. 'The capacity to internalise norms means human agents have *socially programmable* objective functions.' According to Gintis 2003, especially p. 407.
[70] Scheppele 2017, p. 35–66, quote from p. 35.
[71] Graber 2013, p. 214–216.

[...] citizens and elected officials are socialised in ways that lead them to internalise constitutional values and regard constitutional processes as the only legitimate means for resolving legal and policy disputes.[72]

Therefore, ignorance of the constitution on the part of the general public does not necessarily have to be a reason to gloom or despair; it might also be an indicator or constitutional success – the constitution that has become 'habitus'.[73]

---

[72] *Ibid.*, p. 215.

[73] This may also shed a different light on the drab and sober constitution of my country, the Netherlands. It is often alleged that the Dutch constitution is not a living instrument because its extremely rigid revision procedure allows too little modernisation, rendering it outdated. The document also appears to be a lame duck because Dutch judges are – article 120 of the Constitution – barred from reviewing the constitutionality of parliamentary laws. The Netherlands lacks a separate constitutional court whose interpretations could keep constitutional norms 'up-to-date', and the Dutch have little knowledge of the provisions of their constitution. As deplorable as the situation may seem, perhaps this conclusion is precipitate and overly pessimistic. Possibly the Dutch have internalised their constitution (at least its main principles and values), even if it does not quite feel that way. But that is how 'habitus' works: you do not notice it. Outsiders often see the effects of this almost invisible Dutch constitutional system. They see how a bewilderingly fragmented political system – governed by inimitable ground rules involving complicated coalitions, endless negotiations ('poldering') and a predilection for large majorities – somehow manages to keep the manifold minorities on side and also appears able to make decisions reasonably efficiently and effectively. An egalitarian country, which values equality, freedom of expression, and autonomy, coupled with an irreverent respect (often perceived as rudeness or bluntness by other cultures) for other beliefs, lifestyles and sexual orientation. But participation is also held in high regard, sometimes verging on meddlesomeness. And all this is without constitutional courts, legal hair-splitting or major discussions on constitutional principles. A constitutional system that works from the wings or perhaps even more naturally as the backdrop.

29

Once upon a Time ... There Was the Constitution

It was chilly. The wind tugged at the bare branches on that bleak winter day in 431 BCE.[1] The assembled crowd turned their eyes as the Athenian statesman and army commander Perikles slowly rose and hesitantly walked in their direction. Halting momentarily as he was about to speak, he lowered his gaze. The audience's murmur and lamentation died down as he looked up and uttered the first sentences of an oration that was to become legendary.[2]

At the grave Perikles spoke mutedly, his voice rising as he continued the elegy for his comrades who had fallen in the Peloponnesian War – the great conflict which had just broken out between the rival superpowers Athens and Sparta. The assembled mourners had an oppressive, desolate air over them. Over the previous weeks, the dead had been brought back from the battlefield to this public grave near Athens. Their presence was still palpable – the stench added to the lugubriousness. These were the first casualties in what was to become a drawn-out and bitter struggle lasting more than a quarter of a century, eventually laying waste to Athenian glory and hegemony.

Perikles' Funeral Oration primarily addressed the fallen and their relatives but was about infinitely more. This is why it still strikes such a chord with us. He reminds those present what the Athenian constitution stands for:

> If we look to the laws, they afford equal justice to all in their private differences [...]
> The freedom which we enjoy in our government extends also to our ordinary life.
> There, far from exercising a jealous surveillance over each other, we do not feel
> called upon to be angry with our neighbour for doing what he likes [...] But all this

[1] Tracy 2009, p. 68.
[2] Thucydides wrote that it was customary at public funerals in Athens for a prominent person to deliver a funeral oration, a *panegyric*, honouring the war dead. This time the honour went to Perikles, son of Xanthippos. Cf. Thucydides 1998, *Book Two*, 34–46. Text provided by Perseus Digital Library. Original version available for viewing and download at www.perseus.tufts.edu/hopper/. Tracy 2009, p. 68–69.

ease in our private relations does not make us lawless as citizens. Against this fear is our chief safeguard, teaching us to obey the magistrates and the laws, particularly such as regard the protection of the injured. [...] At Athens we live exactly as we please. [...] [We] place the real disgrace of poverty not in owning to the fact but in declining the struggle against it. Our public men have, besides politics, their private affairs to attend to, and our ordinary citizens, though occupied with the pursuits of industry, are still fair judges of public matters. [...] instead of looking on discussion as a stumbling-block in the way of action, we think it an indispensable preliminary to any wise action at all. [... Judge] happiness to be the fruit of freedom and freedom of valour.[3]

Bust of Perikles in the British Museum

The text has retained its appeal and vitality to this day. Particularly striking is how often it speaks of 'we' and 'us' – the core of every constitutional order. It also contains the other basic elements of constitutions, ancient and modern: a legal system, rules for leadership and politics, and their relation to (individual members of) society. But the most important revelation to emerge from oration is the way in which this

---

[3] Thucydides 1998, *Book Two*, 34–46. Cf. Text provided by Perseus Digital Library. Original version available for viewing and download at www.perseus.tufts.edu/hopper/.

happens: the entire Athenian constitution is *a story*. About whom we are, why we are together and how – according to which values and rules – we organise ourselves, and why this is good. Why this imagined constitutional edifice is your home too.

This is the constant of constitutions throughout history: a story that, both in and beyond the text, tries to convince and speak to the audience's soul to make the constitutional system and community it invokes and establishes credible and accept-able. And rightly so, because a community that sends your children to the front and takes your money and worldly goods for an abstract general interest has much to explain – now, as well as in the past. Perikles appreciated this. His text is a siren call to the inner psyche that appeals to our empathy, mutual altruism (equal justice, solidarity in freedom, relinquishing distrust), emotions (shame, lawlessness,[4] hap-piness, courage) and reason (discussion, wise action). Law, leadership and social organisation have become the story itself.

Classical Athens had no *Periklean Papers*, constitutional convention or constitu-ent assembly. Its constitution was certainly not drafted in one go and codified in a single document with a complex revision procedure requiring supermajorities. Let alone a constitutional court packed with Solons. And yet, it was still a consti-tution. Of course, there are huge differences between the Athenian constitution and its modern counterparts. The modern concept of human rights was completely alien to the Greeks; and Athenian and modern conceptions of justice, equality and democracy are like chalk and cheese. Modern constitutions are not contemporary transcriptions of Greek city state constitutions, the Roman state dispensation, medi-aeval charters, or the statutes of the Italian city-states – regardless of how often they are cited in *The Federalist Papers* (1788). However recognisable some of their funda-mental ideas may seem, they have few direct connections to the modern conceptual universe. What the Athenian constitution, which Perikles is speaking about, does share with current constitutions is the basic mechanism: a set of basic rules for politico-legal organisation encompassed in a story. This is what gives an abiding fascination to constitutions: constitutional rules are also a mirror, telling us about who we are and ought to be. 'Constitutions, therefore, show how societies see them-selves',[5] as the German political philosopher Hans Vorländer puts it.

WHY ARE THERE SO MANY CONSTITUTIONS?

This book started with a simple question: why are there so many constitutions? The answer may be equally simple: 'because they provide for the elementary human needs arising from large-scale collaborative arrangements.' Increasing the scale of human cooperation has a self-reinforcing dynamic, but this does not alter the fact that we are poorly disposed in biological terms to collaborate in large communities.

---

[4]   The emotion it evokes is fear.
[5]   Vorländer 2017, p. 210.

Trust and recognition, the pillars of human cooperation, are jeopardised by the magnitude of human societies. Our capacity for collective imagination helps us overcome the obstacles we face when working with strangers. Our narrative transmission of abstract representations of imagined communities, leadership and order, law, contracts and status enables us to artificially trust one another and assign (recognise) roles. The more this succeeds, the more durable the relationship, and the greater the strength and success of the group. And in the never-ending competition between groups of people, the best story always wins – a story we can collectively believe in. So, it is hardly surprising that a successful story about large-scale cooperation is rapidly spreading in a world where ideas can be shared in nanoseconds. Only two modern growth curves seem to have kept pace with the growth of constitutions: the development of communication technology, and world population growth. However little this concurrence might signify.

This outcome to the search for the reasons for the increase in modern constitutions might seem rather inchoate, or perhaps even disappointing. We much prefer, of course, the exquisite messianic humanist vision. Heroic stories about the constitution as a product of the history of civilisation; the corollary of the struggle for a nobler humanity in a better society, arising from traditions, ancient values and the enlightened ideas which showed us our historical destiny. As much as I hail from this tradition, these explanations are essentially no more than stories about the story of the constitution. Constitutional legislators in China have a very different tradition from those in the West; Greek thinkers and characteristically Christian, messianic humanism are marginal in the intellectual history of India; the Saudi Arabian constitution expresses a completely different conceptual universe. They have taken radically different routes to arrive at a constitutional order.

We do not have a common background, but we do share a story. A story that has made us more receptive and seems to have raised its audience as 'constitutional people'.[6] We have used constitutions to develop a grammar allowing us to communicate in different languages about the organisation of large-scale human societies. This has been enormously useful in international intercourse: mutually intelligible grammar has enabled coordination of all manner of actions. And this makes the constitutional elixir more and more irresistible.

Constitutions are everywhere. The explanation is not only in the history of ideas, and economic or politico-strategic processes – it is in the nature of humankind and its ability to share ideas with each other. I hope I have satisfied the general readership, but I can well imagine some feelings of disappointment after such a long read. Barely any mention of the principles of or threats to constitutional democracy; hardly anything about multi-level legal orders or the protection of fundamental

---

[6]   As Elkin says of the United States' 'political fundamentals': '[…] Institutions that […] have shaped us as a people. These institutions have and continue to constitute us as a people, shaping our character in a multitude of ways.' Elkin 2009, p. 1.

freedoms; and nothing about the interplay between state powers, abuse of (open) government, law-making, the role of judges in legal interpretation, judicial activism, judicial independence or constitutional review. 'Useless for legal teaching' somebody has already complained, 'It does not help to understand or improve the practice of the law'.

I take my share of the blame. The reflections in this book do not directly point the way to a more humane immigration policy, or better climate or welfare laws. Nor are they helpful for judges and legal practitioners in setting limits to the freedom of expression, finding criteria for environmental permits or legal principles for public liability. Yet, its insights may help to understand all the things you can and perhaps cannot do with a constitution. They can help you appreciate that a constitutional order is not some arbitrary toolbox a government can use to screw together a society as it wishes; that it is not a question of pressing a few buttons to optimise and steer cooperation. Constitutions are not administrative toys. Appreciating this, and knowing their origin and dynamics, allows you to better direct human cooperation in a constitutional society.

Moreover, is practical relevance the measure of all things in government policy, legal education or research? Not yet, fortunately. And this moral brings this story about the constitution to a close. At least for now, as it is, of course, a never-ending story.

We do not have a common background, but we do share a story. A story that has made us more receptive and seems to have raised its audience as 'constitutional people'.[7] We have used constitutions to develop a grammar allowing us to communicate in different languages about the organisation of large-scale human societies. This has been enormously useful in international intercourse: mutually intelligible grammar has enabled coordination of all manner of actions. And this makes the constitutional elixir more and more irresistible.

Constitutions are ubiquitous nowadays. The explanation for that does not merely ly in the history and genesis of ideas, or their usefulness and appeal for economic or politico-strategic processes – it is held in the nature of humankind and our ability to share ideas by means of 'great' stories with each other. I hope I have satisfied the general readership, but I can well imagine some feelings of disappointment after such a long read. Barely any mention of the principles of or threats to constitutional democracy; hardly anything about multi-level legal orders or the protection of fundamental freedoms; and nothing about the interplay between state powers, abuse of (open) government, law making, the role of judges in legal interpretation, judicial activism, judicial independence or constitutional review. 'Useless for legal teaching' somebody already complained, 'It does not help to understand or improve the practice of the law'.

---

[7] As Elkin says about the 'political fundamentals' of the USA: '[...] Institutions that [...] have shaped us as a people. These institutions have and continue to constitute us as a people, shaping our character in a multitude of ways.' Elkin 2009, p. 1.

I take my share of the blame. The reflections in this book do not directly point the way to a more humane immigration policy, or better climate or welfare laws. Nor are they helpful for judges and legal practitioners in setting limits to the freedom of expression, finding criteria for environmental permits or legal principles for public liability. Yet, its insights may help to understand all the things you can and perhaps cannot do with a constitution. They can help you appreciate that a constitutional order is not some random kind of toolbox a government can use to screw together a society as it wishes; that it is not a question of pressing a few buttons to optimise and steer cooperation. Constitutions are not administrative toys. Appreciating this, and knowing their origin and dynamics, allows you to better direct human cooperation in a constitutional society.

Moreover, is practical relevance the measure of all things in government policy, legal education or research? Not yet, fortunately. And this moral brings this story about the constitution to a close. At least for now, as it is, of course, a *never-ending story*.

References

Abraham, D., 2007, 'Constitutional Patriotism, Citizenship and Belonging in America and Germany', *Temple Political & Civil Rights Law Review*, Vol. 16(2), p. 457–472.

Ackerman, B., 2015, 'Three Paths to Constitutionalism – and the Crisis of the European Union', *British Journal of Political Science*, Vol. 45(4), p. 705–714.

Adolphs, R., 2001, 'The Neurobiology of Social Cognition', *Current Opinion in Neuro-biology*, Vol. 11(2), p. 231–239.

Aiello, L.C., 1996, 'Hominine Preadaptations for Language and Cognition', in: Mellars, P. & Gibson, K. (eds.), *Modelling the Early Human Mind*. Cambridge: McDonald Institute Monographs, p. 89–99.

Albert, R., 2018, 'Constitutional Amendment and Dismemberment', *The Yale Journal of International Law*, Vol. 43(1), p. 1–84.

Albert, R., 2019, *Constitutional Amendments; Making, Breaking, and Changing Constitutions*. Oxford, etc.: Oxford University Press.

Albert, R., Kontiadēs, X. & Fotiadou, A. (eds.), 2017, *The Foundations and Traditions of Constitutional Amendment*. Oxford/London: Hart Publishing.

Alfonso-Gil, J., Lacalle-Calderón, M. & Sánchez-Mangas, R., 2014, 'Civil Liberty and Economic Growth in the World: A Long-run Perspective, 1850–2010', *Journal of Institutional Economics*, Vol. 10(3), p. 427–449.

Alford, J.R., Funk, C.L. & Hibbing, J.R., 2005, 'Are Political Orientations Genetically Transmitted?', *American Political Science Review*, Vol. 99(2), p. 153–167.

Allam, S., 2003, 'Recht im pharaonischen Ägypten', in: Manthe, U. (ed.), *Die Rechtskulturen der Antike: vom Alten Orient bis zum Römischen Reich*. München: Beck, p. 15–54.

Allan, T.R.S., 2001, *Constitutional Justice: A Liberal Theory of the Rule of Law*. Oxford: Oxford University Press.

Allan, T.R.S., 2007, 'Chapter 7: Text, Context, and Constitution; The Common Law as Public Reason', in: Edlin, D.E. (ed.), *Common Law Theory*. Cambridge/New York/Melbourne, etc: Cambridge University Press, p. 185–203.

Alstyne, W.W. van, 1987, 'The Idea of the Constitution as Hard Law', *Journal of Legal Education*, Vol. 37(2), p. 174–183.

Amodio, D.M., Jost, J.T., Master, S.L. & Ye, C.M., 2007, 'Neurocognitive Correlates of Liberalism and Conservatism', *Nature Neuroscience*, Vol. 10(10), p. 1246–1247.

Anderson, B., 1991, *Imagined Communities: Reflections on the Origins and Spread of Nationalism*, orig. 1983, 2nd rev. ed. New York: Verso Books.

Anderson, S., 2010, *How Many Languages Are There in the World?* (with contributions from Harrison, D., Horn, L., Zanuttini, R., and Lightfoot, D.) Washington: Linguistic Society of America.

Andeweg, R.B. & Irwin, G.A., 2014, *Governance and Politics of the Netherlands*. 4th rev. ed. Houndmills, Basingstoke, Hampshire: Palgrave MacMillan.

Aquinas, T., 1265, *De Summa Theologica*.

Arendt, H., 1974, *Über die Revolution (On the Revolution)*. München: Piper.

Arfken, M., 2013, 'Social Justice and the Politics of Recognition', *American Psychologist*, Vol. 68(6), p. 475–480.

Aristotle, 1962, *The Politics*, transl. Sinclair, T.A. London: Penguin.

Aristotle, 2018, *Rhetoric*, transl., intro and notes Reeve, C.D.C. Indianapolis: Hackett Publishing Company.

Asmis, E., 2005, 'A New Kind of Model: Cicero's Roman Constitution in De Republica', *American Journal of Philology*, Vol. 126(3), p. 377–416.

Aunger, R., 1995, 'Storytelling or Science?', *Current Anthropology*, Vol. 36(1), p. 97–130.

Austin, J.L., 1962, *How to Do Things with Words*. London: Oxford University Press.

Aydin, N., Fischer, P. & Frey, D., 2010, 'Turning to God in the Face of Ostracism: Effects of Social Exclusion on Religiousness', *Personality and Social Psychology Bulletin*, Vol. 36(6), p. 742–753.

Balkin, J., 2005, 'Alive and Kicking: Why No One Truly Believes in a Dead Constitution', *Slate Magazine*, 29 August.

Barbalet, J., 2001, *Emotion, Social Theory and Social Structure: A Macrosociological Approach*, orig. 1998. Cambridge/New York, etc.: Cambridge University Press.

Barbalet, J., (ed.) 2002, *Emotions and Sociology*. Oxford: Blackwell Publishing.

Barbalet, J., 2009, 'A Characterization of Trust, and Its Consequences', *Theory and Society*, Vol. 38(4), p. 367–382.

Barber, N.W., 2003, 'The Rechtsstaat and the Rule of Law', (Review of A. Jacobson & B. Schlink, (ed.), Weimar: A Jurisprudence of a Crisis. Berkeley: University of California Press 2000), *University of Toronto Law Journal*, Vol. 53(4), p. 443–454.

Bargh, J.A. & Chartrand, T.L., 1999, 'The Unbearable Automaticity of Being', *The American Psychologist*, Vol. 54(7), p. 462–479.

Barnhart, J., 2017, 'Humiliation and Third-Party Aggression', *World Politics*, Vol. 69(3), p. 532–556.

Barthes, R., 1975, 'An Introduction to the Structural Analysis of Narrative', transl. *Lionel Duisit, New Literary History*, Vol. 6(2), p. 237–272.

Baumeister, R.F. & Leary, M.R., 1995, 'The Need to Belong: Desire for Interpersonal Attachments as Fundamental Human Motivation', *Psychological Bulletin*, Vol. 117(3), p. 497–529.

Bavel, B. van, 2016, *The Invisible Hand? How Market Economies Have Emerged and Declined since AD 500*. Oxford: Oxford University Press.

Beard, M., 2015, *S.P.Q.R.: A History of Ancient Rome*. London: Profile Books.

Beaud, O., 2012, 'Conceptions of the State', in: Rosenfeld & Sajó 2012, p. 269–282.

Beecher Stowe, H., 1852, *Uncle Tom's Cabin or Life among the Lowly*. Boston: Jewett, Proctor & Worthington.

Beer, L.W., 1979, 'Introduction: Constitutionalism in Asia and the United States', in: Beer, L.W. (ed.), *Constitutionalism in Asia: Asian Views of the American Influence*. Berkeley: University of California Press, p. 1–19.

Beetham, D., 1991, *The Legitimation of Power*, 2nd ed. Houndmills, Basingstoke/New York: Palgrave.

Bellamy, R., 2007, *Political Constitutionalism: A Republican Defence of the Constitutionality of Democracy*. Cambridge: Cambridge University Press.

Bentham, J., 2002, 'Nonsense upon Stilts, or Pandora's Box Opened, or The French Declaration of Rights Prefixed to the Constitution of 1791 Laid Open and Exposed', orig. 1795 (first published in French 1816 and in published in English in 1824) reprinted in: Schofield, P., Pease-Watkin, C., Blamires, C. (eds.), The Collected Works of Jeremy Bentham. *Rights, Representation, and Reform: Nonsense Upon Stilts and Other Writings on the French Revolution.* Oxford: Clarendon Press.

Benyishai, A. & Betancourt, R.R., 2010, 'Civil Liberties and Economic Development', *Journal of Institutional Economics*, Vol. 6(3), p. 281–304.

Berezin, M., 2002, 'Secure States: Towards a Political Sociology of Emotion', in: Barbalet 2002, p. 33–52.

Berlin, I., 1969, 'Two Concepts of Liberty', in: Berlin, I. (ed.), *Four Essays on Liberty*. Oxford: Oxford University Press, p. 118–172.

Bernard, G., 2017, *Napoléon et le droit, sous la direction de Thierry Lentz*. Paris: CNRS Editions.

Bernstein, M.J. & Claypool, H.M., 2012, 'Social Exclusion and Pain Sensitivity: Why Exclusion Sometimes Hurts and Sometimes Numbs', *Personality and Social Psychology Bulletin*, Vol. 38(2), p. 185–196.

Besselink, L.F.M., 2014, 'The Kingdom of the Netherlands', in: Besselink, L., Bovend'Eert, P., Broeksteeg, H., De Lange, R. & Voermans, W. (eds.), *Constitutional Law of EU Member States*. Deventer: Kluwer, p. 1187–1241.

Bewes, W.A., 1920, 'The Constitution of Uruguay', *Journal of Comparative Legislation and International Law*, Vol. 2(1), p. 60–63.

Bingham, T., 2010, *The Rule of Law*. Oxford: Oxford University Press.

Bishop, R., 2007, *Taking on the Pledge of Allegiance: The News Media and Michael Newdow's Constitutional Challenge*. Albany: State University of New York Press.

Blokker, P., 2017, 'The Imaginary Constitution of Constitutions', *Social Imaginaries*, Vol. 3(1), p. 167–193.

Blokker, P. & Thornhill, C. (eds.), 2017a, *Sociological Constitutionalism*. Cambridge: Cambridge University Press.

Blokker, P. & Thornhill, C., 2017b, 'Sociological Constitutionalism: An Introduction', in: Blokker & Thornhill 2017, p. 1–32.

Blume, L., Müller, J. & Voigt, S., 2009, 'The Economic Effects of Constitutions: Replicating – and Extending – Persson and Tabellini', *Public Choice*, Vol. 139(1), p. 197–225.

Böckenförde, M., 2017, *Constitutional Amendment Procedures*, Constitution-Building Prime no. 10, International Institute for Democracy and Electoral Assistance (International Idea), second edition. Stockholm: International Idea.

Bodin, J., 1993, *Les six livres de la Republique (The Six Books on the Republic)*, orig. 1576. Paris: Librairie Générale Française.

Bogart, W.A., 2002, *Consequences: The Impact of Law and Its Consequences*. Toronto/London/Buffalo: University of Toronto Press.

Botsman, R., 2017, *Who Can You Trust?: How Technology Brought Us Together – and Why It Could Drive Us Apart*. UK/USA, etc.: Penguin Business.

Bourdieu, P., 1987, *Distinction: A Social Critique of the Judgement of Taste*, transl. Nice, R. Cambridge, MA: Harvard University Press.

Boyd, B., 2009, *On the Origin of Stories: Evolution, Cognition and Fiction*. Cambridge, MA/London: Belknap Press of Harvard University Press.

Braudel, F., 1992, The Wheels of Commerce: Civilization and Capitalism 15th–18th Century (Les Jeux de l'Echange: Civilisation matérielle économie et capitalisme), Vol. II, orig. 1979, transl. Reynolds, R. Berkley: University of California Press.

Brennan, G. & Buchanan, J.M., 1985, *The Reasons of Rules: Constitutional Political Economy*. Cambridge, etc.: Cambridge University Press.

Brest, P., 1980, 'The Misconceived Quest for the Original Understanding', *Boston University Law Review*, Vol. 60(2), p. 204–238.

Brest, P., Levinson, S., Balkin, J.M., Amar, A.R. & Seigel, R.B, 2006, *Processes of Constitutional Decision-making: Cases and Materials*, 6th ed. New York: Aspen.

Breuilly, 2011, 'On the Principle of Nationality', in: Jones, G.S. & Claeys, G. (eds.), *The Cambridge History of Nineteenth-Century Political Thought*. Cambridge: Cambridge University Press, p. 77–109.

Brito Machado, H. de & Machado, R.C.R., 2017, 'Biology, Justice and Hume's Guillotine', *Phenomenology and Mind*, (12), p. 238–246.

Brunner, G., 1977, 'The Functions of Communist Constitutions: An Analysis of Recent Constitutional Developments', *Review of Socialist Law*, Vol. 3(1), p. 121–153.

Buchanan, J.M. & Tullock, G., 2007, *The Calculus of Consent: Logical Foundations of Constitutional Democracy*, orig. 1962. Ann Arbor: Ann Arbor Paperbacks.

Budryté, D., 2011, 'From Ethnic Fear to Pragmatic Inclusiveness? Political Community Building in the Baltic States (1988–2004)', *Ethnicity Studies*, Vol. 4(2), p. 14–41.

Burckhardt, 1979, *Reflections on History*, (Weltgeschichtliche Betrachtungen), orig. 1905, transl. Hottinger, MD/Indianapolis: Liberty Classics.

Burke, E., 2003, *Reflections on the Revolution in France*, orig. 1790. New Haven/London: Yale University Press.

Burke, K., 1945, *The Grammar of Motives*. New York: Prentice-Hall.

Burke, K., 1989, *On Symbols and Society*. Chicago: Chicago University Press.

Caenegem, R.C. van, 1995, repr. 2003, *An Historical Introduction to Western Constitutional Law*. Cambridge: Cambridge University Press.

Cairns, J.W., 2013, 'Watson, Walton, and the History of Legal Transplants', *Georgia Journal of International & Comparative Law*, Vol. 41(3), p. 637–696.

Campbell, T., 2012, 'Legal Studies', in: Goodin, Pettit & Pogge 2012, p. 226–253.

Capoccia, G., 2016, 'Critical Junctures', in: Fioretos, O., Falleti, T.G. & Sheingate, A. (eds.), *The Oxford Handbook of Historical Institutionalism*. Oxford: Oxford University Press, p. 89–106.

Capoccia, G. & Kelemen, D.R., 2007, 'The Study of Critical Junctures: Theory, Narrative, and Counterfactuals in Historical Institutionalism', *World Politics*, Vol. 59(2), p. 341–369.

Capogrossi Colognesi, L., 2014, *Law and Power in the Making of the Roman Commonwealth*, transl. Kopp, L. Cambridge: Cambridge University Press.

Carpenter, D.A., 1990, *The Minority of Henry III*. Berkeley/Los Angeles: University of California Press.

Casson, M. & Della Giusta, M., 2006, 'The Economics of Trust', in: Bachmann, R. & Zaheer, A. (eds.), *Handbook of Trust Research*. Cheltenham, UK/Northampton: Edward Elgar, p. 332–354.

Chang, W.C. & Yeh, J.R., 2012, 'Internationalization of Constitutional Law', in: Rosenfeld & Sajó 2012, p. 1165–1184.

Cheeseman, N., 2015, *Democracy in Africa: Successes, Failures, and the Struggle for Political Reform*. Cambridge: Cambridge University Press.

Choleris, E., Pfaff, D.W. & Kavaliers, M. (eds.), 2013, *Oxytocin, Vasopressin and Related Peptides in the Regulation of Behavior*. Cambridge: Cambridge University Press.

Chomsky, N., 2005, *Language and Mind*, 3rd ed. Cambridge: Cambridge University Press.

Chorvat, T. & McCabe, K., 2006, 'The Brain and the Law', in: Zeki, S. & Goodenough, O. (eds.), *Law and the Brain*. Oxford: Oxford University Press, p. 117–118.

Choudhry, S. (ed.), 2006, *The Migration of Constitutional Ideas*. Cambridge: Cambridge University Press.

Choudhry, S. (ed.), 2010a, *Constitutional Design for Divided Societies: Integration or Accommodation?* Oxford: Oxford University Press.

Choudhry, S., 2010b, 'Intro', 'Bridging Comparative Politics and Comparative constitutional Law: Constitutional Design in Divided Societies', in: Choudhry 2010, p. 3–40.

Choudhry, S. & Ginsburg, T. (eds.), 2016, *Constitution Making*. Northampton: Edward Elgar.

Cicero, Marcus Tullius, 1841–42, 'Treatise on the Republic', transl. Barham, F., *The Political Works of Marcus Tullius Cicero*. London: Edmund Spettigue.

Cicero, Marcus Tullius, 2008, *The Republic and the Laws (De Republica)*, transl. Rudd, N. Oxford: Oxford University Press.

Coan, A., 2011, 'Toward a Reality-Based Constitutional Theory', *Washington University Law Review*, Vol. 89(1), p. 273–286.

Coase, R.H., 1937, 'The Nature of the Firm', *Economica*, Vol. 16(4), p. 386–405.

Coase, R.H., 1960, 'The Problem of Social Cost', *Journal of Law and Economics*, Vol. 3, p. 1–44.

Colenbrander, H.T., 1909, *Ontstaan der grondwet. Bronnenverzameling 1814–1815, deel 2 (The Genesis of the Constitution – Sources 1814–1815, part 2 – in Dutch)*. Gravenhage: Martinus Nijhoff.

Compton, J.W., 2014, *The Evangelical Origins of the Living Constitution*. Cambridge, MA/London: Harvard University Press.

Congleton, R.D., 2010, *Perfecting Parliament*. Cambridge: Cambridge University Press.

Consani, C.F., 2015, 'Constitutional Precommitment and Collective Autonomy: Can They Be Reconciled?', *Revista de Estudos Constitucionais, Hermenêutica e Teoria do Direito*, Vol.7(3), p. 235–242.

Constant, B., 1997, *Principes de politique: Applicables à tous les gouvernements*, orig. 1806–1810, introduction Hofmann, E. Paris: Hachette.

Cooter, R.D., 2000, *The Strategic Constitution*. Princeton: Princeton University Press.

Corwin, E.S., 1936, 'The Constitution as Instrument and as Symbol', *The American Political Science Review*, Vol. 30(6), p. 1071–1085.

Critcher, C.R. & Zayas, V., 2014, 'The Involuntary Excluder Effect: Those Included by an Excluder Are Seen as Exclusive Themselves', *Journal of Personality and Social Psychology*, Vol. 107(3), p. 454–474.

Croissant, A., 2014, 'Ways of Constitution-Making in Southeast Asia: Actors, Interests, Dynamics', *Contemporary Southeast Asia*, Vol. 36(1), p. 23–50.

Cross, F.B., 2005, 'Law and Trust', *Georgetown Law Journal*, Vol. 93(5), p. 1457–1545.

Currie, A. & Sterelny, K., 2017, 'In Defence of Story-telling', *Studies in History and Philosophy of Science*, Vol. 62, p. 14–21.

Czarniwska, B., 2014, *Narratives in Social Science Research*, orig. 2004. London: Sage.

Dafoe, A., Renshon, J. & Huth, P. 2014, 'Reputation and Status as Motives for War', *Annual Review of Political Science*, Vol. 17, p. 371–393.

Dale, W., 1993, 'The Making and Remaking of Commonwealth Constitutions', *International and Comparative Law Quarterly*, Vol. 42(1), p. 67–83.

Daly, E., 2016, 'Ritual and Symbolic Power in Rousseau's Constitutional Thought', *Law, Culture and the Humanities*, Vol. 12(3), p. 620–646.

Darwin, C., 1981, *The Descent of Man, and Selection in Relation to Sex*, orig. 1871. Princeton/Oxford: Princeton University Press.

Dávid-Barrett, T. & Dunbar, R.I.M., 2013, 'Processing Power Limits Social Group Size: Computational Evidence for the Cognitive Costs of Sociality', *Proceedings of the Royal Society B: Biology*, Vol. 280(1765), p. 1–8.

Davis, M.H., 2004, 'Empathy: Negotiating the Border between Self and Other', in: Tiedens, L.Z. & Leach, C.W. (eds.), *The Social Life of Emotions*. Cambridge, etc.: Cambridge University Press, p. 19–42.

Dawkins, R., 2009, *The Greatest Show on Earth: The Evidence for Evolution*. London, etc.: Bantam Books.

Dawkins, R., 2016, *The Selfish Gene*, orig. 1976. Oxford: Oxford University Press.

Dawood, Y., 2007, 'The New Inequality: Constitutional Democracy and the Problem of Wealth', *Maryland Law Review*, Vol. 67(1), p. 123–149.

Deacon, T., 1997, *The Symbolic Species*. London: Penguin Press.

Descartes, R., 1637, *Discours de la Méthode*. Leiden: Jean Maire.

Descartes, R., 1644, *Principa Philosophiae*. Amsterdam: Elsevier.

Diamond, J., 2002, 'Evolution, Consequences and Future of Plant and Animal Domestication', *Nature Magazine*, Vol. 418(6898), p. 700–707.

Diamond, J., 2005, *Guns, Germs and Steel: The Fates of Human Societies*, orig. 1997. New York/London: W. W. Norton & Company.

Diamond, J., 2012, *The World Until Yesterday*. London: Penguin Books.

Diamond, J., 2019, *Upheaval: How Nations Deal with Crisis and Change*. UK/USA/Canada etc.: Allen Lane.

Diamond, L., 1999, *Developing Democracy: Towards Consolidation*. Baltimore: Johns Hopkins University Press.

Diamond, L., 2015a, *Democracy in Decline?* Baltimore: Johns Hopkins University Press.

Diamond, L., 2015b, 'Facing Up to the Democratic Recession', *Journal for Democracy*, Vol. 26(1), p. 141–155.

Dicey, A.V., 1982, *Introduction to the Study of the Law of the Constitution*, orig. 1889. Indianapolis: Liberty Classics.

Dickens, C., 1838, *Oliver Twist: or, the Parish Boy's Progress*. London: Richard Bentley.

Dippel, H. (ed.), 2004, *Constitutions of the World from the Late 18th Century to the Middle of the 19th Century (period 1776–1849)*. Munich: Sauer Verlag.

Dixon, R., 2011, 'Constitutional Amendment Rules: A Comparative Perspective', in: Dixon & Ginsburg 2011, p. 96–111.

Dixon, R. & Ginsburg, T. (eds.), 2011, *Comparative Constitutional Law*. Cheltenham/Northampton: Edward Elgar.

Dixon, R. & Posner, E.A., 2011, 'The Limits of Constitutional Convergence', *Chicago Journal of International Law*, Vol. 11(2), p. 399–424.

Dore, R., Phan, A., Clipperton-Allen, A., Kavaliers, M. & Choleris, E., 2013, 'The Involvement of Oxytocin and Vasopressin in Social Recognition and Social Learning: Interplay with the Sex Hormones', in: Choleris, E., Pfaff, D.W. & Kavaliers, M. (eds.), *Oxytocin, Vasopressin and Related Peptides in the Regulation of Behavior*. Cambridge: Cambridge University Press, p. 232–255.

Douzinas, C. & Nead, L. (eds.), 1999, *Law and the Image: The Authority of Art and the Aesthetics of Law*. Chicago/London: Chicago University Press.

Dreu, C.K.W. de, Shalvi, S., Greer, L.L., Kleef, G.A. van & Handgraaf, M.J.J., 2012, 'Oxytocin Motivates Non-Cooperation in Intergroup Conflict to Protect Vulnerable in Group Members', *Plus One*, Vol. 7(11), p. 1–7.

Duchacek, I.D., 1973, *Power Maps: Comparative Politics of Constitutions*. Santa Barbara: American Bibliographical Center-Clio Press.

Dunbar, R.I.M., 1992, 'Neocortex Size as a Constraint on Group Size in Primates', *Journal of Human Evolution*, Vol. 22(6), p. 469–493.

Dunbar, R.I.M., 1993, 'Coevolution of Neocortical Size, Group Size and Language in Humans', *Behavioral and Brain Sciences*, Vol. 16(4), p. 681–694.

Dunbar, R.I.M., 1998, *Grooming, Gossip and the Evolution of Language*, orig. 1996. Cambridge, MA: Harvard University Press.

Dunn, J., 1990, *Interpreting Political Responsibility: Essays 1981–1989*. Princeton/Oxford: Princeton University Press.

Durkheim, E., 2012, *The Elementary Forms of the Religious Life: A Study in Religious Sociology*, orig. 1915, transl. Swain, J.W., reprinted by Courier Corporation. New York: Dover Publications.

Duverger, M., 1954, *Les partis politiques (Political Parties)*. Paris: Colin.

Dworkin, R.A., 1982, '"Natural" Law Revisited', *University of Florida Law Review*, Vol. 34(2), p. 165–188.

Dworkin, R.A., 1998, *Law's Empire*, orig. 1986. Oxford: Hart Publishing.

Dwyer, S., 2006, 'How Good Is the Linguistics Analogy?', in: Carruthers, P., Laurence, S. & Stich, S. (eds.), *The Innate Mind, Volume II: Culture and Cognition*. Oxford: Oxford University Press, p. 237–255.

Eagleton, T., 2016, *Culture*. New Haven/London: Yale University Press.

Easton, D., 1975, 'A Re-assessment of the Concept of Political Support', *British Journal of Political Science*, Vol. 5(4), p. 435–457.

Edwards, H.L., 2010, 'Once Upon a Time in Law: Myth, Metaphor, and Authority', *Tennessee Law Review*, Vol. 77(4), p. 883–916.

Eisenberger, N.I., 2012, 'The Neural Bases of Social Pain: Evidence for Shared Representations with Physical Pain', *Psychosom Medicine*, Vol. 74(2), p. 126–135.

Eisenberger, N.I. & Lieberman, M., 2004, 'Why Rejection Hurts: A Common Neural Alarm System for Physical and Social Pain', *Trends in Cognitive Sciences*, Vol. 8(7), p. 294–300.

Ekman, P., 1999, 'Basic Emotions', in: Dagliesh, T. & Power, M.J. (eds.), *Handbook of Cognition and Emotion*. New York: John Wiley & Sons, p. 45–60.

Elder-Vass, D., 2012, *The Reality of Social Construction*. Cambridge/New York: Cambridge University Press.

Elias, N., 2000, *The Civilizing Process (Über den Prozeß der Zivilisation: soziogenetische und psychogenetische Untersuchungen)*, orig. 1939, transl. Jephcott, E., eds. Dunning, E., Goudsblom, J. & Menell, S. Malden, MA/Oxford/Carlton: Blackwell Publishing.

Elkin, S.L., 2009, 'Constitutional Collapse: The Faulty Founding', *The Good Society*, Vol. 18(1), p. 1–11.

Elkins, Z. & Simmons, B., 2005, 'On Waves, Clusters and Diffusion: A Conceptual Framework', *Annals of the American Academy of Political and Social Science (apps)*, Vol. 598, p. 33–51.

Elkins, Z., Ginsburg, T. & Melton, J., 2009, *The Endurance of National Constitutions*. New York: Cambridge University Press.

Elkins, Z., Ginsburg, T. & Melton, J., 2016, 'Time and Constitutional Efficacy', in: Ginsburg & Huq 2016, p. 233–267.

Elqayam, S. & Evans, J.St.B.T., 2011, 'Subtracting "ought" from "is": Descriptivism versus Normativism in the Study of Human Thinking', *Behavioral and Brain Sciences*, Vol. 34(5), p. 233–248.

Elster, J., 1979, *Ulysses and the Sirens: Studies in Rationality and Irrationality*. Cambridge: Cambridge University Press.

Elster, J., 1989, *Cement of Society: A Study of Social Order*. Cambridge: Cambridge University Press.

Elster, J., 1995, 'Forces and Mechanisms in the Constitution-Making Process', *Duke Law Journal*, Vol. 45(2), p. 364–396.

Elster, J., 1999, *Alchemies of the Mind: Rationality and the Emotions*. Cambridge: Cambridge University Press.

Elster, J., 2000, *Ulysses Unbound: Studies in Rationality, Precommitment and Constraints*. Cambridge: Cambridge University Press.

Elster, J., 2007, 'The Night of August 4 1789', *Revue Européenne des Sciences Sociales*, Vol. 45(136), p. 71–94.

Elster, J., 2009, *Reason and Rationality*, transl. Rendall, S. Princeton/Oxford: Princeton University Press.

Elster, J., 2017, 'Emotions in Constitution-Making', *Scandinavian Political Studies*, Vol. 40(2), p. 133–156.

Emon, A.E., 2010, 'The Limits of Constitutionalism in the Muslim World: History and Identity in Islamic Law', in: Choudhry 2010, p. 258–286.

Erasmus, D., 1530, *De Civilitate Morum Puerilium Libellus (A Handbook on Good Manners for Children)*.

Ezrahi, Y., 2012, *Imagined Democracies: Necessary Political Fictions*. New York: Cambridge University Press.

Fadel, M., 2016, 'Israeli Law and Constitution Making: The Authoritarian Temptation and the Arab Spring', *Osgoode Hall Law Journal*, Vol. 53(2), p. 472–507.

Fehr, E. & Fischbacher, U., 2003, 'The Nature of Human Altruism', *Nature*, Vol. 425(6960), p. 785–791.

Feldbrugge, F., 2017, *A History of Russian Law: From Ancient Times to the Council Code (Ulozhenie) of Tsar Aleksei Mikhailovich of 1649*. Leiden: Brill/Nijhoff.

Ferguson, N., 2003, *Empire*. London: Penguin Books.

Ferguson, N., 2008, *The War of the World. History's Age of Hatred*. London: Penguin Books.

Ferguson, N., 2009, *The Ascent of Money: A Financial History of the World*. London: Penguin Books.

Ferguson, N., 2016, *Kissinger: 1923–1968: The Idealist*. London: Penguin Books.

Ferguson, N., 2017, *The Square and the Tower: Networks, Hierarchies and the Struggle for Global Power*. London: Allen Lane.

Fierlbeck, K., 2008, *Globalizing Democracy: Power, Legitimacy and the Interpretation of Democratic Ideas*, orig. 1998. Manchester/New York: Manchester University Press.

Figes, O., 2019, *The Europeans: Three Lives and the Making of a Cosmopolitan Culture*. UK/USA/Canada etc.: Allen Lane.

Finkel, I. & Taylor, J., 2015, *Cuneiform*. London: The British Museum Press.

Finnis, J., 2011, 'Law's Authority and Social Theory's Predicament', in: Finnis, J. (ed.), *Philosophy of Law: Collected Essays*, Vol. IV. Oxford: Oxford University Press, p. 46–65.

Fisher, W., 1989, *Human Communication as Narration: Towards a Philosophy of Reason, Value, and Action*, orig. 1987. Columbia: University of South Carolina Press.

Flathman, R.E., 2012, 'Legitimacy', in: Goodin, Pettit & Pogge 2012, p. 678–684.

Fleming, J.E. (ed.), 2013, *Passions and Emotions*. New York/London: New York University Press.

Flinders, M., 2011, 'Daring to be a Daniel: The Pathology of Politicized Accountability in a Monitory Democracy', *Administration & Society*, Vol. 43(5), p. 595–619.

Floyd, J. & Stears, M. (eds.), 2011, *Political Philosophy versus History? Contextualism and Real Politics in Contemporary Political Thought*. Cambridge: Cambridge University Press.

Fombad, C.M., 2014, 'Constitution-Building in Africa: The Never-Ending Story of the Making, Unmaking and Remaking of Constitutions', *African and Asian studies*, Vol. 13(4), p. 429–451.

Foroni, C.F., 2015, 'Constitutional Precommitment and Collective Autonomy: Can They Be Reconciled?', *Revista de Estudos Constitucionais, Hermenêutica e Teoria do Direito*, Vol. 7(3), p. 235–242.

Foucault, M., 1977, *Discipline and Punish: The Birth of the Prison (Surveiller et punir: naissance de la prison)*, orig. 1975, transl. Sheridan, A. London: Allen Lane.

Fowler, J.H. & Schreiber, D., 2008, 'Biology, Politics, and the Emerging Science of Human Nature', *Science*, Vol. 322(5903), p. 912–914.

Frankenberg, G., 2010, 'Constitutional Transfer: The IKEA Theory Revisited', *International Journal for Constitutional Law*, Vol. 8(3), p. 563–579.

Frankopan, P., 2015, *The Silk Roads: A New History of the World*. London/Oxford/ New York/ New Delhi/Sydney: Bloomsbury.

Freedman, A., 2007, *The Party of the First Part: The Curious World of Legalese*. New York: Henry Holt.

Frerichs, S., 2017, 'The Rule of the Market: Economic Constitutionalism Understood Sociologically', in: Blokker & Thornhill 2017, p. 241–264.

Friedland, A.R., 1991, 'Bringing Society Back in: Symbols, Practices, and Institutional Contradictions', in: DiMaggio, P.J. & Powell, W.W. (eds.), *The New Institutionalism in Organizational Analysis*. Chicago: University of Chicago Press, p. 232–267.

Fukuyama, F., 1989, 'The End of History?', The National Interest, Summer, p. 1–18.

Fukuyama, F., 1992, *The End of History and the Last Man*. New York: Free Press.

Fukuyama, F., 2001, 'Differing Disciplinary Perspectives on the Origins of Trust', *Boston University Law Review*, Vol. 81(3), p. 479–494.

Fukuyama, F., 2011, *The Origins of Political Order: From Prehuman Times to the French Revolution*. London: Profile Books.

Fukuyama, F., 2014, *Political Order and Decay: From the Industrial Revolution to the Globalization of Democracy*. New York: Farrar, Strauss & Giroux.

Fukuyama, F., 2018, *Identity: The Demand for Dignity and the Politics of Resentment*. London: Profile Books.

Fuller, L.L., 1969a, *The Morality of Law*, orig. 1964, 2nd rev. ed. New Haven: Yale University Press.

Fuller, L.L., 1969b, 'Human Interaction and the Law', *American Journal of Jurisprudence*, Vol. 14(1), p. 1–36.

Gagliardo, J.G., 1980, *Reich and Nation, The Holy Roman Empire as Idea and Reality, 1763–1806*. Bloomington etc.: Indiana University Press.

Galligan, D.J. & Versteeg, M. (eds.), 2013, *Social and Political Foundations of Constitutions*. New York: Cambridge University Press.

Gardner, W.L., Pickett, C.L. & Brewer, M.B., 2000, 'Social Exclusion and Selective Memory: How the Need to belong Influences Memory for Social Events', *Personality and Social Psychology Bulletin*, Vol. 26(4), p. 486–496.

Gargarella, R., 2014, 'Latin-American Constitutionalism: Social Rights and the "Engine Room" of the Constitution', *Notre Dame Journal of International & Comparative Law*, Vol. 4(1), p. 9–11.

Gargarella, R., 2016, 'When Is a Constitution Doing Well? The Alberdian Test in the Americas', in: Ginsburg & Huq 2016, p. 99–133.

Garner, R., 1990, 'Jacob Burckhardt as a Theorist of Modernity: Reading the Civilization of the Renaissance in Italy', *Sociological Theory*, Vol. 8(1), p. 48–57.

Gellner, E., 1994, *Conditions of Liberty: Civil Society and Its Rivals*. London: Hamish Hamilton.

Gibbon, E., 1985, *The Decline and Fall of the Roman Empire*, orig. part I 1776: II & III 1781: IV, V & VI 1788. New York: Penguin Classics.

Gilbert, M., 2017, 'Entrenchment, Incrementalism, and Constitutional Collapse', *Virginia Law Review*, Vol. 103(4), p. 631–671.

Gill, S., 2007, 'New Constitutionalism, Democratisation and Global Political Economy', *Global Change, Peace & Security*, Vol. 10(1), p. 23–38.

Ginsburg, T., 2011, 'Constitutional Endurance', in: Dixon & Ginsburg 2011, p. 112–125.

Ginsburg, T., 2012, 'Introduction', in: Ginsburg, T. (ed.), *Comparative Constitutional Design*. Cambridge: Cambridge University Press, p. 1–12.

Ginsburg, T., 2012, 'Constitutional Law and Courts', in: Clark, D.S. (ed.), *Comparative Law and Society*, Cheltenham/Northampton: Edward Elgar, p. 290–309.

Ginsburg, T. & Huq, A.Z. (eds.), 2016, *Assessing Constitutional Performance*. Cambridge: Cambridge University Press.

Ginsburg, T. & Huq, A.Z., 2016, 'Intro', in: Ginsburg & Huq 2016, p. 3–35.

Ginsburg, T., Foti, N. & Rockmore, D., 2014, 'We the Peoples: The Global Origins of Constitutional Preambles', *The George Washington International Law Review*, Vol. 46(2), p. 305–340.

Gintis, H., 2003, 'The Hitchhiker's Guide to Altruism: Gene-culture Coevolution and the Internalization of Norms', *Journal of Theoretical Biology*, Vol. 220(4), p. 407–418.

Gintis, H., Bowles, S., Boyd, R. & Fehr, E., 2003, 'Explaining Altruistic Behavior in Humans', *Evolution and Human Behavior*, Vol. 24(3), p. 153–172.

Gladwell, M., 2006, *Blink: The Power of Thinking without Thinking*. London: Penguin Books.

Gladwell, M., 2019, *Talking to Strangers: What We Should Know about the People We Don't Know*. London: Allen Lane.

Go, J., 2002, 'Modeling the State: Postcolonial Constitutions in Asia and Africa', *Southeast Asian Studies*, Vol. 39(4), p. 558–583.

Goderis, B.V.G. & Versteeg, M., 2013, 'The Transnational Origins of Constitutions: Evidence from a New Global Data Set on Constitutional Rights', CentER Discussion Paper, Vol. 2013-010. Tilburg: Economics.

Goldfeder, M., 2013, 'The State of Israel's Constitution: A Comparison of Civilized Nations', *Pace International Law Review*, Vol. 25(1), p. 65–88.

Goldsworthy, A., 2016, *Pax Romana: War, Peace and Conquest in the Roman World*. London: Weidenfeld & Nicolson.

Goldsworthy, J., 2006, 'Questioning the Migration of Constitutional Ideas: Rights, Constitutionalism and the Limits of Convergence', in: Choudhry 2006, p. 115–141.

Goldsworthy, J., 2007, 'The Myth of the Common Law Constitution' (Chapter 8), in: Edlin, D.E. (ed.), *Common Law Theory*. Cambridge/New York/Melbourne, etc.: Cambridge University Press, p. 204–236.

Gommer, H., 2011, *A Biological Theory of Law: Natural Law Theory Revisited*. Seattle: Create Space/Amazon.

Goodenough, O.R. & Prehn, K., 2004, 'A Neuroscientific Approach to Normative Judgment in Law and Justice', *Philosophical Transactions of the Royal Society B: Biological Sciences*, Vol. 359(1451), p. 1709–1726.

Goodhart, D., 2017, *The Road to Somewhere: The Populist Revolt and the Future of Politics*. London: C. Hurst & Co Publishers.

Goodin, R.E., Pettit, P. & Pogge, T. (eds.), 2012, *A Companion to Contemporary Political Philosophy*, orig. 1995, 2nd ed. Oxford: Wiley-Blackwell.

Gottschall, J., 2013, *The Storytelling Animal: How Stories Make Us Human*. New York: Mariner Books.

Graber, M.A., 2013, *A New Introduction to American Constitutionalism*. Oxford/New York: Oxford University Press.

Grau, K., 2002, 'Parliamentary Sovereignty: New Zealand – New Millennium', *Victoria University of Wellington Law Review*, Vol. 33(2), p. 351–377.

Greenberg, J. & Sechler, M.J., 2013, 'Constitutionalism Ancient and Early Modern: The Contributions of Roman Law, Canon Law, and English Common Law', *Cardozo Law Review*, Vol. 34(3), p. 1021–1047.

Grey, T.C., 1979, 'Constitutionalism: An Analytical Framework', in: Pennock, J.R. & Chapman, J.W. (eds.), *Constitutionalism*. New York: New York University Press, p. 189–209.

Grimm, D., 2005, 'Integration by Constitution', *International Journal for Constitutional Law*, Vol. 3(2&3), p. 193–208.

Grimm, D., 2011, 'Verfassung jenseits des Nationaalstaats' (Constitution beyond the Nation State), *Zeitschrift für Rechtssoziologie*, Vol. 32(2), p. 181–188.

Grimm, D., 2012, 'Types of Constitutions', in: Rosenfeld & Sajó 2012, p. 98–132.

Grothe, E., 2005, 'Model or Myth? The Constitution of Westphalia of 1807 and Early German Constitutionalism', *German Studies Review*, Vol. 28(1), p. 1–19.

Gruter, M. & Masters, R.D., 1986, 'Ostracism as a Social and Biological Phenomenon: An Introduction', *Ethology and Sociobiology*, Vol. 7(3), p. 149–158.

Gusfield, J.R. & Michalowicz, J., 1984, 'Secular Symbolism: Studies of Ritual, Ceremony, and the Symbolic Order in Modern Life', *Annual Review of Sociology*, Vol. 101(1), p. 417–443.

Guthrie, C., Rachlinski, J. & Wistrich, A.J., 2007, 'Blinking on the Bench: How Judges Decide Cases', *Cornell Law Review*, Vol. 93(1), p. 1–143.

Guttentag, M.D., 2009, 'Is There a Law Instinct?', *Washington Law Review*, Vol. 87(2), p. 239–328.

Habermas, J., 1993, 'Struggles for Recognition in Constitutional States', *European Journal of Philosophy*, Vol. 1(2), p. 128–155.

Habermas, J., 1996, *Between Facts and Norms*, (*Faktizität und Geltung: Beiträge zur Diskurstheorie des Rechts und des demokratischen Rechtsstaats*), orig. 1992, transl. Rehg, W. Cambridge/Malden MA: Polity Press.

Habermas, J., 1999, 'Braucht Europa eine Verfassung? Eine Bemerkung zu Dieter Grimm' (Does Europe Need a Constitution?: A Note on Dieter Grimm), in: Habermas, J. (ed.), *Die Einbeziehung des Anderen: Studien zur Politischen Theorie (The Inclusion of the Other: Studies in Political Theory)*. Frankfurt am Main: Suhrkamp, p. 185–191.

Habermas, J., 2006, *The Theory of Communicative Action: The Critique of Functionalist Reason*, orig. 1981. Oxford: Blackwell Publishers, p. 309–331.

Hall, E., 2015, *The Ancient Greeks: Ten Ways They Shaped the Modern World*. London: Vintage.

Harari, Y.N., 2011, *Sapiens: A Brief History of Humankind*. London: Vintage.

Harari, Y.N., 2016, *Homo Deus: A Brief History of Tomorrow*. London: Harvill Secker.

Harari, Y.N., 2018, *21 Lessons for the 21st Century*. London: Jonathan Cape/Vintage.

Hardin, R., 2002, *Trust and Trustworthiness*. New York: Russell Sage Foundation.

Hart, H.L.A., 1958, 'Positivism and the Separation of Law and Morals', *Harvard Law Review*, Vol. 71(4), p. 593–629.

Hart, H.L.A., 2012, *The Concept of Law*, 2nd ed., orig. 1961. Oxford: Oxford University Press.

Harth, N.S. & Regner, T., 2017, 'The Spiral of Distrust: (Non-)cooperation in a Repeated Trust Game Is Predicted by Anger and Individual Differences in Negative Reciprocity Orientation', *International Journal of Psychology*, Vol. 52(S1), p. 18–25.

Hartley, L.P., 2014, *The Go-Between*, orig. 1953. London: Penguin Books.

Hauser, M.D., 2006, *Moral Minds*. New York: Harper Collins.

Hayek, F.A., 1960, *The Constitution of Liberty*. London: Routledge & Kegan Paul.

Hegel, G.W.F., 1892, *Lectures on the Philosophy of World History (Vorlesungen über die Philosophie der Weltgeschichte)*, Vol. 1, orig. 1840, transl. Haldane, E.S. London: Kegan Paul, Trench, Trübner & Co.

Hegel, G.W.F, 2018, *The Phenomenology of Spirit (Phänomenologie des Geistes)*, orig. 1807, transl. & ed. Pinkard, T. Cambridge: Cambridge University Press.

Henkin, L., 1994, 'A New Birth of Constitutionalism: Genetic Influences and Genetic Defects', in: Rosenfeld 1994, p. 39–53.

Henrich, J., 2016, *The Secret of Our Success: How Culture Is Driving Human Evolution, Domesticating Our Species, and Making Us Smarter*. Princeton/Oxford: Princeton University Press.

Hensel, S., 2012, 'Constitutional Cultures in the Atlantic World during the "Age of Revolutions"', in: Hensel, S., Block, U., Dircksen, K. & Thamer, H.U. (eds.), *Constitutional Cultures: On the Concept and Representation of Constitutions in the Atlantic World*. Newcastle upon Tyne: Cambridge Scholars Publishing, p. 3–20.

Hessebon, G.T., 2014, 'The Fourth Constitution-Making Wave of Africa: Constitutions 4.0?', *Temple International and Comparative Law Journal*, Vol. 28(2), p. 185–214.

Hirschl, R., 2004, 'The Political Origins of the New Constitutionalism', *Indiana Journal of Global Legal Studies*, Vol. 11(1), p. 71–108.

Hirschl, R., 2009, 'The "Design Sciences" and Constitutional "Success"', *Texas Law Review*, Vol. 87(7), p. 1339–1374.

Hirschl, R., 2013, 'The Strategic Foundations of Constitutions', in: Galligan & Versteeg 2013, p. 157–181.

Hirschl, R., 2014a, 'The Origins of the New Constitutionalism: Lessons from the "old" Constitutionalism', in: Gill, S. & Claire Cutler, A. (eds.), *New Constitutionalism and World Order*. Cambridge: Cambridge University Press, p. 95–108.

Hirschl, R., 2014b, *Comparative Matters: The Renaissance of Comparative Constitutional Law*. Oxford: Oxford University Press.

Hobbes, T., 1651, *On the Citizen*, orig. in Latin (De cive) 1642. Printed by J.C. for R. Royston, at the Angel in Ivie–Lane: London.

Hobbes, T., 1651, *Leviathan, or The Matter, Forme & Power of a Common-Wealth Ecclesiasticall and Civill*. London: printed for Andrew Crooke, at the Green Dragon in St. Pauls Church-yard.

Hobsbawm, E. & Ranger, T. (eds.), 1984, *The Invention of Tradition*, orig. 1983. Cambridge: Cambridge University Press.

Hofman, M.L., 1981, 'Is Altruism Part of Human Nature?', *Journal of Personality and Social Psychology*, Vol. 40(1), p. 121–137.

Hoffman, M.B., 2011, 'Evolutionary Jurisprudence: The End of the Naturalistic Fallacy and the Beginning of Natural Reform?', Chapter 26, in: Freeman, M. (ed.), *Law and Neuroscience*. Oxford: Oxford University Press, p. 403–502.

Holmes, O.W., 1920, *Collected Legal Papers*. New York: Harcourt, Brace & Co.

Holmes, S., 1988, 'Precommitment and the Paradox of Democracy', in: Elster, J. & Slagstad, R. (eds.), *Constitutionalism and Democracy*. Cambridge: Cambridge University Press, p. 195–240.

Holmes, S., 2012, 'Constitutions and Constitutionalism', in: Rosenfeld & Sajó 2012, p. 189–216.

Hominh, Y., 2014, 'The Constitutive Rhetoric of the Preamble to the Australian Constitution as a Performative Utterance', *Australian Journal of Legal Philosophy*, Vol. 39, p. 42–65.

Hopgood, S., 2013, *The Endtimes of Human Rights*. Ithaca, NY: Cornell University Press.

Horowitz, D.L., 1991, *A Democratic South Africa?: Constitutional Engineering in a Divided Society*. Berkeley: University of California Press.

Horowitz, D.L., 2014, 'Ethnic Power Sharing: Three Big Problems', *Journal of Democracy*, Vol. 25(2), p. 5–20.

Hoskin, P., 2008, 'Towards a Written Constitution?', *Coffeeshop-blog*, https://blogsspectator .co.uk/2008/02/towards-a-written-constitution/.

Houston, S. (ed.), 2004, *The First Writing: Script Invention as History and Process*. Cambridge: Cambridge University Press.

Hughes, C., 2018, 'Would Many People Obey Non-coercive Law?', *Jurisprudence*, Vol. 9(2), p. 361–367.

Hughes, S., 2016, 'Donald Trump's Pledge to Defend Article XII of Constitution Raises Eyebrows', *The Wall Street Journal*, 7 July.

Hugo, V., 1862, *Les Misérables*. Paris: Pagnerre.

Hulsker, J., 1989, *Van Gogh en zijn weg: het complete werk*, 6th ed. Amsterdam: Meulenhoff (in Dutch), transl. Hulsker, J., *The Complete Van Gogh*. New York: Abrams, 1980.

Hume, 2004, *A Treatise of Human Nature*, orig. 1739–1740. London: Penguin Classics.

Hunt, L., 2007, *Inventing Human Rights: A History*. New York/London: W.W. Norton & Company.

Huntington, S.P., 1973, *Political Order in Changing Societies*, orig. 1968, 7th ed. New Haven/ London: Yale University Press.

Huntington, S.P., 2011, *The Clash of Civilizations and the Remaking of World Order*, orig. 1996. New York: Simon & Schuster.

Insel, T.R. & Young, L.J., 2000, 'Neuropeptides and the Evolution of Social Behaviour', *Current Opinion in Neurobiology*, Vol. 10(6), p. 784–789.

International Idea (International Institute for Democracy and Electoral Assistance), 2014, *Constitutional Amendment Procedures*. Stockholm: International Idea.

International Idea, 2017, *The Global State of Democracy: Exploring Democracy's Resilience*. Stockholm: International Idea.

Israel, J.I., 2006, *Enlightenment Contested: Philosophy, Modernity, and the Emancipation of Man 1670–1752*. Oxford: Oxford University Press.

Jackson, V., 2012, 'Comparative Constitutional Law: Methodologies', in: Rosenfeld & Sajó 2012, p. 54–74.

Jacobsohn, G.J., 2006, 'Constitutional Identity', *Review of Politics*, Vol. 68(3), p. 361–397.

Jacobsohn, G.J., 2010, *Constitutional Identity*. Cambridge, MA: Harvard University Press.

Jacobsohn, G.J., 2012, 'The Formation of Constitutional Identities', in: Dixon & Ginsburg 2011, p. 129–142.

Jacobsohn, G.J. & Schor, M. (eds.), 2018, *Comparative Constitutional Theory*. Cheltenham/ Northampton: Edward Elgar Publishing.

Jaconelli, J., 2005, 'Do Constitutional Conventions Bind?', *The Cambridge Law Journal*, Vol. 64(1), p. 149–176.

Jenco, L.K., 2010, '"Rule by Man" and "Rule by Law" in Early Republican China: Contributions to a Theoretical Debate', *The Journal of Asian Studies*, Vol. 69(1), p. 181–203.

Jennings, M.M., 1997, 'Clarity of Judgment during Amoral Times in a Society Addicted to Codified Law', *Otolaryngology Head and Neck Surgery*, Vol. 117(1), p. 1–6.

Joyce, R., 2001, *The Myth of Morality*. Cambridge: Cambridge University Press.

Joyce, R., 2006, *The Evolution of Morality*. Cambridge, MA/London: MIT Press.

Joyce, R., 2014, 'The Origins of Moral Judgement', *Behaviour*, Vol. 151(2–3), p. 261–278.

Kahan, D.M., 2003, 'The Logic of Reciprocity: Trust, Collective Action, and Law', *Michigan Law Review*, Vol. 102(1), p. 71–103.

Kahn, P.W., 2003, 'Comparative Constitutionalism in a New Key', *Michigan Law Review*, Vol. 101(8), p. 2677–2705.

Kahneman, D., 2003, 'Maps of Bounded Rationality: A Perspective on Intuitive Judgement and Choice', in: Frängsmyr, T. (ed.), *Les Prix Nobel: The Nobel Prizes 2002*. Stockholm: Nobel Foundation, p. 449–489.

Kahneman, D. 2011, *Thinking, Fast and Slow*. New York: Farrar, Straus and Giroux.

Kant, I., 2011, *Groundwork of the Metaphysics of Morals: A German–English Edition (Grundlegung zur Metaphysik der Sitten)*, orig. 1786, transl. Gregor, M., ed. Timmerman, J. Cambridge/New York/Melbourne etc.: Cambridge University Press.

Keeley, L.H., 1996, *War before Civilization: The Myth of the Peaceful Savage*. New York: W. W. Norton & Company.

Kehoe, D., Ratzan, D.M. & Yiftach, U. (eds.), 2015, *Law and Transaction Costs in the Ancient Economy*. Ann Arbor: University of Michigan Press.

Kelsen, H., 1961, *General Theory of Law and State*, orig. 1945, transl. Wedberg, A. New York: Russell & Russell.

Kelsen, H., 1967, *Pure Theory of Law (Reine Rechtslehre)*, orig. 1960 [1934], transl. Knight, M. Berkeley: University of California Press.

Kelsen, H., 1971, 'What Is Justice?', in: Kelsen, H. (ed.), *What Is Justice? Justice, Law and Politics in the Mirror of Science. Collected Essays*. Berkeley: University of California Press, p. 1–24.

Kelsen, H., 2008, 'Wesen und Entwicklung der Staatsgerichtsbarkeit', orig. 1929, reprint, in: Ooyen, R. Chr. van (ed.), *Wer soll Hüter der Verfassung sein? Abhandlungen zur Theorie der Verfassungsgerichtsbarkeit in der pluralistischen, parlamentarischen Demokratie*. Tübingen: Mohr Siebeck.

Kenny, A., 2003, *Action, Emotion and Will*, orig. 1963. London/New York: Routledge.

Kim, Y., 2007, 'Cosmogony as Political Philosophy', *Philosophy East and West*, Vol. 58(1), p. 108–125.

Knack, S. & Keefer, Ph., 1997, 'Does Social Capital Have an Economic Payoff? A Cross-Country Investigation', *The Quarterly Journal of Economics*, Vol. 112(4), p. 1252–1288.

Knack, S. & Keefer, Ph., 1998, *Law's Empire*, orig. 1986. Oxford and Portland. Oregon: Hart Publishing.

Kokott, J. & Kaspar, M., 2012, 'Ensuring Constitutional Efficacy', in: Rosenfeld & Sajó 2012, p. 795–815.

Kosfeld, M., Heinrichs, M., Zak, P.J., Fischbacher, U. & Fehr, E., 2005, 'Oxycitin Increases Trust in Humans', *Nature*, Vol. 435(7042), p. 673–676.

Krauss, M., 1992, 'The World's Languages in Crisis', *Language*, Vol. 68(1), p. 4–10.

Lacretelle, C., 1814, *Histoire de France pendant les guerres de religion (The History of France during the Religious Wars)*. Tome Deuxième (2nd Volume). Paris: Delauny.

Lakin, J.L., Chartrand, T.L. & Arkin, R.M., 2008, 'I Am Too Just Like You: Nonconscious Mimicry as an Automatic Behavioral Response to Social Exclusion', *Association for Psychological Science*, Vol. 19(8), p. 816–822.

Lane, J.E., 1996, *Constitutions and Political Theory*. New York: Manchester University Press.

Lane, M., 2014, *Greek and Roman Political Ideas*. London: Pelican.

Lanni, A. & Vermeule, A., 2012, 'Constitutional Design in the Ancient World', *Stanford Law Review*, Vol. 64(4), p. 907–949.

LaRue, L.H., 1995a, 'Telling Stories about Constitutional Law', *Texas Tech Law Review*, Vol. 26(4), p. 1275–1286.

LaRue, L.H., 1995b, *Constitutional Law as Fiction: Narrative in the Rhetoric of Authority*. Pennsylvania: The Pennsylvania State University Press.

Laswell, H.D., 1936, *Politics: Who Gets What, When, How?* New York/London/Whittlesey House: McGraw-Hill Book.

Law, D.S., 2010, 'Constitutions', in: Cane, P. & Kritzer, H.M. (eds.), *The Oxford Handbook of Empirical Legal Research*. Oxford: Oxford University Press, p. 376–395.

Law, D.S., 2016, 'Constitutional Archetypes', *Texas Law Review*, Vol. 95(2), p. 153–243.

Law, D.S. & Versteeg, M., 2011, 'The Evolution and Ideology of Global Constitutionalism', *California Law Review*, Vol. 99(5), p. 1163–1258.

Law, D.S. & Versteeg, M., 2012, 'The Declining Influence of the United States Constitution', *New York University Law Review*, Vol. 87(3), p. 762–838.

Law, D.S. & Versteeg, M., 2013, 'Sham Constitutions', *California Law Review*, Vol. 101(4), p. 863–952.

Lawday, D., 2007, *Napoleon's Master: A Life of Prince Talleyrand*. London: Pimlico.

Laws, J., 2012, 'The Good Constitution', *The Cambridge Law Journal*, Vol. 71(3), p. 567–582.

Legrand, P., 1996, 'European Legal Systems Are Not Converging', *The International and Comparative Law Quarterly*, Vol. 45(1), p. 52–81.

Legrand, P., 1997, 'The Impossibility of Legal Transplants', *Maastricht Journal of European and Comparative Law*, Vol. 4(2), p. 111–124.

Leitzel, J., 2015, *Concepts in Law and Economics: A Guide for the Curious*. New York: Oxford University Press.

Levenson, R.W., 1994, 'Human Emotion: A Functional View', in: Ekman, P. & Davidson, R.J. (eds.), *The Nature of Emotion: Fundamental Questions*. New York, etc.: Oxford University Press, p. 123–126.

Levinson, S., 2012, *Framed: America's 51 Constitutions and the Crisis of Governance*. New York: Oxford University Press.

Levitsky, S. & Way, L., 2010, *Competitive Authoritarianism: Hybrid Regimes After the Cold War*. New York: Cambridge University Press.

Lewis, J.D., & Weigert, A.J., 2012, 'The Social Dynamics of Trust: Theoretical and Empirical Research, 1985–2012', *Social Forces*, Vol. 91(1), p. 25–31.

Lijphart, A., 1999, *Patterns of Democracy: Government Forms and Performance in Thirty-Six Countries*. New Haven/London: Yale University Press.

Lijphart, A., 2004, 'Constitutional Design for Divided Societies' *Journal of Democracy*, Vol. 15(2), p. 96–109.

Lindahl, H., 2007, 'Constituent Power and Reflexive Identity: Towards an Ontology of Collective Selfhood', in: Loughlin, M. & Walker, N. (eds.), *The Paradox of Constitutionalism: Constituent Power and Constitutional Form*. Oxford: Oxford University Press, p. 9–24.

Lindahl, H., 2013a, 'We and Cyberlaw: The Spatial Unity of Constitutional Orders', *Indiana Journal of Global Legal Studies*, Vol. 20(2), p. 697–730.

Lindahl, H., 2013b, *Fault Lines of Globalization: Legal Order and the Politics of A-Legality*. Oxford: Oxford University Press.

Linz, J.J. & Stephan, A., 1996, *Problems of Democratic Transition and Consolidation*. Baltimore: Johns Hopkins University Press.

Lipset, S.M., 1959, 'Some Social Requisites of Democracy: Economic Development and Political Legitimacy', *The American Political Science Review*, Vol. 53(1), p. 69–105.

Lipset, S.M., 1963, *Political Man: The Social Bases of Politics*. Garden City: Anchor Books.

Locke, J., 1689, *Two Treatises of Government. Second Treatise*. London: Awnsham Churchill.

Loewenstein, K., 1951, 'Reflections on the Value of Constitutions in Our Revolutionary Age', in: Zurcher, A.J. (ed.), *Constitutions and Constitutional Trends Since World War II: An Examination of Significant Aspects of Postwar Public Law with Particular Reference to the New Constitutions of Western Europe*. New York: New York University Press, p. 191–224.

Loewenstein, K., 1957, *Political Power and the Governmental Process*. Chicago: University of Chicago Press.

Lombardi, C.B., 2013, 'Designing Islamic Constitutions: Past Trends and Options for a Democratic Future', *International Journal of Constitutional Law*, Vol. 11(3), p. 615–645.

Loon, A.J. van, 2014, *Law and Order in Ancient Egypt: The Development of Criminal Justice from the Pharaonic New Kingdom until the Roman Dominate*. MA-thesis. Leiden: Leiden University.

Loughlin, M., 2015, 'The Constitutional Imagination', *The Modern Law Review*, Vol. 78(1), p. 1–25.

Luhmann, N., 1969, *Legitimation durch Verfahren (Legitimation by Procedure)*. Neuwied am Rhein & Berlin: Herman Luchterhand Verlag.

Luhmann, N., 2017, Trust and power, orig. 1973 & 1975, rev. & intr. Morger, C. & King, M., transl. Davis, H., Raffan, J. & Rooney K. Cambridge, UK/Medford, MA, USA: Polity Press.

Maarseveen, H. van & Tang, G. van der, 1978, *Written Constitutions: A Computerized Comparative Study*. New York/Alphen aan den Rijn: Oceana Publications/Sijthoff & Noordhoff.

MacDonald, G. & Leary, M.R., 2005, 'Why Does Social Exclusion Hurt? The Relationship Between Social and Physical Pain', *Psychological Bulletin*, Vol. 131(2), p. 202–223.

MacGregor, N., 2018, *Living with the Gods: On Beliefs and Peoples*. UK/USA/Canada etc.: Penguin Books.

Mackie, J.L., 1977, *Ethics: Inventing Right and Wrong*. New York: Penguin Books.

Madison, J., 1987, 'Federalist Papers, no. 48', in: *The Federalist Papers: Alexander Hamilton, James Madison, John Jay*, orig. 1788, ed. by Karmnick, I. London: Penguin Classics.

Maine, H., 1917, *Ancient Law*, orig. 1861. London, etc.: Dutton.

Mak, G., 2007, *In Europe: Travels through the Twentieth Century*, orig. 2004, transl. Garrett, S. London: Vintage Books.

Mallat, C., 2012, 'Islam and the Constitutional Order', in: Rosenfeld & Sajó 2012, p. 1287–1303.

Malthus, T., 1798, *An Essay on the Principle of Population*. London: J. Johnson.

Mann, T., 1960, *The Magic Mountain (Der Zauberberg)*, orig. 1924, transl. Lowe-Porter, H.T. Harmondsworth, Middlesex, England: Penguin Books.

Marcus, G.E., 2013, 'Reason, Passion, and Democratic Politics: Old Conceptions – New Understandings – New Possibilities', in: Fleming 2013, p. 127–188.

Marquez, X., 2017, *Non-democratic Politics: Authoritarianism, Dictatorships, and Democratization*. London: Palgrave Macmillan.

Marshall, G., 1984, *Constitutional Conventions: The Rules and Forms of Political Accountability*. Oxford: Oxford University Press.

Marx, K., 1844, 'Zur Kritik der Hegelschen Rechts-Philosophie' (A critique on Hegelian legal philosophy), in: *Deutsch-Französische Jahrbücher* (German-French Yearbook), 1/2. Paris: Arnold Ruge & Karl Marx.

Marx, K. & Engels, F., 1888, *The Communist Manifesto*, transl. Samuel Moore in cooperation with Frederick Engels, orig. 1848.

Matheson, C., 1987, 'Weber and the Classification of Forms of Legitimacy', *The British Journal of Sociology*, Vol. 38(2), p. 199–215.

Mattei, U. & Pes, L.G., 2008, 'Civil Law and Common Law: Toward Convergence?', in: Caldeira, G.A., Kelemen, R.D. & Whittington, K.E. (eds.), *The Oxford Handbook of Law and Politics*, p. 268–279.

May, J., 2018, *Regard for Reason in the Moral Mind*. Oxford: Oxford University Press.

Mazur, J. & Ursu, A.E., 2011, 'China's Disinterested Government and the Rule of Law', *Asia & the Pacific Policy Studies*, Vol. 4(2), p. 376–382.

Mbaku, J.M., 2013, 'What Should Africans Expect from Their Constitutions?', *Denver Journal of International Law & Policy*, Vol. 41(2), p. 149–183.

McAllister, I., 1999, 'The Economic Performance of Governments', in: Norris, P. (ed.), *Critical Citizens: Global Support for Democratic Governance*. Oxford: Oxford University Press, p. 188–203.

McCloskey, D.N., 2006, *The Bourgeois Virtues: Ethics for an Age of Commerce*. Chicago: University of Chicago Press.

McLean, J., 2018, 'The Unwritten Constitution', in: Jacobsohn & Schor 2018, p. 395–414.

McLynn, F., 2010, *Marcus Aurelius: Warrior, Philosopher, Emperor*, orig. 2009. London: Vintage.

Meadwell, H., 2001, 'The Long Nineteenth Century in Europe', *Review of International Studies*, Vol. 27(5), p. 165–189.

Meigs, R. & Lewis, D.M., 1969, *A Selection of Greek Historical Inscriptions to the End of the Fifth Century B.C.*, no. 2. London: Clarendon Press.

Rocha Menocal, A., Fritz, V. & Rakner, L., 2008, 'Hybrid Regimes and the Challenges of Deepening and Sustaining Democracy in Developing Countries', *The South African journal of international affairs*, Vol. 15(1), p. 29–40.

Mikhail, J., 2017, *Elements of Moral Cognition: Rawls' Linguistic Analogy and the Cognitive Science of Moral and Legal Judgment*, orig. 2011. Cambridge/New York, etc.: Cambridge University Press.

Mill, J.S., 2002, *On Liberty*, orig. 1859. Mineola, NY: Dover Publications.

Mirow, M.C., 2015, *Latin American Constitutions: The Constitution of Cádiz and its Legacy in Spanish America*. Cambridge: Cambridge University Press.

Mittal, S. & Weingast, B.R., 2011, 'Self-Enforcing Constitutions: With an Application to Democratic Stability in America's First Century', *The Journal of Law, Economics, & Organization*, Vol. 29(2), p. 278–302.

Mizonni, J., 2009, 'The Social Instincts Naturally Lead to the Golden Rule: The Ethics of Charles Darwin', *Teorema: Revista Internacional de Filosofía*, Vol. 28(2), p. 123–133.

Möllering, G., 2006, *Trust, Reason, Routine, Reflexivity*. Amsterdam: Elsevier.

Montenegro, A., 1995, 'Constitutional Design and Economic Performance', *Constitutional Political Economy*, Vol. 6(2), p. 161–169.

Montesquieu, Charles de Secondat, baron de, 2001, *The Spirit of Laws (L'esprit des Lois)*, transl. Thomas Nugent (1752), orig. 1748. Kitchener Ontario Canada: Batoche Books.

Morawetz, T., 1997, 'Law's Essence: Lawyers as Tellers of Tales', (Review of Brooks, P. & Gerwitz, P. (eds.), 1996, *Law's Stories: Narrative and Rhetoric in the Law*. Yale University Press). *Connecticut Law Review*, Vol. 29, p. 899–917.

Morris, N., 2008, 'The Big Question: Why Doesn't the UK Have a Written Constitution, and Does It Matter?' *Independent*, 14 February.

Moyn, S., 2018, *Not Enough: Human Rights in an Unequal World*. Cambridge, MA: The Belknap Press of Harvard University.

Mueller, D.C., 2003, *Public Choice III*. New York: Cambridge University Press.

Mueller, J., 2014, 'Did History End? Assessing the Fukuyama Thesis', *Political Science Quarterly*, Vol. 129(1), p. 35–54.

Müller, J.W., 2010, *Verfassungspatriotismus*. Berlin: Suhrkamp.

Müller, J.W., 2018, 'Militant Democracy and Constitutional Identity', in: Jacobsohn & Schor 2018, p. 415–435.

Murphy, K.M., Shleifer, A. & Vishny, R.W., 1991, 'The Allocation of Talent: Implications for Growth', *The Quarterly Journal of Economics*, Vol. 106(2), p. 503–530.

Murphy, W.F., 2007, *Constitutional Democracy: Creating and Maintaining a Just Political Order*. Baltimore: Johns Hopkins University Press.

Murrow, G.B. & Murrow, R.W., 2013, 'A Biosemiotic Body of Law: The Neurobiology of Justice', *International Journal for the Semiotics of Law – Revue Internationale de Sémiotique Juridique*, Vol. 26(2), p. 275–314.

Nash, J., 1950, 'Equilibrium Points in n-person Games', *Proceedings of the National Academy of Sciences*, Vol. 36(1), p. 48–49.

Nash, J., 1951, 'Non-Cooperative Games', *The Annals of Mathematics*, Vol. 54(2), p. 286–295.

Newton, S., 2006, 'Constitutionalism and Imperialism Sub Specie Spinozae', *Law and Critique*, Vol. 17(3), p. 325–355.

Niezen, R., 2010, *Public Justice and the Anthropology of Law*. Cambridge: Cambridge University Press.

Nogales, M.T. & Zelaya-Fenner, S. (eds.), 2013, *Democratic Governance in Latin America: A Regional Discussion*. Washington: International Republican Institute.

Nooteboom, B., 2002, *Trust: Forms, Foundations, Functions, Failures and Figures*. Cheltenham/Northampton: Edward Elgar.

North, D.C., 1989, 'Institutions and Economic Growth: An Historical Introduction', *World Development*, Vol. 17(9), p. 1319–1332.

North, D.C., 1990, *Institutions, Institutional Change and Economic Performance*. Cambridge: Cambridge University Press.

North, D.C. & Weingast, B.R., 1989, 'Constitutions and Commitment: The Evolution of Institutions Governing Public Choice in Seventeenth-Century England', *The Journal of Economic History*, Vol. 49(4), p. 803–883.

North, D.C., Wallis, J.J. & Weingast, B.R., 2009, *Violence and Social Orders: A Conceptual Framework for Interpreting Recorded Human History*. Cambridge: Cambridge University Press.

Norwich, J., 2012, *The Popes: A History*, orig. 2011. London: Vintage.

Nozick, R., 2002, *Anarchy, State and Utopia*, orig. 1974. Oxford/Malden: Blackwell Publishing.

Nussbaum, M.C., 2013, *Political Emotions: Why Love Matters for Justice*. Cambridge, etc.: Harvard University Press.

O'Scannlain, D., 2004, 'Rediscovering the Common Law', *Notre Dame Law Review*, Vol. 79(2), p. 755–764.

O'Scannlain, D., 2005, 'Is a Written Constitution Necessary?', *Pepperdine Law Review*, Vol. 32(4), p. 793–800.

Öktem, K. & Akkoyunlu, K., 2016, 'Exit from Democracy: Illiberal Governance in Turkey and Beyond', *Southeast European and Black Sea Studies*, Vol. 16(4), p. 469–480.

Omrani, B., 2017, *Caesar's Footprints: Journeys to Roman Gaul*. London: Head Zeus.

Oomen, B.M. & Lelieveldt, H.T., 2008, 'Onbekend maar niet onbemind. Wat weet en vindt de Nederlander van de Grondwet?' (Unkown Makes Unbeloved; What Do the Dutch Think and Know of Their Constitution?), *Nederlands Juristenblad (Dutch Lawyers Journal)*, Vol. 83(10). p. 577–578.

Ortiz-Ospina, E. & Roser, M., 2018, *International Trade*, https://ourworldindata.org/international-trade.

Otten, S., Sassenberg, K. & Kessler, T. (eds.), 2009, *Intergroup Relations: The Role of Motivation and Emotion*. Hove/New York: Psychology Press.

Paine, T., 1969, *Rights of Man*, orig. 1791, ed. by Collins, H. London: Pelican Books.

Papuashvili, G., 2017, 'Post-World War I Comparative Constitutional Developments in Central and Eastern Europe', *International Journal of Constitutional Law*, Vol. 15(1), p. 137–172.

Passchier, R., 2015, *Exploring the Function and Use of Requirements of Amendability in Global Constitutional Design*, https://ssrn.com/abstract=2693493.

Passchier, R., 2017, *Informal Constitutional change: Constitutional Change Without Formal Constitutional Amendment in Comparative Perspective*, PhD-thesis. Universiteit Leiden. Leiden.

Penn, T., 2012, *Winter King: The Dawn of Tudor England*, orig. 2011. London: Penguin Books.

Persson, T. & Tabellini, G., 2003, *The Economic Effects of Constitutions*. Cambridge, MA: MIT Press.

Persson, T. & Tabellini, G., 2004, 'Constitutions and Economic Policy', *Journal of Economic Perspectives*, Vol. 18(1), p. 75–98.

Peters, A., 2007, 'The Globalization of State Constitutions', in: Nijman, J.E. & Nollkaemper, A. (eds.), *New Perspectives on the Divide Between National and International Law*. Oxford: Oxford University Press.

Picado, S., 2004, 'The Evolution of Democracy and Human Rights in Latin America: A Ten Year Perspective', *Human Rights Brief*, Vol. 11(3), p. 28–31.

Piketty, T., 2014, *Capital in the Twenty-first Century*. Cambridge, MA: The Belknap Press of Harvard University Press.

Pinker, S., 2003, *The Blank Slate: The Modern Denial of Human Nature*, orig. 2002. London: Penguin Books.

Pinker, S., 2007a, *The Language Instinct: How the Mind Creates Language*, orig. 1994. New York: Harper Perennial Modern Classics.

Pinker, S., 2007b, *The Stuff of Thought*. London: Allen Lane.

Pinker, S., 2009, *How the Mind Works*, orig. 1999. New York/London: W.W. Norton.

Pinker, S., 2011, *The Better Angels of Our Nature: Why Violence Has Declined*. London: Penguin Books.

Pinker, S., 2018, *Enlightenment Now: The Case for Reason, Science, Humanism, and Progress*. New York, NY: Viking.

Pirie, F., 2013, *The Anthropology of Law*. Oxford: Oxford University Press.

Pitkin, H.F., 1987, 'The Idea of a Constitution', *Journal of Legal Education*, Vol. 37(2), p. 167–169.

Plato, 1983, *The Republic*, transl. Lee, D., 2nd rev. ed. London: Penguin Books.

Plinius Minor (Pliny the Younger), 1969, *Epistulae (The letters of the younger Pliny)*, transl. Radice, B. Harmondsworth: Penguin Books.

Pocock, J.G.A., 1987, *The Ancient Constitution and the Feudal Law: A Study of English Historical Thought in the Seventeenth Century*. Cambridge: Cambridge University Press.

Polkinghorne, D.E., 1988, *Narrative Knowing and the Human Sciences*. Albany: State University of New York Press.

Polybius, 1923, repr. 1979, *The Histories*, transl. Paton, W.R. Cambridge, MA/London: Harvard University Press/William Heinemann.

Posner, R., 1999, 'Emotion versus Emotionalism in Law', in: Bandes, S. (ed.), *The Passions of Law*. New York: New York University Press, p. 309–239.

Posner, R. 2007, *Economic Analysis of Law*, orig. 1972, 7th ed. Austin, TX, etc.: Wolters Kluwer Law & Business.

Pound, R., 1908, 'Common Law and Legislation', *Harvard Law Review*, Vol. 21(6), p. 383–407.

Pozas Loyo, A., 2016, 'What Is "Constitutional Efficacy"? Conceptual Obstacles for Research on the Effects of Constitutions', *Mexican Law Review*, Vol. X(1), p. 23–44.

Price, R., 1776, *Observations on the Nature of Civil Liberty, the Principles of Government, and the Justice and Policy of the War with America*. London: Edward & Charles Dilly and Thomas Cadell.

Prinz, J.J., 2013, 'Constructive Sentimentalism: Legal and Political Implications', in: Fleming 2013, p. 3–18.

Prooijen, J.W. van, Bos, K. van den & Wilke, H. A. M., 2004, 'Group Belongingness and Procedural Justice: Social Inclusion and Exclusion by Peers Affects the Psychology of Voice', *Journal of Personality and Social Psychology*, Vol. 87(1), p. 66–79.

Puddington, A., 2015, 'A Return to the Iron Fist', *Journal of Democracy*, Vol. 26(2), p. 122–138.

Putnam, R. D., 1995a, 'Bowling Alone: America's Declining Social Capital', *Journal of Democracy*, Vol. 6(1), p. 65–78.

Putnam, R. D., 1995b, 'Tuning In, Tuning Out: The Strange Disappearance of Social Capital in America', *PS: Political Science and Politics*, Vol. 28(4), p. 664–683.

Pyysiäinen, I., 2001, 'Cognition, Emotion, and Religious Experience', in: Andresen, J. (ed.), *Religion in Mind: Cognitive Perspectives on Religious Belief, Ritual, and Experience.* Cambridge/New York, etc.: Cambridge University Press, p. 70–93.

Rawls, J., 1999, *A Theory of Justice*, orig. 1971. Cambridge, MA/London: Harvard University Press.

Raz, J., 1982, 'The Claims of Reflective Equilibrium', *Inquiry*, Vol. 25(3), p. 307–330.

Rehnquist, W.H., 2006, 'The Notion of a Living Constitution', *Harvard Journal of Law & Public Policy*, Vol. 29(2), p. 401–415 (revised edition of the article in *Texas Law Review*, Vol. 54(4), 1976, p. 693–706).

Reisenzein, R., 2009, 'Emotions as Metarepresentational States of Mind: Naturalizing the Belief–desire Theory of Emotion', *Cognitive Systems Research*, Vol. 10(1), p. 6–20.

Renan, E., 2018, *What Is a Nation? and Other Political Writings (Qu'est-ce qu'une nation?)*, orig. 1882, transl. Giglioli, M.F.N. New York: Columbia University Press.

Ribner, J.P., 1993, *Broken Tablets: The Cult of the Law in French Art from David to Delacroix.* Berkeley/Los Angeles: University of California Press.

Richter, D., Grün, R., Joannes-Boyau, R., Steele, T.E., Amani, F., Rué, M., Fernandes, P., Raynal, J.-P., Geraads, D., Ben-Ncer, A., Hublin, J.-J. & McPherron, S.P., 2017, 'The Age of the Hominin Fossils from Jebel Irhoud, Morocco, and the Origins of the Middle Stone Age', *Nature*, Vol. 546, p. 293–296.

Ricoeur, P., 1992, *Oneself as Another*, transl. Blamey, K. Chicago: Chicago University Press.

Riker, W.H., 1976, 'Comments on Vincent Ostrom's Paper', *Public Choice*, Vol. 27(1), p. 13–19.

Rizzolatti, G., Sinigaglia, C. & Anderson, F., 2008, *Mirrors in the Brain: How Our Minds Share Actions and Emotions.* Oxford: Oxford University Press.

Roberts, J.M. & Westad, O.A., 2014, *The Penguin History of the World*, orig. 1976, 6th ed. London: Penguin Books.

Robinson, P. & Darley, J.M., 2003, 'The Role of Deterrence in the Formulation of Criminal Law Rules: At Its Worst When Doing Its Best', *Georgetown Law Journal*, Vol. 91(5), p. 949–1002.

Roll, R. & Talbott, J., 2003, 'Political Freedom, Economic Liberty, and Prosperity', *Journal of Democracy*, Vol. 14(3), p. 75–89.

Rommen, H.A., 1947, *Natural Law: A Study in Legal and Social History and Philosophy*, transl. Hanley, T.R. St. Louis: B. Herder Book Co.

Rosas, A. & Armati, L., 2012, *EU Constitutional Law: An Introduction*, 2nd ed. London: Hart Publishing.

Rosenfeld, M. (ed.), 1994, *Constitutionalism, Identity, Difference and Legitimacy: Theoretical Perspectives.* Durham, NC/London: Duke University Press.

Rosenfeld, M., 2010, *The Identity of the Constitutional Subject: Selfhood, Citizenship, Culture and Community.* London/New York: Routledge.

Rosenfeld, M., 2011, *Law, Justice, Democracy, and the Clash of Cultures: A Pluralist Account.* Cambridge: Cambridge University Press.

Rosenfeld, M., 2012, 'Constitutional Identity', in: Rosenfeld & Sajó 2012, p. 756–776.

Rosenfeld, M. & Sajó, A. (eds.), 2012, *The Oxford Handbook of Comparative Constitutional Law.* Oxford: Oxford University Press.

Rosenfeld, M. & Sajó, A., 2012-intro, 'Introduction', in: Rosenfeld & Sajó 2012, p. 1–21.

Rousseau, J.J., 1755, *Discours sur l'origine et les fondements de l'inégalité parmi les hommes (Discourse on the Origin and Foundations of Inequality among Men)*, orig. 1754, transl. Rey, M.M. Amsterdam: Marc-Michel Rey.

Rousseau, J.J., 1762, *Du contrat social ou principes du droit politique (On the Social Contract or the Principles of Public Law)*. Amsterdam: Marc-Michel Rey.

Runciman, D., 2013, *The Confidence Trap: A History of Democracy in Crisis from World War I to the Present.* Princeton/Oxford: Princeton University Press.

Sabato, H., 2018, *Republics of the New World: The Revolutionary Political Experiment in the 19th-Century Latin America*. Princeton/Oxford: Princeton University Press.

Sacconi, L., 2007, 'A Social Contract Account for CSR as an Extended Model of Corporate Governance (ii): Compliance, Reputation and Reciprocity', *Journal of Business Ethics*, Vol. 75(1), p. 77–96.

Sajó, A., 2005, 'Constitution without the Constitutional Moment: A View from the New Member States', *International Journal of Constitutional Law*, Vol. 2(2–3), p. 243–261.

Sajó, A., 2011, *Constitutional Sentiments*. New Haven/London: Yale University Press.

Saler, B., 2001, 'On What We May Believe about Beliefs', in: Andresen J. (ed.), *Religion in Mind: Cognitive Perspectives on Religious Belief, Ritual and Experience*. Cambridge: Cambridge University Press, p. 47–69.

Samuels, K., 2006, 'Post-conflict Peace-building and Constitution-making', *Chicago Journal of International Law*, Vol. 6(2), p. 663–682.

Sartor, G., 1962, 'Constitutionalism: A Preliminary Discussion', *The American Political Science Review*, Vol. 56(4), p. 853–864.

Sassen, S., 2008, *Territory, Authority, Rights: From Medieval to Global Assemblages*. Princeton/Oxford: Princeton University Press.

Saunders, C., 2009, 'Towards a Global Constitutional Gene Pool', *National Taiwan University Law Review*, Vol. 4(3), p. 1–38.

Schaik, C. van & Michel, K., 2016, *The Good Book of Human Nature: An Evolutionary Reading of the Bible*. New York: Basic Books.

Schama, S., 1977, *Patriots and Liberators: Revolution in the Netherlands 1780–1813*. New York: Alfred A. Knopf.

Schama, S., 1989, *Citizens: A Chronicle of the French Revolution*. UK/USA: Penguin Books.

Schechtman, M., 1996, *The Constitution of Selves*. Cornell: Cornell University Press.

Scheppele, K.L., 2008, 'A Constitution between Past and Future', *William and Mary Law Review*, Vol. 49(4), p. 1377–1407.

Scheppele, K.L., 2017, 'The Social Lives of Constitutions', in: Blokker & Thornhill 2017, p. 35–66.

Scheuermann, W.E., 2002, 'Constitutionalism in an Age of Speed', *Constitutional Commentary*, Vol. 19(2), p. 353–813.

Schmitt, C., 2007, *The Concept of the Political*, orig. 1933, transl. Schwab, G. Chicago, etc.: University of Chicago Press.

Schneiderman, 2011, 'A New Global Constitutional Order?', in: Dixon & Ginsburg 2011, p. 189–207.

Schofield, N., 2002, 'Evolution of the Constitution', *British Journal of Political Science*, Vol. 32(1), p. 1–20.

Schwartzberg, M., 2014, *Counting the Many: The Origins and Limits of Supermajority Rule*. Cambridge: Cambridge University Press.

Scott, J.C., 2017, *Against the Grain: A Deep History of the Earliest States*. New Haven/London: Yale University Press.

Scott, M., 2016, *Ancient Worlds: An Epic History of East and West*. London: Windmill Books.

Searle, J.R., 1995, *The Social Construction of Reality*. New York: The Free Press.

Searle, J.R., 2004, *Freedom and Neurobiology: Reflections on Free Will, Language, and Political Power*, 3rd ed. New York: Colombia University Press.

Seidman, R.B., 1975, 'Book Review Legal Transplants', *Boston University Law Review*, Vol. 55, p. 682–683.

Sejersted, F., 1997, 'Democracy and the Rule of Law: Some Historical Experiences of Contradictions in the Striving for Good Government', in: Elster, J. & Slagstad, R. (eds.), *Constitutionalism and Democracy*, orig. 1988. Cambridge: Cambridge University Press, p. 131–152.

Sen, A., 2007, *Identity & Violence: The Illusion of Destiny*. London: Penguin Books.

Sen, A., 2010, *The Idea of Justice*, orig. 2009. London: Penguin Books.

Seppänen, S., 2016, *Ideological Conflict and the Rule of Law in Contemporary China: Useful Paradoxes*. Cambridge: Cambridge University Press.

Service, E.R., 1975, *Origins of the State and Civilization: The Process of Cultural Evolution*. New York: W.W. Norton.

Service, E.R., 1976, *Primitive Social Organization: An Evolutionary Perspective*. Chicago: Random House.

Shapiro, M. & Sweet, A.S., 2002, *On Law, Politics, and Judicialization*. Oxford: Oxford University Press.

Sheehan, J.J., 2015, 'Political History: History of Politics', in: Wright, J.D. (ed.), *International Encyclopedia of the Social and Behavioral Sciences*, 2nd ed. Amsterdam: Elsevier Science, p. 380–385.

Shuo, E. & Josephs, R.A., 2017, 'Psychological Consequences of Social Rejection', in: Williams & Nida 2017, p. 81–94.

Siedentop, L., 2001, *Democracy in Europe*, orig. 2000. London: Penguin Books.

Siedentop, L., 2014, *Inventing the Individual: The Origins of Western Liberalism*. Cambridge, MA: Belknap Press of Harvard University Press.

Sieyès, E.J., 1794, 'Opinion de Sieyès sur les attributions et l'organisation du jury constitutionnaire proposé le 2 thermidor', prononcée à la Convention nationale le 18 du même, l'an iii de la République, dans Moniteur, Séance du 18 thermidor an III, p. 1311.

Simmons, W.P., 2011, *Human Rights Law and the Marginalized Other*. Cambridge: Cambridge University Press.

Simon, S.A., 2014, *Universal Rights and the Constitution*. New York: University of New York Press.

Simons, W.B. (ed.), 1980, *The Constitutions of the Communist World*. Alphen aan den Rijn/ Germantown: Sijthoff & Noordhoff.

Singer, T., Seymour, B., O'Doherty, J.P., Stephan, K.E., Dolan, R.J. & Frith, C.D., 2006, 'Empathic Neural Responses Are Modulated by the Perceived Fairness of Others', *Nature*, Vol. 439(7075), p. 466–469.

Skinner, Q., 1978, *The Foundations of Modern Political Thought: Vol. 1: The Renaissance*. Cambridge, etc.: Cambridge University Press.

Smilov, D., 2013, 'Constitutionalism of Shallow Foundations: The Case of Bulgaria', in: Galligan & Versteeg 2013, p. 611–636.

Smith, A., 2003, *The Wealth of Nations*, orig. 1776. New York: Bantam Classic.

Snell, D.C., 2007, 'The Invention of the Individual', in: Snell, D.C. (ed.), *A Companion to The Ancient Near East*. Carlton, Victoria, Australia: Blackwell Publishing, p. 379–391.

Snyder, J., 2000, *From Voting to Violence: Democratization and Nationalist Conflict*. New York, etc.: W. W. Norton & Company.

Solomon, R.C. & Flores, F., 2001, *Building Trust in Business, Politics, Relationships, and Life*. Oxford: Oxford University Press.

Somos, M., 2010, 'Saint Augustine of Hippo, Step-father of Liberalism', *History of European Ideas*, Vol. 36(2), p. 237–250.

Soullier, C., 1852, Napoléon Ier (empereur des Français 1769–1821). *Maximes et pensées de Napoléon, suivies d'un poème résumant toute l'histoire du grand homme (Napoleon I – Emperor of the French 1769–1821. Axioms and Thoughts Followed by a Poem Summarizing the Whole History of the Great Man)*. Paris: Imprimerie de Madame Lacombe.

Sperber, J., 2005, *The European Revolutions, 1848–1851*. Cambridge: Cambridge University Press.

Spigelman, J., 2015, 'Magna Carta: The Rule of Law and Liberty', *Policy: A Journal of Public Policy and Ideas*, Vol. 31(2), p. 24–31.

Spinoza, B., 2002, *Complete Works*, transl. Shirley, S. ed. Morgan, M.L. Indianapolis, IN: Hackett.

Spinoza, B., 2008, *Ethics: ethica ordine geometrico demonstrata*, orig. 1677, transl. Elwes, R.H.M. Auckland, NZ: Floating Press.

Spinoza, B., 2017, *Treatise on Theology and Politics (Tractatus Theologico-Politicus)*, orig. 1670, transl. Bennett, J. www.earlymoderntexts.com/assets/pdfs/spinoza1669.pdf

Spiro, H.J., 1959, *Government by Constitution: The Political System of Democracy*. New York/Toronto: Random House.

Statman, D., 2000, 'Humiliation, Dignity and Self-respect', *Philosophical Psychology*, Vol. 13(4), p. 523–540.

Steinkeller, P., 2004, 'The Function of Written Documentation in the Administrative Praxis of Early Babylonia', in: Hudson, M. & Wunsch, C. (eds.), *Creating Economic Order, Record-Keeping, Standardization, and the Development of Accounting in the Ancient Near East*, Vol. 5, Bethesda, Maryland: CDL, p. 65–88.

Sterelny, K., 2016, 'Contingency and History', *Philosophy of Science*, Vol. 83(4), p. 521–539.

Stolker, C., 2014, *Rethinking the Law School: Education, Research, Outreach and Governance*. Cambridge: Cambridge University Press.

Strautman, B., 2015, *Law in the State of Nature: The Classical Foundations of Hugo Grotius' Natural Law*, transl. Cooper, B. Cambridge: Cambridge University Press.

Stringham, E.P., 2015, *Private Governance: Creating Order in Economic and Social Life*. Oxford: Oxford University Press, p. 9–20.

Strong, C.F., 1963, *History of Modern Political Constitutions*. New York: Capricorn Books.

Suhler, C.L. & Churchland, P., 2011, 'Can Innate, Modular "Foundations" Explain Morality? Challenges for Haidt's Moral Foundations Theory', *Journal of Cognitive Neuroscience*, Vol. 23(9), p. 2103–2116.

Sunstein, C. R., 2001, *Designing Democracy: What Constitutions Do*. New York: Oxford University Press.

Sunstein, C. R., 2009, *A Constitution of Many Minds: Why the Founding Document Doesn't Mean What It Meant Before*. Princeton, NJ: Princeton University Press.

Sunstein, R.C. & Thaler, R.H., 2008, *Nudge: Improving Decisions About Health, Wealth and Happiness*. New Haven: Yale University Press.

Sunstein, R.C., Jolls, C. & Thaler, R.H., 1998, 'A Behavioral Approach to Law and Economics', *Stanford Law Review*, Vol. 50(5), p. 1471–1550.

Swaab, D., 2014, *We Are Our Brains: From the Womb to Alzheimer's (Wij zijn ons brein: van baarmoeder tot Alzheimer)*, orig. 2000, transl. Hedley-Prole, J.A. London: Allen Lane.

Tan, K.Y.L., 2002, 'Comparative Constitutionalism: The Making and Remaking of Constitutional Orders in Southeast Asia', *Singapore Journal of International and Comparative Law*, Vol. 6(1), p. 1–41.

Tay, W.T.V., 2019, 'Basic Structure Revisited: The Case of Semenyih Jaya and the Defence of Fundamental Constitutional Principles in Malaysia', *Asian Journal of Comparative Law*, Vol. 14(1), p. 113–145.

Taylor, C., 1994, 'The Politics of Recognition', in: Gutmann, A. (ed.), *Multiculturalism and the Politics of Recognition*. Princeton/Oxford: Princeton University Press, p. 25–73.

Taylor, C., 2007, *A Secular Age*. Cambridge, MA: Belknap Press of Harvard University Press.

Tchalova, K. & Eisenberger, N.I., 2017, 'The Shared Neural Substrates of Physical and Social Pain', in: Williams & Nida 2017, p. 61–80.

Ten, C.L., 2012, 'Constitutionalism and the Rule of Law', in: Goodin, Pettit, & Pogge 2012, p. 493–510.

Terpstra, T.T., 2013, *Trading Communities in the Roman World: A Micro-Economic and Institutional Perspective*. Leiden: Brill.

Teubner, G., 1987, *Juridification of Social Spheres: A Comparative Analysis in the Areas of Labor, Corporate, Antitrust, and Social Welfare Law*. Berlin/New York: De Gruyter.

Teubner, G., 1998, 'Legal Irritants: Good Faith in British Law or How Unifying Law Ends up in New Divergences', *The Modern Law Review*, Vol. 61(1), p. 11–32.

Teubner, G., 2004, 'Societal Constitutionalism: Alternatives to State-Centered Constitutional Theory?', in: Joerges, C., Sand, I.J. & Teubner, G. (eds.), *Transnational Governance and Constitutionalism*. Oxford/Portland: Hart Publishing, p. 3–28.

Thaler, R.H., 2015, *Misbehaving: The Making of Behavioral Economics*. New York/ London: W. W. Norton & Company.

Thaler, R.H. & Sunstein, C.R., 2009, *Nudge*, orig. 2008. London/New York: Penguin Books.

Theiss-Morse, E. & Barton, D.G., 2017, 'Emotion, Cognition, and Political Trust', in: Zmerli & Van der Meer 2017, p. 160–175.

Thio, L.-A., 2012, 'Constitutionalism in Illiberal Polities', in: Rosenfeld & Sajó 2012, p. 133–152.

Thomassen, J., Andeweg, R. & Ham, C., 2017, 'Political Trust and the Decline of Legitimacy Debate: A Theoretical and Empirical Investigation into Their Interrelationship', in: Zmerli & Van der Meer 2017, p. 509–525.

Thornhill, C., 2010, 'Legality, Legitimacy and the Constitution: A Historical-functionalist Approach', in: Thornhill & Ashenden 2010, p. 29–56.

Thornhill, C., 2011, *A Sociology of Constitutions: Constitutions and State Legitimacy in Historical-Sociological Perspective*. Cambridge: Cambridge University Press.

Thornhill, C. & Ashenden, S. (eds.), 2010, *Legality and Legitimacy: Normative and Sociological Approaches*. Baden-Baden: Nomos.

Thucydides, 1998, *The Peloponnesian War*, transl. Lattimore, S. Indianapolis/Cambridge: Hackett Publishing.

Thürer, D. & Burri, T., 2008, 'Self-determination', Max Planck Encyclopedia of Public International Law. http://opil.ouplaw.com/view/10.1093/law:epil/9780199231690/law-9780199231690-e873.

Tiedens, L.Z. & Leach, C.W. (eds.), 2004, *The Social Life of Emotions*. Cambridge etc.: Cambridge University Press.

Tocqueville, A. de, 2002, *Democracy in America (De la démocratie en Amérique)*, orig. Vol. I – 1835, Vol. II – 1840, transl. Reeve, H. Pennsylvania: Pennsylvania State University Press.

Tomasi di Lampedusa, G., 2007, *The Leopard (Il Gattopardo)*, orig. 1958, transl. Colquhoun, A. London: Vintage.

Tomlinson, R.A., 2006, 'Adoption', in: Wilson, N. (ed.), *Encyclopedia of Ancient Greece*. New York/London: Routledge.

Torres, G. & Guinier, L., 2012, 'The Constitutional Imaginary: Just Stories About We the People', *Maryland Law Review*, Vol. 71(4), p. 1052–1072.

Towfigh, E.V., 2017, 'The Economic Paradigm', in: Towfigh, E.V. & Petersen, N. (eds.), *Economic Methods for Lawyers*. Cheltenham/Northampton: Edward Elgar, p. 18–31.

Tracy, S.V., 2009, *Pericles: A Sourcebook and Reader*. Berkley, LA/London: University of California Press.

Tremmel, J., 2017, 'Constitutions as Intergenerational Contracts: Flexible or Fixed?', *Intergenerational Justice Review*, Vol. 10(1), p. 4–17.

Tribe, L., 1983, 'A Constitution We Are Amending: In Defense of a Restrained Judicial Role', *Harvard Law Review*, Vol. 97(2), p. 443–445.

Troper, M., 2005, 'Marshall, Kelsen, Barak and the Constitutionalist Fallacy', *International Journal of Constitutional Law*, Vol. 3(1), p. 24–38.

Troper, M., 2010, 'Behind the Constitution? The Principles of Constitutional Identity in France', in: Sajó, A. & Uitz, R. (eds.), *Constitutional Topography: Values and Constitutions*. Portland: Eleven International Publishing, p. 187–203.

Tsebelis, G., 2017, 'The Time Inconsistency of Long Constitutions: Evidence from the World', *European Journal of Political Research*, Vol. 56(4), p. 820–845

Tsebelis, G. & Nardi, D.J., 2016, 'A Long Constitution Is a (Positively) Bad Constitution: Evidence from OECD Countries', *British Journal of Political Science*, Vol. 46(2), p. 457–478.

Tuchman, B.W., 2004, *The Guns of August*, orig. 1962. USA: Presidio Press.

Turnbull, C.M., 1992, 'The Individual, Community and Society: Rights and Responsibilities from an Anthropological Perspective', in: Sack, P. & Aleck, J., (eds.), *Law and Anthropology*. Aldershot, Hong Kong, C.A.: Dartmouth Publishing, p. 212–216.

Turnbull, N., 2010, 'Legitimation in Terms of Questioning: Integrating Political Rhetoric and the Sociology of Law', in: Thornhill & Ashenden, Vol. 2010, p. 29–56.

Turner, R., 2009, *King John: England's Evil King?* Stroud: UK History Press.

Tushnet, M., 1997, 'Constituting We the People', *Fordham Law Review*, Vol. 65(4), p. 1557–1564.

Tushnet, M., 2006, 'Some Reflections on Method in Comparative Constitutional Law', in: Choudhry 2006, p. 67–83.

Tushnet, M., 2009a, 'The Inevitable Globalization of Constitutional Law', *Virginia Journal of International Law*, Vol. 49(4), p. 985–1006.

Tushnet, M., 2009b, *The Constitution of the United States; A Contextual Analysis*. Oxford: Hart Publishing.

Tushnet, M., 2012, 'Constitution', in: Rosenfeld & Sajó, Vol. 2012, p. 217–232.

Tyler, T.R., 2006, *Why do People Obey the Law?* Princeton/Oxford: Princeton University Press.

Uslaner, E.M., 2008, 'Trust as a Moral Value', in: Castiglione, D. et al. (eds.), *The Handbook of Social Capital*. Oxford: Oxford University Press.

Uslaner, E.M., 2017, 'Political Trust, Corruption, and Equality', in: Zmerli & Van der Meer 2017, p. 302–315.

Veblen, Th., 2000, *The Higher Learning in America*, orig. 1918, intro. by Berg, I. New Jersey: Transaction Publishers.

Veblen, Th., 2007, *The Theory of the Leisure Class: An Economic Study of Institutions*, orig. 1899. Oxford/New York: Oxford University Press.

Velde, H. te, 2010, *Van regentenmentaliteit tot populisme: politieke tradities in Nederland (From Regent Mentality to Populism; Political Traditions in the Netherlands)*. Amsterdam: Bert Bakker.

Velde, H. te, 2015, *Sprekende politiek: redenaars en hun publiek in de parlementaire Gouden Eeuw (Political Speech: Orators and Their Audience in the Golden Age of Parliament)*, English translation forthcoming. Amsterdam: Prometheus.

Veljanovski, C., 2010, 'Economic Approaches to Regulation', in: Baldwin, R., Cave, M. & Lodge, M. (eds.), *The Oxford Handbook of Regulation*. Oxford: Oxford University Press, p. 17–38.

Verdonck, E., 2018, De Roeping en Doelstellingen van Hammoerabi (The Calling and Mission of Hammurabi), http://users.belgacom.net/verdonck.eric/law/hammoe.html.

Vermeule, A., 2007, 'Common Law Constitutionalism and the Limits of Reason', *Columbia Law Review*, Vol. 107(6), p. 1482–1532.

Versteeg, M., 2014, 'Unpopular Constitutionalism', *Indiana Law Journal*, Vol. 89(1), p. 1–56.

Versteeg, M. & Zackin, E., 2014, 'American Constitutional Exceptionalism Revisited', *University of Chicago Law Review*, Vol. 81(4), p. 1641–1707.

Vikør, K.S., 2016, 'Islamic Law in the Modern World: States, Laws, and Constitutions', in: Buskens, L. & Sandwijk, A. van (eds.), *Islamic Studies in the Twenty-first Century: Transformations and Continuities*. Amsterdam: Amsterdam University Press, p. 205–222.

Voermans, W, 2018, 'A 200-Year-Old Constitution: Relic or Enigma?', in: Ferrari, G.F., Passchier R. & Voermans W., *The Dutch Constitution Beyond 200 Years: Tradition and Innovation in a Multilevel Legal Order*. The Hague: Eleven International Publishing, p. 11–28.

Voermans, W., Stremler, M. & Cliteur, P., 2017, *Constitutional Preambles: A Comparative Analysis*. Cheltenham/Northampton: Edward Elgar.

Voigt, S., 2011, 'Positive Constitutional Economics II – A Survey of Recent Developments', *Public Choice*, Vol. 146(1), p. 205–256.

Voltaire, 1829, *Essai sur les moeurs et l'esprit des nations (An Essay on Universal History, the Manners, and Spirit of Nations)*, Vol. I (Tome I), orig. 1761, Paris: Werdet & Lequien fils.

Vorländer, H., 2017, 'Constitutions as Symbolic Order: The Cultural Analysis of Constitutionalism', in: Blokker & Thornhill 2017, p. 209–240.

Waal, F. de (ed.), 2015, *Evolved Morality: The Biology and Philosophy of Human Conscience*. Leiden: Brill.

Waal, F. de, 2019, *The Age of Empathy. Nature's Lessons for a Kinder Society*, orig. 2009. London: Souvenir Press.

Waerzeggers, C., 2012, 'The Babylonian Chronicles: Classification and Provenance', *Journal of Near Eastern Studies*, Vol. 71(2), p. 285–298.

Waerzeggers, C., 2017, De wilde jeugd der assyriologie (The Wild Youth of Assyriology), Leiden inaugural address, http://persia-babylonia.org/wp/wp-content/uploads/Oratie–Waerzeggers .pdf (In Dutch).

Waldron, J., 1987, *Nonsense Upon Stilts: Bentham, Burke, and Marx*. London: Methuen & Co.

Waldron, J., 1999, *The Dignity of Legislation*. Cambridge: Cambridge University Press.

Wallis, J., 2014, *Constitution Making during State Building*. Cambridge/New York: Cambridge University Press.

Warren, M., 1989, 'Liberal Constitutionalism as Ideology: Marx and Habermas', *Political Theory*, Vol. 17(4), p. 511–534.

Watanabe, N. & Yamamoto, M., 2015, 'Neural Mechanisms of Social Dominance', *Frotiers in Neuroscience*, Vol. 9(154), p. 1–14.

Watson, A., 1974, *Legal Transplants: An Approach to Comparative Law*. Charlottesville: University Press of Virginia.

Wauters, B. & Benito, M. de, 2017, *The History of Law in Europe: An Introduction*. Cheltenham/Northampton: Edward Elgar.

Weber, E., 1959, *The Nationalist Revival in France, 1905–1914*. Berkeley: University of California Press.

Weber, E., 1976, *Peasants into Frenchmen*. Stanford, CA: Stanford University Press.

Weber, M., 1964, *The Theory of Social and Economic Organization*, orig. 1922, transl. Henderson, A.M. & Parsons, T., Parsons, T. (ed.). New York: Free Press.

Weber, M., 1972, *Wirtschaft und Gesellschaft. Grundriß der verstehenden Soziologie*, orig. 1922, Winckelmann, J. (ed.), 5th rev. ed. Tübingen: Mohr.

Weber, M., 1973, *Science as a Vocation (Wissenschaft als Beruf)*, orig. 1917, uit: Gesammelte Aufsätze zur Wissenschaftslehre, bew. Winckelmann, J.F. Tübingen: Mohr 1973, p. 524–555.

Weber, M., 1976, *Agrarian Sociology of Ancient Civilizations*, orig. 1909, transl. Frank, R.I. London: New Left Books.

Weber, L.R. & Carter, A.I., 2004, *The Social Construction of Trust*, orig. 2003. New York: Springer Science + Business.

Weiler, J.H.H., 1999, *The Constitution of Europe: Do the New Clothes Have an Emperor?* Cambridge/New York: Cambridge University Press.

Weiler, J.H.H., 2003, 'In Defence of the Status Quo: Europe's Constitutional Sonderweg', in: Weiler, J.H.H. & Wind, M. (eds.), *European Constitutionalism Beyond the State*. Cambridge: Cambridge University Press, p. 7–23.

Weiler, J.H.H., 2005, 'On the Power of the Word: Europe's Constitutional Iconography', *International Journal of Constitutional Law*, Vol. 3(2–3), p. 173–190.

Weiler, J.J., 2001, 'Federalism without Constitutionalism: Europe's Sonderweg', in: Nicolaïdis, K. & Howse, R. (eds.), *The Federal Vision. Legitimacy and Levels of Governance in the United States and the European Union*. Oxford: Oxford University Press, p. 54–72.

Weingast, B.R., 1993, 'Constitutions as Governance Structures: The Political Foundations of Secure Markets', *Journal of Institutional and Theoretical Economics*, Vol. 149(1), p. 286–311.

Weingast, B.R., 1995, 'The Economic Role of Institutions: Market-Preserving Federalism and Economic Development', *Journal of Law, Economics, and Organization*, Vol. 11(1), p. 1–31.

Weingast, B.R., 1997, 'The Political Foundations of Democracy and the Rule of Law', *The American Political Science Review*, Vol. 91(2), p. 245–263.

Weingast, B.R., 2016a, 'Capitalism, Democracy, and Countermajoritarian Institutions', *Supreme Court Economic Review*, Vol. 23(1), p. 255–277.

Weingast, B.R., 2016b, 'Exposing the Neoclassical Fallacy: McCloskey on Ideas and the Great Enrichment', *Scandinavian Economic History Review*, Vol. 64(3), p. 189–201.

Weingast, B.R., 2017, *Adam Smith's Constitutional Theory*, https://ssrn.com/abstract=2890639, 14 February.

Weisberg, R.H., 1986, 'Text into Theory: A Literary Approach to the Constitution', *Georgia Law Review*, Vol. 20(4), p. 939–994.

Wen-Chen, C. & Law, D.S., 2018, 'Constitutional Dissonance in China', in: Jacobsohn & Schor 2018, p. 476–513.

Wenzel, M., 2009, 'Social Identity and Justice: Implications for Intergroup Relations', in: Otten, S., Sassenberg, K. & Kessler, T. (eds.), *Intergroup Relations: The Role of Motivation and Emotion*. Hove/New York: Psychology Press, p. 61–79.

Wet, E. de, 2012, 'The Constitutionalization of Public International Law', in: Rosenfeld & Sajó 2012, p. 1209–1230.

Wheare, K.C., 1966, *Modern Constitutions*, 2nd ed. Oxford: Oxford University Press/Oxford Paperbacks University Series.

White, J.D., 2011, 'An Old-Fashioned View of the Nature of Law', *Theoretical Inquiries in Law*, Vol. 12(1), p. 381–402.

Whitman, J.Q., 1996, 'At the Origins of Law and the State: Supervision of Violence, Mutilation of Bodies, or Setting of Prices?' *Chicago-Kent Law Review*, Vol. 71(84), p. 41–84.

Whittington, K.E., 2008, 'Constitutionalism', in: Caldeira, G.A., Kelemen, R.D. & Whittington, K.E. (eds.), *The Oxford Handbook of Law and Politics*. Oxford: Oxford University Press, p. 282–296.

Wickham, C., 2010, *The Inheritance of Rome: A History of Europe from 400–1000*, orig. 2009. London: Penguin Books.

Wilkin, P., 2018, 'The Rise of "Illiberal" Democracy: The Orbánization of Hungarian Political Culture', *Journal of World-Systems Research*, Vol. 24(1), p. 5–42.

Will, G.J., Crone, E.A., Lier, P.A.C. van & Güroğlu, B., 2016, 'Neural Correlates of Retaliatory and Prosocial Reactions to Social Exclusion: Associations with Chronic Peer Rejection', *Developmental Cognitive Neuroscience*, Vol. 19, p. 288–297.

Williams, K.D., Forgas, J.P. & Von Hippel, W. (eds.), 2005, *The Social Outcast: Ostracism, Social Exclusion, Rejection, and Bullying*. New York: Psychology Press.

Williams, K.D., 2007, 'Ostracism: The Kiss of Social Death', *Social and Personality Psychology Compass*, Vol. 1(1), p. 236–247.

Williams, K.D. & Nida, S.A., 2011, 'Ostracism: Consequences and Coping', *Current Directions in Psychological Science*, Vol. 20(2), p. 71–75.

Williams, K.D. & Nida, S.A. (eds.), 2017, *Ostracism, Exclusion, and Rejection*. New York/ London: Routledge.

Wilson, P.H., 2017, *The Holy Roman Empire: A Thousand Years of Europe's History*, orig. 2016. London: Penguin Books.

Wingrove, T., Korpas, A.L. & Weisz, V., 2011, 'Why Were Millions of People *not* Obeying the Law? Motivational Influences on Non-compliance with the Law in the Case of Music Piracy', *Psychology, Crime & Law*, Vol. 17(3), p. 261–276.

Wittberg, L., 2006, 'Can Communication Activities Improve Compliance?', in: Elffers, H., Verboon, P. & Huisman, W. (eds.), *Managing and Maintaining Compliance*. Den Haag: Boom Legal Publishers, p. 25–43.

Wu, J., Balliet, D. & Lange, P.A.M. van, 2016, 'Reputation Management: Why and How Gossip Enhances Generosity', *Evolution and Human Behavior*, Vol. 37(3), p. 193–201.

Yoder, K.J. & Decety, J., 2014, 'The Good, the Bad, and the Just: Justice Sensitivity Predicts Neural Response during Moral Evaluation of Actions Performed by Others', *Journal of Neuroscience*, Vol. 34(12), p. 4161–4166.

Young, E.A., 2007, 'The Constitution Outside the Constitution', *Yale Law Journal*, Vol. 117(3), p. 408–473.

Zakaria, F., 1997, 'The Rise of Illiberal Democracy', *Foreign Affairs*, Vol. 76(6), p. 22–43.

Zakaria, F., 2004, 'Islam, Democracy, and Constitutional Liberalism', *Political Science Quarterly*, Vol. 119(1), p. 1–20.

Zakaria, F., 2007, *The Future of Freedom: Illiberal Democracy at Home and Abroad*. New York/London: W.W. Norton.

Zamyoski, A., 2014, *Phantom Terror: The Threat of Revolution and the Repression of Liberty 1789–1848*. London: William Collins.

Zane, J.M., 1998, *The Story of Law*, orig. 1927, 2nd ed. Indianapolis: Liberty Fund.

Zmerli, S. & Meer, T.W.G. van der (eds.), 2017, *Handbook on Political Trust*. Cheltenham/ Northampton: Edward Elgar.

Zolberg, A.R., 1972, 'Moments of Madness', *Politics & Society*, Vol. 2(2), p. 183–207.

Name & Author Index

Subject Index

Subject Index

humanism, 114, 115, 129, 180, 197, 343
Hume's guillotine, 308, 309
Hundred Years' War, 113
hunter-gatherer, 47–50, 52, 59, 65
hybrid democracy, 36
hybrid regime, 187
hybrid system, 38

icon, 322
iconography, 330
identification, 92, 228, 300, 337, 338
identity, 8, 17, 59, 63, 72, 118, 156, 164, 166,
    234–236, 313, 317, 320, 331
identity claim, 313
idyll, 305
Iliad, 323
illiberal democracy, 184, 185
imagery, 322, 338
imagination, 1, 14, 15, 17, 18, 51, 56, 87, 95, 100, 134,
    165, 234, 294, 295, 297, 314, 322, 323, 327, 343
imagined reality, 14, 15, 29, 71, 294, 318, 319, 321
imitation, 297, 307, 335
imperial constitution, 155, 158, 160, 161
inalienable rights, 24, 215, 319
increasing scale, 51, 65, 113, 114
independence of the judiciary, 137, 209, 213
individual freedom, 11, 73, 110, 122, 126–128, 159,
    174, 186, 192, 259, 275
individual freedom postulate, 122
individuality, 57, 94, 122, 128, 129, 196, 320, 331
Indonesia, 175
industrialisation, 261
inefficiency, 264
inequality, 253, 261
information provision, 250
instinct, 58, 62, 296
institutes, 102
institution, 2, 7, 12–15, 21, 26, 27, 38–40, 43, 51, 56,
    58, 64, 66, 83, 84, 86, 94, 102, 114, 122, 143, 164,
    166, 176, 182, 183, 187, 194, 195, 206, 225, 228,
    230–232, 235, 239, 242, 244, 248, 250–252, 255,
    260, 261, 263–268, 278, 286, 293, 298, 301, 305,
    312, 320, 323, 338
Instrument of Government, 131, 132, 211
intentionality, 15, 41
internal market, 182
internalisation, 64, 300
international human right, 20, 192, 232
International Journal of Constitutional Law, 10
international law, 100, 102, 123, 232, 241
intervention, 89, 152, 175, 203, 245, 260, 261
interwar period, 164, 165, 167
intra-imperial isomorphism, 176
irrational, 276, 293, 316
Islam, 185, 188, 189

Islamic constitution, 188
is-ought problem, 309
Israel, 6, 121, 122, 204
iudice, 101

Jacobin, 141, 145
Japan, 171–173, 179, 219, 247, 275
Japanese constitution, 171
Japanese Self-Defense Forces, 247
Joyous Entry, 111
judge, 14, 15, 27, 28, 72, 80, 85, 96, 101, 106, 110,
    125, 177, 228, 235, 242–244, 254, 256, 264, 286,
    302, 309, 322, 323, 331, 334, 337, 341, 344, 345
judicialisation, 280
justice, 2, 24, 34, 58, 66, 78, 81, 85, 88, 90, 92, 96,
    101, 105, 106, 112, 113, 120, 139, 142, 143, 146, 159,
    160, 166, 172, 198, 259, 275, 283, 286, 301–303,
    318, 319, 323, 340, 342

Kesavananda Bharati v. State of Kerala, 209
king, 42, 44, 54, 77, 78, 80–83, 85, 88, 90, 98, 109,
    110, 113, 118, 132, 135, 136, 139, 143, 146, 148, 149,
    151, 156, 157, 158, 166, 204, 211, 274, 319, 320, 329,
    330, 332, 334
kingship, 52, 53, 66
knight, 139
kosmoi, 87

labour movement, 164
labour productivity, 267
Laeken Declaration, 191
language instinct, 296, 308
large-C constitution, 214
Law of the Twelve Tables, 82
law of war, 116
law's authority, 41
League of Nations, 164
legal borrowing, 229
legal certainty, 262, 266
legal community, 53, 195, 211, 241, 335
legal humanism, 115, 116
legal norm, 206, 209, 239, 240, 292, 302, 307
legal philosopher, 14, 22, 206, 300
legal principle, 2, 20, 40, 96, 189, 212, 302,
    344, 345
legal rule, 11, 17, 19, 20, 33, 66, 71, 72, 75, 76, 78,
    80, 81, 85, 86, 95, 113, 115, 125, 131, 132, 145, 194,
    206, 240, 241, 250, 262, 263, 275, 298, 299, 301,
    307, 308
legal system, 2, 4, 9, 12, 18, 19, 33, 41, 44, 72, 75, 82,
    95, 99, 101, 102, 104, 106, 112, 114, 115, 132, 144,
    188, 192, 194, 197, 206, 211, 213, 214, 216, 228, 229,
    234, 241, 244–246, 250, 262, 264, 299, 300–302,
    307, 312, 320, 341
legal transplants, 229

Subject Index

Made in the USA
Middletown, DE
03 April 2024

52533730R00225